Dictionary

of

AMERICAN MAXIMS

Dictionary

of

AMERICAN MAXIMS

Edited by DAVID KIN

With an Introduction
by
J. DONALD ADAMS

PHILOSOPHICAL LIBRARY
New York

Printed in the United States of America

INTRODUCTION

by

J. Donald Adams

This dictionary must have been a long time in the making. My suspicion is that Mr. Kin began collecting these maxims (and wisecracks) soon after he stopped playing with his alphabet blocks. The range of the sources from which they have been drawn is remarkable. Everybody is here, with his pennyworth, silver dollar, or gold piece of wisdom, from George Washington down to Walter Winchell. There is surprisingly little dross in so large a collection, and some of that is amusing, though not to be accepted as a guide to confident living. As for those maxims, and they are many, which occupy the highest level of man's periodic intelligence, we would, if we could translate all of them into action in our daily lives, create the millennium in a jiffy.

Homo sapiens, that most contradictory of all animate beings, has in the course of the centuries lorded it over creation, set down for the guidance of his fellows an accumulation of acute and succinct wisdom potentially as valuable and reliable as the instinctive lore which is handed down, on the lower levels of brute creation, from one generation of animals to another. Unlike them, however, he has been much less consistent in putting into practice the precepts which the best minds of his species have bequeathed him. He is a fast learner and an equally speedy forgetter. For that reason, he cannot too often be reminded of those tried and proven truths about life which observation and that gift of reason in which he so blindly trusts have awarded him. It is reason enough to justify Mr. Kin's dictionary.

You will have observed that the maxims he has collected here are American maxims; I do not believe that generally speaking, you will find that they differ fundamentally from similar maxims which are the heritage of other peoples. You will, of course, often find a marked difference in the manner in which these truths or half-truths are expressed, for we do have our own way of putting things, and Mr. Kin's dictionary, on many of its pages, has a distinctly native flavor. And that is all to the good; we are much more likely to accept truth if it is addressed to us in the language and the terms to which we are accustomed.

I admire very much the catch-all quality which is the result of Mr. Kin's diligence and perceptiveness. I could wish that in a work so titled and so weighty with wisdom, he had for-sworn such mentally adolescent flippancies as Clarence Dar-row's "I don't believe in God because I don't believe in Mother Goose," such quarter-truths as Logan Pearsall Smith's "A best-seller is a gilded tomb of a mediocre talent," or such witty but shallow reflections as Mencken's definition of adultery, "democracy applied to love." But in such a welter of high-planed thinking as Mr. Kin has set before us, perhaps these irreverent asides serve the purpose of lighting the repast and of adding salt to substance.

Here and there my gorge rose, as when I re-encountered Franklin Roosevelt's fatuous remark: "A conservative is a man with two perfectly good legs who, however, has never learned to walk." I might with equal truth observe that a radical is a man with one good leg who has never learned to use the other. Much more to my taste are such profound bits of wisdom as Robert Frost's "The best way out is always through," or E. W. Howe's "A good scare is worth more to a man than good advice."

But it is needless for me to quote. Mr. Kin's dictionary

speaks for itself, and in no uncertain accents. If you digest its contents you should be a wiser, if not a happier person. But one word of caution: this is rich fare, and high in protein content. Take it easy, a little at a time.

New York City.

A

ABILITY

It is almost as presumptuous to think you can do nothing as to think you can do everything. —*Phillips Brooks.*

Exigencies create the necessary ability to meet and to conquer them. —*Wendell Phillips.*

No man gets the ability to do an impossibility before he does it; the power comes with the effort. It is because of this law that moral obligations are binding. —*Dr. Frank Crane.*

Every man has his own organic gift of disposition, faculty, ability. —*J. F. Clarke.*

The ability to deal with people is as purchasable a commodity as sugar or coffee. And I pay more for that ability than for any other under the sun. —*John D. Rockefeller.*

Consider the postage stamp: its usefulness consists in the ability to stick to one thing till it gets there. —*Josh Billings.*

We judge ourselves by what we feel capable of doing, while others judge us by what we have already done.

—*H. W. Longfellow.*

There is something that is much more scarce, something finer far, something rarer than ability. It is the ability to recognize ability. —*Elbert Hubbard.*

In the last analysis ability is commonly found to consist mainly in a high degree of solemnity. —*Ambrose Bierce.*

One machine can do the work of fifty ordinary men. No machine can do the work of one extraordinary man. —*Elbert Hubbard.*

ABOLITIONISM

Emancipation can be as triumphantly defended on the ground

1

of political economy and material prosperity as it can be on moral
and religious principles. —*W. L. Garrison.*

ABSENCE

The absent are never without fault, nor the present without
excuse. —*B. Franklin.*

ABSINTHE

Absinthe makes the heart grow fonder. —*Addison Mizner.*

ABSOLUTE

The constitution does not recognize an absolute and uncontrollable liberty. —*Charles Evans Hughes.*

Neither property rights nor contract rights are absolute; for
government cannot exist if the citizen may at will use his property
to the detriment of his fellows, or exercise his freedom of contract
to work them harm. —*Owen J. Roberts.*

ABSOLUTISM

The wastes of democracy are among the greatest obvious wastes,
but we have compensations in democracy which far outweigh that
waste, and make it more efficient than absolutism.

—*Louis D. Brandeis.*

ABSTAINER

Abstainer: a weak person who yields to the temptation of denying himself a pleasure. —*Ambrose Bierce.*

ABSTINENCE

Abstaining is favorable both to the head and the pocket.

—*Horace Greeley.*

Always rise from the table with an appetite, and you will never
sit down without one. —*Wm. Penn.*

ABUSE

Abuse is the weapon of the vulgar. —*S. G. Goodrich.*

Whipping and abuse are like laudanum: you have to double the
dose as the sensibilities decline. —*H. B. Stowe.*

Abuse of anyone generally shows that he has marked traits of
character. The stupid and indifferent are passed by in silence.

—*Tryon Edwards.*

ABYSS

Men build their cultures by huddling together, nervously loqua-
cious, at the edge of an abyss. —*Kenneth Burke.*

ACCIDENTS

Nothing with God is accidental.   *—H. W. Longfellow.*

ACCOMPLISHMENT

About all some men accomplish in life is to send a son to Harvard.   *—E. W. Howe.*

We have got but one life here . . . It pays, no matter what comes after it, to try and do things, to accomplish things in this life, and not merely to have a soft and pleasant time.

—Theodore Roosevelt.

Anything approaching accomplishment grows wearisome.

—Sherwood Anderson.

ACCURACY

Accuracy of statement is one of the elements of truth; inaccuracy is a near kin to falsehood.   *—Tryon Edwards.*

Accuracy is the twin brother of honesty; inaccuracy of dishonesty.   *—Charles Simmons.*

ACHIEVEMENT

Mere longevity is a good thing for those who watch Life from the side lines. For those who play the game, an hour may be a year, a single day's work an achievement for eternity.

—Gabriel Heatter.

Finish every day and be done with it. Tomorrow is a new day.

—R. W. Emerson.

My greatest inspiration is a challenge to attempt the impossible.

—Albert A. Michelson.

ACQUAINTANCE

Acquaintance: a degree of friendship called slight when its object is poor or obscure, and intimate when he is rich or famous.

—Ambrose Bierce.

Acquaintance: a person whom we know well enough to borrow from, but not well enough to lend to.   *—Ibid.*

ACTION

The judgment of the world has been that Pilate did not do enough. There is no vigor in expressing an opinion and then washing your hands.   *—Heywood Broun.*

We are passing from a period of extreme individualistic action into a period of associated activities.   *—Herbert Hoover.*

Nothing we ever do is, in strict scientific literalness, wiped out.
　　　　　　　　　　　　　　　　　　　—William James.

Not what man does but how he does it is decisive.
　　　　　　　　　　　　　　　　　—Pierre Van Paassen.

Thought is the seed of action.　　　　*—R. W. Emerson.*

Act—act in the living Present!　　　　*—H. W. Longfellow.*

Until there be correct thought, there cannot be any action, and when there is correct thought, right action will follow.
　　　　　　　　　　　　　　　　　　　—Henry George.

The government of the Union, though limited in its powers, is supreme within its sphere of action.　　*—John Marshall.*

The margin between that which men naturally do, and that which they can do, is so great that a system which urges men on to action and develops individual enterprise and initiative is preferable, in spite of the wastes that necessarily attend that process.
　　　　　　　　　　　　　　　　—Louis D. Brandeis.

Where nothing prompts to action, nothing will be done; where sufficient inducements are presented, every thing will be done, which is within the grasp of human power.　*—Timothy Dwight.*

We are taught by great actions that the universe is the property of every individual in it.　　　　*—R. W. Emerson.*

A man's action is only a picture book of his creed.　*—Ibid.*

An ounce of performance is worth more than a pound of preachment.　　　　　　　　　　　*—Elbert Hubbard.*

Positive anything is better than negative nothing.　*—Ibid.*

Every man feels instinctively that all the beautiful sentiments in the world weigh less than a single lovely action.　*—J. R. Lowell.*

The happiness of love is in action; its test is what one is willing to do for others.　　　　　　　*—Lew Wallace.*

We want men of original perception and original action, who can open their eyes wider than to a nationality, (who) can act in the interest of civilization.　　　　*—R. W. Emerson.*

What a man does, compared with what he is, is but a small part.　　　　　　　　　　　　*—H. D. Thoreau.*

One may well feel chagrined when he finds he can do nearly all he can conceive.　　　　　　　　*—Ibid.*

Thought is the blossom; language the bud; action the fruit behind it.　　　　　　　　　　*—R. W. Emerson.*

Essentially, culture should be for action, and its effect should be to divest labor from the associations of aimless toil.

—*A. N. Whitehead.*

Celibacy does not suit a university. It must mate itself with action.   —*Ibid.*

What a man does, that he has. In himself is his might.

—*R. W. Emerson.*

A society will bear down most heavily upon those actions towards which its members are most vividly drawn, but which some ghostly superstition causes them to fear.   —*Ludwig Lewisohn.*

We may believe that our words—which we assume to express our principles—represent us more truly even than our actions, but to outsiders it is the actions that are more eloquent than the words.

—*H. S. Commager.*

Our actions are the results of our intentions and our intelligence.

—*E. S. Jones.*

Actions lie louder than words.   —*Carolyn Wells.*

Lose no time; be always employed in something useful, but avoid all unnecessary actions.   —*B. Franklin.*

Every action done in company ought to be with some sign of respect to those that are present.   —*G. Washington.*

ACTIVITY

Nobody has any right to find life uninteresting or unrewarding who sees within the sphere of his own activity a wrong he can help to remedy or within himself an evil he can hope to overcome.

—*Chas. W. Eliot.*

Every noble activity makes room for itself.   —*R. W. Emerson.*

Active natures are rarely melancholy: Activity and sadness are incompatible.   —*C. N. Bovee.*

Nothing, says Goethe, is so terrible as activity without insight. Look before you leap is a maxim for the world.   —*E. P. Whipple.*

In all that the people can individually do well for themselves, government ought not to interfere.   —*A. Lincoln.*

A man, like a watch is to be valued for his going.   —*Wm. Penn.*

ACTORS

An actor is a sculptor who carves in snow. —*Lawrence Barrett.*

ACTRESSES

Actresses will happen in the best-regulated families.

—*Oliver Herford.*

ACTS

A decent and manly examination of the acts of Government should be not only tolerated, but encouraged.   —*W. H. Harrison.*

ADAGES

Some of the rough facts of life must be compressed into adages in order to conserve for youth the experience of mankind.

—*Gelett Burgess.*

ADAM

Adam and Eve had many advantages, but the principal one was, that they escaped teething.   —*Mark Twain.*

ADDRESS

Give a boy address and accomplishments, and you give him the mastery of palaces and fortunes where he goes.

—*R. W. Emerson.*

ADJECTIVE

As to the Adjective; when in doubt, strike it out.   —*Mark Twain.*

ADJUSTMENT

Maladjustment is darkness. Adjustment is light. —*Scott Nearing.*

ADMIRATION

Admiration: our polite recognition of another man's resemblance to ourselves.   —*Ambrose Bierce.*

Admiration is a youthful fancy which scarcely ever survives to mature years.   —*H. W. Shaw.*

Admiration is the daughter of ignorance.   —*B. Franklin.*

I never knew a man so mean that I was not willing he should admire me.   —*E. W. Howe.*

ADULTERY

Adultery: democracy applied to love.   —*H. L. Mencken.*

ADVANCE

Advance or decadence are the only choices offered to mankind. The pure conservative is fighting against the essence of the Universe.   —*A. N. Whitehead.*

Social advance depends as much upon the process through which it is secured as upon the result itself.   —*Jane Addams.*

Perhaps we must always advance a little by zigzags; only we must always advance; and the zigzags should go toward the right goal.   —*Theodore Roosevelt.*

ADVANTAGE
We should not wrap ourselves in a banner of so-called principle when we are really concerned only with economic advantage.
—*J. L. McCaffrey.*

ADVENTURE
Adventure is not outside a man; it is within.   —*David Grayson.*

Without adventure civilization is in full decay.
—*A. N. Whitehead.*

To be curious and brave and eager,—is to know the adventure of life.   —*Randolph Bourne.*

ADVERSARIES
In all matters of opinion, our adversaries are insane.
—*Mark Twain.*

ADVERSITY
I'll say this for adversity: people seem to be able to stand it, and that's more than I can say for prosperity.   —*Kin Hubbard.*

No life is so hard that you can't make it easier by the way you take it.   —*Ellen Glasgow.*

You can bear anything if it isn't your own fault.
—*K. F. Gerould.*

Little minds are tamed and subdued by misfortunes; but great minds rise above them.   —*Washington Irving.*

Know how sublime a thing it is to suffer and be strong.
—*H. W. Longfellow.*

By trying we can easily learn to endure adversity—another man's I mean.   —*Mark Twain.*

Adversity . . . is sure to bring a season of sober reflection. Men see clearer at such times. Storms purify the atmosphere.
—*H. W. Beecher.*

As the flint contains the spark, unknown to itself, which the steel alone can awaken to life, so adversity often reveals to us hidden gems, which prosperity or negligence would forever have hidden.   —*H. W. Shaw.*

ADVERTISING

If you don't advertise yourself you will be advertised by your loving enemies.   —*Elbert Hubbard.*

Business today consists in persuading crowds.   —*G. S. Lee.*

Advertising is the life of trade.   —*Calvin Coolidge.*

Sanely applied, advertising could remake the world.
—*Stuart Chase.*

The business that considers itself immune to the necessity for advertising, sooner or later finds itself immune to business.
—*Derby Brown.*

The advertisements in a newspaper are more full of knowledge in respect to what is going on in a state or community than the editorial columns are.   —*H. W. Beecher.*

Advertisements contain the only truths to be relied on in a newspaper.   —*T. Jefferson.*

Advertising is the mouthpiece of business.   —*James R. Adams.*

ADVICE

A bad cold wouldn't be so annoying if it weren't for the advice of our friends.   —*Kin Hubbard.*

It is as easy to give advice to yourself as to others, and as useless.
—*Austin O'Malley.*

"Be yourself!" is about the worst advice you can give to some people.   —*Tom Masson.*

Ask no man. Go out into the night and look straight up to the stars. Take comfort and counsel of them.   —*John P. Altgeld.*

We give advice by the bucket, but take it by the grain.
—*W. R. Alger.*

Advice: the smallest current coin.   —*Ambrose Bierce.*

We are apt to be pert at censoring others, where we will not endure advice ourselves.   —*Wm. Penn.*

Advice is a drug in the market; the supply always exceeds the demand.   —*H. W. Shaw.*

A good scare is worth more to a man than good advice.
—*E. W. Howe.*

Advice is like castor oil, easy enough to give but dreadful uneasy to take.   —*Josh Billings.*

When a man comes to me for advice, I find out the kind of advice he wants, and I give it to him.   —*Ibid.*

Advice is like kissing; it costs nothing and is a pleasant thing to do.   —*Ibid.*

Do not give to thy friends the most agreeable counsels, but the most advantageous.   —*H. T. Tuckerman.*

They that will not be counselled cannot be helped.
—*B. Franklin.*

An empty stomach is not a good political adviser.
—*Albert Einstein.*

AESTHETIC

Without education man is incapable of aesthetic feeling in regard to nature as well as in regard to art.   —*Mathurin Dondo.*

AFFECTATION

Affectation hides three times as many virtues as charity does sins.   —*Horace Mann.*

AFFECTION

Talk not of wasted affection; affection never was wasted.
—*H. W. Longfellow.*

Of all the music that reached farthest into heaven, it is the beating of a loving heart.   —*H. W. Beecher.*

Caresses, expressions of one sort or another, are necessary to the life of the affections as leaves are to the life of a tree. If they are wholly restrained, love will die at the roots.
—*Nathaniel Hawthorne.*

There are moments of mingled sorrow and tenderness, which hallow the caresses of affection.   —*Washington Irving.*

AFFINITY

Truth never yet fell dead in the streets; it has such affinity with the soul of man, the seed however broadcast will catch somewhere and produce its hundredfold.   —*Theodore Parker.*

AFFIRMATION

Through affirmation and denial we make a zigzag path toward reform.   —*Gelett Burgess.*

AFFLICTION

Affliction comes to us, not to make us sad but sober; not to make us sorry but wise.   —*H. W. Beecher.*

The furnace of affliction produces refinement in states as well as in individuals.   *—John Adams.*

To bear other people's afflictions, everyone has courage and enough to spare.   *—B. Franklin.*

Affliction, like the iron-smith, shapes as it smites.   *—C. N. Bovee.*

What seem to us but dim funereal tapers may be heaven's distant lamps.   *—H. W. Longfellow.*

It is the crushed grape that gives out the blood-red wine: it is the suffering soul that breathes the sweetest melodies.
    —Gail Hamilton.

AFRAID

Too many people are afraid of Tomorrow—their happiness is poisoned by a phantom.   *—W. L. Phelps.*

AGE

Age does not endow all old things with strength and virtue, nor are all new things to be despised.   *—Henry W. Grady.*

You are not permitted to kill a woman who has injured you but nothing forbids you to reflect that she is growing older every minute. You are avenged 1440 times a day.   *—Ambrose Bierce.*

We do not count a man's years until he has nothing else to count.   *—R. W. Emerson.*

Grow up as soon as you can. It pays. The only time you really live fully is from thirty to sixty.   *—Hervey Allen.*

Age is not a question of years but of constitution and temperament.   *—Chauncey Depew.*

If wrinkles must be written upon our brows, let them not be written upon the heart. The spirit should not grow old.
    —James A. Garfield.

At 20 years of age the will reigns; at 30 the wit; at 40 the judgement.   *—B. Franklin.*

Respect for age is the natural religion of childhood; it becomes in men a sentiment of the soul.   *—G. E. Woodberry.*

Middle age is the time when a man is always thinking that in a week or two he will feel as good as ever.   *—Don Marquis.*

Age . . . is a matter of feeling, not of years.   *—G. W. Curtis.*

When one finds company in himself and his pursuits, he cannot feel old, no matter what his years may be.   *—A. B. Alcott.*

A person is always startled when he hears himself seriously called old for the first time.   —*O. W. Holmes.*

The easiest things for our friends to discover in us, and the hardest thing for us to discover in ourselves, is that we are growing old.   —*H. W. Shaw.*

Youth is the age of striving and selfishness; old age the period of dreaming dreams for the young and for the future that age is not to see.   —*Arthur Brisbane.*

In our civilization the trouble is that all is planned for youth and too little for age.   —*Ibid.*

At fifty a man's real life begins. He has acquired upon which to achieve; received from which to give; learned from which to teach; cleared upon which to build.   —*E. W. Bok.*

Wrinkles should merely indicate where smiles have been.
                                                        —*Mark Twain.*

The same sorrows rise and set in every age.   —*H. W. Beecher.*

Some old women and men grow bitter with age; the more their teeth drop out, the more biting they get.   —*G. D. Prentice.*

When a woman tells you her age, it's all right to look surprised, but don't scowl.   —*Wilson Mizner.*

At a certain age some people's minds close up; they live on their intellectual fat.   —*W. L. Phelps.*

To me, old age is always fifteen years older than I am.
                                                        —*B. M. Baruch.*

If you want to know how old a woman is, ask her sister-in-law.
                                                        —*E. W. Howe.*

Men, like peaches and pears, grow sweet a little while before they begin to decay.   —*O. W. Holmes.*

Our age is a study in pathology, both psychiatrically and sociologically.   —*Samuel D. Schmalhausen.*

We must produce a great age, or see the collapse of the upward striving of our race.   —*A. N. Whitehead.*

Tranquillity is the *summum bonum* of old age.   —*T. Jefferson.*
Age is no cause for veneration. An old crocodile is still a menace and an old crow sings not like a nightingale.
                                                        —*Dagobert D. Runes*

AGGRESSION

No man has a natural right to commit aggression on the equal rights of another, and this is all from which the laws ought to restrain him; every man is under the natural duty of contributing to the necessities of society, and this is all the laws should enforce on him; and no man having the natural right to be the judge between himself and another, it is his natural duty to submit to the umpirage of an impartial third.   —*T. Jefferson.*

AGITATION

Agitation is that part of our intellectual life where vitality results; there ideas are born, breed and bring forth.
—*G. E. Woodberry.*

Without incessant agitation of ideas, public free discussion, the state is dead.   —*Ibid.*

Agitation prevents rebellion, keeps the peace, and secures progress.   —*Wendell Phillips.*

Agitation is the method that plants the school by the side of the ballot-box.   —*Ibid.*

AGNOSTICISM

I am an agnostic; I do not pretend to know what many ignorant men are sure of.   —*Clarence Darrow.*

Agnosticism is the philosophical, ethical and religious dry-rot of the modern world.   —*F. E. Abbot.*

AGREEMENT

When two men in a business always agree one of them is unnecessary.   —*Wm. Wrigley, Jr.*

Marriage is an honorable agreement among men as to their conduct toward women, and it was devised by women.   —*Don Herold.*

The sheep and the wolf are not agreed upon a definition of the word liberty; and precisely the same difference prevails today among us human creatures.   —*A. Lincoln.*

AGRICULTURE

Blessed be agriculture! if one does not have too much of it.
—*C. D. Warner.*

AILMENTS

One of the commonest ailments of the present day is premature formation of opinion.   —*Kin Hubbard.*

AID

While the people should patriotically and cheerfully support their Government, its functions do not include the support of the people.   —*Grover Cleveland.*

AIM

If I shoot at the sun I may hit a star.   —*P. T. Barnum.*

Perhaps the reward of the spirit who tries is not the goal but the exercise.   —*E. V. Cooke.*

There are two things to aim at in life: first, to get what you want; and after that, to enjoy it. Only the wisest of mankind achieve the second.   —*Logan Pearsall Smith.*

Our aim should be to make art serve man as a thing of action and not man serve art as a thing of escape.   —*V. F. Calverton.*

He who aims high must dread an easy home and popular manners.   —*R. W. Emerson.*

Not failure, but low aim, is crime.   —*J. R. Lowell.*

Man is not so wedded to his own interest that he can make the common good the mark of his aim.   —*John Weiss.*

ALARM CLOCK

Even the most materialistic man has for his alarm clock a shamefaced personal regard.   —*Joyce Kilmer.*

America will never really be a decadent nation until its alarm clocks are jeweled and soft-voiced.   —*Ibid.*

The alarm clock is the symbol of civilization, that is, of voluntary submission, of free-will obedience.   —*Ibid.*

ALIENATION

No one knows the worth of woman's love till he sues for alienation.   —*Oliver Herford.*

ALIENIST

The alienist is not a joke: he finds you cracked, and leaves you broke.   —*Keith Preston.*

ALIMONY

You never realize how short a month is until you pay alimony.
                                    —*John Barrymore*

The wages of sin is alimony.   —*Carolyn Wells*

Alimony is like buying oats for a dead horse.

—Arthur ("Bugs") Baer.

ALL

If your Constitution does not guarantee freedom for all, it is not a Constitution I can subscribe to. *—W. L. Garrison.*

Liberty for each, for all, for ever. *—Ibid.*

It is the government of all; its powers are delegated by all; it represents all, and acts for all. *—John Marshall.*

No man may have all that he pleases. *—Brander Matthews.*

ALLEGIANCE

I know no south, no north, no east, no west to which I owe any allegiance. *—Henry Clay.*

One should never be at peace to the shame of his own soul,—to the violation of his integrity or of his allegiance to God.

—E. H. Chapin.

ALLIANCES

Peace, commerce, and honest friendship with all nations— entangling alliances with none. *—T. Jefferson.*

'Tis our true policy to steer clear of permanent alliances, with any portion of the foreign world—as far, I mean, as we are now at liberty to do it. *—G. Washington.*

ALMONER

The Government is not an almoner of gifts among people, but an instrumentality by which the people's affairs should be conducted upon business principles, regulated by the public need.

—Grover Cleveland.

ALONE

Many people live alone and like it, but most of them live alone and look it. *—Gelett Burgess.*

In Genesis it says that it is not good for a man to be alone, but sometimes it is a great relief. *—John Barrymore.*

ALPHABET

When a talk is made and put down it is good to look at it afterward. *—Sequoyah.*

ALTAR

In olden times sacrifices were made at the altar—a custom which is still continued. *—Helen Rowland.*

ALTRUISM

Altruism is a noble sentiment but no lasting social order has ever been built upon it alone.   —*James T. Shotwell.*

AMATEURS

The world is too full of amateurs who can play the golden rule as an aria with variations.   —*H. D. Lloyd.*

AMBITION

Hitch your wagon to a star.   —*R. W. Emerson.*

Most people would succeed in small things if they were not troubled by great ambitions.   —*H. W. Longfellow.*

Every man is said to have his peculiar ambition. . . . I have no other so great as that of being truly esteemed of my fellow-men, by rendering myself worthy of their esteem.   —*A. Lincoln.*

The tallest trees are most in the power of the winds, and ambitious men of the blasts of fortune.   —*Wm. Penn.*

High seats are new but uneasy, and crowns are always stuffed with thorns.   —*James Gordon Brooks.*

Ambition is like hunger: it obeys no law but its appetite.
—*H. W. Shaw.*

AMERICA

The child of two continents, America can be explained in its significant traits by neither alone.   —*V. L. Parrington.*

I am certain that, however great the hardships and the trials which loom ahead, our America will endure and the cause of human freedom will triumph.   —*Cordell Hull.*

Our America is Here, is Now, and beckons on before us, and this glorious assurance is not only our living hope, but our dreams to be accomplished.   —*Thomas Wolfe.*

The true discovery of America is before us.   —*Ibid.*

Intellectually I know that America is no better than any other country; emotionally I know she is better than every other country.
—*Sinclair Lewis.*

America is a tune. It must be sung together. ....   —*G. S. Lee.*

I was born an American; I live an American; I shall die an American.   —*Daniel Webster.*

Only those Americans who are willing to die for their country are fit to live.   —*Douglas MacArthur.*

This generation of Americans has a rendevous with destiny.
—*F. D. Roosevelt.*

Some Americans need hyphens in their names, because only part of them has come over.   —*Woodrow Wilson.*

America is already the first world-federation in miniature.
—*Randolph Bourne.*

There is nothing wrong with America that the faith, love of freedom, intelligence and energy of her citizens cannot cure.
—*D. D. Eisenhower.*

America lives in the heart of every man everywhere who wishes to find a region where he will be free to work out his destiny as he chooses.   —*Woodrow Wilson.*

Lift up America O lift green freedom to the evening sun.
—*Archibald MacLeish.*

America is the youngest of the nations, and inherits all that went before in history. . . . Mine is the whole majestic past, and mine the shining future.   —*Mary Antin.*

As long as we can all stand up together, God will bless America.
—*C. H. Kopf.*

Whether God blesses America or not does not depend so much upon God as it does upon us Americans.   —*Ibid.*

It was wonderful to find America, but it would have been more wonderful to miss it.   —*Mark Twain.*

Don't sell America short.   —*J. P. Morgan.*

America is the country where you buy a lifetime supply of aspirin for one dollar, and use it up in two weeks.
—*John Barrymore.*

In America with a stubborn world to conquer . . . unremitting labor was the price of survival.   —*Stuart Chase.*

Let America be America again,
Let it be the dream it used to be.
—*Langston Hughes.*

America is the most democratic of all nations; at least so they say.   —*Thorstein Veblen.*

America is but another name for opportunity. Our whole history appears like a last effort of divine Prudence on behalf of the human race.   —*R. W. Emerson.*

America is rising with a giant's strength. Its bones are yet but
cartilages.   —*Fisher Ames.*

Our country, right or wrong. When right, to be kept right; when
wrong, to be put right.   —*Carl Schurz.*

Here individuals of all nations are melted into a new race of
men, whose labor and posterity will one day cause great changes
in the world.   —*J. Hector St. John de Crèvecoeur.*

America is not a mere body of traders; it is a body of free men.
                                                          —*Woodrow Wilson.*

Our greatness is built upon our freedom—is moral, not material.
We have a great ardor for gain; but we have a deep passion for the
rights of man.   —*Ibid.*

Anglo-Saxon civilization has taught the individual to protect his
own rights; American civilization will teach him to respect the
rights of others.   —*W. J. Bryan.*

Great has been the Greek, the Latin, the Slav, the Celt, the
Teuton, and the Anglo-Saxon, but greater than any of these is the
American, in whom are blended the virtues of them all.
                                                             —*W. J. Bryan.*

Put none but Americans on guard tonight.
                                               —*Ascribed to G. Washington.*

I know only two tunes; one of them is "Yankee Doodle", and
the other isn't.   —*U. S. Grant.*

America calls for government with a soul.   —*F. D. Roosevelt.*

My folks didn't come over on the Mayflower, but they were
there to meet the boat.   —*Will Rogers.*

Just what is it that America stands for? If she stands for one
thing more than another it is for the sovereignty of self-governing
people.   —*Woodrow Wilson.*

AMERICAN

To be an American is of itself almost a moral condition, an education, and a career.   —*George Santayana.*

American life is a powerful solvent. It seems to neutralise every
intellectual element, however tough and alien it may be, and to
fuse it in the native good-will, complacency, thoughtlessness, and
optimism.   —*Ibid.*

It is by making himself one with human nature in America, its
faith, its methods, and the controlling purposes in our life among

nations, and not by birth merely, that a man becomes an American.
—*G. E. Woodberry.*

The American is a new man who acts on new principles; he must therefore entertain new ideas and form new opinions.
—*J. Hector St. Jean de Crèvecoeur.*

Americans are the western pilgrims, who are carrying along with them the great mass of arts, sciences, vigor, and industry which began long since in the East.
—*Ibid.*

I am not a Virginian, but an American. —*Patrick Henry.*

Thank God, I—I also—am an American! —*Daniel Webster.*

The American Dream . . . has been a dream of being able to grow to the fullest development as man and woman.
—*James Truslow Adams.*

It will never be possible for any length of time for any group of the American people, either by reason of wealth or learning or inheritance or economic power, to retain any mandate, any permanent authority to arrogate to itself the political control of American public life. —*F. D. Roosevelt.*

You cannot dedicate yourself to America unless you become in every respect and with every purpose of your will thorough Americans. —*Woodrow Wilson.*

Some Americans need hyphens in their names because only part of them has come over. —*Ibid.*

I am an American and therefore what I do, however small, is of importance. —*Struthers Burt.*

Rome endured as long as there were Romans. America will endure as long as we remain American in spirit and in thought.
—*D. S. Jordan.*

An American is one who loves justice and believes in the dignity of man. —*H. L. Ickes.*

An American is one who will fight for his freedom and that of his neighbor. —*Ibid.*

An American is one who will sacrifice property, ease and security in order that he and his children may retain the rights of free men. —*Ibid.*

I am still American enough to feel that it is always worth while at least to try both to have your cake and eat it.
—*Charlotte Muret.*

Franklin was the typical American.   —*Ludwig Lewisohn.*

The American is nomadic in religion, in ideas, in morals.
—*J. R. Lowell.*

Good Americans, when they die, go to Paris.   —*T. G. Appleton.*

I am a one hundred per cent American!—I am, God damn, I am!
—*W. W. Woollcott.*

The American people never carry an umbrella. They prepare to
walk in eternal sunshine.   —*Alfred E. Smith.*

AMERICANISM

When an Office Holder, or one that has been found out, can't
think of anything to deliver a speech on, he always falls back on
the good old subject, Americanism.   —*Will Rogers.*

Americanism consists in utterly believing in the principles of
America.   —*Woodrow Wilson.*

AMIABILITY

Natural amiableness is too often seen in company with sloth,
with uselessness, with the vanity of fashionable life.
—*W. E. Channing.*

AMUSEMENT

The only way to amuse some people is to slip and fall on an
icy pavement.   —*E. W. Howe.*

Christian discipleship does not involve the abandonment of
any innocent enjoyment. . . . diversion or amusement.
—*W. Gladden.*

The church has been so fearful of amusement that the devil has
had the charge of them.   —*H. W. Beecher.*

ANARCHISTS

The anarchists are simply unterrified Jeffersonian Democrats.
—*Benj. B. Tucker.*

ANARCHY

It is not much in the American vein to construct private little
anarchies in the haze of a smoking-room.   —*Stuart P. Sherman.*

ANCESTORS

The pride of ancestry increases in the ratio of distance.
—*G. W. Curtis.*

Every man is an omnibus in which his ancestors ride.
—*O. W. Holmes.*

I don't know who my grandfather was; I am much more concerned to know what his grandson will be. —*A. Lincoln.*

Pedigrees seldom improve by age: the grandson is too often a weak infringement on the grandsire's patent. —*H. W. Shaw.*

The Colonial Dames and the Daughters of the American Revolution organized in 1890 to recreate the social distinctions their ancestors had fled and defend the shibboleths their ancestors had attacked. —*H. S. Commager.*

There is no king who has not had a slave among his ancestors, and no slave who has not had a king among his. —*Helen Keller.*

It would be more honorable to our ancestors to praise them in words less, but in deeds to imitate them more. —*Horace Mann.*

ANCESTRY

America is full of religious confusion and contradiction. How could it be otherwise in a nation with our ancestry?

—*Elizabeth Jackson.*

Think of your forefathers! Think of your posterity!

—*John Q. Adams.*

ANCIENT

A democracy is the most ancient and the most probable.

—*John Wise.*

ANGELS

An actually existing fly is more important than a possibly existing angel. —*R. W. Emerson.*

If a man is only a little lower than the angels, the angels should reform. —*M. W. Little.*

Man was created a little lower than the angels, and has been getting a little lower ever since. —*Josh Billings.*

Earth has one angel less and heaven one more, since yesterday. —*Nathaniel Hawthorne.*

Let us hope that the angels look tenderly down on the sins of too much love. —*H. B. Stowe.*

If men were angels, no government would be necessary.

—*Alexander Hamilton.*

If angels were to govern men, neither external or internal controls on government would be necessary. —*Ibid.*

ANGER

When angry count ten before you speak; if very angry, a hundred.   —*T. Jefferson.*

Never forget what a man says to you when he is angry.
—*H. W. Beecher.*

The worst tempered people I've ever met were people who knew they were wrong.   —*Wilson Mizner.*

When angry count four; when very angry, swear.
—*Mark Twain.*

People always say that they are not themselves when tempted by anger into betraying what they really are.   —*E. W. Howe.*

Whatever is begun in anger ends in shame.   —*B. Franklin.*

Anger is never without a reason, but seldom with a good one.
—*B. Franklin.*

Men often make up in wrath what they want in reason.
—*W. R. Alger.*

Anger blows out the lamp of the mind.   —*R. G. Ingersoll.*

It is he who is in the wrong who first gets angry.   —*Wm. Penn.*

ANIMAL

My feeling toward the animal is that he is our younger brother, and that we are our brother's keeper.   —*Mary Johnston.*

I think I could turn and live with animals, they are so placid and self-contained.   —*Walt Whitman.*

Only two great groups of animals, men and ants, indulge in highly organized mass warfare.   —*C. H. Haskins.*

Animals have their own place and their own meaning in the universal order. The spirit of God is with them, as it is with us.
—*F. H. Hedge.*

Personally I would not give a fig for any man's religion whose horse, cat and dog do not feel its benefits.   —*S. P. Cadman.*

Beyond domestic animals and our response to their fealty and affection, we have a peculiar charge concerning the wild animals which supply our clothes, food and adornments.   —*Ibid.*

We are all in the same boat, both animals and men. You cannot promote kindness to one without benefiting the other.
—*E. E. Hale.*

A mule has neither pride of ancestry nor hope of posterity.
—*R. G. Ingersoll.*

ANT

None preaches better than the ant, and she says nothing.
—*B. Franklin.*

Ants are good citizens—they place group interest first.
—*Clarence Day.*

ANTICIPATION

Sorrow itself is not so hard to bear as the thought of sorrow
coming. —*T. B. Aldrich.*

ANTIQUITY

Cities, unlike human creatures, may grow to be so old that at
last they will become new. —*William Winter.*

How cunningly Nature hides every wrinkle of her inconceivable
antiquity under roses and violets and morning dew!
—*R. W. Emerson.*

ANTI-SEMITISM

There is not the slightest ground for anti-Semitism among us.
—*Wm. Howard Taft.*

ANTISEPTIC

What an antiseptic is a pure life! —*J. R. Lowell.*

ANTI-VIVISECTIONIST

An anti-vivisectionist is one who gags at a guinea pig and swallows a baby. —*H. L. Mencken.*

ANXIETY

The thinner the ice, the more anxious is everyone to see whether
it will bear. —*Josh Billings.*

Do not anticipate trouble, or worry about what may never happen. Keep in the sunlight. —*B. Franklin.*

How much have cost us the evils that never happened!
—*T. Jefferson.*

The misfortunes hardest to bear are these which never came.
—*J. R. Lowell.*

APATHY

The apathy of the people is enough to make every statue leap
from its pedestal and hasten the resurrection of the dead.
—*W. L. Garrison.*

Apathy is a sort of living oblivion.   —*Horace Greeley.*

APHORISMS

Aphorisms are portable wisdom, the quintessential extracts of thought and feeling.   —*W. P. Alger.*

Sensible men show their sense by saying much in few words.
                                                        —*Charles Simmons.*

Almost every wise saying has an opposite one, no less wise, to balance it.   —*George Santayana.*

APOLOGY

Apology is only egotism wrong side out.   —*O. W. Holmes.*

No sensible person ever made an apology.   —*R. W. Emerson.*

APPEARANCES

The world is governed more by appearances than by realities, so that it is fully as necessary to seem to know something as to know it.   —*Daniel Webster.*

APPETITE

Any young man with good health and a poor appetite can save up money.   —*J. M. Bailey.*

APPLAUSE

Applause is the echo of a platitude.   —*Ambrose Bierce.*

The silence that accepts merit as the most natural thing in the world, is the highest applause.   —*R. W. Emerson.*

Applause waits on success.   —*B. Franklin.*

About the only person we ever heard of that wasn't spoiled by being lionized was a Jew named Daniel.   —*G. D. Prentice.*

APPLICATION

The greatest homage to truth is to use it.   —*R. W. Emerson.*

APPLIED

It is by means of applied science that the earth can be made habitable and a decent human life made possible.
                                                        —*E. E. Slosson.*

APPOINTMENT

Unfaithfulness in the keeping of an appointment is an act of clear dishonesty. You may as well borrow a person's money as his time.   —*Horace Mann.*

APPRECIATION

If a man can write a better book, preach a better sermon, or make a better mouse-trap than his neighbor, though he builds his house in the woods, the world will make a beaten pathway to his door. —*R. W. Emerson.*

Next to invention is the power of interpreting invention; next to beauty is the power of appreciating beauty. —*Margaret Fuller.*

We never know a greater character unless there is in ourselves something congenial to it. —*W. E. Channing.*

A work of real merit finds favor at last. —*A. B. Alcott.*

Nature and books belong to the eyes that see them.
—*R. W. Emerson.*

ARCHBISHOP

Archbishop: a Christian ecclesiastic of a rank superior to that attained by Christ. —*H. L. Mencken.*

ARCHITECT

Architect: one who drafts a plan of your house, and plans a draft of your money. —*Ambrose Bierce.*

ARCHITECTURE

The surest test of the civilization of a people—at least, as sure as any— afforded by mechanical art, is to be found in their architecture, which presents so noble a field of the grand and the beautiful, and which, at the same time, is so intimately connected with the essential comforts of life. —*William H. Prescott.*

Architecture is a mirror, though not a passive one, reflecting the forces and ideas of a time. —*R. M. Bennett.*

Great architecture is the flowering of geometry.
—*R. W. Emerson.*

ARGUMENT

Many can argue; not many converse. —*A. B. Alcott.*

Neither irony nor sarcasm is argument. —*Rufus Choate.*

Insolence is not logic; epithets are the arguments of malice.
—*R. G. Ingersoll.*

Keep cool—anger is not argument. —*Daniel Webster.*

Great authorities are arguments. —*Ibid.*

If you lose in an argument, you can still call your opponent names. —*Elbert Hubbard.*

The only way to get the best of an argument is to avoid it.
—*Dale Carnegie.*

Behind every argument is someone's ignorance.
—*Louis D. Brandeis.*

Prejudices are rarely overcome by arguments; not being founded in reason they cannot be destroyed by logic.   —*Tryon Edwards.*

There is no good in arguing with the inevitable. The only argument available with an east wind is to put on your greatcoat.
—*J. R. Lowell.*

The true philosophical mind never wishes to win an argument but rather the truth. And the way to the truth is the way of hesitancy.   —*Dagobert D. Runes.*

ARISTOCRACY

An aristocracy is a dangerous constitution in the church of Christ.   —*John Wise.*

God and wise nature were never propitious to the birth of this monster (aristocracy).   —*Ibid.*

Some will always be above others. Destroy the equality today, and it will appear again tomorrow.   —*R. W. Emerson.*

A monied aristocracy in our country . . . has already set the government at defiance.   —*T. Jefferson.*

There is a natural aristocracy among men. The grounds of this are virtue and talent.   —*Ibid.*

Aristocracy is always cruel.   —*Wendell Phillips.*

An aristocracy of wealth (is) of more harm and danger than benefit to society.   —*T. Jefferson.*

An aristocracy is a combination of many powerful men for the purpose of maintaining and advancing their own particular interests. It is consequently a concentration of all the most effective parts of a community for a given end; hence its energy, efficiency and success.   —*James F. Cooper.*

ARISTOCRAT

The aristocrat is the democrat ripe and gone to seed.
—*R. W. Emerson.*

ARMAGEDDON

We stand at Armageddon and we battle for the Lord.
—*Theodore Roosevelt.*

ARMOR

Armor is the kind of clothing worn by a man whose tailor was a blacksmith. —*Ambrose Bierce.*

ARSENAL

We must be the great arsenal of democracy. —*F. D. Roosevelt.*

ART

Art is long, and Time is fleeting. —*H. W. Longfellow.*

As long as art is the beauty parlor of civilization, neither art nor civilization is secure. —*John Dewey.*

The whole art of government consists in the art of being honest. —*T. Jefferson.*

In art of all kinds the moral lesson is a mistake. —*F. M. Crawford.*

The life of art is fruitful only within the framework of our virtue. —*Howard Mumford Jones.*

Real art is illumination . . . It adds stature to life. —*Brooks Atkinson.*

The chief value of history consists in its proper employment for the purposes of art. —*W. G. Simms.*

Life too near paralyzes art. —*R. W. Emerson.*

The world will never understand our spirit except in terms of art. —*Randolph Bourne.*

Art is not a figuration but a transfiguration of matter. —*Mathurin Dondo.*

Art will once more be the great spiritual stimulant, the dynamic power in the endless fight of man against nature. —*Ibid.*

To suppress the liberty of art is like Herod's slaughter of the innocents—an attempt to kill off the alteration of the ideas, ideals, and ways and works of men at the source. —*H. M. Kallen.*

Art is intelligibility become an immediate delight and freedom enjoyed. —*Irwin Edman.*

Each school, each age, each race has its own art, often highly individualized and peculiar to itself. —*G. E. Woodberry.*

Art is the place of the soul's freedom; there it forgets its dream unhampered; there, age after age, race after race, it gives its dream to the world that is. —*Ibid.*

All good art—at least all good literary art—has a thesis. Its thesis is that life is larger than life . . . the life we have been leading day by day.   —*Malcolm Cowley.*

The revolutionary movement is a boon to art, and art even in its purest forms, for it drags artists out of their studios and opens new ranges of ideas, passions and sensations to them.

—*Max Eastman.*

Art belongs with life itself.   —*Ibid.*

Art is power.   —*H. W. Longfellow.*

In art the hand can never execute anything higher than the heart can inspire.   —*R. W. Emerson.*

Art is nature passed through the alembic of men.   —*Ibid.*

Alas, alas! for art in America. It has a hard stubby row to hoe.
—*Theodore Dreiser.*

Art is the stored honey of the human soul, gathered on wings of misery and travail.   —*Ibid.*

Every artist was first an amateur.   —*R. W. Emerson.*

Great art is as irrational as great music. It is mad with its own loveliness.   —*George Jean Nathan.*

ARTIFICE

There is a certain artificial polish which is purchased at the expense of all original and sterling traits of character.

—*Washington Irving.*

ARTIST

An artist may visit a museum, but only a pedant can live there.
—*George Santayana.*

An artist is a dreamer consenting to dream of the actual world.
—*Ibid.*

The artists must be sacrificed to their art. Like the bees, they must put their lives into the sting they give.   —*R. W. Emerson.*

It is the artist only who is the true historian.   —*W. G. Simms.*

The artist is . . . a vessel of freedom.   —*H. M. Kallen.*

Of all men the artist has been perhaps the most insecure.
—*Leo Gurko.*

The artist does not illustrate science (but) he frequently responds to the same interests that a scientist does.

—*Lewis Mumford.*

There is no clearer line of demarcation among human types than that between the artist and the man of action. —*Max Eastman.*

The defining function of the artist is to cherish consciousness. —*Ibid.*

Artists may deceive themselves, but I do not cherish the opinion that they must. —*Ibid.*

Comic-strip artists do not make good husbands, and God knows they do not make good comic strips. —*Don Herold.*

ASCENT

When you are climbing a mountain, don't talk; silence gives ascent. —*R. J. Burdette.*

Hitch your wagon to a star. —*R. W. Emerson.*

ASPIRATION

To hear the lark sing we must be
At heaven's gate with the lark.

—*Alice Cary.*

If a man constantly aspires, is he not elevated? Did ever a man try heroism, magnanimity, truth, sincerity, and find that there was not advantage in them—that it was a vain endeavor?

—*H. D. Thoreau.*

The heavens are as deep as our aspirations are high. —*Ibid.*

No man can ever rise above that at which he aims.

—*A. A. Hedge.*

There is not a single heart but has its moments of longing.

—*H. W. Beecher.*

ASSERTION

A bare assertion is not necessarily the naked truth.

— *G. D. Prentice.*

ASSETS

A tranquil mind and quiet conscience are assets of no mean value. —*Lyman Abbott.*

ASSIDUITY

Whatever I do study ought to be engaged in with all my soul, for I will be eminent in something. —*H. W. Longfellow.*

ASSOCIATION

To associate with very rich people involves sacrifices.

—*Edward S. Martin.*

Associate yourself with men of good quality if you esteem your reputation, for it is better to be alone than in bad company.

—*G. Washington.*

The company in which you will improve most will be least expensive to you.   —*Ibid.*

Concert fires people to a certain fury of performance they can rarely reach alone.   —*R. W. Emerson.*

There are many objects of great value to man which cannot be attained by unconnected individuals, but must be attained, if attained at all, by association.   —*Daniel Webster.*

ASSURANCE

In the assurance of strength there is strength.   —*C. N. Bovee.*

ATHEISM

I don't believe in God because I don't believe in Mother Goose.
—*Clarence Darrow.*

Thank Heaven, the female heart is untenantable by atheism.
—*Horace Mann.*

To wish there should be no God is to wish that the things which we love and strive to realize and make permanent, should be only temporary and doomed to frustration and destruction.

—*W. P. Montague.*

Atheism leads not to badness but only to an incurable sadness and loneliness.   —*Ibid.*

ATHEIST

Nobody talks so constantly about God as those who insist that there is no God.   —*Heywood Broun.*

The atheist has no hope.   —*J. F. Clarke.*

ATOMIC ENERGY

The fear that atomic energy will become a weapon of universal destruction rather than a tool of planetary health and prosperity is a realistic fear—indispensable; as a matter of fact, for the planning of new strategies to master the social and economic dangers of our day.   —*Joshua Loth Liebman.*

There will one day spring from the brain of science a machine or force so fearful in its potentialities, so absolutely terrifying, that even man, the fighter, who will dare torture and death in order

to inflict torture and death, will be appalled, and will abandon
war for ever.   *—Thomas A. Edison.*

ATTAINMENT

The rarest attainment is to grow old happily and gracefully.
     —L. M. Child.

ATTEMPT

We lose much by fearing to attempt.   *—J. N. Maffitt.*

ATTENTION

When you can do the common things of life in an uncommon
way you will command the attention of the world.
     —George W. Carver.

Attention is the stuff that memory is made of and memory
is accumulated genius.   *—J. R. Lowell.*

ATTENTIONS

When a girl marries she exchanges the attentions of many men
for the inattention of one.   *—Helen Rowland.*

AUTHOR

A great writer does not reveal himself here and there, but
everywhere.   *—J. R. Lowell.*

The worst intrusion I know is represented in the author who
forgets that you are only a reader, and starts to put on a show.
     —Wilson Mizner.

The Great Author of All made everything out of nothing, but
many a human author makes nothing out of everything.
     —G. D. Prentice.

The only happy author in this world is he who is below the
care of reputation.   *—Washington Irving.*

Authors must not, like Chinese soldiers, expect to win victories
by turning somersaults in the air.   *—H. W. Longfellow.*

A writer who attempts to live on the manufacture of his imagination is continually coquetting with starvation.   *—E. P. Whipple.*

The motives and purposes of authors are not always as pure and
high as, in the enthusiasm of youth, we sometimes imagine.
     —H. W. Longfellow.

A pin has as much head as some authors, and a good deal more
point.   *—G. D. Prentice.*

A writing man is something of a black sheep, like the village
fiddler.   —*E. W. Howe.*

AUTHORITY

Authority in all its modes, is the bond of the Commonwealth.
                                                —*G. E. Woodberry.*

All authority belongs to the people.   —*T. Jefferson.*

He who is firmly seated in authority soon learns to think security, and not progress, the highest lesson of statescraft.
                                                        —*J. R. Lowell.*

The encouragement and protection of the good subjects of any
state, and the suppression and punishment of bad ones, are the
principal objects for which all authority is instituted, and the line
in which it ought to operate.   —*T. Paine.*

The Deity has not given any order or family of men authority
over others, and if any men have given it they only could give it
for themselves.   —*Samuel Adams.*

AUTOCRACY

It is so common to point out the absurdity of conducting a war
for political democracy which leaves industrial and economic
autocracy practically untouched.   —*John Dewey.*

AUTOGRAPH

The most important autograph in a book is your own.
                                                —*Christopher Morley.*

AVAIL

What shall it avail a nation to save the whole of a miserable
trade and lose its liberties?   —*Henry Clay.*

AVARICE

What must be the wealth that avarice aided by power cannot
exhaust.   —*James Otis.*

A man sometimes covers up the entire disc of eternity with a
dollar.   —*E. H. Chapin.*

AVERAGE

We will not have great individuals or great leaders, but a great
average bulk, unprecedentedly great.   —*Walt Whitman.*

AVIATION

Armies do not protect against the aerial war.
                                            —*Alexander Graham Bell.*

B

BABIES

A babe is a mother's anchor. She cannot swing far from her moorings. —*H. W. Beecher.*

The vast majority of babies will have to put up with being born when their time comes, and make the best of it.
—*Agnes Repplier.*

Th' worst feature of a new baby is its mother's singing.
—*Kin Hubbard.*

BACHELOR

A bachelor gets tangled up with a lot of woman in order to avoid getting tied up to one. —*Helen Rowland.*

A bachelor never quite gets over the idea that he is a thing of beauty and a boy forever. —*Ibid.*

Never trust a husband too far, nor a bachelor too near. —*Ibid.*

A single man has not nearly the value he would have in a state of union. He is an incomplete animal. He resembles the odd half of a pair of scissors. —*B. Franklin.*

The only good husbands stay bachelors; they're too considerate to get married. —*F. P. Dunne.*

Bachelors know more about woman than married men; if they didn't, they'd be married too. —*H. L. Mencken.*

BAD

The bad man is the man who no matter how good he *has* been is beginning to deteriorate, to grow less good. —*John Dewey.*

A man is as good as he has to be, and a woman as bad as she dares. —*Elbert Hubbard.*

Except the Flood, nothing was ever as bad as reported.
                                                —*E. W. Howe.*

I am as bad as the worst but, thank God, I am as good as the best.   —*Walt Whitman.*

BAIT

The best bait for bedbugs is to sleep three in a bed.
                                                —*Josh Billings.*

BALD

Better a bald head than none at all.   —*Austin O'Malley.*

BALLADS

> Open my ears to music; let
>   Me thrill with Spring's first flutes and drums—
> But never let me dare forget
>   The bitter ballads of the slums.

                                                —*Louis Untermeyer.*

BALLOT

Among free men, there can be no successful appeal from the ballot to the bullet.   —*A. Lincoln.*

The ballot is stronger than the bullet.   —*Ibid.*

Ballots are the rightful and peaceful successors of bullets.
                                                —*Ibid.*

BANKER

A banker is a fellow who lends you his umbrella when the sun is shining and wants it back the minute it begins to rain.
                                                —*Mark Twain.*

BANKRUPTCY

One could always begin in America, even again and again. Bankruptcy, which in the fixed society of Europe was the tragic end of a career, might be merely a step in personal education.
                                                —*J. A. Krout.*

BANKS

Banking establishments are more dangerous than standing armies.   —*T. Jefferson.*

BAR

The difference between chirping out of turn and a faux pas depends on what kind of a bar you're in.   —*Wilson Mizner.*

BARGAIN

One of the difficult tasks in this world is to convince a woman that even a bargain costs money. —*E. W. Howe.*

Matrimony is a bargain, and somebody has to get the worst of the bargain. —*Helen Rowland.*

BARGAINING

Collective bargaining has become, with surprising swiftness, one of the greatest forces of our society. —*J. M. Clark.*

All government employees should realize that the process of collective bargaining as we understand it cannot be transplanted into the public service. —*F. D. Roosevelt.*

BASENESS

Blindness we may forgive, but baseness we will smite.
—*William Vaughn Moody.*

There is a law of neutralization of forces, which hinders bodies from sinking beyond a certain depth in the sea; but in the ocean of baseness, the deeper we get, the easier the sinking.
—*J. R. Lowell.*

BATTLE

The battle, sir, is not to the strong alone; it is to the vigilant, the active, the brave. —*Patrick Henry.*

Battle knows only three realities: enemy, rifle, life.
—*Edwin Rolfe.*

Recognize in your little fight against your avarice or your untruthfulness or your laziness, only one skirmish in that battle whose field covers the earth, and whose clamor rises and falls from age to age, but never wholly dies. —*Phillips Brooks.*

We have heard of men celebrating their country's battles who in war were celebrated for keeping out of them. —*G. D. Prentice.*

Don't fire until you see the whites of their eyes.
—*William Prescott.*

Battle . . . a method of untying with the teeth a political knot that would not yield to the tongue. —*Ambrose Bierce.*

BEASTS

We have learned to recognize emotional qualities in beasts we know, or know about. —*Agnes Repplier.*

We and the beasts are kin. Man has nothing that the animals have not at least a vestige of; the animals have nothing that man does not in some degree share.   —*E. T. Seton.*

Your people, sir—your people is a great *beast!*
                                                    —*Alexander Hamilton.*

BEAUTIFUL

Though we travel the world over to find the beautiful, we must carry it with us, or we find it not.   —*R. W. Emerson.*

The human heart yearns for the beautiful in all ranks of life.
                                                    —*H. B. Stowe.*

BEAUTY

Truth and beauty are but different faces of the same All.
                                                    —*R. W. Emerson.*

> He thought it happier to be dead,
> To die for beauty, than to live for bread.
>
> —*Ibid.*

Beauty is its own excuse for being.   —*Ibid.*

Not only does beauty fade, but it leaves a record upon the face as to what became of it.   —*Elbert Hubbard.*

The perception of beauty is a moral test.   —*H. D. Thoreau.*

There is in every creature a fountain of life, which, if not choked back by stones and other dead rubbish, will create a fresh atmosphere, and bring to life beauty.   —*Margaret Fuller.*

The beauty seen, is partly to him who sees it.   —*C. N. Bovee.*

No man receives the full culture of a man in whom the sensibility to the beautiful is not cherished.   —*W. E. Channing.*

Beauty is the mark God sets on virtue.   —*R. W. Emerson.*

The soul, by an instinct stronger than virtue, ever associates beauty with truth.   —*H. T. Tuckerman.*

Beauty is the index of a larger fact than wisdom.
                                                    —*O. W. Holmes.*

The good is always beautiful, the beautiful is good.
                                                    —*J. G. Whittier.*

Beauty is the wealth of the eye, and a cat may gaze upon a king.   —*Theodore Parker.*

Beauty is a pledge of the possible conformity between the soul

and nature, and consequently a ground of faith in the supremacy
of the good. —*George Santayana.*

Beauty intoxicates the eye, as wine does the body; both are
morally fatal if indulged. —*J. G. Saxe.*

Beauty, like truth and justice, lives within us; like virtue and like
moral law, it is a companion of the soul. —*George Bancroft.*

Fitness is so inseparable an accompaniment of beauty, that it
has been taken for it. —*R. W. Emerson.*

Beauty is the pilot of the young soul. —*Ibid.*

The best books have most beauty. —*W. E. Channing.*

In every man's heart there is a secret nerve that answers to
the vibrations of beauty. —*Christopher Morley.*

We are living in a world of beauty but how few of us open our
eyes to see it! —*Lorado Taft.*

The greatest truths are wronged if not linked with beauty.
—*W. E. Channing.*

Beauty is excrescence, superabundance, random ebullience, and
sheer delightful waste to be enjoyed in its own high right.
—*D. C. Peattie.*

Beauty is like a rainbow—full of promise but short-lived.
—*Josh Billings.*

Beauty without grace is the hook without the bait.
—*R. W. Emerson.*

Beauty in a woman's face, like sweetness in a woman's lips, is
a matter of taste. —*M. W. Little.*

BED

> Early to bed and early to rise,
> Makes a man healthy, wealthy, and wise.
>
> —*B. Franklin.*

No civilized person ever goes to bed the same day he gets up.
—*Richard Harding Davis.*

BEDFELLOWS

Civilization, like politics, makes strange bedfellows.
—*Charles A. Beard.*

BEE

No good sensible working bee listens to the advice of a bedbug
on the subject of business. —*Elbert Hubbard.*

A bee is never as busy as it seems; it's just that it can't buzz any slower. —*Kin Hubbard.*

BEGGAR

Beggar: one who has relied on the assistance of his friends.

—*Ambrose Bierce.*

BEHAVIOR

I don't say we all ought to misbehave, but we ought to look as if we could. —*Orson Welles.*

Behavior which appears superficially correct but is intrinsically corrupt always irritates those who see below the surface.

—*James Conant.*

The reason the way of the transgressor is hard is because it's so crowded. —*Kin Hubbard.*

Let us treat men and women well; treat them as if they were real; perhaps they are. —*R. W. Emerson.*

Woe to him who seeks to please rather than to appall!

—*Herman Melville.*

BELIEF

I believe in this damn mixed-up country of ours. In an odd way I'm in love with it. —*Sherwood Anderson.*

We are born believing. A man bears beliefs, as a tree bears apples. —*R. W. Emerson.*

I believe it is my duty to my country to love it, to support its Constitution, to obey its laws, to respect its flag and to defend it against all enemies. —*William T. Page.*

People believe only in the commonplace, that which they are accustomed to see. —*Robert L. Ripley.*

Go home and believe in yourselves more. —*Phillips Brooks.*

Our democracy in this country had its roots in religious belief, and we had to acknowledge soon after its birth that differences in religious belief are inherent in the spirit of true Democracy.

—*Eleanor Roosevelt.*

That belief which inspires a man to higher life, which moves him to trample down his besetting sins, to help his weaker brother, to rise into communion with God, is to him a Divine voice.

—*G. S. Merriam.*

We do not want cynicism, we want belief.

—*Sherwood Anderson.*

The use we make of mechanical instrumentalities is not due to these instruments alone but to their entanglement with a texture of beliefs and ideals that matured in a pre-industrial age.

—John Dewey.

When men think and believe in one set of symbols and act in ways which are contrary to their professed and conscious ideas, confusion and insincerity are bound to result. *—Ibid.*

A believing love will relieve us of a vast load of care.

—R. W. Emerson.

I do not believe today everything I believed yesterday; I wonder will I believe tomorrow everything I believe today.

—Isaac Goldberg.

When everyone begins to believe anything it ceases to be true; for example, the notion that the homeliest girl in the party is the safest. *—H. L. Mencken.*

A man is accepted into church for what he believes and he is turned out for what he knows. *—Mark Twain.*

Belief is not a matter of choice but of connection.

—R. G. Ingersoll.

Belief without evidence is what is told by one who speaks without knowledge, of things without parallel. *—Ambrose Bierce.*

It hurts more to have a belief pulled than to have a tooth pulled, and no intellectual novocain is available. *—Elmer Davis.*

BENEFACTOR

Benefactor: one who makes two smiles grow where one grew before. *—Chauncey Depew.*

BENEFICENCE

The tenure of power by man is, in the moral purposes of his Creator, upon condition that it shall be exercised to ends of beneficence, to improve the condition of himself and his fellow-men.

—John Q. Adams.

Money spent on ourselves may be a millstone about the neck; spent on others it may give us wings like eagles.

—R. D. Hitchcock.

BENEFITS

The benefit we receive must be rendered again line for line, deed for deed to somebody. Beware of too much good staying in thy hand. *—R. W. Emerson.*

He is great who confers the most benefits.   *—Ibid.*

BENEVOLENCE

Benevolence towards mankind excites wishes for their welfare, and such wishes endear the means of fulfilling them.

—John Dickinson.

A noble deed is a step towards heaven.   *—J. G. Holland.*

The lower a man descends in his love the higher he lifts his life.   *—W. R. Alger.*

Every charitable act is a stepping stone toward heaven.

—H. W. Beecher.

The higher mortal ought to mourn that it has thus far lived having helped so few with its friendship, having uttered so few cheering words to so few fainting spirits.   *—David Swing.*

No grace or blessing is truly ours till we are aware that God has blessed someone else with it through us.   *—Phillips Brooks.*

BEST

Early to bed and early to rise, and you'll meet very few of our best people.   *—George Ade.*

The best way out is always through.   *—Robert Frost.*

The best government rests on the people, and not on the few, on persons and not on property, on the free development of public opinion, and not on authority.   *—George Bancroft.*

It is a simple formula: do your best and somebody might like it.
—Dorothy Baker.

BEST-SELLER

A best-seller is the gilded tomb of a mediocre talent.

—Logan Pearsall Smith.

BET

The race is not always to the swift, nor the battle to the strong—but that's the way to bet.   *—Damon Runyon.*

BETTER

It is better no doubt to give crumbs than the loaf.

—Robinson Jeffers.

To be as good as our fathers we must be better.

—Wendell Phillips.

From every civilized part of the earth men have come to America in search of a better life. For centuries life promised more in the new world than in the old. —*V. F. Calverton.*

BIBLE

Hold fast to the Bible as the sheet-anchor of your liberties. Write its precepts in your hearts, and practise them in your lives.
—*U. S. Grant.*

If we abide by the principles taught by the Bible, our country will go on prospering. —*Daniel Webster.*

Sinful and sorrowing men have come to the Bible and have found the way of forgiveness and peace. —*Joshua Bloch.*

The Bible is one mighty representative of the whole spiritual life of humanity. —*Helen Keller.*

A knowledge of the Bible without a college course is more valuable than a college course without the Bible. —*W. L. Phelps.*

The Bible is a window in this prison-world, through which we may look into eternity. —*Timothy Dwight.*

A Bible and a newspaper in every house, a good school in every district—all studied and appreciated as they merit—are the principal support of virtue, morality and civil liberty.
—*B. Franklin.*

The inspiration of the Bible depends upon the ignorance of the gentleman who reads it. —*R. G. Ingersoll.*

It is impossible to mentally or socially enslave a Bible-reading people. The principles of the Bible are the groundwork of human freedom. —*Horace Greeley.*

BIBLES

Bibles and religions proceed out of the heart of man.
—*O. L. Triggs.*

BIG BUSINESS

We demand that big business give people a square deal.
—*Theodore Roosevelt.*

Somehow or other we shall have to work out methods of controlling the big corporation without paralyzing the energies of the business community. —*Ibid.*

Big Business is not dangerous because it is big, but because its bigness is an unwholesome inflation created by privilege and exemptions which it ought not to enjoy.   —*Woodrow Wilson.*

There is in every line of business a unit of greatest efficiency. The unit of greatest efficiency is reached when the disadvantages of size counterbalance the advantages.   —*Louis D. Brandeis.*

The corporation is undoubtedly of impressive size. But we must adhere to the law and the law does not make mere size an offense or the existence of power an offense.   —*Joseph McKenna.*

America can no more survive and grow without big business than it can survive and grow without small business.
                                                                —*Benjamin Franklin.*

There used to be a certain glamour about big things. Big things may be very bad and mean.   —*Louis D. Brandeis.*

Today it is not big business that we have to fear. It is big government.   —*Wendell L. Willkie.*

BIGOTRY

Bigotry is chronic dogmatism.   —*Horace Greeley.*
There is no bigotry like that of "free thought" run to seed.
                                                                        —*Ibid.*

Bigotry, intolerance, contempt, and spiritual pride are more fatal sins than sins of wild and passionate indulgence.
                                                                —*H. S. Bradley.*

Bigotry dwarfs the soul by shutting out the truth.
                                                                —*E. H. Chapin.*

All bigotries hang to one another.   —*T. Jefferson.*

BIGOTS

In totalitarian governments the bigots rule.   —*Lyman Bryson.*
Democracies do not put bigots in office.   —*Ibid.*

The mind of the bigot is like the pupil of the eye; the more light you pour upon it, the more it will contract.   —*O. W. Holmes.*

All are bigots who limit the divine within the boundaries of their present knowledge.   —*Margaret Fuller.*

BIOGRAPHY

One anecdote of a man is worth a volume of biography.
                                                                —*W. E. Channing.*

No department of literature is so false as biography.   —*Ibid.*

A life that is worth writing at all, is worth writing minutely and faithfully. *—H. W. Longfellow.*

Biography, especially of the great and good . . . is an inspiring and ennobling study. Its direct tendency is to reproduce the excellence it records. *—Horace Mann.*

Biography is an exit from history. It is only when a man is through with history that he thinks of writing his biography.

—Leon Samson.

There is properly no history, only biography. *—R. W. Emerson.*

Biography is the best form of history. *—H. W. Shaw.*

BIRDS

Every little bird that droops and dies in its nest falls as softly into God's hand as do His saints and martyrs. *—J. F. Clarke.*

The birds, God's poor who cannot wait. *—H. W. Longfellow.*

Hast thou named all the birds without a gun? *—R. W. Emerson.*

The bird that constructs its beautiful nest with nature's materials is greater than the wanton hand that destroys it, though less powerful. *—E. W. Wilcox.*

BIRTH

Why is it that we rejoice at a birth and grieve at a funeral? Is it because we are not the person concerned? *—Mark Twain.*

The only bird that gives the poor a real tumble is the stork.

—Wilson Mizner.

There is two things in this life for which we are never fully prepared, and that is—twins. *—Josh Billings.*

BIRTHDAYS

Marriage is the alliance of two people, one of whom never remembers birthdays and the other never forgets them.

—Ogden Nash.

BITTEN

A man bitten by a dog, no matter whether the animal is mad or not, is apt to get mad himself. *—G. D. Prentice.*

BLACKOUT

Western culture is covered by a blackout.

—P. A. Sorokin.

BLAME

When a man does all he can though he succeed not well, blame not him that did it. —*G. Washington.*

Every country tries to blame every other country for actions which they themselves might take if the situation were reversed.
  —*Jerome Davis.*

BLESSINGS

Possessing ourselves the combined blessing of liberty and order, we wish the same to other countries. —*T. Jefferson.*

Our blessings are the least heeded, because the most common events of life. —*Hosea Ballou.*

BLINDNESS

The only lightless dark in the night of darkness is ignorance and insensibility. —*Helen Keller.*

Those that think it permissible to tell white lies soon grow colorblind. —*Austin O'Malley.*

BLONDES

Gentlemen prefer blondes, but take what they can get.
  —*Don Herold.*

BLOOD

The best blood will at some time get into a fool or a mosquito.
  —*Austin O'Malley.*

Some men give their blood to their country; others their spleen.
  —*Gelett Burgess.*

Some kind of pace may be got out of the veriest jade by the near prospect of oats; but the thoroughbred has the spur in his blood.
  —*J. R. Lowell.*

BLUNDERS

Nature never makes any blunders; when she makes a fool she means it. —*Josh Billings.*

A blunder at the right moment is better than cleverness at the wrong time. —*Carolyn Wells.*

BLUSTERING

Blustering is the characteristic manners of cowardice.
  —*Edward Everett.*

The devil may be bullied, but not the Deity. —*W. R. Alger.*

BOARDINGHOUSE

It must be nice to run a boardinghouse and not have to worry about something different for dinner every day.   —*Kin Hubbard.*

BOASTING

Fools carry their daggers in their open mouths.   —*H. W. Shaw.*

BODY

No knowledge can be more satisfactory to a man than that of his own frame, its parts, their functions and actions.

—*T. Jefferson.*

If anything is sacred, the human body is sacred.

—*Walt Whitman.*

The body decays, but the soul continues to go onward and upward till the body drops from it and leaves it more alive than ever.   —*J. F. Clarke.*

God made the human body, and it is by far the most exquisite and wonderful organization which has come to us from the Divine hand.   —*H. W. Beecher.*

BOLONEY

No matter how thin you slice it, it's still boloney.

—*Alfred E. Smith.*

BOMB

The hydrogen bomb does not recognize national boundaries.

—*Brien McMahon.*

I do not believe that civilization will be wiped out in a war fought with the atomic bomb. Perhaps two-thirds of the people of the earth might be killed, but enough men capable of thinking, and enough books, would be left to start again, and civilization could be restored.   —*Albert Einstein.*

Work and status must be guaranteed to every child on earth because that lack of status and of security and the presence of joblessness and hunger can become the percussion cap on the atomic bombs of earth's destruction.   —*Joshua Loth Liebman.*

We human beings who can invent and produce such incredible machines of war can become and must become no less ingenious in social engineering to eliminate the economic fears in the hearts of men and women.   —*Ibid.*

BOND

There are two classes of persons whose word is as good as their bond: those whose word is never broken, and those whose bond is good for nothing. —*G. D. Prentice.*

BONDAGE

We would rather die on our feet than live on our knees.
—*F. D. Roosevelt.*

Familiarize yourselves with the chains of bondage and you prepare your own limbs to wear them. —*A. Lincoln.*

No body of men ever had the right to guarantee the holding of human beings in bondage. —*W. L. Garrison.*

BONE

Know your own bone; gnaw at it, bury it, unearth it, and gnaw at it still. —*H. D. Thoreau.*

BOOKS

To produce a mighty book, you must choose a mighty theme. No great and enduring volume can ever be written on the flea, though many there be that have tried it. —*Herman Melville.*

God be thanked for books. They are the voices of the distant and the dead, and make us heirs of the spiritual life of past ages.
—*W. E. Channing.*

A book is the only immortality. —*Rufus Choate.*

Camerade, this is no book.
Who touches this, touches a man.

—*Walt Whitman.*

For people who like that kind of a book, that is the kind of a book they will like. —*A. Lincoln.*

In the main, there are two sorts of books: those that no one reads and those that no one ought to read. —*H. L. Mencken.*

A war of ideas can no more be won without books than a naval war can be won without ships. —*F. D. Roosevelt.*

The books which help you most are those which make you think the most. —*Theodore Parker.*

Books must be read as deliberately and reservedly as they were written. —*H. D. Thoreau.*

Read the best books first, or you may not have the chance to read them at all.   *—Ibid.*

That is a good book which is opened with expectation and closed with profit.   *—A. B. Alcott.*

Books are not men and yet they are alive.   *—Stephen V. Benét.*

Society is a strong solution of books. It draws its virtue out of what is best worth reading, as hot water draws the strength of tea-leaves.   *—O. W. Holmes.*

A house is not home unless it contains food and fire for the mind as well as the body.   *—Margaret Fuller.*

Books are chiefly useful as they help us to interpret what we see and experience.   *—W. E. Channing.*

Books are the best things, well used; abused, among the worst.   *—R. W. Emerson.*

If we encounter a man of rare intellect, we should ask him what books he reads.   *—Ibid.*

We prize books, and they prize them most who are themselves wise.   *—Ibid.*

Many readers judge the power of a book by the shock it gives their feelings—as some savage tribes determine the power of muskets by their recoil; that being considered best which fairly prostrates the purchaser.   *—H. W. Longfellow.*

I would never read a book if it were possible for me to talk half an hour with the man who wrote it.   *—Woodrow Wilson.*

I cannot live without books.   *—T. Jefferson.*

BOOM

The starting of a boom by printing press techniques is the guarantee of the bust to follow.   *—Bradford Smith.*

BOOZE

Here we are in the midst of the greatest crisis since the Civil War and the only thing the two national parties seem to want to debate is booze.   *—John Dewey.*

BORE

The bore is the same eating dates under the cedars of Lebanon as over baked beans in Beacon Street.   *—O. W. Holmes.*

A bore is a man who spends so much time talking about himself that you can't talk about yourself.   *—M. D. Landon.*

All men are bores, except when we want them. —*O. W. Holmes.*

There are few wild beasts more to be dreaded than a communicative man having nothing to communicate.   —*C. N. Bovee.*

Bores are not to be got rid of except by rough means. They are to be scraped off like scales from a fish.   —*Ibid.*

Bore, n. A person who talks when you wish him to listen.

—*Ambrose Bierce.*

The basic fact about human existence is not that it is a tragedy, but that it is a bore.   —*H. L. Mencken.*

BORN

Poets are born, not paid.   —*Addison Mizner.*

BORROWING

If you would know the value of money, go try to borrow some; for he that goes a-borrowing goes a-sorrowing.   —*B. Franklin.*

Th' feller that calls you "brother" generally wants something that don't belong to him.   —*Kin Hubbard.*

Let us all be happy and live within our means, even if we have to borrow the money to do it with.   —*Artemus Ward.*

Never call a man a fool; borrow from him.   —*Addison Mizner.*

Getting into debt is getting into a tanglesome net. —*B. Franklin.*

Lots of fellows think a home is only good to borrow money on.

—*Kin Hubbard.*

BOSS

The boss has the courage of the brute, or he would not be boss; but when it comes to a moral issue he is the biggest coward in the lot. The bigger the brute the more abject its terror at what it does not understand.   —*Jacob Riis.*

The American government is a rule of the people, by the people, for the boss.   —*Austin O'Malley.*

More powerful than all the success slogans ever penned by human hand is the realization for every man that he has but one boss. That boss is the man—he—himself.   —*Gabriel Heatter.*

BOSTON

You may know a Boston man by two traits . . . he thinks he knows and he thinks he is right.   —*G. E. Woodberry.*

And this is good old Boston,
The home of the bean and the cod,
Where the Lowells talk to the Cabots,
And the Cabots talk only to God.
                                    —*J. C. Bossidy.*

BOTTLES

What is home without a hot-water bottle?   —*Don Herold.*

Many social visits you think paid to yourself are paid to your bottles.   —*Austin O'Malley.*

BOUNDARIES

Sooner or later every man finds his boundaries.   —*H. E. Fosdick.*

BOY

A boy is Truth with dirt on its face, Beauty with a cut on its finger.   —*Allan Beck.*

A boy is a magical creature—you can lock him out of your workshop, but you can't lock him out of your heart.   —*Ibid.*

Men die by millions now, because God blunders,
Yet to have made this boy He must be wise.

                                    —*Sara Teasdale.*

There is nothing so aggravating as a fresh boy who is too old to ignore and too young to kick.   —*Kin Hubbard.*

One of the best things in the world to be is a boy; it requires no experience, but needs some practice to be a good one.
                                    —*C. D. Warner.*

A boy has a natural genius for combining business with pleasure.
                                    —*Ibid.*

You can take a boy out of the country but you can't take the country out of a boy.   —*Arthur ("Bugs") Baer.*

Boys will be boys, and so will a lot of middle-aged men.

                                    —*Kin Hubbard.*

The fact that boys are allowed to exist at all is evidence of a remarkable Christian forbearance among men.   —*Ambrose Bierce.*

BRAG

Cunning egotism: if I cannot brag of knowing something, then I brag of not knowing it; at any rate, brag.   —*R. W. Emerson.*

BRAIN

Brain: the apparatus with which we think we think.
—*Ambrose Bierce.*

The brain is a wonderful organ; it starts working the moment you get up in the morning, and does not stop until you get into the office.   —*Robert Frost.*

It is astonishing what an effort it seems to be for many people to put their brains definitely and systematically to work. They seem to insist on somebody else doing their thinking for them.
—*Thomas A. Edison.*

BRAVE

None but the brave can live with the fair.   —*Kin Hubbard.*
None but the brave desert the fair.   —*Addison Mizner.*

BRAVERY

At the bottom of not a little of the bravery that appears in the world, there lurks a miserable cowardice. Men will face powder and steel because they have not the courage to face public opinion.
—*E. H. Chapin.*

BREAD

Three things must a man possess if his soul would live . . . Bread, Beauty and Brotherhood.   —*Edwin Markham.*

If you can't get half a loaf take a whole one—a whole loaf is better than no bread.   —*Josh Billings.*

Were we directed from Washington when to sow, and when to reap, we should soon want bread.   —*T. Jefferson.*

We in America especially cannot live by bread alone precisely because we have too much bread, and too much bread kills the spirit.   —*H. M. Kallen.*

BREAKDOWN

Maladjustment to the new tempo (of American life) is reaching the point of possible breakdown.   —*James Truslow Adams.*

BREAKFAST

Never work before breakfast; if you have to work before breakfast, get your breakfast first.   —*Josh Billings.*

BREEDING

Good breeding consists in concealing how much we think of ourselves and how little we think of the other person.
—*Mark Twain.*

Good breeding requires time, application, and expense, and can therefore not be compassed by those whose time and energy are taken up with work. *—Thorstein Veblen.*

BREVITY

As man is now constituted, to be brief is almost a condition of being inspired. *—George Santayana.*

Brevity is the soul of lingerie. *—Dorothy Parker.*

The wisdom of nations lies in their proverbs, which are brief and pithy. *—Wm. Penn.*

The one prudence in life is concentration. *—R. W. Emerson.*

You may get a large amount of truth into a brief space.
—H. W. Beecher.

Brevity and conciseness are the parents of correction.
—Hosea Ballou.

Never be so brief as to become obscure. *—Tryon Edwards.*

BRIBERY

Not the politician, not the bribe-taker, but the bribe-giver, the man we are too proud of, our successful business man—he is the source of sustenance of bad government. *—Lincoln Steffens.*

The taking of a bribe or gratuity should be punished with as severe penalties as the defrauding of the state. *—Wm. Penn.*

Not only do both bribe-givers and bribe-takers rot down, but their innocent families are destroyed by the leprosy that comes from tainted dollars. *—John P. Altgeld.*

BRIDGE

I say banish bridge; let's find some pleasanter way of being miserable together. *—Don Herold.*

BROAD-MINDEDNESS

Broad-mindedness is the result of flattening high-mindedness out.
—George Santayana.

BROADWAY

Broadway is a main artery of New York life—the hardened artery.
—Walter Winchell.

BROKE

Next to a city the loneliest place in the world when you're broke is among relatives. *—Kin Hubbard.*

BROTHERHOOD

Brotherhood is not just a Bible word. Out of comradeship can come and will come the happy life for all.   —*Heywood Broun.*

Blow, bugles; blow—not for the unknown dead, but for the plain and palpable brotherhood of life.   —*Ibid.*

Humanity cannot go forward, civilization cannot advance, except as the philosophy of force is replaced by that of human brotherhood.   —*F. B. Sayre.*

Grant us brotherhood, not only for this day but for all our years —a brotherhood not of words but of acts and needs.

—*Stephen V. Benét.*

The need of the human race is for a World International Team.

—*Basil Mathews.*

While there is a lower class I am in it. While there is a criminal class I am of it. While there is a soul in prison I am not free.

—*E. V. Debs.*

> The crest and crowning of all good,
> Life's final star, is Brotherhood.

—*Edwin Markham.*

If civilization is to survive, we must cultivate the science of human relationships—the ability of all peoples, of all kinds, to live together, in the same world at peace.   —*F. D. Roosevelt.*

BUDGET

The modern governmental budget is, and must be, the balance wheel of the economy.   —*Douglas Abbott.*

BUILDING

Our building may fall, but if we have built aright, some of the foundation stones will remain and become part of the structure that will ultimately abide.   —*Dwight Morrow.*

If we build with wisdom, and with courage, and with patience, those that come after us will be helped by our work.   —*Ibid.*

BULLFIGHT

It is impossible to believe the emotional and spiritual intensity and pure, classic beauty that can be produced by a man, an animal, and a piece of scarlet serge draped over a stick.

—*Ernest Hemingway.*

BURDEN

I would rather have a big burden and a strong back, than a weak back and a caddy to carry life's luggage.   —*Elbert Hubbard.*

BUREAUCRACY

The moment responsibilities of any community, particularly in economics and social questions, are shifted from any part of the nation to Washington, then that community has subjected itself to a remote bureaucracy. It has lost a large part of its voice in the control of its own destiny.   —*H. C. Hoover.*

The proposal is frequently made that the government ought to assume the risks that are "too great for private industry." This means that bureaucrats should be permitted to take risks with the tax-payers' money that no one is willing to take with his own.

—*Henry Hazlitt.*

BURLESQUE

Burlesque is the guerilla weapon of political warfare.

—*Horace Greeley.*

Burlesque is often most telling and often most unfair; stimulated by want of a juster argument.   —*W. R. Alger.*

Burlesque—the keenest of political weapons.

—*Wm. Cullen Bryant.*

BUSINESS

The business of America is business.   —*Calvin Coolidge.*

Business is religion and religion is business.   —*M. Babcock.*

There are two times in a man's life when he should not speculate: when he can't afford it, and when he can.   —*Mark Twain.*

The fundamental principle which governs the handling of postage stamps and of millions of dollars is the same.   —*F. D. Armour.*

Anybody can cut prices, but it takes brains to produce a better article.   —*Ibid.*

A man's success in business today turns upon his power of getting people to believe that he has something that they want. —*G. S. Lee.*

It is not the crook in modern business that we fear, but the honest man who does not know what he is doing.

—*Owen D. Young.*

The way to stop financial "joy-riding" is to arrest the chauffeur, not the automobile.   —*Woodrow Wilson.*

The best investment a young man starting out in business could possibly make is to give all his time, all his energies to work, just plain, hard work.   —*C. M. Schwab.*

The government is a tyrant living by theft, and therefore has no business to engage in any business.   —*Benj. R. Tucker.*

Christmas is over and Business is Business.   —*F. P. Adams.*

Business will be either better or worse.   —*Calvin Coolidge.*

The man who is above his business may one day find his business above him.   —*Daniel Drew.*

Small business is the biggest business of them all. —*J. E. Murray.*

If small business goes, big business does not have any future except to become the economic arm of a totalitarian state.
                                                                      —*P. D. Reed.*

The man who talks business at home is in danger of getting well-meant but risky advice.   —*H. H. Vreeland.*

What is everybody's business is nobody's business—except the journalist's.   —*Joseph Pulitzer.*

Drive thy Business, let not that drive thee.   —*B. Franklin.*

It is very easy to manage our neighbor's business, but our own sometimes bothers us.   —*Josh Billings.*

No man knows where his business ends and his neighbor's begins
                                                                    —*E. W. Howe.*

No business is above Government; and Government must be empowered to deal adequately with any business that tries to rise above Government.   —*F. D. Roosevelt.*

BUSINESSMEN

The man who is employed for wages is as much a businessman as his employer.   —*W. J. Bryan.*

The business ability of the man at the head of any business concern, big or little, is usually the factor which fixes the gulf between striking success and hopeless failure. —*Theodore Roosevelt.*

Men on the inside of business know how business is conducted.
                                                                —*Woodrow Wilson.*

One of the rarest phenomena is a really pessimistic businessman.
                                                                   —*Miriam Beard.*

Most are engaged in business the greater part of their lives, because the soul abhors a vacuum and they have not discovered any continuous employment for man's nobler faculties.

—H. D. Thoreau.

BUSY

A really busy person never knows how much he weighs.

—E. W. Howe.

The successful people are the ones who can think up things for the rest of the world to keep busy at.   *—Don Marquis.*

BUSYBODIES

Busy souls have no time to be busybodies.   *—Austin O'Malley.*

BUY

It makes no difference what it is, a woman will buy anything.she thinks a store is losing money on.   *—Kin Hubbard.*

C

CALAMITY

Calamities are of two kinds: misfortune to ourselves, and good fortune to others. —*Ambrose Bierce.*

I never knew a man to be drowned who was worth the saving. —*Ibid.*

CALUMNY

To persevere in one's duty and to be silent is the best answer to calumny. —*G. Washington.*

Calumny is a vice of curious constitution; trying to kill it keeps it alive; leave it to itself and it will die a natural death. —*T. Paine.*

I laid it down as a law to myself, to take no notice of the thousand calumnies issued against me, but to trust my character to my own conduct, and the good sense and candor of my fellow citizens. —*T. Jefferson.*

CALVINISM

There is no system which equals Calvinism in intensifying, to the last degree, ideas of moral excellence and purity of character. It has always worked for liberty. —*H. W. Beecher.*

The promulgation of Calvin's theology was one of the longest steps that mankind has taken towards personal freedom. —*John Fiske.*

He who will not respect the influence of Calvin knows but little of the origin of American independence. —*George Bancroft.*

I have read the fathers, and the schoolmen, and Calvin too: but I find that he that has Calvin has them all. —*John Cotton.*

The ethical rigor of Calvinism and the sect ideal which animated American church life in its pioneer days have combined to produce a temper of ethical activism in American Protestantism of particularly robust quality. —*R. Niebuhr.*

Calvinism with its central tenet of the corruption of the natural is one of the most dangerous of the central superstitions of mankind. —*Ludwig Lewisohn.*

The central difficulty of a Calvinistic business civilization (is) its inability to integrate experience, which it despised, with creative expression. —*Ibid.*

CANT

Cant is the twin sister of hypocrisy. —*H. W. Beecher.*

Cant is good to provoke common sense. —*R. W. Emerson.*

CAPITAL

Capital is that part of wealth which is devoted to obtaining further wealth. —*Alfred Marshall.*

Capital is condensed labor. It is nothing till labor takes hold of it. —*David Swing.*

Capital still pats Labor on the back—with an ax. —*F. P. Dunne.*

From the first institution of government to the present time there has been a struggle going on between capital and labor for a fair distribution of profits resulting from their joint capacities. —*Martin Van Buren.*

Today, in order to provide customers for business, your Government uses Government capital to provide jobs, to prevent farm prices from collapsing and to build up purchasing power when private capital fails to do it. —*F. D. Roosevelt.*

Capital must be free in order that people may be free. —*N. B. Gaskill.*

When capital is brought under government control, people are brought under control also, their activity is limited and their development depends . . . on the purposes of economic dictatorship. —*Ibid.*

A dollar invested in industry by the government . . . carries with it a threat of government dictation or outright nationalization of the industry in which it is invested. —*J. H. McGraw, Jr.*

The accumulation of capital is not harmful to society; the harm lies rather in the fact that capital serves the interests of a few. —*Joseph Wedemeyer.*

Capital is a result of labor, and is used by labor to assist it in further production. Labor is the active and initial force and labor is therefore the employer of capital. —*Henry George.*

We cannot destroy the capital supply—whether by taxation or by other ill-advised policies designed to redistribute the wealth . . . without paying the piper. —*Carl Snyder.*

Labor is prior to, and independent of, capital. —*A. Lincoln.*

Capital is only the fruit of labor, and could never have existed if labor had not first existed. —*Ibid.*

Labor is the superior of capital, and deserves much the higher consideration. —*Ibid.*

CAPITALISM

Capitalism here has moved from outpost to outpost, much in the manner that the utopians have conceived that socialism would.

—*Leon Samson.*

A few men that own capital hire a few others, and these establish the relation of capital and labor rightfully. —*A. Lincoln.*

Capitalism is dying and its extremities are already decomposing. The blotches upon the surface show that the blood no longer circulates. The time is near when the cadaver will have to be removed and the atmosphere purified. —*E. V. Debs.*

The dynamo of our economic system is self-interest which may range from mere petty greed to admirable types of self-expression.
—*Felix Frankfurter.*

What we mean when we say we are for or against capitalism is that we like or dislike a certain civilization or scheme of life.
—*J. A. Schumpeter.*

The fundamental idea of modern capitalism is not the right of the individual to possess and enjoy what he has earned, but the thesis that the exercise of this right redounds to the general good.
—*R. B. Perry.*

Our capitalism in the '80's and '90's was a buccaneer capitalism, and our labor leaders during the formative years of the American Federation of Labor were primitive tribal chieftains, each craft a tribe, who fought back with desperate guerilla tactics.

—*Benjamin Stolberg.*

It is quite conceivable today, as it was not when capitalism began, that production and distribution could be carried on at least as well if all the legal owners should be buried in an earth-quake. —*George Soule.*

Capitalism cannot be rejuvenated. Its sanctions have been destroyed. Its loyalties are daily more anti-social and unlovely. Its institutions grow steadily weaker save as they acquire the feverish strength of fascism. —*Norman Thomas.*

CAPITALIST

The hated capitalist is simply a mediator, the prophet, the adjustor according to his divination of the future desire.

—*O. W. Holmes, Jr.*

If you are looking for a Moses to lead you out of the capitalist wilderness, you will stay right where you are.

—*E. V. Debs.*

The American worker is merely a capitalist without money.

—*George Sokolsky.*

CARDS

There are no friends at cards or world politics. —*F. P. Dunne.*

CAREER

An artist's career always begins tomorrow. —*J. M. Whistler.*

Democracy has its great career for the first time in our national being, and exhibits here most purely its formative powers, and unfolds destiny on the grand scale. —*G. E. Woodberry.*

CARELESSNESS

Carelessness does more harm than a want of knowledge.

—*B. Franklin.*

For want of a nail the shoe was lost; for want of a shoe the horse was lost; and for want of a horse the rider was lost, being overtaken and slain by the enemy; and all for want of care about a horseshoe nail. —*Ibid.*

CARES

Cares are only cravings of that immortal hunger which the swine's food of earthly things cannot satisfy. —*Horace Bushnell.*

Our cares are the mothers, not only of our charities and virtues, but of our best joys and most cheering and enduring pleasures.

—*W. G. Simms.*

The night shall be filled with music
And the cares that infest the day
Shall fold their tents like the Arabs,
And silently steal away.

—*H. W. Longfellow.*

CASUISTRY
Casuistry is useful for purposes of defense, and a skillful apologist can explain away much.   —*V. L. Parrington.*

CAT
The cat, having sat upon a hot stove lid, will not sit upon a hot stove lid again. Nor upon a cold stove lid.   —*Mark Twain.*

CAUSALITY
Our lives are haunted by a Georgia slattern, because a London cutpurse went unhung.   —*Thomas Wolfe.*

We have penetrated far less deeply into the regularities obtaining within the realm of living things, but deeply enough nevertheless to sense at least the rule of fixed necessity.

—*Albert Einstein.*

CAUSE
The probability that we may fail in the struggle ought not to deter us from the support of a cause we believe to be just.

—*A. Lincoln.*

No cause can command the deepest loyalties and the greatest sacrifices of men till it is presented under a moral aspect.

—*Arthur M. Schlesinger, Sr.*

Christian Science explains all cause and effects as mental, not physical.   —*Mary Baker Eddy.*

That cause is strong, which has not a multitude but a strong man behind it.   —*J. R. Lowell.*

We are tired of great causes.   —*F. Scott Fitzgerald.*

Ours is an abiding faith in the cause of human freedom. We know it is God's cause.   —*Thomas E. Dewey.*

I am permitted to die for a cause, not merely to pay the debt of nature—as all must.   —*John Brown.*

CAUTION
Little boats should keep near shore.   —*B. Franklin.*

Put all thine eggs in the one basket and—watch that basket.
—*Mark Twain.*

Caution, though very often wasted, is a good risk to take.
—*H. W. Shaw.*

CENSORSHIP

Damn all expurgated books, the dirtiest book of all is the expurgated book. —*Walt Whitman.*

Pontius Pilate was the first great censor and Jesus Christ the first great victim of censorship. —*Ben Lindsay.*

He is always the severest censor of the merit of others who has the least worth of his own. —*E. L. Magoon.*

Every burned book enlightens the world. —*R. W. Emerson.*

I am mortified to be told, in the United States of America, the sale of a book can become a subject of inquiry, and of criminal inquiry too. —*T. Jefferson.*

I have sworn upon the altar of God eternal hostility against every form of tyranny over the mind of man. —*Ibid.*

I am opposed to censorship. Censors are pretty sure to be fools. I have no confidence in the suppression of every-day facts.
—*James Harvey Robinson.*

CERTITUDE

Certitude is not the test of certainty. We have been cocksure of many things that were not so. —*O. W. Holmes, Jr.*

CHANCE

Those who trust to chance must abide by the results of chance. They have no legitimate complaint against anyone but themselves.
—*Calvin Coolidge.*

We are not at the mercy of any wave of chance.
—*R. W. Emerson.*

Young man, sit down and keep still; you will have plenty of chances yet to make a fool of yourself before you die.
—*Josh Billings.*

CHANGE

Action and reaction, ebb and flow, trial and error, change—this is the rhythm of living. Out of our over-confidence, fear; out of our fear, clearer vision, fresh hope. And out of hope—progress.
—*Bruce Barton.*

The world hates change, yet it is the only thing that has brought progress.   —*C. F. Kettering.*

What we can do is to get new mental images. We can do that. We can move out into better spiritual relationships until we are changed.   —*H. E. Fosdick.*

All things must change to something new, to something strange.
                                                              —*H. W. Longfellow.*

Revolutions are not made; they come.   —*Wendell Phillips.*

We cannot save this world without changing it.
                                                              —*H. E. Fosdick.*

We cannot save our economic system without changing it.
                                                              —*Ibid.*

We cannot save ourselves without being changed.   —*Ibid.*

Change is the password of growing states.   —*G. E. Woodberry.*

Our age was destined to experience a decisive change . . . the revival of religious wars in the form of warfare between political ideologies, with the concomitant torture, punishment, and extermination of the dissenters.   —*Hans J. Morgenthau.*

The problem is not whether business will survive in competition with business, but whether any business will survive at all in the face of social change.   —*L. J. McGinley.*

Change of heart is no more redemption than hunger is dinner. We must have honesty, love, justice in the heart of the business world, but for these we must also have the (institutional) forms which will fit them.   —*H. D. Lloyd.*

Whether social change is fast or lazy, whether it is achieved by violence or by Fabian reform, it leads forward, but never quite up to the perfect system or the perfect state.   —*Lyman Bryson.*

There is a certain relief in change, even though it be from bad to worse; as I have found in traveling in a stage-coach, that it is often a comfort to shift one's position and be bruised in a new place.   —*Washington Irving.*

CHARACTER

Make the most of yourself, for that is all there is of you.
                                                              —*R. W. Emerson.*

A character is like an acrostic—read it forward, backward, or across, it still spells the same thing.   —*Ibid.*

Character is that which can do without success. —*Ibid.*

Character is what you are in the dark. —*D. L. Moody.*

Some lives are like an ebbing tide in a harbor; the farther they go out, the more mud they expose. —*Austin O'Malley.*

Character is much easier kept than recovered. —*T. Paine.*

How can we expect a harvest of thought who have not had a seed-time of character? —*H. D. Thoreau.*

Character is a by-product; it is produced in the great manufacture of daily duty. —*Woodrow Wilson.*

The principal advantage of a democracy is a general elevation in the character of the people. —*James F. Cooper.*

There never has been a great and beautiful character which has not become so by filling well the ordinary and smaller offices appointed of God. —*Horace Bushnell.*

The world thinks more of condition than of character. —*Ibid.*

In our barbarous society the influence of character is in its infancy. —*R. W. Emerson.*

Character is what God and the angels know of us; reputation is what men and women think of us. —*Horace Mann.*

Character lives in a man, reputation outside of him.
—*J. G. Holland.*

Character is the spiritual body of the person. —*E. P. Whipple.*

A man's character is the reality of himself. —*H. W. Beecher.*

The character inherent in the American people has done all that has been accomplished; and it would have done something more, if the government had not sometimes got in its way.
—*H. D. Thoreau.*

Grandeur of character lies wholly in force of soul, in the force of thought, moral principles, and love, and this may be found in the humblest conditions of life. —*W. E. Channing.*

The finest qualities of our characters do not come from trying but from that mysterious and yet most effective capacity to be inspired. —*H. E. Fosdick.*

Many people have character who have nothing else.
—*Don Herold.*

The great hope of society is individual character.
—*W. E. Channing.*

In this world a man must either be anvil or hammer.
—H. W. Longfellow.

It is by presence of mind in untried emergencies that the native metal of a man is tested. *—J. R. Lowell.*

The true greatness of a nation is in those qualities which constitute the greatness of the individual. *—Charles Sumner.*

The Napoleonic test of character is success, and the final test of success is permanence. *—Austin Phelps.*

The grand aim of man's creation is the development of a grand character. *—Ibid.*

Grand character is, by its very nature, the product of probationary discipline. *—Ibid.*

We boil at different degrees. *—R. W. Emerson.*

Character is moral order seen through the medium of an individual nature. *—Ibid.*

Never does a man portray his own character more vividly than in his manner of portraying another's. *—Ibid.*

Character shows itself apart from genius as a special thing. The first point of measurement of any man is that of quality.
—J. W. Higginson.

Character is the basis of happiness and happiness the sanction of character. *—George Santayana.*

CHARITY

Charity: a thing that begins at home, and usually stays there.
—Elbert Hubbard.

With malice toward none, with charity for all, with firmness in the right as God gives us to see the right, let us finish the work we are in. *—A. Lincoln.*

> Behold, I do not give lectures or a little charity,
> When I give I give myself.
>
> *—Walt Whitman.*

Knowledge puffeth up, charity buildeth up; one makes a balloon of us, the other a temple. *—Horace Bushnell.*

Take egotism out, and you would castrate the benefactors.
—R. W. Emerson.

Charity uncovers a multitude of sins.   —*Carolyn Wells.*

Every charitable act is a stepping stone towards heaven.

—*H. W. Beecher.*

Charity may even be used as a means for administering a sop to one's social conscience while at the same time it buys off the resentment which might otherwise grow up in those who suffer from social injustice.   —*John Dewey.*

Hope is all right and so is Faith, but what I would like to see is a little Charity.   —*Don Marquis.*

A bone to the dog is not charity. Charity is the bone shared with the dog, when you are just as hungry as the dog.

—*Jack London.*

In charity to all mankind, bearing no malice or ill-will to any human being, and even compassionating those who hold in bondage their fellow-men, not knowing what they do.

—*John Q. Adams.*

CHASTITY

Female virtue is like a tender and delicate flower; let but the breath of suspicion rest upon it, and it withers and perhaps perishes forever.   —*Andrew Jackson.*

A man defines his standing at the court of chastity by his views of women.   —*A. B. Alcott.*

CHEATING

Nobody loves to be really cheated, but it does seem as though everyone is anxious to see how near he could come to it.

—*Josh Billings.*

We know that there are chiselers. At the bottom of every case of criticism and obstruction we have found some selfish interest, some private axe to grind.   —*F. D. Roosevelt.*

Don't steal; thou'lt never thus compete
Successfully in business. Cheat.

—*Ambrose Bierce.*

Three things are men most likely to be cheated in: a horse, a wig, and a wife.   —*B. Franklin.*

CHEERFULNESS

Cheer up, the worst is yet to come.   —*Philander Johnson.*

Let us be of good cheer, remembering that the misfortunes hardest to bear are those which never happen.   —*J. R. Lowell.*

The true source of cheerfulness is benevolence.   —*P. Godwin.*

God is glorified, not by our groans, but by our thanksgivings.
—*E. P. Whipple.*

CHILDREN

A child is a beam of sunlight from the Infinite and Eternal, with possibilities of virtue and vice—but as yet unstained.
—*Lyman Abbott.*

A child's education should begin at least one hundred years before he is born.   —*O. W. Holmes.*

The schools of democracy should be concerned to give each child opportunity to express himself in that kind of purposeful functioning which is mind.   —*John L. Childs.*

It must be a hard life to be the child of a psychologist.
—*Tom Masson.*

Many children, many cares; no children, no felicity.
—*C. N. Bovee.*

Children are God's apostles, sent forth, day by day, to preach of love, and hope, and peace.   —*J. R. Lowell.*

You cannot teach a child to take care of himself unless you will let him take care of himself. He will make mistakes, and out of these mistakes will come his wisdom.   —*H. W. Beecher.*

The mistakes of children are often better than their no-mistakes.
—*Ibid.*

It's a wise child that owes his own father.   —*Carolyn Wells.*

Your little child is your only true democrat.   —*H. B. Stowe.*

The children of today will be the architects of our country's destiny in 1900.   —*James A. Garfield.*

A torn jacket is soon mended; but bad words bruise the heart of a child.   —*H. W. Longfellow.*

The potential possibilities of any child are the most intriguing and stimulating in all creation.   —*Ray L. Wilbur.*

We are the children of our age, but children who can never know their mother.   —*Logan Pearsall Smith.*

Men are generally more careful of their horses and dogs than of their children.   —*Wm. Penn.*

Children have one great advantage. Eventually they will grow up and sometime even they will learn better.   —*H. W. Van Loon.*

Better to be driven out from among men than to be disliked of children.   —*R. H. Dana.*

Teach your child to hold his tongue; he'll learn fast enough to speak.   —*B. Franklin.*

Imitate little children and trust.   —*O. L. Frothingham.*

There is little use to talk about your child to anyone; other people either have one or haven't.   —*Don Herold.*

Be gentle in old age; peevishness is worse in second childhood than in first.   —*G. D. Prentice.*

Our children are delivered to schools in automobiles. But whether that adds to their grades is doubtful.   —*Will Rogers.*

Don't take up a man's time talking about the smartness of your children; he wants to talk to you about the smartness of his children.   —*E. W. Howe.*

Pretty much all the honest truthtelling there is in the world is done by children.   —*O. W. Holmes.*

Again, many possessions, if they do not make a man better, are at least expected to make his children happier; and this pathetic hope is behind many exertions.   —*George Santayana.*

CHOICE

When you have to make a choice and don't make it, that is in itself a choice.   —*William James.*

God offers to every mind its choice between truth and repose.   —*R. W. Emerson.*

Remember that nature makes every man love all women, and trusts the trivial matter of special choice to the commonest accident.   —*O. W. Holmes.*

Of two evils choose the prettier.   —*Carolyn Wells.*

Follow then thy choice.   —*Wm. Cullen Bryant.*

He who chooses the beginning of a road chooses the place it leads to. It is the means that determine the end.   —*H. E. Fosdick.*

CHRIST

Everyone in the world is Christ and they are all crucified.
—*Sherwood Anderson.*

Jesus Christ, the condescension of divinity, and the exaltation of humanity.   —*Phillips Brooks.*

The idea of Christ is much older than Christianity.
                                                    —*George Santayana.*

There was a God before Christ.   —*Dagobert D. Runes.*

CHRISTIAN

Every Stoic was a Stoic; but in Christendom, where is the Christian?   —*R. W. Emerson.*

Christians and camels receive their burdens kneeling.
                                                    —*Ambrose Bierce.*

A Christian is like a locomotive: a fire must be kindled in the heart of the thing before it will go.   —*M. W. Jacobus.*

A Christian is nothing but a sinful man who has put himself to school to Christ for the honest purpose of becoming better.
                                                    —*H. W. Beecher.*

Christians never were meant to be respectable.   —*H. E. Fosdick.*

I have only two comforts to live upon. The one is the perfection of Christ; the other is the imperfection of all Christians.
                                                    —*Nathaniel Ward.*

To be like Christ is to be a Christian.   —*Wm. Penn.*

Whatever makes men good Christians, makes them good citizens.
                                                    —*Daniel Webster.*

To become a Christian in the early days was to step out of caste, to reject conventional standards, to put oneself in opposition to the prevailing customs of the social order, to sever both intimate and public ties which bound one to the world.   —*C. C. Morrison.*

To become a Christian was to court disrepute, to be numbered with those whom society held suspect and even despised.   —*Ibid.*

To become a Christian is, for us, the most respectable act a man can perform. It involves no slightest loss of caste. The convert loses nothing. He risks nothing. He gains every point.   —*Ibid.*

CHRISTIANITY

Christianity is a battle, not a dream.   —*Wendell Phillips.*

He who shall introduce into public affairs the principle of primitive Christianity will revolutionize the world.   —*B. Franklin.*

Christianity is a life, not a creed; a spirit, not a form.
                                                    —*C. L. Goodell*

Christianity won't work long in our day. The organization of society is against it.   —*Lincoln Steffens.*

Bear witness, O Thou strong and merciful One,
That earth's most hateful crimes have in Thy name
been done.   —*J. G. Whittier.*

CHRISTIAN SCIENCE

Christian Science reveals incontrovertibly that Mind is All-in-all, that the only realities are the divine Mind and idea.
—*Mary Baker Eddy.*

CHRISTMAS

No Santa Claus! Thank God, he lives, and he lives forever.
—*Francis P. Church.*

Blow, bugles of battle, the marches of peace.   —*J. G. Whittier.*

CHURCH

A church is a place in which gentlemen who have never been to heaven brag about it to persons who will never get there.
—*H. L. Mencken.*

It takes *men,* not a creed, to make a church.   —*C. B. McAfee.*

To prove that a church was needed for a medieval system of society does not prove that it is needed for ours.
—*Kenneth Burke.*

The Christian culture has been all but absorbed into the body of our secular culture, retaining no ethical marks to distinguish it. The church is actually patronized by the social order as a means of stabilizing and perpetuating the existing system.
—*C. C. Morrison.*

The church must assert its own ethical autonomy.   —*Ibid.*

In vain is church and prayer. In vain is praise and form, if it does not inspire an *enthusiasm* for humanity, if it does not inspire a love of men shown in *justice, righteousness,* and *service.*
—*Lyman Abbott.*

More people would go to church if they hadn't observed what sanctity had done for the dull deacons.   —*Wilson Mizner.*

If you have a church, judge your own church by this standard: does this help toward the coming of the universal community?
—*Josiah Royce.*

CIGAR

What this country needs is a good five cent cigar.
                                                    —*Thomas R. Marshall.*

Our country has plenty of good five-cent cigars, but the trouble is they charge fifteen cents for them.   —*Will Rogers.*

More than one cigar at a time is excessive smoking.
                                                    —*Mark Twain.*

CIRCUMSTANCES

A man is what the winds and tide have made him.   —*Jim Tully.*

The same wind that carries one vessel into port may blow another off shore.   —*C. N. Bovee.*

Circumstances alter faces.   —*Carolyn Wells.*

CIRCUS

If a circus is half as good as it smells, it's a great show.
                                                    —*Fred Allen.*

The first one to catch a circus in a lie is a boy.
                                                    —*Kin Hubbard.*

CITIES

Cities have always been the fireplaces of civilization, whence light and heat radiated out into the dark. —*Theodore Parker.*

The thing generally raised on city land is taxes.
                                                    —*C. D. Warner.*

A great city is that which has the greatest men and women.
                                                    —*Walt Whitman.*

The great cities rest upon our broad and fertile prairies.
                                                    —*W. J. Bryan.*

City life: millions of people being lonesome together.
                                                    —*H. D. Thoreau.*

Cities make men talkative and entertaining, but they make them artificial.   —*R. W. Emerson.*

I always seem to suffer some loss of faith on entering cities.
                                                    —*Ibid.*

CITIZENS

Let us at all times remember that all American citizens are brothers of a common country, and should dwell together in bonds of fraternal feeling.   —*A. Lincoln.*

The largeness of nature or the nation were monstrous without a corresponding largeness and generosity of spirit of the citizen.
—Walt Whitman.

If you will help run our government in the American way, then there will never be danger of our government running America in the wrong way. *—Omar N. Bradley.*

If once the people become inattentive to the public affairs, you and I and Congress and Assemblies, Judges and Governors, shall all become wolves. *—T. Jefferson.*

If destruction be our lot we must ourselves be its author and finisher. As a nation of freemen we must live through all time, or die by suicide. *—A. Lincoln.*

Every citizen owes to the country a vigilant watch and close scrutiny of its public servants and a fair and reasonable estimate of their fidelity and usefulness. *—Grover Cleveland.*

The typical business-man is a bad citizen; he is busy . . . He is the one that has no use and therefore no time for politics.
—Lincoln Steffens.

In a government bottomed on the will of all, the liberty of every individual citizen becomes interesting to all. *—T. Jefferson.*

The first requisite of a good citizen in this republic of ours is that he should be able and willing to pull his weight.
—Theodore Roosevelt.

The constitution does not provide for first and second class citizens. *—Wendell L. Willkie.*

The humblest citizen of all the land, when clad in the armor of a righteous cause is stronger than all the hosts of Error.
—W. J. Bryan.

What keeps a republic on its legs, is good citizenship.
—Mark Twain.

The power of citizenship is relinquished by those who have a livelihood to make, to those who make politics their livelihood.
—H. D. Lloyd.

In this country of ours the man who has not raised himself to be a soldier, and the woman who has not raised her boy to be a soldier for the right—neither one of them is entitled to citizenship in the Republic. *—Theodore Roosevelt.*

CITY LIFE

City life: millions of people being lonesome together.

—*H. D. Thoreau.*

CIVILITY

The highest proof of civility is that the whole public action of the State is directed on securing the greatest good of the greatest number.   —*R. W. Emerson.*

If a civil word or two will render a man happy, he must be a wretch, indeed, who will not give them to him.   —*Wm. Penn.*

CIVILIZATION

Civilization is order and freedom promoting cultural activity.

—*Will Durant.*

Civilization begins with order, grows with liberty and dies with chaos.   —*Ibid.*

A living civilization requires learning, but it lies beyond it.

—*A. N. Whitehead.*

The true test of civilization is, not the census, nor the size of the cities, nor the crops, but the kind of man that the country turns out.   —*R. W. Emerson.*

A sufficient and sure method of civilization is the influence of good women.   —*Ibid.*

We must succeed in providing a rational co-ordination of impulses and thoughts, or for centuries civilization will sink into a mere welter of minor excitements.   —*A. N. Whitehead.*

Civilization is more of the heart than of the mind.

—*David Swing.*

Civilization is not a burden. It is an opportunity.

—*A. Meiklejohn.*

The end of the human race will be that it will eventually die of civilization.   —*R. W. Emerson.*

I think it probable that civilization somehow will last as long as I care to look ahead—perhaps with smaller numbers, but perhaps also bred to greatness and splendor by science.

—*O. W. Holmes, Jr.*

Like human behavior, civilization is made and not born. Like life itself, it must be nourished day by day, ceaselessly, with new energy and new materials, or it sickens and dies.

—*Charles A. Dorsey.*

Less race phobia, more intelligent understanding of the nature of civilization. —*Ibid.*

No true civilization can be expected permanently to continue which is not based on the great principles of Christianity.
—*Tryon Edwards.*

Civilization is a constant quest for non-violent means of solving conflicts; it is a common quest for peace. —*Max Ascoli.*

Civilization is sitting awkwardly on a volcano. The clash between the pretenses and the practises is so vividly real as to be patent even to the dullest mind. —*Samuel D. Schmalhausen.*

Civilization is a hideous thing. Blessed is savagery.
—*Lafcadio Hearn.*

The path of civilization is paved with tin cans.
—*Elbert Hubbard.*

Civilization, or that which is so called, has operated two ways to make one part of society more affluent and the other part more wretched than would have been the lot of either in natural state.
—*T. Paine.*

We think our civilization near its meridian, but we are yet only at the cock-crowing and the morning star. —*R. W. Emerson.*

Unless man has the wit and the grit to build his civilization on something better than material power, it is surely idle to talk plans for a stable peace. —*F. B. Sayre.*

CIVILIZED

To be a civilized man in America is measurably less difficult . . . than it used to be, say, in 1890. —*H. L. Mencken.*

CLASSES

No matter what class of society you may select from—taking a corresponding number from each—the individuals from all classes will be equal in their native capacity for knowledge.
—*Lester Ward.*

Other lands have their vitality in a few, a class, but we have it in the bulk of our people. —*Walt Whitman.*

I will not have the laborer sacrificed to my convenience and pride, nor to that of a great class of such as me. —*R. W. Emerson.*

Those who hold and those who are without property have ever formed distinct interests in society. —*James Madison.*

A landed interest, a manufacturing interest, with many lesser interests, grow up of necessity into different classes, actuated by different sentiments and views.   *—Ibid.*

Class and group divisions based on property lie at the basis of modern governments; and politics and constitutional law are inevitably a reflex of these contending interests.

—Charles A. Beard.

The rise of a new governing class is always synonymous with a social revolution and a redistribution of property.

—Charles A. Madison.

The real danger of democracy is, that the classes which have the power under it will assume all the rights and reject all the duties—that is, that they will use the political power to plunder those who have.   *—W. G. Sumner.*

There are only two classes of men who live in history: those who crowd a thing to its extreme limit, and those who then arise and cry, "Hold!"   *—Elbert Hubbard.*

We do not intend that this Republic should ever fail as those republics of the olden times failed, in which there finally came to be a government by classes, which resulted either in the poor plundering the rich or in the rich . . . exploiting the poor.

—Theodore Roosevelt.

The distinctions separating the social classes are false; in the last analysis they rest on force.   *—Albert Einstein.*

The dominant classes . . . must perforce obtain from the government such rules as are consonant with the larger interests necessary to the continuance of their economic processes, or they must themselves control the organs of government.   *—Charles A. Beard.*

The mass of mankind has not been born with saddles on their backs, nor a favored few booted and spurred, ready to ride them legitimately, by the grace of God.   *—T. Jefferson.*

The innocent class are always the victim of the few; they are in all countries and at all times the inferior agents, and must toil, and bleed and are always sure of meeting with oppression and rebuke. It is for the sake of the great leaders on both sides that so much blood must be spilt; that of the people is counted as nothing.   *—Hector St. Jean de Crèvecoeur.*

All communities divide themselves into the few and the many. The first are the rich and well-born, the other the mass of the people.   —*Alexander Hamilton.*

It is as unjust to require that men of refinement and training should defer in their habits and associations to the notions of those who are their inferiors in these particulars, as it is to insist that political power should be the accompaniment of birth.

                —*James F. Cooper.*

CLASSIC

A classic is something that everybody wants to have read and nobody wants to read.   —*Mark Twain.*

CLEANLINESS

Clean your finger before you point at my spots.   —*B. Franklin.*

Who would appear clean, must be clean all through.

                —*Alice Cary.*

We've a country, and we've made it, and we're going to keep it clean.   —*J. K. Bangs.*

Above all things, keep clean. It is not necessary to be a pig in order to raise one.   —*R. G. Ingersoll.*

Tolerate no uncleanliness in body, clothes, or habitation.

                —*B. Franklin.*

CLEMENCY

Look upon the errors of others in sorrow, not in anger.

                —*H. W. Longfellow.*

Levity will operate with greater force, in some instances, than rigor.   —*G. Washington.*

CLERGYMAN

Clergyman: a ticket speculator outside the gates of heaven.

                —*H. L. Mencken.*

If you would lift me you must be on a higher ground.

                —*R. W. Emerson.*

As a career, the business of an orthodox preacher is about as successful as that of a celluloid dog chasing an asbestos cat through Hell.   —*Elbert Hubbard.*

A congregation who can't afford to pay a clergyman enough want a missionary more than they do a clergyman.

                —*Josh Billings.*

A clergyman is a man who undertakes the management of our spiritual affairs as a method of bettering his temporal ones.

—*Ambrose Bierce.*

Perfect obedience to the moral law would abolish clergymen.

—*O. B. Frothingham.*

The clergy have not been ethical innovators.

—*James Harvey Robinson.*

CLOTHES

Do not conceive that fine clothes make fine men, anymore than fine feathers make fine birds.   —*G. Washington.*

If thou art clean and warm it is sufficient, for more doth but rob the poor and please the wanton.   —*Wm. Penn.*

COERCION

Millions of innocent men, women and children since the introduction of Christianity, have been burned, tortured, fined and imprisoned, yet we have not advanced one inch toward uniformity. What has been the effect of coercion? To make one-half of the world fools and the other half hypocrites.   —*T. Jefferson.*

Experience has taught us that men will not adopt and carry into execution measures the best calculated for their own good without the intervention of a coercive power.   —*G. Washington.*

COLLEGE

Some men are graduated from college cum laude, some are graduated summa cum laude, and some are graduated mirabile dictu.   —*Wm. Howard Taft.*

You can lead a boy to college but you cannot make him think.

—*Elbert Hubbard.*

COMFORTS

The comforts of life, at the rate they are increasing, bid fair to buy us soon.   —*Edward S. Martin.*

Most of the luxuries, and many of the so-called comforts, of life are not only not indispensable, but positive hindrances to the elevation of mankind.   —*H. D. Thoreau.*

COMMAND

No man is fit to command another that cannot command himself.   —*Wm. Penn.*

COMMERCE

Commerce links all mankind in one common brotherhood of mutual dependence and interests. *—James A. Garfield.*

The only type of economic structure in which government is free and in which the human spirit is free is one in which commerce is free. *—Thurman Arnold.*

Perfect freedom is as necessary to the health and vigor of commerce, as it is to the health and vigor of citizenship.

—Patrick Henry.

The hope of commercial gain has done nearly as much for the cause of truth as even the love of truth itself. *—C. N. Bovee.*

Commerce defies every wind, outrides every tempest, and invades every zone. *—George Bancroft.*

Commerce is entitled to a complete and efficient protection in all its legal rights, but the moment it presumes to control a country, or to substitute its fluctuating expedients for the high principles of natural justice that ought to lie at the root of every political system, it should be frowned on, and rebuked.

—James F. Cooper.

The selfish spirit of commerce knows no country, and feels no passion or principle but that of gain. *—T. Jefferson.*

COMMITTEE

If you want to kill any idea in the world today, get a committee working on it. *—C. F. Kettering.*

COMMON SENSE

Common sense is very uncommon. *—Horace Greeley.*

Common sense is instinct, and enough of it is genius.

—H. W. Shaw.

Common sense is the knack of seeing things as they are, and doing things as they ought to be done. *—Ibid.*

COMMUNISM

Communism means barbarism. *—J. R. Lowell.*

Bolshevism is a menace to absentee ownership. That is its unpardonable sin. *—Thorstein Veblen.*

Bolshevism . . . is the sin against the Holy Ghost of established Law and Order. *—Ibid.*

The communism of combined wealth and capital, the outgrowth of overweening cupidity and selfishness which assiduously undermines the justice and integrity of free institutions, is not less dangerous than the communism of oppressed poverty and toil which, exasperated by injustice and discontent, attacks with wild disorder the citadel of misrule.   *—Grover Cleveland.*

Were it possible to have a community of property, it would soon be found that no one would toil, but that men would be disposed to be satisfied with barely enough for the supply of their physical wants, since none would exert themselves to obtain advantages solely for the use of others.   *—James F. Cooper.*

COMPANY

Associate yourself with men of good quality if you esteem your own reputation; for 'tis better to be alone than in bad company.
    —G. Washington.

I have three chairs in my house: one for solitude, two for friendship, three for company.   *—H. D. Thoreau.*

A holding company is a thing where you hand an accomplice the goods while the policeman searches you.   *—Will Rogers.*

Misery loves company, but company does not reciprocate.
    —Addison Mizner.

The man who lives by himself and for himself is apt to be corrupted by the company he keeps.   *—C. H. Parkhurst.*

COMPASSION

The mind is no match with the heart in persuasion; constitutionality is no match with compassion.
    —E. M. Dirksen.

Far from being a handicap to command, compassion is the measure of it. For unless one values the lives of his soldiers and is tormented by their ordeals, he is unfit to command.
    —Omar N. Bradley.

COMPENSATION

Evermore in the world is this marvellous balance of beauty and disgust, magnificence and rats.   *—R. W. Emerson.*

Curses always recoil on the head of him who imprecates them. If you put a chain around the neck of a slave, the other end fastens itself around your own.   *—Ibid.*

Earth gets its price for what earth gives us, the beggar is taxed for a corner to die in; the priest has his fee who comes and shrives us, we bargain for the graves we lie in. *—J. R. Lowell.*

If the poor man cannot always get meat, the rich man cannot always digest it. *—Henry Giles.*

No success can be a compensation for the wound inflicted on a nation's mind by renouncing right as the Supreme Law.

—W. E. Channing.

COMPETITION

Anybody can win unless there happens to be a second entry.
—George Ade.

The only competition worthy of a wise man is with himself.
—Washington Allston.

Do unto the other feller the way he'd like to do unto you an' do it fust. *—E. N. Westcott.*

We believe in competition, in the excitement of conflict and the testing of man against man in a fair fight. *—Felix Frankfurter.*

I am firmly opposed to the Government entering into any business the major purpose of which is competition with our citizens.
—Herbert Hoover.

Our present competitive system is as necessary, as firmly founded in experience, as our system of eating three meals a day.

—E. W. Howe.

The tides of economic life are sweeping us on towards socialization. The competitive system is breaking down. *—Kirby Page.*

Competition should not extend to fields where it has demonstrably bad social and economic consequences. The exploitation of child labor, the chiseling of workers' wages, the stretching of workers' hours, are not necessary, fair, or proper methods of competition. *—F. D. Roosevelt.*

The idea of imposing restrictions on a free economy to assure freedom of competition is like breaking a man's leg to make him run faster. *—M. R. Sayre.*

Competition is the keen cutting edge of business, always shaving away at costs. *—Henry Ford II.*

Competition comes in place of monopoly; and intelligence and industry ask only for fair play and an open field.

—Daniel Webster.

Of all human powers operating on the affairs of mankind, none is greater than that of competition.   —*Henry Clay.*

Without competition, we would be clinging to the clumsy and antiquated processes of farming and manufacture and the methods of business of long ago, and the twentieth would be no further advanced than the eighteenth century.   —*William McKinley.*

The purpose of our competitive system . . . is to maintain that degree of competition which induces progress and protects the consumer.   —*Herbert Hoover.*

Every implement or utensil, every mechanical device is a triumph of mind over the physical forces of nature in ceaseless and aimless competition.   —*Lester Ward.*

Competition enslaves, monopoly liberates. We must, therefore, have the greatest possible monopoly, one that includes the whole people economically as they are now included politically.

—*W. D. Howells.*

Competitors continually seek to limit competition and to obtain for themselves some measure of monopoly power.

—*Dewey Anderson.*

The very notion of competition assumes monopoly, in the sense that what we get the rest cannot get.   —*H. P. Fairchild.*

There could be no adequate civilization, no Christianity, until cooperation had displaced competition, and men were become equal in economic rights as they were in franchise rights.

—*V. L. Parrington.*

The carpenter or plumber or painter, the butcher or baker or candlestick maker who would naturally prosper is he who does the same work better than his competitors.   —*H. M. Kallen.*

The best of truth is the power of the thought to get itself accepted in the competition of the market.   —*O. W. Holmes, Jr.*

Competition is the very life of science.   —*H. M. Kallen.*

COMPLAINING

The wheel that squeaks the loudest is the one that gets the grease.   —*Josh Billings.*

Constant complaint is the poorest sort of pay for all the comforts we enjoy.   —*B. Franklin.*

Married men live longer than single men, or at least they complain more about it.   —*Don Herold.*

COMPLIMENTS

Some people pay a compliment as if they expected a receipt.
—Kin Hubbard.

I can live for two months on a good compliment.
—Mark Twain.

When you cannot get a compliment in any other way, pay yourself one. *—Ibid.*

To compliment often implies an assumption of superiority in the complimenter. It is, in fact, a subtle detraction.
—H. D. Thoreau.

When a man makes a woman his wife, it's the highest compliment he can pay her, and it's usually the last. *—Helen Rowland.*

COMPROMISE

Compromise is but the sacrifice of one right or good in the hope of retaining another, too often ending in the loss of both.
—Tryon Edwards.

It is the weak man who urges compromise—never the strong man. *—Elbert Hubbard.*

> From compromise and things half done,
> Keep me with stern and stubborn pride;
> And when at last the fight is won,
> God, keep me still unsatisfied.
>
> *—Louis Untermeyer.*

Compromise makes a good umbrella, but a poor roof; it is temporary expedient, often wise in party politics, almost sure to be unwise in statesmanship. *—J. R. Lowell.*

It is time to . . . revive the devoted patriotism and spirit of compromise which distinguished the sages of the Revolution and the fathers of our Union. *—Andrew Jackson.*

From the beginning of our history the country has been afflicted with compromise. It is by compromise that human rights have been abandoned. *—Charles Sumner.*

I insist that this (compromise) shall cease. The country needs repose after all its trials; it deserves repose. And repose can only be found in everlasting principles. *—Ibid.*

CONCEIT

Conceit is God's gift to little men. *—Bruce Barton.*

The average man plays to the gallery of his own self-esteem.
                                                —*Elbert Hubbard.*

And so we plough along, as the fly said to the ox.
                                                —*H. W. Longfellow.*

Conceited men often seem a harmless kind of men, who, by an overweening self-respect, relieve others from the duty of respecting them at all.   —*H. W. Beecher.*

He that falls in love with himself will have no rival.
                                                —*B. Franklin.*

Truly, this world can get on without us, if we would but think so.   —*H. W. Longfellow.*

A man—poet or prophet or whatever he may be—readily persuades himself of his right to all the worship that is voluntarily tendered.   —*Nathaniel Hawthorne.*

Solitude is almost the only condition in which the acorn of conceit can grow to the oak of perfect self-delusion.
                                                —*E. P. Whipple.*

Conceit is to human character what salt is to the ocean: it keeps it sweet and renders it endurable.   —*O. W. Holmes.*

Most men are like eggs, too full of themselves to hold anything else.   —*Josh Billings.*

When some men discharge an obligation, you can hear the report for miles around.   —*Mark Twain.*

CONDUCT

The ultimate test for us of what a truth means is the conduct it dictates or inspires.   —*William James.*

The force that rules the world is conduct, whether it be moral or immoral.   —*N. M. Butler.*

Great is the conduct of a man who lets rewards take care of themselves—come if they will or fail to come—but goes on his way, true to the truth simply because it is true, strongly loyal to the right for its pure righteousness.   —*Phillips Brooks.*

Come not near the books or writings of any one so as to read them unasked.   —*G. Washington.*

Every action in company ought to be some sign of respect to those present.   —*Ibid.*

Life is not so short but that there is always time for courtesy.
—*R. W. Emerson.*

Speak not when others speak. —*G. Washington.*

When another speaks be attentive yourself, and disturb not the audience. —*Ibid.*

It is a dear and lovely disposition and a most valuable one,— that can brush away indignities and discourtesies and seek and find the pleasanter features of an experience. —*Mark Twain.*

A good musical comedy consists largely of disorderly conduct occasionally interrupted by talk. —*George Ade.*

Where the routine is rigorously prescribed by law, the law, and not the man, must have the credit of the conduct.
—*William H. Prescott.*

The supreme rule of life, both individual and collective, must be that utterance of Jesus which is truly the foundation stone of liberty and civilization: "Therefore, all things whatsoever ye would that men should do to you do ye even so to them."
—*Harold L. Ickes.*

CONFERENCE

The United States never lost a war or won a conference.
—*Will Rogers.*

A conference is a gathering of important people who singly can do nothing, but together can decide that nothing can be done.
—*Fred Allen.*

CONFESSION

When a woman writes her confessions she is never further from the truth. —*J. G. Huneker.*

It is the duty of nations as well as of men to confess their sins and transgressions in humble sorrow, yet with assured hope that genuine repentance will lead to mercy and pardon. —*A. Lincoln.*

CONFIDENCE

All you need in this life is ignorance and confidence, and then success is sure. —*Mark Twain.*

If you once forfeit the confidence of your fellow-citizens, you can never regain their respect and esteem. —*A. Lincoln.*

Be courteous to all, but intimate with few; and let those few be well tried before you give them your confidence.
—*G. Washington.*

Only trust thyself, and another shall not betray thee.
                                                         —*Wm. Penn.*

A man can be too confiding in others, but never too confident
in himself.   —*H. H. Vreeland.*

Confidence . . . thrives only on honesty, on honor, on the sacredness of obligations, on faithful protection and on unselfish performance. Without them it cannot live.   —*F. D. Roosevelt.*

Trust men and they will be true to you; treat them greatly
and they will show themselves great.   —*R. W. Emerson.*

Disregard the old maxim "Do not get others to do what you
can do yourself." My motto is, do not do that which others can
do as well.   —*Booker T. Washington.*

Fields are won by those who believe in winning.
                                                       —*J. W. Higginson.*

Confidence is a thing not to be produced by compulsion. Men
cannot be forced into trust.   —*Daniel Webster.*

CONFORMITY

Singularity in the right hath ruined many; happy those who
are convinced of the general opinion.   —*B. Franklin.*

CONGRESS

Some members of Congress would best promote the country's
peace by holding their own.   —*G. D. Prentice.*

There are two periods when Congress does no business: one
is before the holidays, and the other after.   —*Ibid.*

I never lack material for my humor column when Congress is
in session.   —*Will Rogers.*

It could probably be shown by facts and figures that there is
no distinctly native American criminal class except Congress.
                                                       —*Mark Twain.*

Every man in it is a great man, an orator, a critic, a statesman;
and therefore every man upon every question must show his oratory, his criticism, and his political abilities.   —*John Adams.*

Fleas can be taught nearly everything that a Congressman can.
                                                       —*Mark Twain.*

Some statesmen go to congress and some go to jail. It is the
same thing after all.   —*Eugene Field.*

With Congress, every time they make a joke it's a law, and every time they make a law it's a joke.   —*Will Rogers.*

I took the Canal Zone and let Congress debate, and while the debate goes on the canal does too.   —*Theodore Roosevelt.*

CONQUEST

The more acquisitions the government makes abroad, the more taxes the people have to pay at home.   —*T. Paine.*

Amalgamations by conquest have always brought agony to the conquered. There lies our danger.   —*Brooks Adams.*

If there be one principle more deeply rooted than any other in the mind of every American, it is that we should have nothing to do with conquest.   —*T. Jefferson.*

CONSCIENCE

Courage without conscience is a wild beast.   —*R. G. Ingersoll.*

Religions are the great fairy tales of the conscience.

—*George Santayana.*

Labor hard to keep alive in your breast that little spark of celestial fire called conscience.   —*G. Washington.*

Civilization is simply applied conscience, and Progress is a widening conscience.   —*H. D. Lloyd.*

A guilty conscience is the mother of invention.

—*Carolyn Wells.*

The world stands or falls with the laws of life which Heaven has written in the human conscience.   —*Pierre Van Paassen.*

Conscience is God's viceregent on earth, . . . a divine voice in the human soul.   —*Francis Bowen.*

A good conscience is a continual Christmas.   —*B. Franklin.*

We never do evil so thoroughly and heartily as when led to it by an honest but perverted, because mistaken, conscience.

—*Tryon Edwards.*

Conscience tells us that we ought to do right, but it does not tell us what right is—that we are taught by God's word.

—*H. C. Trumbull.*

A disciplined conscience is a man's best friend. It may not be his most amiable, but it is his most faithful monitor.

—*Austin Phelps.*

Good-nature is the harmonious act of conscience.

—*H. W. Beecher.*

When a government takes the life of a man without the consent of his conscience, it is an audacious government, and is taking a step towards its own dissolution.   —*H. D. Thoreau.*

A conscience void of offense, before God and man, is an inheritance for eternity.   —*Daniel Webster.*

It is far more important to me to preserve an unblemished conscience than to compass any object however great.
—*W. E. Channing.*

'Tis the business of little minds to shrink; but he whose heart is firm, and whose conscience approves his conduct, will pursue his principles unto death.   —*T. Paine.*

What we call conscience, in many instances, is only a wholesome fear of the constable.   —*C. N. Bovee.*

What dungeon is so dark as one's own heart? What jailer so inexorable as one's self?   —*Nathaniel Hawthorne.*

Conscience is the mirror of our souls, which represents the errors of our lives in their full shape.   —*George Bancroft.*

Men of character are the conscience of the society to which they belong.   —*R. W. Emerson.*

These have been men whom no power in the universe could turn from the right, by whom death in its most dreadful forms has been less dreadful than transgression of the inward law.
—*W. E. Channing.*

Conscience: an inner voice that warns us somebody is looking.
—*H. L. Mencken.*

If you would sleep soundly, take a clear conscience to bed with you.   —*B. Franklin.*

You may bend conscience to your dealings, but the Ten Commandments will not budge.   —*J. R. Lowell.*

The doctrine of persecution for cause of conscience is proved guilty of all the blood of the souls crying for vengeance under the altar.   —*Roger Williams.*

It is the will and command of God that (since the coming of his Son, the Lord Jesus) a permission of the most paganish, Jewish, Turkish or Antichristian consciences and worships be granted to all men in all nations and countries.   —*Ibid.*

Driven from every corner of the earth, freedom of thought and the right of private judgment in matters of conscience direct their course to this happy country as their last asylum.

—Samuel Adams.

Churches come and go, but there has ever been but one religion. The only religion is conscience in action. *—H. D. Lloyd.*

The church of the social conscience will be a church that will not only preach Christ but do Christ. *—Ibid.*

Man's conscience is the supreme judge of what is true or false, good or evil. A person who lives professing a belief he does not hold has lost the only true, the only immutable thing—his conscience. *—Dagobert D. Runes.*

The moral sense, or conscience, is as much a part of man as his leg or arm. It is given to all human beings in a stronger or weaker degree, as force of members is given them in a greater or less degree. *—T. Jefferson.*

We are bound, you, I, and every one, to make common cause, even with error itself, to maintain the common right of freedom of conscience. *—Ibid.*

The most miserable pettifogging in the world is that of a man in the court of his own conscience. *—H. W. Beecher.*

I desire so to conduct the affairs of this administration that if at the end, when I come to lay down the reins of power, I have lost every other friend on earth, I shall at least have one friend left, and that friend shall be down inside me. *—A. Lincoln.*

Government being, among other purposes, instituted to protect the consciences of men from oppression, it certainly is the duty of rulers, not only to abstain from it themselves but, according to their stations, to prevent it in others. *—G. Washington.*

CONSECRATION

. . . The world will little note, nor long remember, what we say here, but it can never forget what they did here. *—A. Lincoln.*

CONSERVATION

Conservation means the wise use of the earth and its resources for the lasting good of men. *—Gifford Pinchot.*

World-wide practice of Conservation and the fair and continued access by all nations to the resources they need are the two indis-

pensable foundations of continuous plenty and of permanent peace.
—Ibid.

CONSERVATISM

There is always a certain meanness in the argument of conservatism, joined with a certain superiority in its fact.
—R. W. Emerson.

What is conservatism? Is it not adherence to the old and tried, against the new and untried? *—A. Lincoln.*

Conservatism is the maintenance of conventions already in force.
—Thorstein Veblen.

A conservative is a statesman who is enamored of existing evils, as distinguished from the Liberal, who wishes to replace them with others. *—Ambrose Bierce.*

A conservative is a man with two perfectly good legs who, however, has never learned to walk. *—F. D. Roosevelt.*

Religion is the source of both radicalism and conservatism.
—R. Niebuhr.

Men are conservative after dinner. *—R. W. Emerson.*

Men are conservative when they are least vigorous, or when they are most luxurious. *—Ibid.*

A conservative is a man who is too cowardly to fight and too fat to run. *—Elbert Hubbard.*

No man can be a conservative until he has something to lose.
—James P. Warburg.

A conservative is a man who just sits and thinks, mostly sits.
—Woodrow Wilson.

We have conservatives enough. *—W. E. Channing.*

CONSISTENCY

A foolish consistency is the hobgoblin of little minds, adored by little statesmen and philosophers and divines.
—R. W. Emerson.

With consistency great souls have nothing to do. *—Ibid.*
Don't be consistent but be simply true. *—Ibid.*

Victorious living can be consistent with occasional failure.
—E. S. Jones.

Civilizations are never made up of wholly consistent parts.
—Lyman Bryson.

We feel something like respect for consistency even in error.

—*T. Paine.*

Do I contradict myself? Very well then I contradict myself. (I am large, I contain multitudes).　　　　—*Walt Whitman.*

CONSTITUTION

Man is more than constitution.　　　　—*J. G. Whittier.*

Constitutions should consist only of general provisions; the reason is that they must necessarily be permanent, and that they cannot calculate for the possible change of things.

—*Alexander Hamilton.*

We are under a Constitution, but the Constitution is what the judges say it is.　　　　—*Charles Evans Hughes.*

In questions of power let no more be heard of confidence in man, but bind him down from mischief by the chains of the constitution.　　　　—*T. Jefferson.*

Liberty under the Constitution is necessarily subject to the restraints of due process.　　　　—*Ibid.*

Our Constitution professedly rests upon the good sense and attachment of the people. This basis, weak as it may appear, has not yet been found to fail.　　　　—*John Q. Adams.*

Our Constitution is so simple and practical that it is possible always to meet extraordinary needs by changes in emphasis and arrangement without loss of essential form. —*F. D. Roosevelt.*

There is a higher law than the Constitution.　—*W. H. Seward.*

The constitution is not a mere lawyer's document; it is a vehicle of life, and its spirit is always the spirit of the age.

—*Woodrow Wilson.*

Not the Constitution but free land, and an abundance of natural resources open to a fit people, made the democratic type of society in America for three centuries.　　　　—*F. J. Turner.*

The Constitution is the supreme law of the land ordained and established by the people. All legislation must conform to the principles it lays down.　　　　—*Pierce Butler.*

I consider the foundation of the Constitution as laid on this ground—that all powers not delegated to the United States, by the Constitution, nor prohibited by it to the states, are reserved to the states, or to the people. To take a single step beyond . . . is to take possession of a boundless field of power.　—*T. Jefferson.*

A Constitution is not intended to embody a particular economic theory, whether of paternalism and the organic relation of the citizen to the state or laissez faire.   —*O. W. Holmes, Jr.*

The basis of our political system is the right of the people to make or alter their Constitution of government.
                                                           —*G. Washington.*

Let the end be legitimate, let it be within the scope of the Constitution, and all means which are appropriate, which are plainly adapted to that end, which are not prohibited, but consist with the letter and spirit of the Constitution, are constitutional.
                                                           —*John Marshall.*

The Constitution was essentially an economic document based upon the concept that the fundamental rights of private property are anterior to government and morally beyond the reach of popular majorities.
                                                           —*Charles H. Beard.*

The basis of our political systems is the right of the people to make and to alter their constitutions of government. But the constitution which at any time exists, until changed by an explicit and authentic act of the whole people, is sacredly obligatory upon all.
                                                           —*G. Washington.*

A constitution is a thing antecedent to a government, and a government is only the creature of a constitution. The constitution of a country is not the act of its government, but of the people constituting a government.
                                                           —*T. Paine.*

CONSULT

Consult: to seek another's approval of a course already decided on.
                                                           —*Ambrose Bierce.*

CONSUMPTION

Consumer ignorance acts as a subsidy to inefficient plants.
                                                           —*S. H. Slichter.*

Human desires are the stream which makes the social machine work.
                                                           —*E. L. Bernays.*

In so far as liberty is organizable, consumer cooperation is the organization of liberty.

—H. M. Kallen.

CONTEMPT

It is impossible to think well of the mind of a girl who treats one with tacit contempt.

—W. D. Howells.

I have unlearned contempt.—It is a sin that is engendered earliest in the soul, and doth beset it like a poison worm, feeding on all its beauty.

—N. P. Willis.

CONTENTMENT

We should be content with what we have, but never with what we are.

—Channing Pollock.

Content is the philosophers's stone, that turns all it touches into gold.   *—B. Franklin.*

To the discontented man no chair is easy.   *—Ibid.*

A man looking at the present in the light of the future, and taking his whole being into account, may be contented with his lot: that is Christian contentment.   *—H. W. Beecher.*

One who is contented with what he has done will never become famous for what he will do.—He has lain down to die, and the grass is already over him.   *—C. N. Bovee.*

They that deserve nothing shall be content with anything.

—Erskine Mason.

If a man is not content in the state he is in, he will not be content in the state he would be in.   *—Ibid.*

Do good with what thou hast or it will do thee no good.

—Wm. Penn.

One should be either sad or joyful. Contentment is a warm sty for eaters and sleepers.   *—Eugene O'Neill.*

CONTRACT

Pretty much all law consists in forbidding men to do some things they want to do, and contract is no more exempt from law than other acts.   *—O. W. Holmes, Jr.*

CONTROL

In framing a government which is to be administered by men over men, the great difficulty lies in this: You must first enable the government to control the governed; and in the next place oblige it to control itself.   —*Alexander Hamilton.*

We must find practical controls over blind economic forces as well as over blindly selfish men.   —*F. D. Roosevelt.*

The old days of laissez faire are gone. A new age or system is in the making, . . . in which control and planning are largely in the hands of government and only routine management to any great extent remains to private business.   —*H. M. Larson.*

We cannot succeed with a controlled and regulated society under a Government which destroys initiative, chokes production, fosters disunity, and discourages men with vision and imagination from creating employment and opportunity.
                                                —*Thomas E. Dewey.*

It will never be possible for any length of time for any group of the American people, either by reason of wealth or learning or inheritance or economic power, to retain any mandate, any permanent authority to arrogate to itself the political control of American public life.   —*F. D. Roosevelt.*

CONTROVERSY

No great advance has been made in science, politics or religion without controversy.   —*Lyman Beecher.*

Labor controversy is a part of free economy. It cannot be determined from the top down without destroying freedom.
                                                —*Clarence Randall.*

No man believes his creed who is afraid to hear it attacked.
                                                —*Wendell Phillips.*

Most controversies would soon be ended, if those engaged in them would first accurately define their terms and then adhere to their definitions.   —*Tryon Edwards.*

CONVERSATION

Conversation is an art in which a man has all mankind for competitors.   —*R. W. Emerson.*

Lettuce is like conversation; it must be fresh and crisp, so sparkling that you scarcely notice the bitter in it.
                                                —*C. D. Warner.*

A man of no conversation should smoke.   —*R. W. Emerson.*

Debate is masculine, conversation feminine.   —*A. B. Alcott.*

All bitter feelings are avoided, or at least greatly reduced, by prompt face-to-face discussion.   —*Walter B. Pitkin.*

Conversation warms the mind and enlivens the imagination.
—*B. Franklin.*

Apart from conversation, from discourse and communication, there is no thought and no meaning, only just events, dumb, preposterous, destructive.   —*John Dewey.*

A good memory and a tongue tied in the middle is a combination which gives immortality to conversation.   —*Mark Twain.*

Be sincere. Be simple in words, manners and gestures. Amuse as well as instruct. If you can make a man laugh you can make him think and make him like and believe you.   —*Alfred E. Smith.*

Generally speaking, poverty of speech is the outward evidence of poverty of mind.   —*Bruce Barton.*

Speak well of everyone—none of us are so very good.
—*Elbert Hubbard.*

Conversation is the slowest form of human communication.
—*Don Herold.*

Conversation is an abandonment to ideas, a surrender to persons.
—*A. B. Alcott.*

Conversation is the vent of character as well as of thought.
—*R. W. Emerson.*

Many can argue, not many converse.   —*A. B. Alcott.*

Debate is angular, conversation circular, and radiant of the underlying unity.   —*Ibid.*

Conversation is the laboratory and workshop of the student.
—*R. W. Emerson.*

When two minds of a high order, interested in kindred subjects, come together, their conversation is chiefly remarkable for the summariness of its allusions and the rapidity of its transitions.
—*William James.*

CONVICTION

It does not take great men to do great things; it only takes consecrated men.   —*Phillips Brooks.*

The only faith that wears well and holds its color in all weathers is that which is woven of conviction and set with the sharp mordant of experience. —*J. R. Lowell.*

Speak your latent conviction, and it shall be the universal sense.
—*R. W. Emerson.*

COOPERATION

Men can do jointly what they cannot do singly; and the union of minds and hands, the concentration of their power, becomes almost omnipotent. —*Daniel Webster.*

We must all stand together, or assuredly we shall all hang separately. —*B. Franklin.*

Man is not naturally solitary; he must have something he belongs to. He has a basic urge to work with his fellows, to gain their approval, and to be a member of a group in good standing.
—*J. M. Clarke.*

There is no limit, other than our own resolve, to the temporal goals we set before ourselves—as free individuals joined in a team with our fellows; as a free nation in the community of nations.
—*D. D. Eisenhower.*

We must needs band together if we would achieve a higher life.
—*Felix Adler.*

Either . . . take our place as one of the leading industrial nations organized for the highest efficiency possible under cooperative industrial production, or we . . . merely become a field of exploitation, a sphere of European influence, to be parcelled out like China. —*Charles Steinmetz.*

The highest and best form of efficiency is the spontaneous cooperation of a free people. —*Woodrow Wilson.*

COOPERATIVE

The alternative to the totalitarian state is the cooperative commonwealth. —*Norman Thomas.*

COQUETTE

A coquette is a young lady of more beauty than sense.
—*H. W. Longfellow.*

Every line in her face is the line of least resistance.
—*I. S. Cobb.*

CORPORATION

A corporation is an artificial being, invisible, intangible, and existing only in contemplation of law. —*John Marshall.*

Our aim is not to do away with corporations. . . . We draw the line against misconduct, not against wealth.

—*Theodore Roosevelt.*

CORRUPT

He is a man of splendid abilities, but utterly corrupt. He shines and stinks like a rotten mackerel by moonlight.

—*John Randolph.*

CORRUPTION

The time to guard against corruption and tyranny is before they shall have gotten hold of us. —*T. Jefferson.*

It is better to keep the wolf out of the fold than to trust to drawing his teeth and talons after he shall have entered. —*Ibid.*

There is something in corruption which, like a jaundiced eye, transfers the color of itself to the object it looks upon, and sees everything stained and impure. —*T. Paine.*

COST

Government—Federal and State and local—costs too much.

—*F. D. Roosevelt.*

We have been proud of our industrial achievements, but we have not hitherto stopped thoughtfully enough to count the human cost, the cost of lives snuffed out, or energies overtaxed and broken, the fearful physical and spiritual cost to the men and women and children upon whom the dead weight and burden of it all has fallen pitilessly the years through.

—*Woodrow Wilson.*

After all, doesn't free love cost the most? —*Tom Masson.*

The rising cost of living can be controlled, providing that all elements making up the cost of living are controlled at the same time. —*F. D. Roosevelt.*

I haven't heard of anybody who wants to stop living on account of the cost. —*Kin Hubbard.*

COUNSEL

He that won't be counselled can't be helped.

—*B. Franklin.*

Good counsel failing men can give, for why?
He that's aground knows where the shoal doth lie.

—*Ibid.*

COUNTRY

This country, with its institutions, belongs to the people who inhabit it.   —*A. Lincoln.*

Each one of us can make our country seem as it truly is—determined to do its part to carry the free world forward to strength and security.   —*Dean Acheson.*

This country and this people seem to have been made for each other.   —*John Jay.*

Our country! in her intercourse with foreign nations may she always be in the right; but our country right or wrong!
—*Stephen Decatur.*

Where liberty dwells, there is my country.   —*B. Franklin.*

Love your neighbor as yourself, and your country more than yourself.   —*T. Jefferson.*

How can a man be said to have a country when he has not right of a square inch of it.   —*Henry George.*

Indeed I tremble for my country when I reflect that God is just.
—*T. Jefferson.*

Let our object be, our country, our whole country, and nothing but our country.   —*Daniel Webster.*

Our country is too large to have all its affairs directed by a single government.   —*T. Jefferson.*

I consider it the best part of an education to have been born and brought up in the country.   —*A. B. Alcott.*

Of all places in the world where life can be lived to its fullest and freest, where it can be met in its greatest variety and beauty, there is none to equal the open country, or the country town.
—*Ray S. Baker.*

COURAGE

One man with courage makes a majority.
—*Andrew Jackson.*

Far better it is to dare mighty things, to win glorious triumphs, even though checkered by failure, than to take rank with those poor spirits who neither enjoy much nor suffer much, because they live in the grey twilight that knows not victory nor defeat.
—*Theodore Roosevelt.*

The soul little suspects its own courage.   —*Frank Crane.*

We have had to tear men's bodies to pieces, to burn, crush,

strangle and crucify them to find that last wonderful drop of courage. —*Ibid.*

We lack the courage to be where we are:—
We live too much to travel in old roads,
To triumph in old fields. —*E. A. Robinson.*

Conscience in the soul is the root of all true courage. If a man would be brave, let him learn to obey his conscience.

—*J. F. Clarke.*

Courage is always greatest when blended with meekness.

—*E. H. Chapin.*

Religion gives a man courage . . . the courage that can face a world full of howling and of scorn. —*Theodore Parker.*

No man in the world has more courage than the man who can stop after eating one peanut. —*Channing Pollock.*

Hold the Fort! I am coming. —*W. T. Sherman.*

Half a man's wisdom goes with his courage. —*R. W. Emerson.*

Courage makes a man more than himself; for he is then himself plus his valor. —*W. R. Alger.*

To bear other people's afflictions, everyone has courage enough and to spare. —*B. Franklin.*

The most sublime courage I have ever witnessed has been among the class too poor to know they possessed it, and too humble for the world to discover it. —*H. W. Shaw.*

> Do you fear the force of the wind,
> The slash of rain?
> Go face them and fight them,
> Be savage again. —*Hamlin Garland.*

I would define true courage to be a perfect sensibility of the measure of danger, and a mental willingness to endure it.

—*W. T. Sherman.*

Courage considered in itself or without reference to its causes, is no virtue, and deserves no esteem. It is found in the best and the worst, and is to be judged according to the qualities from which it springs and with which it is conjoined.

—*W. E. Channing.*

Courage without conscience is a wild beast. —*R. G. Ingersoll.*

A coward is much more exposed to quarrels than a man of spirit.

—*T. Jefferson.*

COURTESY

The small courtesies sweeten life; the greater ennoble it.
—*C. N. Bovee.*

Life is not so short but that there is always time enough for courtesy.   —*R. W. Emerson.*

We must be courteous to a man as we are to a picture, which we are willing to give the advantage of a good light.   —*Ibid.*

COURTSHIP

A chap ort t' save a few o' the' long evenings he spends with his girl till after they're married.   —*Kin Hubbard.*

I profess not to know how women's hearts are wooed and won. To me they have always been matters of riddle and admiration.
—*Washington Irving.*

> Men seldom make passes
> At girls who wear glasses.
>
> —*Dorothy Parker.*

If I am not worth the wooing I surely am not worth the winning.
—*H. W. Longfellow.*

COVETOUSNESS

The only gratification a covetous man gives to his neighbors, is to let them see that he himself is as little better for what he has, as they are.   —*Wm. Penn.*

COWARDICE

The craven's fear is but selfishness, like his merriment.
—*J. G. Whittier.*

At the bottom of a good deal of the bravery that appears in the world there lurks a miserable cowardice. Men will face powder and steel because they cannot face public opinion.
—*E. H. Chapin.*

Coward: one who in perilous emergency thinks with his legs.
—*Ambrose Bierce.*

He who loves and runs away may live to love another day.
—*Carolyn Wells.*

There are several good protections against temptation, but the surest is cowardice.   —*Mark Twain.*

It is better to make a thousand mistakes and suffer a thousand reverses than to run away from battle.   —*H. Van Dyke.*

CREATION

Man was made at the end of the week's work when God was tired.   *—Mark Twain.*

In a dying world creation is revolution.   *—Waldo Frank.*

The Creation is a museum, all full, and crowded with wonders and beauties and glories.   *—Horace Mann.*

CREATOR

All I have seen teaches me to trust the Creator for all I have not seen.   *—R. W. Emerson.*

CREDIT

Credit is like chastity, they can both stand temptation better than suspicion.   *—Josh Billings.*

If a feller screwed up his face when he asked fer credit like he does when he's asked t' settle, he wouldn't git it.

    —Kin Hubbard.

Public credit is suspicion asleep.   *—T. Paine.*

As a very important source of strength and security, cherish public credit. One method of preserving it is to use it as sparingly as possible.   *—G. Washington.*

There is no power to compel a nation to pay its just debts. Its credit depends on its honor.   *—R. B. Hayes.*

In this institution of credit . . . always some neighbor stands ready to be bread and land and tool and stock to the young adventurer.   *—R. W. Emerson.*

As William James said of the boarder: "It is much more important for the landlady to know his philosophy than his income."
    —Harry Scherman.

Creditors have a better memory than debtors, and creditors are a superstitious sect, great observers of set days and fines.

    —B. Franklin.

The most trifling actions that affect a man's credit are to be regarded.   *—Ibid.*

Some folks get credit for having horse sense that hain't ever had enough money to make fools of themselves.

    —Kin Hubbard.

Credit is the life blood of industry, and the control of credit is the control of all society.   *—Upton Sinclair.*

The private control of credit is the modern form of slavery.

—Ibid.

No man's credit is so good as his money.   *—E. W. House.*

It takes man to make a devil; and the fittest man for such a purpose is a snarling, waspish, red-hot fiery creditor.

—H. W. Beecher.

CREDO

I believe in one God, and no more; and ·I hope for happiness beyond this life. I believe in the equality of man; and I believe that religious duties consist in doing justice, loving mercy, and endeavoring to make our fellow creatures happy.   *—T. Paine.*

> Justice is the only worship;
> Love is the only priest;
> Ignorance is the only slavery;
> Happiness is the only good;
> The time to be happy is now
> The place to be happy is here,
> The way to be happy is to make others so.
>
> *—R. G. Ingersoll.*

CREDULITY

Credulity is belief in slight evidence, with no evidence, or against evidence.   *—Tryon Edwards.*

I cannot spare the luxury of believing that all things beautiful are what they seem.   *—Fitz-Greene Halleck.*

The more gross the fraud the more greedily will it be swallowed since folly will always find faith wherever imposters will find impudence.   *—C. N. Bovee.*

CREED

Call your opinion your creed, you will change it every day. Make your creed simply and broadly out of the revelation of God, and you may keep it to the End.   *—Phillips Brooks.*

The world is my country; all mankind are my brethren; to do good is my religion; I believe in one God and no more.   *—T. Paine.*

Creeds grow so thick along the way, their boughs hide God.

—Lizette W. Reese.

I would rather be a superb meteor, every atom of me in magnificent glow, than a sleepy and permanent planet.

—Jack London.

I would rather be ashes than dust! I would rather that my spark would burn out in a brilliant blaze than it should be stifled by dry-rot. —*Ibid.*

> So many gods, so many creeds—
> So many paths that wind and wind
> While just the art of being kind
> Is all the sad world needs.
> —*E. W. Wilcox.*

CRIME

No greater calamity can befall a people than to prosper by crime. —*W. E. Channing.*

If you do big things they print your face, and if you do little things they print only your thumbs. —*Arthur "Bugs" Baer.*

I, John Brown, am quite certain that the crimes of this guilty land will never be purged away but with Blood. —*John Brown.*

There is no den in the wide world to hide a rogue. Commit a crime and the earth is made of glass. —*R. W. Emerson.*

Purposelessness is the fruitful mother of crime.
—*C. H. Parkhurst.*

Wherever a man commits a crime, God finds a witness.
—*R. W. Emerson.*

CRIMINALS

The reason there are so many imbeciles among imprisoned criminals is that an imbecile is so foolish even a detective can detect him. —*Austin O'Malley.*

A criminal is a person with predatory instincts who has not sufficient capital to form a corporation.
—*Howard Scott.*

We enact many laws that manufacture criminals, and then a few that punish them. —*Benj. R. Tucker.*

CRISIS

These are the times that try men's souls. —*T. Paine.*

Every great crisis of human history is a pass of Thermopylae, and there is always a Leonidas and his three hundred to die in it, if they can not conquer. —*G. W. Curtis.*

We live amidst one of the greatest crises in human history.
—*P. A. Sorokin.*

The crisis is omnipresent and involves almost the whole of culture and society from top to bottom.   —*Ibid.*

Every crisis offers you extra desired power.   —*W. M. Marston.*

The nearer any disease approaches to a crisis, the nearer it is to cure.   —*T. Paine.*

Man is not imprisoned by habit. Great changes in him can be wrought by crisis—once that crisis can be recognized and understood.   —*Norman Cousins.*

A crisis is expected to be followed by a depression, the depression by revival, the revival by prosperity, and prosperity by a new crisis.   —*W. C. Mitchell.*

CRITIC

A drama critic is a person who surprises the playwright by informing him what he meant.   —*Wilson Mizner.*

Critics are a kind of freebooters in the republic of letters.
                                              —*Washington Irving.*

Nature, when she invented, manufactured, and patented her authors, contrived to make critics out of the chips that were left.
                                              —*O. W. Holmes.*

A critic is a legless man who teaches running.
                                              —*Channing Pollock.*

Critics are constantly carrying on a guerilla warfare of their own, and discovering anew the virtues of individuality, modernity, Puritanism, the Romantic Spirit or the spirit of the Middle West.
                                              —*Joel Spingarn.*

> The stones that critics hurl with harsh intent
> A man may use to build his monument.
>   —*Arthur Guiterman.*

Critics are sentinels in the grand army of letters, stationed at the corners of newspapers and reviews to challenge every new author.   —*H. W. Longfellow.*

> Nature fits all her children with something to do,
> He who would write and can't write, can surely review.
>   —*J. R. Lowell.*

A critic is a man who expects miracles.   —*J. G. Huneker.*

A wise scepticism is the first attribute of a good critic.
                                              —*J. R. Lowell*

The public is the only critic whose opinion is worth anything at all. —*Mark Twain.*

CRITICISM

Criticism in a free man's country is made on certain assumptions, one of which is the assumption that the government belongs to the people and is at all times subject to the people's correction and criticism. —*Archibald MacLeish.*

The artist, without respect to medium, is interested in criticism because it is a form of public opinion. Also, because it *creates* public opinion. —*John Gassner.*

The legitimate aim of criticism is to direct attention to the excellent. —*C. N. Bovee.*

Criticism is dangerous, because it wounds a man's precious pride, hurts his sense of importance and arouses his resentment. —*Dale Carnegie.*

The strength of criticism lies in the weakness of the thing criticized. —*H. W. Longfellow.*

To avoid criticism, do nothing, say nothing, be nothing. —*Elbert Hubbard.*

Don't abuse your friends and expect them to consider it criticism. —*E. W. Howe.*

The wise man always throws himself on the side of his assailants. It is more to his interest than it is theirs to find his weak points. —*R. W. Emerson.*

A critic is a necessary evil, and criticism is an evil necessity. —*Carolyn Wells.*

In the periods of basic cultural transition the criticism that does not start out from metaphysics and a true understanding of religious experience is idle, irrelevant, impotent, and anti-social. —*Waldo Frank.*

You do not get a man's most effective criticism until you provoke him. Severe truth is expressed with some bitterness. —*H. D. Thoreau.*

Show me the man who insists that he welcomes criticism if only it is "constructive", and I will show you a man who does not want any criticism at all. —*H. L. Ickes.*

I have always very much despised the artificial canons of criticism. When I have read a work in prose or poetry, or seen a painting, a statue, etc., I have only asked myself whether it gives me pleasure, whether it is animating, interesting, attaching? If it is, it is good for these reasons.   —*T. Jefferson.*

CROSS

We can't cross a bridge until we come to it; but I always like to lay down a pontoon ahead of time.   —*B. M. Baruch.*

CRUELTY

Cruelty is a part of nature, at least of human nature, but it is the one thing that seems unnatural to us.   —*Robinson Jeffers.*

An angel with a trumpet said, "Forever more forever more, the reign of violence is o'er."   —*H. W. Longfellow.*

CULTURE

Culture means the perfect and equal development of man on all sides.   —*John Burroughs.*

Real culture lives by sympathies and admirations, not by dislikes and disdains; under all misleading wrappings it pounces unerringly upon the human cure.   —*William James.*

That is true culture which helps us to work for the social betterment of all.   —*H. W. Beecher.*

Our culture must not omit the arming of the man. . . . let him take both reputation and life in his hand, and, with perfect urbanity, dare the gibbet and the mob by the absolute truth of his speech, and the rectitude of his behavior.   —*R. W. Emerson.*

Culture, with us, ends in headache.   —*Ibid.*

Culture is what your butcher would have if he were a surgeon.
                                          —*Mary Pettibone Peele.*

Our cultural humility before the civilizations of Europe is the chief obstacle which prevents us from producing any true indigenous culture of our own.   —*Randolph Bourne.*

When shall we learn that "culture," like the kingdom of heaven, lies within us, in the heart of our national soul, and not in foreign galleries and books?   —*Ibid.*

Culture is one thing and varnish another.   —*R. W. Emerson.*

There is another culture in the world than this immoral, so-called moral culture which your business men and statesmen prate about and march their armies all over.   —*Lincoln Steffens.*

CUNNING

Cunning is to wisdom as an ape to a man.

—*Wm. Penn.*

The cunning of the fox is as murderous as the violence of the wolf, and we ought to guard equally against both.

—*T. Paine.*

CURE

There is no cure for birth or death save to enjoy the interval.

—*George Santayana.*

There's another advantage of being poor—a doctor will cure you faster. —*Kin Hubbard.*

One of the best temporary cures for pride and affectation is seasickness: a man who wants to vomit never puts on airs.

—*Josh Billings.*

CURIOSITY

Creatures whose mainspring is curiosity enjoy the accumulating of facts, far more than the pausing at times to reflect on those facts.

—*Clarence Day.*

CURSE

Labor is the curse of the world, and nobody can meddle with it without becoming proportionately brutalized.

—*Nathaniel Hawthorne.*

The sole solution for the human race lies in the removal of the primal curse, the sentence of hard labor for life that was imposed on man as he left Paradise. —*E. E. Slosson.*

CUSTOM

Custom meets us at the cradle and leaves us only at the tomb.

—*R. G. Ingersoll.*

Have a place for everything and keep the thing somewhere else; this is not advice, it is merely custom. —*Mark Twain.*

There is no tyrant like custom, and no freedom where its edicts are not resisted. —*C. N. Bovee.*

CYNIC

Cynic: a blackguard whose faulty vision sees things as they are, not as they ought to be. —*Ambrose Bierce.*

A cynic is a man who looks at the world with a monocle in his mind's eye. —*Carolyn Wells.*

A cynic is a man who, when he smells flowers, looks around for a coffin.   —*H. L. Mencken.*

It takes a clever man to turn cynic and a wise man to be clever enough not to.   —*Fannie Hurst.*

In his heart of hearts the cynic knows that he is a defeated man and that his cynicism is merely an expression of the fact that he has lost courage and is beaten.   —*George E. Vincent.*

The cynic puts all human actions into two classes: openly bad and secretly bad.   —*H. W. Beecher.*

The cynic is one who never sees a good quality in a man, and never fails to see a bad one. He is the human owl, vigilant in darkness, and blind to light, mousing for vermin, and never seeing noble game.   —*Ibid.*

Watch what people are cynical about, and one can often discover what they lack, and subconsciously, beneath their touchy condescension, deeply wish they had.   —*H. E. Fosdick.*

CYNICISM

Still the mind smiles at its own rebellions.   —*Robinson Jeffers.*

D

DANCING

Dancing is wonderful training for girls; it's the first way you learn to guess what a man is going to do before he does it.

—Christopher Morley.

Social dissipation as witnessed in the ball-room . . . is the avenue of lust and it is the curse of every town in America.

—Thomas D. Talmadge.

I don't think much of a dance step where the girl looks like she was being carried out of a burning building.   *—Kin Hubbard.*

The true idea of dancing entitles it to favor. Its end is to realize perfect grace in motion.   *—W. E. Channing.*

DANDRUFF

Everybody has something; a man has dandruff, and a woman has cold feet.   *—E. W. Howe.*

DANDY

Clothes form the intellect of the dandy.   *—H. W. Shaw.*

DANGER

There is danger that the individual, whether farmer, worker, manufacturer, lawyer, or doctor, soon will be pulling an economic oar in the galley of the state.   *—J. F. Byrnes.*

It is in wealth, in incorporated, combining, perpetuated wealth, that the danger of labor lies.   *—Wendell Phillips.*

There's nothing so comfortable as a small bank roll; a big one is always in danger.   *—Wilson Mizner.*

In the face of great perils never before encountered, our strong purpose is to protect and to perpetuate the integrity of democracy.

—F. D. Roosevelt.

DANGEROUS

There is no such thing as a dangerous woman; there are only susceptible men.   —*J. W. Krutch.*

Democracy is a dangerous form of government. The United States of America is a democracy.   —*Gerald W. Johnson.*

DANIEL

About the only person we ever heard of that wasn't spoiled by being lionized, was a Jew named Daniel.   —*G. D. Prentice.*

DARING

And what they dare to dream of, dare to do.   —*J. R. Lowell.*

DARKNESS

The love game is never called off on account of darkness.
                                                            —*Tom Masson.*

DARLING

Darling: the popular form of address used in speaking to a person of the opposite sex whose name you cannot at the moment recall.   —*Oliver Herford.*

DARWINISM

If we do not like the survival of the fittest, we have only one possible alternative, and that is, the survival of the unfittest. The former is the law of civilization; the latter is the law of anti-civilization.   —*W. G. Sumner.*

DAUGHTER

We never know how a son is going to turn out or when a daughter is going to turn in.   —*Kin Hubbard.*

A rich man and his daughter are soon parted.   —*Ibid.*

DAY

A Day is a miniature Eternity.   —*R. W. Emerson.*

April 1 is the day upon which we are reminded of what we are on the other 364.   —*Mark Twain.*

There is no day born but comes like a stroke of music into the world and sings itself all the way through.   —*H. W. Beecher.*

There is more real life in the average man's day than there was in a nobleman's decade only a hundred years ago.
                                                          —*Gabriel Heatter.*

Finish every day and be done with it.   —*R. W. Emerson.*

DEAD

Early to rise and early to bed makes a male healthy and wealthy and dead. —*James Thurber.*

Isolation ends at the edge of the grave. Whatever the estate of the dead, they are not divided by prejudice of race or nationality. To them, at least, all things are common. —*Heywood Broun.*

The dead . . . do not need us, but forever and forever more we need them. —*James A. Garfield.*

Many a live wire would be a dead one except for his connections. —*Wilson Mizner.*

DEAL

A man who is good enough to shed his blood for his country is good enough to be given a square deal afterward. More than that no man is entitled to, and less than that no man shall have.
—*Theodore Roosevelt.*

I pledge . . . a New Deal for the American People.
—*F. D. Roosevelt.*

DEARNESS

What we obtain too cheap, we esteem too lightly:—'Tis dearness only that gives every thing its value. —*T. Paine.*

DEATH

He that lives to live forever, never fears dying. —*Wm. Penn.*

Death is but crossing the world, as friends do the seas; they live in one another still. —*Ibid.*

In order to write tellingly about death you have to have the principle of life, and those that have it will make it felt in spite of everything. —*Edmund Wilson.*

We do not die of death: we die of vertigo.
—*Archibald MacLeish.*

Death: to stop sinning suddenly. —*Elbert Hubbard.*

Those who welcome death have only tried it from the ears up.
—*Wilson Mizner.*

Nothing can happen more beautiful than death.
—*H. W. Longfellow.*

We owe a deep debt of gratitude to Adam, the first great benefactor of the human race: he brought death into the world.
—*Mark Twain.*

Death is strong, but life is stronger.   —*Phillips Brooks.*

The young may die, but the old must.   —*H. W. Longfellow.*

> Death comes not to the living soul,
> Nor age to the loving heart.
> —*Phoebe Cary.*

All say, "How hard it is that we have to die"—a strange complaint to come from the mouths of people who have had to live.
—*Mark Twain.*

There is no fireside however defended but has one vacant chair.
—*H. W. Longfellow.*

The body of the Unknown Soldier has come home, but his spirit will wander with that of his brothers. There will be no rest for his soul until the great democracy of death has been translated into the unity of life.   —*Heywood Broun.*

Even death may prove unreal at the last, and stoics be astounded into heaven.   —*Herman Melville.*

Death is not an end. It is a new impulse.   —*H. W. Beecher.*

One may live as a conqueror, a king, or a magistrate: but he must die as a man.   —*Daniel Webster.*

Who ever really saw anything but horror in the smile of the dead?   —*Edgar Allan Poe.*

The bodies of those that made such a noise and tumult when alive, when dead, lie as quietly among the graves of their neighbors as any others.   —*Jonathan Edwards.*

Our civilization is founded on the shambles, and every individual existence goes out in a lonely spasm of helpless agony.
—*William James.*

DEBATE

In all debates, let Truth be thy aim, not victory, or an unjust interest: And endeavor to gain, rather than to expose thy Antagonist.   —*Wm. Penn.*

DEBT (NATIONAL)

Debt is the fatal disease of republics, the first thing and the mightiest to undermine governments and corrupt the people.
—*Wendell Phillips.*

A national debt, if not excessive, will be to us a national blessing.
—*Alexander Hamilton.*

If the debt should once more be swelled to a formidable size, its entire discharge will be despaired of, and we shall be committed to the English career of debt, corruption and rottenness, closing with revolution.   —*T. Jefferson.*

To preserve their independence, we must not let our rulers load us with perpetual debt. We must make our election between economy and liberty, or profusion and servitude.   —*Ibid.*

Permanent debts pertain to monarchial governments; and tending to monopolies, perpetuities, and class legislation, are totally irreconciliable with free institutions.   —*Andrew Johnson.*

Our national debt, after all, is an internal debt, owed not only by the nation but to the nation. If our children have to pay the interest they will pay that interest to themselves.
     —*F. D. Roosevelt.*

Our capacity to carry a large debt in a post-war period without undue hardship depends mainly on our ability to maintain a high level of employment and income.   —*Ibid.*

DEBT (PERSONAL)

In the midst of life we are in debt.   —*E. W. Mumford.*

If I owe Smith ten dollars, and God forgives me, that doesn't pay Smith.   —*R. G. Ingersoll.*

Rather go to bed supperless than rise in debt.   —*B. Franklin.*

Debt is like any other trap, easy enough to get into, but hard enough to get out of.   —*H. W. Shaw.*

Debt, grinding debt . . . is a preceptor whose lessons cannot be foregone.   —*R. W. Emerson.*

Always pay; for first or last you must pay your entire debt.
     —*Ibid.*

A habit of debt is very injurious to the memory.
     —*Austin O'Malley.*

Some people use one half their ingenuity to get into debt, and the other half to avoid paying it.   —*G. D. Prentice.*

Never run into debt, not if you can find anything else to run into.   —*Josh Billings.*

A church debt is the devil's salary.   —*H. W. Beecher.*

Wilt thou seal up the avenues of ill?
Pay every debt as if God wrote the bill.
                                                        —*R. W. Emerson.*

If you want the time to pass quickly, just give your note for ninety days.   —*R. B. Thomas.*

DEBUNKING

We are standing at the end of an era of debunking. . . . We carried it too far. In our efforts to smash false façades, we smashed some of the solid old foundations.   —*Wm. B. Huie.*

DECALOGUE

Say what you will about the Ten Commandments, you must always come back to the pleasant fact that there are only ten of them.   —*H. L. Mencken.*

The Decalogue and the Golden Rule have no place in a political campaign.   —*J. J. Ingalls.*

DECAY

Man passes away . . . his very monument becomes a ruin.
                                                   —*Washington Irving.*

DECEIT

You can fool some of the people all the time, and all of the people some of the time, but you cannot fool all of the people all of the time.   —*A. Lincoln.*

Men, like musical instruments, seem made to be played upon.
                                                        —*C. N. Bovee.*

Many an honest man practises on himself an amount of deceit, sufficient, if practised on another, and in a little different way, to send him to the State prison.   —*Ibid.*

Every crowd has a silver lining.   —*P. T. Barnum.*

Nothing needs a trick but a trick; sincerity loathes one.
                                                        —*Wm. Penn.*

There is less misery in being cheated than that kind of wisdom which perceives, or thinks it perceives, that all mankind are cheats.   —*E. H. Chapin.*

Hateful to me, as are the gates of hell, is he who, hiding one thing in his heart, utters another.   —*Wm. Cullen Bryant.*

The worst deluded are the self-deluded.   —*C. N. Bovee.*

There's a sucker born every minute.   —*P. T. Barnum.*

DECENCY

Don't overestimate the decency of the human race.

—H. L. Mencken.

The standard of decency is higher, class for class and this requirement of decent appearance must be lived up to on pain of losing caste. *—Thorstein Veblen.*

We are decent 99 per cent of the time, when we could easily be vile. *—R. W. Riis.*

DECISION

It does not take much strength to do things, but it requires great strength to decide on what to do. *—Elbert Hubbard.*

Decide not rashly. The decision made can never be recalled.

—H. W. Longfellow.

He only is a well-made man who has a good determination.

—R. W. Emerson.

Take time to deliberate; but when the time for action arrives, stop thinking and go on. *—Andrew Jackson.*

Decision of character will often give to an inferior mind command over a superior. *—William Wirt.*

The least thing a weak personality wants to do is to decide.

—Frank Crane.

Once to every man and nation comes the moment to decide,
In the strife of Truth and Falsehood, for the good or evil side.
—J. R. Lowell.

DECORUM

A breach of faith may be condoned, but a breach of decorum cannot! Manners maketh man! *—Thorstein Veblen.*

The barbarian of the quasi-peacable stage of industry is notoriously a more high-bred gentleman, in all that concerns decorum, than any but the very exquisite among the men of a later age.

—Ibid.

Decorum is a product and an exponent of leisure-class life.

—Ibid.

Decorum is supreme for the humanist. *—Irving Babbitt.*

DEEDS

A noble deed is a step toward God. *—J. G. Holland.*

There is no more contemptible type of human character than

that of the nerveless sentimentalist and dreamer who spends his life in a weltering sea of sensibility and emotion, but who never does a manly concrete deed.   —*William James.*

Don't take the will for the deed; get the deed.
                                                        —*E. W. Mumford.*

Whose sons sat silent when base deeds were done.
                                                            —*J. R. Lowell.*

Deeds survive the doers.   —*Horace Mann.*

Put your creed into your deed.   —*R. W. Emerson.*

When a deed is done, it cannot be undone, nor can our thoughts reach out to all the mischiefs that may follow.
                                                        —*H. W. Longfellow.*

No matter what a man's aims, or resolutions, or professions may be, it is by one's deeds that he is to be judged, both by God and man.   —*H. W. Beecher.*

Great deeds cannot die.   —*R. W. Emerson.*

The man's whole life preludes the single deed.   —*J. R. Lowell.*

> Little deeds of kindness, little words of love,
> Make our earth an Eden like the heaven above.
>   —*Julia F. Carney.*

DEFEAT
It is defeat that turns bone to flint; it is defeat that turns gristle to muscle; it is defeat that makes men invincible.
                                                        —*H. W. Beecher.*

What is defeat? Nothing but education, nothing but the first step to something better.   —*Wendell Phillips.*

Defeat is a school in which truth always grows strong.
                                                        —*H. W. Beecher.*

Defeat is not the worst of failures. Not to have tried is the true failure.   —*G. E. Woodberry.*

Many a good man have I seen go under.   —*Walt Whitman.*

The greatest test of courage on earth is to bear defeat without losing heart.   —*R. G. Ingersoll.*

Believe you are defeated, believe it long enough, and it is likely to become a fact.   —*N. V. Peale.*

Train your mind never to accept the thought of defeat about anything.   —*Ibid.*

Defeat never comes to any man until he admits it.

—*Josephus Daniels.*

There is a defeatist notion current among liberals that to stress socialism is to invite fascism. —*Norman Thomas.*

In the long run all battles are lost and so are all wars.

—*H. L. Mencken.*

DEFECT

As no man ever had a point of pride that was not injurious to him, so no man had ever a defect that was not somewhere made useful to him. —*R. W. Emerson.*

DEFENSE

Our first line of defense is a sound, solvent American economy.

—*J. F. Byrnes.*

Millions for defense but not one cent for tribute.

—*Charles C. Pinckney.*

It is one of the greatest reproaches to human nature that wars are sometimes just. The defence of nations sometimes causes a just war against the injustice of other nations. —*Daniel Webster.*

No man can suffer too much, and no man can fall too soon, if he suffer, or if he fall, in the defense of the liberties and constitution of his country. —*Ibid.*

The liberties of our country, the freedom of our civil constitution, are worth defending at all hazards; and it is our duty to defend them against all attacks. —*Samuel Adams.*

DEFICITS

Let us have the courage to stop borrowing to meet continuing deficits—stop the deficits! —*F. D. Roosevelt.*

No country needs deficit spending when private enterprise, either through its own efforts or in cooperation with government, is able to maintain employment. —*H. A. Wallace.*

In a period of high prosperity it is not sound public policy for the Government to operate at a deficit. —*H. S. Truman.*

We have operated in red ink so long that the pages of the Federal ledger look like a slaughter-house. —*K. B. Keating.*

DEGRADE

Whoever degrades another, degrades me. —*Walt Whitman.*

DELAY

Do not delay: the golden moments fly.   —*H. W. Longfellow.*

Each of us must do his part. We cannot delay, individually or nationally, while we suspiciously scrutinize the sacrifices made by our neighbor, and through a weasling logic seek some way to avoid our own duties.   —*D. D. Eisenhower.*

Do not put off till tomorrow what can be enjoyed today.
                                              —*Josh Billings.*

Ah! nothing is too late till the tired heart shall cease to palpitate.
                                              —*H. W. Longfellow.*

Where duty is plain, delay is both foolish and hazardous; where it is not, delay may be both wisdom and safety.
                                              —*Tryon Edwards.*

DELIGHT

Society would be delightful were all women married and all men single.   —*Edgar Saltus.*

A sip is the most that mortals are permitted from any goblet of delight.   —*A. B. Alcott.*

DELUSION

Love is the delusion that one woman differs from another.
                                              —*H. L. Mencken.*

No man is happy without a delusion of some kind. Delusions are as necessary to our happiness as realities.   —*C. N. Bovee.*

The whole people is hugging the delusion that law is a panacea.
                                              —*Samuel Gompers.*

DEMAGOGUE

The demagogue is usually sly, a detractor of others, . . . appeals to passions and prejudices rather than to reason, and is in all respects a man of intrigue and deception, of sly cunning and management.   —*James F. Cooper.*

The demagogue, whether of the Right or Left, is consciously or unconsciously, an undetected liar.   —*Walter Lippmann.*

Expect to be called a demagogue, but don't be a demagogue.
                                              —*Calvin Coolidge.*

To be the favorite of an ignorant multitude, a man must descend to their level.   —*Fisher Ames.*

He (the demagogue) must desire what they desire, and detest all they do not approve: he must yield to their prejudices and substitute them for principles. —*Ibid.*

The demagogue is one who preaches doctrines he knows to be untrue to men he knows to be idiots. —*H. L. Mencken.*

The demagogue is usually sly, a detractor of others, a professor of humility and disinterestedness, a great stickler for equality as respects all above him, a man who acts in corners, and avoids open and manly expositions of his course, calls blackguards gentlemen, and gentlemen folks, appeals to passions and prejudices rather than to reason, and is in all respects a man of intrigue and deception, of sly cunning and management. —*James F. Cooper.*

The honest man, whether rich or poor, who earns his own living and tries to deal justly by his fellows, has as much to fear from the insincere and unworthy demagogue, promising much and performing nothing, or else performing nothing but evil, who would set on the mob to plunder the rich, as from the crafty corruptionist who, for his own ends, would permit the common people to be exploited by the very wealthy. —*Theodore Roosevelt.*

DEMOCRACY

Democracy is the government of the people, by the people, for the people. —*A. Lincoln.*

Democracy means not "I am as good as you are," but "You are as good as I am." —*Theodore Parker.*

All the ills of democracy can be cured by more democracy. —*Alfred E. Smith.*

I believe in democracy because it releases the energies of every human being. —*Woodrow Wilson.*

The world must be made safe for democracy.

—*Ibid.*

Democracy means that the aggregate of mankind shall be so organized as to create for each man the maximum opportunity of growth in accordance with the dictates of his own genius and aspiration. —*R. B. Perry.*

It would be folly to argue that the people . . . can and do make mistakes, but compared with the mistakes which have been made by every kind of autocracy they are unimportant.

—*Calvin Coolidge.*

Democracy is based upon the conviction that there are extraordinary possibilities in ordinary people.   —*H. E. Fosdick.*

While democracy must have its organization and controls, its vital breath is individual liberty.   —*Charles Evans Hughes.*

You cannot possibly have a broader basis for any government than that which includes all the people, with all their rights in their hands, and with an equal power to maintain their rights.
—*W. L. Garrison.*

Government of the people, by the people, and for the people shall not perish from the earth.   —*A. Lincoln.*

All that Democracy means, is as equal participation in rights as is practicable.   —*James F. Cooper.*

We are committed primarily to democracy. The essential justice for which we are striving is an incident of our democracy, not the main end.   —*Louis D. Brandeis.*

Democracy is a method of our getting ahead without leaving any of us behind.   —*T. V. Smith.*

Democracy, I do not conceive that ever God did ordain as a fit government either for church or commonwealth. If the people be governors, who shall be governed?   —*John Cotton.*

On the whole, with scandalous exceptions, Democracy has given the ordinary worker more dignity than he ever had.
—*Sinclair Lewis.*

A representative democracy . . . will in my opinion, be most likely to be happy, regular and durable.   —*Alexander Hamilton.*

Democracy is a mode of dealing with souls.
—*G. E. Woodberry.*

Democracy is the earthly hope of man.   —*Ibid.*

Every man is wanted, and no man is wanted much.
—*R. W. Emerson.*

Democracy has not failed; the intelligence of the race has failed before the problems the race has raised.
—*Robert M. Hutchins.*

The best government rests on the people, and not on the few, on persons and not on property, on the free development of public opinion and not on authority.   —*George Bancroft.*

As I would not be a slave, so I would not be a master. This expresses my idea of democracy.   —*A. Lincoln.*

Democracy gives every man the right to be his own oppressor.
—J. R. Lowell.

Democracy becomes a government of bullies tempered by editors.   *—R. W. Emerson.*

Democracies being established for the common interests, and the public agents being held in constant check by the people, their general tendency is to serve the whole community, and not small portions of it, as is the case in narrow governments.
—James F. Cooper.

Democracies are less liable to popular tumults than any other polities, because the people having legal means in their power to redress wrongs, have little inducement to employ any other.
—Ibid.

A democracy is more than a form of government; it is primarily a mode of associated living, of conjoint communicated experience.
—John Dewey.

The beauty of democracy is that you never can tell when a youngster is born what he is going to do with you, and that, no matter how humble he is born . . . he has got a chance to master the minds and lead the imaginations of the whole country.
—Woodrow Wilson.

False democracy shouts Every man down to the level of the average. True democracy cries All men up to the height of their fullest capacity for service and achievement.   *—N. M. Butler.*

The government of the Union is emphatically and truly a government of the people. In form and in substance it emanates from them. Its powers are granted by them, and are to be exercised directly on them and for their benefit.   *—John Marshall.*

We of the United States are constitutionally and conscientiously democrats.   *—T. Jefferson.*

The greatest destroyer of democracy in the world is war itself.
—H. E. Fosdick.

Too many people expect wonders from democracy. When the most wonderful thing of all is just having it.   *—Walter Winchell.*

DEMOCRAT

The democrat is a young conservative; the conservative is an old democrat.   *—R. W. Emerson.*

I never said all Democrats were saloonkeepers; what I said was all saloonkeepers were Democrats.   —*Horace Greeley.*

A democrat is incapable of imagining honor in an antagonist, and hence incapable of honor himself.   —*H. L. Mencken.*

Christ was the first true democrat that ever breathed.
                                                        —*J. R. Lowell.*

Your little child is your only true democrat.   —*H. B. Stowe.*

I am all kinds of a democrat, so far as I can discover—but the root of the whole business is this, that I believe in the patriotism and energy and initiative of the average man.
                                                        —*Woodrow Wilson.*

Democrats consider the people as the safest depository of power in the last resort; they cherish them, therefore, and wish to leave in them all the powers to the exercise of which they are competent.
                                                        —*T. Jefferson.*

DEMOCRATIC

It is the weakness of our democratic Governments which is responsible for the chaos and disaster which have come upon ourselves and through us, upon all the nations of the earth.
                                                        —*A. Meiklejohn.*

Democratic government cannot be too strong.
                                                        —*Ibid.*

DENTIST

Dentist: a prestidigitator who, putting metal into your mouth, pulls coins out of your pocket.   —*Ambrose Bierce.*

DEPENDENCE

Dependence begets subservience and venality, suffocates the germ of virtue, and prepares fit tools for the designs of ambition.
                                                        —*T. Jefferson.*

The gentle needs the strong to sustain it, as much as rock-flowers need rocks to grow on, or the ivy the rugged walls which it embraces.   —*H. B. Stowe.*

The ship of heaven guides itself and will not accept a wooden rudder.   —*R. W. Emerson.*

DEPRAVITY

Every prison, and fetter, and scaffold, and bolt, and bar, and chain is evidence that man believes in the depravity of man.
                                                        —*Tryon Edwards.*

The depravity of the business classes of our country is not less than has been supposed but infinitely greater.   *—Walt Whitman.*

DEPRESSION

Depressions may bring people closer to the church—but so do funerals.   *—Clarence Darrow.*

The boom is the ineluctable antecedent of the depression.
                                            —Carl Snyder.

Economists are almost invariably engaged in defeating the last slump.   *—Stuart Chase.*

No one has yet found a sure way of bringing about just a little depression.   *—Allan Sproul.*

DESCENT

Some folks seem to have descended from the chimpanzee much later than others.   *—Kin Hubbard.*

We are descended not only from monkeys, but from monks.
                                            —Elbert Hubbard.

I haven't much doubt that man sprang from the monkey, but where did the monkey spring from?   *—Josh Billings.*

DESIGN

The role of city design in the future can hardly be over-emphasized.   *—Lewis Mumford.*

City design is the art of orchestrating human functions in the community.   *—Ibid.*

DESIRE

It is easier to suppress the first desire than to satisfy all that follow it.   *—B. Franklin.*

The freedom to do some thing awakens the desire to do it.
                                            —Carl Schurz.

In nature the implanting of a desire indicates that the gratification of that desire is in the constitution of the creature that feels it.
                                            —H. W. Beecher.

Every desire bears its death in its very gratification.
                                            —Washington Irving.

DESPAIR

When we are flat on our backs there is no way to look but up.
                                            —Roger W. Babson.

Some noble spirits mistake despair for content.

—*N. P. Willis.*

DESPERATION
The mass of men lead lives of quiet desperation.

—*H. D. Thoreau.*

DESPONDENCY
Nobody ever grew despondent looking for trouble.

—*Kin Hubbard.*

Despondency is ingratitude; hope is God's worship.

—*H. W. Beecher.*

DESPOTISM
It is the old practice of despots to use a part of the people to keep the rest in order.   —*T. Jefferson.*

All despotisms, under whatever name they masquerade, are efforts to freeze history, to stop change, to solidify the human spirit.   —*Charles A. Beard.*

There is only one way by which a despotism can be altered, that is by revolution, by the kind of violence employed in its establishment.   —*Ibid.*

The chief interest in the American crusade against slavery arises from its relation to this general world conflict between liberty and despotism.   —*Jesse Macy.*

Slavery and despotism are in their nature but a species of warfare. They involve the forcing of men to act in violation of their true selves.   —*Ibid.*

Despotic power is (shaken by) the threatened indignation of the whole civilized world.   —*Daniel Webster.*

It would be a dangerous delusion if our confidence in the men of our choice should silence our fears for the safety of our rights. Confidence is everywhere the parent of despotism. Free government is founded in jealousy, not in confidence.   —*T. Jefferson.*

When the white man governs himself, that is self-government; but when he governs himself and also another man, that is more than self-government—that is despotism.   —*A. Lincoln.*

DESPOTS
A genius is democratic and modern . . . Come forth sweet democratic despots of the West.   —*Walt Whitman.*

DESTINY

This generation of Americans has a rendezvous with destiny.
—*F. D. Roosevelt.*

Destiny is no matter of chance, it is a matter of choice: It is not a thing to be waited for, it is a thing to be achieved.
—*W. J. Bryan.*

Every man meets his Waterloo at last. —*Wendell Phillips.*

Our manifest destiny is to overspread the continent.
—*John Louis O'Sullivan.*

Destiny is the product of conduct. —*I. W. Joyce.*

In an age when . . . all Europe was alive with prophets, crying out, in the name of the human spirit, against the cruel advances of capitalist industrialising . . . America, innocent, ignorant, profoundly untroubled, slept the righteous sleep of its own manifest and peculiar destiny. —*Van Wyck Brooks.*

God did not make the American people the mightiest human force of all time simply to feed and die. He has appointed for us a destiny equal to our endowments. —*Albert Beveridge.*

We have one country, one constitution, and one destiny.
—*Daniel Webster.*

There is a destiny that makes us brothers—none goes his way alone. —*Edwin Markham.*

Lots of folks confuse bad management with destiny.
—*Kin Hubbard.*

We are part of a creative destiny, reaching backward and forward to infinity—a destiny that reveals itself, though dimly, in our striving, in our love, our thought, our appreciation.
—*J. E. Boodin.*

The preservation of the sacred fire of liberty and the destiny of the republican model of government are justly considered as deeply, and perhaps finally staked on the experiment entrusted to the American people. —*G. Washington.*

Men are what their mothers made them.
—*R. W. Emerson.*

Would the face of nature be so serene and beautiful if man's destiny were not equally so? —*H. D. Thoreau.*

Every noble scheme, every poetic manifestation, prophesies to man his eventual destiny. —*Margaret Fuller.*

DESTITUTE

He belongs to so many benevolent societies that he is destitute.
—E. W. Howe.

DETERMINATION

The die was now cast; I had passed the Rubicon. Swim or sink, live or die, survive or perish with my country was my unalterable determination.   *—John Adams.*

DETERMINISM

The theory of economic determination has not been tried out in American history, and until it is tried out, it cannot be found wanting.   *—Charles A. Beard.*

DETOUR

Detour: something that lengthens your mileage, diminishes your gas and strengthens your vocabulary.
—Oliver Herford.

DETRACTION

Unjustifiable detraction always proves the weakness as well as the meanness of the one who employs it.
—E. L. Magoon.

DEVIL

If there were only some shorter and more direct route to the devil, it would save an awful lot of sorrow and anxiety in this world.   *—Kin Hubbard.*

God indeed has the Devil in a chain, but has horribly lengthened out the chain.   *—Cotton Mather.*

Resist the devil and he will flee from you; offer him a bold front and he runs away.   *—Horace Bushnell.*

Merely by smashing our enemies we shall not remake the world. By Beelzebub no devils are cast out.   *—B. I. Bell.*

From the wiles of the Devil, I beseech thee deliver and defend Thy most unworthy servant.   *—Cotton Mather.*

I have set myself to countermine the whole plot of the Devil, against New England, in every branch of it.
—Ibid.

That there is a devil is a thing doubted by none but such as are under the influence of the Devil.   *—Ibid.*

It is not enough to tell me you worked hard to get your gold. So does the Devil work hard.   *—H. D. Thoreau.*

If I am the Devil's child, I will live then from the Devil; no law can be sacred to me but that of my nature.   —*R. W. Emerson.*

Give the devil his due, but be careful that there ain't much due him.   —*Josh Billings.*

DEVOTION

All is holy where devotion kneels.   —*O. W. Holmes.*

DEW

There is dew in one flower and not in another, because one opens its cup and takes it in, while the other closes itself and the drop runs off.   —*H. W. Beecher.*

DICE

The best throw of the dice is to throw them away.

—*Austin O'Malley.*

DICTATORSHIP

The dictators . . . will destroy one another, and kill off most of us. But even that disaster will not eradicate the desire of men and women to lay down their lives for that which is more than themselves.   —*B. I. Bell.*

No dictator in history has ever dared to run the gauntlet of a really free election.   —*F. D. Roosevelt.*

It is an axiom of statesmanship, which the successful founders of tyranny have understood and acted upon, that great changes can best be brought about under old forms.   —*Henry George.*

The superiority of democracy over dictatorship, as regards economic advancement, lies in its preference for the accumulation of capital rather than of cannon.   —*Carl Snyder.*

If in the long run the beliefs expressed in proletarian dictatorship are destined to be accepted by the dominant forces in the community, the only meaning of free speech is that they shall be given their chance and have their say.   —*O. W. Holmes, Jr.*

The ultimate failures of dictatorship cost humanity far more than any temporary failures of democracy.   —*F. D. Roosevelt.*

When liberty becomes license, dictatorship is near.

—*Will Durant.*

DIE

To die is different from what anyone supposed and luckier.

—*Walt Whitman.*

I never wanted to see anybody die, but there are a few obituary notices I have read with pleasure. *—Clarence Darrow.*

Let us endeavor so to live that when we come to die even the undertaker will be sorry. *—Mark Twain.*

DIET

In general, mankind, since the improvement of cookery, eat twice as much as nature requires. *—B. Franklin.*

DIFFERENCE

It makes but little difference whether you are committed to a farm or a county jail. *—H. D. Thoreau.*

The difference between the right word and the almost right word is the difference between lightning and the lightning bug.

—Mark Twain.

The difference between a man and his valet: they both smoke the same cigars, but only one pays for them. *—Robert Frost.*

The difference between a moral man and a man of honor is that the latter regrets a discreditable act even when it has worked.

—H. L. Mencken.

The difference between us and our neighbor is that we don't tell half of what we know while he doesn't know half of what he tells.

—G. D. Prentice.

DIFFICULT

Life is only difficult if we think or make it so. *—E. W. Bok.*

The Difficult is that which can be done immediately; the Impossible that which takes a little longer. *—George Santayana.*

DIFFICULTIES

Difficulties are God's errands and trainers, and only through them can one come to the fulness of manhood. *—H. W. Beecher.*

With stout hearts and strong arms we can surmount all our difficulties. *—Henry Clay.*

Difficulties are meant to rouse, not discourage. The human spirit is to grow strong by conflict. *—W. E. Channing.*

Nature, when she adds brain, adds difficulty.

—R. W. Emerson.

Difficulties, by bracing the mind to overcome them, assist cheerfulness as exercise assists digestion. *—C. N. Bovee.*

Difficulty is the excuse history never accepts. *—Samuel Grafton.*

The occasion is piled high with difficulty, and we must rise high with the occasion. —*A. Lincoln.*

DIGNITY

No race can prosper till it learns that there is as much dignity in tilling a field as in writing a poem. —*Booker T. Washington.*

Perhaps the only true dignity of man is his capacity to despise himself. —*George Santayana.*

Dignity belongs to the conquered. —*Kenneth Burke.*

The primal principle of democracy is the worth and dignity of the individual. —*Edward Bellamy.*

That dignity, consisting in the quality of human nature, is essentially the same in all individuals, and therefore equality is the vital principle of democracy. —*Ibid.*

If the equality of individuals and the dignity of man be myths, they are myths to which the republic is committed.
—*Howard Mumford Jones.*

I believe in the dignity of labor, whether with head or hand; that the world owes every man an opportunity to make a living.
—*John D. Rockefeller, Jr.*

In all human beings, if only understanding be brought to the business, dignity will be found. —*H. L. Mencken.*

It is of little use in trying to be dignified, if dignity is no part of your character. —*C. N. Bovee.*

There is a healthful hardiness about real dignity that never dreads contact and communion with others, however humble.
—*Washington Irving.*

DILIGENCE

Diligence is the mother of good luck. —*B. Franklin.*

DIPLOMACY

Diplomacy: lying in state. —*Oliver Herford.*

International arbitration may be defined as the substitution of many burning questions for a smouldering one.
—*Ambrose Bierce.*

American diplomacy is easy on the brain but hell on the feet.
—*Charles G. Dawes.*

Diplomacy is to do and say
The nastiest thing in the nicest way.
                                    —*Isaac Goldberg.*

Diplomacy is a disguised war, in which states seek to gain by
barter and intrigue, by the cleverness of arts, the objectives which
they would have to gain more clumsily by means of war.
                                    —*Randolph Bourne.*

A diplomatic character is the narrowest sphere of society that
man can act in. It forbids intercourse by a reciprocity of suspicion;
and a diplomatist is a sort of unconnected atom, continually re-
pelling and repelled.   —*T. Paine.*

There are three species of creatures who when they seem coming are going, when they seem going they come: diplomats,
women, and crabs.   —*John Hay.*

A diplomat is a man who always remembers a woman's birth-
day but never remembers her age.   —*Robert Frost.*

DIRECTION
The great thing in this world is not so much where we are, but
in what direction we are moving.   —*O. W. Holmes.*

No individual or group will be judged by whether they come up
to or fall short of some fixed result, but by the direction in which
they are moving.   —*John Dewey.*

The good man is the man who, no matter how morally unworthy
he has been, is moving to become better.   —*Ibid.*

The world turns aside to let any man pass who knows whither he
is going.   —*D. S. Jordan.*

One has to know where he is going before he can go about
finding out how he can get there.   —*Joseph Rosenfarb.*

Progress implies direction and that means some conscious purpose.   —*Ibid.*

A person is really alive only when he is moving forward to
something more.   —*Winifred Rhoades.*

The penguin flies backwards because he doesn't care to see
where he's going, but wants to see where he's been.
                                    —*Fred Allen.*

DISAPPOINTMENT
Mean spirits under disappointment, like small beer in a thunderstorm, always turn sour.   —*John Randolph.*

Disappointment is often the salt of life. *—Theodore Parker.*

We mount to heaven mostly on the ruins of our cherished schemes, finding our failures were successes. *—A. B. Alcott.*

DISCIPLINE

Education is what is given and gotten at college,—discipline for life's duties, discipline to life's natural and moral laws, discipline to the rule of life's Great Exemplar. *—J. Edwards.*

It is never wise to slip the hands of discipline.

—Lew Wallace.

No pain, no palm; no thorns, no throne; no gall, no glory; no cross, no crown. *—Wm. Penn.*

In the order named, these are the hardest to control: Wine, Women and Song. *—F. P. Adams.*

DISCONTENT

Restlessness is discontent—and discontent is the first necessity of progress. Show me a thoroughly satisfied man—and I will show you a failure. *—Thomas A. Edison.*

Discontent is the want of self-reliance; it is conformity of will. *—R. W. Emerson.*

DISCOVERY

Early in our experience we made the revolutionary discovery that gentleness and kindliness were more practical than brute strength. *—R. W. Riis.*

I think the true discovery of America is before us. I think the true fulfillment of our spirit, of our people, of our mighty and immortal land is yet to come. *—Thomas Wolfe.*

All great discoveries are made by men whose feelings run ahead of their thinking. *—C. H. Parkhurst.*

DISCRETION

I have never been hurt by anything I didn't say.

—Calvin Coolidge.

When you have got an elephant by the hind leg, and he is trying to run away, it's best to let him run. *—A. Lincoln.*

A sound discretion is not so much indicated by never making a mistake as by never repeating it. *—C. N. Bovee.*

DISCUSSION

Good discussion is a kind of detective uncovering the hidden categories and secret springs of emotions that underlie "opinions" on things.   —*Randolph Bourne.*

A good discussion . . . is fundamentally a cooperation. It progresses towards some common understanding.   —*Ibid.*

A good discussion increases the dimensions of everyone who takes part.   —*Ibid.*

Discussion: a method of confirming others in their errors.
                                                      —*Ambrose Bierce.*

DISEASE

We classify disease as error, which nothing but Truth or Mind can heal.   —*Mary Baker Eddy.*

Because man's emotions are still tied to the past while his ideas move toward the future, he finds himself in a state of division and disease.   —*Samuel D. Schmalhausen.*

We are the carriers of health and disease—either the divine health of courage and nobility or the demonic diseases of hate and anxiety.   —*Joshua Loth Liebman.*

No one can be immunized against us; as long as we live we make the world freer or more enslaved, nobler or more degraded.
                                                                      —*Ibid.*

The fear of life is the favorite disease of the twentieth century.
                                                             —*W. L. Phelps.*

Disease is the retribution of outraged Nature.   —*Hosea Ballou.*

In diagnosing the disease called humanity . . . poets present the most mark'd indications.   —*Walt Whitman.*

The diseases of the present have little in common with the diseases of the past save that we die of them.   —*Agnes Repplier.*

A bodily disease may be but a symptom of some ailment in the spiritual past.   —*Nathaniel Hawthorne.*

Decay and disease are often beautiful, like the pearly tear of shell-fish and the hectic glow of consumption.   —*H. D. Thoreau.*

Priggishness is just like painter's colic or any other trade disease.
                                                           —*William James.*

DISGRACE

It's no disgrace to be poor, but it might as well be.
                                                              —*Kin Hubbard.*

No one can disgrace us but ourselves. *—J. G. Holland.*

DISHONESTY

Dishonesty is so grasping it would deceive God Himself, were it possible. *—George Bancroft.*

DISINFECTANTS

But if men cannot live on bread alone, still less can they do so on disinfectants. *—A. N. Whitehead.*

DISINTEGRATION

We (must) regard crime, mental disorders, family disorganization, juvenile delinquency, prostitution and sex offenses, and much that now passes as the result of pathological processes (e.g., gastric ulcer) as evidence, not of individual wickedness, incompetence, perversity, or pathology, but as human reactions to cultural disintegration. *—Laurence K. Frank.*

DISLOYALTY

There is something peculiarly sinister and insidious in even a charge of disloyalty. Such a charge all too frequently places a stain on the reputation of an individual which is indelible and lasting, regardless of the complete innocence later proved.
—John Lord O'Brian.

Every effort to confine Americanism to a single pattern, to constrain it to a single formula, is disloyalty to everything that is valid to Americanism. *—H. S. Commager.*

DISPUTE

It were endless to dispute upon everything that is disputable.
—Wm. Penn.

DISSENT

In a number of cases dissenting opinions have in time become the law. *—Charles Evans Hughes.*

Those who begin coercive elimination of dissent soon find themselves exterminating dissenters. Compulsory unification of opinion achieves only the unanimity of the graveyard.
—Felix Frankfurter.

If our democracy is to flourish, it must have criticism; if our government is to function it must have dissent.
—H. S. Commager.

DISSOLUTION

I laugh at what you call dissolution,
And I know the amplitude of time.
—*Walt Whitman.*

DISTINCTION

Distinctions in society will always exist under every just government.   —*Andrew Jackson.*

Whether in heaven or in hell, or in whatever state man is supposed to exist hereafter, the good and the bad are the only distinctions.   —*T. Paine.*

DISTRUST

The older I grow, the more I distrust the familiar doctrine that age brings wisdom.   —*H. L. Mencken.*

On one issue at least, men and women agree: they both distrust women.   —*Ibid.*

There is no republican road to safety but in constant distrust.
—*Wendell Phillips.*

Self-distrust is the cause of most of our failures.
—*C. N. Bovee.*

To think and feel we are able, is often to be so.   —*Joel Hawes.*

DIVERSITY

I resist anything more than my own diversity.
—*Walt Whitman.*

DIVORCE

Divorce is like matrimony: a fellow has got to go through it three or four times before he knows how.   —*Edgar Saltus.*

The divorced were never really married.   —*J. L. Basford.*

Desertion—the poor man's method of divorce.   —*A. G. Hays.*

DO

If thou wouldst not be known to do anything, never do it.
—*R. W. Emerson.*

Our chief want in life is somebody who shall make us do what we can.   —*Ibid.*

We can't do for another without at the same time doing for ourselves.   —*R. W. Trine.*

DOCTORS

God heals and the doctor takes the fee.   —*B. Franklin.*

The doctor is not infrequently death's pilot-fish.
  —*G. D. Prentice.*

No profession can boast of so many active men of great age as medicine.   —*Elbert Hubbard.*

Doctors know what you tell them.   —*Don Herold.*

> Joy and Temperance and Repose
> Slam the door on the doctor's nose.
>   —*H. W. Longfellow.*

DOCTRINE

Doctrine is the necessary foundation of duty; if the theory is not correct, the practise cannot be right. Tell me what a man believes, and I will tell you what he will do. —*Tryon Edwards.*

Doctrine is nothing but the skin of truth set up and stuffed.
  —*H. W. Beecher.*

A clash of doctrines is not a disaster—it is an opportunity.
  —*A. N. Whitehead.*

DOG

If you pick up a starving dog and make him prosperous, he will not bite you. That is the principal difference between a dog and a man.   —*Mark Twain.*

When a man's dog turns against him it is time for a wife to pack her trunk and go home to mama.   —*Ibid.*

The dog is the filthiest of the domestic animals. For this he makes up in a servile, fawning attitude towards his master.
  —*Thorstein Veblen.*

The dog commends himself to our favor by affording play to our propensity for mastery.   —*Ibid.*

The dog that snaps the quickest gets the bone.
  —*Daniel Drew.*

A dog is the only thing on this earth that loves you more than he loves himself.   —*Josh Billings.*

The dog that will follow everybody ain't worth a curse.
  —*Ibid.*

A reasonable number of fleas is good for a dog—keeps him from brooding over being a dog.   —*E. N. Westcott.*

About the only thing on a farm that has an easy time is the dog.
—*E. W. Howe.*

DOGMAS

The dogmas of the quiet past are inadequate to the stormy present.   —*A. Lincoln.*

Every dogma must have its day.   —*Carolyn Wells.*

DOGMATIC

It is always safe to be dogmatic about tomorrow.

—*Heywood Broun.*

DOING

Because I cannot do everything, I will not refuse to do the something that I can do.   —*E. E. Hale.*

DOLES

Governing people may prefer to give doles to idle working people . . . but the practice extended over long periods of time is ruinous to economy and morals. It represents the imbecility of defeatism.   —*Charles A. Beard.*

DOLLAR

The Almighty Dollar, that great object of universal devotion throughout our land.   —*Washington Irving.*

The dollar mark is not the stamp of success. You may attain far greater success than that, and leave a much larger legacy.
—*W. E. Mason.*

With all this talk about taking care of the unemployed, what is going to take care of the unemployed employer? Nothing except the consumer's dollar.   —*H. L. Hopkins.*

DOMESTIC

It is not education which makes women less domestic, but wealth.   —*Katherine J. Gallagher.*

DOOM

If we suffer tamely a lawless attack upon our liberty, we encourage it, and involve others in our doom.   —*Samuel Adams.*

DOOMSDAY

No man has learned anything rightly until he knows that every day is doomsday.   —*R. W. Emerson.*

DOT

The dot is simply a bribe designed to overcome the disinclination of the male. —*H. L. Mencken.*

DOUBLE

The safest way to double your money is to fold it over once and put it in your pocket. —*Kin Hubbard.*

DOUBT

More persons, on the whole, are humbugged by believing in nothing, than by believing too much. —*P. T. Barnum.*

Just think of the tragedy of teaching children not to doubt.
—*Clarence Darrow.*

I respect faith, but doubt is what gets you an education.
—*Wilson Mizner.*

When in doubt, tell the truth. —*Mark Twain.*

Don't waste life in doubts and fears. —*R. W. Emerson.*

To have doubted one's own first principles, is the mark of a civilized man. —*O. W. Holmes, Jr.*

Faith keeps many doubts in her pay. If I could not doubt, I should not believe. —*H. D. Thoreau.*

DRAMA

All stories are drama. —*Bernard De Voto.*

The dramatist, like the poet, is born, not made.
—*William Winter.*

DREAMS

The American Dream . . . has been a dream of being able to grow to the fullest development as man and woman.
—*James Truslow Adams.*

If while we sleep, we can have pleasant dreams, it is so much added to the pleasure of life. —*B. Franklin.*

In dreams we are true poets; we create the persons of the drama . . . and we listen with surprise to what they say.
—*R. W. Emerson.*

If one advances confidently in the directions of his dreams, and endeavors to live the life which he has imagined, he will meet with a success unexpected in common hours. —*H. D. Thoreau.*

Dogs dream, horses dream, all animals dream. —*Jack London.*

The smaller the head, the bigger the dream.

—*Austin O'Malley.*

The existing world is not a dream, and cannot with impunity be treated as a dream.   —*R. W. Emerson.*

Dreams are nothing but incoherent ideas, occasioned by partial or imperfect sleep.   —*Benjamin Rush.*

Just because you brought dreams with you, America is more likely to realize dreams such as you brought. You are enriching us if you came expecting us to be better than we are.

—*Woodrow Wilson.*

Let there be dreams, one said. I answered: Yea, Let there be dreams today.   —*Clinton Scollard.*

DRESS

Any garment which is cut to fit you is much more becoming even if it is not so splendid as a garment which has been cut to fit somebody not of your stature.   —*Edna Ferber.*

Beware of all enterprises that require new clothes.

—*H. D. Thoreau.*

Be careless in your dress if you must, but keep a tidy soul.

—*Mark Twain.*

Eat to please thyself, but dress to please others.   —*B. Franklin.*

When a soldier is hit by a cannon-ball, rags are as becoming as purple.   —*H. D. Thoreau.*

No man ever stood lower in my estimation for having a patch in his clothes.   —*Ibid.*

The cat in gloves catches no mice.   —*B. Franklin.*

There is new strength, repose of mind, and inspiration in fresh apparel.   —*Ella W. Wilcox.*

If a man should suddenly be changed to a woman, he couldn't get his clothes off.   —*E. W. Howe.*

No woman should have enough clothes to make her ask, "What'll I wear?"   —*Don Herold.*

Clothes don't make the man, but good clothes have got many a man a good job.   —*H. H. Vreeland.*

It is an interesting question how far men would retain their relative rank if they were divested of their clothes.

—*H. D. Thoreau.*

I hate to see men overdressed; a man ought to look like he's put together by accident, not added up on purpose.

—*Christopher Morley.*

We should have harmony of dress, both sexes participating in a general result of charm that blends to make our artistic whole.

—*Richard Burton.*

Half the human race has been shut out from the privilege of pleasing the taste by dress. —*Ibid.*

DRINKING

There are two things that will be believed of any man whatsoever, and one of them is that he has taken to drink.

—*Booth Tarkington.*

All excess is ill, but drunkenness is of the worst sort.

—*Wm. Penn.*

He that is drunk is not a man, because he is void of reason that distinguishes a man from a beast. —*Ibid.*

A soft drink turneth away company. —*Oliver Herford.*

Drinking makes such fools of people, and people are such fools to begin with, that it's compounding a felony. —*Robert Benchley.*

One swallow doesn't make a summer but too many swallows make a fall. —*G. D. Prentice.*

Many a man keeps on drinking till he hasn't a coat to either his back or his stomach. —*Ibid.*

DRUNKARDS

There are more old drunkards than old doctors. —*B. Franklin.*

A drunkard is like a whisky bottle, all neck and belly and no head. —*Austin O'Malley.*

DUNKING

Dunking is bad taste but tastes good. —*F. P. Adams.*

DUPLICITY

No man, for any considerable period, can wear one face to himself, and another to the multitude, without finally getting bewildered as to which may be the true. —*Nathaniel Hawthorne.*

DURABILITY

A nation may be said to consist of its territory, its people, and laws. The territory is the only part which is of certain durability.

—*A. Lincoln.*

DUTY

Do your duty and leave the consequences to God.
—Wade Hampton.

It is the duty of all public officers to minister according to the plain rules of the public state, and not by their own fancy and wills.   *—John Wise.*

> When Duty whispers low, "Thou must,"
> The youth replies, "I can."
> *—R. W. Emerson.*

Who escapes a duty, avoids a gain.   *—Theodore Parker.*

Do thy duty; that is best; leave unto the Lord the rest.
—H. W. Longfellow.

Reverence the highest; have patience with the lowest; let this day's performance of the meanest duty be thy religion.
—Margaret Fuller.

Human happiness and moral duty are inseparably connected.
—G. Washington.

Religious duties consist in doing justice, loving mercy, and endeavoring to make our fellow-creatures happy.   *—T. Paine.*

It is the duty of those serving the people in public places to closely limit public expenditures to the actual needs of the government economically administered.   *—Grover Cleveland.*

Every man is under the natural duty of contributing to the necessities of society, and this is all the laws should enforce on him.
—T. Jefferson.

There is nothing in the universe that I fear, but that I shall not know all my duty or fail to do it.   *—Mary Lyon.*

Persons are disposed to mount upon some particular duty, as upon a war-horse, and to drive it furiously on and upon and over all other duties that may stand in the way.   *—Daniel Webster.*

There are men who, with clear perceptions, as they think, of their own duty, do not see how too eager a pursuit of one duty may involve them in the violation of others, or how too warm an embracement of one truth may lead to a disregard of other truths equally important.   *—Ibid.*

When you have a number of disagreeable duties to perform, always do the most disagreeable first.   *—Josiah Quincy.*

. . . it is just as hard to do your duty when men are sneering at you as when they are shooting at you.   —*Woodrow Wilson.*

Fellowships we want, that will hold, not religion as a duty, but duty as a religion.   —*Felix Adler.*

All higher motives, ideals, conceptions, sentiments in a man are of no account if they do not come forward to strengthen him for the better discharge of the duties which devolve upon him in the ordinary affairs of life.   —*H. W. Beecher.*

The liberties of our country, the freedom of our civil constitution, are worth defending at all hazards, and it is our duty to defend them against all attacks.   —*Samuel Adams.*

I am much too good and noble to sacrifice my preferences to my duty.   —*W. D. Howells.*

The most important part of self-culture is to enthrone the sense of duty within us.   —*W. E. Channing.*

Only aim to do your duty, and mankind will give you credit where you fail.   —*T. Jefferson.*

DYNAMIC

We must wish to maintain a dynamic, progressive people. No nation can remain static and survive.   —*Herbert Hoover.*

Dynamic progress is not made with dynamite. And that dynamite today is the geometrical increase of spending by our Governments —federal, state and local.   —*Ibid.*

DYSPEPTIC

A dyspeptic is a man that can eat his cake and have it too.
—*Austin O'Malley.*

E

EARLY

The early morning has gold in its mouth.

—*B. Franklin.*

He who rises late may trot all day, and not overtake his business at night.   —*Ibid.*

EARNEST

A man in earnest finds means, or, if he cannot find, creates them.

—*W. E. Channing.*

EARNESTNESS

Earnestness is the devotion of all the faculties.

—*C. N. Bovee.*

The earnestness of life is the only passport to the satisfaction of life.   —*Theodore Parker.*

EARNING

A man who accepts any share which he has not earned in another man's capital cannot be an independent citizen.

—*W. G. Sumner.*

EARTH

The earth and its resources belong of right to its people.

—*Gifford Pinchot.*

There is many a man whose strength is renewed like that of the wrestler of Irrassa every time his feet touch the earth.

—*Ray S. Baker.*

Our earth is but a small star in the great universe. Yet of it we can make, if we choose, a planet unvexed by war, untroubled by hunger or fear, undivided by senseless distinctions of race, color or theory.   —*Stephen V. Benét.*

The earth is given as a common for men to labor and live in.
—T. Jefferson.

This whole earth which we inhabit is but a point in space.
—H. D. Thoreau.

Either mankind unites or it will destroy itself; either the earth is governed or it will be blown up. *—Harris Wofford, Jr.*

"The earth is the Lord's and the fullness thereof": this is no longer a hollow dictum of religion, but a directive for economic action toward human brotherhood. *—Lewis Mumford.*

'Tis the same to him who wears a shoe, as if the whole earth were covered with leather. *—R. W. Emerson.*

EASTER

The Easter story is the story of the fundamental fight between life and death, between hope and despair. *—Heywood Broun.*

If the city of our heart is holy with the presence of a living Christ, then the dear dead will come to us, and we shall know that they are not dead but living. *—Phillips Brooks.*

EASTWARD

We go eastward to realize history and study the works of art and literature, retracing the steps of the race; we go westward as into the future, with a spirit of enterprise and adventure.
—H. D. Thoreau.

EASY

Easy, pleasant work does not make robust minds, does not give men a consciousness of their powers, does not train them to endurance, to perseverance, to steady force without which all other acquisitions avail nothing. *—W. E. Channing.*

It is easy in the world to live after the world's opinion; it is easy in solitude to live after our own; but the great man is he who in the midst of the crowd keeps with perfect sweetness the independence of solitude. *—R. W. Emerson.*

EATING

Part of the secret of success in life is to eat what you like and let the food fight it out inside. *—Mark Twain.*

Married life ain't so bad after you get so you can eat things your wife likes. *—Kin Hubbard.*

No man is lonely while eating spaghetti—it requires so much attention.   —*Christopher Morley.*

To eat is human; to digest, divine.   —*C. T. Copeland.*

Fools make feasts, and wise men eat them.   —*B. Franklin.*

One should eat to live, not live to eat.   —*Ibid.*

ECCENTRICITY

Be virtuous and you will be eccentric.   —*Mark Twain.*

Eccentricity is developed monomania.   —*Bayard Taylor.*

Without bigots, eccentrics, cranks and heretics the world would not progress.   —*Gelett Burgess.*

ECHO

Applause is the echo of a platitude.   —*Ambrose Bierce.*

The old echoes are long in dying.   —*C. H. Parkhurst.*

ECONOMIC

The burden of all sensible critiques of modern society must be against its economic structure.   —*C. Hartley Grattan.*

ECONOMICS

Economics and art are strangers.   —*Willa Cather.*

ECONOMY

Beware of little expenses; a small leak will sink a great ship.
—*B. Franklin.*

Ere you consult your fancy, consult your purse.   —*Ibid.*

A man often pays dear for a small frugality.   —*R. W. Emerson.*

They take their pride in making their dinner cost much; I take my pride in making my dinner cost little.   —*H. D. Thoreau.*

Economy is for the poor; the rich may dispense with it.
—*C. N. Bovee.*

I believe that thrift is essential to well ordered living and that economy is a prime requisite of a sound financial structure, whether in government, business or personal affairs.

—*John D. Rockefeller, Jr.*

Our economy is to a considerable extent controlled: it is characterized by group, by organized action. The individual has been, if not dethroned, at least de-emphasized.   —*B. L. Masse.*

Don't give too much for the whistle.   —*B. Franklin.*

The efficiency of most workers is beyond the control of the management and depends more than has been supposed upon the willingness of men to do their best. —*S. H. Slichter.*

I place economy among the first and most important of republican virtues. —*T. Jefferson.*

The life and spirit of the American economy is progress and expansion. —*H. S. Truman.*

EDITOR

Editor: a person employed on a newspaper, whose business it is to separate the wheat from the chaff, and to see that the chaff is printed. —*Elbert Hubbard.*

EDUCATION

When you educate a man you educate an individual; when you educate a woman you educate a whole family. —*R. M. MacIver.*

The educated scamp is a scamp still and all the more dangerous to the community. —*Theodore Roosevelt.*

Education: that which discloses to the wise and disguises from the foolish their lack of understanding. —*Ambrose Bierce.*

If a man empties his purse into his head, no man can take it away from him. An investment in knowledge always pays the best interest. —*B. Franklin.*

Very few can be trusted with an education.
—*Louise I. Guiney.*

There is nothing to which education is subordinate save more education. —*John L. Childs.*

To educate a child perfectly requires profounder thought, greater wisdom, than to govern a state. —*W. E. Channing.*

If a man's education is finished he is finished. —*E. A. Filene.*

Nothing in education is so astonishing as the amount of ignorance it accumulates in the form of inert facts. —*Henry Adams.*

There is not a good work which the hand of man has ever undertaken, which his heart has ever conceived, which does not require a good education for its helper. —*Horace Mann.*

As to education, the greater the need the greater the dislike.
—*L. Gronlund.*

Education is a better safeguard of liberty than a standing army.
—*Edward Everett.*

Education toward a world order must begin at home. We must begin by educating ourselves toward a universal ideal, not by striving to educate all people to our model.   —*Roscoe Pound.*

Education, we are often told, is a drawing out of the faculties.
—*J. R. Lowell.*

If, almost on the day of their landings, our ancestors founded schools and endowed colleges, what obligations do not rest upon us, living under circumstances so much more favorable, both for providing and for using the means of education?
—*Daniel Webster.*

The attainment of knowledge does not comprise all which is contained in the larger term of education.   —*Ibid.*

The best education in the world is that got by struggling to get a living.   —*Wendell Phillips.*

Education is our only political safety. Outside of this ark all is deluge.   —*Horace Mann.*

Do not ask if a man has been through college; ask if a college has been through him—if he is a walking university.
—*E. H. Chapin.*

You can lead a boy to college, but you cannot make him think.
—*Elbert Hubbard.*

Training is everything. The peach was once a bitter almond; cauliflower is but cabbage with a college education.
—*Mark Twain.*

Soap and education are not as sudden as a massacre, but they are more deadly in the long run.   —*Mark Twain.*

I do not desire to drive Europe out of the colleges, I merely insist upon the necessity of putting America in.
—*Howard Mumford Jones.*

There is but one method of preventing crimes, and of rendering a republican form of government durable, and that is, by disseminating the seeds of virtue and knowledge through every part of the state by means of proper places and modes of education, and this can be done effectually only by the interference and aid of the Legislature.   —*Benjamin Rush.*

No mother's mark is more permanent than the mental naevi and moles, and excrescences, and mutilations, that students carry with them out of the lecture room.   —*O. W. Holmes.*

A child's education should begin at least one hundred years before he was born.   —*Ibid.*

We need education in the obvious more than investigation of the obscure.   —*Ibid.*

The best way to combat a campaign of miseducation is to conduct a campaign of education.   —*Thomas A. Edison.*

Our educational system—much of it—belongs in the time when we traveled by horse-back and canal boat.   —*Ibid.*

Only a long and still unfinished education has taught men to separate emotions from things and ideas from their objects.
—*George Santayana.*

I have never let my schooling interfere with my education.
—*Mark Twain.*

The most important method of education always has consisted of that in which the pupil was urged to actual performance.
—*Albert Einstein.*

Humiliation and mental oppression by ignorant and selfish teachers wreak havoc in the youthful mind that can never be undone and often exert a baleful influence in later life.
—*Ibid.*

EFFICIENCY

In the old world that is passing, in the new world that is coming, national efficiency has been and will be a controlling factor in national safety and welfare.   —*Gifford Pinchot.*

EFFORT

The percentage of the national effort which is spent on preparation for war may be indicative of the moral decadence of any civilization.   —*Jerome Davis.*

It is hard to fail, but it is worse never to have tried to succeed. In this life we get nothing save by effort.
—*Theodore Roosevelt.*

Freedom from effort in the present merely means that there has been effort stored up in the past.   —*Ibid.*

You never know what you can do without until you try.
—*F. P. Adams.*

The man who does not learn, early in life, to focus his efforts, to centralize his power, will never achieve marked success in anything.   —*O. S. Marden.*

Man owes his growth, his energy, chiefly to that striving of the will, that conflict with difficulty, which we call effort.

—*W. E. Channing.*

After several years of cold war, we are intensely aware that a military effort cannot be separated from political objectives.

—*Omar N. Bradley.*

Keep the faculty of effort alive in thee by a little gratuitous exercise every day.   —*William James.*

Do every day or two something for no other reason than thou wouldst rather not do it, so that when the hour of dire need draws nigh, it may find thee not unnerved and untrained to stand the test.

—*Ibid.*

EGGS

All the goodness of a good egg cannot make up for the badness of a bad one.   —*Charles A. Dana.*

Most men are like eggs, too full of themselves to hold anything else.   —*Josh Billings.*

One does not need to eat more than part of an egg to know that it is bad.   —*Walter Hines Page.*

EGOTISM

I now know all the people worth knowing in America, and I find no intellect comparable to mine.   —*Margaret Fuller.*

Some of the greatest love affairs I've known have involved one actor—unassisted.   —*Wilson Mizner.*

Take egotism out, and you would castrate the benefactors.

—*R. W. Emerson.*

The man who lives to himself alone lives a little, dwarfed, and stunted life, because he has no part in this larger life of humanity.

—*R. W. Trine.*

Nor do I understand who there can be more wonderful than myself.   —*Walt Whitman.*

The hermit who runs off into the seclusion of the desert or the forest or the cloister or the ivory tower is often less of a saint than an egotistical sinner who tries to strike a special bargain with the Lord or Mephistopheles.   —*Dagobert D. Runes.*

EGOTIST

An egotist is a man who talks so much about himself that he gives me no time to talk about myself.   —*H. L. Wayland.*

Egotist: a person of low taste, more interested in himself than in me.   *—Ambrose Bierce.*

EIGHT-HOUR-DAY
Eight hours to work, eight hours to play, eight hours to sleep, seems to be the ideal division.   *—Andrew Carnegie.*

Any man who wishes his brother to work more than eight hours a day is not a civilized man.   *—R. G. Ingersoll.*

ELECT
The Elect are whosoever will, and the non-elect are whosoever won't.   *—H. W. Beecher.*

ELECTION
No matter whether the Constitution follows the flag or not, the Supreme Court follows the election returns.   *—F. P. Dunne.*

The Republicans have their splits right after election, and Democrats have theirs just before an election.   *—Will Rogers.*

The election isn't very far off when a candidate can recognize you across the street.   *—Kin Hubbard.*

ELEGANCE
Self-command is the main elegance.   *—R. W. Emerson.*

ELEVATORS
There are no elevators in the house of success.

—H. H. Vreeland.

ELIGIBLE
If you are eligible to bad fortune where you stand, you are equally eligible to good fortune there.   *—John Burroughs.*

ELITE
Each honest calling, each walk of life, has its own elite, its own aristocracy based on excellence of performance.   *—James Conant.*

ELOQUENCE
There is no eloquence without a man behind it.

—R. W. Emerson.

Eloquence is logic on fire.   *—Lyman Beecher.*

Eloquence shows the power and possibility of man.

—R. W. Emerson.

False eloquence is exaggeration; true eloquence is emphasis.

—*W. R. Alger.*

True eloquence does not consist in speech. Words and phrases may be marshalled in every way, but they cannot compass it. It must consist in the man, in the subject, and in the occasion. It comes, if it comes at all, like the outbreaking of a fountain from the earth, or the bursting forth of volcanic fires, with spontaneous, original native force.   —*Daniel Webster.*

ELUSIVE

Men like to pursue an elusive woman, like a cake of wet soap in a bathtub—even men who hate baths.   —*Gelett Burgess.*

EMERGENCY

In the emergency of war our nation's powers are unbelievable.

—*Ernie Pyle.*

EMERSON

Thank God for the sun, the moon, and Ralph Waldo Emerson.

—*Theodore Parker.*

EMINENT

That you have enemies you must not doubt, when you reflect that you have made yourself eminent.   —*T. Jefferson.*

EMOTIONS

Self-esteem is the most voluble of the emotions.

—*F. M. Colby.*

The young man who has not wept is a savage, and the old man who will not laugh is a fool.   —*George Santayana.*

An enraged man is a lion, a cunning man is a fox, a firm man is a rock, a learned man is a torch.   —*R. W. Emerson.*

Middle age: when you begin to exchange your emotions for symptoms.   —*I. S. Cobb.*

How many women are born too finely organized in sense and soul for the highway they must walk with feet unshod.

—*O. W. Holmes.*

Emotion is the surest arbiter of a poetic choice, and it is the priest of all supreme unions in the mind.   —*Max Eastman.*

Man became half human while worshipping at the shrine of pure reason; the result was the emotions were captured by perverts and tyrants.   —*Joshua Loth Liebman.*

Since Freud, it is quite clear that emotion is a major part of human life, the mother of reason, the source of art, science, literature and religion.   —*Ibid.*

EMPIRE

A great empire, like a great cake, is most easily diminished at the edges.   —*B. Franklin.*

EMPIRICIST

The really competent critic must be an empiricist. If pills fail, he gets out his saw. If the saw won't cut, he seizes a club.

—*H. L. Mencken.*

EMPLOYER

The time when the employer could ride roughshod over his labor is disappearing with the doctrine of "laissez-faire" in which it was founded. The sooner the fact is recognized, the better for the employer.   —*Herbert Hoover.*

EMPLOYMENT

Not only our future economic soundness but the very soundness of our democratic institutions depends on the determination of our Government to give employment to idle men.

—*F. D. Roosevelt.*

Employment gives health, sobriety and morals.

—*Daniel Webster.*

Life is hardly respectable if it has no generous task, no duties or affections that constitute a necessity of existing.

—*George B. Emerson.*

Each man's task is his life-preserver.   —*Ibid.*

ENCROACHMENTS

There are more instances of the abridgement of the freedom of the people by gradual and silent encroachments of those in power than by violent and sudden usurpation.   —*James Madison.*

END

The final end of government is not to exert restraint but to do good.   —*Rufus Choate.*

The end of good government is to cultivate humanity, and promote the happiness of all.   —*John Wise.*

The end justifies the means only when the means used are such as actually bring about the desired and desirable end.

—John Dewey.

The end, in the sense of consequences, provides the only basis for moral values and action, the only justification that can be found for means employed.   *—Ibid.*

The only ends are the consequences.   *—Ibid.*

The only worthwhile ends in community life are free men who live and exemplify their freedom, in a social and cooperative spirit.

—James T. Farrell.

Freedom is only good as a means; is no end in itself.

—Herman Melville.

If we are but sure the end is right, we are too apt to gallop over all bounds to compass it; not considering the lawful ends may be very unlawfully attained.   *—Wm. Penn.*

The real justification of a rule of law is that it helps to bring about a social end which we desire.   *—O. W. Holmes, Jr.*

Knowledge of means without knowledge of ends is animal training.   *—E. D. Martin.*

ENDEAVOR

Christian endeavor is notoriously hard on female pulchritude.

—H. L. Mencken.

ENDURANCE

One never endures or endeavors to one's self alone.

—W. D. Howells.

Still achieving, still pursuing, learn to labor and to wait.

—H. W. Longfellow.

Endurance is the crowning quality.   *—J. R. Lowell.*

Not in the achievement, but in the endurance of the human soul, does it show its divine grandeur, and its alliance with the infinite God.   *—E. H. Chapin.*

ENEMIES

When you are ill make haste to forgive your enemies, for you may recover.   *—Ambrose Bierce.*

If you have no enemies, you are apt to be in the same predicament in regard to friends.   *—Elbert Hubbard.*

Love your enemies, for they tell you your faults. *—B. Franklin.*

Instead of loving your enemies, treat your friends a little better.
—*E. W. Howe.*

The man who ain't got an enemy is really poor. —*Josh Billings.*

Slavery is the deadly enemy of free labor. —*David Wilmot.*

Those whom I served most essentially have been my greatest enemies. —*Benjamin Rush.*

Any power must be the enemy of mankind which enslaves the individual by terror and force. —*Albert Einstein.*

Life would not be worth living if we didn't keep our enemies.
—*F. P. Dunne.*

There is no little enemy. —*B. Franklin.*

It is from our enemies that we often gain excellent maxims, and are frequently surprised into reason by their mistakes.
—*T. Paine.*

Men will never love their enemies until they cease to have enmities. —*John Dewey.*

ENERGY

Manual labor is a school in which men are placed to get energy of purpose and character. —*W. E. Channing.*

Energy and persistence conquer all things. —*B. Franklin.*

What is woman released from reproductive fulfillment, to do with her pent-up negated energy? What is so often referred to as the restlessness of modern woman is obviously traceable to this major frustration and willed perversion of deep biologic impulses.
—*Samuel D. Schmalhausen.*

Energy, even like the biblical grain of mustard-seed, will remove mountains. —*Hosea Ballou.*

The world belongs to the energetic. —*R. W. Emerson.*

ENFORCEMENT

In enforcing a truth we need severity rather than efflorescence calm. —*Alexander Woollcott.*

ENGLISH

The English have an extraordinary ability for flying into a great of language. —*Edgar Allan Poe.*

ENGLISH LANGUAGE

View'd freely, the English language is the accretion and growth of every dialect, race and range of time, and is both the free and compacted composition of all.   *—Walt Whitman.*

ENJOYMENT

The common stock of intellectual enjoyment should not be difficult of access because of the economic position of him who would approach it.   *—Jane Addams.*

Those who would enjoyment gain must find it in the purpose they pursue.   *—Sarah J. Hale.*

The first half of life consists of the capacity to enjoy without the chance; the last half consists of the chance without the capacity.
—Mark Twain.

ENNUI

Ennui shortens life, and bereaves the day of its light.
—R. W. Emerson.

Ambition itself is not so reckless of human life as ennui; clemency is a favorite attribute of the former; but ennui is the taste of a cannibal.   *—George Bancroft.*

ENTERPRISE

The only enterprise that is really private is intellectual enterprise, and upon this depends all other enterprise.   *—H. S. Commager.*

These men who extol private enterprise in the economic realm are the mortal enemies of private enterprise in the spiritual and the intellectual realm.   *—Ibid.*

Whether political freedom is necessarily dependent on free enterprise is a matter about which reasonable men may differ.
—Alan Barth.

ENTERTAINMENT

The only way to entertain some folks is to listen to them.
—Kin Hubbard.

Some women seem to be able to entertain everybody but their husbands.   *—Ibid.*

A man never does justice to himself as an entertainer when his wife is around.   *—E. W. Howe.*

ENTHUSIASM

Nothing great was ever achieved without enthusiasm.

—R. W. Emerson.

National enthusiasm is the great nursery of genius.

—H. T. Tuckerman.

As the lesser enthusiasms fade and fail, one should take a stronger hold on the higher ones.   *—D. S. Jordan.*

The glory of the Eternal still shines for men, and what have years or forms of flesh to do with the enthusiasm of the soul that has caught the light of it?   *—R. W. Emerson.*

Enthusiasm begets enthusiasm.   *—H. W. Longfellow.*

In things pertaining to enthusiasm no man is sane who does not know how to be insane on proper occasions.

—H. W. Beecher.

Enthusiasts soon understand each other.   *—Washington Irving.*

Nothing great was ever achieved without enthusiasm. The way of life is wonderful; it is by abandonment.   *—R. W. Emerson.*

ENVIRONMENT

The pressure of social influence about us is enormous, and no single arm can resist it.   *—Felix Adler.*

It is only after we have ordered the environment that we can have orderly interior lives.   *—C. Hartley Grattan.*

ENVY

Envy is the most acid fruit that grows on the stock of sin.

—Hosea Ballou.

There is a time in every man's education when he arrives at the conviction that envy is ignorance; that imitation is suicide.

—R. W. Emerson.

Few envy the consideration enjoyed by the oldest inhabitant.

—Ibid.

Envy's memory is nothing but a row of hooks to hang up grudges on.   *—John Foster.*

Virtue is not secure against envy.   *—Wm. Penn.*

Those who despair to rise in distinction by their virtues, are happy if others can be depressed to a level with themselves.

—B. Franklin.

EPIDEMIC

Some people are so sensitive that they feel snubbed if an epidemic overlooks them.   —*Kin Hubbard.*

EPIGRAMS

An epigram is a gag that's played Carnegie Hall.
                                                    —*Oscar Levant.*

Somewhere in the world there is an epigram for every dilemma.
                                                    —*H. W. Van Loon.*

An epigram often flashes light into regions where reason shines but dimly.   —*E. P. Whipple.*

An epigram is a half-truth so stated as to irritate the person who believes the other half.   —*Shailer Mathews.*

Epigrams cover a multitude of sins.   —*Carolyn Wells.*

EPITAPHS

Reading the epitaphs, our only salvation lies in resurrecting the dead and burying the living.   —*Paul Eldridge.*

EQUAL

No man has a natural right to commit aggression on the equal rights of another.   —*Ibid.*

It is the right of the possessor of property to be placed on an equal footing with all his fellow-citizens, in every respect. If he is not to be exalted on account of his wealth, neither is he to be denounced.   —*James F. Cooper.*

All that democracy means is as equal a participation in rights as is practicable.   —*Ibid.*

The equal right of all men to use of land is as clear as their equal right to breathe the air—it is a right proclaimed by the fact of their existence.   —*Henry George.*

We cannot suppose that some men have a right to be in this world, and others no right.   —*Ibid.*

Only a peace between equals can last: only a peace, the very principle of which is equality, and a common participation in a common benefit.   —*Woodrow Wilson.*

We believe, as asserted in the Declaration of Independence, that all men are created equal; but that does not mean that all men are or can be equal in possessions, in ability, or in merit; it simply means that all shall stand equal before the law.   —*W. J. Bryan.*

EQUALITARIANISM

I give the password primeval, I give the sign of democracy. By God, I will accept nothing that all cannot have on equal terms.

—*Walt Whitman.*

EQUALITY

It is no part of the American idea of equality that men should be leveled down, but rather that they should be leveled up.

—*R. B. Perry.*

We hold these truths to be self-evident, that all men are created equal; that they are endowed by their creator with certain inalienable rights; that among these are life, liberty and the pursuit of happiness.   —*T. Jefferson.*

> I celebrate myself, and sing myself,
> And what I assume you shall assume,
> For every atom belonging to me as good
> as belongs to you.
>
> —*Walt Whitman.*

Every improvement in education, science, art, or government expands the chances of man on earth. Such expansion is no guarantee of equality.   —*W. G. Sumner.*

Equality of talents, of education or of wealth cannot be produced by human institutions.   —*Andrew Jackson.*

Liberty, like equality, is a word more used than understood. Perfect and absolute liberty is as incompatible with the existence of society as equality of condition.   —*James F. Cooper.*

I essayed to prevent Indians and Negroes being rated with horses and hogs; but could not prevail.   —*Samuel Sewall.*

The natural equality of men against men must be duly favored; in that government has never established by God or nature, to give one man a prerogative to insult over another.   —*John Wise.*

Complete equality means universal irresponsibility.

—*T. S. Eliot.*

I believe in social equality because it is impossible to believe anything else.   —*H. J. Kester.*

In the gates of eternity, the black hand and the white hand hold each other with an equal clasp.   —*H. B. Stowe.*

The mass of mankind has not been born with saddles on their backs, nor a favored few booted and spurred, ready to ride them legitimately, by the grace of God. —*T. Jefferson.*

Legal equality calls for equal rights in courts of law.
—*H. M. Groves.*

America was created to break every kind of monopoly, and to set men free, upon a footing of equality. —*Woodrow Wilson.*

I believe in the equality of men. —*T. Paine.*

The good and the bad are the only distinctions. —*Ibid.*

Social equality calls for the respectful treatment of all men by each other in their social intercourse. —*H. M. Groves.*

I think with the Romans of old, that the general of today should be a common soldier tomorrow, if necessary. —*T. Jefferson.*

Equality, in a social sense, may be divided into that of condition and that of rights. Equality of condition is incompatible with civilization, and is found only to exist in those communities that are but slightly removed from the savage state. In practice, it can only mean a common misery. —*James F. Cooper.*

Certainly the Negro is not our equal in color—perhaps not in many other respects; still, in the right to put into his mouth the bread that his own hands have earned he is the equal of every other man, white or black. —*A. Lincoln.*

EQUANIMITY
Equanimity is the gem in virtue's chaplet, and St. Sweetness the loveliest in her calendar. —*A. B. Alcott.*

EQUITY
Justice and equity were before time, and will be after it.
—*Nathaniel Ward.*

The dream of equity will win. —*Carl Sandburg.*

EQUIVOCATION
There is no possible excuse for a guarded lie. Equivocation is malice prepense. —*Hosea Ballou.*

I am in earnest—I will not equivocate—I will not excuse—I will not retreat a single inch—and I will be heard.
—*W. L. Garrison.*

ERROR

Error of opinion may be tolerated where reason is left free to combat it.   —*T. Jefferson.*

Truth is the proper and sufficient antagonist to error and has nothing to fear from the conflict, unless by human interposition, disarmed of her natural weapons, free argument and debate.

—*Ibid.*

It takes less time to do a thing right than it does to explain why you did it wrong.   —*H. W. Longfellow.*

Sometimes we may learn more from a man's errors, than from his virtues.   —*Ibid.*

One of the most pernicious errors of modern times is the belief in the goodness of nature, considered as the origin and fount of all physical, moral and aesthetic perfection.   —*Mathurin Dondo.*

Errors may be opposed to errors; but truths, upon all subjects, mutually support each other.   —*Benjamin Rush.*

Great minds . . . begin by breaking with the vulgar errors and delusions of their times.   —*Ludwig Lewisohn.*

It is one of the fatalest errors of our lives, when we spoil a good cause by ill management.   —*Wm. Penn.*

It is only an error of judgment to make a mistake, but it argues an infirmity of character to adhere to it when discovered.

—*C. N. Bovee.*

ESTATE

There are few grave legal questions involved in a poor estate.
—*E. W. Howe.*

Many a man would have been worse if his estate had been better.   —*B. Franklin.*

ESTEEM

What we obtain too cheaply we esteem too lightly.

—*T. Paine.*

ESTHETICS

Esthetics gives us fact, not truth.   —*Leo Stein.*

ETERNAL

Love is woman's eternal spring and man's eternal fall.
—*Helen Rowland.*

Nature is too thin a screen: the glory of the Eternal breaks through everywhere.   —*R. W. Emerson.*

ETERNITY

I leave eternity to Thee; for what is man that he could live the lifetime of his God?   —*Herman Melville.*

All great natures delight in stability; all great men find eternity affirmed in the very promise of their faculties.   —*R. W. Emerson.*

ETHICS

All the religion we have is the ethics of one or another holy person.   —*R. W. Emerson.*

Ethics is the science of human duty.   —*David Swing.*

ETIQUETTE

We must conform, to a certain extent, to the conventionalities of society, for they are the refined results of a varied and long experience.   —*A. A. Hodge.*

EUGENICS

It takes as much time to breed a libertarian as it takes to breed a race horse.   —*H. L. Mencken.*

EVE

Eve was the first woman who fooled her man.

—*Josh Billings.*

EVEN

The best you get is an even break.   —*F. P. Adams.*

EVENTS

The three most important events of human life are equally devoid of reason: birth, marriage, and death.   —*Austin O'Malley.*

I claim not to have controlled events, but confess plainly that events have controlled me.   —*A. Lincoln.*

It may be that some larger world process is working through each series of historical events; but ultimate causes lie beyond a trout in the milk.   —*H. D. Thoreau.*

While I talk and the flies buzz, a sea-gull catches a fish at the mouth of the Amazon, a tree falls in the Adirondack wilderness, a man sneezes in Germany, a hope dies in Tartary, and twins are born.   —*Charles A. Beard.*

EVERYWHERE

Some persons can be everywhere at home; others can sit musingly at home and be everywhere. *—G. D. Prentice.*

EVIDENT

I delight in telling what I think; but if you ask me how I dare say so, or why it is so, I am the most helpless of men.

—R. W. Emerson.

What our enemies say ought not to be taken as evidence.

—Olive Logan.

It is for ordinary minds, and not for psychoanalysts, that our rules of evidence are framed. They have their source very often in considerations of administrative convenience, of practical expediency, and not in rules of logic. *—Benjamin Cardozo.*

EVIL

It is a sin to believe evil of others, but it is seldom a mistake. *—H. L. Mencken.*

The frenzied and thoughtless are always prone to fly from evils at hand to greater evils which they cannot imagine until a more cruel fate has closed in upon them. *—Charles A. Beard.*

The first lesson of history is the good of evil. *—R. W. Emerson.*

I think it a less evil that some criminals should escape than that the government should play an ignoble part.

—Justice O. W. Holmes.

It is privilege that causes evil in the world, not wickedness, and not men. *—Lincoln Steffens.*

One of our national deficiencies is ignorance of evil.

—Elizabeth Jackson.

It is some compensation for great evils that they enforce great lessons. *—C. N. Bovee.*

There are no necessary evils in government. Its evils exist only in its abuses. *—Andrew Jackson.*

To do evil, that good may come of it, is for bunglers in politics, as well as morals. *—Wm. Penn.*

Evil is something that comes to us in our own doing of evil.

—Lyman Bryson.

Evil propels me and reform of evil propels me.

—Walt Whitman.

What is called good is perfect and what is called evil is just as perfect.   —*Ibid.*

Evils, like poisons, have their uses, and there are diseases which no other remedy can reach.   —*T. Paine.*

Evil is merely privative not absolute; it is like cold, which is the privation of heat.   —*R. W. Emerson.*

There are a thousand hacking at the branches of evil to one who is striking at the root.   —*H. D. Thoreau.*

Of two evils, choose to be the least.   —*Ambrose Bierce.*

Every sweet hath its sour, every evil its good. —*R. W. Emerson.*

Constantly, without our knowing it, we are sources of infection for good and evil.   —*Joshua Loth Liebman.*

All experience hath shown that mankind are more disposed to suffer while evils are sufferable, than to right themselves by abolishing the forms to which they are accustomed.   —*T. Jefferson.*

If you do what you should not, you must bear what you would not.   —*B. Franklin.*

Evil is inevitable, but it is also remediable.   —*Horace Mann.*

In the history of man it has been very generally the case, that when evils have grown insufferable, they have touched the point of cure.   —*E. H. Chapin.*

Evil is not what you do to yourself, only what you do to others. If you deal wrongly with yourself you are foolish or careless or shortsighted, but if you deal wrongly with others you have done evil.   —*Dagobert D. Runes.*

EVOLUTION

We must remember that there are no short cuts in evolution.
                                                   —*Louis D. Brandeis.*

The goal of evolution is self-conquest.   —*Elbert Hubbard.*

The office of the leisure class in social evolution is to retard the movement and to conserve what is obsolescent.
                                                   —*Thorstein Veblen.*

The law over all, the law of laws, is the law of successions; for what is the present, after all, but a growth out of the past?
                                                   —*Walt Whitman.*

As ages roll on there is doubtless a progression in human nature.
                                                   —*J. McCosh.*

It is no longer strength of body that prevails, but strength of mind; while the law of God proclaims itself superior to both.

—Ibid.

Creative evolution is at last becoming conscious.

—E. E. Slosson.

Concerning what ultimately becomes of the individual it (evolution) has added nothing and subtracted nothing.

—R. A. Millikan.

EXAGGERATION

There are people so addicted to exaggeration that they can't tell the truth without lying. *—Josh Billings.*

Exaggeration is a blood relation to falsehood and nearly as blamable. *—Hosea Ballou.*

Those who exaggerate in their statements belittle themselves.

—Charles Simmons.

EXAMPLE

The rotten apple spoils his companion. *—B. Franklin.*

Few things are harder to put up with than the annoyance of a good example. *—Mark Twain.*

We can do nothing for our fellow man. But still it is good to know that we can be something for them; to know (and this we may know surely) that no man or woman of the humblest sort can really be strong, gentle, pure and good, without the world being better for it, without somebody being helped and comforted by the very existence of goodness. *—Phillips Brooks.*

The United States government cannot consistently recommend sound policies to foreign governments as a condition for loans, when it is not following such policies itself. It can preach effectively only by example. *—Henry Hazlitt.*

Other men are lenses through which we read our own minds.

—R. W. Emerson.

First find the man in yourself if you will inspire manliness in others. *—A. B. Alcott.*

What you learn from bad habits and in bad society you will never forget, and it will be a lasting pang to you.

—John B. Gough.

EXCESS

Too much plenty makes mouth dainty. *—B. Franklin.*

There can be no excess to love, none to knowledge, none to beauty, when these attributes are considered in the purest sense.
—*R. W. Emerson.*

There seems to be an excess of everything except parking space and religion. —*Kin Hubbard.*

EXCHANGE

Commerce is the great civilizer. We exchange ideas when we exchange fabrics. —*R. G. Ingersoll.*

EXCLUSIVENESS

Any one—a fool or an idiot—can be exclusive. —*R. W. Trine.*

Only the man or the woman of a small, personal, self-centered, self-seeking nature is exclusive. —*Ibid.*

Exclusiveness is a characteristic of recent riches, high society, and the skunk. —*Austin O'Malley.*

EXCUSES

Excellence is the perfect excuse. Do it well, and it matters little what. —*R. W. Emerson.*

Don't make excuses—make good. —*Elbert Hubbard.*

He that is good for making excuses is seldom good for anything else. —*B. Franklin.*

EXERCISE

Whenever I feel like exercise, I lie down until the feeling passes.
—*Robert M. Hutchins.*

I get my exercise acting as a pallbearer to my friends who exercise. —*Chauncey Depew.*

EXISTENCE

The existence of human society is a much surer fact of experience than the existence of Betelgeuse. —*Lewis Mumford.*

We are weary of the unreal and untrue existence we are forced to lead. —*Felix Adler.*

The biggest and most pertinent lesson in history—at least for democracies—is that they cannot take their existence for granted.
—*Norman Cousins.*

In the battle for existence, talent is the punch, and tact is the clever footwork. —*Wilson Mizner.*

EXPECTANCY

If there is anything this nation has to give the world beyond its technological and organizational skill, it is surely that sense of expectancy which has possessed us and which, up to this time, we have never completely lost.   —*J. Donald Adams.*

EXPEDIENCY

I believe the moral losses of expediency always far outweigh the temporary gains. And I believe that every drop of blood saved through expediency will be paid for by twenty drawn by the sword.
—*Wendell L. Willkie.*

Expedients are for the hour, principles for the ages.
—*H. W. Beecher.*

EXPERIENCE

Only so much do I know, as I have lived.   —*R. W. Emerson.*

Skill to do comes of doing.   —*Ibid.*

Experience keeps a dear school, but fools will learn in no other.
—*B. Franklin.*

One thorn of experience is worth a whole wilderness of warning.
—*J. R. Lowell.*

Love is based on a view of women that is impossible to those who have had any experience with them.   —*H. L. Mencken.*

The years teach much which the days never know.
—*R. W. Emerson.*

Life is adventure in experience.
—*D. C. Peattie.*

The multitude are more effectually set right by experience, than kept from going wrong by reasoning with them.
—*B. Franklin.*

Theory may mislead us; experience must be our guide.
—*H. S. Commager.*

Beyond this planet and apart from the human race, experience is too little imaginable to be interesting.   —*George Santayana.*

God sends experience to paint men's portraits.
—*H. W. Beecher.*

Nobody will use other people's experience, nor have of his own, till it is too late to use it.   —*Nathaniel Hawthorne.*

Experience is a safe light to walk by, and he is not a rash man

who expects to succeed in future from the same means which have
secured it in times past. —*Wendell Phillips.*

We should be careful to get out of an experience only the wisdom that is in it—and stop there. —*Mark Twain.*

All experience is an arch to build upon. —*Henry Adams.*

Some people have had nothing else but experience.
—*Don Herold.*

Experience increases our wisdom but doesn't reduce our follies.
—*Josh Billings.*

Experience is a revelation in the light of which we renounce our
errors of youth for those of age. —*Ambrose Bierce.*

There is but one substitute for imagination, and that is experience. —*Gelett Burgess.*

To get things done an ounce of faith is worth a ton of experience.
—*Frank Crane.*

I have but one lamp by which my feet are guided, and that is
the lamp of experience. I know of no way of judging of the future
but by the past. —*Patrick Henry.*

All experience is against state regulation and in favor of liberty.
—*W. G. Sumner.*

The story of any one man's real experience finds its startling
parallel in that of every one of us. —*J. R. Lowell.*

EXPERIMENT

That which we call sin in others is experiment for us.
—*R. W. Emerson.*

Democracy is nothing more than an experiment in government,
more likely to succeed in a new soil, but likely to be tried in all
soils, which must stand or fall on its own merits as others have
done before it. —*J. R. Lowell.*

If it should be proclaimed that our example has become an
argument against the (democratic) experiment, the knell of popular
liberty would be sounded throughout the earth.
—*Daniel Webster.*

Our Constitution is an experiment, as all life is an experiment.
—*O. W. Holmes, Jr.*

There must be power in the states and the nation to remould, through experimentation, our economic practices and institutions to meet changing social and economic needs. *—Louis D. Brandeis.*

Denial of the right to experiment may be fraught with serious consequences to the nation. *—Ibid.*

It is common sense to take a method and try it. If it fails, admit it frankly and try another. But above all, try something.
—F. D. Roosevelt.

EXPERT

An expert is one who knows more and more about less and less.
—N. M. Butler.

An expert is a man who avoids the small errors as he sweeps on to the grand fallacy. *—Benjamin Stolberg.*

EXPLANATIONS

I fear explanations explanatory of things explained.
—A. Lincoln.

It takes less time to do a thing right than to explain why you did it wrong. *—H. W. Longfellow.*

EXPLOITATION

No system has ever existed which did not in some form involve the exploitation of some human beings for the advantage of others.
—John Dewey.

EXPRESSION

The expression a woman wears on her face is far more important than the clothes she wears on her back. *—Dale Carnegie.*

EXPURGATED

The war was not expurgated for those who went through it.
—Christopher Morley.

EXTORTION

There is too much extortion being practiced by American business. *—Philip Murray.*

EXTRAORDINARY

All the extraordinary men I have ever known were chiefly extraordinary in their own estimation. *—Woodrow Wilson.*

EXTRAVAGANCE

Public extravagance begets extravagance. *—Grover Cleveland.*

There is hope in extravagance; there is none in routine.

—*R. W. Emerson.*

EXTREMISTS

The extremists of both parts of this country are violent; they mistake loud and violent talk for eloquence and for reason. They think he who talks loudest reasons best.   —*Daniel Webster.*

We must not overlook the important role that extremists play. They are the gadflies that keep society from being too complacent or self-satisfied; they are, if sound, the spearhead of progress.

—*Abraham Flexner.*

A free country like England or America is almost always a middle-of-the-road country, but to keep in the middle of the road a nation must have not only conservatives who know the value of tradition and habit, but extremists who underrate the importance of both.   —*Ibid.*

EYES

Men of cold passion have quick eyes.

—*Nathaniel Hawthorne.*

The eyes of other people are the eyes that ruin us.

—*B. Franklin.*

The eye of the master will do more work than both his hands.

—*Ibid.*

The eye is the window of the soul; the intellect and will are seen in it.   —*Hiram Powers.*

The animal looks for man's intentions right into his eyes.—Even a rat, when you hunt and bring him to bay, looks you in the eye.

—*Ibid.*

F

FABLE

Fiction or fable allures to instruction.   —*B. Franklin.*

FACE

The scale of the intellect is not to be measured by inches in a man's face.   —*Benjamin West.*

Every man over forty is responsible for his face.

—*A. Lincoln.*

A quarter century of living should put a great deal into a woman's face besides a few wrinkles and some unwelcome folds around the chin.   —*Frances P. Keyes.*

A man will inevitably be a little less of a bear in trying to wear the face of a Christian.   —*Helen Hunt Jackson.*

The face, in youth, is the artless index of the mind.

—*Horace Mann.*

I have always considered my face a convenience rather than an ornament.   —*O. W. Holmes.*

What is in a man's heart is on his face, and is shortly written all over him.   —*Irving Bacheller.*

It matters more what's in a woman's face than what's on it.

—*Claudette Colbert.*

FACES

Some faces are books in which not a line is written, save perhaps a date.   —*H. W. Longfellow.*

FACILITIES

The world ain't getting no worse; we've only got better facilities.

—*Kin Hubbard.*

FACTION

United we stand: divided we fall. Let us not split into factions which must destroy this union upon which our existence depends.
—*Patrick Henry.*

Lines are being drawn between devotion to justice and adherance to a faction, between fair play and love of darkness that is reactionary in effect no matter what banner it floats.
—*John Dewey.*

The most common and durable source of factions has been the various and unequal distribution of property. Those who hold and those who are without property have ever formed distinct interests in society.   —*James Madison.*

Liberty is to faction what air is to fire, an element without which it instantly expires.   —*Ibid.*

A feeble government produces more factions than an oppressive one.   —*Fisher Ames.*

FACTORY

By linking the soil with the factory we are forming an alliance capable of resisting every onslaught.   —*Henry Ford.*

The United States is the greatest factory the world has ever known.   —*E. E. Hughes.*

FACTS

The fact that man possessed the capacity to rise from bestial savagery to civilization, at a time when it had never before been done, is the greatest fact in the history of the universe as known to us.   —*James H. Breasted.*

The basic fact is economic insecurity. The correlative fact is the mind's despair.   —*Samuel D. Schmalhausen.*

It is a strange fact that the impractical among mankind are remembered.   —*Hans Zinsser.*

The whole worth of education is directed towards cultivating the capacity of framing associations of ideas that conform to objective facts. It is thus that life is guided.   —*John Fiske.*

To the wise a fact is true poetry and the most beautiful of fables.
—*R. W. Emerson.*

Every natural fact is a symbol of some spiritual fact.
—*Ibid.*

Some people have a peculiar faculty for denying facts.

—*G. D. Prentice.*

We do not deal much in facts when we are contemplating ourselves.   —*Mark Twain.*

Facts, if they are assembled upon a sufficiently partisan basis, can be made to document any case one wishes to establish.

—*J. H. McGraw, Jr.*

Social facts are themselves natural facts.   —*John Dewey.*

You can't put the facts of experience in order while you are getting them, especially if you are getting them in the neck.

—*Lincoln Steffens.*

No facts to me are sacred; none are profane.

—*R. W. Emerson.*

Get your facts first, and then you can distort them as much as you please.   —*Mark Twain.*

The answer to political failure is "more facts," and the accumulation of more facts but leads to more political failures.

—*Hans S. Morgenthau.*

Facts had little to do with the convictions of Cotton Mather. He carved his devils in his heart.   —*Ludwig Lewisohn.*

FAILURE

They fail, and they alone, who have not striven.

—*T. B. Aldrich.*

A failure is a man who has blundered but is not able to cash in the experience.   —*Elbert Hubbard.*

Never give a man up until he has failed at something he likes.

—*Lewis E. Lawes.*

Not failure, but low aim, is crime.   —*J. R. Lowell.*

The only time you don't fail is the last time you try anything—and it works.   —*Wm. Strong.*

There is nothing, after all, like a good thorough failure for making people happy.   —*W. D. Howells.*

Fear of failure may be paralyzing instead of a fillip to activity.

—*Joseph Rosenfarb.*

Nothing succeeds like—failure.   —*Oliver Herford.*

Far better it is to dare mighty things, to win glorious triumphs, even though checkered by failure, than to take rank with those

poor spirits who neither enjoy much nor suffer much, because they
live in the gray twilight that knows neither victory nor defeat.

—Theodore Roosevelt.

The failure of the artist must strike close to the identity and
potency of the man.   *—Bernard De Voto.*

At times, to fail in life is to succeed, and to succeed is to fail.

—F. M. Isserman.

He (Isaiah) assumed the task of failure. He had the courage
. . . to fail in life . . . that he might become a tribune of the people.

—Ibid.

Self-distrust is the cause of most of our failures.

—C. N. Bovee.

Ninety-nine percent of the failures come from people who have
the habit of making excuses.   *—George W. Carver.*

It is an interesting commentary on the business judgment of
government that failures of big companies have been most common
among those most subjected to government regulation.

—Raymond Moley.

Some men are going to get beaten because they have not the
brains, they have not the initiative, they have not the skills, and
they have not the knowledge, they have not the same capacity
that other men have.   *—Woodrow Wilson.*

FAIR

If you want a man to do fair work for you, let him have fair play.

—G. D. Prentice.

FAITH

Faith is beyond us—our better part; it is the complement of the
American ideal, its atmosphere and heavenly sustenance.

—G. E. Woodberry.

The faith of one age is the fact of the next; and then how
differently it looks!   *—Ibid.*

The idea that the faith of science is a belief that the world is
already in itself completely rational is not so much inspiration to
work as it is a justification for acquiescence.

—John Dewey.

The core of faith is the Beloved Community. There is nothing
else under heaven whereby men have been saved or can be saved.

—Josiah Royce.

The essence of all faith for people of my belief is that man's life can be, and will be, better.   —*Thomas Wolfe.*

The truth-seeking spirit and the spirit of faith, instead of being opposed, are in the deepest harmony. The man whose faith is most genuine is most willing to have its assertions tested by the severest scrutiny.   —*G. S. Merriam.*

Faith is false to itself when it dreads truth, and the desire for truth is prompted by an inner voice of faith.   —*Ibid.*

The smallest seed of faith is better than the largest fruit of happiness.   —*H. D. Thoreau.*

They are the weakest, however strong, who have no faith in themselves or their powers.   —*C. N. Bovee.*

Our society in America is founded . . . upon a faith in man as an end in itself.   —*David L. Lilienthal.*

We are a people who have built upon a faith in the spirit of man.
                                                                —*Ibid.*

Let us have faith that right makes might; and in that faith let us to the end dare to do our duty as we understand it.
                                                                —*A. Lincoln.*

Humanity will live by the faith and the hope, the love and the suffering, of a smaller number of men . . . who say: "Nevertheless and in spite of everything, and whatever may come, I believe."
                                                        —*Pierre Van Paassen.*

Faith may be defined briefly as an illogical belief in the occurrence of the improbable.   —*H. L. Mencken.*

We have kept faith with the founders of our country and their God.   —*John D. Rockefeller, Jr.*

Faith is courage; it is creative while despair is always destructive.
                                                                —*D. S. Muzzey.*

Don't lose faith in humanity: think of all the people in the United States who have never played you a single nasty trick.
                                                                —*Elbert Hubbard.*

So long as our young people are steadfast in their faith, we can be assured of the vitality of our society, and its ability to go on meeting the challenges of the future.   —*Dean Acheson.*

Observe good faith and justice towards all nations. Cultivate peace and harmony with all.   —*G. Washington.*

If it wasn't for faith, there would be no living in this world; we couldn't even eat hash with any safety.   —*Josh Billings.*

Faith: belief without evidence in what is told by one who speaks without knowledge, of things without parallel.

—*Ambrose Bierce.*

The old faiths light their candles all about, but burly Truth comes by and blows them out.   —*L. W. Reese.*

Faith loves to lean on time's destroying arm.

—*O. W. Holmes.*

Faith is among men what gravity is among planets and suns.
—*Charles A. Parkhurst.*

When faith is lost, when honor dies, the man is dead.
—*J. G. Whittier.*

Faith is not contrary to reason, but rather "reason grown courageous."   —*Sherwood Eddy.*

Without faith we are without horizons, a line of march, something ahead. All great rallying cries are in the future.
—*G. E. Woodberry.*

FALLACY

To regard the making of money as more important than producing goods—that is the central fallacy on which government and finance agree.   —*Henry Ford.*

FALSEHOOD

Be sure not to tell a first falsehood, and you needn't fear being detected in any subsequent ones.   —*G. D. Prentice.*

I believe it is an established maxim in morals that he who makes an assertion without knowing whether it is true or false is guilty of falsehood, and the accidental truth of the assertion does not justify or excuse him.   —*A. Lincoln.*

Falsehood is cowardice.   —*Hosea Ballou.*

Not the least misfortune in a prominent falsehood is the fact that tradition is apt to repeat it for truth.   —*Ibid.*

Falsehoods not only disagree with truths, but usually quarrel among themselves.   —*Daniel Webster.*

Truth shuns not the light; but falsehood deals in sly and dark insinuations, and prefers darkness, because its deeds are evil.
—*Andrew Jackson.*

Falsehoods which we spurn today were the truths of long ago.
—J. G. Whittier.

Truth never turns to rebuke falsehood; her own straightforward-
ness is the severest correction. *—H. D. Thoreau.*

FALSTAFF

You can't have Falstaff and have him thin.

—George Santayana.

FAME

Fame is that parasite of pride, ever scornful to meekness, and
ever obsequious to insolent power. *—John Q. Adams.*

What's fame after all? 'Tis apt to be what someone writes on
your tombstone. *—F. P. Dunne.*

If a man can write a better book, preach a better sermon, or
make a better mouse-trap, than his neighbor, though he builds his
house in the woods, the world will make a beaten path to his door.
—R. W. Emerson.

Fame is proof that people are gullible. *—Ibid.*

Fame is a fickle food
Upon a shifting plate.

—Emily Dickinson.

How prudently we proud men compete for nameless graves,
while now and then some starveling of Fate forgets himself into
immortality. *—Wendell Phillips.*

Fame is what you have taken, character's what you give.

—Bayard Taylor.

The highest form of vanity is love of fame.

—George Santayana.

The fame of a great man is not rigid and stony like his bust.
It changes with time. It needs time to give it due perspective.
—R. W. Emerson.

Fame lives, though dust decays. *—Clinton Scollard.*

I have come to regard this matter of Fame as the most transparent of all vanities. *—Herman Melville.*

Even the best things are not equal to their fame.

—H. D. Thoreau.

No true and permanent fame can be founded except in labors
which promote the happiness of mankind. *—Charles Sumner.*

An earthly immortality belongs to a great and good character.
—*Edward Everett.*

Fame is the beauty-parlor of the dead.

—*Benjamin DeCasseres.*

> A little heap of dust,
> A little streak of rust,
> A stone without a name—
> Lo! hero, sword and fame!

—*Ambrose Bierce.*

Fame usually comes to those who are thinking about something else.   —*O. W. Holmes.*

FAMILIARITY

Familiarity breeds contempt—and children.   —*Mark Twain.*

Familiarity so dulls the edge of perception as to make us least acquainted with things forming part of our daily life.

—*Julia W. Howe.*

FAMILY

Families with babies and families without babies are sorry for each other.   —*E. W. Howe.*

The family is the miniature commonwealth upon whose integrity the safety of the larger commonwealth depends.   —*Felix Adler.*

We express the noblest longings of the human heart when we speak of a time to come in which all mankind will be united in one family.   —*Ibid.*

He that raises a large family does, indeed, while he lives to observe them, stand a broader mark for sorrow; but then he stands a broader mark for pleasure too.   —*B. Franklin.*

> Join the United States and join the family—
> But not much in between unless a college.

—*Robert Frost.*

We are to be grouped together, and brooded by love, and reared day by day in that first of churches, the family.

—*H. W. Beecher.*

FAMOUS

After a fellow gets famous it doesn't take long for someone to bob up that used to sit by him at school.   —*Kin Hubbard.*

FANATICISM

Fanaticism consists in redoubling your efforts when you have forgotten your aim.   —*George Santayana*.

What is fanaticism today is the fashionable creed of tomorrow, and trite as the multiplication table a week later.
—*Wendell Phillips*.

Fanaticism is religion caricatured.   —*E. P. Whipple*.

The downright fanatic is nearer to the heart of things than the cool and slippery disputant.   —*E. H. Chapin*.

Religious fanatics have done more to prejudice the cause they advocate than have its opponents.   —*Hosea Ballou*.

FANTASTIC

There is nothing, however fantastic, that (given competent organization) a team of engineers, scientists and administrators cannot do today.   —*David E. Lilienthal*.

FAREWELL

The air is full of farewells to the dying and mournings for the dead.   —*H. W. Longfellow*.

FARMING

One good thing about living on a farm is that you can fight your wife without being heard.   —*Kin Hubbard*.

Burn down your cities and leave our farms, and your cities will spring up again as if by magic; but destroy our farms and the grass will grow in the streets of every city in the country.
—*W. J. Bryan*.

Corruption of morals in the mass of cultivators is a phenomenon of which no age or nation has furnished an example.   —*Ibid*.

When tillage begins, other arts follow. The farmers therefore are the founders of human civilization.   —*Daniel Webster*.

The first farmer was the first man; and all historic nobility rests on possession and use of land.   —*R. W. Emerson*.

> Give fools their gold, and knaves their power;
>   Let fortune's bubbles rise and fall;
> Who sows a field, or trains a flower,
>   Or plants a tree, is more than all.
>
> —*J. G. Whittier*.

Those who labor in the earth are the chosen people of God, if He ever had a chosen people, whose breasts He has made His peculiar deposit for substantial and genuine virtue.

—T. Jefferson.

FASCISM

Fascism is not dead in America. On the contrary, it is now in the process of post-war reconversion.   *—O. John Rogge.*

Cure the evils of Democracy by the evils of Fascism! Funny therapeutics! I've heard of their curing syphilis by giving the patient malaria, but I've never heard of their curing malaria by giving the patient syphilis.   *—Sinclair Lewis.*

The immediate alternative to Fascism is the rapid growth of a democratic Socialism.   *—Norman Thomas.*

Fascism . . . like all real revolutions (is) but the receiver of the bankrupt age that preceded it.   *—Hans J. Morgenthau.*

Fascism . . . in its mastery of technological attainments is truly progressive—were not the propaganda machines of Goebbels and the gas chambers of Himmler models of technical rationality?

—Ibid.

Fascism is a product of economic collapse and intense suffering, accompanied by national frustration and bitterness. *—Kirby Page.*

There is no such thing as total peace, but there is such a thing as total war and total annihilation of rights. Totality, which is inhuman, belongs to fascism, not to us.   *—Max Ascoli.*

FASHION

The law of fashion is the law of life.   *—O. W. Holmes, Jr.*

I never truckled; I never took off the hat to Fashion, and held it out for pennies.   *—Frank Norris.*

Fashion: a despot whom the wise ridicule and obey.

—Ambrose Bierce.

Every generation laughs at the old fashions, but follows religiously the new.   *—H. D. Thoreau.*

Fashion is the science of appearances, and it inspires one with the desire to seem rather than to be.   *—E. H. Chapin.*

We smile at the women who are eagerly following the fashions in dress whilst we are as eagerly following the fashions in thought.

—Austin O'Malley.

Fashion must be forever new or she becomes insipid.

—*J. R. Lowell.*

Fashion is something barbarous, for it produces innovation without reason and imitation without benefit.

—*George Santayana.*

FAST

The world is moving so fast these days that the man who says it can't be done is generally interrupted by someone doing it.

—*Elbert Hubbard.*

FASTIDIOUSNESS

Fastidiousness is only another form of egotism.

—*J. R. Lowell.*

FAT

I find no sweeter fat than sticks to my own bones.

—*Walt Whitman.*

FATAL

How fatal are the effects of idleness and intemperance among the rich, and of hard labor and penury among the poor?

—*Benjamin Rush.*

FATALISM

Even when Americans had believed in the doctrine of pre-destination, they had not accepted it fatalistically or logically abandoned efforts to merit salvation.   —*H. S. Commager.*

The major heresies from Christianity have always been lapses back towards fatalism.   —*Isabel Paterson.*

We're all poor nuts. And things happen. And we just get mixed in wrong, that's all.   —*Eugene O'Neill.*

FATE

What a man thinks of himself, that it is which determines, or rather indicates, his fate.   —*H. D. Thoreau.*

Fate is character.   —*William Winter.*

There is no good arguing with the inevitable.   —*J. R. Lowell.*

In our likeness still we shape our fate.   —*Ibid.*

This day we fashion destiny, our web of fate we spin.

—*J. G. Whittier.*

We are spinning our own fates, good or evil, and never to be undone.   —*William James.*

Fate is a name for facts not yet passed under the fire of thought; for causes that are unpenetrated.   —*R. W. Emerson.*

If you believe in fate, believe in it, at least, for your good.
                                                                        —*Ibid.*

I am ready for my fate.   —*John Brown.*

Should mankind discover the law of its own historical unfolding, then it would be imprisoned in its own fate, and powerless to change it.   —*Charles A. Beard.*

Let us then be up and doing, with a heart for any fate.
                                                              —*H. W. Longfellow.*

Man has the capacity of almost complete control of fate. If he fails it will be by the ignorance or folly of men.
                                                                  —*E. L. Thorndike.*

In two senses we are precisely what we worship. Ourselves are Fate.   —*Herman Melville.*

Every path of your own is the path of fate. Keep on your own track then.   —*H. D. Thoreau.*

FATHER

The worst misfortune that can happen to an ordinary man is to have an extraordinary father.   —*Austin O'Malley.*

FAULTS

To find out a girl's faults, praise her to her girl friends.
                                                                      —*B. Franklin.*

Nothing shows our weakness more than to be so sharp-sighted at spying other men's faults, and so purblind about our own.
                                                                        —*Wm. Penn.*

The cardinal method with faults is to overgrow them and choke them out with virtues.   —*John Bascom.*

A woman will sometimes confess her sins, but I never knew one to confess her faults.   —*Josh Billings.*

FEAR

The only thing we have to fear is fear itself.
                                                              —*F. D. Roosevelt.*

Our fear is all we have to fear.   —*Alice Cary.*

The basest of all things is to be afraid.   —*William Faulkner.*

I learned that fear was inspired in men and women who could not reconcile themselves to the possibility that hardship and sacrifice might confront them in battling for the right.

—George W. Norris.

It does not help the clarity or concentration of a man's thinking if he is oppressed by the fear of a needy or precarious old age.

—Abraham Flexner.

I cannot know fear. I fear that it is impossible for danger to awe me. *—W. L. Garrison.*

I tremble at nothing but my own delinquencies as one is bound to be perfect, even as my heavenly Father is perfect.

—Ibid.

Don't be afraid! Fear means destruction. It makes the hand tremble and the mind waver. *—Frank Crane.*

Fear and lack of faith go hand in hand. The one is born of the other. Tell me how much one is given to fear, and I will tell you how much he lacks in faith. *—R. W. Trine.*

He has not learned the lesson of life who does not every day surmount a fear. *—R. W. Emerson.*

The most terrible fear that any artist can feel (is) the fear that his talent has been drained away, that his spark has been quenched, that his achievement is over forever. *—Bernard De Voto.*

We shall never be able to remove suspicion and fear as potential causes of war until communication is permitted to flow, free and open, across international boundaries. *—H. S. Truman.*

They (the European nations) do not propagandize war fears or war psychosis such as we get out of Washington.

—Herbert Hoover.

He has but one great fear who fears to do wrong.

—C. N. Bovee.

If a man harbors any sort of fear, it percolates through all his thinking, damages his personality, makes him landlord to a ghost.

—Lloyd Douglas.

Fear clogs; Faith liberates. *—Elbert Hubbard.*

Fear is a kind of bell . . . it is the soul's signal for rallying.

—H. W. Beecher.

Half our fears are baseless and the other half discreditable.

—C. N. Bovee.

Mutual fear is a principal link in the chain of mutual love.

—T. Paine.

FEARLESSNESS

I do not tremble with all the states and churches and political economies at my heels.   *—Horace Traubel.*

FEASTING

Feast, and your halls are crowded; Fast, and the world goes by.

—Ella W. Wilcox.

He who feasts every day, feasts no day.   *—Charles Simmons.*

FEATURES

Features—the great soul's apparent seat.   *—Wm. Cullen Bryant.*

FEELINGS

It is part of my religion not to hurt any man's feelings.

—W. D. Howard.

The head best leaves to the heart what the heart alone divines.

—A. B. Alcott.

Some feelings are quite untranslatable; no language has yet been found for them.   *—H. W. Longfellow.*

After thirty-five a man begins to have thoughts about women; before that age he has feelings.   *—Austin O'Malley.*

The hardest thing is to disguise your feelings when you put a lot of relatives on the train for home.   *—Kin Hubbard.*

A man will be what his most cherished feelings are.

—H. W. Beecher.

FELICITY

Human felicity is produced not so much by great pieces of good fortune that seldom happen, as by little advantages that occur every day.   *—B. Franklin.*

FELLOW-MEN

Many times I realize how much my own outer and inner life is built upon the labors of my fellow-men, both living and dead, and how earnestly I must exert myself in order to give in return as much as I have received.   *—Albert Einstein.*

FELLOWSHIP

What men call good fellowship is commonly but the virtue of pigs in a litter which lie close together to keep each other warm.

—H. D. Thoreau.

Fellowship in devotion to the moral ideal is the source of sustained power and enthusiasm. —*Felix Adler.*

It is men's moral nature, longing to be fed and strengthened, that urges them into fellowship. —*Ibid.*

The victory of a fellowship of free men requires an end of the ancient division of men and nations into the House of Have and Have-not. —*Norman Thomas.*

FEMALES

The venom of the female viper is more poisonous than that of the male viper. —*Benj. F. Butler.*

Without excluding yourself from the other sex, let it occupy but a small portion of your time. —*Timothy Pickering.*

The females of all species are most dangerous when they appear to retreat. —*Don Marquis.*

FENCE

The fence around a cemetery is foolish, for those inside can't come out and those outside don't want to get in.

—*Arthur Brisbane.*

Good fences make good neighbors. —*Robert Frost.*

Farmers ought to learn to make better fences; why not establish a fencing school for their benefit? —*G. D. Prentice.*

FETISH

The New Humanists make a fetish of morality precisely as the New Mechanists made a fetish of the machine.

—*Lewis Mumford.*

FEW

Though the culture bestowed on many should be successful only with a few, yet the influence of those few and the service in their power may be very great. —*B. Franklin.*

FICTION

Truth is said to be stranger than fiction; it is to most folks.

—*Josh Billings.*

Truth is stranger than fiction; fiction is obliged to stick to possibilities, truth isn't. —*Mark Twain.*

The foundation of good fiction and good poetry seems to be ethic rather than aesthetic. —*F. M. Crawford.*

Reading fiction is as hard to me as trying to hit a target by hurling feathers at it. —*William James.*

The truth of fiction is the necessity of what happens.

—*Bernard De Voto.*

The illusion of fiction has attributes that might justify us in calling it a hallucination. —*Ibid.*

Wondrous strong are the shells of fiction.

—*H. W. Longfellow.*

There is little truth we get so true as that which we find in fiction. —*J. G. Holland.*

FIDELITY

Fidelity is seven-tenths of business success.

—*James Parton.*

FIGHT

The way to fight a woman is with your hat—grab it and run.

—*John Barrymore.*

Whether we fight tomorrow or on a later day, we shall before long close our ranks and fight to win. —*Alexander Woollcott.*

You can refuse to love a man or to lend him money, but if he wants to fight, you've got to oblige him. —*F. P. Dunne.*

"Thrice is he armed that has his quarrel just"—
But four times he who gets the blow in fust.

—*Josh Billings.*

I propose to fight it out on this line if it takes all summer.

—*U. S. Grant.*

I have not yet begun to fight. —*John Paul Jones.*

There is such a thing as a man being too proud to fight.

—*Woodrow Wilson.*

Americans have always known how to fight for their rights and their way of life. Americans are not afraid to fight. They fight joyously in a just cause. —*H. L. Ickes.*

You cannot preserve liberties such as we enjoy, save by willingness to fight for them if need be. —*Frank Knox.*

I am sure that, from among America's fighting men and others, warriors will appear to fight the unending battle for good government. —*George W. Norris.*

To preserve his freedom of worship, his equality before the law,

Figure 182

his liberty to speak and act as he sees fit, subject only to provisions that he trespass not upon similar rights of others—a Londoner will fight. So will a citizen of Abilene.   —*D. D. Eisenhower.*

Do not get into a fight if you can possibly avoid it. If you get in, see it through. Don't hit if it is honorably possible to avoid hitting, but never hit soft. Don't hit at all if you can help it; don't hit a man if you can possibly avoid it; but if you do hit him, put him to sleep.   —*Theodore Roosevelt.*

FIGURE

Few girls are as well shaped as a good horse.

—*Christopher Morley.*

FIND

He who hunts for flowers will find flowers; and he who loves weeds may find weeds.   —*H. W. Beecher.*

FINITUDE

Let a' man once overcome his selfish teror at his own finitude, and his finitude is, in one sense, overcome.   —*George Santayana.*

FIRMNESS

Real firmness is good for anything; strut is good for nothing.

—*Alexander Hamilton.*

The greatest firmness is the greatest mercy.

—*H. W. Longfellow.*

FIRST

Make it a rule to get there first with the most men.

—*Gen. N. B. Forrest.*

FISHING

There are more fish taken out of a stream than ever were in it.

—*Oliver Herford.*

There is no use in your walking five miles to fish when you can depend on being just as unsuccessful near home.   —*Mark Twain.*

I would rather fish than eat, particularly eat fish.

—*Corey Ford.*

The biggest fish he ever caught were those that got away.

—*Eugene Field.*

Fishing is a delusion entirely surrounded by liars in old clothes.

—*Don Marquis.*

It's good fishing in troubled waters.   —*Daniel Drew.*

FIT

Be fit for more than the thing you are now doing.

—*James A. Garfield.*

FLAG

A thoughtful mind when it sees a nation's flag, sees not the flag, but the nation itself.   —*H. W. Beecher.*

The American flag has been a symbol of Liberty, and men rejoiced in it.   —*Ibid.*

This flag, which we honor and under which we serve, is the emblem of our unity, our power, our thought and purpose as a nation.   —*Woodrow Wilson.*

The things that the flag stands for were created by the experience of a great people. Everything that it stands for was written by their lives.   —*Ibid.*

No matter what happens to you, no matter who flatters you or who abuses you, never look at another flag, never let a night pass but you pray God to bless that flag.   —*E. E. Hale.*

The less a statesman amounts to, the more he loves the flag.

—*Kin Hubbard.*

Accompany your own flag throughout the world under the protection of your own cannon.   —*Daniel Webster.*

If any one attempts to haul down the American flag, shoot him on the spot.   —*John A. Dix.*

A flag is an emblem of warfare; when unfurled it is a challenge to combat.   —*Charles T. Sprading.*

The flag is the embodiment, not of sentiment, but of history.

—*Woodrow Wilson.*

White is for purity, red for valor, blue for justice.

—*Charles Sumner.*

FLATTERY

Avoid flatterers, for they are thieves in disguise.   —*Wm. Penn.*

Be no flatterer.   —*G. Washington.*

When a man is really important, the worst adviser he can have is a flatterer.   —*Gerald W. Johnson.*

You know what a fan letter is—it's just an inky raspberry.

—*Bob Hope.*

Men are not flattered by being shown that there has been a difference of purpose between the Almighty and them.

—*A. Lincoln.*

Knavery and flattery are blood relations. —*Ibid.*

Flattery is like cologne water, to be smelt of, not swallowed.

—*Josh Billings.*

No man flatters the woman he truly loves. —*H. T. Tuckerman.*

We love flattery, even when we see through it, and are not deceived by it, for it shows that we are of importance enough to be courted. —*R. W. Emerson.*

FLAVOR

The flavor of frying bacon beats orange blossoms.

—*E. W. Howe.*

FLAX

Get your spindle and your distaff ready, and God will send you flax. —*J. G. Holland.*

FLESH

Poor flesh, to fight the calendar so long. —*E. A. Robinson.*

FLIES

Do what we can, summer will have its flies.

—*R. W. Emerson.*

FLIRTING

A flirt is like a dipper at a hydrant: Everyone is at liberty to drink from it, but no one desires to carry it away.

—*N. P. Willis.*

Flirtation is a circulating library in which we seldom ask twice for the same volume. —*C. N. Bovee.*

Alas, the transports beauty can inspire. —*Ibid.*

FLOWERS

Flowers are love's truest language. —*P. Benjamin.*

Die when I may, I want it said of me by those who knew me best, that I always plucked a thistle and planted a flower where I thought a flower would grow. —*A. Lincoln.*

Whatever a man's age, he can reduce it several years by putting a bright-colored flower in his buttonhole. —*Mark Twain.*

Flowers are the sweetest things that God ever made and forgot
to put a soul into.   —*H. W. Beecher.*

Flowers may beckon towards us, but they speak toward heaven
and God.   —*Ibid.*

FLY

A fly is as untamable as a hyena.   —*R. W. Emerson.*

FOE

Welcome, new duties! We sheathe no sword. We only turn the
front of the army upon a new foe.   —*Wendell Phillips.*

FOLLY

A good folly is worth whatever you pay for it.

—*George Ade.*

We spend half our lives unlearning the follies transmitted to us
by our parents, and the other half transmitting our own follies to
our offspring.   —*Isaac Goldberg.*

It is folly to endeavor to make ourselves shine before we are
luminous.   —*Horace Bushnell.*

Levity of behavior, always a weakness, is far more unbecoming
in a woman than a man.   —*Wm. Penn.*

When folly is bliss, 'tis ignorance to be otherwise.

—*E. W. Mumford.*

One man's folly is another man's wife.   —*Helen Rowland.*

FOOD

If we could help the people of the Orient to get . . . three
square meals a day . . . that one change alone would have more
impact on the whole world than all the armies and battles in
history.   —*H. S. Truman.*

There's somebody at every dinner party who eats all the celery.
—*Kin Hubbard.*

FOOLS

Nobody can describe a fool to the life, without much patient
self-inspection.   —*F. M. Colby.*

A fellow who is always declaring he's no fool, usually has his
suspicions.   —*Wilson Mizner.*

Tricks and treachery are the practice of fools that have not wit
enough to be honest.   —*B. Franklin.*

Let us be thankful for the fools; but for them the rest of us could not succeed. —*Mark Twain.*

God save the fools, and don't let them run out, for if it weren't for them, wise men couldn't get a living. —*Josh Billings.*

Every single forward step in history has been taken over the bodies of empty-headed fools who giggled and snickered.
—*Bruce Barton.*

A fool and her money are soon courted. —*Helen Rowland.*

Money never made a fool of anybody; it only shows 'em up.
—*Kin Hubbard.*

A learned fool is one who has read everything, and simply remembered it. —*Josh Billings.*

Most everyone seems to be willing to be a fool himself, but he can't bear to have anybody else one. —*Ibid.*

The best way to convince a fool that he is wrong is to let him have his own way. —*Ibid.*

Too clever is dumb. —*Ogden Nash.*

The cleverest woman on earth is the biggest fool on earth with a man. —*Dorothy Parker.*

Hain't we got all the fools in town on our side? And hain't that a big enough majority in any town. —*Mark Twain.*

He that teaches himself hath a fool for a master. —*B. Franklin.*

To be a man's own fool is bad enough; but the vain man is everybody's. —*Wm. Penn.*

It takes one woman twenty years to make a man of her son, and another woman twenty minutes to make a fool of him.
—*Helen Rowland.*

Experience is a school where a man learns what a big fool he has been. —*Josh Billings.*

The best way to silence any friend of yours whom you know to be a fool is to induce him to hire a hall. —*Woodrow Wilson.*

Every man is a damn fool for at least five minutes every day. Wisdom consists in not exceeding the limit. —*Elbert Hubbard.*

The learned fool writes his nonsense in better language than the unlearned, but still 'tis nonsense. —*B. Franklin.*

Men are called fools in one age for not knowing what they were called fools for averring in the age before. —*H. W. Beecher.*

FORBIDDEN

Adam was human; he didn't want the apple for the apple's sake; he wanted it because it was forbidden.   —*Mark Twain.*

FORCE

There is such a thing as a nation being so right that it does not need to convince others by force that it is right.
—*Woodrow Wilson.*

Power politics can be defined as the foreign policy of a state when based on the use or the threat of force.   —*Ely Culbertson.*

There is a force that drives us on and yet we are that force, and sometimes have controlled it.   —*Paul Engle.*

There is not a greater fallacy on earth than the doctrine of force, as applied to government.   —*Walt Whitman.*

Government by force is a contradiction in terms and an impossibility in physics. Force is what is governed. Government originates in the moral faculty.   —*Isabel Paterson.*

It is inconceivable that we should follow the evil path of Europe and place our reliance upon triumphant force.
—*W. J. Turner.*

Right reason is stronger than force.   —*James A. Garfield.*

FORCES

Forces work; they are not, like mathematical concepts, exhausted in description.   —*George Santayana.*

The natural forces crush and destroy man when he transgresses them, as they destroy or neutralize one another.
—*John Burroughs.*

Forces rather than men are still doing most of our planning for us.   —*E. B. George.*

FORD

Did he who made the Ford make thee?   —*Ogden Nash.*

FOREDOOMED

We live and act like men foredoomed to destruction.
—*Paul Hutchinson.*

FOREIGN

Against the insidious wiles of foreign influence the jealousy of a free people ought to be constantly awake.   —*G. Washington.*

History and experience prove that foreign influence is one of the most baneful foes of republican government. —*Ibid.*

FOREIGN POLICY

The division of the empire into states is for our own convenience, but abroad this distinction ceases. —*T. Paine.*

FOREIGN RELATIONS

It is the sincere wish of United America to have nothing to do with the political intrigues, or the squabbles of European nations.
—*G. Washington.*

FOREIGNERS

Most of the men I respect are foreigners. —*H. L. Mencken.*

FOREST

American democracy was born of no theorist's dream . . . It came out of the American forest, and it gained new strength each time it touched a new frontier. —*F. J. Turner.*

FORGETTING

A retentive memory may be a good thing, but the ability to forget is the true token of greatness. —*Elbert Hubbard.*

FORGIVENESS

"I can forgive, but I cannot forget," is only another way of saying, "I cannot forgive." —*H. W. Beecher.*

Reversing your treatment of the man you have wronged is better than asking his forgiveness. —*Elbert Hubbard.*

We never ask God to forgive anybody except where we haven't.
—*Ibid.*

Nobuddy ever fergits where he buried a hatchet.
—*Kin Hubbard.*

There is no revenge so complete as forgiveness.
—*H. W. Shaw.*

His heart was as great as the world, but there was no room in it to hold the memory of a wrong. —*R. W. Emerson.*

FORGOTTEN

It's sweet to be remembered, but it's often cheaper to be forgotten. —*Kin Hubbard.*

FORMULA

Labor peace is a relationship between human beings—which is the prime reason that it cannot be established by formula.

—*J. L. McCaffrey.*

FORTITUDE

There is strength of quiet endurance as significant of courage as the most daring feats of prowess.   —*H. T. Tuckerman.*

FORTUNE

Fortune is the rod of the weak, and the staff of the brave.

—*J. R. Lowell.*

"Fortune knocks at every man's door once in a life," but in a good many cases, the man is in a neighboring saloon and does not hear her.   —*Mark Twain.*

Fortune is like a coquette: if you don't run after her, she will run after you.   —*H. W. Shaw.*

Fortune, like a coy mistress, loves to yield her favors, though she makes us wrest them from her.   —*C. N. Bovee.*

FOSSIL

Government has been a fossil; it should be a plant.

—*R. W. Emerson.*

FOUNDATIONS

If you have built castles in the air, your work need not be lost; that is where they should be. Now put the foundations under them.   —*H. D. Thoreau.*

FOUNDERS

A science which hesitates to forget its founders is lost.

—*A. N. Whitehead.*

I deem it a great thing for a nation, in all the periods of its fortunes, to be able to look back to a race of founders.

—*Rufus Choate.*

FRAUD

Keep a cow, and the milk won't have to be watered but once.

—*Josh Billings.*

For the most part fraud in the end secures for its companions repentance and shame.   —*Charles Simmons.*

FREE

Free men set themselves free.   —*James Oppenheim.*

Who are a free people? . . . Those who live under a government so constitutionally checked and controlled that proper provision is made against its being otherwise exercised.

—John Dickinson.

The doctrine that all men should be free means that all men should be free of oppressive government. *—R. M. MacIver.*

Where the artists keep free no other sort or condition of man long remains bound. *—H. M. Kallen.*

All might be free if they valued freedom, and defended it as they ought. *—Samuel Adams.*

Every American is a free member of a mighty partnership that has at its command all the pooled strength of Western Civilization —spiritual ideals, political experience, social purpose, scientific wealth, industrial prowess. *—D. D. Eisenhower.*

They who seem to be pulling and hauling, jostling, and clamoring, have done a day's work that is somehow good. But they only are as competent and wise as they are free. *—William A. White.*

As he died to make men holy, let us die to make men free.

—Julia W. Howe.

If you would liberate me you must be free.

—R. W. Emerson.

Where the press is free, and every man able to read, all is safe.

—T. Jefferson.

The man is free who is protected from injury.

—Daniel Webster.

In giving freedom to the slave we assure freedom to the free.

—A. Lincoln.

All men everywhere should be free. *—Ibid.*

Where free speech is stopped miasma is bred, and death comes fast. *—H. W. Beecher.*

FREEDOM

Education is the first resort as well as the last, for a world-wide solution of the problem of freedom. *—H. M. Kallen.*

Heaven knows how to put a proper price upon its goods; and it would be strange indeed if so celestial an article as freedom should not be highly rated. *—T. Paine.*

Those who expect to reap the blessings of freedom, must, like men, undergo the fatigue of supporting it. *—Ibid.*

Those who deny freedom to others deserve it not for themselves, and, under a just God, cannot long retain it.   —*A. Lincoln.*

As long as you have freedom, freedom of capital and freedom in the lines of business, you are safe; and if you have not freedom you cannot be safe under any circumstances.
                                                      —*Louis D. Brandeis.*

Human freedom is . . . an achievement by men, and, as it was gained by vigilance and struggle, it can be lost by indifference and supineness.   —*H. F. Byrd.*

Freedom is an indivisible word. If we want to enjoy it, and fight for it, we must be prepared to extend it to everyone, whether they are rich or poor, whether they agree with us or not, no matter what their race or the color of their skin.   —*Wendell L. Willkie.*

The community cannot prosper without permitting, nay encouraging, the far-reaching exercise of individual freedom.
                                                      —*H. S. Commager.*

War and freedom cannot live together . . . peace too is the organization of liberty.   —*H. M. Kallen.*

Freedom is the going and the goal of world peace.
                                                                —*Ibid.*

Not a grave of the murder'd for freedom but grows seed for freedom in its turn to bear seed.   —*Walt Whitman.*

Man seeks freedom as the magnet seeks the pole or water its level, and society can have no peace until every member is really free.   —*Josiah Warren.*

I do not believe we can have any freedom at all in the philosophical sense, for we act not only under external compulsion but also by inner necessity.   —*Albert Einstein.*

Political freedom gives purpose and happiness to the community that succeeds in working out freedom in its politics.
                                                      —*Max Ascoli.*

The only freedom worth possessing is that which gives enlargement to a people's energy, intellect and virtues.
                                                      —*W. E. Channing.*

I believe in freedom—social, economic, domestic, political, mental and spiritual.   —*Elbert Hubbard.*

The only freedom worth achieving is a freedom which puts each of us at something he can do and sets before him as a personal and individual responsibility the management of his activity, relations, and possession so that in the end "he owes not any man."   —*Alexander Hamilton.*

Freedom is not caprice, but room to enlarge.   —*C. A. Bartol.*

A bird in a cage is not half a bird.   —*H. W. Beecher.*

Knowledge is essential to freedom.   —*W. E. Channing.*

Show me the steps of freedom, and her feet turn never backward.   —*J. R. Lowell.*

This nation, under God, shall have a new birth of freedom.

—*A. Lincoln.*

The liberties of our country, the freedom of our civil constitution are worth defending at all hazards; and it is our duty to defend them against all attacks. We have received them as a fair inheritance.   —*Samuel Adams.*

Freedom will never want her hearts of oak!

—*Philip M. Freneau.*

Under God we are determined that wheresoever, whensoever, or howsoever we shall be called to make our exit, we will die free men.   —*Josiah Quincy.*

Freedom hath been hunted round the globe. Asia and Africa have long expelled her. Europe regards her like a stranger, and England hath given her warning to depart. Oh, receive the fugitive, and prepare in time an asylum for mankind!   —*T. Paine.*

Since the general civilization of mankind, I believe there are more instances of the abridgment of the freedom of the people by gradual and silent encroachments of those in power than by violent and sudden usurpations.   —*James Madison.*

My faith in the proposition that each man should do precisely as he pleases with all which is exclusively his own lies at the foundation of the sense of justice there is in me. I extend the principle to communities of men as well as to individuals. I so extend it because it is politically wise, as well as naturally just: politically wise in saving us from broils about matters which do not concern us.   —*A. Lincoln.*

Those who deny freedom to others deserve it not for themselves, and, under a just God, cannot long retain it.   —*Ibid.*

The freedom of a government does not depend upon the quality of its laws, but upon the power that has the right to create them.   —*Thaddeus Stevens.*

Freedom exists only where the people take care of the government.
                                                    —*Woodrow Wilson.*

I am for freedom of religion and against all maneuvers to bring about a legal ascendancy of one sect over another.
                                                    —*T. Jefferson.*

The United States, knowing no distinction of her own citizens on account of religion or nativity, naturally believes in a civilization the world over which will secure the same universal views.
                                                    —*U. S. Grant.*

There is always one man to state the case for freedom. That's all we need, one.   —*Clarence Darrow.*

Slaves cannot teach freedom.   —*A. Meiklejohn.*

FREEDOM (OF THE PRESS)
Freedom of the press is the staff of life for any vital democracy.
                                                    —*Wendell L. Willkie.*

Our liberty depends on the freedom of the press, and that cannot be limited without being lost.   —*T. Jefferson.*

The freedom of the press is one of the great bulwarks of liberty and can never be restrained but by despotic governments.
                                                    —*George Mason.*

Freedom of conscience, of education, of speech, of assembly are among the very fundamentals of democracy and all of them would be nullified should freedom of the press ever be successfully challenged.   —*F. D. Roosevelt.*

A free press maintains the Majesty of the People.
                                                    —*John Adams.*

Of all times in time of war the press should be free.
                                                    —*William E. Borah.*

With all its licentiousness and all its evil, the entire and absolute freedom of the press is essential to the preservation of government on the basis of a free constitution.   —*Daniel Webster.*

Our liberty cannot be guarded but by the freedom of the press, nor that be limited without danger of losing it.
                                                    —*T. Jefferson.*

In America we talk about freedom of the press but in reality . . . we slant the news the way we want it to be understood.
                                                    —*Eugene A. Simon.*

Hail to the Press! chosen guardian of freedom!
Strong sword-arm of justice! bright sunbeam of truth!
—Horace Greeley.

FREEDOM (OF RELIGION)

I am mortified to be told that, in the United States of America, the sale of a book can become a subject of inquiry, and of criminal inquiry too, as an offense against religion; that a question like this can be carried before the civil magistrate. Is this then our freedom of religion? *—T. Jefferson.*

FREEDOM OF SPEECH

Personally I have no enthusiasm for organized jeering sections, but I hold that the spontaneous right of raspberry should be denied to no one in America. *—Heywood Broun.*

FREE ENTERPRISE

Agriculture, manufacture, commerce and navigation, the four pillars of our prosperity, are the most thriving when left most free to individual enterprise. *—T. Jefferson.*

The private enterprise system really consists of harnessing men, money and ideas, and the genius of inventors and technologists with the savings of the thousands. *—Malcolm Muir.*

The war has been a crucible for all of the economic systems of the world, for our own, for Communism, Fascism, Nazism, all the others. And the American system has outproduced the world.
—B. M. Baruch.

The free enterprise system is a way of economic life, open to hope—an economy open to new ideas, new products, new jobs, new men. *—W. B. Benton.*

The free enterprise system is not, never has been, and never should be a system of complete laissez faire.

—Ibid.

If there is a high percentage of people with superior capacity and a moderately good level of general competence, this makes private enterprise workable. *—J. M. Clarke.*

If free enterprise is to be saved, it must be shared.
—W. F. Bennett.

The very survival of free enterprise depends upon a rising standard of living and an expanding economy. *—H. S. Truman.*

Essential to a system of free enterprise is a climate in which new, small, and independent business can be conceived and born, can grow and prosper.   —*W. B. Benton.*

FRIEND

"Stay" is a charming word in a friend's vocabulary.
                                                    —*A. B. Alcott.*

Every man should keep a fair-sized cemetery in which to bury the faults of his friends.   —*H. W. Beecher.*

The only way to have a friend is to be one. —*R. W. Emerson.*

A friend is a person with whom I may be sincere.   —*Ibid.*

If you want to make a dangerous man your friend, let him do you a favor.   —*Lewis E. Lawes.*

The best way to keep your friends is not to give them away.
                                                    —*Wilson Mizner.*

A home-made friend wears longer than one you buy in the market.   —*Austin O'Malley.*

Friends made fast seldom remain fast.   —*Ibid.*

We need new friends; some of us are cannibals who have eaten their old friends up; others must have ever-renewed audiences before whom to re-enact an ideal version of their lives.
                                            —*Logan Pearsall Smith.*

A friend that ain't in need is a friend indeed.
                                                    —*Kin Hubbard.*

Friend: one who knows all about you and loves you just the same.   —*Elbert Hubbard.*

Actions, not words, are the true criterion of the attachment of friends.   —*G. Washington.*

A man must get friends as he would get food and drink for nourishment and sustenance.   —*Randolph Bourne.*

He must keep them (friends) as he would health and wealth, as the infallible safeguards against misery and poverty of spirit.
                                                    —*Ibid.*

It is better to make friends fast than to make fast friends.
                                                    —*E. W. Mumford.*

Nothing makes the earth seem so spacious as to have friends at a distance; they make the latitudes and longitudes.
                                                    —*H. D. Thoreau.*

If you would win a man to your cause, first convince him that you are his sincere friend. —*A. Lincoln.*

There are three faithful friends—an old wife, an old dog, and ready money. —*B. Franklin.*

Friends: people who borrow my books and set wet glasses on them. —*E. A. Robinson.*

All we can do is to make the best of our friends, love and cherish what is good in them, and keep out of the way of what is bad. —*T. Jefferson.*

I never considered a difference of opinion in politics, in religion, in philosophy, as cause for withdrawing from a friend.
—*T. Jefferson.*

The most I can do for my friend is simply to be his friend.
—*H. D. Thoreau.*

I never met a man I didn't like. —*Will Rogers.*

A real friend is one who walks in when the rest of the world walks out. —*Walter Winchell.*

I find as I grow older that I love those most whom I loved first.
—*T. Jefferson.*

FRIENDSHIP

Show me a genuine case of platonic friendship, and I shall show you two old or homely faces. —*Austin O'Malley.*

Friendship is a plant of slow growth, and must undergo and withstand the shocks of adversity before it is entitled to the appellation. —*G. Washington.*

What is commonly called friendship is only a little more honor among rogues. —*H. D. Thoreau.*

Friendship is a union of spirits, a marriage of hearts, and the bond thereof of virtue. —*Wm. Penn.*

Friendship is never established as an understood relation.—It is a miracle which requires constant proofs. It is an exercise of the purest imagination and the rarest faith. —*H. D. Thoreau.*

It should be our endeavor to cultivate the peace and friendship of every nation, even of that which has injured us most, when we shall have carried our point against her. —*T. Jefferson.*

The holy passion of friendship is of so sweet and steady and loyal and enduring a nature that it will last through a whole lifetime, if not asked to lend money. —*Mark Twain.*

About the only thing in life that makes it worth while is the enjoyment of friendly relations.   —*George W. Norris.*

When friendships are real, they are not glass threads or frost work, but the solidest things we can know.   —*R. W. Emerson.*

We should thank God that He did not give us the power of hearing through walls; otherwise there would be no such thing as friendship.   —*Austin O'Malley.*

Friendship is the only cement that will ever hold the world together.   —*Woodrow Wilson.*

There can be no friendship where there is no freedom. Friendship loves a free air, and will not be fenced up in straight and narrow enclosures.   —*Wm. Penn.*

FRONTIER

Moving westward, the frontier became more and more American.   —*F. J. Turner.*

The advance of the frontier has meant a steady movement away from the influence of Europe, a steady growth of independence on American lines.   —*Ibid.*

The temptations of our vast interior keep our society in a constant state of transition.   —*W. G. Simms.*

The frontier was a moving social laboratory and bears the imprint of experimentalism, of adventurism, of blueprintism, that is of the essence of the utopian mode of advance.

—*Leon Samson.*

In nearly every case the unit working on the frontier was a young married couple.   —*F. L. Paxson.*

The frontier, for all its savage brutal habits, had created . . . if only now and then, characters that rose superior to destiny.

—*Ellen Glasgow.*

After the geographical frontier was closed, we carried over its spirit of individualism and adventure into finance, industry and labor.   —*Benjamin Stolberg.*

FRONTIERSMAN

The frontiersman who set himself up as a final authority, who despised the wisdom of savants, who looked upon himself as the equal of all men, provided that prototype from which Whitman's great "I" was derived.   —*V. F. Calverton.*

FRUGALITY

Make no expense but to do good to others, or yourself—i.e., waste nothing. —*B. Franklin.*

FUN

Spinning a rope's a lot of fun—providing your neck ain't in it. —*Will Rogers.*

The only good in pretending is the fun we get out of fooling ourselves that we fool somebody. —*Booth Tarkington.*

Fun is like life insurance: the older you get, the more it costs. —*Kin Hubbard.*

Take all the fools out of this world, and there wouldn't be any fun or profit living in it. —*Josh Billings.*

FUNCTION

The economic function of the producer is not to employ labor but to produce goods. —*J. H. Williams.*

FUNERALS

Funerals are a lost art in the big cities. —*Don Herold.*

What men prize most is a privilege, even if it be that of chief mourner at a funeral. —*J. R. Lowell.*

FUNNY

Everything is funny, as long as it is happening to somebody else. —*Will Rogers.*

FUTURE

The immediate future of the world has been laid on the doorstep of the individual American. —*Wm. B. Huie.*

Our national future depends upon our national character—that is, whether it is spiritually or materially minded.
—*Roger W. Babson.*

What will be, is. —*Austin O'Malley.*

The future is not important any more. —*Gertrude Stein.*

I have been over into the future and it works. —*Lincoln Steffens.*

We should all be concerned about the future because we will have to spend the rest of our lives there. —*C. F. Kettering.*

I never think of the future. It comes soon enough.
—*Albert Einstein.*

The whole future of the increased standard of living depends on somebody saving—whether it is corporations, whether it is individuals.   —*R. A. Taft.*

Democracy is a prophecy, and looks to the future; it is for this reason that it has its great career.   —*G. E. Woodberry.*

The land belongs to the future . . . we come and go but the land is always here.   —*Willa Cather.*

Don't lay any certain plans for the future; it is like planting toads and expecting to raise toadstools.   —*Josh Billings.*

The program for the future demands a change in the economic foundations of society.   —*Max Eastman.*

We are today far short of the industrial capacity we need for a growing future.   —*H. S. Truman.*

Neither race, nor tradition, nor the actual past, binds the American to his countryman, but rather the future which together they are building.   —*Hugo Munsterberg.*

The fruition of democracy, on aught like a grand scale, resides altogether in the future.   —*Walt Whitman.*

It is easy to see, hard to foresee.   —*B. Franklin.*

When all else is lost, the future still remains.

—*C. N. Bovee.*

I know of no way of judging the future but by the past.

—*Patrick Henry.*

I like the dreams of the future better than the history of the past.   —*T. Jefferson.*

The future is more uncertain than the present.

—*Walt Whitman.*

G

GAIN

It is always sound business practice to take any obtainable net gain, at any cost and at any risk to the rest of the community.

—Thorstein Veblen.

There are no gains without pains. *—B. Franklin.*

GAMBLING

There are two times in a man's life when he should not speculate: when he can't afford it, and when he can. *—Mark Twain.*

Gambling is the child of avarice, the brother of iniquity, and the father of mischief. *—G. Washington.*

Gambling with cards, or dice, or stocks, is all one thing—it is getting money without giving an equivalent for it.

—H. W. Beecher.

The best throw with the dice is to throw them away.

—Charles Simmons.

Gambling is an ancient and universal form of play.

—Stuart Chase.

Gambling is a revolt against boredom. *—Ibid.*

It may be that the race is not always to the swift, nor the battle to the strong—but that's the way to bet. *—Damon Runyon.*

Nothing between human beings is one to three. In fact, I long ago came to the conclusion that all life is six to five against. *—Ibid.*

The only man who makes money following the races is the one who does so with a broom and shovel. *—Elbert Hubbard.*

The gambling known as business looks with austere disfavor upon the business known as gambling. *—Ambrose Bierce.*

If a "tinhorn" in the West was caught cheating, he would never play another game—and there was no coroner's inquest.

—*Fiorello La Guardia.*

The urge to gamble is so universal and its practice so pleasurable that I assume it must be evil.   —*Heywood Broun.*

Man is the only animal that plays poker.   —*Don Herold.*

GAME

Possibly the game of Life cannot be won; but if it can be won, it will be the players in the game who win it, not the superior people who pride themselves on not knowing the difference between a fair ball and a foul, to say nothing of those in the grandstand or in the bleachers whose contribution is throwing pop bottles at the umpire.   —*Max Otto.*

To beat some one else in a game, or to be beaten, may mean much or little. To beat our own game means a great deal.

—*M. D. Babcock.*

When the One great Scorer comes to write against your name —He marks—not that you won or lost—but that you played the game.   —*Grantland Rice.*

Games lubricate the body and the mind.   —*B. Franklin.*

GANGSTERISM

Gangsterism . . . flourishes wherever men doubt the efficacy of reasonableness and intelligence.   —*A. Meiklejohn.*

GARBAGE

Dumping a little of everything into the school makes of education intellectual garbage.   —*E. D. Martin.*

GARDENING

In order to live off a garden, you practically have to live in it.
—*Kin Hubbard.*

What a man needs in gardening is a cast-iron back with a hinge in it.   —*C. D. Warner.*

GARTER

Garter: an elastic band intended to keep a woman from coming out of her stockings and desolating the country. —*Ambrose Bierce.*

GAYETY

Gayety is often the reckless ripple over depths of despair.

—*E. H. Chapin.*

GEHENNA

A woman's last resort is henna; a man's Gehenna.

—*Helen Rowland.*

GENEALOGY

Genealogy: an account of one's descent from an ancestor who did not particularly care to trace his own. —*Ambrose Bierce.*

GENERALS

Generals are human; I know of none immune to error.

—*Omar N. Bradley.*

In generals, as in all other men, capabilities cannot always obscure weakness, nor can talents hide faults. —*Ibid.*

GENERATION

The generation now in the driver's seat hates to make anything, wants to live and die in an automobile. —*Willa Cather.*

Every new generation contrives to find some new way of being puritanical. —*Randolph Bourne.*

The wrong-doing of one generation lives into the successive one and . . . becomes a pure and uncontrollable mischief.

—*Nathaniel Hawthorne.*

Every new generation is a fresh invasion of savages.

—*Hervey Allen.*

Upon our generation is laid the heavy task of building a more secure and more gracious life, not only for the few, but for the multitude as well. —*Paul Douglas.*

GENEROSITY

Generosity during life is a very different thing from generosity in the hour of death; one proceeds from genuine liberality and benevolence, the other from pride or fear. —*Horace Mann.*

A man is sometimes more generous when he has but little money than when he has plenty, perhaps thro' fear of being thought to have but little. —*B. Franklin.*

There is a bastard kind of generosity, which being extended to all men, is as fatal to society, on one hand, as the want of true generosity is on the other. —*Thomas Paine.*

GENIUS

Every genius is a child, every child is a genius. —*Lester Ward.*

Inventive genius requires pleasurable mental activity as a condition for its vigorous exercise.   —*A. N. Whitehead.*

If a man can have only one kind of sense, let him have common sense. If he has that and uncommon sense too, he is not far from genius.   —*H. W. Beecher.*

Genius is one per cent inspiration and ninety-nine per cent perspiration.   —*Thomas A. Edison.*

In every work of genius we recognize our own rejected thoughts.
                                                        —*R. W. Emerson.*

It is with rivers as it is with people: the greatest are not always the most agreeable nor the best to live with.   —*H. Van Dyke.*

It is the privilege of genius that to it life never grows commonplace as to the rest of us.   —*J. R. Lowell.*

These are the prerogatives of genius: to know without having learned; to draw just conclusions from unknown premises; to discern the soul of things.   —*Ambrose Bierce.*

Genius is infinite painstaking.   —*H. W. Longfellow.*

Genius is an infinite capacity for giving pains. —*Don Herold.*

Some people's genius lies in giving infinite pains.
                                                    —*Addison Mizner.*

No man ever followed his genius till it misled him.
                                                    —*H. D. Thoreau.*

Genius, all over the world, stands hand in hand, and one shock of recognition runs the whole circle round.   —*Herman Melville.*

Genius, in truth, means little more than the faculty of perceiving in an unhabitual way.   —*William James.*

To appreciate thoroughly the work of what we call genius, is to possess all the genius by which the work was produced.
                                                    —*Edgar Allan Poe.*

Genius may have its limitations, but stupidity is not thus handicapped.   —*Elbert Hubbard.*

To believe your own thought, to believe that what is true for you in your private heart is true for all men—that is genius.
                                                        —*R. W. Emerson.*

Genius is inconsiderate, self-relying, and, like unconscious beauty, without any intention to please.   —*Isaac Mayer Wise.*

Genius may be almost defined as the faculty of acquiring poverty. —*E. P. Whipple.*

Genius is lonely without the surrounding presence of people to inspire it. —*T. W. Higginson.*

There are geniuses in trade as well as in war, or the state, or letters; and the reason why this or that man is fortunate is not to be told. It lies in the man: that is all anybody can tell you about it. —*R. W. Emerson.*

There is no genius in life like the genius of energy and industry. —*D. G. Mitchell.*

Genius is always in advance of its time—the pioneers for the generation which it precedes. —*W. G. Simms.*

Genius (has) the power of lighting its own fire. —*John Foster.*

Great geniuses have the shortest biographies. Their cousins can tell you nothing about them. —*R. W. Emerson.*

There are two kinds of geniuses. The first and highest may be said to speak out of the eternal to the present, and must compel the age to understand it; the second understands the age, and tells it what it wishes to be told. —*J. R. Lowell.*

Genius is no snob. It does not run after titles or seek by preference the high circles of society. —*Woodrow Wilson.*

Geniuses are commonly believed to excel other men in their power of sustained attention . . . But it is their genius making them attentive, not their attenion making geniuses of them.
—*William James.*

GENOCIDE
Weapons of the genocide are not placed on parade.
—*Lewis Mumford.*

GENTLEMAN
To ignore, to disdain to consider, to overlook, are the essence of the gentleman. —*William James.*

When Adam delved and Eve span, the Devil was the gentleman. —*New England Primer.*

This is the final test of a gentleman: his respect for those who can be of no possible service to him. —*W. L. Phelps.*

One of the embarrassments of being a gentleman is that you are not permitted to be violent in asserting your rights.
—*N. M. Butler.*

Living blood, and a passion of kindness, does at last distinguish God's gentleman from Fashion's. —*R. W. Emerson.*

A gentleman is one who never strikes a woman without provocation. —*H. L. Mencken.*

Here (in Kentucky) is the old idea, somewhat current still in England, that the highest mark of the gentleman is not cultivation of mind, not intellect, not knowledge, but elegant living.
—*J. L. Allen.*

The time to test a true gentleman is to observe him when he is in contact with individuals of a race that is less fortunate than his own. —*Booker T. Washington.*

The flowering of civilization is the finished man . . . the gentleman. —*R. W. Emerson.*

The flowering of civilization is the finished man . . . the gentlemind an offender of a wrong he may have committed against him. He can not only forgive, he can forget; and he strives for that nobleness of self and mildness of character which impart sufficient strength to let the past be but the past. A true man of honor feels humbled himself when he cannot help humbling others.
—*Robert E. Lee.*

GENTLENESS

We are indebted to Christianity for gentleness, especially toward women. —*Charles Simmons.*

GEOPOLITICS

Neither history nor economics can be intelligently studied without a constant reference to the geographical surroundings which have affected different nations. —*Brooks Adams.*

GIFT

The only gift is a portion of thyself. —*R. W. Emerson.*

It is better to deserve without receiving, than to receive without deserving. —*R. G. Ingersoll.*

It takes all the fun out of a bracelet if you have to buy it yourself. —*Peggy Joyce.*

The greatest grace of a gift, perhaps, is that it anticipates and admits of no return. —*H. W. Longfellow.*

'Tis more blessed to give than to receive; for example, wedding presents. —*H. L. Mencken.*

If it were not for the presents, an elopement would be preferable. —*George Ade.*

Natural liberty is a gift of the beneficent Creator, to the whole human race. —*Alexander Hamilton.*

Examples are few of men ruined by giving. Men are heroes in spending, cravens in what they give. —*C. N. Bovee.*

Give what you have. To some one it may be better than you dare to think. —*H. W. Longfellow.*

GIGOLO

A gigolo is a fee-male. —*Isaac Goldberg.*

GIRLS

I never saw an athletic girl that thought she was strong enough to do indoor work. —*Kin Hubbard.*

Little girls are the nicest things that happen to people.
—*Allan Beck.*

A girl is Innocence playing in the mud, Beauty standing on its head, and Motherhood dragging a doll by the foot. —*Ibid.*

Love is the delightful interval between meeting a beautiful girl and discovering that she looks like a haddock.
—*John Barrymore.*

Some girls never know just what they are going to do from one husband to another. —*Tom Masson.*

Some girls get all there is out of life in one summer.
—*Kin Hubbard.*

I never expected to see the day when girls would get sunburned in the places they now do. —*Will Rogers.*

GIVING

He gives only the worthless gold who gives from a sense of duty. —*J. R. Lowell.*

> Not what we give, but what we share,
> For the gift without the giver is bare.

—*Ibid.*

> Behold, I do not give lectures or a little charity,
> When I give I give myself.

—*Walt Whitman.*

The beauty of the sunbeam lies partly in the fact that God does not keep it; He gives it away to us all.   —*David Swing.*

If it is more blessed to give than to receive, then most of us are content to let the other fellow have the greater blessing.
                                                            —*Shailer Mathews.*

GLASS

Those who live in stone houses should not throw glass.
                                                            —*Austin O'Malley.*

GLEAM

Say the gleam was not for us, but never say we doubted it.
                                                            —*E. A. Robinson.*

GLORY

There is glory enough for all.   —*W. S. Schley.*
True glory is a flame lighted at the skies.   —*Horace Mann.*

GLUTTONY

The miser and the glutton are two facetious buzzards: one hides his store and the other stores his hide.   —*Josh Billings.*

As for me, give me turtle or give me death. What is life without turtle? Nothing. What is turtle without life? Nothinger still.
                                                            —*Artemus Ward.*

GOAL

It is for us to pray not for tasks equal to our powers, but for powers equal to our tasks, to go forward with a great desire forever beating at the door of our hearts as we travel towards our distant goal.   —*Helen Keller.*

It is only through strife, through hard and dangerous endeavor, that we shall ultimately win the goal of true national greatness.
                                                            —*T. Roosevelt.*

There is no limit, other than our own resolve, to the temporal goals we set before ourselves—as free individuals joined in a team of our fellows; as a free nation in the community of nations.
                                                            —*D. D. Eisenhower.*

GOD

God, as some cynic has said, is always on the side which has the best football coach.   —*Heywood Broun.*

God will not look you over for medals, degrees, or diplomas, but for scars.   —*Elbert Hubbard.*

An honest God is the noblest work of man.   —*R. G. Ingersoll.*

My concern is not whether God is on our side; my great concern is to be on God's side, for God is always right. —*A. Lincoln.*

God is incorporeal, divine, supreme, infinite Mind, Spirit, Soul, Principle, Life, Love. —*Mary Baker Eddy.*

God is not a cosmic bell-boy for whom we can press a button to get things. —*H. E. Fosdick.*

> An' you've gut to git up airly
> Ef you want to take in God.
> —*J. R. Lowell.*

The existence of God can never be proved satisfactorily to a doubting intellect, for the proof rests on spontaneous insights. —*J. F. Clarke.*

He (God) is in His world making it right. —*Lyman Abbott.*

I hear and behold God, in every object, yet understand not God in the least. —*Walt Whitman.*

Our age cries for the living God. —*F. M. Isserman.*

God enters by a private door into every individual. —*R. W. Emerson.*

Men talk of "finding God," but no wonder it is difficult; He is hidden in that darkest hiding-place, your own heart. You yourself are a part of Him. —*Christopher Morley.*

O my brothers, God exists! —*R. W. Emerson.*

God was feeling mightily good when he made Gene Debs, and he didn't have anything else to do all day. —*James Whitcomb Riley.*

God is continually giving. He will not withhold from you or me. —*Theodore Parker.*

The influence of God in Nature, in its mechanical, vital, or instructive action, is beautiful. —*Ibid.*

God is attracting our regard in and through all things. Every flower is a hint of his beauty; every grain of wheat is a token of his beneficence; every atom of dust is a revelation of his power. —*W. H. Furness.*

It is hard to believe in God, but it is far harder to disbelieve in Him. —*H. E. Fosdick.*

The existence of God means that we are living in a moral order, and in a moral order we can no more sin and get away with it than we can break all physical laws and escape the penalty.   —*Ibid.*

I see the marks of God in the heavens and the earth; but how much more in a liberal intellect, in magnanimity, in unconquerable rectitude.   —*W. E. Channing.*

It is impossible to govern the world without God.
                                                        —*G. Washington.*

God governs the world and we have only to do our duty wisely, and leave the issue to him.   —*John Jay.*

I cannot imagine a God of the universe made happy by my getting down on my knees and calling Him "great."
                                                        —*Susan B. Anthony.*

God is simply the hero of a religious novel.   —*H. D. Lloyd.*

God reigns and the government at Washington still lives.
                                                        —*James A. Garfield.*

GOD Almighty will not give up a people to military destruction, or leave them unsupportedly to perish, who had so earnestly and so repeatedly sought to avoid the calamities of war, by every decent method which wisdom could invent.   —*T. Paine.*

No people can be bound to acknowledge and adore the invisible hand, which conducts the affairs of men, more than the people of the United States.   —*G. Washington.*

The lilies are redolent of God. God is the mind of man. He is the Soul of All.   —*Theodore Parker.*

The universe, broad, oval, deep, and high, is a handful of God, which God enchants. He is the mysterious magic which possesses the world.   —*Ibid.*

Man is, and always has been, a maker of gods. It has been the most serious and significant occupation of his sojourn in the world.
                                                        —*John Burroughs.*

In the faces of men and women I see God.   —*Walt Whitman.*

The deities of one age are the by-words of the next.
                                                        —*R. G. Ingersoll.*

GOLD

Gold has worked from Alexander's time down . . . When something holds good for two thousand years I do not believe it can be so because of prejudice or mistaken theory.   —*B. M. Baruch.*

I shall not help crucify mankind upon a cross of gold. I shall not aid in pressing down upon the brow of labor this crown of thorns. —*W. J. Bryan.*

Gold is good in its place, but living, brave, patriotic men are better than gold. —*A. Lincoln.*

The poetical instinct turns whatever it touches into gold.
—*J. G. Holland.*

GOLDEN RULE

Do unto the other feller the way he'd like to do unto you, an' do it fust. —*E. N. Westcott.*

GOLDFISH

No one can feel as helpless as the owner of a sick goldfish.
—*Kin Hubbard.*

GOLF

Rail splitting produced an immortal President in Abraham Lincoln; but Golf, with 29 thousand courses, hasn't produced even a good A Number-1 Congressman. —*Will Rogers.*

GOOD

Be not simply good; be good for something. —*H. D. Thoreau.*

Be good and you will be lonesome. —*Mark Twain.*

The good die young—because they see it's no use living if you've got to be good. —*John Barrymore.*

We have a call to do good, as often as we have the power and occasion. —*Wm. Penn.*

The Good is that which satisfies want, craving, which fulfills or makes complete the need which stirs to action. —*John Dewey.*

The good of society as a whole cannot be better served than by the preservation against arbitrary restraint of the liberties of its constituent members. —*George Sutherland.*

> To one fixed trust my spirit clings;
> I know that God is good.
> —*J. G. Whittier.*

Roaming in thought over the Universe, I saw the little that is Good steadily hastening towards immortality.
—*Walt Whitman.*

All religion has relation to life, and the life of religion is to do good. —*Lyman Abbott.*

The good life is not only good for one's conscience; it is good for art, good for knowledge, good for health, good for fellowship.
                                                —*Lewis Mumford.*

Business interests are the public good and in serving business the state is serving society.   —*V. L. Parrington.*

In the United States, doing good has come to be, like patriotism, a favorite device of persons with something to sell.
                                                —*H. L. Mencken.*

Be good even at the cost of your self-respect.   —*Don Herold.*

The Good, the True, the Beautiful! Alas, the Good is so often untrue, the True so often unbeautiful, the Beautiful so often not good.   —*Isaac Goldberg.*

The larger view always and through· all shams, all wickednesses, discovers the Truth that will, in the end, prevail, and all things surely, inevitably, resistlessly work together for good.
                                                —*Frank Norris.*

The good must triumph.   —*Fannie Hurst.*

It is vain to ask God to make us good. He never makes any one good. We may ask Him to help us to become good; that He always does.   —*W. Gladden.*

What a sublime doctrine it is that goodness cherished now is Eternal Life already entered upon!   —*W. E. Channing.*

Scream as we may at the bad, the good prevails.
                                                —*C. A. Bartol.*

Everything good in a man thrives best when properly recognized.   —*J. G. Holland.*

Goodness is the only investment that never fails.
                                                —*H. D. Thoreau.*

I believe . . . that every human mind feels pleasure in doing good to another.   —*T. Jefferson.*

GOOD BREEDING
Good breeding consists in concealing how much we think of ourselves and how little we think of the other person.
                                                —*Mark Twain.*

Good-breeding is surface Christianity.   —*O. W. Holmes.*

GOOD CHEER

Let us be of good cheer, remembering that the misfortunes hardest to bear are those which never come.   —*Amy Lowell.*

GOOD HUMOR

Good-humor makes all things tolerable.   —*H. W. Beecher.*

Good-nature is stronger than tomahawks.   —*R. W. Emerson.*

Good-humor, gay spirits, are the liberators, the sure cure for spleen and melancholy.   —*A. B. Alcott.*

When good-natured people leave us, we look forward with extra pleasure to their return.   —*H. W. Shaw.*

GOSPEL

The gospel assures us that love is stronger than hatred, peace than war, holiness than evil, truth than error. It is the marriage of the goodness of motive and the goodness of attainment;—heaven hereafter and heaven here.   —*J. F. Clarke.*

As science is now constituted a literal adherence to the moral precepts throughout the gospels would mean sudden death.
     —*A. N. Whitehead.*

GOSSIP

What people say behind your back is your standing in the community.   —*E. W. Howe.*

Gossip is vice enjoyed vicariously.   —*Elbert Hubbard.*

People like to tell tales. If I take the rap for what they tell me, they'll tell a lot.   —*Walter Winchell.*

Everybody says it, and what everybody says, must be true.
     —*James F. Cooper.*

Gossip is always a personal confession either of malice or imbecility.   —*J. G. Holland.*

Gossip: sociologists on a mean and petty scale.
     —*Woodrow Wilson.*

The only time people dislike gossip is when you gossip about them.   —*Will Rogers.*

So live that you wouldn't be ashamed to sell the family parrot to the town gossip.   —*Ibid.*

There isn't much to be seen in a little town, but what you hear makes up for it.   —*Kin Hubbard.*

Whatever is done or said, returns at last to me.

—*Walt Whitman.*

Gossip is the art of saying nothing in a way that leaves practically nothing unsaid.   —*Walter Winchell.*

GOVERNMENT

Democracy is not a way of governing, whether by majority or otherwise, but primarily a way of determining who shall govern and, broadly, to what end.   —*R. M. MacIver.*

If people do not possess the capacity to govern themselves, they are, inevitably governed by others.   —*Felix Morley.*

No man is good enough to govern another man without that other's consent.   —*A. Lincoln.*

Government is at best an expedient; but most governments are usually, and all governments are sometimes, unexpedient.

—*H. D. Thoreau.*

Governments, like clocks, go from the motion men give them, and, as governments are made and moved by men, so by them they are ruined, too.   —*Wm. Penn.*

The natural progress of things is for liberty to yield and government to gain ground.   —*T. Jefferson.*

The function of Government must be to favor no small group at the expense of its duty to protect the rights of personal freedom and of private property of all its citizens.   —*F. D. Roosevelt.*

The office of government is not to confer happiness, but to give men opportunity to work out happiness for themselves.

—*W. E. Channing.*

The whole of government consists in the art of being honest.

—*T. Jefferson.*

Government, even in its best state, is but a necessary evil; in its worst state, an intolerable one.   —*T. Paine.*

That particular form of government is necessary which best suits the temper and inclination of a people.   —*John Wise.*

As long as our government is administered for the good of the people, and is regulated by their will; as long as it secures to us the rights of persons and of property, liberty of conscience and of the press, it will be worth defending.   —*Andrew Jackson.*

Every form of government tends to perish by excess of its basic principles.   —*Will Durant.*

Government, like dress, is the badge of lost innocence.

—*T. Paine.*

Government is not reason, it is not eloquence—it is force.

—*G. Washington.*

Government is force.　　　　　　　　　　　—*J. J. Ingalls.*

The people's government, made for the people, made by the people, (is) answerable to the people.　　—*Daniel Webster.*

The Government that shakes its fist first and its finger afterwards falls into contempt.　　　　　　—*Elihu Root.*

The essence of free Government is an effectual control of rivalry.

—*John Adams.*

We admit of no government by divine right.—The only legitimate right to govern is an express grant of power from the governed.　　　　　　　　　　　　—*W. H. Harrison.*

Good government is not a substitute for self-government.

—*Dwight Morrow.*

The final end of government is not to exert restraint but to do good.　　　　　　　　　　　　　　—*Rufus Choate.*

Government began in tyranny and force, began in the feudalism of the soldier and the bigotry of the priest, and the ideas of justice and humanity have been fighting their way, like a thunderstorm, against the organized selfishness of human nature.

—*Wendell Phillips.*

Government is itself an art, one of the subtlest of the arts. It is the art of making man live together in peace and with reasonable happiness.　　　　　　　　　　—*Felix Frankfurter.*

Whatever government is not a government of laws is a despotism, let it be called what it may.　　　—*Daniel Webster.*

All free governments are managed by the combined wisdom and folly of the people.　　　　　　　—*James A. Garfield.*

Governments exist to protect the rights of minorities.

—*Wendell Phillips.*

Government is only a necessary evil, like other go-carts and crutches.　　　　　　　　　　　　　　　—*Ibid.*

If men be good government cannot be bad.

—*Wm. Penn.*

No government can be free that does not allow all its citizens to participate in its formation and execution of her laws. There are

degrees of tyranny; but every other government is a despotism.
—*Thaddeus Stevens.*

Government over all, by all, and for the sake of all.
—*Theodore Parker.*

The will of the people is the only legitimate foundation of any government, and to protect its free expression should be our first object.   —*T. Jefferson.*

The basis of our political systems is the right of the people to make and alter their constitutions of government.
—*G. Washington.*

The national government possesses those powers which it can be shown the people have conferred on it, and no more. All the rest belongs to the state governments, or to the people themselves.
—*Daniel Webster.*

With all the imperfections of our present government, it is without comparison the best existing, or that ever did exist.
—*T. Jefferson.*

The firm basis of government is justice, not pity.
—*Woodrow Wilson.*

The government is us; we are the government, you and I.
—*Theodore Roosevelt.*

Good government, and especially the government of which every American citizen boasts, has for its objects the protection of every person within its care in the greatest liberty consistent with the good order of society, and his perfect security in the enjoyment of his earnings with the least possible diminution for public needs.
—*Grover Cleveland.*

Government is a trust, and the officers of the government are trustees; and both the trust and the trustees are created for the benefit of the people.   —*Henry Clay.*

While all other sciences have advanced, that of government is at a standstill—little better understood, little better practised now than three or four thousand years ago.   —*John Adams.*

That government is the strongest of which every man feels himself a part.   —*T. Jefferson.*

It is for the good of nations, and not for the emolument or aggrandizement of particular individuals, that government ought to be established, and that mankind are at the expense of supporting it. The defects of every government and constitution both as to principle and form, must, on a parity of reasoning, be as open to discussion as the defects of a law, and it is a duty which every man owes to society to point them out. —*T. Paine.*

In framing a government which is to be administered by men over men the great difficulty lies in this: You must first enable the government to control the governed, and in the next place, oblige it to control itself. —*Alexander Hamilton.*

When a people shall have become incapable of governing themselves, and fit for a master, it is of little consequence from what quarter he comes. —*G. Washington.*

Society is produced by our wants and government by our wickedness; the former promotes our happiness *positively* by uniting our affections, the latter *negatively* by restraining our vices. The one encourages intercourse, the other creates distinctions. The first is a patron, the last a punisher. —*T. Paine.*

All governments depend upon the good will of the people.
—*John Adams.*

All free governments are the creatures of volition—a breath can make them and a breath can destroy them. —*A. H. Stephens.*

Experience teaches us to be most on our guard to protect liberty when the government's purposes are beneficent.
—*Louis D. Brandeis.*

Governments exist to protect the rights of minorities. The loved and the rich need no protection—they have many friends and few enemies. —*Wendell Phillips.*

GOWN

> Where's the man could ease a heart
> Like a satin gown?
>
> —*Dorothy Parker.*

GRACE

Grace is savage and must be savage in order to be perfect.
—*C. W. Stoddard.*

Beauty and grace command the world. —*Park Benjamin.*

A beautiful form is the finest of the fine arts.

—*R. W. Emerson.*

GRADUATE

The college graduate is presented with a sheepskin to cover his intellectual nakedness.   —*Robert M. Hutchins.*

No intelligent person in the eighteenth century would have thought a modern highschool graduate in any sense an educated person.   —*E. D. Martin.*

GRAMMAR

Grammar is the grave of letters.   —*Elbert Hubbard.*

Why care for grammar as long as we are good?
                                                —*Artemus Ward.*

Grammar school never taught me anything about grammar.
                                                —*Isaac Goldberg.*

I've never heard a blue jay use bad grammar, but very seldom; and when they do. they are as ashamed as a human.
                                                —*Mark Twain.*

> Any fool can make a rule
> And every fool will mind it.
>   —*H. D. Thoreau.*

GRASS

> Pile the bodies high at Austerlitz and Waterloo.
> Shovel them under and let me work—
>   I am the grass: I cover all.
>
>   —*Carl Sandburg.*

GRASSHOPPERS

We are as willing to sit on the fence and lecture to the grasshoppers about our superior objectivity as we ever were.
                                                —*Michael Straight.*

GRATITUDE

If you pick up a starving dog and make him prosperous, he will not bite you. This is the principal difference between a dog and a man.   —*Mark Twain.*

Next to ingratitude, the most painful thing to bear is gratitude.
                                                —*Hosea Ballou.*

Gratitude is the fairest blossom which springs from the soul.
                                                —*H. W. Beecher.*

> Two kinds of gratitude: the sudden kind
> We feel for what we take, the larger kind
> We feel for what we give.
>
> —*E. A. Robinson.*

GRAVE

The only difference between a rut and a grave is their dimensions.   —*Ellen Glasgow.*

The grave wherever found, preaches a short and pithy sermon.
—*Nathaniel Hawthorne.*

The grave of those we love, what a place for meditation!
—*Washington Irving.*

The battle of our life is brief; the alarm, the struggle, the relief, then sleep we side by side.   —*H. W. Longfellow.*

All that tread the globe are but a handful to the tribes that slumber in its bosom.   —*Wm. Cullen Bryant.*

It is wrong to walk on a grave.   —*A. M. Giovannitti.*

There is but one easy place in this world, and that is the grave.
—*H. W. Beecher.*

A grave is such a quiet place.   —*Edna St. Vincent Millay.*

GRAVEYARDS

The graveyards are full of people the world could not do without.
—*Elbert Hubbard.*

GRAVITY

There is gravity in wisdom, but no particular wisdom in gravity.
—*H. W. Shaw.*

GREAT

Every man, in every condition, is great.   —*W. E. Channing.*

The world's great men have not commonly been great scholars, nor its great scholars great men.   —*O. W. Holmes.*

Every great man is unique.   —*R. W. Emerson.*

A great city is that which has the greatest men and women.
—*Walt Whitman.*

The pure in heart are free of suspicion; the great cannot be humiliated.   —*Eleanor Roosevelt.*

> Lives of great men all remind us
> We can make our lives sublime.
>
> —*H. W. Longfellow.*

It is to be lamented that great characters are seldom without a blot.   —*G. Washington.*

Great men stand like solitary towers in the city of God.
—*H. W. Longfellow.*

To be great is to be misunderstood.   —*R. W. Emerson.*

There never was yet a truly great man that was not at the same time truly virtuous.   —*B. Franklin.*

Great men are rarely isolated mountain peaks; they are the summits of ranges.   —*T. W. Higginson.*

Great minds have purposes, others have wishes.
—*Washington Irving.*

The final proof of greatness lies in being able to endure contumely without resentment.   —*Elbert Hubbard.*

Artists have rarely greatness except in the depth of their plunge or copiousness of their grasp of human experience.
—*Max Eastman.*

To feel themselves in the presence of true greatness many men find it necessary to be alone.   —*Tom Masson.*

Greatness is its own torment.   —*Theodore Parker.*

The most useful is the greatest.   —*Ibid.*

A solemn and religious regard to spiritual and eternal things is an indispensable element of all true greatness.   —*Daniel Webster.*

No man has come to true greatness who has not felt in some degree that his life belongs to his race, and that what God gives him he gives him for mankind.   —*Phillips Brooks.*

GREED

Avarice and happiness never saw each other, how then should they become acquainted?   —*B. Franklin.*

The most pitiful human ailment is a birdseed heart.
—*Wilson Mizner.*

We expect more than belongs to us; take all that's given us though never meant us; and fall out with those that are not as full of us as we are of ourselves.   —*Wm. Penn.*

GRIEF

If misery loves company, misery has company enough.
—*H. D. Thoreau.*

Great grief makes sacred those upon whom its hand is laid.—
Joy may elevate, ambition glorify, but only sorrow can consecrate.
—*Horace Greeley.*

There is no grief like the grief that does not speak.
—*H. W. Longfellow.*

Crying widows are easiest consoled.   —*O. W. Holmes.*

GROUP

It will never be possible for any length of time for any group of
the American people, either by reason of wealth or learning or
inheritance or economic power, to retain any mandate, any permanent authority to arrogate to itself the political control of American public life.   —*F. D. Roosevelt.*

America does not consist of groups. A man who thinks of himself as belonging to a particular national group in America has not
yet become an American.   —*Woodrow Wilson.*

Committee: A group which succeeds in getting something done
only when it consists of three members, one of whom happens to
be sick and another absent.   —*H. W. Van Loon.*

Culture (is) the patterning of human behavior into orderly conduct in accidence with the basic assumptions and beliefs and
sensibilities of each group.   —*Laurence K. Frank.*

GROVES

The groves were God's first temples.   —*W. C. Bryant.*

GROWTH

We grow best when clouds hang over us because clouds bear
rain and rain refreshes us.   —*H. W. Beecher.*

GRUDGE

Some men feel that the only thing they owe the woman who
marries them is a grudge.   —*Helen Rowland.*

GRUMBLER

The chronic grumbler is a church social compared to the fellow
that agrees with everything you say.   —*Kin Hubbard.*

GUARD

It is of great importance in a republic not only to guard the
society against the oppression of its rulers, but to guard one part
of the society against the injustice of the other part.
—*James Madison.*

GUEST

Nobody can be as agreeable as an uninvited guest.

—Kin Hubbard.

GUILT

It is often the essence of the institutions of liberty that it be recognized that guilt is personal and cannot be attributed to the holding of opinion or to mere intent in the absence of overt acts.

—Charles Evans Hughes.

The crimes of this guilty land will never be purged away but with blood.   *—John Brown.*

Whatever punishment does to a nation, it does not induce a sense of guilt.   *—Anne O'Hare McCormick.*

There is no refuge from confession but suicide; and suicide is confession.   *—Daniel Webster.*

God hath yoked to guilt her pale tormentor, misery.

—W. C. Bryant.

This doctrine of guilt by association (is) a device for subverting our constitutional principles and practices, for destroying our constitutional guarantees, and for corrupting our faith in ourselves and in our fellow men.   *—H. S. Commager.*

Action and care will in time wear down the strongest frame, but guilt and melancholy are poisons of quick dispatch.

—T. Paine.

What other dungeon is so dark as one's own heart! What jailor so inexorable as one's self!   *—Nathaniel Hawthorne.*

Let no guilty man escape.   *—U. S. Grant.*

GUN

The policeman ought to have a gun. It is better that he should have the gun than that the gangster should have it.

—Raymond Clapper.

GUSTO

I live with constantly increasing gusto and excitement. I am sure it all means something.   *—W. L. Phelps.*

GUTS

What forest of laurel we bring, and the tears of mankind, to those who stood firm against the opinion of their contemporaries.

—R. W. Emerson.

H

HABIT

Chaos often breeds life, when order breeds habit.

—*Henry Adams.*

Each year, one vicious habit rooted out, in time ought to make the worst man good. —*B. Franklin.*

Habit is a cable; we weave a thread of it every day, and at last we cannot break it. —*Horace Mann.*

Habit is habit and not to be flung out of the window by any man, but coaxed downstairs a step at a time. —*Mark Twain.*

Nothing so needs reforming as other people's habits.

—*Ibid.*

A woman marries the first time for love, the second time for companionship, the third time for support, and the rest of the time just from habit. —*Helen Rowland.*

I always have a habit of saying what I think.

—*Wendell L. Willkie.*

The only American habit that can really be called a system is the habit of pluralism and experimentation.

—*H. S. Commager.*

It is easy to assume a habit; but when you try to cast it off, it will take skin and all. —*H. W. Shaw.*

The more of the details of our daily life we can hand over to the effortless custody of automatism, the more our higher powers of mind will be set free for their proper work.

—*William James.*

A single bad habit will mar an otherwise faultless character, as an ink-drop soileth the pure white page. —*Hosea Ballou.*

Habit is the enormous fly-wheel of society, its most precious
conservative agent.   —*William James.*

Habits are to the soul what the veins and arteries are to the
blood, the courses in which it moves.   —*Horace Bushnell.*

In a majority of cases habit is a greater plague than ever afflicted
Egypt.   —*John Foster.*

The man who has daily inured himself to habits of concentrated attention, energetic volition and self-denial in unnecessary
things, will stand like a tower when everything rocks around him,
and when his softer fellow-mortals are winnowed like chaff in the
blast.   —*William James.*

HAIR

Babies haven't any hair;
Old men's heads are just as bare;—
Between the cradle and the grave
Lies a haircut and a shave.

—*Samuel Hoffenstein.*

Not ten yoke of oxen
Have the power to draw us
Like a woman's hair.

—*H. W. Longfellow.*

HALF

Half the world does not know how the other half lives, but is
trying to find out.   —*E. W. Howe.*

I believe the government cannot remain permanently half slave
and half free.   —*A. Lincoln.*

HAM

Nothing helps scenery like ham and eggs.

—*Mark Twain.*

HANDICAP

In difficult situations to stage a comeback, to turn a minus into
a plus, to capitalize a handicap, takes more than the gentler
virtues. It takes the combative spirit.   —*H. E. Fosdick.*

HANDS

Every time a boy shows his hands, someone suggests that he
wash them.   —*E. W. Howe.*

The hand is the mind's perfect vassal.　　　*—H. T. Tuckerman.*

I love a hand that meets my own with a grasp that causes some sensation.　　　*—F. S. Osgood.*

HANG

We must all stand together, or assuredly we shall hang separately.　　　*—B. Franklin.*

HAPPINESS

Happiness is the only good, reason the only torch, justice the only worship, humanity the only religion, and life the only priest.
—R. G. Ingersoll.

The office of government is not to confer happiness, but to give men opportunity to work out happiness for themselves.
—W. E. Channing.

This is a government of the people, for their happiness and prosperity, and not for that of the few, at the expense of the many.
—Andrew Jackson.

A government, in its truest sense, is only a method to bring to humanity the greatest amount of happiness, and is founded, after all, upon the love of man for man.　　　*—George W. Norris.*

Happiness lies not in the mere possession of money; it lies in the enjoyment of achievement, in the thrill of creative effort.
—F. D. Roosevelt.

The public happiness is the true object of legislation, and can be secured only by the masses of mankind themselves awakening to the knowledge and care of their own interests.
—George Bancroft.

Such happiness as life is capable of comes from the full participation of all our powers in the endeavor to wrest from each changing situation of experience its own full and unique meaning.
—John Dewey.

It's pretty hard to tell what does bring happiness; poverty and wealth have both failed.　　　*—Kin Hubbard.*

It is difficult to tell which gives some couples the most happiness, the minister who marries them or the judge who divorces them.　　　*—M. W. Little.*

Happiness sneaks in through a door you didn't know you left open.　　　*—John Barrymore.*

If you ever find happiness by hunting for it, you will find it, as the old woman did her lost spectacles, safe on her own nose all the time.   —*Josh Billings.*

Happiness, to some elation, is to others, mere stagnation.
—*Amy Lowell.*

Men have a much better time of it than women; for one thing, they marry later; for another thing, they die earlier.
—*H. L. Mencken.*

It is the law of our nature to desire happiness. This law is not local, but universal; not temporary, but eternal.
—*Horace Mann.*

To fill the hour, and leave no crevice for a repentance or an approval,—that is happiness.   —*R. W. Emerson.*

The first axiom of democracy . . . all have a right to the pursuit of happiness.   —*G. E. Woodberry.*

Purpose and happiness are not embodied in the mechanism of institutions, but in free men.   —*Max Ascoli.*

Most of the happiness in this world consists in possessing what others can't get.   —*Josh Billings.*

Happiness is not the end of life; character is.
—*H. W. Beecher.*

Happiness is the harvest of a quiet age.   —*Austin O'Malley.*

The foolish man seeks happiness in the distance; the wise grows it under his feet.   —*James Oppenheim.*

Service to a just cause rewards the worker with more real happiness and satisfaction than every other venture of life.
—*Carrie Chapman Cutt.*

Happiness, like every other emotional state, has blindness and insensibility to opposing facts given it as its instinctive weapon for self-protecton against disturbance.   —*William James.*

It is neither wealth nor splendor, but tranquility and occupation, which give happiness.   —*T. Jefferson.*

Man is the artificer of his own happiness.   —*H. D. Thoreau.*

Happiness in this world, when it comes, comes incidentally. Make it the object of pursuit, and it leads us a wild-goose chase, and is never attained. Follow some other object and very possibly we may find that we have caught happiness without dreaming of it.
—*Nathaniel Hawthorne.*

Inherited wealth is a big handicap to happiness. It is as certain death to ambition as cocaine is to morality.

—*William K. Vanderbilt.*

HAPPY

If a man is happy in America it is considered he is doing something wrong. —*Clarence Darrow.*

Seek not to be rich, but happy. —*Wm. Penn.*

Let us all be happy and live within our means, even if we have to borrow the money to do it with. —*Charles F. Browne.*

> The time to be happy is now,
> The place to be happy is here,
> The way to be happy is to make others so.
> —*R. G. Ingersoll.*

We are happy now because God wills it. —*J. R. Lowell.*

It is not the function of the State to make men happy. They must make themselves happy in their own way, and at their own risk. —*W. G. Sumner.*

No one is happy, it is apparent; the successful are driven as relentlessly as the failures by their sense of guilt, their compulsions and their frustrations. —*Laurence K. Frank.*

Happy people die whole, they are all dissolved in a moment, they have had what they wanted. —*Robinson Jeffers.*

I had a pleasant time with my mind, for it was happy.

—*Louisa May Alcott.*

There is no record in history of a happy philosopher: they exist only in romantic legends. —*H. L. Mencken.*

HARDSHIP

A cobweb is as good as the mightiest cable when there is no strain upon it. —*H. W. Beecher.*

Bad times have a scientific value. These are occasions a good learner would not miss. —*R. W. Emerson.*

The times are not so bad as they seem; they couldn't be.

—*Jay Franklin.*

HARDWARE

The fellow that owns his own home is always just coming out of a hardware store. —*F. M. Hubbard.*

HARVEST

In the majority of cases the best fruit of a man's toil is reaped after his death, and oftentimes when he has died hungering for it.

—*Irene C. Safford.*

HASTE

No man who is in a hurry is quite civilized.　　—*Will Durant.*

In skating over thin ice our safety is our speed.

—*R. W. Emerson.*

Fraud and deceit are ever in a hurry.　　—*B. Franklin.*

Take time for all things: great haste makes great waste.

—*Ibid.*

Manners require time, as nothing is more vulgar than haste.

—*R. W. Emerson.*

HAT

Never run after your own hat—others will be delighted to do it; why spoil their fun?　　—*Mark Twain.*

HATE

Hating people is like burning down your own house to get rid of a rat.　　—*H. E. Fosdick.*

Malice can always find a mark to shoot at, and a pretense to fire.

—*Charles Simmons.*

Hate no one; hate their *vices,* not themselves.

—*J. G. Brainard.*

Dislike what deserves it, but never hate, for that is the nature of malice, which is applied to persons, not to things.

—*Wm. Penn.*

I shall never permit myself to stoop so low as to hate any man.

—*Booker T. Washington.*

There is no faculty of the human soul so persistent and universal as that of hatred.　　—*H. W. Beecher.*

Against enemies who preach the principles of hate and practice them, we set our faith in human love and in God's care for us and all men everywhere.　　—*F. D. Roosevelt.*

HEAD

A man with a small head is like a pin without any, very apt to get into things beyond his depth.　　—*Josh Billings.*

Samson with his strong body had a weak head, or he would not have laid it into a harlot's lap.　　—*B. Franklin.*

We do not need to counsel from ourselves that there are varieties of capacities in the world. Some men have heads, but they are not particularly furnished. —*Woodrow Wilson.*

The softer a man's head, the louder his socks.

—*Helen Rowland.*

HEADACHE

If all the people in the world should agree to sympathize with a certain man at a certain hour, they could not cure his headache.

—*E. W. Howe.*

HEALTH

If I had my way I'd make health catching instead of disease.

—*R. G. Ingersoll.*

It is the soundness of the bones that ultimates itself in the peach-bloom complexion. —*R. W. Emerson.*

Ours is a world which brings pain and hardship, suffering and disaster, but then sets in motion ingenious agencies which quietly but steadily repair the damage. —*J. G. Gilkey.*

We must face what we fear; that is the case of the core of the restoration of health. —*Max Lerner.*

Health is the thing that makes you feel that now is the best time of the year. —*F. P. Adams.*

Perfect obedience to the laws of health would abolish the medical profession. —*O. B. Frothingham.*

The receipts of cookery are swelled to a volume; but a good stomach excels them all. —*Wm. Penn.*

All healthy things are sweet-tempered. —*R. W. Emerson.*

Health is not a condition of matter, but of Mind; nor can the material senses bear reliable testimony on the subject of health.

—*Mary Baker Eddy.*

Civilization and comfort, good plumbing, good beds, and good food have made us big and healthy and tough.

—*Elizabeth Jackson.*

There's lots of people in this world who spend so much time watching their health that they haven't the time to enjoy it.

—*Josh Billings.*

The only way to keep your health is to eat what you don't want, drink what you don't like, and do what you'd rather not.

—*Mark Twain.*

Health lies·in labor, and there is no royal road to it but through
toil.   —*Wendell Phillips.*

Half of the mental difficulties men suffer arise from a morbid
state of health.   —*H. W. Beecher.*

Be sober and temperate, and you will be healthy.

—*B. Franklin.*

Some people think that doctors and nurses can put scrambled
eggs back into the shell.   —*Dorothy Canfield.*

Few things are more important to a community than the health
of its women. All men need mothers of strong frames.

—*T. W. Higginson.*

The first wealth is health.   —*R. W. Emerson.*

HEARING

It is a foolish man that hears all he hears.

—*Austin O'Malley.*

HEART

In our own hearts, we mold the whole world's hereafters; and
in our own hearts we fashion our own gods.

—*Herman Melville.*

What your heart thinks is great, is great. The soul's emphasis
is always right.   —*R. W. Emerson.*

An honest heart being the first blessing, a knowing head is the
second.   —*T. Jefferson.*

> A mill-stone and the human heart are turning
> round and round;
> If they have nothing else to grind, they must
> themselves be ground.

—*H. W. Longfellow.*

The head learns new things, but the heart forevermore practices
old experiences.   —*H. W. Beecher.*

The heart of the fool is in his mouth, but the mouth of the wise
man is in his heart.   —*B. Franklin.*

What if my trousers are shabby and worn; they cover a warm
heart.   —*Tom Masson.*

In each human heart are a tiger, a pig, an ass, and a nightingale; diversity of character is due to their unequal activity.

—*Ambrose Bierce.*

The mother's heart is the child's schoolroom.   *—H. W. Beecher.*

Look then, into thine own heart and write! *—H. W. Longfellow.*

The heart is wiser than the intellect.   *—J. G. Holland.*

Home-keeping hearts are happiest.   *—H. W. Longfellow.*

Hearts are stronger than swords.   *—Wendell Phillips.*

The heart is the best logician.   *—Ibid.*

What the heart has once owned and had, it shall never lose.
—H. W. Beecher.

When a young man complains that a young lady has no heart, it is pretty certain that she has his.   *—C. D. Prentice.*

Wealth and want equally harden the human heart.
—Theodore Parker.

Whatever comes from the heart carries the heat and color of its birthplace.   *—O. W. Holmes.*

HEARTHSTONE

Look well to the hearthstone; therein all hope for America lies.
—Calvin Coolidge.

HEAVEN

Heaven goes by favor; if it went by merit, you would stay out and your dog would go in.   *—Mark Twain.*

What a man misses mostly in heaven is company.   *—Ibid.*

The word "heaven" means harmony.   *—R. W. Trine.*

Many might go to heaven with half the labor they go to hell.
—R. W. Emerson.

Heaven lies about us in our infancy—and we lie about heaven later on.   *—C. B. Loomis.*

> I never spoke with God,
> Nor visited in heaven;
> Yet certain am I of the spot
> As if the chart were given.
>
> *—Emily Dickinson.*

> Heaven is not reached by a single bound
> But we build the ladder by which we rise.
>
> *—J. G. Holland.*

> 'Tis Heaven alone that is given away,
> 'Tis only God may be had for the asking.
>
> *—J. R. Lowell.*

Heaven does not make holiness, but holiness makes heaven.
—*Phillips Brooks.*

As much of heaven is visible as we have eyes to see.
—*William Winter.*

What tranquility will there be in heaven!
—*Jonathan Edwards.*

The way to Heaven is ascending; we must be content to travel up hill, though it be hard and tiresome, and contrary to the natural bias of our flesh.   —*Jonathan Edwards.*

HEIRS

We are the heirs of wonderful treasures from the past: treasures of literature and of the arts. They are ours for the asking—all our own to have and to enjoy, if only we desire them enough.
—*Lorado Taft.*

HELL

The wicked work harder to reach hell than the righteous to get to heaven.   —*Josh Billings.*

Hell is both sides of the tomb, and a devil may be respectable and wear good clothes.   —*C. H. Parkhurst.*

The road to hell is thick with taxicabs.

—*Don Herold.*

Kansas has started in to raise hell, and she seems to have an overproduction.   —*William A. White.*

If I owned Texas and Hell, I would rent out Texas and live in Hell.   —*Philip H. Sheridan.*

I say it's spinach, and I say the hell with it.

—*E. B. White.*

If you keep your eyes so fixed on heaven that you never look at the earth, you will stumble into hell.   —*Austin O'Malley.*

My advice to the women's clubs of America is to raise more hell and fewer dahlias.   —*J. M. Whistler.*

A bad woman raises hell with a good many men while a good woman raises hell with only one.   —*E. W. Howe.*

The word "hell" is from the Old English "hell," meaning to build a wall around, to separate. To be helled was to be shut off from.
—*R. W. Trine.*

The sight of hell's torments will exalt the happiness of the saints forever.   —*Jonathan Edwards.*

If there is no hell, a good many preachers are obtaining money
under false pretences.   —*Billy Sunday.*

HELP

God help those who do not help themselves!

—*Addison Mizner.*

If you really want to help your fellow-man, you must not merely
have in you what would do them good if they should take it from
you, but you must be such a man that they can take it from you.
—*Phillips Brooks.*

If you're in trouble, or hurt or need—go to the poor people.
They're the only ones that'll help—the only ones.

—*John Steinbeck.*

He stands erect by bending over the fallen. He rises by lifting
others.   —*R. G. Ingersoll.*

HEN

I go on working for the same reason that a hen goes on laying
eggs.   —*H. L. Mencken.*

HEREAFTER

If God has put into our very reason difficulties which are insoluble here, is not this a promise that they shall be solved hereafter?   —*J. F. Clarke.*

HEREDITY

Heredity is an omnibus in which all our ancestors ride, and
every now and then one of them puts his head out and embar-
rasses us.   —*O. W. Holmes.*

Society through government, may be able to eliminate the
special privileges of money inheritance by "accident of birth." But
government cannot eliminate the disadvantages of weaknesses of
mind or body resulting from the "accident of birth."

—*D. R. Richberg.*

A good cow may have a bad calf.   —*Noah Webster.*

There is something frightful in the way in which not only characteristic qualities but particular manifestations of them, are repeated from generation to generation.   —*O. W. Holmes.*

HERESY

Heresy is what the minority believe; it is the name given by the
powerful to the doctrine of the weak.   —*R. G. Ingersoll.*

In politics as in religion, it is equally absurd to aim at making proselytes by fire and sword. Heresies in either can rarely be cured by persecution. *—Alexander Hamilton.*

HERITAGE

Our American heritage is threatened as much by our own indifference as by the most unscupulous office or by the most powerful foreign threat. *—D. D. Eisenhower.*

HEROISM

The hero is one who kindles a great light in the world, who sets up blazing torches in the dark streets of life for men to see by. The saint is the man who walks through the dark paths of the world, himself a "light." *—Felix Adler.*

A hero is no braver than an ordinary man, but he is brave five minutes longer. *—R. W. Emerson.*

Every man becomes a hero at last. *—Ibid.*

> In the world's broad field of battle,
>   In the bivouac of Life,
> Be not like the dumb, driven cattle!
>   Be a hero in the strife!
> *—H. W. Longfellow.*

The Romantic Hero was no longer the knight, the wandering poet, the cowpuncher, the aviator, not the brave young district attorney, but the great sales-manager, whose title of nobility was "go-getter." *—Sinclair Lewis.*

In war the heroes always outnumber the soldiers ten to one. *—H. L. Mencken.*

How hard it is for us to see the heroic in an act of our neighbor! *—John Burroughs.*

The heroic soul does not sell its justice and its nobleness. *—R. W. Emerson.*

A hero cannot be a hero unless in an heroic world. *—Nathaniel Hawthorne.*

I had never noticed the great fields of heroism lying round about me. I had failed to see it present and alive . . . And yet there it was in the daily lives of the laboring classes. *—William James.*

Self-trust is the essence of heroism. *—R. W. Emerson.*

More heroism has been displayed in the household and the closet, than in the most memorable battlefields of history.

—*H. W. Beecher.*

The greatest obstacle to being heroic is the doubt whether one may not be going to prove one's self a fool; the truest heroism is to resist the doubt, and the profoundest wisdom to know when it ought to be resisted and when to be obeyed.

—*Nathaniel Hawthorne.*

When the will defies fear, when duty throws the gauntlet down to fate, when honor scorns to compromise with death—this is heroism.   —*R. G. Ingersoll.*

Fortunate men! Your country lives because you died.

—*James A. Garfield.*

HESITATE

Don't hesitate to be as reactionary as the multiplication table.

—*Calvin Coolidge.*

HEW

Hew to the line, let the chips fall where they may.

—*R. Conkling.*

HIERARCHY

Some must follow, and some command, though all are made of clay!   —*H. W. Longfellow.*

HIGHBROW

A highbrow is a person educated beyond his intelligence.

—*Brander Matthews.*

HISTORY

History is bunk.   —*Henry Ford.*

The history of the world is the record of man in quest of his daily bread and butter.   —*H. W. Van Loon.*

History is still less rigidly historical than comparative anatomy or social psychology.   —*James Harvey Robinson.*

The history of Liberty is a history of limitations of governmental powers, not the increase of it.   —*Woodrow Wilson.*

The history of ideas is the history of mistakes. But through all mistakes it is also the history of the gradual purification of conduct.

—*A. N. Whitehead.*

History can be written as the record of the follies of the majority.

—*Lindsay Rogers.*

We can know nothing of any nation unless we know its history.
                                                    —*Agnes Repplier.*

We can know nothing of the history of any nation unless we know something of all nations.   —*Ibid.*

The use of history is to give value to the present hour and its duty.   —*R. W. Emerson.*

Fellow citizens, we cannot escape history.   —*A. Lincoln.*

History is moving faster and faster all the time. Machinery and education are speeding up history the way moving pictures speed up the blossoming of a flower.   —*Max Eastman.*

The history of civilization if intelligently conceived may be an instrument of civilization.   —*Charles and Mary Beard.*

The so-called lessons of history are for the most part the rationalization of the victors. History is written by the survivors.
                                                    —*Max Lerner.*

History is but the unrolled scroll of prophecy.
                                                    —*James A. Garfield.*

History is clarified experience.   —*J. R. Lowell.*

The history of the past is a mere puppet-show.
                                                    —*H. W. Longfellow.*

History is but a kind of Newgate calendar, a register of the crimes and miseries that man has inflicted on his fellow-man.
                                                    —*Washingon Irving.*

History: an account mostly false, of events unimportant, which are brought about by rulers mostly knaves, and soldiers mostly fools.
                                                    —*Ambrose Bierce.*

The march of Providence is so slow and our desires so impatient; the work of progress is so immense and our means of aiding it so feeble; the life of humanity is so long, that of the individual so brief, that we often see only the ebb of the advancing ways, and are thus discouraged. It is history that teaches us to hope.
                                                    —*Robert E. Lee.*

Not that which men do worthily, but that which they do successfully, is what history makes haste to record.
                                                    —*H. W. Beecher.*

Man is fed with fables through life, and leaves it in the belief he knows something of what has been passing, when in truth he has known nothing but what has passed under his own eye.

—*T. Jefferson.*

The public history of all countries, and all ages, is but a sort of mask, richly colored. The interior working of the machinery must be foul. —*John Q. Adams.*

A morsel of genuine history is a thing so rare as to be always valuable. —*T. Jefferson.*

History repeats itself, that's one of the things that's wrong with history. —*Clarence Darrow.*

HOG

It's the still hog that eats the most. —*Daniel Drew.*

HOLE

A hole is nothing at all, but you can break your neck in it.

—*Austin O'Malley.*

HOLIDAYS

The holiest of all holidays are those kept by ourselves in silence and apart, the secret anniversaries of the heart, when the full tide of feeling overflows. —*H. W. Longfellow.*

HOLINESS

It seemed to me that holiness brought an inexpressible purity, brightness, peacefulness, and nourishment to the soul; that it made the soul like a field or garden of God, with all manner of pleasant flowers. —*Jonathan Edwards.*

HOLLYWOOD

Hollywood is a place where people from Iowa mistake each other for movie stars. —*Fred Allen.*

Hollywood is no place for a professional comedian; the amateur competition is too great. —*Ibid.*

Hollywood impresses me as being ten million dollars' worth of intricate and highly ingenious machinery functioning elaborately to put skin on baloney. —*George Jean Nathan.*

HOLOCAUST

Millions of men in thousands of years are included in this holocaust of past time—eras of savagery, Assyrian civilization, Christian butcheries, the Czar yet supreme, the Turk yet alive.

—*G. E. Woodberry.*

HOME

Home is the place where, when you have to go there,
They have to take you in.
                                              —*Robert Frost.*

It takes a heap o' livin' in a house t' make it home.
                                              —*E. A. Guest.*

Be it ever so humble, there's no place like home.
                                              —*John H. Payne.*

To stay at home is best.   —*H. W. Longfellow.*

Home is the most popular, and will be the most enduring of all
earthly establishments.   —*Channing Pollock.*

Home is where there's one to love us.   —*Charles Swain.*

I am in favor of cutting up the wild lands into parcels, so that
every poor man can have a home.   —*A. Lincoln.*

If there is anything splendid it is a home where all are equal.
                                              —*R. G. Ingersoll.*

I have come home to myself, behold me.   —*Robinson Jeffers.*

Go where he will, the wise man is at home.
                                              —*R. W. Emerson.*

The man who loves home best, and loves it most unselfishly,
loves his country best.   —*J. G. Holland.*

The sweetest type of heaven is home.   —*Ibid.*

Home interprets heaven. Home is heaven for beginners.
                                              —*C. H. Parkhurst.*

As the homes, so the state.   —*A. B. Alcott.*

The happiness of the domestic fireside is the first boon of
Heaven; and it is well it is so, since it is that which is the lot of
the mass of mankind.   —*T. Jefferson.*

The sweets of home are balanced not only by its tenderer sorrows, but by a thousand artificial prejudices, enmities, and restrictions.   —*George Santayana.*

HOMOSEXUALITY

Overt homosexuality among women (is) a newfangled device
for jazzing up the sexual life and giving it a counterfeit zest to
compensate the contentment that normal mating in sober marriage
once yielded and now no longer appears to promise.
                                    —*Samuel D. Schmalhausen.*

HOMESICKNESS

I'm crazy about America and I want to go home.
—*Thornton Wilder.*

I can't be soul-happy outside my beloved U.S.A. —*Ibid.*

It is to one's own America, wherever it may be, that one always comes back. —*Samuel Putnam.*

HONESTY

I would give no thought of what the world might say of me, if I could only transmit to posterity the reputation of an honest man.
—*Sam Houston.*

'Tis hard (but glorious) to be poor and honest: an empty sack can hardly stand upright; but if it does, 'tis a stout one.
—*B. Franklin.*

Let not any honest man suppress his sentiments concerning freedom, however small their influence is likely to be.
—*John Dickinson.*

Confidence . . . thrives only on honesty, on honor, on the sacredness of obligations, on faithful protection and on unselfish performance. Without them it cannot live. —*F. D. Roosevelt.*

I have not observed men's honesty to increase with their riches.
—*T. Jefferson.*

All men profess honesty as long as they can. To believe all men honest would be folly. To believe none so, is something worse.
—*John Q. Adams.*

Honesty is the rarest wealth anyone can possess, and yet all the honesty in the world ain't lawful tender for a loaf of bread.
—*Josh Billings.*

Authority must have power to make and keep people honest; people, honesty to obey authority. —*Nathaniel Ward.*

Honesty pays, but it don't seem to pay enough to suit some people. —*F. M. Hubbard.*

A shady business never yields a sunny life. —*B. C. Forbes.*

I'd rather know a square guy than own a square mile.
—*Wilson Mizner.*

I consider the most enviable of all titles the character of an "honest man." —*G. Washington.*

Honesty is not only the first step toward greatness,—it is greatness itself. —*C. N. Bovee.*

Let honesty be as the breath of thy soul.   —*B. Franklin.*

HONEY

There is a difference in having a rational judgment that honey is sweet, and having a sense of its sweetness . . . the heart is concerned in the latter.   —*Jonathan Edwards.*

HONEYMOON

Honeymoon: the time during which the bride believes the bridegroom's word of honor.   —*H. L. Mencken.*

The honeymoon is not actually over until we cease to stifle our sighs and begin to stifle our yawns.   —*Helen Rowland.*

HONOR

Honor all men.   —*John Wise.*

Nothing is lost save honor!   —*Jim Fisk.*

National honor is national property of the highest value.
          —*James Monroe.*

Our history honors many names whose morals would not stand the Acid Test, but our History honors no man who betrayed or attempted to betray a Government Trust.   —*Will Rogers.*

The louder he talked of his honor, the faster we counted our spoons.   —*R. W. Emerson.*

The true honor of a nation is to be found only in deeds of justice, and in the happiness of its people.   —*Charles Sumner.*

One of the greatest sources of suffering is to have an inborn sense of honor.   —*B. De Casseres.*

What is life without honor? Degradation is worse than death.
          —*Stonewall Jackson.*

When faith is lost, when honor dies,
     The man is dead!   —*J. G. Whittier.*

The word honor in the mouth of Mr. Webster is like the word love in the mouth of a whore.   —*R. W. Emerson.*

We mutually pledge to each other our lives, our fortunes, and our sacred honor.   —*T. Jefferson.*

HONORABLE

In our age, there can be no peace that is not honorable; there can be no war that is not dishonorable.

          —*Charles Sumner.*

HOPE

He that lives on hope will die fasting. —*B. Franklin.*

Why should there not be a patient confidence in the ultimate justice of the people? Is there any better or equal hope in the world? —*A. Lincoln.*

Girls and boys of America, you are the hope of the world!
—*Hermann Hagedorn.*

The hope of a new world is alive today in millions of hearts the world around. —*Max Otto.*

We, here in America, hold in our hands the hope of the world, the fate of the coming years. —*Theodore Roosevelt.*

Shame and disgrace will be ours if in our eyes the light of high resolve is dimmed, if we trail in the dust the golden hopes of men.
—*Ibid.*

Hope is the only universal liar who never loses his reputation for veracity. —*R. G. Ingersoll.*

Sing to my soul, renew its languishing faith and hope.
—*Walt Whitman.*

Hope is the gay, skylarking pajamas we wear over yesterday's bruises. —*B. De Casseres.*

There is nothing so well known as that we should not expect something for nothing—but we all do and call it Hope.
—*E. W. Howe.*

One does not expect in this world; one hopes and pays carfares.
—*Josephine P. Peabody.*

Youth fades; love droops; the lesson of friendship falls;
A mother's secret hope outlives them all. —*O. W. Holmes.*

God puts the excess of hope in one man in order that it may be a medicine to the man who is despondent. —*H. W. Beecher.*

Hope is life and life is hope. —*Adele Shreve.*

Hope proves a man deathless. —*Herman Melville.*

It (hope) is the struggle of the soul, breaking loose from what is perishable, and attesting her eternity. —*Ibid.*

> You made me what I am to-day,
> I hope you're satisfied.
>
> —*Henry Fink.*

HORROR

There will one day spring from the brain of science a machine or force so fearful in its potentialities, so absolutely terrifying, that even man, the fighter, who will dare torture and death, will be appalled, and so will abandon war forever.

—*Thomas A. Edison.*

HORSES

It is not best to swap horses while crossing the stream.

—*A. Lincoln.*

HOSPITALITY

Hospitality: the virtue which induces us to feed and lodge certain persons who are not in need of food and lodging.

—*Ambrose Bierce.*

HOUR

Some people can stay longer in an hour than others can in a week.   —*W. D. Howells.*

Nothing can move a man who is paid by the hour; how sweet the flight of time seems to his calm mind.   —*C. D. Warner.*

There is more room for the actual play of originality, daring, imagination, courage and real conquest in an hour of our lives than there was in centuries of sword tilting.   —*Gabriel Heatter.*

The first hour of the morning is the rudder of the day.

—*H. W. Beecher.*

Lost, yesterday, somewhere between Sunrise and Sunset, two golden hours, each set with sixty diamond minutes. No reward is offered for they are gone forever.   —*Horace Mann.*

HOUSE

Your house is your fortress in a warring world, where a woman's hand buckles on your armor in the morning and soothes your fatigue and wounds at night.   —*Frank Crane.*

The maker of a house, of a real human house, is God himself, the same who made the stars and built the world.

—*Ibid.*

A man's house is his castle, and whilst he is quiet, he is as well guarded as a prince in his castle.   —*James Otis.*

A big house is one of the greediest cormorants which can light upon a little income.   —*Edward S. Martin.*

HUMAN

A human being is an ingenious assembly of portable plumbing.
—*Christopher Morley.*

All that I care to know is that a man is a human being—that is enough for me; he can't be any worse. —*Mark Twain.*

Every human heart is human. —*H. W. Longfellow.*

HUMANISM

After all, all things are man's. Before God created man, man created God. —*G. Hartley Grattan.*

The central assumption of Humanism is that of a dualism of man and nature. —*Norman Foerster.*

An organic attitude towards life can truly be called humanism.
—*Lewis Mumford.*

I retain my belief in the nobility and excellence of the human. I believe that spiritual sweetness and unselfishness will conquer the gross gluttony of today. —*Jack London.*

Humanism is in the end futile without religion.
—*T. S. Eliot.*

Every human being has an individuality that can be made socially effective. —*Isidor Schneider.*

Democracy is humanism, humanism is democracy.
—*H. M. Kallen.*

HUMANIST

The humanist exercises the will to refrain. —*Irving Babbitt.*

HUMANITARIANISM

I call that mind free which sets no bounds to its love . . . and offers itself up a willing victim to the cause of mankind.
—*W. E. Channing.*

HUMANITY

Humanity is the Sin of God. —*Theodore Parker.*

Even if we should be borne down again and again, the voice of humanity will arise from the dust and drive the money changers out of the temple and the traitors out of the land.
—*John P. Altgeld.*

Every man belongs to the race and owes a duty to mankind.
—*W. E. Channing.*

The law of humanity must reign over the assertion of all human rights.   —*Ibid.*

Year after year the gates of prison-hells return to the world an emaciated, deformed, will-less shipwrecked crew of humanity, with the Cain mark on their foreheads, their hopes crushed, all their natural inclinations thwarted.   —*Emma Goldman.*

Humanity has become a distorted image of its own noble self.
                                                          —*P. A. Sorokin.*

There are times when one would like to hang the whole human race, and finish the farce.   —*Mark Twain.*

The age of chivalry has gone; the age of humanity has come.
                                                          —*Charles Sumner.*

HUMBUG

Take the humbug out of this world, and you haven't much left to do business with.   —*Josh Billings.*

HUMILITY

Extremes meet and there is no better example than the haughtiness of humility.   —*R. W. Emerson.*

He who admits that he, himself, is a worm ought not to complain when he is trodden on.   —*Elbert Hubbard.*

Be humble or you'll stumble.   —*Dwight L. Moody.*

Humility is the first of the virtues—for other people.
                                                          —*O. W. Holmes.*

Humbleness is always grace, always dignity.   —*J. R. Lowell.*

Imitate Jesus and Socrates.   —*B. Franklin.*

Light is the same in the sun and in the candle.
                                                          —*G. E. Woodberry.*

The humblest life may be a life of sacrifice, and the poorer it is, generally, the greater the sacrifice.   —*Ibid.*

Humility must always be the portion of any man who receives acclaim earned in the blood of his followers and the sacrifices of his friends.   —*D. D. Eisenhower.*

The true way to be humble is not to stoop till thou art smaller than thyself, but to stand at thy real height against some higher nature that shall show thee what the real smallness of thy greatest greatness is.   —*Phillips Brooks.*

The more humble a man is before God, the more he will be

exalted; the more humble he is before man, the more he will get rode roughshod. —*Josh Billings.*

It is the mark of nobleness to volunteer the lowest service, the greatest spirit only attaining to humility. —*R. W. Emerson.*

Humility, like darkness, reveals the heavenly lights.
—*H. D. Thoreau.*

Never be haughty to the humble; never be humble to the haughty. —*Jefferson Davis.*

At moments she discovered she was grotesquely wrong, and then she treated herself to a week of passionate humility.
—*Henry James.*

HUMOR

The secret source of humor is not joy but sorrow; there is no humor in heaven. —*Mark Twain.*

Men will confess to treason, murder, arson, false teeth, or a wig. How many of them will own up to a lack of humor?
—*F. M. Colby.*

The longer I live the more I think of humor as in truth the saving sense. —*Jacob Riis.*

There are no things by which the troubles and difficulties of this life can be resisted better than with wit and humor.
—*H. W. Beecher.*

There are very few good judges of humor, and they don't agree.
—*Josh Billings.*

Whenever you find Humor, you find Pathos close by his side.
—*E. P. Whipple.*

HUMORIST

A humorist is a man who feels bad but who feels good about it.
—*Don Herold.*

He must not laugh at his own wheeze: a snuff box has no right to sneeze. —*Keith Preston.*

Think of what would happen to us in America if there were no humorists; life would be one long Congressional Record.
—*Tom Masson.*

HUNGER

An empty stomach is not a good political adviser.
—*Albert Einstein.*

In the workingman's house hunger looks in, but dares not enter.
—*B. Franklin.*

Children dying of pellagra must die because a profit cannot be taken from an orange. And coroners must fill in the certificates— deeds of malnutrition—because the food must rot, must be forced to rot.   —*John Steinbeck.*

The great companies did not know that the line between hunger and anger is a thin line.   —*Ibid.*

Hunger does not breed reform; it breeds madness, and all the ugly distempers that make an ordered life impossible.
—*Woodrow Wilson.*

HUSBANDS

The only time that most women give their orating husbands undivided attention is when the old boys mumble in their sleep.
—*Wilson Mizner.*

One good husband is worth two good wives; for the scarcer things are, the more they're valued.   —*B. Franklin.*

My idea of walking into the jaws of death is marrying some woman who's lost three husbands.   —*Kin Hubbard.*

Most wives are nicer than their husbands, but that's nothing; I am nice to everybody from whom I get money.
—*Don Herold.*

French husbands often give their wives a companionship which American women can only find in one another.
—*Charlotte Muret.*

HUSTLES

Everything comes to him who hustles while he waits.
—*Thomas A. Edison.*

HYDRA

Slavery is a Hydra Sin, and includes in it every violation of the precepts of the Law and the Gospel.   —*Benjamin Rush.*

HYPHEN

The hyphenated American always hoists the American flag undermost.   —*Theodore Roosevelt.*

HYPOCRISY

Behavior which appears superficially correct but is intrinsically corrupt always irritates those who see below the surface.
—*James Conant.*

No man, for any considerable period, can wear one face to himself, and another to the multitude, without finally getting bewildered as to which may be the true.   —*Nathaniel Hawthorne.*

The man who murdered both his parents . . . pleaded for mercy on the grounds that he was an orphan.   —*A. Lincoln.*

Business has its fixed standard of hypocrisy.

—*Lafcadio Hearn.*

Boston has carried the practice of hypocrisy to the nth degree of refinement, grace and failure.   —*Lincoln Steffens.*

We are companions in hypocrisy.   —*W. D. Howells.*

The world consists almost exclusively of people who are one sort and who behave like another sort.   —*Zona Gale.*

Hypocrisy is oftenest clothed in the garb of religion.

—*Hosea Ballou.*

Some of the most arrant pirates of . . . capitalism, like Carnegie and Rockefeller, were pious Christians.   —*C. Hartley Grattan.*

I hate it (slavery) because it enables the enemies of free institutions to taunt us as hypocrites.   —*A. Lincoln.*

If you cultivate piety as an end and not as a means, you will become a hypocrite.   —*Austin O'Malley.*

Nerves die that hypocrites can double their profits.

—*Elizabeth Jackson.*

If the world despises a hypocrite, what must they think of him in heaven?   —*Josh Billings.*

I

IDEALISM

Words without actions are the assassins of idealism.
                                        —Herbert Hoover.

Absolute idealism (is) the last, boldest and most grandiose systematic defense of God, immortality and eternal values.
                                        —May Brodbeck.

Imbedded in idealism is the wisdom of the race, the insight that from our hopes and fears, expectations and suspicions, we form our own world. But to mistake the inner landscape for the outer is madness.   *—Ibid.*

IDEALISTS

An idealist is a person who helps other people to be prosperous.
                                        —Henry Ford.

When they come downstairs from their Ivory Towers, idealists are apt to walk straight into the gutter.
                                        —Logan Pearsall Smith.

The American is the great idealist among mankind.
                                        —Leon Samson.

Pare an idealist to the quick and you'll find a Nero.
                                        —Benjamin De Casseres.

Sometimes people call me an idealist. Well, that is the way I know I am an American. America is the only idealistic nation in the world.   *—Woodrow Wilson.*

IDEALS

Ideals are like the stars: we never reach them, but like the mariners of the sea, we chart our course by them.
                                        —Carl Schurz.

Ideals are our better selves. —*A. B. Alcott.*

Man can never come up to his ideal standard.

—*Margaret Fuller.*

It is the nature of the immortal spirit to raise that standard (of ideals) higher and higher as it goes from strength to strength still upward and onward. —*Ibid.*

A man's ideal, like his horizon, is constantly receding from him as he advances toward it. —*W. G. T. Shedd.*

Great objects form great minds. —*Nathaniel Emmons.*

What we need most, is not so much to realize the ideal as to idealize the real. —*F. H. Hedge.*

Ideals were not archaic things, beautiful and impotent; they were the real sources of power among men. —*Willa Cather.*

To have greatly dreamed precludes low ends. —*J. R. Lowell.*

There can be—there is—no conflict between human rights and property rights when exercised by men dedicated to our American ideals. —*M. R. Sayre.*

What are the American ideals? They are the development of the individual through liberty and the attainment of the common good through democracy and social justice. —*Louis D. Brandeis.*

There is this benefit in brag, that the speaker is unconsciously expressing his own ideal. —*R. W. Emerson.*

A large proportion of human beings live not so much in themselves as in what they desire to be. —*E. P. Whipple.*

Every life has its actual blanks which the ideal must fill up, or which else remain bare and profitless forever. —*J. W. Howe.*

Ideals are the world's masters. —*J. G. Holland.*

Be true to your own highest conviction. —*W. E. Channing.*

The true ideal is not opposed to the real but lies in it; and blessed are the eyes that find it. —*J. R. Lowell.*

I am not celebrating high ideals, lofty aims, fine purposes, grand resolutions. One of the most dangerous things in the world is to accept them and think you believe in them, and then neglect the day-by-day means that lead to them. —*H. E. Fosdick.*

Every genuine American holds to the ideals of justice for all men, of independence, including free speech and free action within the limits of law, of obedience to law, of universal education, of material well-being for all the well-behaving and industrious, of peace and goodwill among men.   —*C. E. Norton.*

Some men can live up to their loftiest ideals without ever going higher than a basement.   —*Theodore Roosevelt.*

Some people never have anything except ideals. —*E. W. Howe.*

Let us be true to our democratic ideals . . . by living in such a manner as to show that democracy can be efficient in promoting the public welfare.   —*Austin O'Malley.*

There is no force so democratic as the force of an ideal.
                                                  —*Calvin Coolidge.*

IDEAS

Every society needs a continuous flow of new ideas.
                                                  —*H. S. Commager.*

An Idea isn't responsible for the people who believe in it.
                                                  —*Don Marquis.*

For an idea ever to be fashionable is ominous, since it must afterwards be always old-fashioned.   —*George Santayana.*

To create man was a fine and original idea; but to add the sheep was a tautology.   —*Mark Twain.*

Man is ready to die for an idea, provided that idea is not quite clear to him.   —*Paul Eldridge.*

We must fight our way through not alone to the destruction of our enemies but to a new world idea. We must win the peace.
                                                  —*Wendell L. Willkie.*

The world stands on ideas, not on iron or cotton.
                                                  —*R. W. Emerson.*

The policy of repression of ideas cannot work and never has worked.   —*Robert M. Hutchins.*

These antagonistic ideas, if so they may be called, are equally true and neither can be spared . . . In a healthy mind they live together.   —*W. E. Channing.*

The ideas and images in men's minds are the invisible powers that constantly govern them; and to these they all pay universally a ready submission.   —*Jonathan Edwards.*

Ideas are booming through the world louder than cannon.
                                                  —*W. M. Paxton.*

The kind of man who demands that government enforce his ideas is always the kind whose ideas are idiotic. —*H. L. Mencken.*

New England has never shown the slightest sign of a genuine enthusiasm for ideas. —*Ibid.*

Ideas control the world. —*James A. Garfield.*

Great ideas come when the world needs them. —*Austin Phelps.*

Events are only the shells of ideas. —*E. H. Chapin.*

Present ideas of love, marriage, and the family are almost exclusively masculine constructions. —*John Dewey.*

Many ideas grow better when transplanted into another mind than in the one where they sprung up. —*O. W. Holmes.*

Ideas in the head set hands about their several tasks.
—*A. B. Alcott.*

One has to dismount from an idea and get into saddle again at every parenthesis. —*O. W. Holmes.*

An idea to be suggestive, must come to the individual with the force of a revelation. —*William James.*

There is no adequate defense, except stupidity, against the impact of a new idea. —*P. W. Bridgman.*

An idea that is not dangerous is unworthy of being called an idea at all. —*Elbert Hubbard.*

Every idea is an incitement. It offers itself for belief and if believed it is acted on unless some other belief outweighs it or some failure of energy stifles the movement at its birth.
—*O. W. Holmes, Jr.*

Three ideas stand out above all others in the influence they have exerted and are destined to exert upon the development of the human race: The idea of the Golden Rule; the idea of natural law; the idea of age-long growth or evolution. —*R. A. Millikan.*

In many ways ideas are more important than people—they are much more permanent. —*C. F. Kettering.*

IDIOTS

In the first place God made idiots; this was for practice; then he made school boards. —*Mark Twain.*

IDLENESS

Troubles spring from idleness, and grievous toils from needless ease. —*B. Franklin.*

If you are idle you are on the way to ruin, and there are few stopping places upon it.—It is rather a precipice than a road.

—*H. W. Beecher.*

Sloth, like rust, consumes faster than labor wears, while the used key is always bright.   —*B. Franklin.*

Sloth makes all things difficult, but industry, all things easy.

—*Ibid.*

Idleness is paralysis.   —*R. D. Hitchcock.*

There are but few men who have character enough to lead a life of idleness.   —*Josh Billings.*

I loaf and invite my soul.   —*Walt Whitman.*

Idleness is emptiness: the tree in which the sap is stagnant remains fruitless.   —*Hosea Ballou.*

The work of the Lord cannot wait upon sluggards.

—*V. L. Parrington.*

American workers comprehended the great fact that an idle man, whether he be a worker, or a millionaire, harms all.

—*Thomas A. Edison.*

IGNORANCE

To be ignorant of one's ignorance is the malady of the ignorant.

—*A. B. Alcott.*

I honestly believe it is better to know nothing than to know what ain't so.   —*Josh Billings.*

If a nation expects to be be ignorant and free, in a state of civilization, it expects what never was and never will be.

—*T. Jefferson.*

The compounding of individual ignorances in masses (cannot) produce a continuous directing force in public affairs.

—*Walter Lippmann.*

Genuine ignorance is . . . profitable because it is likely to be accompanied by humility, curiosity, and open-mindedness; whereas ability to repeat catch-phrases, cant terms, familiar propositions, gives the conceit of learning and coats the mind with varnish waterproof to new ideas.   —*John Dewey.*

In order to have wisdom we must have ignorance.

—*Theodore Dreiser.*

Where ignorance is bliss it's foolish to borrow your neighbor's newspaper.   —*Kin Hubbard.*

Ignorance is preferable to error; and he is less remote from truth who believes nothing, than he who believes what is wrong.
—*T. Jefferson.*

There is a modern delusion, cultivated by the lazy and the arty, that originality is the prerogative of ignorance.
—*H. M. Kallen.*

Ignorance is the enemy of originality.   —*Ibid.*

Inspiration springs more readily from knowledge than from ignorance.   —*Ibid.*

It takes a lot of things to prove you are smart, but only one thing to prove you are ignorant.   —*Don Herold.*

The older we grow the greater becomes our wonder at how much ignorance one can contain without bursting one's clothes.
—*Mark Twain.*

Ignorance is the wet-nurse of prejudice.   —*H. W. Shaw.*

Ignorance breeds monsters to fill up the vacancies of the soul that are unoccupied by the verities of knowledge. —*Horace Mann.*

The ignorant classes are the dangerous classes. Ignorance is the womb of monsters.   —*H. W. Beecher.*

The more one endeavors to sound the depth of his ignorance the deeper the chasm appears.   —*A. B. Alcott.*

Everybody is ignorant, only on different subjects. —*Will Rogers.*

He who knows nothing is nearer the truth than he whose mind is filled with falsehoods and errors.   —*T. Jefferson.*

There are many things of which a wise man might wish to be ignorant.   —*R. W. Emerson.*

A man's ignorance is as much his private property, and as precious in his own eyes, as his family Bible.   —*O. W. Holmes.*

Ignorance is of a peculiar nature; once dispelled, it is impossible to reestablish it. It is not originally a thing of itself, but is only the absence of knowledge; and though man may be kept ignorant, he cannot be made ignorant.   —*T. Paine.*

The trouble with most folks isn't so much their ignorance, as knowing so many things that ain't so.   —*Josh Billings.*

ILL-NATURE
Ill-nature is a sort of running sore of the disposition.
—*H. W. Shaw.*

Think of a man in a chronic state of anger.

—H. W. Beecher.

ILLUSION

Better a dish of illusion and a hearty appetite for life, than a feast of reality and indigestion therewith.   *—H. A. Overstreet.*

Don't part with your illusions. When they are gone you may still exist, but you have ceased to live.   *—Mark Twain.*

Things are not what they seem.   *—H. W. Longfellow.*

It is an amiable illusion, which the shape of our planet prompts, that every man is at the top of the world.   *—R. W. Emerson.*

A man loses his illusions first, his teeth second, and his follies last.   *—Helen Rowland.*

A pleasant illusion is better than a harsh reality.

—C. N. Bovee.

IMAGINATION

Imagination, creative imagination, is an action of the mind that produces a new idea or insight.   *—R. W. Gerard.*

The soul without imagination is what an observatory would be without a telescope.   *—H. W. Beecher.*

Imagination is the organ through which the soul within us recognizes a soul without us.   *—H. N. Hudson.*

It is the divine attribute of the imagination that it can create a world for itself.   *—Washington Irving.*

The quality of the imagination is to flow and not to freeze.

—R. W. Emerson.

Keep the imagination sane—that is one of the truest conditions of communion with heaven.   *—Nathaniel Hawthorne.*

The imagination is the very eye of faith.   *—H. W. Beecher.*

Science does not know its debt to imagination.

—R. W. Emerson.

Solitude is as needful to the imagination as society is wholesome for the character.   *—J. R. Lowell.*

Love is the triumph of imagination over intelligence.

—H. L. Mencken.

IMBECILES

The reason there are so many imbeciles among imprisoned criminals is that an imbecile is so foolish even a detective can detect him.   *—Austin O'Malley.*

IMITATION

Insist on yourself; never imitate. —*R. W. Emerson.*

Imitation belittles. —*C. N. Bovee.*

Imitation forms our manners, our opinions, our very lives.
—*John Weiss.*

Men will lessen what they will not imitate.
—*Wm. Penn.*

There is much difference between imitating a good man and counterfeiting him. —*B. Franklin.*

To be as good as our fathers, we must be better. Imitation is not discipleship. —*Wendell Phillips.*

Imitation cannot go above its model. The imitator dooms himself to hopeless mediocrity. —*R. W. Emerson.*

IMMANENCE

God is not outside of His world, He is inside. He is perpetually leading it on from instant to instant. —*Phillips Brooks.*

IMMIGRANTS

All of our people—except full-blooded Indians—are immigrants, or descendants of immigrants, including even those who came here on the Mayflower. —*F. D. Roosevelt.*

This country was built up by immigrants who, in the vast majority of cases, came here to escape poverty, oppression, and lack of opportunity at home. —*Alfred E. Smith.*

IMMIGRATION

When a single country is peacefully invaded by millions of men from scores of other countries . . . we have something new in history. —*R. E. Park.*

If there are any abroad who desire to make this the land of their adoption, it is not in my heart to throw ought in their way to prevent them from coming to the United States. —*A. Lincoln.*

We send missionaries to China so the Chinese can get to heaven, but we won't let them into our country. —*Pearl Buck.*

The admitted right of a government to prevent the influx of elements hostile to its internal peace and security may not be questioned, even where there is no treaty stipulation on the subject. —*Grover Cleveland.*

IMMORAL

What is moral is what you feel good after and what is immoral
is what you feel bad after.   *—Ernest Hemingway.*

IMMORALITY

Give up money; give up fame, give up science, give the earth
itself and all it contains, rather than do an immoral act.
                                               —T. Jefferson.

All the things I really like to do are either immoral, illegal, or
fattening.   *—Alexander Woollcott.*

This story is slightly immoral, but so I guess, are all stories
based on truth.   *—Ring Lardner.*

IMMORTALITY

Our Creator would never have made such lovely days, and have
given us the deep hearts to enjoy them, above and beyond all
thought, unless we were meant to be immortal.
                                               —Nathaniel Hawthorne.

> Dust thou art, to dust returnest,
> Was not spoken of the soul.
>   *—H. W. Longfellow.*

I swear I think now that everything without exception has an
eternal soul!   *—Walt Whitman.*

I believe in the immortality of the soul, not in the sense in
which I accept the demonstrable truths of science, but as a supreme act of faith in the reasonableness of God's work.
                                               —John Fiske.

I think it is not improbable that man . . . may have cosmic
destinies that he does not understand. And so beyond the vision
of battling races and an impoverished earth, I catch a dreaming
glimpse of peace.   *—O. W. Holmes, Jr.*

I know I am deathless.   *—Walt Whitman.*

I swear I think there is nothing but immortality.   *—Ibid.*

The smallest sprout shows there is really no death.   *—Ibid.*

I believe in the immortality of the soul because I have within
me immortal longings.   *—Helen Keller.*

I know of no arguments to prove the immortality of the soul,
but such as are derived from the Christian revelation.
                                               —Benjamin Rush.

Millions long for immortality who do not know what to do with themselves on a rainy Sunday afternoon. —*Susan Ertz.*

All men desire to be immortal. —*Theodore Parker.*

The immortality of the soul is assented to rather than believed, believed rather than lived. —*O. A. Brownson.*

An earthly immortality belongs to a great and good character. —*Edward Everett.*

> To be eternal—to vegetate through all eternity—
> No such everlasting for me!
> God, if He can, keep me from such a blight!
> —*Louis Untermeyer.*

It is equally true of the pen as the pencil, that what is drawn from life and the heart alive bears the impress of immortality. —*H. T. Tuckerman.*

The lords of Europe paid off the slaves of Europe with immortality, a cheap currency indeed, while they themselves pursued their hedonistic way of life in sumptuous palaces built with the same blood and sweat and terror that erected their grandiose cathedrals. —*Dagobert D. Runes.*

Our hope of immortality does not come from any religions, but nearly all religions come from that hope. —*R. G. Ingersoll.*

The insatiableness of our desires asserts our personal imperishableness. —*A. B. Alcott.*

IMPARTIALITY

My spear knows no brother. —*Theodore Roosevelt.*

IMPERFECTION

There is a crack in everything God has made. —*R. W. Emerson.*

Great men are apt to have great faults, and the faults appear the greater by their contrast with their excellencies.
—*Charles Simmons.*

IMPIETY

Impiety: Your irreverence toward my deity.
—*Ambrose Bierce.*

IMPORTANCE

There's nothing that you and I make so many blunders about, and the world so few, as the actual amount of our importance.
—*Josh Billings.*

The deepest urge in human nature is the desire to be important.
—*John Dewey.*

IMPORTS

We must recognize that imports do not hurt us, but enrich us, both as individuals and as a nation. They bring us goods that we could not otherwise have or afford.   —*P. G. Hoffman.*

IMPOSSIBILITY

The word "impossible" is to a scientist much like the spur to a horse.   —*Wm. D. Coolidge.*

Every man is an impossibility until he is born.
—*R. W. Emerson.*

Apparently there is nothing that cannot happen.
—*Mark Twain.*

If politics means anything today it must become the "art of the impossible."   —*Lewis Mumford.*

The "impossible" is World Government: the road to life.
—*Ibid.*

IMPOSSIBLE

The Difficult is that which can be done immediately; the Impossible that which takes a little longer.   —*George Santayana.*

IMPROVEMENT

A democratic society aims at its own social improvement, not the preservation of the status quo.   —*John L. Childs.*

Undoubtedly a man is to labor to better his condition, but first to better himself.   —*W. E. Channing.*

Look up, and not down; look forward and not back; look out and not in; and lend a hand.   —*E. H. Hale.*

IMPULSES

The creative impulses of men are always at war with the possessive impulses.   —*Van Wyck Brooks.*

Beautiful impulses are good in themselves, but we Americans are inclined to trust them too exclusively.   —*Elizabeth Jackson.*

INCLINATION

In this world the inclination to do things is of more importance than the mere power.   —*E. H. Chapin.*

INCOME

An increasing proportion of the expanding total income must go to those in the lower levels of income, where consumption wants are less satisfied. —*H. G. Moulton.*

INCREDULITY

Incredulity robs us of many pleasures, and gives us nothing in return. —*J. R. Lowell.*

Incredulity is the wisdom of a fool. —*H. W. Shaw.*

More persons, on the whole, are humbugged by believing in nothing than by believing in too much. —*P. T. Barnum.*

INDECISION

It is small wonder where the shepherds hesitate and stumble, that the sheep draw back affrighted. —*Scott Nearing.*

A man without decision can never be said to belong to himself. —*John Foster.*

There is no more miserable human being than one in whom nothing is habitual but indecision. —*William James.*

INDEPENDENCE

I would rather sit in a pumpkin and have it all to myself than be crowded on a velvet cushion. —*H. D. Thoreau.*

Let independence be our boast ever mindful what it cost. —*Joseph Hopkinson.*

There is often as much independence in not being led as in not being driven. —*Tryon Edwards.*

There is no more independence in politics than there is in jail. —*Will Rogers.*

A man who accepts any share which he has not earned in another man's capital cannot be an independent citizen. —*W. G. Sumner.*

Independence now and forever. —*John Adams.*

I am for those who have never been master'd. —*Walt Whitman.*

The declaration of Independence blew Europe off its moral base. —*Mary Cohen.*

Independence is the only bond that can tie and keep us together. —*T. Paine.*

The greatest of all human benefits is independence.
                                                        —*Parke Godwin.*

There is something better, if possible, that a man can give than his life. That is his living spirit to a service that is not easy, to resist counsels that are hard to resist, to stand against purposes that are difficult to stand against.   —*Woodrow Wilson.*

Neither the clamor of the mob nor the voice of power will ever turn me by the breadth of a hair from the course I mark out for myself, guided by such knowledge as I can obtain, and controlled and directed by a solemn conviction of right and duty.
                                                    —*Robert M. LaFollette.*

Declarations of Independence make nobody really independent.
                                                    —*George Santayana.*

INDIAN
I believe the Indian to be in body and mind equal to the white man.   —*T. Jefferson.*

INDIFFERENCE
Selfish people, with no heart to speak of, have the best time of it.
                                                        —*H. W. Shaw.*

INDIGNATION
Righteous indignation: your own wrath as opposed to the shocking bad temper of others.   —*Elbert Hubbard.*

As a people we possess a phenomenal capacity for righteous indignation.   —*Elizabeth Jackson.*

The capacity of indignation makes an essential part of the outfit of every honest man.   —*J. R. Lowell.*

INDISPENSABLE
There is no indispensable man.   —*F. D. Roosevelt.*

INDIVIDUALISM
No one ever heard of state freedom, much less did anyone ever hear of state morals. Freedom and morals are the exclusive possession of individuals.   —*H. M. Wriston.*

In every culture the individual is of necessity cribbed, cabined and confined within the limitations of what his culture tells him to see, to believe, to do and to feel.   —*Laurence K. Frank.*

Is it so hard for men to stand by themselves,
They must hang on Marx or Christ, or mere Progress?
                                        —*Robinson Jeffers.*

The country attracted the restless individualist. The frontier itself and then the memory of it defeated for many years the inexorable collectivist logic of the machine process.
                                        —*Lillian Symes.*

There is nothing . . . will make a man better understand his interests than the independent management of his own affairs on his own responsibility.   —*Carl Schurz.*

Individualism may be regarded . . . as the system in which human stupidity can do the least harm.   —*J. M. Clark.*

Our American individualism has been far too simple, far too childish a theory of human experience to account for the facts.
                                        —*A. Meiklejohn.*

As we teach a young person it is not enough to teach him to "be himself." We must teach him to "be himself in an organized society."   —*Ibid.*

Both individualism and socialism are true and ever-active principles, and . . . the very idea of the state implies both.
                                        —*Francis Lieber.*

The protagonist of freedom is the individual, but its production is always a social venture.   —*Max Ascoli.*

The ancient dichotomy of the individual and society will sooner or later be dissolved as we understand that society is in each individual and what we call "social adjustment" is essentially the individual's relation to himself.   —*Laurence K. Frank.*

I never submitted the whole system of my opinions to the creed of any party of men whatever, in religion, in philosophy, in politics, or in anything else, where I was capable of thinking for myself. Such an addiction is the last degradation of a free and moral agent. If I could not go to Heaven but with a party, I would not go there at all.   —*T. Jefferson.*

Individuality is the aim of political liberty. By leaving to the citizen as much freedom of action and of being as comports with order and the rights of others, the institutions render him truly a freeman. He is left to pursue his means of happiness in his own manner.   —*James F. Cooper.*

Any power must be the enemy of mankind which enslaves the individual by terror and force, whether it arises under a Fascist or Communist flag. All that is valuable in human society depends upon the opportunity for development accorded to the individual.

—*Albert Einstein.*

INDIVIDUALITY

There will never be a really free and enlightened state until the state comes to recognize the individual as a higher and independent power, from which all its own power and authority are derived, and treats him accordingly.   —*H. D. Thoreau.*

Surely the individual, the person in the singular number, is the more fundamental phenomenon, and the social institution, of whatever grade, is but secondary and ministerial.

—*William James.*

Modern life has become so highly integrated, so inextricably socialized, so definitely organic, that the very concept of the individual is becoming obsolete.   —*H. P. Fairchild.*

The present is the time of all times for the individual man: the individual will: the individual mind: the individual energy.

—*E. W. Bok.*

More than ever before, in our country, this is the age of the individual.   —*D. D. Eisenhower.*

The free individual has been justified as his own master; the state as his servant.   —*Ibid.*

Historically, society is prior to the individual. In America, the individual is prior to society.   —*Leon Samson.*

Society is a concrete organism . . . Its life is inseparable from the lives of individuals.   —*Benj. R. Tucker.*

The whole theory of the universe is directed unerringly to one single individual.   —*Walt Whitman.*

Nothing, not God, is greater to one than one's self is.

—*Ibid.*

You are not thrown to the winds, you gather certainly and safely around yourself! yourself! yourself! forever and ever.

—*Ibid.*

Individuality is founded in feeling; and the recesses of feeling, the darker, blinder strata of character, are the only places in the world in which we catch real fact in the making.

—*William James.*

INDIVISIBLE

If we cannot get peace, plenty, and freedom together, we shall get none of them. To achieve liberty, equality and fraternity is an indivisible task. *—Norman Thomas.*

INDOCTRINATION

We have no thoughts of our own, no opinions of our own; they are transmitted to us, trained into us. *—Mark Twain.*

INDOLENCE

Nothing is so injurious as un-occupied time. If you are idle, you are on the road to ruin. *—H. W. Beecher.*

INDUSTRY

Lose no time; be always employed in something useful; cut off all unnecessary action. *—B. Franklin.*

The most important product of industry is what it does to the lives of the people who work in it; and for its own safety it needs to contribute to making well-balanced individuals whose social faculties are neither atrophied nor perverted. *—J. M. Clark.*

Keep your working power at its maximum. *—W. R. Alger.*

Industry need not wish, and he that lives upon Hope will die fasting. *—B. Franklin.*

Plough deep while sluggards sleep. *—Ibid.*

The great menace to the life of an industry is industrial self-complacency. *—David Sarnoff.*

INEQUALITY

To base on a state of most glaring social inequality political institutions under which men are theoretically equal, is to stand a pyramid on its apex. *—Henry George.*

One half of the world must sweat and groan that the other half may dream. *—H. W. Longfellow.*

INFANCY

Infancy is the perpetual Messiah, which comes into the arms of fallen men, and pleads with them to return to paradise.
—R. W. Emerson.

INFATUATION

The evil of infatuation is illustrated by the drunkard.
—John B. Gough.

INFERIORITY

I am the inferior to any man whose rights I trample under foot.
—*R. G. Ingersoll.*

The surrender of life is nothing to sinking down into acknowledgement of inferiority.   —*John C. Calhoun.*

Some men appear to feel that they belong to a pariah caste. They fear to offend, they bend and apologize, and walk through life with a timid step.   —*R. W. Emerson.*

INFINITY

Man's moral range and reach is practically infinite.
—*Phillips Brooks.*

Each of us is all the sums he has not counted: subtract us into nakedness and night again, and you shall see in Crete four thousand years ago the love ended yesterday in Texas.   —*Thomas Wolfe.*

INFLATION

Inflation is repudiation.   —*Calvin Coolidge.*

No civilized country in the world has ever voluntarily adopted the extreme philosophies of either fascism or communism, unless the middle class was first liquidated by inflation.
—*H. W. Prentis.*

Inflation is a form of hidden taxation which it is almost impossible to measure.   —*John Beckley.*

A little inflation is like a little pregnancy—it keeps growing.
—*Leon Henderson.*

The first panacea for a mismanaged nation is inflation of the currency; the second is war. Both bring a temporary prosperity; both bring a permanent ruin.   —*Ernest Hemingway.*

INFLUENCE

Woman's influence is powerful, especially when she wants anything.   —*Josh Billings.*

Men are what their mothers made them.   —*R. W. Emerson.*

We perceive and are affected by changes too subtle to be described.   —*H. D. Thoreau.*

He is the greatest whose strength carries up the most hearts by the attraction of his own.   —*H. W. Beecher.*

The humblest individual exerts some influence, either for good or evil, upon others.   —*Ibid.*

Influence is not government. —*G. Washington.*

The blossom cannot tell what becomes of his odor; and no man can tell what becomes of his influence. —*H. W. Beecher.*

INFORMAL

Informal's what woman always say they're going to be and never are. —*Christopher Morley.*

INGRATITUDE

Next to ingratitude, the most painful thing to bear is gratitude. —*H. W. Beecher.*

A proud man is seldom a grateful man, for he never thinks he gets as much as he deserves. —*Ibid.*

INHERITANCE

To inherit property is not to be born—is to be still-born, rather. —*H. D. Thoreau.*

INHUMANITY

The only sin against God is inhumanity, for you can only injure God by injuring his children. —*Lyman Abbott.*

INITIATIVE

The initiative of a mere minority has yielded unparalleled results. What tremendous horizons loom if we fully develop the initiative of the majority! —*L. P. Shield.*

Machines move mountains, but initiative moves men. —*Ibid.*

America cannot have both security of occupations and unlimited private initiative. —*W. A. Brown, Jr.*

INJURY

The natural principle of war is to do the most harm to our enemy with the least harm to ourselves; and this of course is to be effected by stratagem. —*Washington Irving.*

Never does the human soul appear so strong as when it foregoes revenge and dares to forgive an injury. —*H. E. Chapin.*

Christianity commands us to pass by injuries; policy, to let them pass by us. —*B. Franklin.*

The Constitution does not secure to anyone liberty to conduct his business in such fashion as to inflict injury upon the public at large, or upon any substantial group of the people.
—*Owen J. Roberts.*

Lay silently the injuries you receive upon the altar of oblivion.
—Hosea Ballou.

INJUSTICE

Our law says well, to delay Justice is Injustice.

—Wm. Penn.

Injustice is relatively easy to bear; what stings is justice.

—H. L. Mencken.

It is absurd to claim that injustice committed by muscle should be regulated, while that committed by brain should be unrestrained.   *—Lester Ward.*

When the law undertakes to . . . grant titles, gratuities, and exclusive privileges, to make the rich richer and the potent more powerful, the humbler members of society—the farmers, mechanics and laborers . . . have a right to complain of the injustice of their government.   *—Andrew Jackson.*

Those who commit injustice bear the greatest burden.

—Hosea Ballou.

Whatever the human law may be, neither an individual nor a nation can commit the least act of injustice against the obscurest individual without having to pay the penalty for it.

—H. D. Thoreau.

The only government that I recognize . . . is that power which establishes justice in the land, and not that which establishes injustice.   *—Ibid.*

It is time that public interest should no longer hallow injustice, and fortify governments in making the weak their prey.

—W. E. Channing.

Did the mass of men know the actual selfishness and injustice of their rulers, not a government would stand a year. The world would ferment with revolution.   *—Theodore Parker.*

There is but one blasphemy, and that is injustice.

—R. G. Ingersoll.

INK

In these days the greater part of whitewashing is done with ink.
—G. D. Prentice.

INNOCENCE

I dare to be as brave as I am innocent.   *—Nathaniel Bacon.*

To be innocent is to be not guilty; but to be virtuous is to overcome our evil inclinations.   *—Wm. Penn.*

The innocence that feels no risk and is taught no caution, is more vulnerable than guilt, and oftener assailed.   —*N. P. Willis.*

INQUEST

Whenever a husband and wife begin to discuss their marriage, they are giving evidence at an inquest.   —*H. L. Mencken.*

INQUIRY

It is error only, and not truth, that shrinks from inquiry.
                                                                —*T. Paine.*

History tells us (and the lesson is invaluable) that the physical force which has put down free inquiry has been the main bulwark of the superstitions and illusions of past ages.
                                                        —*W. E. Channing.*

True Democracy makes no inquiry about the color of the skin, or place of nativity.   —*A. Lincoln.*

Any science, such as economics, which has to do with human conduct, becomes a genetic inquiry into the human scheme of life.   —*Thorstein Veblen.*

The science (of economics) is necessarily an inquiry into the life-history of material civilization.   —*Ibid.*

The moment philosophy supposes it can find a final and comprehensive solution, it ceases to be inquiry and becomes bitter apologetics or propaganda.   —*John Dewey.*

INSANITY

The human race consists of the dangerously insane and such as are not.   —*Mark Twain.*

What garlic is to salad, insanity is to art.
                                                —*Augustus Saint-Gaudens.*

These who are urging with utmost ardor what are called the greatest benefits to mankind, are narrow, self-pleasing, conceited men, and affect us as the insane do.   —*R. W. Emerson.*

INSECT

Was ever insect flying between two flowers
Told less than we are told of what we are?
                                                —*E. A. Robinson.*

INSIGHT

Real genius of moral insight is a motor which will start any engine.   —*Edmund Wilson.*

INSINCERITY

Insincerity in a man's own heart must make all his enjoyments, all that concerns him, unreal; so that his whole life must seem like a merely dramatic representation.   *—Nathaniel Hawthorne.*

INSOLVENCY

The truth is that we are fast people, bound to beat the world, even in the abyss of our insolvency.   *—G. F. Train.*

INSOMNIACS

Insomniacs don't sleep because they worry about it, and they worry about it because they don't sleep.   *—F. P. Adams.*

INSPIRATION

Inspiration must find answering inspiration.   *—A. B. Alcott.*

INSTINCT

Deeper than all theories, apart from all discussion, the mighty instinct for social justice shapes the hearts that are ready to receive it.   *—Vida D. Scudder.*

A goose flies by a chart which the Royal Geographical Society could not mend.   *—O. W. Holmes.*

Things rooted deep in human instinct—that were rooted in animal instinct before we became human—are not to be uprooted in any such instant of infinity as a generation or a mere millennium.
     —Channing Pollock.

It is the rooted instinct in men to admire what is better and more beautiful than themselves.   *—J. R. Lowell.*

Animals, which build by instinct, build only what they need.
     —Edward S. Martin.

Man's building instinct, if it gets a chance to spread itself at all, is boundless, just as all his instincts are.   *—Ibid.*

The world is governed and kept going by a few strong instincts.
     —Frank Crane.

A few strong instincts and a few plain rules suffice us.
     —R. W. Emerson.

Instinct is animal strength.   *—Daniel Webster.*

INSTITUTIONS

An institution is the lengthened shadow of one man.
     —R. W. Emerson.

What are lands, and seas, and skies, to civilized man, without society, without knowledge, without morals, without religious culture and how can these be enjoyed, in all their extent and all their excellence, but under the protection of wise institutions and free government. —*Daniel Webster.*

The female woman is one of the greatest institutions of which this land can boast. —*Artemus Ward.*

It is a requisite of liberty that the body of a nation should retain the power to modify its institutions as circumstances shall require. —*James F. Cooper.*

I am not to be bullied by institutions. I am not to be frightened by parchments. Form and theories are nothing to me. —*Wendell Phillips.*

The institutions established for self-government have been founded with intent to secure justice and independence for all. —*C. E. Norton.*

It is idle to talk of institutions as sacred. They are but human means adapted to human ends. —*C. N. Bovee.*

If after trial they (institutions) are found to work satisfactorily, it is well; if imperfectly, then the sooner they are modified, or swept away the better. —*Ibid.*

Business and industry have a political problem and responsibility. The problem is to gain and maintain the confidence of the American people so as to survive as free institutions. —*Henry Ford II.*

Civilization laughs at institutions. —*G. E. Woodberry.*

I shall not have much faith in our institutions if they are fitted only to sail in serene seas and wholly unable to withstand the storm. —*William E. Borah.*

Republican institutions will go down before monied corporations. —*Wendell Phillips.*

Man is as the Lord made him. But we can change our institutions. —*Louis D. Brandeis.*

INSTRUCTION

A good newspaper and Bible in every house, a good schoolhouse in every district, and a church in every neghborhood, all appreciated as they deserve, are the chief support of virtue, morality, civil liberty, and religion. —*B. Franklin.*

INSUFFERABLE

In the history of man it has been very generally the case that when evils have grown insufferable they have touched the point of cure.   —*E. H. Chapin.*

INSULT

There should be more in American liberty than the privilege we enjoy of insulting the President with impunity.
                                              —*Austin O'Malley.*

A gentleman will not insult me, and no man not a gentleman can insult me.   —*Frederick Douglass.*

INSURANCE

If you don't have social insurance you are going to have relief.
                                              —*S. H. Slichter.*

INTEGRITY

Nothing is at last sacred but the integrity of your own mind.
                                              —*R. W. Emerson.*

INTELLECT

Intellect is stronger than cannon.   —*Theodore Parker.*

The whole world is becoming a common field for intellect to act in. Energy of mind, genius, power wherever it exists, may speak out in any tongue, and the world will hear it.
                                              —*Daniel Webster.*

If a man's eye is on the Eternal, his intellect will grow.
                                              —*R. W. Emerson.*

The intellect has only one failing.—It has no conscience.
                                              —*J. R. Lowell.*

Every man should use his intellect (as) a lighthouse that those afar off on the sea may see the shining, and learn the way.
                                              —*H. W. Beecher.*

There are one-story intellects, two-story intellects, and three-story intellects with skylights.   —*O. W. Holmes.*

INTELLECTUALS

Intellectuals should never marry; they won't enjoy it, and besides, they should not reproduce themselves.   —*Don Herold.*

Nature is hitting back. She's taking the world away from the intellectuals and giving it back to the apes.
                                              —*Robert E. Sherwood.*

It is time that we should cease to limit to professed scholars the titles of thinkers, philosophers. Whoever seeks truth with an earnest mind, no matter when or how, belongs to the school of intellectual men. —*W. E. Channing*.

INTELLIGENCE

The sum of the moral intelligence of the community should rule the State. —*George Bancroft*.

It is impossible to underrate human intelligence—beginning with one's own. —*Henry Adams*.

There is nobody so irritating as somebody with less intelligence and more sense than we have. —*Don Herold*.

The greatest of all the arts in political economy is to change a consumer into a producer; and the next greatest is to increase the producing power,—and this is to be directly obtained by increasing his intelligence. —*Horace Mann*.

That (idea) which was a weed in one intelligence becomes a flower in the other, and a flower again dwindles down to a mere weed by the same change. —*O. W. Holmes*.

Intelligence . . . is inherently involved in action.
—*John Dewey*.

Intelligence, heretofore a growth, is destined to become a manufacture. —*Lester Ward*.

Intelligence increases mere physical labor one half.—The use of the head intrigues the labor of the hands. —*H. W. Beecher*.

INTEMPERANCE

Intemperance weaves the winding-sheet of souls.
—*John B. Gough*.

The smaller the drink, the clearer the head. —*Wm. Penn*.

The habit of using ardent spirits, by men in office, has occasioned more injury to the public and more trouble to me than all other causes! —*T. Jefferson*.

INTENTIONS

The hardest task of a girl's life is to prove to a man that his intentions are serious. —*Helen Rowland*.

Good intentions are very mortal and very perishable things; like very mellow and choice fruit they are difficult to keep.
—*Charles Simmons*.

INTERDEPENDENCE

If our brothers are oppressed, then we are oppressed. If they hunger, we hunger. If their freedom is taken away our freedom is not secure.   —*Stephen V. Benét.*

INTEREST

Only free peoples can hold their purpose and their honor steady to a common end and prefer the interest of mankind to any narrow interest of their own.   —*Woodrow Wilson.*

In our own interest, we must assume greater responsibilities in the future for political and economic security among nations.
                                                —*Thomas E. Dewey.*

During strikes it must always be remembered that the public interest is paramount.   —*Fiorello La Guardia.*

Interest springs from the power of increase which the reproductive forces of nature give to capital.   —*Henry George.*

In investing money the amount of interest you want should depend on whether you want to eat well or sleep well.
                                                —*J. Kenfield Morley.*

The obvious interests of the majority of the people . . . lead to the democratizing of the national economic system to accord with the political system.   —*Edward Bellamy.*

'Tis against some men's principle to pay interest, and seems against others' interest to pay the principal.   —*B. Franklin.*

Men will pursue their interests.   —*Alexander Hamilton.*

INTERNATIONALISM

We are participants whether we would or not, in the life of the world. The interests of all nations are our own also.
                                                —*Woodrow Wilson.*

Arts and letters, like science, spontaneously orchestrate to one another so that no sooner does a land mature a variant in its culture than it is imported by other lands, for the most part without passport and without tariff.   —*H. M. Kallen.*

Every local or national culture has an international cultivation.
                                                —*Ibid.*

International minds are integral to the being of the arts and sciences.   —*Ibid.*

My country is the world and my religion is to do good.
—*T. Paine.*

Our country is the world—our countrymen are all mankind.
—*W. L. Garrison.*

The man who loves other countries as much as his own stands on a level with the man who loves other women as much as he loves his own wife. —*Theodore Roosevelt.*

INTIMACY

The thing which in the subway is called congestion is highly esteemed in the night spots as intimacy. —*Simeon Strunsky.*

INTOLERANCE

Racial and religious intolerance in the United States is dynamite—guaranteed, if it explodes, to blow up everyone.
—*H. S. Canby.*

Nothing dies so hard, or rallies so often as intolerance.
—*H. W. Beecher.*

It were better to be of no church than to be bitter for any.
—*Wm. Penn.*

The devil loves nothing better than the intolerance of reformers, and dreads nothing so much as their charity and patience.
—*J. R. Lowell.*

Bigotry and intolerance, silenced by argument, endeavors to silence by persecution, in old days by fire and sword, in modern days by the tongue. —*Charles Simmons.*

INTUITION

Woman's intution is the result of millions of years of not thinking. —*Rupert Hughes.*

What passes for woman's intuition is often nothing more than man's transparency. —*George Jean Nathan.*

INVENTION

The greatest invention of the nineteenth century was the invention of the method of invention. —*A. N. Whitehead.*

The march of invention has clothed mankind with powers of which a century ago the boldest imagination could not have dreamt. —*Henry George.*

The right of an inventor to his invention is no monopoly . . .
in any other sense than as a man's own house is a monopoly.
                                                    —*Daniel Webster.*

It would be a jolly good thing to declare a moratorium on inventions for at least a decade, and treat all inventors as dangerous
lunatics, with proper care and supervision.   —*Stuart Chase.*

He who invents a machine augments the power of a man and
the well-being of mankind.   —*H. W. Beecher.*

High heels were invented by a woman who had been kissed
on the forehead.   —*Christopher Morley.*

Only an inventor knows how to borrow, and every man is or
should be an inventor.   —*R. W. Emerson.*

America is a nation that conceives many odd inventions for getting somewhere but can think of nothing to do when it gets there.
                                                    —*Will Rogers.*

If the works of the great poets teach anything, it is to hold mere
invention somewhat cheap. It is not the finding of a thing, but the
making something out of it after it is found, that is of consequence.
                                                    —*J. R. Lowell.*

INVESTIGATION

There's always room at the top—after the investigation.
                                                    —*Oliver Herford.*

Congressional investigations are for the benefit of photographers.
                                                    —*Will Rogers.*

INVESTMENT

Investment consists in the placing of capital into some form
wherefrom an income is expected.   —*J. E. Meeker.*

However the owners of capital may grumble, they will invest
if they think they see a chance of profit plus a reasonable assurance of safety.   —*George Soule.*

Save for gold, jewels, works of art, perhaps good agricultural
land, and a very few other things, there ain't no such animal as
a permanent investment.   —*B. M. Baruch.*

INVINCIBLE

There is, hidden deep within each one of us, a secret self which
is ultimately invincible.   —*J. G. Gilkey.*

INWARD

Without this inward spiritual freedom, outward liberty is of little worth. —*W. E. Channing.*

IRISH

The Irish are the cry-babies of the Western world. Even the mildest quip will set them off into resolutions and protests.

—*Heywood Broun.*

An Irishman can be worried by the consciousness that there is nothing to worry about. —*Austin O'Malley.*

IRONY

Irony is an insult conveyed in the form of a complaint.

—*E. P. Whipple.*

Irony is jesting hidden behind gravity. —*John Weiss.*

IRRELIGION

The conscious irreligion of the polital radical, at war with his unconscious religiosity, is a source of confusion in our civilization.

—*R. Niebuhr.*

ISOLATIONISM

We cannot protect ourselves by withdrawing from the rest of the world. Operation Withdrawal is Operation Suicide.

—*Thomas E. Dewey.*

If you wish to avoid foreign collision, you had better abandon the ocean. —*Henry Clay.*

We have learned that we cannot live alone, in peace; that our own well-being is dependent on the well-being of other nations, far away. —*F. D. Roosevelt.*

ISRAEL

Freud, in blasting the idea of human aloneness, has revived the intuitive wisdom of the prophets of Israel who sang the song of man's relatedness to man. —*Joshua Loth Liebman.*

ISSUES

Give the people issues, and you will not have to sell your souls for campaign funds. —*William E. Borah.*

ITALIANS

Civilization might just disappear everywhere: though we hope that Italians might go on singing their operas superbly and providing excellent cream-ices. —*T. S. Eliot.*

J

JACKALS

Democracy is also a form of religion; it is the worship of jackals by jackasses. —*H. L. Mencken.*

JACKPOT

When the stork picked you up, slung you comfortably from his bill, and began winging his way earthward with you, the chances were fifteen to one against you. You hit the jackpot. You live in the United States of America! —*Phelps Adams.*

JAIL

While there is a lower class, I am in it; while there is a criminal element, I am of it; while there is a soul in jail, I am not free. —*E. V. Debs.*

JANUARY

January in New England is a mixture of rheumatism, chilblains, frozen water pipes, mittens, overshoes, blocked trains, and automobile troubles by the hoodful. —*Dallas L. Sharp.*

JAPAN

If Europe and America were absolutely devastated, Japan with her present equipment in libraries, laboratories, and technology could begin the work of occupying the vacant area using the machine process in the operation. —*Charles A. Beard.*

JAZZ

Every one needs a solid classical basis before they can embark on jazz. —*Benny Goodman.*

Jazz will endure just as long as people hear it through their feet instead of their brains. —*J. P. Sousa.*

The chief trouble with jazz is that there is not enough of it; some of it we have to listen to twice.   *—Don Herold.*

JEALOUSY

Confidence is everywhere the parent of despotism. Free government is founded in jealousy, not in confidence.   *—T. Jefferson.*

Jealousy is one of lovers' parasites.   *—H. W. Shaw.*

Jealousy is the forerunner of love and often its awakener.
    —F. M. Crawford.

There is never jealousy where there is not strong regard.
    —Washington Irving.

Truth is sensitive and jealous of the least encroachment upon its sacredness.   *—A. B. Alcott.*

Lots of people know a good thing the minute the other fellow sees it first.   *—Job E. Hedges.*

JEERING

A sneer is the weapon of the weak.   *—J. R. Lowell.*

Who can refute a sneer? It is independent of proof, reason, argument or sense.   *—Charles Simmons.*

JEFFERSON

The principles of Jefferson are the definitions and axioms of free society.   *—A. Lincoln.*

JEREMIAD

I do not know where we are going, nor do I see any light ahead. There seems to me to be no headway on the ship, and that we are going on the rocks.   *—Brooks Adams.*

JERUSALEM

New England before the Civil War was full of idealists who were going to build each his own brand of New Jerusalem.
    —Elizabeth Jackson.

JESUS

Time has no power over the name and deeds and words of Jesus Christ.   *—W. E. Channing.*

The system of morals and His religion, as He left them to us, is the best the world ever saw, or is likely to see.   *—B. Franklin.*

Political economy and social science cannot teach any lessons that are not embraced in the simple truths that were taught to poor fishermen and Jewish peasants by One who, eighteen hundred years ago was crucified.   —*Henry George.*

The notion that the Jews became a mere shadow of themselves after their most exalted Word had become manifest in Jesus Christ is refuted by the bare facts of history.   —*Waldo Frank.*

He who studies Christ deeply does not deal in the past so much as in the future.   —*David Swing.*

What the world unwittingly is groping after is allegiance to the eternal, the compassionate, the completely integrating Christ.
—*B. I. Bell.*

Jesus was crucified as a revolutionist.   —*Shailer Mathews.*

Jesus identifies Himself with the downmost, the most oppressed.
—*J. N. Sayre.*

There is no better way to try a doctrine by than the question, is it merciful or is it unmerciful? If the character is that of mercy, it has the image of Jesus, who is the way, the truth, and the life.
—*Hosea Ballou.*

JEWELS
Not consistency but persistence is the jewel.
—*Louis D. Brandeis.*

The first thing to turn green in the spring is Christmas jewelry.
—*Kin Hubbard.*

JEWS
The Jews had far more missionary ardor than used to be supposed.   —*James Harvey Robinson.*

The Jew can survive only as the bearer of a religious idea, as the organ of a spiritual force.   —*I. S. Moses.*

When with true American enthusiasm we recall the story of our war for independence . . . we should not fail to remember how well the Jews in America performed their part in the struggle.
—*Grover Cleveland.*

The Jews of the United States . . . have become indissolubly incorporated in the great army of American Citizenship.
—*Theodore Roosevelt.*

No individual should be subjected anywhere, by reason of the fact that he is a Jew, to a denial of any common right or opportunity enjoyed by non-Jews.   —*Louis D. Brandeis.*

They are not Jews in America; they are American citizens.

—Woodrow Wilson.

Jews are different because they issue from a great and potent tradition which for more than three thousand years . . . has kept its continuous identity and its one general direction.

—Waldo Frank.

The most extraordinary trait of the Jews was that they actually strove to make the vision of their prophets into the common deeds of their lives.   *—Ibid.*

We Jews are not bound together by a spoken vow or a watery baptism administered in a physical church. In fact, we do not even have an organized physical church. What binds us is neither vows, nor water, nor paper. It is something more binding than any of these. It is our consciousness of belonging together, of being one.   *—Dagobert D. Runes.*

The bond that has united the Jews for thousands of years and that unites them today is, above all, the democratic ideal of social justice, coupled with the ideal of mutual aid and tolerance among all men.   *—Albert Einstein.*

JINGLE

Another bad thing about "prosperity" is that you can't jingle any money without bein' under suspicion.   *—Kin Hubbard.*

JINGOISM

In every part of the world the good desire of men for peace and decency is undermined by the dynamite of jingoism.

—Robert E. Sherwood.

JIU-JITSU

Turning the other cheek is a kind of mind jiu-jitsu.

—G. S. Lee.

JOBS

It is easier to do a job right than to explain why you didn't.

—Martin Van Buren.

When a man's pursuit gradually makes his face shine and grow handsome, be sure it is a worthy one.   *—William James.*

Men are vain, but they won't mind women working so long as they get smaller salaries for the same job.   *—I. S. Cobb.*

Few of us understand what a big job a little job may be.

—Channing Pollock.

Under our present system we will have to face indefinitely the fact that many people will want jobs who cannot find them.
—*H. L. Hopkins.*

The liberty of a democracy is not safe if its business system does not provide employment and produce and distribute goods in such a way as to sustain an acceptable standard of living.
—*F. D. Roosevelt.*

Government cannot guarantee a living to millions of people when unemployed, even if they have paid part of the cost by taxes on their wages, without something to say about where people work, and their wages.
—*B. C. Marsh.*

Fair Employment Practice Acts may prevent a Negro or Jew from getting fired for racial reasons, but they will not go far toward getting him a job in the first place.
—*H. S. Commager.*

The American at war can do as good a job as the next man, with machines or without.
—*Elizabeth Jackson.*

Our jobs today are less active . . . All-round development, such as the pioneer and the craftsman knew, is increasingly a thing of the past.
—*Stuart Chase.*

Just because a man is sacred, no rich class has the right to enjoy the prodigal life and to hold huge fortunes in its possession while millions of decent, honest industrious men are jobless, breadless, and devoid of the elementary necessities of life.
—*P. A. Sorokin.*

The promotion of revolution in America has always been an uphill job.
—*Lillian Symes.*

JOIN

Lots of times you have to pretend to join a parade in which you're not really interested in order to get where you're going.
—*Christopher Morley.*

Those whom God has put asunder no man can join together.
—*Elbert Hubbard.*

We are a nation of joiners, and it is by joining that we get most of the business of democracy done.
—*H. S. Commager.*

JOINT

The human knee is a joint and not an entertainment.
—*Percy Hammond.*

JOKES

We love a joke that hands us a pat on the back while it kicks the other fellow downstairs. —*C. L. Edson.*

Joking often loses a friend, and never gains an enemy. —*Charles Simmons.*

If you think before you speak, the other fellow gets in his joke first. —*E. W. Howe.*

A poet in history is divine, but a poet in the next room is a joke. —*Max Eastman.*

Some people are so dry that you might soak them in a joke for a month and it would not get through their skins. —*H. W. Beecher.*

Granting our wish is one of Fate's saddest jokes. —*J. R. Lowell.*

I don't make jokes; I just watch the government and report the facts. —*Will Rogers.*

There are only three basic jokes, but since the mother-in-law joke is not a joke but a very serious question, there are only two. —*George Ade.*

JOLT

The worst jolt most of us ever get is when we fall back on our own resources. —*Kin Hubbard.*

A man without mirth is like a wagon without springs, in which one is caused disagreeably to jolt by every pebble over which it runs. —*H. W. Beecher.*

JONAH

When down in the mouth, remember Jonah: he came out all right. —*Thomas A. Edison.*

JOT

A man is a great thing upon the earth and through eternity, but every jot in the greatness of man is unfolded out of woman. —*Walt Whitman.*

JOURNALISM

Journalism has become . . . the most important function in the community. —*Henry George.*

It is the newspaper owner's business to sell information and not advice nor propaganda. —*Walter B. Pitkin.*

A news sense is really a sense of what is important, what is vital, what has color and life—what people are interested in. That's Journalism.   —*Burton Rascoe.*

Journalism will kill you, but it will keep you alive while you're at it.   —*Horace Greeley.*

Journalism is organized gossip.   —*Edward Eggleston.*

Journalism consists in buying white paper at two cents a pound and selling it at ten cents a pound.   —*Charles A. Dana.*

JOURNEY

I tramp a perpetual journey . . . You must travel it for yourself.
                                            —*Walt Whitman.*

JOY

When we speak of joy, we do not speak of something we are after, but of something that will come to us when we are after God and duty.   —*Horace Bushnell.*

The joy of heaven will begin as soon as we attain the character of heaven, and do its duties.   —*Theodore Parker.*

Joy comes, grief goes, we know not how.   —*J. R. Lowell.*

Melancholy attends the best joys of an ideal life.
                                            —*Margaret Fuller.*

The masters painted for joy, and knew not that virtue had gone out of them.   —*R. W. Emerson.*

The sun does not shine for a few trees and flowers, but for the wide world's joy.   —*H. W. Beecher.*

Joys divided are increased.   —*J. G. Holland.*

Memory brings us joys faint as is the perfume of the flowers, faded and dried, of the summer that is gone.   —*H. W. Beecher.*

There is the laughter which is born out of the pure joy of living, the spontaneous expression of health and energy—the sweet laughter of the child. This is a gift of God.   —*J. E. Boodin.*

Joy in one's work is the consummate tool.   —*Phillips Brooks.*

In this world, full often, our joys are only the tender shadows which our sorrows cast.   —*H. W. Beecher.*

Eat with the Rich, but go to the play with the Poor, who are capable of Joy.   —*Logan Pearsall Smith.*

One can endure sorrow alone, but it takes two to be glad.
                                            —*Elbert Hubbard.*

JUDAISM

The equivalence of Judaism and life is a central characteristic of the Jewish religion. *—Isidor Singer.*

Judaism is by its very nature a missionary religion, which means growth, expansion, universality. *—I. S. Moses.*

The builders of Judaism utilized emotion in order to sublimate the passions, the angers, the dreams, of the people.
—Joshua Loth Liebman.

Jews expressed, rather than repressed, their shortcomings and inadequacies and sins . . . Passover represented the passion for freedom, and Shevvoth the joy and the acceptance of the Law.
—Ibid.

JUDEA

On a map of the world you may cover Judea with your thumb, Athens with a finger tip; but they still lead it in the thought and action of every civilized man. *—J. R. Lowell.*

JUDGES

Make not thyself the judge of any man. *—H. W. Longfellow.*

A judge is a law student who marks his own examination papers.
—H. L. Mencken.

The man who can't tell a lie thinks he is the best judge of one.
—Mark Twain.

A man cannot speak but be judged himself.
—R. W. Emerson.

The jurists of today . . . insist upon study of the actual social effects of legal institutions and legal doctrines. *—Roscoe Pound.*

Judges are apt to be naive, simple-minded men, and they need something of the Mephistopheles. *—O. W. Holmes, Jr.*

When a court decides a case upon grounds of public policy, the judge becomes, in effect, a legislator. The question then involved is no longer one for lawyers only. *—Louis D. Brandeis.*

A woman in love is a very poor judge of character.
—J. G. Holland.

JUDGMENT

Man's capacities have never been measured. Nor are we to judge of what he can do by any precedents, so little has been tried.
—H. D. Thoreau.

We all have to assume a standard of judgment in our own minds either of things or persons.   —*O. W. Holmes.*

At twenty years of age the will reigns; at thirty the wit; at forty the judgment.   —*B. Franklin.*

Common sense is, of all kinds, the most uncommon.
                    —*Tryon Edwards.*

You cannot see the mountain near.   —*R. W. Emerson.*

We judge ourselves by what we feel capable of doing; others judge us by what we have done.   —*H. W. Longfellow.*

Enthusiasm for a cause sometimes warps judgment.
                    —*Wm. Howard Taft.*

The average man's judgment is so poor, he runs a risk every time he uses it.   —*E. W. Howe.*

The very thing that men think they have got the most of, they have got the least of; and that is judgment.   —*H. W. Shaw.*

Human judgment is finite, and it ought always to be charitable.
                    —*William Winter.*

Outward judgment often fails, inward judgment never.
                    —*Theodore Parker.*

The right of private judgment is absolute in every American citizen.   —*James A. Garfield.*

Knowledge is the treasure, but judgment is the treasurer of a wise man.   —*Wm. Penn.*

Objectivity became the watchword of progress, and men began to be ashamed of intruding their subjective emotions into the realms of human judgment.   —*Joshua Loth Liebman.*

We must get away from employment policies based on cold arithmetical averages and take advantage of the skills and judgment of older people.   —*B. M. Baruch.*

It is reckless to make hasty adverse judgments on far-reaching revolutionary movements before those tradition-shattering up-surges of peoples and nations have had an opportunity to work themselves out, to correct their cruelties and crudities, to fulfill the ideals of their founders.   —*Corliss Lamont.*

Less judgment than wit is more sail than ballast.
                    —*Wm. Penn.*

Where judgment has wit to express it, there is the best orator.
                    —*Ibid.*

Hesitancy in judgment is the only true mark of the thinker.

—*Dagobert D. Runes.*

JUDICIARY

Courts cannot control nature, though by trying to do so they may, like the Parliament of Paris, create a friction which shall induce an appalling catastrophe.   —*Brooks Adams.*

JUDICIOUS

That was a judicious mother who said: I obey my children for the first year of their lives, but ever after I expect them to obey me.   —*H. W. Beecher.*

JUNE

What is so rare as a day in June?   —*J. R. Lowell.*

JUNGLE

The American jungle is rich in denatured elements of a transplanted world.   —*Waldo Frank.*

In what Concentrated Wealth means by free enterprise—freedom to use and abuse the common man—I do not believe. I object to the law of the jungle.   —*Gifford Pinchot.*

JURISPRUDENCE

The law is made to protect the innocent by punishing the guilty.

—*Daniel Webster.*

The criminal law is not founded on the principle of vengeance; it uses evil only as a means of preventing greater evil.

—*Ibid.*

JURY

Whenever a jury . . . suffer the guilty to escape, they become responsible for the augmented danger of the innocent.

—*Daniel Webster.*

A jury consists of twelve persons chosen to decide who has the better lawyer.   —*Robert Frost.*

The efficiency of our criminal jury system is only marred by the difficulty of finding twelve men every day who don't know anything and can't read.   —*Mark Twain.*

JUST

I can conceive of no God except a just God.

—*George W. Norris.*

Man is unjust, but God is just: and finally justice triumphs.
—*H. W. Longfellow.*

Then conquer we must, when our cause it is just,
And this be our motto,—"In God is our trust."
—*Francis Scott Key.*

Under a government which imprisons any unjustly, the true
place for a just man is also a prison.   —*H. D. Thoreau.*

JUSTICE

Justice is the great interest of man on earth.
—*Daniel Webster.*

Unless justice be done to others it will not be done to us.
—*Woodrow Wilson.*

Has justice ever grown in the soil of absolute power? Has not
justice always come from the . . . heart and spirit of men who
resist power?   —*Ibid.*

Whoever pleads for justice helps to keep the peace and whoever tramples upon the plea for justice, temperately made in the
name of peace, only outrages peace and kills something fine in
the heart of man which God put there when we got our manhood.
—*William A. White.*

Governments cannot accept liberty as their fundamental basis
for justice, because governments rest upon authority and not upon
liberty.   —*Charles T. Sprading.*

Justice is no respecter of persons.   —*John Wise.*

It is impossible to tell where the law stops and justice begins.
—*Arthur ("Bugs") Baer.*

Peace, if possible, but justice at any rate.   —*Wendell Phillips.*

The books are balanced in heaven, not here.   —*H. W. Shaw.*
Pity and forbearance should characterize all acts of justice.
—*B. Franklin.*

Justice is the ligament which holds civilized beings and civilized
nations together.   —*Daniel Webster.*

Wrong none by doing injuries, or omitting the benefits that are
your duty.   —*B. Franklin.*

My country will do justice to those who serve her.
—*Sam Houston.*

No peace is lasting until it is founded upon that essential equitable compromise between the contending forces—capital and labor—known as justice. —*William A. White.*

All things come to him who waits—even justice.
—*Austin O'Malley.*

Lenity has always wisdom and justice on its side.
—*Hosea Ballou.*

Justice is the tolerable accommodation of the conflicting interests of society. —*Learned Hand.*

The firm basis of government is justice, not pity.
—*Woodrow Wilson.*

> Fear not, then thou child infirm,
> There's no god dare wrong a worm.
> —*R. W. Emerson.*

The administration of justice is the firmest pillar of government.
—*G. Washington.*

Observe good faith and justice toward all nations; cultivate peace and harmony with all. —*Ibid.*

Liberty means Justice, and Justice is the law of health and strength, of fraternity and cooperation. —*Henry George.*

Our primary social adjustments are a denial of Justice.
—*Ibid.*

Justice demands that we right this wrong; Justice that cannot be denied; that cannot be put off; that with the scales carries the sword. —*Ibid.*

Injustice is relatively easy to bear; what stings is justice.
—*H. L. Mencken.*

Justice is the end of government. It is the end of civil society. It ever has been and ever will be pursued until it be obtained, or until liberty be lost in the pursuit. —*Alexander Hamilton.*

The sword of the law should never fall but on those whose guilt is so apparent as to be pronounced by their friends as well as foes. —*T. Jefferson.*

I believe that justice is instinct and innate, that the moral sense is as much a part of our constitution as that of feeling, seeing or hearing. —*Ibid.*

Justice has nothing to do with expediency. It has nothing to do with any temporary standard whatever. It is rooted and grounded in the fundamental instincts of humanity.   —*Woodrow Wilson.*

Justice, though due to the accused, is due to the accuser also. The concept of fairness must not be strained till it is narrowed to a filament. We are to keep the balance true.

—*Benjamin Cardozo.*

JUSTIFICATION

The preservation of the spirit and faith of the nation does, and will, furnish the highest justification for every sacrifice that we may make in the cause of national defense.   —*F. D. Roosevelt.*

K

KANT

Kant was led to balance the world upon thought—oblivious to the scanty supply of thinking. —*A. N. Whitehead.*

KEEN

For health and the constant enjoyment of life, give me a keen and ever present sense of humor; it is the next best thing to an abiding faith in providence. —*G. B. Cheever.*

KEEP

"Thou shalt not get found out" is not one of God's commandments; and no man can be saved by trying to keep it.
—*Leonard Bacon.*

KEY

The used key is always bright. —*B. Franklin.*

The key to every man is his thought. He can only be reformed by showing him a new idea which commands his own.
—*R. W. Emerson.*

Many a treasure besides Ali Baba's is unlocked with a verbal key. —*H. Van Dyke.*

KEYNOTE

Moderation is the keynote of lasting enjoyment.
—*Hosea Ballou.*

Our American keynote . . . a hatred of the sordid . . . an ability to forget the past for the sake of the whole; a desire for largeness; a willingness to stand exposed. —*Ezra Pound.*

KICKING

Truth is tough. It will not break, like a bubble at a touch; nay,

you may kick it about all day, like a football, and it will be round
and full at evening.   —*O. W. Holmes.*

Men ain't apt to get kicked out of good society for being rich.
                                                            —*Josh Billings.*

KILL

It is not hard work that kills men, it is worry.   —*H. W. Beecher.*

Death cannot kill what never dies, nor can spirits ever be divided that love and live in the same divine principle. —*Wm. Penn.*

To keep your friends, treat them kindly; to kill them, treat them
often.   —*G. D. Prentice.*

All governing overmuch kills the self-help and energy of the
governed.   —*Wendell Phillips.*

When differences are sufficiently far-reaching we try to kill the
other man rather than let him have his way.   —*O. W. Holmes.*

There are more ways of killing a man's love than by strangling
it to death, but that's the usual way.   —*Helen Rowland.*

Nations and peoples can work together to kill much better than
they can to live.   —*Raymond Clapper.*

In organized world murder, men show magnificent courage, invention, and ability to work together. But not when you try to
leave the murder out of it and try to organize civilization for living
instead of killing.   —*Ibid.*

A great many political speeches are literary parricides: they kill
their fathers.   —*G. D. Prentice.*

I do not wish to kill or be killed, but I can foresee circumstances
in which both of these things would be by me unavoidable. In
extremities I would even be killed.   —*H. D. Thoreau.*

Much smoking kills live men and cures dead swine.
                                                            —*G. D. Prentice.*

KIND

The law can make you quit drinking; but it can't make you
quit being the kind that needs a law to make you quit drinking.
                                                            —*Don Marquis.*

> The two kinds of people on earth that I mean
> Are the people who lift and the people who lean.
>   —*E. W. Wilcox.*

The man who gives his life for a principle has done more for his kind than he who discovers a new metal or names a new gas.

—*J. R. Lowell.*

KINDERGARTEN

The world is a kind of spiritual kindergarten where bewildered infants are trying to spell God with the wrong blocks.

—*E. A. Robinson.*

KINDNESS

I shall pass through life but once. Let me show kindness now as I shall not pass this way again. —*Wm. Penn.*

Kindness is a language the dumb can speak and the deaf can hear and understand. —*C. E. Bovee.*

Be kind and considerate to others, depending somewhat upon who they are. —*Don Herold.*

Be kind to dumb people. —*Ibid.*

A kind heart is a fountain of gladness, making everything in its vicinity freshen into smiles. —*Washington Irving.*

It is the strength of holy purpose, infused into the kind affections, which raises them into virtues. —*W. E. Channing.*

A word of kindness is seldom spoken in vain, while witty sayings are as easily lost as the pearls slipping from a broken string.

—*G. D. Prentice.*

There is no beautifier of complexion or form of behavior like the wish to scatter joy, and not pain, around us. —*R. W. Emerson.*

> Let me be a little kinder,
> Let me be a little blinder
> To the faults of those around me.
>
> —*E. A. Guest.*

Kindness goes a long ways lots of times when it ought to stay at home. —*Kin Hubbard.*

He that has done you a kindness will be more ready to do you another, than he whom you yourself have obliged.

—*B. Franklin.*

If you can make people kind, not merely respectable, the problem will be solved. —*Elbert Hubbard.*

Perfect obedience to the law of kindness would abolish government and the State. —*O. B. Frothingham.*

Human kindness has never weakened the stamina or softened

the fiber of a free people. A nation does not have to be cruel in
order to be tough.   —*F. D. Roosevelt.*

KINGDOMS

Nature, through all her kingdoms, insures herself.
                                            —*R. W. Emerson.*

All things unrevealed belong to the kingdom of mystery.
                                            —*J. G. Holland.*

All minds that reason and all hearts that beat act in one empire
of one King: and of that vast kingdom the law the most sweeping,
most eternal, is the law of loving-kindness.   —*David Swing.*

The kingdom of God is the only absolute monarchy that is free
from despotism.   —*Charles Simmons.*

The kingdom in this world must be established by redeeming
men, one by one, to their higher destiny.   —*John Haynes Holmes.*

There is nothing stronger than human prejudice. A crazy
sentimentalism, like that of Peter the Hermit, hurled half of
Europe upon Asia, and changed the destinies of kingdoms.
                                            —*Wendell Phillips.*

KINGS

Every chair should be a throne and hold a king.
                                            —*R. W. Emerson.*

The problem of democracy is not the problem of getting rid of
kings. It is the problem of clothing the whole people with the
elements of kingship. To make kings and queens out of a hundred
million people! That is the problem of American democracy.
                                            —*F. C. Morehouse.*

Every man a king.   —*Huey P. Long.*

A king that lives by law, lives by love.   —*Nathaniel Ward.*

Implements of war and subjugation are the last arguments to
which kings resort.   —*Patrick Henry.*

Slavery it is that makes slavery; freedom, freedom. The slavery
of women happened when the men were slaves of kings.
                                            —*R. W. Emerson.*

The modern king has become a vermiform appendix: useless
when quiet; when obtrusive, in danger of removal.
                                            —*Austin O'Malley.*

One of the strongest natural proofs of the folly of hereditary
right in kings is that Nature disapproves of it; otherwise she

would not so frequently turn it into ridicule by giving mankind an ass instead of a lion. —*T. Paine.*

Idleness and pride tax with a heavier hand than kings and parliaments. —*B. Franklin.*

Those arguments that are made, that the inferior race are to be treated with as much allowance as they are capable of enjoying . . . are the arguments kings have made for enslaving the people in all ages of the world. —*A. Lincoln.*

All the arguments in favor of kingcraft . . . always bestride the necks of the people—not that they wanted to do it, but because the people were better off for being ridden. —*Ibid.*

The kingliest being ever born in the flesh lay in a manger.
—*E. H. Chapin.*

We must have kings, we must have nobles; nature is always providing such in every society, only let us have the real instead of the titular. —*R. W. Emerson.*

Kings, in this chiefly, should imitate God; their mercy should be above all their works. —*Wm. Penn.*

Chaos is King! —*Samuel D. Schmalhausen.*

There is not a crowned head in Europe whose talents or merits would entitle him to be elected a vestryman by the people of any parish in America. —*T. Jefferson.*

Kings is mostly rapscallions. —*Mark Twain.*

KINSHIP

Justice is the minimum requirement of reverence for personality and recognition of kinship. —*Kirby Page.*

KISSES

All the legislation in the world will not abolish kissing.
—*Elinor Glyn.*

To a woman the first kiss is just the end of the beginning; to a man it is the beginning of the end. —*Helen Rowland.*

A man snatches the first kiss, pleads for the second, demands the third, takes the fourth, accepts the fifth—and endures all the rest.
—*Ibid.*

When women kiss, it always reminds me of prize-fighters shaking hands. —*H. L. Mencken.*

A kiss from my mother made me a painter. —*Benjamin West.*

You cannot analyze a kiss anymore than you can dissect the fragrance of flowers.   —*H. W. Shaw.*

God pardons like a mother who kisses the offense into everlasting forgetfulness.   —*H. W. Beecher.*

Passion looks not beyond the moment of its existence.—Better, it says, the kisses of love today, than the felicities of heaven afar off.   —*C. N. Bovee.*

KNAVERY

Slavery and knavery go as seldom asunder, as tyranny and cruelty!   —*Nathaniel Ward.*

There is nothing seems so like an honest man as an artful knave.
—*Charles Simmons.*

KNEES

I have been driven many times to my knees by the overwhelming conviction that I had nowhere else to go. My own wisdom, and that of all about me seemed insufficient for the day.
—*A. Lincoln.*

KNIVES

Mishaps are like knives, that either serve us or cut us, as we grasp them by the blade or the handle.   —*J. R. Lowell.*

The value of a dollar is to buy just things.—A dollar is worth more in a law-abiding community than in some sink of crime, where dice, knives, and arsenic are in constant play.
—*R. W. Emerson.*

KNOT

A man will joyfully pay a lawyer five hundred dollars for untying the knot that he begrudged a clergyman fifty dollars for tying.   —*Helen Rowland.*

KNOW

Only what we partly know already inspires us with a desire to know more.   —*William James.*

What one knows is, in youth, of little moment; they know enough who know how to learn.   —*Henry Adams.*

Men who know the same things are not long the best company for each other.   —*R. W. Emerson.*

Responsibilities gravitate to the person who can shoulder them, and power flows to the man who knows how.   —*Elbert Hubbard.*

All I know is what I read in the newspapers.   —*Will Rogers.*

He who knows little, and knows it, knows much. —*C. D. Stewart.*

Many men know how to flatter; few men know how to praise.
—*Wendell Phillips.*

The first dawn of smartness is to stop buying things you don't
know anything about—especially if they run to anything over a
dollar.   —*Wilson Mizner.*

It's a relief to be of the common clay, after all, and to know it.
If I get broken, I can be easily replaced.   —*W. D. Howells.*

To cease smoking is the easiest thing I ever did; I ought to
know because I've done it a thousand times.   —*Mark Twain.*

Ours is a world where people don't know what they want and
are willing to go through hell to get it.   —*Don Marquis.*

It's what a fellow thinks he knows that hurts him.
—*Kin Hubbard.*

A man never knows how to say good-by; a woman never knows
when to say it.   —*Helen Rowland.*

He mastered whatever was not worth the knowing.
—*J. R. Lowell.*

Of all the scamps society knows best, the traditional good fellow
is the most despicable.   —*J. G. Holland.*

KNOW-HOW

The economic machinery of the world . . . must be repaired and
started again. We have tools and parts. We have what is just as
important—the know-how.   —*John W. Snyder.*

KNOWLEDGE

It is better to know nothing than to know what ain't so.
—*H. W. Shaw.*

To the small part of ignorance that we arrange and classify we
give the name knowledge.   —*Ambrose Bierce.*

Knowledge exists to be imparted.   —*R. W. Emerson.*

Knowledge is the field of freedom, of choice, decision, new
expression.   —*H. M. Kallen.*

Anything that may be called knowledge, or a known object,
marks a question answered, a difficulty disposed of, a confusion
cleared up, an inconsistency reduced to coherence, a perplexity
mastered.   —*John Dewey.*

Knowledge is possible as far as we can develop instrumentalities of inquiry, measurement, symbolization, calculations, and testing.
—*Ibid.*

We do not need more knowledge, we need more character!
—*Calvin Coolidge.*

Knowledge is the only fountain, both of the love and the principles of human liberty.   —*Daniel Webster.*

Knowledge, in truth, is the great sun in the firmament. Life and power are scattered with all its beams.   —*Ibid.*

Knowledge is the knowing that we cannot know.
—*R. W. Emerson.*

In whatever direction the future moves, whether the earthquake is long in coming or not, we must from now onward learn to live and act in the knowledge that we are all responsible to and for one another, because we have one common eternal destiny and because we are dependent on the one Father, who made brothers of us all.   —*Pierre Van Paassen.*

There was never a nation great, until it came to the knowledge that it had nowhere in the world to go for help.   —*C. D. Warner.*

The great demand of the world is knowledge. The great problem is the equalization of intelligence, to put all knowledge in possession of every human being.   —*Lester Ward.*

To know that we know what we know, and that we do not know what we do not know, that is true knowledge.   —*H. D. Thoreau.*

If you have knowledge, let others light their candles at it.
—*Margaret Fuller.*

Knowledge and timber shouldn't be much used till they are seasoned.   —*O. W. Holmes.*

Short cuts to specific knowledge are delusions.   —*E. D. Martin.*

Knowledge is power, if you know it about the right person.
—*E. W. Mumford.*

The best corrective of American provincialism is not merely a knowledge of Europe, but also a richer knowledge of the struggle of the republic to become what it has dreamt of becoming.
—*Howard Mumford Jones.*

Knowledge may belong to the brain of the scholar; but wisdom is the breath of the people.   —*G. E. Woodberry.*

Knowledge is the idea volatile and abstract, but wisdom is the idea dipped in the dyer's vat of life. —*Ibid.*

It is in knowledge as in swimming; he who flounders and splashes on the surface, makes more noise, and attracts more attention, than the pearl-diver who quietly dives in quest of treasures to the bottom. —*Washington Irving.*

The chief knowledge that a man gets from reading books is the knowledge that very few of them are worth reading.
—*H. L. Mencken.*

Knowledge of our duties is the most essential part of the philosophy of life. If you escape duty you avoid action. The world demands results. —*G. W. Goethals.*

If a man empties his purse into his head no one can take it away from him. —*B. Franklin.*

The love of knowledge in a young man is almost a warrant against the inferior excitement of passions and vices.
—*H. W. Beecher.*

Knowledge of politics, as Dante knew, is knowledge of perspectives and proportions which, when observed, sustain society, and when violated, wreck it. —*Max Ascoli.*

A good woman is known by what she does; a good man by what he doesn't. —*Helen Rowland.*

There is always a bond of peace that is both permanent and enriching; the increasing knowledge of the world in which experiment occurs. —*Walter Lippmann.*

Knowledge is like money: the more a man gets, the more he craves. —*H. W. Shaw.*

Contemplation is to knowledge what digestion is to food—the way to get life out of it. —*Tryon Edwards.*

A learned man is a tank; a wise man is a spring. —*W. R. Alger.*

An investment in knowledge always pays the best interest.
—*B. Franklin.*

Fullness of knowledge always means some understanding of the depths of our ignorance; and that is always conducive to humility and reverence. —*R. H. Millikan.*

Banish me from Eden when you will, but first let me eat of the fruit of the tree of knowledge. —*R. G. Ingersoll.*

Knowledge is the great sun of the firmament. Life and power are scattered with all its beams.   *—Daniel Webster.*

Of all kinds of knowledge that we can ever obtain, the knowledge of God and the knowledge of ourselves are the most important.   *—Jonathan Edwards.*

KNOW-NOTHING

I am not a Know-Nothing; that is certain. How could I be? How could anyone who abhors the oppression of Negroes be in favor of degrading classes of white people.   *—A. Lincoln.*

KNUCKLES

If you do not hear reason, she will rap you over the knuckles.
   —B. Franklin.

L

LABOR

Labor is prior to, and independent of, capital. Capital is only the fruit of labor and could never have existed if labor had not first existed.   —*A. Lincoln.*

I have faith in labor, and I see the goodness of God in placing us in a world where labor alone can keep us alive.
—*W. E. Channing.*

Capital is a result of labor. And is used by labor to assist it in further production. Labor is the active and initial force, and labor is therefore the employer of capital.   —*Henry George.*

Labor disgraces no man; unfortunately you occasionally find men disgrace labor.   —*U. S. Grant.*

Without labor there would be no government, and no leading class, and nothing to preserve.   —*Ibid.*

It is only through labor and painful effort, by grim energy and resolute courage, that we move on to better things.
—*Theodore Roosevelt.*

Labor, the creator of wealth, is entitled to all it creates.
—*Wendell Phillips.*

Labor is man's great function. He is nothing, he can be nothing, he can achieve nothing, he can fulfil nothing, without working.
—*Orville Dewey.*

It has so happened, in all ages of the world, that some have labored, and others have without labor enjoyed a large proportion of the fruits. This is wrong and should not continue.
—*A. Lincoln.*

Labor: one of the processes by which A acquires property for B.
—*Ambrose Bierce.*

Industry cannot flourish if labor languish.   —*Calvin Coolidge.*

Labor humanizes, exalts.   —*A. B. Alcott.*

Labor is a school of benevolence as well as justice.

—*W. E. Channing.*

Labor—the expenditure of vital effort in some form—is the measure, nay, it is the maker of values.   —*J. G. Holland.*

Labor was appointed at the creation.   —*Horace Mann.*

Labor is the handmaid of religion.   —*C. H. Parkhurst.*

Labor in this country is independent and proud. It has not to ask the patronage of capital, but capital solicits the aid of labor.

—*Daniel Webster.*

Loves makes labor light.   —*J. G. Holland.*

The concept of labor as a "commodity" is so outmoded that we don't even talk about it today.   —*Ira Mosher.*

Love labor; for if thou dost not want it for food, thou mayst for physic.   —*Wm. Penn.*

Genius may conceive but patient labor must consummate.

—*Horace Mann.*

Labor is one of the great elements of society—the great substantial interest on which we all stand.   —*Daniel Webster.*

Labor is the capital of our workingmen.   —*Grover Cleveland.*

As labor is the common burden of our race, so the effort of some to shift their share of the burden on to the shoulders of others is the great durable curse of the race.   —*A. Lincoln.*

> Let us then be up and doing
> With a heart for any fate;
> Still achieving, still pursuing,
> Learn to labor and to wait.
>
> —*H. W. Longfellow.*

LABORER

When the day is done, when the work of a life is finished, when the fold of evening meets the dusk of night, beneath the silent stars the tired laborer should fall asleep.   —*R. G. Ingersoll.*

The laborer is the author of all greatness and wealth.

—*U. S. Grant.*

If any continue through life in the condition of the hired laborer, it is not the fault of the system, but because of either a dependent nature which prefers it, or improvidence, folly, or singular misfortune. —*A. Lincoln.*

LACE

It is difficult to see why lace should be so expensive; it is mostly holes. —*M. W. Little.*

LADY

A true lady or gentleman remains at home with a grouch same as if they had pneumonia. —*Kin Hubbard.*

LAMB

(Progressive education) is confronted with the choice of becoming an avowed experiment of democracy or else becoming a set of ingenious devices for tempering the wind to the shorn lamb.
—*Boyd H. Bode.*

LAND

The land is the only thing we have in the world which ungrudgingly yields abundance, and asks for nothing more in return than diligence. —*Henry Ford.*

The wilderness through which we are passing to the Promised Land is all over filled with fiery flying serpents. —*Cotton Mather.*

To waste, to destroy, our natural resources, to skin and exhaust the land instead of using it so as to increase its usefulness, will result in undermining in the days of our children the very prosperity which we ought by right to hand down to them amplified and developed. —*Theodore Roosevelt.*

The equal right of all men to the use of land is as clear as their equal right to breathe the air—it is a right proclaimed by the fact of their existence. For we cannot suppose that some men have a right to be in this world, and others no right. —*Henry George.*

As labor cannot produce without the use of land, the denial of the equal right to the use of land is necessarily the denial of the right of labor to its own product. —*Ibid.*

Man must have access to land or be a slave. —*Jerry Simpson.*

The man who owns the earth owns the people, for they must buy the privilege of living on his earth. —*Ibid.*

If a man own land, the land owns him. —*R. W. Emerson.*

LANDSCAPE

To an American, American literature is part of his native landscape, and so' veiled with associations that he cannot always see what the author is really saying.   —*Edmund Wilson.*

We are now slowly learning to do as communities what rich individuals do occasionally as "country gentlemen"—revivify and restore the whole landscape, returning with love what we destroyed in our haste and our greedy, short-sighted financial exploitation.   —*Lewis Mumford.*

Some persons suppose that landscape has no power to communicate human sentiment; but this is a great mistake. —*George Innes.*

There is a property in the horizon which no man has, but he whose eyes can integrate all the parts,—that is, the poet.
                                                   —*R. W. Emerson.*

Every antique farmhouse and moss-grown cottage is a picture.
                                                   —*Washington Irving.*

This is grand! 'tis solemn! 'tis an education in itself to look upon!
                                                   —*James F. Cooper.*

LANGUAGE

Language, as well as the faculty of speech, was the immediate gift of God.   —*Noah Webster.*

Every language is a temple in which the soul of those who speak it is enshrined.   —*O. W. Holmes.*

The vernacular tongue of the country has become greatly vitiated, depraved, and corrupted by the style of our Congressional debates.   —*Daniel Webster.*

All the languages in the world are but local differentiations of one planetary tongue.   —*Thornton Wilder.*

Language is the blood of the soul into which thoughts run and out of which they grow.   —*O. W. Holmes.*

Language is a city in the building of which every human being brought a stone.   —*R. W. Emerson.*

The language denotes the man.   —*C. N. Bovee.*

Language is but little better than the croak and cackle of fowls and other utterances of brute nature—sometimes not so adequate.
                                                   —*Nathaniel Hawthorne.*

Language was given us that we might say pleasant things to each other.   —*C. N. Bovee.*

There are cases which cannot be overdone by language.
                                                   —*T. Paine.*

As there is now nothing new to be learned from the dead languages, all the useful books being already translated, the languages are becoming useless, and the time expended in teaching and learning them is wasted. So far as the study of languages may contribute to the progress and communication of knowledge, it is only in the living languages that new knowledge is to be found. —*T. Paine.*

LAST

When liberty goes out of a place, it is not the first to go, nor the second or third to go. It waits for all the rest to go—it is the last. —*Walt Whitman.*

LATITUDE

Every man thinks a latitude safe for himself which is nowise to be indulged to another. —*R. W. Emerson.*

LAUGHTER

I can usually judge a fellow by what he laughs at.
—*Wilson Mizner.*

Everything is funny as long as it is happening to somebody else.
—*Will Rogers.*

Morally considered, laughter is next to the Ten Commandments.
—*H. W. Shaw.*

Alas for the worn and heavy soul if it has outlived its privilege of springtime and sprightliness. —*Nathaniel Hawthorne.*

The laughter of man is the contentment of God. —*John Weiss.*

No man feels like laughing when he bumps his funny bone.
—*M. W. Little.*

Laughing is the sensation of feeling good all over, and showing it principally in one spot. —*Josh Billings.*

> Laugh and the whole world laughs with you,
> Weep and you weep alone.
> —*Ella W. Wilcox.*

You grow up the day you have the first real laugh—at yourself.
—*Ethel Barrymore.*

With the fearful strain that is on me night and day, if I did not laugh I should die. —*A. Lincoln.*

The penalty for laughing in a courtroom is six months in jail; if it were not for this penalty, the jury would never hear the evidence.   —*H. L. Mencken.*

Progress is nothing but the victory of laughter over dogma.
                                                   —*Benjamin De Casseres.*

LAW

Let reverence of the law . . . become the political religion of the nation.   —*A. Lincoln.*

I sometimes wish that people would put a little more emphasis upon the observance of the law than they do upon its enforcement.
                                                   —*Calvin Coolidge.*

Men do not make laws. They do but discover them.   —*Ibid.*

Man became free when he recognized that he was subject to law.   —*Will Durant.*

Laws that do not embody public opinion can never be enforced.
                                                   —*Elbert Hubbard.*

Without law there is freedom only for the most powerful and chaos prevails.   —*Joseph Rosenfarb.*

The life of the law has not been logic; it has been experience.
                                                   —*O. W. Holmes, Jr.*

The law is made up of the rules for decision which the courts lay down.   —*John Chapman Gray.*

The law is not the place for the artist or the poet.
                                                   —*O. W. Holmes, Jr.*

Law is whatever is boldly asserted and plausibly maintained.
                                                   —*Aaron Burr.*

The law of heaven is love.   —*Hosea Ballou.*

I believe that the law was made for man and not man for the law; that government is the servant of the people and not their master.   —*John D. Rockefeller, Jr.*

He that lives above law, shall live under hatred, do what he can.
                                                   —*Nathaniel Ward.*

Ignorance of the law excuses no man—from practicing it.
                                                   —*Addison Mizner.*

The absolute justice of the State enlightened by the perfect reason of the State, that is law.   —*Rufus Choate.*

I know no method to secure the repeal of bad or obnoxious laws so effective as their stringent execution.   —*U. S. Grant.*

Law is merely the expression of the will of the strongest for the time being, and therefore laws have no fixity, but shift from generation to generation.   *—Charles A. Madison.*

The law of human progress, what is it but the moral law?
    —Henry George.

There should be a law prohibiting over three Americans going anywhere abroad together.   *—Will Rogers.*

The first duty of law is to keep sound the society it serves.
    —Woodrow Wilson.

Laws can not create and superimpose the ideals sought, they can only free people from the shackles and give them a chance to work out their own salvation.   *—Samuel Gompers.*

There is no end to the laws, and no beginning to the execution of them.   *—Mark Twain.*

We should not employ the statutes to accomplish by indirection what Congress never empowered us to accomplish.
    —William O. Douglas.

He who dethrones the idea of law bids chaos welcome in its stead.   *—Horace Mann.*

The same law which rots down the weak sneak sooner or later overtakes his brainier brother. But this does not right wrong nor does it restore stolen goods.   *—John P. Altgeld.*

The people's safety is the law of God.   *—James Otis.*

It is only rogues who feel the restraints of law. *—J. G. Holland.*

A law is not a law without coercion behind it.
    —James A. Garfield.

With us law is nothing unless close behind it stands a warm, living public opinion.   *—Wendell Phillips.*

When any people are ruled by laws, in framing which they have no part, that are to bind them to all intents and purposes, without, in the same manner, binding the legislators themselves, they are, in the strictest sense, slaves; and the government, with respect to them, is despotic.   *—Alexander Hamilton.*

We bury men when they are dead, but we try to embalm the dead body of laws, keeping the corpse in sight long after the vitality has gone. It usually takes a hundred years to make a law; and then, after it has done its work, it usually takes a hundred years to get rid of it.   *—H. W. Beecher.*

It is difficult to make our material condition better by the best laws, but it is easy enough to ruin it by bad laws.

—Theodore Roosevelt.

While there is still doubt, while opposite convictions still keep a battlefront against each other, the time for law has not come.

—O. W. Holmes, Jr.

It is not only vain, but wicked, in a legislator to frame laws in opposition to the laws of nature, and to arm them with the terrors of death. This is truly creating crimes in order to punish them.

—T. Jefferson.

LAWSUIT

A successful lawsuit is the one worn by a policeman.

—Robert Frost.

LAWYERS

Every man should know something of law; if he knows enough to keep out of it, he is a pretty good lawyer.   *—Josh Billings.*

When there's a rift in the lute, the business of the lawyer is to widen the rift and gather the loot.   *—A. G. Hays.*

Lawyer: the only man in whom ignorance of the law is not punished.   *—Elbert Hubbard.*

Necessity has no law; I know some attorneys of the same.

—B. Franklin.

> Why does a hearse horse snicker
> Hauling a lawyer away?
>
> *—Carl Sandburg.*

No man can be a sound lawyer who is not well-read in the laws of Moses.   *—Fisher Ames.*

If a man dies and leaves his estate in an uncertain condition, the lawyers become his heirs.   *—E. W. Howe.*

Lawyers earn a living by the sweat of their browbeating.

—J. G. Huneker.

Young lawyers attend the courts, not because they have business there but because they have no business anywhere else.

—Washington Irving.

I've had ample contact with lawyers, and I'm convinced that the only fortune they ever leave is their own.   *—Wilson Mizner.*

The trouble with law is lawyers.   *—Clarence Darrow.*

You cannot live without the lawyers and certainly you cannot die without them. —*Joseph H. Choate.*

A countryman between two lawyers is like a fish between two cats. —*B. Franklin.*

It is the trade of lawyers to question everything, yield nothing, and to talk by the hour. —*T. Jefferson.*

LAZINESS

Humanity is constitutionally lazy. —*J. G. Holland.*

Laziness travels so slowly that poverty soon overtakes him.
—*B. Franklin.*

Lazy folk's stummucks don't git tired. —*Joel Chandler Harris.*

Easy street is a blind alley. —*Wilson Mizner.*

You never see no "To Let" signs on Easy Street.
—*Kin Hubbard.*

Laziness is a good deal like money—the more a man has of it, the more he seems to want. —*H. W. Shaw.*

LEADERS

He must be a born leader or misleader of men, who, in age, has as strong a confidence in his opinions and in the necessity of bringing the universe into conformity with them as he had in youth. —*J. R. Lowell.*

The happiest men I know in all this unhappy life of ours, are those leaders who, brave, loyal, and sometimes in tears, are serving their fellow men. —*Lincoln Steffens.*

Wherever the people have found a leader who was loyal to them, brave, and not too far ahead, there they have followed him.
—*Ibid.*

No party is as bad as its leaders. —*Will Rogers.*

Surely, whoever speaks to me in the right voice, him or her I shall follow. —*Walt Whitman.*

It is no loss of liberty to subordinate ourselves to a natural leader. —*George Santayana.*

LEADERSHIP

New scientific knowledge is dangerous today because it comes at a time when spiritual leadership has failed to make clear the connection between belief and practice. —*John Foster Dulles.*

The predominant power of the civilized world has migrated to our country. Surely we will use this power wisely and thus earn and preserve the moral leadership with which our authority and our wisdom so rightly and so fortunately have vested us.

—Lewis W. Douglas.

In the great mass of our people there are plenty of individuals of intelligence from among whom leadership can be recruited.

—Herbert Hoover.

LEARNING

The brighter you are, the more you have to learn.

—Don Herold.

There is four hundred times as much learning in the world as there is wisdom.   *—Josh Billings.*

The secret of education lies in respecting the pupil.

—R. W. Emerson.

Drudgery is as necessary to call out the treasures of the mind, as harrowing and planting those of the earth.   *—Margaret Fuller.*

I've known countless people who were reservoirs of learning yet never had a thought.   *—Wilson Mizner.*

Thought, intelligence, is the dignity of a man, and no man is rising but in proportion as he is learning to think clearly and forcibly, or directing the energy of his mind to the acquisition of truth.   *—W. E. Channing.*

Alas, for the man who has not learned to work! He is a poor creature. He does not know himself.   *—Ibid.*

We should live and learn; but by the time we've learned, it's too late to live.   *—Carolyn Wells.*

Learning, to be of much use, must have a tendency to spread itself among the common people.   *—H. W. Beecher.*

If you want learning, you must work for it.   *—J. G. Holland.*

The wisest mind hath something yet to learn.

—George Santayana.

Bees are sometimes drowned (or suffocated) in the honey which they collect. So some writers are lost in their collected learning.

—Nathaniel Hawthorne.

LECTURER

Lecturer: one with his hand in your pocket, his tongue in your ear, and his faith in your patience.   *—Ambrose Bierce.*

LEGISLATION

The public happiness is the true object of legislation and can be secured only by the masses of mankind themselves awakening to the knowledge and care of their own interests.

—George Bancroft.

The wise know that foolish legislation is a rope of sand, which perishes in the twisting. *—R. W. Emerson.*

We are not legislating for this moment only, or for the present generation, or for the present populated limits of the United States, but our acts must embrace a wider scope—reaching northward to the Pacific and southwardly to the river Del Norte.

—Henry Clay.

Before progressive legislation can become a success, every legislature must become, as it were, a polytechnic school, a laboratory of philosophic research, into the laws of society and of human nature. *—Lester Ward.*

LEGISLATOR

No legislator is qualified to vote on or propose measures designed to affect the destinies of millions of social units until he masters all that is known of the science of society.

—Lester Ward.

Every true legislator must be a sociologist. *—Ibid.*

LEGISLATURE

Now and then an innocent man is sent to the legislature.

—Kin Hubbard.

LEISURE

The democratic faith is that every human being born is born to live as a gentleman of leisure. *—H. M. Kallen.*

They talk of the dignity of work. Bosh. True work is the necessity of poor humanity's earthly condition. The dignity is in leisure.

—Herman Melville.

I loaf and invite my soul. *—Walt Whitman.*

We want margin to our lives. *—H. D. Thoreau.*

Employ thy time well, if thou meanest to gain leisure.

—B. Franklin.

LENDING

If you would lose a troublesome visitor, lend him money.

—B. Franklin.

Don't borrow or lend; but if you must do one, lend.

—Josh Billings.

The government never lends or gives anything to business that it does not take away from business. *—Henry Hazlitt.*

Lend not beyond thy ability, nor refuse to lend out of thy ability.

—Wm. Penn.

LENT

A blunderer is a man who starts a meat market during Lent.

—J. M. Bailey.

LETTERS

There are certain people whom one almost feels inclined to urge to hurry up and die so that their letters can be published.

—Christopher Morley.

I have received no more than one or two letters in my life that were worth the postage. *—H. D. Thoreau.*

When truth, in its outward flow joins beauty, the two rivers make a new flood called "letters." *—David Swing.*

The lover of letters loves power too. *—R. W. Emerson.*

A profusion of fancy and quotations is out of place in a love-letter. *—C. N. Bovee.*

LEVITY

A light and trifling mind never takes in great ideas, and never accomplishes anything great or good. *—W. R. Sprague.*

LEWDNESS

Lewdness is a very broad way to death, ornamented with artful flowers. *—Charles Simmons.*

LIARS

No man has a good enough memory to make a successful liar.

—A. Lincoln.

Liar: one who tells an unpleasant truth. *—Oliver Herford.*

I would guarantee that if enough liars talked to you, you would get the truth; because the parts that they did not invent would match one another, and the parts that they did invent would not match one another. *—Woodrow Wilson.*

All press agents belong to a club of which Ananias is the honorary president. *—J. K. Bangs.*

What a dull world this would be if every imaginative maker of legends was stigmatized as a liar!   —*Heywood Broun.*

LIBERAL

A liberal is a man who is willing to spend somebody else's money.   —*Carter Glass.*

To be a liberal one doesn't have to be a wastrel.
—*P. H. Douglas.*

It is an uncompromising devotion to the idea of equal liberty as both the means and the end of life that characterizes the liberal spirit.   —*H. M. Kallen.*

I'm liberal . . . I mean, so altruistically moral, I never take my own side in a quarrel.   —*Robert Frost.*

The liberals, whose thinking once had an economic and political base are now off base.   —*Max Lerner.*

The liberal . . . is Mr. Janus Facing-Both Ways. He sees two sides to every question.   —*Ibid.*

In all those things which deal with people, be liberal, be human. In all those things which deal with the people's money or their company, or their form of government, be conservative— and don't be afraid to use the word.   —*D. D. Eisenhower.*

LIBERALISM

Liberalism is a force truly of the spirit proceeding from the deep realization that economic freedom cannot be sacrificed if political freedom is to be preserved.   —*Herbert Hoover.*

The liberal philosophy is based on the conviction that, except in emergencies and for military purposes, the division of labor cannot be regulated successfully by coercive authority.
—*Walter Lippmann.*

Liberalism in general means the opening up of opportunities in all fields of human endeavor.   —*M. R. Cohen.*

Liberalism will not die. It is as indispensable to life as the pure air all around about.   —*George W. Norris.*

If liberalism means anything, it means complete and courageous devotion to the freedom of inquiry.   —*John Dewey.*

Liberalism seeks to govern primarily by applying and perfecting reciprocal relations; whereas authoritarianism governs primarily by the handing down of decrees.   —*Walter Lippmann.*

We are witnessing a concerted attempt to drive America from the open highway of liberalism and into retreat towards the caves of an all-powerful reaction.   *—James A. Michener.*

American liberalism from the very start was reactionary in that it defended competition instead of offering it, thereby helping to hold back the progressive advance of our economic life.
—V. F. Calverton.

Our task is to show that a militant collectivist democracy differs from passive liberalism, and that it means not a weakening but a renewal of the energies that once made liberalism a fighting world movement.   *—Max Lerner.*

LIBERALITY

Be rather bountiful than expensive; do good with what thou hast, or it will do thee no good.   *—Wm. Penn.*

That which is called liberality is frequently nothing more than the vanity of giving.   *—Theodore Parker.*

LIBERATION

If you would liberate me, you must be free.   *—R. W. Emerson.*

The history of the pre-democratic world . . . does not record a single instance of free men fighting for the liberation of slaves.
—H. M. Kallen.

Americans (believed) that the world was beginning afresh with them, that they were appointed to liberate the masses of mankind.
—Van Wyck Brooks.

LIBERTINES

I worship in the Synagogue of the Libertines.   *—Jim Fiske.*

LIBERTY

Give me liberty, or give me death!   *—Patrick Henry.*

Natural liberty is a gift of the beneficent Creator, to the whole human race, and . . . civil liberty is founded in that, and cannot be wrested from any people without the most manifest violation of justice.   *—Alexander Hamilton.*

Liberty exists in proportion to wholesome restraint.
—Daniel Webster.

The passion for liberty cannot be strong in the breasts of those who are accustomed to deprive their fellow-creatures of liberty.
—Susan B. Anthony.

American liberty is a religion. It is a thing of the spirit. It is an aspiration on the part of people for not alone a free life but a better life.   *—Wendell L. Willkie.*

Liberty, like charity, must begin at home.   *—James Conant.*

The notion of liberty on which the Republic was founded, the spirit of America that animated Emerson and Whitman, is vividly alive today only in the unassimilated foreigner, in that pathetic pilgrim to a forgotten shrine.   *—Ludwig Lewisohn.*

Where liberty dwells, there is my country.   *—B. Franklin.*

Liberty is the fullest opportunity for man to be and do the very best that is possible for him.   *—Phillips Brooks.*

The foundation stone of democracy, indeed of all our liberties, is the free enterprise system; we cannot long enjoy political and religious liberty unless we likewise possess economic liberty.
—H. F. Byrd.

The liberty of the artist is the avatar of all the liberties of man.
—H. M. Kallen.

Doing what we please is not freedom, is not liberty; rather, it is the abuse of true liberty and freedom.   *—Patrick Joseph Hayes.*

Liberty is the one thing you can't have unless you give it to others.   *—William A. White.*

Civil liberty, while it resigns a part of natural liberty, retains the free and generous exercise of all the human faculties, so far as it is compatible with the public welfare.   *—James Wilson.*

Liberty! let others despair of you! I never despair of you.
—Walt Whitman.

What light is to the eyes—what air is to the lungs—what love is to the heart, liberty is to the soul of man.   *—R. G. Ingersoll.*

The God who gave us life, gave us liberty at the same time.
—T. Jefferson.

Eternal vigilance is the price of liberty.   *—Wendell Phillips.*

Liberty, when it begins to take root, is a plant of rapid growth.
—G. Washington.

Those who would give up essential liberty to purchase a little temporary safety, deserve neither liberty nor safety. *—B. Franklin.*

I have always in my own thought summed up individual liberty,

and business liberty, and every other kind of liberty, in the phrase that is common in the sporting world, "A free field and no favor."
                                                        —*Woodrow Wilson.*

The liberties of our country, the freedom of our civil constitution, are worth defending at all hazards; and it is our duty to defend them against all attacks.   —*Samuel Adams.*

American liberty is derived from nature or it is derived from God. But never from the social order.   —*Leon Samson.*

God grants liberty only to those who love it, and are always ready to guard and defend it.   —*Daniel Webster.*

The tidal wave of God's providence is carrying liberty throughout the globe.   —*H. W. Beecher.*

The greatest dangers to liberty lurk in insidious encroachment by men of zeal, well-meaning but without understanding.
                                                        —*Louis D. Brandeis.*

The history of liberty is a history of resistance. The history of liberty is a history of limitations of governmental power, not the increase of it.   —*Woodrow Wilson.*

The more liberty you give away the more you will have.
                                                        —*R. G. Ingersoll.*

Four score and seven years ago our fathers brought forth on this continent a new nation, conceived in liberty and dedicated to the proposition that all men are created equal.   —*A. Lincoln.*

The things required for prosperous labor, prosperous manufacturers, and prosperous commerce are three. First, liberty; second, liberty; third, liberty.   —*H. W. Beecher.*

I am for the people of the whole nation doing just as they please in all matters which concern the whole nation; for that of each part doing just as they choose in all matters which concern no other part; and for each individual doing just as he chooses in all matters which concern nobody else.   —*A. Lincoln.*

The ball of liberty is now so well in motion that it will roll round the globe.   —*T. Jefferson.*

We are not to expect to be translated from despotism to liberty in a featherbed.   —*Ibid.*

The tree of liberty must be refreshed from time to time with the blood of patriots and tyrants. It is its natural manure.
                                                        —*Ibid.*

Is life so dear or peace so sweet as to be purchased at the price of chains and slavery? Forbid it, Almighty God! I know not what course others may take, but as for me, give me liberty, or give me death. —*Patrick Henry.*

Natural liberty is a gift of the beneficent Creator to the whole human race, and . . . civil liberty is founded in that, and cannot be wrested from any people without the most manifest violation of justice. —*Alexander Hamilton.*

Liberty in itself is not government. —*B. M. Baruch.*

It is no longer open to doubt that the liberty of the press and of speech is within the liberty safeguarded from invasion by state action. —*Charles Evans Hughes.*

Liberty is the only thing you cannot have unless you are willing to give it to others. —*William A. White.*

We not only praise individual liberty but our constitution has the unique distinction of insuring it. —*Charles Evans Hughes.*

LIBRARIES

There are seventy million books in American libraries, but the one you want to read is always out. —*Tom Masson.*

Every library should try to be complete on something, if it were only the history of pinheads. —*O. W. Holmes.*

The richest minds need not large libraries. —*A. B. Alcott.*

A library is but the soul's burial ground. —*H. W. Beecher.*

Shelved around me lie the mummied authors. —*Bayard Taylor.*

A library is a land of shadows. —*H. W. Beecher.*

LICENSE

Corporations engaged in interstate commerce should be regulated if they are found to exercise a license working to the public injury. —*Theodore Roosevelt.*

LIES

A lie has always a certain amount of weight with those who wish to believe it. —*E. W. Rice.*

The lie of fear is the refuge of cowardice, and the lie of fraud the device of the cheat. —*Edward Bellamy.*

The inequalities of men and the lust of acquisition are a constant premium on lying. —*Ibid.*

Sin has many tools, but a lie is the handle which fits them all.
—*O. W. Holmes.*

LIFE

Life is not a spectacle or a feast; it is a predicament.
—*George Santayana.*

Oh, to live out such a life as God appoints—how great a thing it is!   —*Horace Bushnell.*

God asks no man whether he will accept life; that is not the choice. You must take it; the only choice is how. —*H. W. Beecher.*

The ladder of life is full of splinters, but they always prick the hardest when we're sliding down.   —*W. L. Brownell.*

With us of the younger generation of the South . . . pretty much the whole of life has been merely not dying.   —*Sidney Lanier.*

The obstinate insisting that tweedledum is not tweedledee is the bone and marrow of life.   —*William James.*

Human life and turnips remain cheap and plentiful.
—*Kin Hubbard.*

Life should be an alternation of employments, so diversified as to call the whole man into action.   —*W. E. Channing.*

The life, the life! O, my God! shall the life never be sweet?
—*Margaret Fuller.*

Life is short, but it is long enough to ruin any man who wants to be ruined.   —*Josh Billings.*

We find in life exactly what we put in it.   —*R. W. Emerson.*

The good life is the healthful life, the merry life. Life is health, joy, laughter.   —*J. E. Boodin.*

Life is made up of sobs, sniffles, and smiles, with sniffles predominating.   —*O. Henry.*

Life is real! Life is earnest!
And the grave is not its goal.
—*H. W. Longfellow.*

It takes life to love Life.   —*E. L. Masters.*

Life is just one damned thing after another.
—*Frank Ward O'Malley.*

Every man's life is a plan of God.   —*Horace Bushnell.*

The first task of life is to live. Men begin with acts, not with thoughts.   —*W. G. Sumner.*

We live as fully as we can the fragment of life that is our own life. —*Max Ascoli.*

I see life—for most at least—as a very grim and dangerous contest, relieved . . . by a sense or by an illusion of pleasure, which is the bait, and the lure for all in this internecine contest.
—*Theodore Dreiser.*

If man's life is great, let him count more precious all its winters and summers. —*David Swing.*

The fact of life ought to imply a fitness to live. —*Ibid.*

Only a blind man would deny that characteristic traits of present life are a mad scramble for material commodities, a devotion to attainment of external power, and an insensate love of foolish luxuries and idle display. —*John Dewey.*

Be a life long or short, its completeness depends on what it was lived for. —*D. S. Jordan.*

The problem of life is not to make life easier, but to make men stronger. —*Ibid.*

No one is really miserable who has not tried to cheapen life.
—*Ibid.*

The first place is held by life. —*G. E. Woodberry.*

Men differ in place, honor, and influence, but there is one seamless garment of life for all. —*Ibid.*

Life is not to be spent anticipating a reward or not, or endured, or anything of the kind, but it is to be enjoyed to the last detail.
—*Theodore Dreiser.*

Do not take life too seriously; you will never get out of it alive.
—*Elbert Hubbard.*

Every life is a march from innocence, through temptation, to virtue or to vice. —*Lyman Abbott.*

Be not afraid of life. Believe that life is worth living, and your belief will help create the fact. —*William James.*

Life is work, and everything you do is so much more experience.
—*Henry Ford.*

Life itself, without the assistance of colleges and universities, is becoming an advanced institution of learning. —*Thomas A. Edison.*

Is life so dear, or peace so sweet, as to be purchased at the price of chains and slavery? Forbid it, Almighty God!
—*Patrick Henry.*

Into each life some rain must fall.   —*H. W. Longfellow.*

Life is a matter of energy and faith. Our energy is distracted, dissipated, tormented. Our faith is a dream enacting a nightmare.
                                   —*Samuel D. Schmalhausen.*

Life's a tough proposition, and the first hundred years are the hardest.   —*Wilson Mizner.*

Life is too strong for you!—It takes life to love life.
                                          —*E. L. Masters.*

Life is a foreign language: all men mispronounce it.
                                       —*Christopher Morley.*

Life isn't a spurt, but a long, steady climb.   —*G. H. Lorimer.*

Life is a series of little deaths, out of which life always returns.
                                     —*Charles Feidelson, Jr.*

Life in any form is our perpetual responsibility.
                                          —*S. P. Cadman.*

Life is a fatal complaint, and an eminently contagious one.
                                          —*O. W. Holmes.*

You cannot philosophize your life and live it too.
                                          —*Don Herold.*

Born in throes, 'tis fit that man should live in pains and die in pangs.   —*Herman Melville.*

Man's real life is happy, chiefly because he is ever expecting that it soon will be so.   —*Edgar Allan Poe.*

All life is an experiment. Every year if not every day we have to wager our salvation upon some prophecy based upon imperfect knowledge.   —*O. W. Holmes, Jr.*

Life is made up of marble and mud.   —*Nathaniel Hawthorne.*

Were it offered to my choice, I should have no objection to a repetition of the same life from its beginning, only asking the advantages authors have in a second edition to correct some faults of the first.   —*B. Franklin.*

What is life, I ask myself, is it a gracious gift? No, it is too bitter; a gift means something valuable conferred, but life appears to be a mere accident, and of the worst kind: we are born to be victims of diseases and passions, of mischances and death.
                                —*Hector St. Jean de Crèvecoeur.*

The art of life is the art of avoiding pain.   —*T. Jefferson.*

I wish to preach, not the doctrine of ignoble ease, but the doctrine of strenuous life.   —*Theodore Roosevelt.*

Life is like a cash register, in that every account, every thought, every deed, like every sale, is registered and recorded.
                                                                  —*Fulton J. Sheen.*

The more abundant life.   —*F. D. Roosevelt.*

In spite of everything, life is good.   —*H. W. Van Loon.*

Life consists not simply in what heredity and environment do to us but in what we make out of what they do to us.
                                                                  —*H. E. Fosdick.*

LIFE-PRESERVER

Every man's task is his life-preserver.   —*R. W. Emerson.*

LIFESAVER

For parlor use, the vague generality is a lifesaver. —*George Ade.*

LIGHT

Light is the symbol of truth.   —*J. R. Lowell.*

The thing to do is to supply light and not heat.
                                                                  —*Woodrow Wilson.*

LIGHTNING

The mattock will make a deeper hole in the ground than lightning.   —*Horace Mann.*

LIKED

He liked to like people, therefore people liked him.
                                                                  —*Mark Twain.*

LIMITATIONS

I seldom think about my limitations, and they never make me sad. Perhaps there is just a touch of yearning at times; but it is vague, like a breeze among flowers.   —*Helen Keller.*

LIMITS

The only limit to our realization of tomorrow will be our doubts of today.   —*F. D. Roosevelt.*

The limits of our American way are only those vast expanses of 150 million creative minds—150 million creative minds which the spark of individual initiative awaits only to release.—*L. P. Shield.*

LINCOLN

His heart was as great as the world, but there was no room in it to hold the memory of wrong.   —*R. W. Emerson.*

As long as he lived he was the guiding star of a whole brave nation, and when he died the little children cried in the streets.

—*J. L. Motley.*

LION

There may come a time when the lion and the lamb will lie down together, but I am still betting on the lion. —*Josh Billings.*

LIQUOR

Liquor talks mighty loud when it gets loose from the jug.

—*J. C. Harris.*

LISTENING

A good listener is not only popular everywhere, but after a while he knows something. —*Wilson Mizner.*

When it comes to making love, a girl can always listen so much faster than a man can talk. —*Helen Rowland.*

LITERATURE

Literature is an investment of genius which pays dividends to all subsequent times. —*John Burroughs.*

The whole of modern literature is corrupted by what I call secularism. —*T. S. Eliot.*

Great literature is simply language charged with meaning to the utmost possible degree. —*Ezra Pound.*

Literature is the orchestra of platitudes. —*Thornton Wilder.*

It takes a great deal of history to produce a little literature.

—*Henry James.*

Literature is that part of thought that is wrought out in the name of the beautiful. —*David Swing.*

Literature is not a source of moral precepts; nor a source of a pseudo-religious discipline; it is a phase of experience.

—*C. Hartley Grattan.*

All literature is one expression of one human life-experience.

—*Thornton Wilder.*

Literature cannot be cured by exhortation. If it could, any pulpeteer would be able to father a renaissance the like of which would stagger Pericles. —*John Chamberlain.*

Our American professors like their literature clear, cold, pure, and very dead. —*Sinclair Lewis.*

It is the life of literature that acts upon life. —*J. G. Holland.*

Our authors and scholars are generally men of business, and make their literary pursuits subservient to their interests.

—*Benjamin Rush.*

Literature is a noble calling, but only when the call obeyed by the aspirant issues from a world to be enlightened and blessed, not from a void stomach clamoring to be gratified and filled.

—*Horace Greeley.*

LITTLE

A great man is always willing to be little.   —*R. W. Emerson.*

Tremendous consequences come from little things.—I am tempted to think . . . these are no little things.   —*Bruce Barton.*

In great matters men show themselves as they wish to be seen; in small matters, as they are.   —*Gamaliel Bradford.*

Man wants but little here below, but wants that little strong.

—*O. W. Holmes.*

LIVE

I think some folks are foolish to pay what it costs to live.

—*Kin Hubbard.*

It is easy to live for others; everybody does.   —*R. W. Emerson.*

We are always getting ready to live, but never living.

—*Ibid.*

Not to love is not to live, or it is to live a living death.

—*R. W. Trine.*

LIVES

Our lives are merely strange dark interludes in the electrical display of God the Father.   —*Eugene O'Neill.*

The first half of our lives is ruined by our parents and the second half by our children.   —*Clarence Darrow.*

LIVING

We live ruins amidst ruins.   —*R. W. Emerson.*

Our sciences, our ideologies, and our arts are essential to humane living; and their expression in wholeness furthers and effectuates life.   —*Lewis Mumford.*

We put too much emphasis and importance and advertising on our so-called High standard of living.   —*Will Rogers.*

To live and let live, without clamor for distinction or recognition; to wait on divine Love; to write truth first on the tablet of

one's own heart,—this is the sanity and perfection of living, and my
human ideal.   —*Mary Baker Eddy.*

To live is to function. That is all there is in living.
                                                —*O. W. Holmes, Jr.*

Initiative, aggressive conviction, enlightened self-interest, are the
characteristics that must be dominant among the people if the
nation is to make substantial progress toward better living and
higher ideals.   —*Samuel Gompers.*

A decent standard of living in return for their labor must obviously include provision for illness, accident, old age and death.
. . . This is a legitimate cost of production.   —*Philip Murray.*

The resources of the nation can be made to produce a far higher
standard of living for the masses if only government is intelligent
and energetic in giving the right directions to economic life.
                                                —*F. D. Roosevelt.*

A man who does not learn to live while he is getting a living,
is a poorer man after his wealth is won, than he was before.
                                                —*J. G. Holland.*

Living, you let live and help live.   —*H. M. Kallen.*

The person who limits his interests to the means of living without consideration of the content or meaning of his life is defeating
God's great purpose when he brought into existence a creature
with the intelligence and godlike powers that are found in man.
                                                —*A. H. Compton.*

Don't believe the world owes you a living; the world owes you
nothing—it was here first.   —*R. J. Burdette.*

No ceremonies salute the time clock and the steam whistle, no
hierophants unveil the mysteries of the counting house, no myths
attend the tractor and the reaper-binder . . . For multitudes the art
of living is detached from the business of living. —*R. M. MacIver.*

Perhaps it would be a good idea, fantastic as it sounds, to muffle
every telephone, stop every motor and halt all activity for an hour
some day, to give people a chance to ponder for a few minutes on
what it is all about, why they are living and what they really want.
                                                —*James Truslow Adams.*

LOAFING

Even if a farmer intends to loaf, he gets up in time to get an
early start.   —*E. W. Howe.*

If a loafer is not a nuisance to you, it is a sign that you are somewhat of a loafer yourself.   *—Ibid.*

The only undignified job I know is loafing. *—G. H. Lorimer.*

LOANS
The man who won't loan money isn't going to have many
friends—or need them.   *—Wilson Mizner.*

When the government makes loans or subsidies to business,
what it does is to tax successful private businesses in order to support unsuccessful private business.   *—Henry Hazlitt.*

LOCOMOTION
Methods of locomotion have improved greatly in recent years,
but places to go remain about the same.   *—Don Herold.*

LOGIC
Logic: an instrument used for bolstering a prejudice.
                                              —Elbert Hubbard.

The mind has its own logic but does not often let others in on it.
                                              —Bernard De Voto.

Whatever our characteristic American virtues are, logic isn't one
of them. We share with the other English-speaking peoples a genius for living happily with contradictions, anomalies, and compromises.   *—Elizabeth Jackson.*

You can't be logical and complimentary at the same time. It is
too much to ask.   *—W. D. Howells.*

Man is not logical and his intellectual history is a record of
mental reserves and compromises. He hangs on to what he can in
his old beliefs even when he is compelled to surrender their
logical basis.   *—John Dewey.*

A page of history is worth a volume of logic. *—O. W. Holmes.*

It is logical that the United States should do whatever it is able
to do to assist in the return of normal economic health in the
world, without which there can be no political stability and no
assured peace.   *—George Marshall.*

LONELINESS
Loneliness is stamped on the American face; it rises like an
exhalation from the American landscape.   *—Van Wyck Brooks.*

Why should I feel lonely? Is not our planet in the Milky Way?
—*H. D. Thoreau.*

The whole conviction of my life now rests upon the belief that loneliness, far from being a rare and curious phenomenon, peculiar to myself and to a few other solitary men, is the central and inevitable fact of human existence.   —*Thomas Wolfe.*

LONESOME

Be virtuous and you will be happy; but you will be lonesome sometimes.   —*E. W. Nye.*

Be good and you will be lonesome.   —*Mark Twain.*

LONGING

In us is the longing for unity.   —*J. H. Bodin.*

LOOK

Very few people look the part and are it too.   —*Don Herold.*

Love looks through a telescope; envy, through a microscope.
—*Josh Billings.*

LORD

Mine eyes have seen the glory of the coming of the Lord.
—*Julia W. Howe.*

LOOSE

Everything nailed down is comin' loose.

—*Marc Connolly.*

LOSE

Give me the heart to fight and lose.   —*Louis Untermeyer.*

LOSS

We are threatened with the loss of the people's confidence, the very foundation of democratic government.

—*David E. Lilienthal.*

I have lived . . . with the sense of having suffered a vast and indefinite loss . . . what I have lost was a country.

—*H. D. Thoreau.*

'Tis better to have loved and lost than never to have been sued.
—*Kin Hubbard.*

LOVE

Love is like the measles; we can have it but once, and the later in life we have it, the tougher it goes with us.   —*Josh Billings.*

The ability to make love frivolously is the chief characteristic which distinguishes human beings from the beasts.

—Heywood Broun.

Love, we say, is life; but love without hope and faith is agonizing death. *—Elbert Hubbard.*

There is no remedy for love but to love more. *—H. D. Thoreau.*

Our reliance is in the love of liberty which God has planted in us. *—A. Lincoln.*

Love is ownership. *—H. W. Beecher.*

Love is more just than justice. *—Ibid.*

Every man's life, practically speaking, is shaped by his love. If it is a downward, earthly love, then his actions will be tinged by it; all his life will be as his reigning love. *—Horace Bushnell.*

Love is like war: easy to begin but very hard to stop.

—H. L. Mencken.

The love of freedom is the ultimate human impulse.

—O. L. Triggs.

Love is a wonderful thing and highly desirable in marriage.

—Rupert Hughes.

In the last analysis, love is only the reflection of a man's own worthiness from other men. *—R. W. Emerson.*

Only from the exuberant is it possible to get an enlivening return in the execution of the Commandment: "Love thy neighbor as thyself." *—Heywood Broun.*

Love, and you shall be loved. *—R. W. Emerson.*

Love makes obedience lighter than liberty. *—W. R. Alger.*

Love is the hardest lesson in Christianity; but, for that reason, it should be most our care to learn it. *—Wm. Penn.*

What we most love and revere generally is determined by early associations. *—O. W. Holmes, Jr.*

I believe that love is the greatest thing in the world; that it alone can overcome hate; that right can and will triumph over might. *—John D. Rockefeller, Jr.*

That strange phenomenon love . . . pops up in the strangest places. *—Thornton Wilder.*

Love cannot be forced, love cannot be coaxed and teased. It comes out of Heaven, unasked and unsought. *—Pearl Buck.*

Love is strongest in pursuit; friendship, in possession.

—*R. W. Emerson.*

The life that goes out in love to all is the life that is full, and rich, and continually expanding in beauty and in power.

—*R. W. Trine.*

The more one loves the nearer he approaches to God, for God is the spirit of infinite love.   —*Ibid.*

They that love beyond the world cannot be separated by it.

—*Wm. Penn.*

I never knew how to worship until I knew how to love.

—*H. W. Beecher.*

You can always get someone to love you—even if you have to do it yourself.   —*Tom Masson.*

Perhaps they were right in putting love into books . . . Perhaps it could not live anywhere else.   —*William Faulkner.*

Love has never known a law beyond its own sweet will.

—*J. G. Whittier.*

Love is the life of the soul. It is the harmony of the universe.

—*W. E. Channing.*

He that falls in love with himself will have no rivals.

—*B. Franklin.*

In your amours you should prefer old women to young ones. This you call a paradox, and demand my reasons. They are: . . . 8th and lastly: they are so grateful.   —*B. Franklin.*

I don't know how the people will feel toward me, but I will take to my grave my love for them which has sustained me through life.   —*Robert M. La Follette.*

LOVELY

The secret of being loved is being lovely; and the secret of being lovely is being unselfish.   —*J. G. Holland.*

LOVERS

Scratch a lover, and find a foe.   —*Dorothy Parker.*

A husband is what is left of the lover after the nerve has been extracted.   —*Helen Rowland.*

It is easier to keep half a dozen lovers guessing than to keep one lover after he has stopped guessing.   —*Ibid.*

LOYALTY

Enlightened loyalty means harm to no man's loyalty.

—Josiah Royce.

It is a gross perversion not only of the concept of loyalty but of the concept of Americanism to identify it with a particular economic system. *—H. S. Commager.*

If loyalty and private enterprise are inextricably associated, what is to preserve loyalty if private enterprise fails? *—Ibid.*

Loyalty . . . is a realization that America was born of revolt, flourished in dissent, became great through experimentation.*—Ibid.*

We join ourselves to no party that does not carry the American flag, and keep step to the music of the Union. *—Rufus Choate.*

We mutually pledge to each other our lives, our fortunes, and our sacred honor. *—T. Jefferson.*

A true friend of his country loves her friends and benefactors and thinks it no degradation to commend and commemorate them.

—Daniel Webster.

We must announce our loyalty . . . to those religious, political and humanitarian principles which seem best calculated to see a man or a nation through a period of darkness.*—James A. Michener.*

Loyalty means nothing unless it has at its heart the absolute principle of self-sacrifice. *—Woodrow Wilson.*

LUCK

The best you get is an even break. *—F. P. Adams.*

The only sure thing about luck is that it will change.

—Wilson Mizner.

A pound of pluck is worth a ton of luck. *—James A. Garfield.*

As long as we are lucky we attribute it to our smartness; our bad luck we give the gods credit for. *—Josh Billings.*

Diligence is the mother of good luck. *—B. Franklin.*

Watch out when you're getting all you want; fattening hogs ain't in luck. *—J. C. Harris.*

Shallow men believe in luck.—Strong men believe in cause and effect. *—R. W. Emerson.*

As for what you're calling hard luck—well, we made New England out of it, that and codfish. *—Stephen Vincent Benét.*

LUNCH

You can always judge a man by what he eats, and therefore a country in which there is no free lunch is no longer a free country.
—Arthur ("Bugs") Baer.

LUST

Husbands have been forced to prostitute their wives, and mothers their daughters, to gratify the brutal lust of a (slave) master.
—Benjamin Rush.

Pride goes with cruelty and cruelty with lust.
—Elizabeth Jackson.

LUXURY

Give us the luxuries of life and we will dispense with necessaries.
—O. W. Holmes.

Freedom for Americans is not a luxury of peace to be "sacrificed" in war-time. It is necessary at all times, but above all in war; then it becomes an instant matter of life and death. *—Isabel Paterson.*

Sedition is bred in the lap of luxury. *—George Bancroft.*

Luxury and learning are ill bedfellows. *—Charles W. Eliot.*

Most of the luxuries, and many of the so-called comforts of life, are not only not indispensable, but positive hindrances to the elevation of mankind. *—H. D. Thoreau.*

LYING

The truth that survives is simply the lie that is pleasantest to believe. *—H. L. Mencken.*

A lie in time saves nine. *—Addison Mizner.*

One of the striking differences between a cat and a lie is that a cat has only nine lives. *—Mark Twain.*

No man lies consistently, and he cannot lie about everything if he talks to you long. *—Woodrow Wilson.*

It is twice as hard to crush a half-truth as a whole lie.
—Austin O'Malley.

A lie with a purpose is one of the worst kind, and the most profitable. *—F. P. Dunne.*

With a man, a lie is a last resort; with women, it's First Aid.
—Gelett Burgess.

Telling lies is a fault in a boy, an art in a lover, an accomplishment in a bachelor, and second nature in a married woman.
—Helen Rowland.

Truth is beautiful without doubt, and so are lies.

—R. W. Emerson.

The devil is the father of lies, but he neglected to patent the idea, and the business now suffers from competition.

—Josh Billings.

The perjurer's mother told white lies.   *—Austin O'Malley.*

Falsehoods not only disagree with truth, but they usually quarrel among themselves.   *—Daniel Webster.*

There is no worse lie than a truth misunderstood by those who hear it.   *—William James.*

The hardest tumble a man can make is to fall over his own bluff.

—Ambrose Bierce.

The most intangible, and therefore the worst kind of a lie is a half truth.   *—Washington Allston.*

Speak the truth.—Equivocation is half way to lying, and lying is whole way to hell.   *—Wm. Penn.*

The man who fears no truths has everything to fear from lies.

—T. Jefferson.

M

MACHINERY

A machine cannot be either enslaved or liberated. The term applies only to human beings. —*Isabel Paterson.*

He that invents a machine augments the power of man and the well-being of mankind. —*H. W. Beecher.*

One machine can do the work of fifty ordinary men. No machine can do the work of one extraordinary man. —*Elbert Hubbard.*

Men have become the tools of their tools. —*H. D. Thoreau.*

It is to the supernatural agency, the divinity in machinery, that we must look for the salvation of society. —*E. E. Slosson.*

The machine age began . . . with the domination of engineering as the supreme art. —*Lewis Mumford.*

To curb the machine and limit art to handicraft is a denial of opportunity. —*Ibid.*

To extend the machine into provinces where it has no function to perform is likewise a denial of opportunity. —*Ibid.*

The machine age has resulted in a transferring of the locus of the ideal of a larger and more evenly distributed happiness and leisure from heaven to earth. —*John Dewey.*

In those countries where machinery has been developed to little or no purpose poverty reigns, ignorance is the prevailing condition, and civilization consequently far in the rear.
—*C. D. Wright.*

He is a workman only because and so far as he effectually shares in this common stock of technological equipment.
—*Thorstein Veblen.*

The machines are not driving men out of work. —*Henry Ford.*

As the machine age is perfected and extended more, more men and women will have work to provide the innumerable comforts which the machine age will make possible to everybody.

—Ibid.

The cultural growth dominated by the machine industry is of a sceptical matter-of-fact complexion, materialistic, immoral, unpatriotic, undevout. *—Thorstein Veblen.*

MADNESS

Insanity is often the logic of an accurate mind overtaxed.

—O. W. Holmes.

The insane, for the most part, reason correctly, but from false principles, while they do not perceive that their premises are incorrect. *—Tryon Edwards.*

We go by the majority vote, and if the majority are insane, the sane must go to the hospital. *—Horace Mann.*

When a young American writer seems mad, it is usually because an old one drives him crazy. *—F. M. Colby.*

When you see a married couple coming down the street, the one who is two or three steps ahead is the one that's mad.

—Helen Rowland.

MAIDENHOOD

Maidens' hearts are always soft:
Would that men's were truer!

—Wm. Cullen Bryant.

Nature has thrown a veil of modest beauty over maidenhood and moss roses. *—N. P. Willis.*

MAINE

I lived in Maine like a bird of the air, so perfect was the freedom I enjoyed. But it was there I got my cursed habits of solitude.

—Nathaniel Hawthorne.

As Maine goes, so goes the nation. *—A political maxim.*

As Maine goes, so goes Vermont. *—James A. Farley.*

MAJORITY

One with the law is a majority. *—Calvin Coolidge.*

It is my principle that the will of the majority should always prevail. *—T. Jefferson.*

One, on God's side, is a majority. *—Wendell Phillips.*

One and God make a majority.   —*Frederick Douglass.*

The great majority of people are neither one thing nor the other, but are living in a no man's land.   —*T. S. Eliot.*

The voice of the majority saves bloodshed, but it is no less the arbitrament of force than is the decree of the most absolute of despots backed by the most powerful of armies.   —*Benj. R. Tucker.*

If the fools do not control the world, it isn't because they are not in the majority.   —*E. W. Howe.*

Any man more right than his neighbors, constitutes a majority of one.   —*H. D. Thoreau.*

Justice, not the majority, should rule.   —*C. N. Bovee.*

The moment a mere numerical superiority by either states or voters in this country proceeds to ignore the needs and desires of the minority, and for their own selfish purpose or advancement, hamper or oppress that minority, or debar them in any way from equal privileges and equal rights—that moment will mark the failure of our constitutional system.   —*F. D. Roosevelt.*

If by the mere force of numbers a majority should deprive a minority of any clearly written constitutional right, it might, in a moral point of view, justify revolution—certainly would if such a right were a vital one.   —*A. Lincoln.*

Though the will of the majority is in all cases to prevail, that will, to be rightful, must be reasonable; the minority possess their equal rights, which equal laws must protect, and to violate would be oppression.   —*T. Jefferson.*

On a candid examination of history, we shall find that turbulence, violence, and abuse of power, by the majority trampling on the rights of the minority, have produced factions and commotions which, in republics, have, more frequently than any other cause, produced despotism.   —*James Madison.*

The thing we have to fear in this country, to my way of thinking, is the influence of the organized minorities, because somehow or other the great majority does not seem to organize. They seem to feel that they are going to be effective because of their known strength, but they give no expression of it.   —*Alfred E. Smith.*

The history of most countries has been that of majorities—mounted majorities, clad in iron, armed with death, treading down the tenfold more numerous minorities.   —*O. W. Holmes.*

MALICE

With malice towards none, with charity for all.   —*A. Lincoln.*

But for that blindness which is inseparable from malice, what terrible powers of evil would it possess!   —*W. G. Simms.*

MALNUTRITION

The short skirts of today reveal the malnutrition of yesterday.
—*Don Herold.*

MAN

Man, biologically considered, . . . is the most formidable of all the beasts of prey, and, indeed, the only one that preys systematically on its own species.   —*William James.*

Every man is a volume, if you know how to read him.
—*W. E. Channing.*

Man is a piece of the universe made alive.   —*R. W. Emerson.*

Man's the bad child of the universe.   —*James Oppenheim.*

I am an acme of things accomplished, and I am encloser of things to be.   —*Walt Whitman.*

> When faith is lost, when honor dies,
> The man is dead!
>
> —*J. G. Whittier.*

Man is a special being, and if left to himself, in an isolated condition, would be one of the weakest creatures; but associated with his kind, he works wonders.   —*Daniel Webster.*

The forgotten Man is delving away in patient industry . . . he works, he votes, generally he prays—but he always pays—yes, above all, he pays.   —*W. G. Sumner.*

A man is a god in ruins.   —*R. W. Emerson.*

The cheapness of man is every day's tragedy.   —*Ibid.*

Man passes away; his name perishes from record and recollection; his history is as a tale that is told, and his very monument becomes a ruin.   —*Washington Irving.*

Man has ever distrusted those influences which threatened to interfere with the task of providing sufficient money or food for himself and his family.   —*H. W. Van Loon.*

God save the Rights of Man!   —*Philip M. Freneau.*

The biggest thing about a principle or a battle or an army is a man.   —*F. W. Bok.*

That man has absolute dominion, . . . is true not of physical man, but of spiritual man.   —*R. W. Trine.*

Take even a common man, the commonest, and beat and bruise him enough and you will see his soul rise God-like.

—*Frank Crane.*

The ablest man I ever met is the man you think you are.

—*F. D. Roosevelt.*

Man has made his bedlam; let him lie in it.   —*Fred Allen.*

Man is Creation's masterpiece; but who says so?—Man.

—*Elbert Hubbard.*

Man is a political animal by nature; he is a scientist by chance or choice; he is a moralist because he is a man.

—*Hans J. Morgenthau.*

I am frankly daring to proclaim myself the American Man.

—*Sherwood Anderson.*

I never met a man I didn't like.   —*Will Rogers.*

I believe that man will not merely endure; he will prevail.

—*William Faulkner.*

Never before in human history has *homo sapiens* felt so un-solved, dissolved so completely in a state of irresolution.

—*Samuel D. Schmalhausen.*

There is no indispensable man.   —*F. D. Roosevelt.*

Man was destined for society.   —*T. Jefferson.*

For some generations now man has been trying to decide whether he is merely a high-grade simian or a son of God.

—*Wilbur Urban.*

The soul of man createth his own destiny and power.

—*N. P. Willis.*

What a Bedlamite is man!   —*T. Jefferson.*

Man is, at one and the same time, a solitary being and a social being.   —*Albert Einstein.*

The bulk of mankind are schoolboys through life.

—*T. Jefferson.*

I am the inferior of any man whose rights I trample under foot. Men are not superior by reason of the accidents of race or color. They are superior who have the best heart—the best brain. The superior man . . . stands erect by bending above the fallen. He rises by lifting others. —*R. G. Ingersoll.*

MANAGEMENT

In the last analysis management has to manage, if any concern is to be a success financially or in any other way.

—*Philip Murray.*

The philosophy . . . that labor should join with management . . . cannot be accepted. It is contradictory of American traditions and free enterprise. —*William Green.*

Management is the marshaling of manpower, resources and strategy in getting a job done. —*M. E. Dimock.*

Management . . . must be concerned first with the opportunity for a decent living. —*Hugh Comer.*

MANKIND

To live in mankind is far more than to live in a name.

—*Vachel Lindsay.*

The time of isolated states is past and Mankind is already one interacting community. —*P. A. Sorokin.*

Mankind is a tribe of animals, living by habits and thinking in symbols; and it can never be anything else.

—*George Santayana.*

Mankind is being reformed, but conditions among the lower animals are frightful. —*Don Marquis.*

The capacities of mankind can go on developing, improving, perfecting, as long as the cycles of eternity revolve.

—*Horace Mann.*

No man is so great as mankind. —*Theodore Parker.*

Mankind are very odd creatures: one half censure what they practice, the other half practice what they censure. —*B. Franklin.*

The last hopes of mankind . . . rest with us. —*Daniel Webster.*

America has lifted high the light which will shine unto all generations and guide the feet of mankind to the goal of justice and liberty and peace. —*Woodrow Wilson.*

Mankind are earthen jugs with spirits in them.

—*Nathaniel Hawthorne.*

Take mankind in general: they are vicious, their passions may be operated upon. —*Alexander Hamilton.*

There are times when one would like to hang the whole human race, and finish the farce.   —*Mark Twain.*

MANNERS

Manners are an expression of the relation of status—a symbolic pantomime of mastery on the one hand and of subservience on the other.   —*Thorstein Veblen.*

Bad manners simply indicate that you care a good deal more for the food than for the society at the table.   —*Gelett Burgess.*

It is a mistake that there is no bath that will cure people's manners, but drowning would help.   —*Mark Twain.*

Good manners are made up of petty sacrifices.
                                                        —*R. W. Emerson.*

Manners are the happy ways of doing things.   —*Ibid.*

A bad man with good manners often outdoes a good man with bad manners.   —*H. H. Vreeland.*

Savages we call them because their manners differ from ours.
                                                        —*B. Franklin.*

Fine manners need the support of fine manners in others.
                                                        —*R. W. Emerson.*

Manners easily and rapidly mature into morale.
                                                        —*Horace Mann.*

I don't believe in the goodness of disagreeable people.
                                                        —*Orville Dewey.*

The prince of darkness may be a gentleman, as we are told he is, but whatever God of earth and heaven is, he can never be a gentleman.   —*William James.*

MARCH

In the march of life, do not heed the order "right about" when you know you are about right.   —*O. W. Holmes.*

March without the people, and you march into night.
                                                        —*R. W. Emerson.*

MARKET

Opportunity is generated by the enforcement of the free market.
                                                        —*Thomas Hewes.*

MARRIAGE

Marriage is a great institution, and no family should be without it.   —*Channing Pollock.*

In marriage do thou be wise; prefer the Person before Money; Virtue before Beauty; the Mind before the Body. —*Wm. Penn.*

Harmony in the married state is the very first object to be aimed at. —*T. Jefferson.*

The satisfactions of normal married life do not decline but mount. —*Charles W. Eliot.*

I think if people marry it ought to be for life; the laws are altogether too lenient with them. —*F. P. Dunne.*

They stood before the altar and supplied
The fires themselves in which their fat was fried.

—*Ambrose Bierce.*

One has no business to be married unless, waking and sleeping, one is conscious of the responsibility. —*Abraham Flexner.*

Where there's marriage without love, there will be love without marriage. —*B. Franklin.*

If it were not for the Presents, an Elopement would be Preferable. —*George Ade.*

Marriage is that relation between man and woman in which the independence is equal, the dependence mutual, and the obligation reciprocal. —*L. K. Anspacher.*

Marriage: a community consisting of a master, a mistress, and two slaves, making in all, two. —*Ambrose Bierce.*

The days just prior to marriage are like a snappy introduction to a tedious book. —*Wilson Mizner.*

A person's character is but half formed till after wedlock.

—*Charles Simmons.*

Marriages are best made of dissimilar material.

—*Theodore Parker.*

Deferred marriages are temptations to wickedness.

—*H. W. Beecher.*

It isn't tying himself to one woman that a man dreads when he thinks of marrying; it's separating himself from all the others.

—*Helen Rowland.*

Marriage suffers most from our regarding it a failure whenever it falls below a perfect score. —*Channing Pollock.*

Marriage is the greatest educational institution on earth. —*Ibid.*

By the legal fiction of divorce, marriage has become a relation dissoluble at will.   —*Brooks Adams.*

Wedding: the point at which a man stops toasting a woman and begins roasting her.   —*Helen Rowland.*

Marriage is the only known example of the happy meeting of the immovable object and the irresistible force.   —*Ogden Nash.*

There is more of good nature than of good sense at the bottom of most marriages.   —*H. D. Thoreau.*

Love, the quest; marriage, the conquest; divorce, the inquest.
—*Helen Rowland.*

Marriage is neither heaven nor hell; it is simply purgatory.
—*A. Lincoln.*

Before marriage, a man will lie awake all night thinking about something you said; after marriage, he'll fall asleep before you finish saying it.   —*Helen Rowland.*

Marriage: a souvenir of love.   —*Ibid.*

The sanctity of marriage and the family relation make the corner-stone of our American society and civilization.
—*James A. Garfield.*

It's as hard to get a man to stay home after you've married him as it was to get him to go home before you married him.
—*Helen Rowland.*

Never marry but for love; but see that thou lovest what is lovely.
—*Wm. Penn.*

Think of your ancestors and your posterity, and you will never marry.   —*E. W. Mumford.*

Such a large sweet fruit is a comfortable marriage, that it needs a very long summer to ripen in and then a long winter to mellow and sweeten in.   —*Theodore Parker.*

Matrimony is the root of all evil.   —*Addison Mizner.*

When billing and cooing results in matrimony, the billing always comes after the cooing.   —*Tom Masson.*

A chap ought to save a few of the long evenings he spends with his girl till after they're married.   —*Kin Hubbard.*

It takes a man twenty-five years to learn to be married; it's a wonder women have the patience to wait for it.   —*C. B. Kelland.*

Marriage, by making us more contented, causes us often to be less enterprising.   —*C. N. Bovee.*

A fellow never knows what he would have done till he's been married a couple of years. —*Kin Hubbard.*

Don't try to marry an entire family or it may work out that way. —*George Ade.*

Those who marry to escape something usually find something else. —*Ibid.*

> Some pray to marry the man they love,
> My prayer will somewhat vary:
> I humbly pray to Heaven above
> That I love the man I marry.
> —*Rose Pastor Stokes.*

MARTYRS

I cannot now better serve the cause I love so much than to die for it; and in my death I may do more than in my life.
—*John Brown.*

Some that will hold a creed unto martyrdom will not hold the truth against a sneering laugh. —*Austin O'Malley.*

It is more difficult, and calls for higher energies of soul, to live a martyr than to die one. —*Horace Mann.*

There are daily martyrdoms occurring of more or less self-abnegation, and of which the world knows nothing.
—*E. H. Chapin.*

The heralds of freedom . . . are also its martyrs.
—*Vida D. Scudder.*

MARVELOUS

Marvelous is the providence of the law that equalizes all, even in mind and sentiment. —*A. M. Giovannitti.*

MASSACHUSETTS

The love of freedom has always been a dangerous possession in Massachusetts. —*V. L. Parrington.*

Have faith in Massachusetts. —*Calvin Coolidge.*

MASSES

There is a growing unrest among the masses.
—*Henry George.*

The masses . . . do most of the dying for both sides of every conflict. —*Joseph Rosenfarb.*

MASTER

Do not worry over the charge of treason to your masters but be concerned with the treason that involves yourself.—*E. V. Debs.*

From this hour I ordain myself loos'd of limits and imaginary lines. Going where I list, my own master total and absolute.
—*Walt Whitman.*

The measure of a master is his success in bringing all men round to his opinion twenty years later.   —*R. W. Emerson.*

Our employers can no more afford to be absolute masters of their employees than they can afford to submit to the mastery of their employees.   —*Louis D. Brandeis.*

MATERIALISM

Kind words will never die—neither will they buy groceries.
—*E. W. Nye.*

MATHEMATICS

Mathematics deals exclusively with the relations of concepts to each other without consideration of their relation to experience.
—*Albert Einstein.*

MATURITY

Maturity is often more absurd than youth and very frequently is most unjust to youth.   —*Thomas A. Edison.*

MAXIMS

Maxims are like lawyers who must needs see but one side of the case.   —*Gelett Burgess.*

Maxims . . . are little sermons.   —*Ibid.*

Precepts and maxims are of great weight; and a few useful ones at hand, do more forward a wise and happy life, than whole volumes of cautions that we know not where to find.
—*Charles Simmons.*

The value of a maxim depends on its intrinsic excellence and the ease with which it may be applied to practise. —*Charles Hodge.*

Maxims are strongly stamped, medallion-like sayings.
—*R. W. Emerson.*

It is more trouble to make a maxim than it is to do right.
—*Mark Twain.*

It is time that the low maxims of policy, which have ruled for ages, should fall.   —*W. E. Channing.*

No matter how full a reservoir of maxims one may possess . . . if one has not taken advantage of every concrete opportunity to act, one may remain entirely unaffected for the better.

—*William James.*

With mere good intentions, hell is proverbially paved. —*Ibid.*

MEAL

Marriage is a meal where the soup is better than the dessert.

—*Austin O'Malley.*

MEANNESS

When some folks don't know nothing mean about some one, they switch the subject. —*Kin Hubbard.*

A nation cannot afford to do a mean thing.

—*Charles Sumner.*

There is something in meanness which excites a species of resentment that never subsides. —*T. Paine.*

I have a great hope of a wicked man; slender hope of a mean one. —*H. W. Beecher.*

The mean is the divine if we make it so. —*John Burroughs.*

MEANS

There's too many folks of limited means who think that nothing's too good for them. —*Kin Hubbard.*

MEASURE

Whether a man lives or dies in vain can be measured only by the way he faces his own problems, by the success or failure of the inner conflict within his own soul. And of this no one may know save God. —*James Conant.*

MECHANIC

The people have a saying that God Almighty is himself a mechanic. —*B. Franklin.*

MEDICINES

He's the best physician that knows the worthlessness of the most medicines. —*B. Franklin.*

The best of all medicines are rest and fasting. —*Ibid.*

I firmly believe that if the whole materia medica could be sunk to the bottom of the sea, it would be all the better for mankind, and all the worse for the fishes. —*O. W. Holmes.*

The best medicine I know for rheumatism is to thank the Lord
it ain't the gout.   —*Josh Billings.*

MEDIOCRITY

How many minds you must leave as you find—in permanent
mediocrity.   —*John Foster.*

Most people would succeed in small things, if they were not
troubled by great ambitions.   —*H. W. Longfellow.*

MEDITATION

Meditation is the nurse of thought and thought the food for
meditation.   —*Charles Simmons.*

MEEKNESS

Meekness is not a contemplative virtue; it is maintaining peace
and patience in the midst of pelting provocation.
                                                          —*H. W. Beecher.*

Selfish men may possess the earth; it is the meek only who
inherit it from the Heavenly Father, free from all the defilement
and perplexities of unrighteousness.   —*John Woolman.*

It's goin' t' be fun t' watch an' see how long th' meek kin keep
the earth after they inherit it.   —*Kin Hubbard.*

MEETING

The joy of meeting, not unmixed with pain.
                                                    —*H. W. Longfellow.*

Every once in a while you meet a fellow in some honorable
walk of life that was once admitted to the bar.   —*Kin Hubbard.*

Ah me! the world is full of meetings such as this—a thrill, a
voiceless challenge and reply, and sudden parting after!
                                                          —*N. P. Willis.*

MELANCHOLY

Melancholy looks upon a beautiful face and sees but a grin-
ning skull.   —*C. N. Bovee.*

Melancholy attends the best joys of an ideal life.
                                                       —*Margaret Fuller.*

MELIORISM

If the condition of man is to be progressively ameliorated, as we
fondly hope and believe, education is to be the chief instrument in
effecting it.   —*T. Jefferson.*

Life will have little meaning for me except as I am able to contribute toward some ideal of social betterment, if not, in deed, then in word. —*Randolph Bourne.*

MEMBERS

There are ten church members by inheritance for one by conviction. —*Austin O'Malley.*

MEMORY

Grant but memory to us and we can lose nothing by death.
—*J. G. Whittier.*

Memory is not so brilliant as hope but it is more beautiful, and a thousand times more true. —*G. D. Prentice.*

There is a remembrance of the dead, to which we turn even from the charms of the living. —*Washington Irving.*

Memory can glean but never renew. —*H. W. Beecher.*

Nothing now is left but a majestic memory.
—*H. W. Longfellow.*

I would not wish you to possess that kind of memory which retains with accuracy and certainty all names and dates. I never knew it to accompany much invention or fancy. It is almost the exclusive blessing of dullness. —*Aaron Burr.*

MEN

All men in the abstract are just and good. —*R. W. Emerson.*

God give me men! A time like this demands strong minds, great hearts, true faith and ready hands! —*J. G. Holland.*

We must have many Lincoln-hearted men. —*Vachel Lindsay.*

It's the little men, fighting behind, who win wars.
—*Channing Pollock.*

Everybody likes and respects self-made men. It is a great deal better to be made in that way than not to· be made at all.
—*O. W. Holmes.*

Men are like trees, each one must put forth the leaf that is created in him. —*R. W. Emerson.*

We are the hollow men
We are the stuffed men
Leaning together.

—*T. S. Eliot.*

Men are not superior by reason of the accidents of race or color. They are superior who have the best heart—the best brain.
—*R. G. Ingersoll.*

Men are but grown-up boys after all.   —*W. D. Howells.*

Great men stand like solitary towers in the city of God.
—*H. W. Longfellow.*

MERCY

Let us be merciful as well as just.   —*H. W. Longfellow.*

Lenity will operate with greater force, in some instances, than rigor.   —*G. Washington.*

Mercy among the virtues is like the moon among the stars.—It is the light that hovers above the judgment seat.
—*E. H. Chapin.*

Mercy more becomes a magistrate than the vindictive wrath which men call justice.   —*H. W. Longfellow.*

Hate shuts her soul when dove-eyed Mercy pleads.
—*Charles Sprague.*

The sooner we recognize the fact that the mercy of the All-Merciful extends to every creature endowed with life, the better it will be for us as men and Christians.   —*J. G. Whittier.*

Mercy uplifts the soul and purifies the life.   —*A. W. S. Garden.*

It is the madness of folly, to expect mercy from those who have refused to do justice . . .   —*T. Paine.*

MERIT

The best evidence of merit is the cordial recognition of it whenever and wherever it may be found.   —*C. N. Bovee.*

Merit is never so conspicuous as when coupled with an obscure origin, just as the moon never appears so lustrous as when it emerges from a cloud.   —*Ibid.*

MESSIANISM

Nor are we acting for ourselves alone, but for the whole human race.   —*T. Jefferson.*

METHOD

Each mind has its own method.   —*R. W. Emerson.*

Method goes far to prevent trouble in business.   —*Wm. Penn.*

Method facilitates every kind of business, and by making it easy makes it agreeable, and also successful.   —*Charles Simmons.*

Method is the architecture of success.   —*H. W. Shaw.*

The poet's method is that of life itself, which is just awakened by the beauty without to thought and feeling; he expresses the state evoked by that beauty and absorbing it.

—*G. E. Woodberry.*

A new method of thinking has arisen.   —*T. Paine.*

What else, as a social instrument, is the method of science but the art of bringing liberty of conscience, liberty of thought and of expression to power and sufficiency?   —*H. M. Kallen.*

The measure of civilization is the degree in which the method of cooperative intelligence replaces the method of brute conflict.

—*John Dewey.*

MID-AMERICA

The place between mountain and mountain I call Mid-America is my land. Good or bad, it's all I'll ever have.

—*Sherwood Anderson.*

MIDDLE AGE

From middle age on everything of interest is either illegal, immoral or fattening.   —*Alexander Woollcott.*

MIDDLE-CLASS

This is a middle-class country and the middle class will have its will and way.   —*William A. White.*

The disintegration of capitalism is squeezing out the middle-class.   —*Norman Thomas.*

The middle-class . . . is like Boston, "a State of Mind."   —*Ibid.*

MIGHT

Let us have faith that right makes might, and in that faith let us to the end dare to do our duty as we understand it.

—*A. Lincoln.*

The white man as yet is a half-tamed pirate, and avails himself as much as ever of the maxim, might makes right.

—*Margaret Fuller.*

MILITARISM

The spirit of this country is totally adverse to a large military force.   —*T. Jefferson.*

MILK-COW

A new milk-cow is stepmother to every man's baby.

—Josh Billings.

MILLION

In national affairs a million is only a drop in the budget.

—Burton Rascoe.

MIND

A government of equal rights must . . . rest upon mind; not upon wealth, not brute force.   *—George Bancroft.*

God is Mind, and God is infinite; hence all is Mind.

—Mary Baker Eddy.

Every human mind feels pleasure in doing good to another.

—T. Jefferson.

The living world of the mind is as dynamic as the material world (they are one).   *—Waldo Frank.*

Watch the mind as you would eye a mean dog.

—Kenneth Burke.

Mind is acquired through a continuous process of interaction with physical and social affairs.   *—John L. Childs.*

The mind celebrates a little triumph whenever it can formulate a truth.   *—G. Santayana.*

There can never be any idea, thought, or act of the mind, unless the mind first received some idea from sensation.

—Jonathan Edwards.

Mind is the great lever of all things; human thought is the process by which human evils are ultimately answered.

—Daniel Webster.

There is no separate "mind" gifted in and of itself with a faculty of thought.   *—John Dewey.*

Many a man that can't direct you to a corner drugstore will get a respectful hearing when age has further impaired his mind.

—F. P. Dunne.

To pass from a mirror-mind to a mind with windows is an essential element in the development of real personality.

—H. E. Fosdick.

New light is added to the mind in proportion as it uses that which it has.   *—R. W. Emerson.*

God hath created the mind free.   *—T. Jefferson.*

All attempts to influence it (the mind), by temporal punishments or burdens, or by civil incapacitations tend only to beget habits of hypocrisy and meanness. —*Ibid.*

No exertion of the legs can bring two minds much nearer to one another. —*H. D. Thoreau.*

What the country needs is dirtier fingernails and cleaner minds. —*Will Rogers.*

Don't despair of a student if he has one clear idea. —*N. Emmons.*

Few minds wear out; more rust out. —*C. N. Bovee.*

Old minds are like old horses; you must exercise them if you wish to keep them in working order. —*John Adams.*

The mind does not know what diet it can feed on until it has been brought to the starvation point. —*O. W. Holmes.*

Mind is the great leveller of all things. —*Daniel Webster.*

MINORITY

The minority possess their equal rights, which equal law must protect, and to violate would be oppression. —*T. Jefferson.*

Never be afraid of minorities, so that minorities are based on principles. —*H. W. Beecher.*

The thing we have to fear in this country, is the influence of the organized minorities, because somehow or other, the great majority does not seem to organize. —*Alfred E. Smith.*

The totalitarian technique is to separate minorities, not bring them together. —*Norman Cousins.*

Since America is minorities, totalitarianism in this country may in all likelihood represent one of the most disastrous, costly and chaotic episodes ever recorded. —*Ibid.*

There can be no such thing in America as a selective minority persecution. —*Ibid.*

The smallest number, with God and truth on their side, are weightier than thousands. —*Charles Simmons.*

The minority of a country is never known to agree, except in its efforts to reduce and oppress the majority. —*James F. Cooper.*

MIRACLE

A miracle: an event described by those to whom it was told by men who did not see it. —*Elbert Hubbard.*

Marriage is the miracle that transforms a kiss from a pleasure
into a duty, and a life from a luxury into a necessity.
                                                    —*Helen Rowland.*

We must not sit down and look for miracles. Up, and be doing,
and the Lord will be with thee.   —*John Eliot.*

MIRTH

Mirth is God's medicine.   —*H. W. Beecher.*

Mirth is the sweet wine of human life. It should be offered
sparkling with zestful life unto God.   —*Ibid.*

Mirth is a Proteus, changing its shape and manner from most
superfluous gayety to the deepest humor.   —*E. P. Whipple.*

The gift of gayety may itself be the greatest good fortune, and
the most serious step toward maturity.   —*Irwin Edman.*

Mirthfulness is in the mind and you cannot get it out.—It is just
as good in its place as conscience or veneration. —*H. W. Beecher.*

MISANTHROPY

The peculiarity of the New England hermit has not been his
desire to get near to God, but his anxiety to get away from man.
                                                    —*H. W. Mabie.*

The opinions of the misanthropical rest upon the very partial
basis, that they adopt the bad faith of a few as evidence of the
worthlessness of all.   —*C. N. Bovee.*

It seems such a pity that Noah and his party did not miss the
boat.   —*Mark Twain.*

MISCHIEFS

Men wish to be saved from the mischiefs of their virtues, but
not from their vices.   —*R. W. Emerson.*

MISER

Punishment of a miser—to pay the drafts of his heir in his tomb.
                                                    —*Nathaniel Hawthorne.*

The miser, poor fool, not only starves his body, but also his own
soul.   —*Theodore Parker.*

Through life's dark road his sordid way he wends; an incarna-
tion of fat dividends.   —*Charles Sprague.*

MISERY

If misery loves company, misery has company enough.
—*H. D. Thoreau.*

Threescore years and ten is enough; if a man can't suffer all the misery he wants in that time, he must be numb.   —*Josh Billings.*

It is difficult to make a man miserable while he feels he is worthy of himself and claims kindred to the great God who made him.
—*A. Lincoln.*

Half the misery in the world comes of want of courage to speak, and to bear the truth plainly, and in a spirit of love.
—*H. B. Stowe.*

A people driven to desperation by want and misery is a constant threat of disorder and chaos, both internal and external.
—*Cordell Hull.*

MISFORTUNES

Little minds are tamed and subdued by misfortunes; but great minds rise above it.   —*Washington Irving.*

Let us be of good cheer, however, remembering that the misfortunes hardest to bear are those which never come.
—*J. R. Lowell.*

Misfortunes and twins never come singly.   —*Josh Billings.*

Our bravest lessons are not learned through success, but misfortune.   —*A. B. Alcott.*

Some souls are ennobled and elevated by seeming misfortunes, which then become blessings in disguise.   —*E. H. Chapin.*

MISSION

To establish liberty for mankind is the highest mission on earth.
—*John P. Altgeld.*

Here is the mission of the present: We are to reconcile spirit and matter.   —*R. W. Emerson.*

The mission of government, henceforth, in civilized lands, is not repression alone, and not authority alone, not even of law . . . but . . . to train communities through all their grades, beginning with individuals and ending there again, to rule themselves.
—*Walt Whitman.*

MISTAKE

The first mistake in public business is going into it.
—*B. Franklin.*

There is one excuse for every mistake a man can make, but only one.   —*G. H. Lorimer.*

When a fellow makes the same mistake twice he's got to throw up both hands and own up to carelessness or cussedness.   —*Ibid.*

> There is a glory
> In a great mistake.
>   —*Nathalia Crane.*

The individual is always mistaken.   —*R. W. Emerson.*

The greatest mistake you can make in this life is to be continually fearing you will make one.   —*Elbert Hubbard.*

The only man who never makes a mistake is the man who never does anything.   —*Theodore Roosevelt.*

I have made mistakes, but I have never made the mistake of claiming that I never made one.   —*J. G. Bennett.*

MOB

The mob is man voluntarily descending to the nature of the beast.   —*R. W. Emerson.*

A mob (without intoxicating drinks) would be as impossible as combustion without oxygen.   —*Horace Mann.*

There is no grievance that is a fit object of redress by mob rule.
                                          —*A. Lincoln.*

The nose of a mob is its imagination. By this, at any time, it can be quietly led.   —*Edgar Allan Poe.*

Mob law does not become due process of law by securing the assent of a terrorized jury.   —*O. W. Holmes, Jr.*

MODERATION

A thing moderately good is not so good as it ought to be.
                                               —*T. Paine.*

Moderation in temper is always a virtue; but moderation in principle is always a vice.   —*Ibid.*

Human strength lies not in extremes, but in avoiding extremes.
                                          —*R. W. Emerson.*

Avoid extremes; forbear resenting injuries as much as you think they deserve.   —*B. Franklin.*

Tranquil pleasures last the longest.   —*C. N. Bovee.*

Let a man take time enough for the most trivial deed, though it be but the paring of his nails. —*H. D. Thoreau.*

MODERNITY

For modern man to prefer safety to freedom is to betray his modernity. —*H. F. Kallen.*

MODERNS

Each generation produces its squad of "moderns" with pea-shooters to attack Gibraltar. —*Channing Pollock.*

MODESTY

Modesty died when false modesty was born. —*Mark Twain.*

The statue that advertises its modesty with a fig leaf really brings its modesty under suspicion. —*Ibid.*

Modest expression is a beautiful setting to the diamond of talent and genius. —*E. H. Chapin.*

A woman in love is less modest than a man; she has less to be ashamed of. —*H. L. Mencken.*

Modesty is bred of self-reverence. Fine manners are the mantle of fair minds. None are truly great without this ornament.
—*A. B. Alcott.*

MOMENT

Each moment is the fruit of forty thousand years.
—*Thomas Wolfe.*

The last moment belongs to us—that agony is our triumph.
—*Bartolomeo Vanzetti.*

MONARCHY

Our government grows more intolerable every day. I wish it might be changed to a monarchy. —*Nathaniel Hawthorne.*

Monarchy would not have continued so many ages in the world had it not been for the abuses it protects. It is the master fraud, which shelters all others. —*T. Paine.*

MONEY

It is our task to bring together the men, machines and money.
—*F. D. Roosevelt.*

I cannot afford to waste my time making money.
—*L. Agassiz.*

Put not your trust in money, but put your money in trust.
                                                            —*O. W. Holmes.*

If you would know the value of money, go and try to borrow
some.   —*B. Franklin.*

Never ask of money spent where the spender thinks it went.
                                                            —*Robert Frost.*

Desire for money will produce hard-fistedness and not enterprise.   —*A. N. Whitehead.*

Now money's the measure of all.   —*Grant Allen.*

Man is more valuable than money.   —*Wendell Phillips.*

Covetous men need money least, yet most effect it; and prodi-
gals, who need it most, do least regard it.   —*Theodore Parker.*

Money can beget money, and its offspring can beget more, and
so on.   —*B. Franklin.*

When a fellow says it hain't the money but the principle o' the
thing, it's th' money.   —*Kin Hubbard.*

Money never made a fool of anybody; it only shows 'em up.
                                                            —*Ibid.*

Money is like an arm or leg—use it or lose it.   —*Henry Ford.*

Bad money, even in small doses, is poison to the economic sys-
tem.   —*W. Randolph Burgess.*

I am appalled at the magnitude of my bank account.
                                                            —*Alexander Woollcott.*

What this country needs is a good five-cent nickel.
                                                            —*Ed Wynn.*

A man's soul may be buried under a pile of money.
                                                            —*Nathaniel Hawthorne.*

Money represents the price of life.   —*R. W. Emerson.*

The modern capitalist not only thinks in terms of money, but
he thinks in terms of money more exclusively than the French
aristocrat or lawyer ever thought in terms of caste.
                                                            —*Brooks Adams.*

Money is the only substance which can keep a cold world from
nicknaming a citizen "Hey, you!"   —*Wilson Mizner.*

Money is not required to buy one necessity of the soul.
                                                            —*H. D. Thoreau.*

Nobody works as hard for his money as the man who marries it.
—*Kin Hubbard.*

To possess money is very well; to be possessed by it, is to be possessed by a devil.   —*Tryon Edwards.*

The people of the United States are entitled to a sound and stable currency.   —*Grover Cleveland.*

Save whatever is current at the moment, except currency.
—*I. S. Cobb.*

The use of money is all the advantage there is in having it.
—*B. Franklin.*

The darkest hour in any man's life is when he sits down to plan how to get money without earning it.   —*Horace Greeley.*

The plainest print cannot be read through a gold eagle.
—*A. Lincoln.*

Broadway is a place where people spend money they haven't earned to buy things they don't need to impress people they don't like.   —*Walter Winchell.*

Money often costs too much.   —*R. W. Emerson.*

A power has risen up in the government greater than the people themselves, consisting of many and various and powerful interests, combined into one mass, and held together by the cohesive power of the vast surplus in the banks.   —*John C. Calhoun.*

MONKEY

Our Heavenly Father invented man because he was disappointed in the monkey.   —*Mark Twain.*

The monkey is an organized sarcasm upon the human race.
—*H. W. Beecher.*

MONOMANIA

Adhesion to one idea is monomania; to a few, slavery.
—*C. N. Bovee.*

MONOPOLY

The man who argues that there is an economic advantage in private monopoly is aiding socialism.   —*W. J. Bryan.*

Business monopoly in America paralyzes the system of free enterprise on which it is grafted, and it is as fatal to those who manipulate it as the people who suffer its impositions.
—*F. D. Roosevelt.*

Monopoly is as deadly an enemy of free enterprise as managed economy.   *—H. M. Wristen.*

Monopoly power, within the meaning of the antitrust laws, is the ability to impose unreasonable restraints on competition.
—T. C. Clark.

MONROE DOCTRINE

We should consider any attempt on their (European nations) part to extend their system to any portion of this hemisphere, as dangerous to our peace and safety.   *—James Monroe.*

If the American nation will speak softly and yet build and keep a pitch of the highest training a thoroughly efficient navy, the Monroe Doctrine will go far.   *—Theodore Roosevelt.*

MONUMENTS

Peace has its victories no less than war, but it doesn't have as many monuments to unveil.   *—Kin Hubbard.*

Monuments and eulogy belong to the dead.
—Daniel Webster.

Monuments are only valuable for the characters which they perpetuate.   *—James A. Garfield.*

No man who needs a monument ever ought to have one.
—Nathaniel Hawthorne.

MOODS

Women need not look at those dear to them to know their moods.   *—W. D. Howells.*

MOON

If you go expressly to look at the moon, it becomes tinsel.
—R. W. Emerson.

Everyone is a moon, and has a dark side which he never shows to anybody.   *—Mark Twain.*

MORAL

The moral sense is as much a part of man as his leg or his arm.
—T. Jefferson.

Nature hath implanted in our breast a love of others, a sense of duty to them, a moral instinct, in short, which prompts us irresistibly to feel and to succor their distresses.   *—Ibid.*

Cruelty to brute animals is another means of destroying moral sensibility.   *—Benjamin Rush.*

What is moral is what you feel good after and what is immoral is what you feel bad after.   *—Ernest Hemingway.*

Literature, has been, and probably always will be judged by moral standards.   *—T. S. Eliot.*

Man's moral nature is a riddle which only eternity can solve.
—H. D. Thoreau.

The crown of iron, the fire of fire, the ether and source of all elements, is moral force.   *—R. W. Emerson.*

The true grandeur of humanity is in moral elevation, sustained, enlightened and decorated by the intellect of man.
—Charles Sumner.

I believe that the world's moral laws are the outcome of the world's experience. It needed no God to come out of heaven to tell men that murder and theft and the other immoralities were bad both for the individual who commits them, and for society which suffers from them.   *—Mark Twain.*

The moral experience of men has everywhere and in all ages been the same.   *—John Haynes Holmes.*

MORALITY

A passion for the primitive is a sign of archaism in morals.
—George Santayana.

Morals is not a catalogue of acts nor a set of rules to be applied like drugstore prescriptions or cook-book recipes. The need in morals is for specific methods of inquiry and of contrivance.
—John Dewey.

Morality and religion are but words to him who fishes in gutters for the means of sustaining life, and crouches behind barrels in the street for shelter from the cutting blast of a winter night.
—Horace Greeley.

Morality is a private and costly luxury.   *—H. B. Adams.*

I never did, or countenanced, in public life, a single act inconsistent with the strictest good faith; having never believed there was one code of morality for a public, and another for a private man.   *—T. Jefferson.*

Aim above morality. Be not simply good; be good for something.
—H. D. Thoreau.

Conventional morality is a drab morality, in which the only fatal thing is to be conspicuous.   *—John Dewey.*

We Americans cannot conceive of a war without a moral background. . . . Any weak, saddle-colored nation that happens to be situated near us . . . had better look out. We have our moral eye on such people and are likely to introduce American morality at any moment.   —*W. E. Woodward.*

Again and again we let the world down by our moral impotence.   —*Lillian Smith.*

The more knowledge man has the more sensible he will be of the benefits of morality.   —*Cadwallader Colden.*

A man's acts are usually right, but his reasons seldom are.
—*Elbert Hubbard.*

Men imagine that they communicate their virtue and vice only by overt actions, and do not see that virtue or vice emit a breath every moment.   —*R. W. Emerson.*

Where there is no free agency, there can be no morality.
—*William H. Prescott.*

Religion is the root, without which morality would die.
—*C. A. Bartol.*

Morality without religion is only a kind of dead reckoning.
—*H. W. Longfellow.*

Morality is the vestibule of religion.   —*E. H. Chapin.*

Reason and experience both forbid us to expect that national morality can prevail in exclusion of religious principle.
—*G. Washington.*

There can be no high civility without a deep morality.
—*R. W. Emerson.*

Behind the pretensions of conventional morality are entrenched large scale vested interests whose security is maintained by getting the existing code clothed with the sanctity of religion.
—*C. C. Morrison.*

The nation, being in effect a licensed predatory concern, is not bound by the decencies of that code of law and morals that governs private conduct.   —*Thorstein Veblen.*

MORALS
What can laws do without morals?   —*B. Franklin.*

It is not best that we use our morals weekdays; it gets them out of repair for Sundays.   —*Mark Twain.*

Moralizing and morals are two entirely different things and are always found in entirely different people. *—Don Herold.*

The frequent use of capital punishments never mended the morals of a people. *—Benjamin Rush.*

MORE

Whoever seeks more will get less. *—Hans J. Morgenthau.*

MORMONS

Their religion is singular, but their wives are plural.
—Artemus Ward.

MORNING

Remember when old December's darkness is all about you, that the world is really in every minute and point as full of life as in the most joyous morning you ever lived through. *—William James.*

The morning hour has gold in its mouth. *—B. Franklin.*

MORTALITY

Human beings and human institutions are mortal. They grow, expand and die with the regularity of trees and shrubs.
—H. W. Van Loon.

The mortality of mankind is but a part of the process of living—a step on the way to immortality. *—Tryon Edwards.*

Man weeps to think that he will die so soon; woman, that she was born so long ago. *—H. L. Mencken.*

When I think what we can be if we must, I can't believe that the least of us shall finally perish. *—W. D. Howells.*

It's all a world where bugs and emperors
Go singularly back to the same dust,
Each in his time.

—E. A. Robinson.

MOSQUITO

If a mosquito bite thee on one hand, give him the other—palm downward. *—M. W. Little.*

MOTHER

A man never sees all that his mother has been to him, until it is too late to let her know that he sees it. *—W. D. Howells.*

Men are what their mothers made them. *—R. W. Emerson.*

What is home without a mother? *—Alice Hawthorne.*

All that I am or hope to be, I owe to my angel mother.
—*A. Lincoln.*

All that I am my mother made me. —*John Adams.*

The old-time mother who used to wonder where her boy was now has a grandson who wonders where his mother is.
—*Kin Hubbard.*

The mother's heart is the child's schoolroom. —*H. W. Beecher.*

Mothers are, indeed, the affectionate and effective teachers of the human race. —*Daniel Webster.*

They (mothers) work, not upon the canvas that shall perish, nor the marble that shall crumble into dust, but upon mind, upon spirit, which is to last forever, and which is to bear, for good or evil, throughout its duration, the impress of a mother's plastic hand. —*Ibid.*

The hand that rocks the cradle is the hand that rules the world.
—*W. S. Ross.*

MOTHER-IN-LAW

When mother-in-law comes in at the door, love flies out at the window. —*Helen Rowland.*

Don't undertake to live with your mother-in-law, but if worst comes to worst, let your mother-in-law live with you.
—*Josh Billings.*

Be kind to your mother-in-law, and if necessary pay for her board at some good hotel. —*Ibid.*

MOTIVE

God made man to go by motives, and he will not go without them any more than a boat without steam, or a balloon without gas. —*H. W. Beecher.*

Whatever touches the nerves of motive, whatever shifts man's moral position, is mightier than steam, or caloric, or lightning.
—*E. H. Chapin.*

Pure motives do not insure perfect results. —*C. N. Bovee.*

A good intention clothes itself with sudden power.
—*R. W. Emerson.*

When shallow critics denounce the profit motive inherent in our system of private enterprise, they ignore the fact that it is an economic support of every human right we possess and without it, all rights would soon disappear. —*D. D. Eisenhower.*

Never fear to bring the sublimest motive to the smallest duty.
—*Phillips Brooks.*

He that does good for good's sake seeks neither praise nor reward, though sure of both at last. —*Wm. Penn.*

MOULD

Mould conditions aright and men will grow good to fit them.
—*Horace Fletcher.*

MOURNING

Men mourn for what they have lost, women for what they ain't got. —*Josh Billings.*

Sorrows when shared are less burdensome, though joys divided are increased. —*J. G. Holland.*

MOUTH

Mouth: In man the gateway to the soul; in woman, the outlet of the heart. —*Ambrose Bierce.*

If you keep your mouth shut you will never put your foot in it.
—*Austin O'Malley.*

If a woman could talk out of the two sides of her mouth at the same time, a great deal would be said on both sides.
—*G. D. Prentice.*

MOVEMENT

The great thing in this world is not so much where we stand, as in what direction we are moving. —*O. W. Holmes.*

To reach the port of heaven, we must sail sometimes with the wind and sometimes against it,—but we must sail, and not drift, nor lie at anchor. —*Ibid.*

MUCK-RAKING

Men with the muck-rake are often indispensable to the well-being of society, but only if they know when to stop raking the muck. —*Theodore Roosevelt.*

MULE

A mule has neither pride of ancestry nor hope of posterity.
—*R. G. Ingersoll.*

The mule is half horse and half jackass, and then comes to a full stop, nature discovering her mistake. —*Josh Billings.*

MURDER

Every unpunished murder takes away from the security of every man's life.   —*Daniel Webster.*

To murder character is as truly a crime as to murder the body; the tongue of the slanderer is brother to the dagger of the assassin.   —*Tryon Edwards.*

MUSES

To call the Muses to mine aid is the unchristian use and trade.
—*M. W. Wigglesworth.*

MUSIC

Music is another lady that talks charmingly and says nothing.
—*Austin O'Malley.*

Sweet music—sacred tongue of God.   —*C. G. Leland.*

Madame de Stael pronounced architecture to be frozen music; so is statuary crystallized spirituality.   —*A. B. Alcott.*

Classical music is the kind that we keep hoping will turn into a tune.   —*Kin Hubbard.*

There is no day born but comes like a stroke of music into the world and sings itself all the way through.   —*H. W. Beecher.*

Music causes us to think eloquently.   —*R. W. Emerson.*

If a man does not keep pace with his companion, perhaps it is because he hears a different drummer. Let him step to the music he hears, however measured or far away.   —*H. D. Thoreau.*

Good music has the emotion that is appropriate already in it, and it is a sin to drown by gross unmusical bawling and screaming. That is why almost all singers nowadays are so unmusical, so crude and so violent.   —*George Santayana.*

Music is the only language in which you cannot say a mean or sarcastic thing.   —*John Erskine.*

Music is the universal language of mankind.
—*H. W. Longfellow.*

Wagner's music is better than it sounds.   —*E. W. Nye.*

. . . I am saddest when I sing. So are those who hear me. They are sadder even than I am.   —*Artemus Ward.*

Where painting is weakest, namely in the expression of the highest moral and spiritual ideas, there music is sublimely strong.
—*H. B. Stowe.*

MUSICIAN

No musician is any good to me unless he's a good musician. You work with a man because he's a good man—that's all.

—*Benny Goodman.*

MUTTER

A girl's best friend is her mutter. —*Dorothy Parker.*

MUTUALISM

A man might profess to be perfectly independent, and to set at naught the opinions and wishes of others; but he could not get along without soon finding the inconvenience to himself of such a system. And so with nations. —*John Q. Adams.*

MYSELF

I celebrate myself, and sing myself. —*Walt Whitman.*

MYSTERY

There is generally something that requires hiding at the bottom of a mystery. —*Nathaniel Hawthorne.*

The most beautiful thing we can experience is the mysterious. It is the source of all true art and power. —*Albert Einstein.*

He who can no longer pause to wonder and stand rapt in awe, is as good as dead; his eyes are closed. —*Ibid.*

Mystery and innocence are not akin. —*Hosea Ballou.*

MYSTICISM

Mysticism is the very pinnacle of individualism.

—*Bernard Smith.*

Mysticism is sentimentality taken seriously. —*Leo Stein.*

N

NAME

To live in mankind is far more than to live in a name.
—*Vachel Lindsay*.

When a woman says, "I don't wish to mention any names," it ain't necessary. —*Kin Hubbard*.

Some men do as much begrudge others a good name, as they want one themselves: and perhaps that is the reason of it.
—*Wm. Penn*.

Take not God's name in vain; select a time when it will have effect. —*Ambrose Bierce*.

The name of political economy has continually been invoked against every effort of the working classes to increase their wages or decrease their hours of labour. —*Henry George*.

The Pythagoreans were used to change names with each other—fancying that each would share the virtues they admired in the other. —*H. D. Thoreau*.

Men are the constant dupes of names, while their happiness and well-being mainly depend on things. —*James Cooper*.

NARCOTICS

It is not inspiration which we owe to narcotics; it is merely counterfeit excitement and fury. —*R. W. Emerson*.

NATION

The nation blessed with the largest portion of liberty must in proportion to its numbers be the most powerful nation upon earth.
—*John Q. Adams*.

Territory is but the body of a nation. The people who inhabit its hills and valleys are its soul, its spirit, its life.
—*James A. Garfield*.

A nation never falls but by suicide.   —*R. W. Emerson.*

It is a base truth to say that happy is the nation that has no history. Thrice happy is the nation that has a glorious history.
                                              —*Theodore Roosevelt.*

It is by no means necessary that a great nation should always stand at the heroic level. But no nation has the root of greatness in it unless in time of need it can rise to the heroic level.   —*Ibid.*

We are a rebellious nation.   —*Theodore Parker.*

Our nation, the immortal spirit of our domain, lives in us—in our hearts and minds and consciences. There it must find its nutriment or die.   —*Grover Cleveland.*

A live nation can always cut a deep mark and can have the best authority the cheapest . . . namely from its own soul.
                                              —*Walt Whitman.*

I am for the whole people doing just as they please in all matters which concern the whole nation.   —*A. Lincoln.*

In a world which has dreamt of internationalism, we find that we have all unawares been building up the first international nation.   —*Randolph Bourne.*

America has been the intellectual battleground of the nations.
                                              —*Ibid.*

The saying of Shelley, "The mind in creation is a fading coal," seems to be true of nations.   —*G. E. Woodberry.*

A highwayman is as much a robber when he plunders in a gang as when single; and a nation that makes an unjust war is only a *great gang.*   —*B. Franklin.*

A nation's character is the sum of its splendid deeds; they constitute one common patrimony, the nation's inheritance. They awe foreign powers, they arouse and animate our own people.
                                              —*Henry Clay.*

The true grandeur of nations is in those qualities which constitute the true greatness of the individual.   —*Charles Sumner.*

A nation cannot afford to do a mean thing.   —*Ibid.*

I love to think of a glorious nation built upon the will of free men, set apart for the propagation and cultivation of humanity's best ideal of a free government, and made ready for the growth and fruitage of the highest aspirations of patriotism.
                                              —*Grover Cleveland.*

No nation can be destroyed while it possesses a good home life.
—*J. G. Holland.*

Without a humble imitation of the divine Author of our blessed religion we can never hope to be a happy nation.
—*G. Washington.*

A nation may be said to consist of its territory, its people and its laws. The territory is the only part which is of certain durability.
—*A. Lincoln.*

Nations, like individuals, are subjected to punishments and chastisements in this world.   —*Ibid.*

A nation, like a person, has a mind—a mind that must be kept informed and alert, that must know itself, that understands the hopes and the needs of its neighbors—all the other nations that live within the narrowing circle of the world.   —*F. D. Roosevelt.*

NATIONAL

Great literatures, or periods in them, have usually marked the culmination of national power.   —*G. E. Woodberry.*

The love for our native land strengthens our individual and national character.   —*Alexander Hamilton.*

NATIONALISM

Nationalism is an infantile disease. It is the measles of mankind.
—*Albert Einstein.*

Born in iniquity and conceived in sin, the spirit of nationalism has never ceased to bend human institutions to the service of dissension and distress.   —*Thorstein Veblen.*

There is a higher form of patriotism than nationalism, and that higher form is not limited by the boundaries of one's country; but by a duty to mankind to safeguard the trust of civilization.
—*Oscar S. Straus.*

NATURAL

Civilization is artificial, the work of the artificer, the priest, the teacher, the poet, the artist, all of whom are engaged in the endless battle against the natural.   —*Mathurin Dondo.*

The natural alone is permanent.   —*H. W. Longfellow.*

A government of our own is our natural right.   —*T. Paine.*

NATURALIST

There is no avoiding that dilemma; you must be either a naturalist or a supernaturalist. —*T. S. Eliot.*

NATURAL LAW

The philosopher knows that the laws of the Creator have never changed with respect either to the principles of science or the properties of matter. Why, then, is it supposed they have changed with respect to man? —*T. Paine.*

NATURE

A life in harmony with nature, the love of truth and virtue, will purge the eyes to understand her text. —*R. W. Emerson.*

Government is not formed by nature, as other births or productions. —*John Wise.*

I enter a swamp as a sacred place—a sanctum sanctorum. There is the strength, the marrow of Nature. —*H. D. Thoreau.*

Nature is mutable cloud which is always and never the same. —*R. W. Emerson.*

Conventionalities are all very well in their proper place, but they shrivel at the touch of nature like stubble in the fire. —*J. R. Lowell.*

The conquest of nature, not the imitation of nature, is the whole duty of man. —*E. E. Slosson.*

In nature femaleness is fundamental and maleness accidental or variational. —*J. Q. Dealey.*

Nature encourages no looseness, pardons no errors. —*R. W. Emerson.*

Nature has no one distinguishable ultimate tendency with which it is possible to feel a sympathy. —*William James.*

Nature is very rarely right; to such an extent even, that it might also be said that nature is usually wrong. —*J. M. Whistler.*

A world of nature, teeming with abundance, produces for the nasses of mankind the misery of poverty, disease and death. —*John Haynes Holmes.*

To him who in the love of Nature holds
Communion with her visible forms, she speaks
A various language.
—*Wm. Cullen Bryant.*

Nature makes boys and girls lovely to look upon so they can be tolerated until they acquire some sense.   —*W. L. Phelps.*

I love to think of nature as an unlimited broadcasting station, through which God speaks to us every hour, if we will only tune in.   —*George W. Carver.*

Man must go back to Nature for information.   —*T. Paine.*

Moon, planet, gas, crystal are concrete geometry and numbers.
                                                                        —*R. W. Emerson.*

It is not what nature does with a man that matters but what he does with nature.   —*Ray S. Baker.*

We talk of our mastery of nature, which sounds very grand; but the fact is we respectfully adapt ourselves, first, to her ways.
                                                                            —*Clarence Day.*

There are no discontinuities in nature.   —*C. Hartley Grattan.*

Nature and spirit are inseparable, and are best studied as a unit . . . The idealist's point of view is the obverse of the naturalist's.   —*A. B. Alcott.*

As soon as you say Me, a God, or Nature, so soon you jump off your stool and hang from the beam.   —*Herman Melville.*

Nature is man's religious book, with lessons for every day.
                                                                        —*Theodore Parker.*

Nature cannot be surprised in undress. Beauty breaks in everywhere.   —*R. W. Emerson.*

Go forth under the open sky and list to nature's teachings.
                                                                      —*Wm. Cullen Bryant.*

At times there is nothing so unnatural as nature.
                                                                          —*Carolyn Wells.*

Nature and man shall be disjoin'd and diffused no more.
                                                                          —*Walt Whitman.*

Everything in nature tells a different story to all eyes that see and to all ears that hear.   —*R. G. Ingersoll.*

It is a false dichotomy to think of nature and man. Mankind is that factor in nature which exhibits in its most intense form the plasticity of nature.   —*A. N. Whitehead.*

Nature knows nothing of rights. She knows only laws. Man, on the other hand, has ideals and aspirations.
                                                                  —*James Truslow Adams.*

NATURE (Human)

There's a good deal of human nature in man.

—*Artemus Ward.*

The badness of good people . . . is the revenge taken by human nature for the injuries heaped upon it in the name of morality.

—*John Dewey.*

The moral nature of woman, as maintained in this rudimentary stage by her economic dependence, is a continual check to the progress of the human soul.   —*Charlotte P. Gilman.*

Human nature is the same everywhere.   —*John Brown.*

Moral principles that exalt themselves by degrading human nature are in effect committing suicide.   —*John Dewey.*

The elements of human nature are indeed so fixed that favorable or unfavorable circumstances have little effect upon its essential constitution, but prosperity or the reverse brings different traits into prominence.   —*C. E. Norton.*

The inquiry of truth, which is the lovemaking of it; the knowledge of truth, which is the presence of it, and the belief of truth, which is the enjoying of it, is the sovereign good of human nature.

—*J. G. Whittier.*

It is as easy to change human nature as to oppose the strong current of selfish passions.   —*Alexander Hamilton.*

It seems to be inherent in human nature to want a deity to worship and a devil to abhor. Machinery has become the devil of a widespread cult.   —*John Dewey.*

Science and Christianity are at one in abhorring the natural man and calling upon the civilized man to fight and subdue him.

—*E. E. Slosson.*

The best way to study human nature is when nobody else is present.   —*Tom Masson.*

Human nature loses its most precious quality when it is robbed of the sense of things beyond, unexplored and yet insistent.

—*A. N. Whitehead.*

No law can be sacred to me but that of my nature.

—*R. W. Emerson.*

Fascism failed as a practical philosophy because it did not understand the nature of man, who is not only the object of political manipulation but also a moral person, endowed with resources which do not yield to manipulation.   —*Hans J. Morgenthau.*

Knowledge of human nature is the beginning and end of political education.   —*Henry Adams.*

We school ourselves to despise human nature. But God did not make us despicable.   —*W. D. Howells.*

Human nature has a much greater genius for sameness than for originality.   —*J. R. Lowell.*

A true man never frets about his place in the world, but just slides into it by the gravitation of his nature, and swings there as easily as a star.   —*E. H. Chapin.*

There is something in human nature which makes an individual recognize and reward merit, no matter under what color of skin merit is found.   —*Booker T. Washington.*

Nature will not change. In any future great national trial, compared with the men of this, we shall have as weak and as strong, as silly and as wise, as bad and as good.   —*A. Lincoln.*

While a fox is a fox and a wolf is a wolf and a bear is a bear, man can be a lamb today and a wolf tomorrow, play dove in the morning and hawk in the evening, talk like a parrot or be mute as a fish.   —*Dagobert D. Runes.*

NAZISM
Nazism was above all a mighty and magnificently organized assault upon human freedom and democracy. —*Stephen S. Wise.*

NEATNESS
As a general thing, an individual who is neat in his person is neat in his morals.   —*H. S. Shaw.*

NECESSITY
Necessity has no law.   —*B. Franklin.*

Necessity can sharpen the wits even of children.
                                                    —*Timothy Dwight.*

Our necessities are few but our wants are endless.
                                                       —*H. W. Shaw.*

A man's power is hooped in by necessity, which, by many experiments, he touches on every side, until he learn its arc.
                                                      —*R. W. Emerson.*

Necessity is our lot in nature; the world of art is the place of the spirit's freedom. —*G. E. Woodberry.*

A people never fairly begins to prosper till necessity is treading on its heels. —*W. G. Simms.*

Necessity never made a good bargain. —*B. Franklin.*

"Necessity is the mother of invention," is a silly proverb. "Necessity is the mother of futile dodges" is much nearer the truth.
—*A. N. Whitehead.*

The sin and sorrow and suffering of the world are a necessary part of the natural course of things. —*John Borroughs.*

Without death and decay, how could life go on? —*Ibid.*

Make yourself necessary to somebody. —*R. W. Emerson.*

The argument of necessity is not only the tyrant's plea, but the patriot's defense, and the safety of the state. —*James Wilson.*

NECKLACE
Many a necklace becomes a noose. —*Paul Eldridge.*

NEED
In too many countries—including our own—too many people are too willing to put party loyalty and personal privilege above the needs of their nation. —*Paul Hoffman.*

Our greatest need is to regain confidence in our spiritual heritage. —*John Foster Dulles.*

The only way to discover a need is in terms of a pattern or scheme of values or an inclusive philosophy of some kind.
—*Boyd H. Bode.*

What we need is fewer stump-speakers and more stump-pullers —less talk and more work—fewer ginmills and more gins—fewer men at the front and more men at the hoe.
—*Henry W. Grady.*

The government is not an almoner of gifts among the people, but an instrumentality by which the people's affairs should be conducted upon business principles, regulated by the public need.
—*Grover Cleveland.*

A man of courage never needs weapons, but he may need bail.
—*E. W. Mumford.*

It has been pointed out by historical materialists, that crusades succeed only when they fill economic needs; but it could as well be said that crusades succeed only when they fill moral needs. The two motives are inseparable, and the presence of the one does not discredit the other.   —*Arthur M. Schlesinger, Jr.*

NEGATIVE

A cold is both positive and negative; sometimes the Eyes have it and sometimes the Nose.   —*W. L. Phelps.*

Reform is affirmative, conservatism negative; conservatism goes for comfort, reform for truth.   —*R. W. Emerson.*

NEGLECT

A little neglect may breed great mischief.   —*B. Franklin.*

NEGRO

The blackamoor's darkness differs not in the dark from the fairest white.   —*Roger Williams.*

If the Negro is a man . . . there can be no moral right in connection with one man's making a slave of another.

—*A. Lincoln.*

In our greedy haste to make profit of the Negro, let us beware lest we "cancel and tear in pieces" even the white man's charter of freedom.   —*Ibid.*

Beautiful also are the souls of my people.   —*Langston Hughes.*

The Negroes are a suffering people, and we as a civil society are they by whom they have suffered.   —*John Woolman.*

A heavy account lies against us as a civil society for oppressions committed against people who did not injure us.   —*Ibid.*

The Negro is an exotic of the most gorgeous and superb countries of the world, and he has deep in his heart a passion for all that is splendid, rich and fanciful.   —*H. B. Stowe.*

I have supposed the black man, in his present state, might not be in body and mind equal to the white man; but it would be hazardous to affirm that, equally cultivated for a few generations, he would not become so.   —*T. Jefferson.*

If he knows enough to be hanged, he knows enough to vote.
—*Frederick Douglass.*

All I ask for the Negro is that if you do not like him, let him alone. If God gave him but little, that little let him enjoy.
—*A. Lincoln.*

I protest against the counterfeit logic which concludes that, because I do not want a black woman for a slave I must necessarily want her for a wife. I need not have her for either. I can just leave her alone. In some respects she certainly is not my equal; but in her natural right to eat the bread she earns with her own hands without asking leave of any one else, she is my equal, and the equal of all others. —*A. Lincoln.*

NEIGHBORS

Love your neighbor, yet don't pull down your hedge.
—*B. Franklin.*

The love of humanity as such is mitigated by violent dislike of the next-door neighbor. —*A. N. Whitehead.*

Some men are like a clock on a roof; they are useful only to the neighbors. —*Austin O'Malley.*

Every man takes care that his neighbor shall not cheat him. But a day comes when he begins to care that he does not cheat his neighbor. —*R. W. Emerson.*

Good fences make good neighbors. —*Robert Frost.*

The best part of a real estate bargain is the neighbor.
—*Austin O'Malley.*

A good neighbor is a fellow who smiles at you over the back fence but doesn't climb over it. —*Arthur ("Bugs") Baer.*

Let the heathen go to hell; help your neighbor. —*E. W. Howe.*

In the field of world policy I would dedicate this nation to the policy of the good neighbor. —*F. D. Roosevelt.*

No one can love his neighbor on an empty stomach.
—*Woodrow Wilson.*

NEST

God gives every bird its food, but He does not throw it into the nest. —*J. G. Holland.*

NET

Marriage: a woman's hair net tangled in a man's spectacles on top of the bedroom dresser. —*Don Herold.*

The biggest word in the language of business is not gross, but net. —*Herbert Casson.*

NEUROTIC

Contemporary civilization is neurotic through and through and

compels woman to occupy the position of instability she now peril-
ously holds amid the welter of modernity.

—Samuel Schmalhausen.

NEUTRALITY

A wise neuter joins with neither, but uses both, as his honest
interest leads him.   *—Wm. Penn.*

People who demand neutrality in any situation are usually not
neutral but in favor of the status quo.   *—Max Eastman.*

Great art *can* be neutral. Great dramas can be written, and have
been, by dramatists seeing a conflict as equal-sided and eternally
unresolved.   *—Ibid.*

In this world today there is no such thing as neutrality. You
are either for Hitler or against him. You either fight him or you
help him.   *—Alexander Woollcott.*

NEW

As our case is new, so we must think anew and act anew.

—A. Lincoln.

Every new discovery must necessarily raise in us a fresh sense
of the greatness, wisdom, and power of God.

—Jonathan Edwards.

What is valuable is not new, and what is new is not valuable.

—Daniel Webster.

No truth so sublime but it may seem trivial tomorrow in the
light of new thought.   *—R. W. Emerson.*

He is an American who, leaving behind him all his ancient prejudices and manners, receives the new government he obeys, and
the new rank he holds.   *—Hector St. Jean de Crèvecoeur.*

Every newly discovered truth judges the world, separates the
good from the evil, and calls on faithful souls to make sure of
their election.   *— Julia W. Howe.*

Truth always has a bewitching flavor of newness in it.

—J. R. Lowell.

The Old World has had the poems of myths, fictions, feudalism,
conquest, caste, dynastic wars, and splendid exceptional characters
and affairs, which have been great; but the New World needs the
poems of realities and science and of the democratic average,
which shall be greater.   *—Walt Whitman.*

The wonder is always new that any sane man can be a sailor.
—*R. W. Emerson.*

NEW ENGLAND

The New Englanders are a people of God, settled in those which were once the Devil's territories.   —*Cotton Mather.*

When England grew corrupt, God brought over a number of pious persons, and planted them in New England, and this land was planted with a noble vine.   —*Jonathan Edwards.*

But how is the gold become dim. How greatly have we forsaken the pious example of our fathers!   —*Ibid.*

The sway of the clergy in New England is indeed formidable. No mind beyond mediocrity dares there to develop itself.
—*T. Jefferson.*

NEWS

What's ancient history to you may be news to me.
—*Channing Pollock.*

If a man bites a dog, that is news.   —*John Bogart.*

NEWSPAPERS

The man who reads nothing at all is better educated than the man who reads nothing but newspapers.   —*T. Jefferson.*

People read the tabloid papers because they think that these papers deal with "real life."   —*E. D. Martin.*

Do not read newspapers column by column; remember they are made for everybody, and don't try to get what isn't meant for you.   —*R. W. Emerson.*

The most truthful part of a newspaper is the advertisements.
—*T. Jefferson.*

A newspaper is a circulating library with high blood pressure.
—*Arthur ("Bugs") Baer.*

The morning paper is just as necessary for an American as dew is to the grass.   —*Josh Billings.*

The world before and after the Deluge were not more different than our republics of letters after the late (Civil) War. For ten years the new generation read nothing but newspapers.
—*E. C. Stedman.*

Take away the newspaper and this country of ours would become a scene of chaos.   —*Harry Chandler.*

The daily newspaper sustains the same relation to the young writer as the hospital to the medical student.

—*G. H. Lorimer.*

We live under a government of men and morning newspapers.

—*Wendell Phillips.*

To the press alone, chequered as it is with abuses, the world is indebted for all the triumphs which have been gained by reason and humanity over error and oppression.   —*James Madison.*

If words were invented to conceal thought, newspapers are a great improvement on a bad invention.   —*H. D. Thoreau.*

Blessed are they who never read a newspaper, for they shall see Nature, and through her God.   —*Ibid.*

In the long, fierce struggle for freedom of opinion, the press, like the Church, counted the martyrs by thousands.

—*James A. Garfield.*

Were it left to me to decide whether we should have a government without newspapers or newspapers without government, I should not hesitate a moment to prefer the latter.   —*T. Jefferson.*

Let me make the newspapers, and I care not what is preached in the pulpit or what is enacted in Congress.   —*Wendell Phillips.*

All I know is what I see in the papers.   —*Will Rogers.*

The careful reader of a few good newspapers can learn more in a year than most scholars do in their great libraries.

—*F. B. Sanborn.*

NEW YORK

There is nothing distinctive about living in New York; over eight million other people are doing it.   —*Don Herold.*

NEW YORKERS

New Yorkers are nice about giving you street directions; in fact, they seem quite proud of knowing where they are themselves.

—*Katharine Brush.*

NIAGARA

War and Niagara thunder to a music of their own.

—*Wendell Phillips.*

NICE

Be nice to people on your way up because you'll meet them on your way down.   —*Wilson Mizner.*

Most nice things are silly.   —*W. D. Howells.*

NICKEL

What this country needs is a good five cent nickel.

—*F. P. Adams (also attributed to Ed Wynn).*

NIGHT

The nearer the dawn the darker the night.

—*H. W. Longfellow.*

NIGHTSTICK

There is more law at the end of a policeman's nightstick than in a decision of the Supreme Court.   —*"Clubber" Williams.*

NIHILISM

Nihilism is the righteous and honorable resistance of a people crushed under an iron rule.   —*Wendell Phillips.*

NINETEEN

Nobody is as sophisticated as a boy of nineteen who is just recovering from a baby-grand passion.   —*Helen Rowland.*

NOBILITY

There is in every man something greater than he had begun to dream of. Men are nobler than they think themselves.

—*Phillips Brooks.*

Be noble in every thought and in every deed.

—*H. W. Longfellow.*

Noble souls, through dust and heat, rise from disaster and defeat.

—*Ibid.*

God has put something noble and good into every heart which His hand created.   —*Mark Twain.*

It is better to inspire the heart with a noble sentiment than to teach the mind a truth of science.   —*Phillips Brooks.*

> Be noble! And the nobleness that lies
> In other men, sleeping, but never dead,
> Will rise in majesty to meet thine own.
>
> —*J. R. Lowell.*

To be good is noble, but to teach others how to be good is nobler—and less trouble.   —*Mark Twain.*

Nature's noblemen are everywhere, in town and out of town, gloved and rough-handed, rich and poor.   —*N. P. Willis.*

Nature makes all the nobleman; wealth, education, or pedigree never made one yet.   —*H. W. Shaw.*

Noble by birth, yet nobler by great deeds.

—*H. W. Longfellow.*

We read noble stories merely to escape from our own ignoble lives.   —*Elizabeth Jackson.*

When a noble deed is done, who is likely to appreciate it? They who are noble themselves.   —*H. D. Thoreau.*

Earth's noblest thing—a woman perfected.   —*J. R. Lowell.*

It was not nobility that gave land, but the possession of land that gave nobility.   —*Henry George.*

NOISE

Noise proves nothing; often a hen who has merely laid an egg cackles as if she had laid an asteroid.   —*Mark Twain.*

Many an irksome noise, go a long way off, is heard as music.
—*H. D. Thoreau.*

He who sleeps in continual noise is wakened by silence.
—*W. D. Howells.*

Noise is a stench in the ear.   —*Ambrose Bierce.*

NON-CHRISTIANS

The deadliest thing that ever can happen to Christianity is that non-Christians should beat Christians at what the Master intended to be their own game, pouring mankind from vessel to vessel.

—*H. E. Fosdick.*

NONCONFORMIST

Whoso would be a man must be a nonconformist.

—*R. W. Emerson.*

NONSENSE

Nonsense is to sense, as shade to light; it heightens effect.
—*Frederick Saunders.*

I express many absurd opinions, but I am not the first man to do it; American freedom consists largely in talking nonsense.
—*E. W. Howe.*

The learned fool writes his nonsense in better language than the unlearned, but still 'tis nonsense.   —*B. Franklin.*

NORMALCY

We must stabilize and strive for normalcy.   —*W. G. Harding.*

NORMALITY

Gladness is to the soul what health is to the body, what sanity is to the mind, the test of normality.   —*Bliss Carman.*

NORMS

All norms are broken. Mental, moral, aesthetic, and social anarchy reigns supreme.   —*P. S. Sorokin.*

Society is the norm for mental health. Only a sane society can create sane individuals, dedicated to the life of Reason.

—*D. G. Kin.*

NOSES

When you're down and out, something always turns up—and it's usually the noses of your friends.   —*Orson Welles.*

NOTHING

Absolute nothing is the aggregate of all the contradictions in the world.   —*Jonathan Edwards.*

Half a loaf is better than none.   —*Helen Rowland.*

Blessed are they who have nothing to say, and who cannot be persuaded to say it.   —*J. R. Lowell.*

NOTION

There are many humorous things in the world: among them the white man's notion that he is less savage than the other savages.
—*Mark Twain.*

The notion of civil liberty is that each man is guaranteed the use of all his own powers exclusively, for his own welfare.

—*W. G. Sumner.*

NOVEL

It is dangerous to write a novel. Parts of the personality resist expression, sometimes with powerful weapons of defense.

—*Bernard De Voto.*

Legitimately produced and truly inspired, fiction interprets humanity; informs the understanding and quickens the affections.
—*H. T. Tuckerman.*

The novel obeys pretty well the laws of its era, and in many ways, especially in the variety of its development, represents the time.   —*C. D. Warner.*

NOVELIST

A novelist has made a fictional representation of life. In doing so he has revealed to us more significance, it may be, than we could find in life by ourselves.   —*Bernard De Voto.*

The function of the novelist of this present day is to comment upon life as he sees it.   —*Frank Norris.*

NUMBER

It is always in the power of a small number to make a great clamor.   —*B. Franklin.*

Never one thing and seldom one person can make for a success. It takes a number of them merging into one perfect whole.
—*Marie Dressler.*

O

OATH

Oaths are the fossils of piety.   *—George Santayana.*

You can have no oath registered in heaven to destroy the government; while I shall have the most solemn one to "preserve, protect and defend it."   *—A. Lincoln.*

They also swear who only stand and wait.

—Addison Mizner.

OBEDIENCE

Justice is the insurance which we have on our lives and property . . . Obedience is the premium which we pay for it.

—Wm. Penn.

Obedience alone gives the right to command.   *—R. W. Emerson.*

Let thy child's first lesson be obedience, and the second will be what thou wilt.   *—B. Franklin.*

There are two kinds of men who never amount to much: those who cannot do what they are told, and those who can do nothing else.   *—C. H. K. Curtis.*

God, eternally real, estimates the nations of the earth by one standard: obedience or non-obedience to the moral law.

—B. I. Bell.

True obedience is true liberty.   *—H. W. Beecher.*

Everywhere the flower of obedience is intelligence. Obey a man with cordial loyalty and you will understand him.

—Phillips Brooks.

Obedience to God is the most infallible evidence of sincere and supreme love of him.   *—N. Emmons.*

Obedience to the will of Man is the most infallible evidence of supreme love of God.   *—D. G. Kin.*

The very idea of power of the people to establish a government presupposes the duty of every individual to obey the established government.   —*G. Washington.*

OBJECT

While I have always recognized that the object of business is to make money in an honorable manner, I have endeavored to remember that the object of life is to do good.   —*Peter Cooper.*

The legitimate object of government is to do for a community of people whatever they need to have done, but cannot do at all, in their separate and individual capacities.   —*A. Lincoln.*

The care of human life and happiness, and not their destruction, is the first and only legitimate object of good government.
—*T. Jefferson.*

The great object of the institution of civil government is the improvement of the condition of those who are parties to the social compact.   —*John Q. Adams.*

Let our object be our country, our whole country, and nothing but our country.   —*Daniel Webster.*

The great objects of the framers of the Constitution should be kept steadily in view in the interpretation of any clause of it; and when it is susceptible of various interpretations that construction should be preferred which tends to promote the objects of the framers of the Constitution, to the consolidation of the Union.
—*Henry Clay.*

OBLIGATION

When some men discharge an obligation you can hear the report for miles around.   —*Mark Twain.*

I always considered my first obligation to be to my patients, and therefore made every other duty to Society yield to them.
—*Benjamin Rush.*

Most men remember obligations, but not often to be grateful for them.   —*W. G. Simms.*

The bond of obligation is transmuted into liberty.
—*W. R. Alger.*

OBLIVION

Fame is a vapor; popularity an accident; riches take wings; the only certainty is oblivion.   —*Horace Greeley.*

The oblivions of time will be the reminiscences of eternity.
—*Charles Simmons.*

OBSCURITY

He is the happiest of whom the world says the least, good or bad. —*T. Jefferson.*

OBSERVATION

The great sources of wisdom are experience and observation, and these are denied to none. —*W. E. Channing.*

Only so much do I know as I have lived. —*R. W. Emerson.*

Observation—activity of both eyes and ears. —*Horace Mann.*

OBSTACLES

No business or study which does not present obstacles, tasking to the full the intellect and the will, is worthy of a man.
—*W. E. Channing.*

Some minds seem almost to create themselves, springing up under every disadvantage, and working their solitary but irresistible way through a thousand obstacles. —*Washington Irving.*

OBSTINACY

The difference between perseverance and obstinacy is that one often comes from a strong will, and the other from a strong won't.
—*H. W. Beecher.*

Firmness in adherence to truth and duty is sometimes mistaken for obstinacy by those who do not comprehend its nature and motive. —*Tryon Edwards.*

OBVIOUS

It requires a very unusual mind to understand the analysis of the obvious. —*A. N. Whitehead.*

The obvious is that which is never seen until someone expresses it simply. —*Kahlil Gibran.*

OCCUPATION

Nature fits all her children with something to do.
—*J. R. Lowell.*

The crowning fortune of a man is to be born to some pursuit which finds him employment and happiness, whether it be to make baskets, or broadswords, or canals, or statues, or songs.
—*R. W. Emerson.*

No amount of preaching, exhortation, sympathy, benevolence, will render the condition of our working women what it should be, so long as the kitchen and needle are substantially their only resources.   —*Horace Greeley.*

ODOR

Perfume: any smell that is used to drown a worse one.
                                                            —*Elbert Hubbard.*

OFFENSE

To apologize is to lay the foundation for a future offense.
                                                            —*Ambrose Bierce.*

No human being, man or woman, can act up to a sublime standard without giving offense.   —*W. E. Channing.*

OFFICE

The very essence of a free government consists in considering offices as public trusts, bestowed for the good of the country, and not for the benefit of an individual or a party.
                                                            —*John C. Calhoun.*

If a due participation of office is a matter of right, how are vacancies to be obtained? Those by death are few; by resignation, none.   —*T. Jefferson.*

This struggle and scramble for office, for a way to live without work, will finally test the strength of our institutions.
                                                            —*A. Lincoln.*

Public office is the last refuge of the incompetent.
                                                            —*Boise Penrose.*

A public office is a public trust.   —*Grover Cleveland.*

Every man who takes office in Washington either grows or swells.   —*Woodrow Wilson.*

I shall never ask, never refuse, nor ever resign an office.
                                                            —*T. Jefferson.*

The post office, with its educating energy, . . . is a first measure of civilization.   —*R. W. Emerson.*

OFFICERS

Every lawful magistrate, whether succeeding or elective, is not only the minister of God, but the minister or servant of the people also.   —*Roger Williams.*

Public officers are the trustees of the people.

—*Grover Cleveland.*

Bad officials are elected by good citizens who do not vote.

—*George Jean Nathan.*

Five things are requisite to a good officer—ability, clean hands, despatch, patience, and impartiality. —*Wm. Penn.*

Government is a trust and the officers of the government are trustees; and both the trust and the trustees are created for the benefit of the people. —*Henry Clay.*

OLD

Nowadays most women grow old gracefully; most men, dis-gracefully. —*Helen Rowland.*

Let us not be too particular; it is better to have old secondhand diamonds than none at all. —*Mark Twain.*

We are idolators of the old. —*R. W. Emerson.*

Being an old maid is like death by drowning, a really delightful sensation after you cease to struggle. —*Edna Ferber.*

An old maid has one consolation: she can never be a widow no matter who dies. —*C. B. Loomis.*

All would live long, but none would be old. —*B. Franklin.*

Some men are born old, and some never seem so.

—*Tryon Edwards.*

Youthful follies growing on old age, are like the few young shoots on the bare top of an old stump of an oak. —*John Foster.*

Old age is wise for itself but not for the community.

—*Wm. Cullen Bryant.*

So long as you are learning, you are not growing old. It's when a man stops learning that he begins to grow old.

—*Joseph Hergesheimer.*

ONE

People will buy anything that's one to a customer.

—*Sinclair Lewis.*

One good thing about having one suit of clothes—you've always got your pencil. —*Kin Hubbard.*

Marry one woman and you get six. —*Don Herold.*

ONIONS

Life is like an onion: you peel off layer after layer and then you find there is nothing in it.   —*J. G. Huneker.*

Onions can make even heirs and widows weep.   —*B. Franklin.*

When a couple of young people strongly devoted to each other commence to eat onions, it is safe to pronounce them engaged.
—*J. M. Bailey.*

OPERA

I would rather sing grand opera than listen to it.
—*Don Herold.*

Opera in English is, in the main, just about as sensible as base-ball in Italian.   —*H. L. Mencken.*

OPINION

In proportion as the structure of a government gives force to public opinion, it is essential that public opinion should be enlightened.   —*G. Washington.*

We live in an age when there has been established among the nations a more elevated tribunal than ever before existed on earth; I mean the tribunal of the enlightened public opinion of the world.
—*Daniel Webster.*

We must make our own public opinion, to buoy us up in every loftier aspiration.   —*Felix Adler.*

All free governments, whatever their name, are in reality governments by public opinion, and it is on the quality of this public opinion that their prosperity depends.   —*J. R. Lowell.*

The pressure of the public opinion is like the pressure of the atmosphere; you can't see it—but, all the same, it is sixteen pounds to the square inch.   —*Ibid.*

Empty wine bottles have a bad opinion of women.
—*Ambrose Bierce.*

People seem not to realize that their opinion of the world is also a confession of character.   —*R. W. Emerson.*

Every man has a perfect right to his opinion, provided it agrees with ours.   —*Josh Billings.*

The only sin which we never forgive in each other is difference of opinion.   —*R. W. Emerson.*

It is the difference of opinion that makes horse races.
—*Mark Twain.*

To be positive: to be mistaken at the top of one's voice.
—*Ambrose Bierce.*

The foolish and the dead alone never change their opinion.
—*J. R. Lowell.*

Private opinion is weak, but public opinion is almost omnipotent.
—*H. W. Beecher.*

It is rare that the public sentiment decides immorally or unwisely, and the individual who differs from it ought to distrust and examine his own opinion.   —*T. Jefferson.*

Public opinion, though often formed upon a wrong basis, yet generally has a strong underlying sense of justice.   —*A. Lincoln.*

In the modern world the intelligence of public opinion is the indispensable condition of social progress.   —*Charles W. Eliot.*

What plays the mischief with the truth is that men will insist upon the universal application of a temporary feeling or opinion.
—*Herman Melville.*

There is no generation of mankind whose opinions are not subject to be influenced by what appears to them to be their present emergent and exigent interests.   —*Daniel Webster.*

We should be eternally vigilant against any attempts to check the expression of opinions which we loathe and believe to be fraught with death.   —*O. W. Holmes, Jr.*

The legislature may forbid or restrict any business when it has a sufficient force of public opinion behind it.   —*Ibid.*

In any age of authority and spiritual bondage, the opinions of an individual are often important,—sometimes decisive.
—*W. E. Channing.*

Law is nothing unless close behind it stands a warm, living public opinion.   —*Wendell Phillips.*

You can afford to have a decent regard for public opinion: but you can never afford to let yourself get into the pathetic condition where what they say or may say will keep you from doing what ought to be done.   —*Bruce Barton.*

I do not regret having braved public opinion when I knew it was wrong and was sure it would be merciless. —*Horace Greeley.*

Public opinion is a weak tyrant, compared with our private opinion.—What a man thinks of himself, that it is which determines, or rather indicates his fate.   —*H. D. Thoreau.*

No man can have a reasonable opinion of women until he has long lost interest in hair restorers.   —*Austin O'Malley.*

I will alter what I believe today, if it should contradict all I said yesterday.   —*Wendell Phillips.*

He who is master of all opinions can never be the bigot of any.   —*W. R. Alger.*

Real political issues cannot be manufactured by the leaders of political parties. The real political issues of the day declare themselves, and come out of the depths of that deep which we call public opinion.   —*James A. Garfield.*

In Boston they say, How much does he know? In New York, How much is he worth? in Philadelphia, Who were his parents?   —*Mark Twain.*

There is, and always has been, one tremendous ruler of the human race—and that ruler is that combination of the opinions of all, the levelling up of universal sense which is called public sentiment. That is the ever-present regulator and police of humanity.   —*Thomas B. Reed.*

OPPORTUNITY

Opportunity: a favorable occasion for grasping a disappointment.   —*Ambrose Bierce.*

Seek the first possible opportunity to act on every good resolution you make.   —*William James.*

Opportunities should never be lost, because they can hardly be regained.   —*Wm. Penn.*

Equality of opportunity as we have known it no longer exists.   —*F. D. Roosevelt.*

Just as freedom to farm has ceased, so also the opportunity in business has narrowed. It still is true that man can start small enterprises, trusting to native shrewdness and ability to keep abreast of competitors, but area after area has been preempted altogether by the great corporations.   —*Ibid.*

I believe that every right implies a responsibility; every opportunity, an obligation; every possession, a duty.   —*John D. Rockefeller, Jr.*

The world does not owe men a living, but business, if it is to fulfill its ideal, owes men an opportunity to earn a living.   —*Owen D. Young.*

Applied to world affairs, democracy means that the aggregate of mankind shall be so organized as to create for each man the maximum opportunity of growth in accordance with the dictates of his own genius and aspiration. —*R. B. Perry.*

You cannot make your opportunities concur with the opportunities of people whose incomes are ten times greater than yours.
—*Edward S. Martin.*

A great many men, if put in the right position, would be Luthers and Columbuses. —*E. H. Chapin.*

There can be no equality of opportunity, the first essential of justice in the body politic, if men and women and children be not shielded in their lives, their very vitality, from the consequences of great industrial and social processes which they cannot alter, control, or singly cope with. —*Woodrow Wilson.*

The very essence of equality of opportunity and of American individualism . . . demands economic justice as well as political and social justice. It is no system of laissez faire. —*Herbert Hoover.*

Plough deep while sluggards sleep. —*B. Franklin.*

Some of us miss opportunity because we are too dull to try. Others let opportunity go by, too much startled when they see it to take hold of it. —*Arthur Brisbane.*

The commonest form, one most often neglected, and the safest opportunity for the average man to seize, is hard work. —*Ibid.*

The lure of the distant and the difficult is deceptive. The great opportunity is where you are. —*John Borroughs.*

Let not the opportunity that is so fleeting, yet so full, pass neglected away. —*O. L. Frothingham.*

Man's importunity is woman's opportunity. —*Carolyn Wells.*

Great opportunities come to all, but many do not know they have met them. —*W. E. Dunning.*

The best men are not those who have waited for chances but who have taken them; besieged the chance; conquered the chance; and made chance the servitor. —*E. H. Chapin.*

Occasions are rare; and those who know how to seize upon them are rarer. —*H. W. Shaw.*

OPPOSITION

Democracy cannot exist without conflict, and it becomes mean-

ingless when one party can suppress all opposition.
                                    —*Arthur M. Schlesinger, Jr.*

Opposition strengthens the manly will.   —*A. B. Alcott.*

There is no possible success without some opposition as a fulcrum.   —*O. W. Holmes.*

A strenuous soul hates cheap success; it is the ardor of the assailant that makes the vigor of the defendant.   —*R. W. Emerson.*

We oppose despotism and slavery, whether imposed by state or individual.   —*B. M. Baruch.*

In the long run, truth is aided by nothing so much as by opposition.   —*W. E. Channing.*

OPPRESSION

If to plead the cause of the oppressed be treason, Lord Almighty, judge and let the guilty die!   —*Nathaniel Bacon.*

It is of great importance in a republic not only to guard the society against the oppression of its rulers, but to guard one part of the society against the injustice of the other part.

                                    —*James Madison.*

Assistance given to the weak makes the one who gives it strong; and oppression of the unfortunate makes one weak.

                                    —*Booker T. Washington.*

The oppression of any people for opinion's sake has rarely had any other effect than to fix those opinions deeper and render them more important.   —*Hosea Ballou.*

I am not a friend to a very energetic government. It is always oppressive. It places the governors indeed more at their ease, at the expense of the people.   —*T. Jefferson.*

You can't hold a man down without staying down with him.
                                    —*Booker T. Washington.*

He that would make his own liberty secure must guard even his enemy from oppression; for if he violates this duty, he establishes a precedent that will reach to himself.   —*T. Paine.*

Every spot of the old world is over-run with oppression. Freedom hath been hunted round the world . . . O! receive the fugitive, and prepare in time an asylum for mankind.   —*Ibid.*

Slavery and oppression must cease, or American liberty must perish.   —*A. Lincoln.*

OPTIMISM

The older I grow . . . the more I am confirmed in my optimism, in democracy. —*Walt Whitman.*

No matter how temporarily dark and depressing the skies may be, social progress, despite its setbacks, always has been ,upward and onward. —*George W. Norris.*

The optimist proclaims that we live in the best of all possible worlds; and the pessimist fears this is true. —*Branch Cabell.*

I am an optimist because I believe in God. Those who have no faith are quite naturally pessimists and I do not blame them. —*W. L. Phelps.*

Do not expect the world to look bright, if you habitually wear gray-brown glasses. —*Charles H. Eliot.*

So of cheerfulness, or a good temper, the more it is spent, the more of it remains. —*R. W. Emerson.*

Optimism is a kind of heart stimulant—the digitalis of failure. —*Elbert Hubbard.*

Keep your face to the sunshine and you cannot see the shadow. —*Helen Keller.*

Every cloud has its silver lining, but it is sometimes a little difficult to get it to the mint. —*Don Marquis.*

An optimist is a girl who mistakes a bulge for a curve. —*Ring Lardner.*

A pessimist is a man who thinks all women are bad. An optimist is one who hopes they are. —*Chauncey Depew.*

Two men look out through the same bars:
One sees the mud, and one the stars. —*Frederick Langbridge.*

The only limit to our realization of tomorrow will be our doubts of today. —*F. D. Roosevelt.*

Animal optimism is a great renovator and disinfectant in the world. —*George Santayana.*

ORATORY

Here comes the orator, with his flood of words and his drop of reason. —*B. Franklin.*

A man never becomes an orator if he has anything to say. —*F. P. Dunne.*

There is no power like that of true oratory.   —*Henry Clay*.

Foreign relations are not sudden things created by books or speeches or banquets. The history of nations is more important than their oratory.   —*Herbert Hoover*.

Orators should take a lesson from nature: she often gives us the lightning without the thunder, but never the thunder without the lightning.   —*E. Burrit*.

ORCHESTRA

The orchestra hurls me wider than Uranus does.
                                                —*Walt Whitman*.

ORCHESTRATION

The orchestration of mankind goes on.   —*H. M. Kallen*.

ORDER

The art of progress is to preserve order amid change, and to preserve change amid order. Life refuses to be embalmed alive.
                                                —*A. N. Whitehead*.

The more prolonged the halt in some unrelieved system of order, the greater the crash of the dead society.   —*Ibid*.

The individual is, in American theory, the free, the voluntary originator and organizer of the social order, is superior to it in every way.   —*Leon Samson*.

Order which society enjoins and old men love, is a low conception.   —*G. E. Woodberry*.

Order means acquiescence, content, a halt; persisted in, it means the atrophy of life, a living death; it is the abdication of progress.
                                                —*Ibid*.

The order that every state upholds is an order based on the existing distribution of property.   —*R. M. MacIver*.

A great part of that order which reigns among mankind is not the effect of government. It had its origin in the principles of society, and the natural constitution of men. It existed prior to government, and would exist if the formality of government were abolished.   —*T. Paine*.

I believe that truth and justice are fundamental to an enduring social order.   —*John D. Rockefeller, Jr*.

Atomic energy . . . may intimidate the human race into bringing order into its international affairs, which, without the pressure of fear, it would not do.   —*Albert Einstein*.

Let all your things have their places; let each part of your business have its time. —*B. Franklin.*

It is time for America and the world to move on from a social order in which unregulated profit is the driving force. It is time to move up to a social order in which equality of opportunity will cease to be a dream and actually come to pass.

—*Gifford Pinchot.*

The existence of a moral order is an argument not against God but for him. —*H. E. Fosdick.*

Social order is in man; it is that which man himself creates and maintains by what he believes and assumes.

—*Laurence K. Frank.*

Social order is man's self-chosen design for living. —*Ibid.*

Social order is not something that is given, as a part of the cosmos, but is always that which is sought. —*Ibid.*

Man himself must courageously and hopefully look forward to an unending endeavor to achieve social order and to create a human way of life. —*Ibid.*

ORGANISM

The real problem of life, both for men and societies, is to keep the organism and the environment, the inner world and the outer, the personality and its creative sources, in the state of tension wherein growth and renewal may continually take place.

—*Lewis Mumford.*

ORGANIZATION

It is not the organization that creates. Man creates: organization builds. —*R. W. Emerson.*

The business of government is to see that no other organization is as strong as itself; to see that no body or group of men no matter what their private interest is, may come into competition with the authority of society. —*Woodrow Wilson.*

We are facing the necessity of fitting a new social organization, as we did once fit the old organization, to the happiness and prosperity of the great body of citizens. —*Ibid.*

Modern democracy does not mean individualism. It means a system in which private, voluntary organizations function under general, and mostly indirect governmental control. —*A. H. Hansen.*

Organization taught the laborer discussion, investigation, consideration, and it taught some employers that justice is the best policy.   —*John P. Altgeld.*

The organization of freedom is increasingly complex; yet its final results, its achievements and failures, are to be seen and felt by everybody.   —*Max Ascoli.*

The religion of the modern man is postulated on the . . . organization of liberty.   —*H. M. Kallen.*

Let us play the free man's part in the modern organization of freedom.   —*Ibid.*

ORIGINAL

The only original thing about some men is original sin.
—*Helen Rowland.*

I think the enemy is old as time and evil as Hell, and that he has been here with us from the beginning.   —*Thomas Wolfe.*

ORIGINALITY

Originality is simply a pair of fresh eyes.   —*T. W. Higginson.*

Though old the thought and oft exprest,
'Tis his at last who says it best.
—*J. R. Lowell.*

Great men are more distinguished by range and extent than by originality.   —*R. W. Emerson.*

All thoughtful men are solitary and original in themselves.
—*J. R. Lowell.*

This gives force to the strong—that the multitude have no habit of self-reliance or original action.   —*R. W. Emerson.*

What a good thing Adam had—when he said a good thing, he knew nobody had said it before.   —*Mark Twain.*

ORNAMENT

Show is not substance; realities govern wise men.   —*Wm. Penn.*

We all originally came from the woods; it is hard to eradicate from any of us the old taste for the tattoo and the war-paint.
—*E. P. Whipple.*

The moment that money gets into our pockets, it breaks out in ornaments on our person, without always giving refinement to our manners.   —*Ibid.*

ORTHODOXY

No official, high or petty, can prescribe what shall be orthodox in politics, nationalism, religion, or other matters of opinion, or force citizens to confess by word or act their faith therein.

—Robert E. Jackson.

OSTENTATION

Do what good thou canst unknown, and be not vain of what ought rather to be felt than seen. *—Wm. Penn.*

Ostentation is the signal flag of hypocrisy. *—E. H. Chapin.*

OUGHT

Resolve to perform what you ought; perform without fail what you resolve. *—B. Franklin.*

OVERCENTRALIZATION

The cumulative effect of overcentralization of administration in a national capital is greatly to reduce the effectiveness of government. *—David E. Lilienthal.*

OVEREMPHASIS

We have overemphasized what might be called political or Bill-of-Rights democracy. *—H. A. Wallace.*

OVERSTATEMENT

The chief error in philosophy is overstatement.

—A. N. Whitehead.

Sensitive patriotism, in a country made from a group of colonies and more conscious of its future than its past, has been ready with overstatement, and provincial critics have given attributes belonging to Shakespeare or Cervantes to authors differing from the great in kind as well as in degree. *—H. S. Canby.*

OVERTRAINED

A college education is a good thing, but many a graduate finds himself overtrained. *—H. H. Vreeland.*

OWNERSHIP

The fiscal strength of a nation lies not in what government owns but in what its people own. The sinews of war are not dollars—they are efforts. *—B. M. Baruch.*

The true gravitation-hold of liberalism in the United States will be a more universal ownership of property, general homesteads, general comfort—a vast intertwining reticulation of wealth.

—*Walt Whitman.*

If carried to the logical extreme, the final concentration of ownership in the hands of government gives to it, in all practical effects, absolute power over our lives.   —*D. D. Eisenhower.*

The objections to unlimited private ownership are sentimental or political, not economic.   —*O. W. Holmes, Jr.*

The established businesslike system of ownership and control will no longer work.   —*Thorstein Veblen.*

I would rather sit on a pumpkin and have it all to myself than be crowded on a velvet cushion.   —*H. D. Thoreau.*

OX

It depends upon whose ox is gored.   —*Noah Webster.*

Where can the laboring ox go that the plough will not be heavy to drag? And unless he drag it, how shall the seed be sown?

—*Junipero Serra.*

P

PACIFISM

What is the design of military masters? To make men skilful murderers. I cannot consent to become a pupil in this sanguinary school. —*W. L. Garrison.*

The way to stop war is to stop going to war; stop supporting it and it will fall, just as slavery did, just as the Inquisition did.
—*Charles T. Sprading.*

PAGAN

Perhaps no one can be really a good appreciating pagan, who has not once been a bad puritan. —*Randolph Bourne.*

PAIN

Pain dies quickly, and lets her weary prisoners go; the fiercest agonies have shortest reign. —*Wm. Cullen Bryant.*

Pain is no longer pain when it is past.
—*Margaret J. Preston.*

There's a pang in all rejoicing, and a joy in the heart of pain.
—*Bayard Taylor.*

The only folks who give us pain are those we love the best.
—*Ella W. Wilcox.*

> Never a lip is curved with pain
> That can't be kissed into smiles again.
>
> —*Bret Harte.*

PAINTING

Pictures must not be too picturesque. —*R. W. Emerson.*

The love of gain never made a painter; but it has marred many.
—*Washington Allston.*

The painter who is content with the praise of the world in

respect to what does not satisfy himself is not an artist, but an artisan; for though his reward is only praise, his pay is that of a mechanic.   *—Ibid.*

The first merit of pictures is the effect which they can produce upon the mind.   *—H. W. Beecher.*

Every time I paint a portrait I lose a friend.   *—J. S. Sargent.*

PANIC

A panic is a sudden desertion of us, and a going over to the enemy of our imagination.   *—C. N. Bovee.*

PARADISE

Man finds his paradise when he is imparadised in God.
—Horace Bushnell.

Gentleness and kindness will make our home a paradise upon our earth.   *—C. A. Bartol.*

Every man has a paradise around him till he sins, and the angel of an accusing conscience drives him from his Eden.
—H. W. Longfellow.

PARADOX

We never come so near to a truly well rounded view of any truth, as when it is offered paradoxically; that is under contradictions.   *—Horace Bushnell.*

There is that glorious Epicurean paradox: 'Give me the luxuries of life, and we will dispense with its necessaries.'
—O. W. Holmes.

PARDON

Nothing in this low and ruined world bears the meek impress of the Son of God so surely as forgiveness.   *—Alice Cary.*

Pardon, not wrath, is God's best attribute.   *—Bayard Taylor.*

To obtain pardon from God you must cease to sin.
—H. W. Beecher.

PARENTS

There is no friendship, no love, like that of the parent for the child.   *—H. W. Beecher.*

The first half of our lives is ruined by our parents and the second half by our children.   *—Clarence Darrow.*

Next to God, thy parents.   *—Wm. Penn.*

There is no such penalty for error and folly as to see one's children suffer for it.   —*W. G. Sumner.*

We never know the love of the parent till we become parents ourselves.   —*H. W. Beecher.*

Parents were invented to make children happy by giving them something to ignore.   —*Ogden Nash.*

Reverence and cherish your parents.   —*T. Jefferson.*

PARIS
Good Americans, when they die, go to Paris.

—*T. G. Appleton.*

PARTY
Political parties serve to keep each other in check, one keenly watching the other.   —*Henry Clay.*

Party honesty is party expediency.   —*Grover Cleveland.*

He serves his party best who serves the country best.

—*R. B. Hayes.*

Now is the time for all good men to come to the aid of the party.   —*C. E. Weller.*

If I could not go to Heaven but with a party I would not go there at all.   —*T. Jefferson.*

America has outgrown parties; henceforth it is too large, and they too small.   —*Walt Whitman.*

I place no reliance upon any old party nor upon any new party.
—*Ibid.*

The Democratic Party ain't on speaking terms with itself.

—*F. P. Dunne.*

These has ever been, and will always be, two dominant parties in politics.   —*Daniel Webster.*

We must drive far away the demon of party spirit and local reproach.   —*G. Washington.*

A fire not to be quenched, it (party spirit) demands a uniform vigilance to prevent it bursting into flame, lest, instead of warming it shall consume.   —*Ibid.*

PASSIONS
The passions are too much engrossed by their objects to meditate on themselves; and none are more ignorant of their growth and subtle workings than their own victims.   —*W. E. Channing.*

Passion, though a bad regulator, is a powerful spring.
—*R. W. Emerson.*

The blossoms of passion are bright and full of fragrance, but they beguile us and lead us astray, and their odor is deadly.
—*H. W. Longfellow.*

Strong passions are the life of manly virtues.   —*W. G. Simms.*

Why has government been instituted at all? Because the passions of men will not conform to the dictates of reason and justice, without constraint.   —*Alexander Hamilton.*

The way to avoid evil is not by maiming our passions, but by compelling them to yield their vigor to our moral nature.
—*H. W. Beecher.*

They (curbed passions) become, as in the ancient fable, the harnessed steeds that bear the chariot of the sun.   —*Ibid.*

Passion (is) the mob of the man, that commits a riot upon his reason.   —*Wm. Penn.*

True passion is a consuming flame, and either it must find fruition or it will burn the human heart to dust and ashes.
—*William Winter.*

A genuine passion is like a mountain stream; it admits of no impediment; it cannot go backward; it must go forward.
—*C. N. Bovee.*

Bee to the blossom, moth to the flame; each to his passion; what's in a name?   —*Helen Hunt Jackson.*

PAST

Let the dead Past bury its dead.   —*H. W. Longfellow.*

Those who cannot remember the past are condemned to repeat it.   —*George Santayana.*

The past is a bucket of ashes.   —*Carl Sandburg.*

The best prophet of the future is the past.   —*John Sherman.*

The past has little serious value save as a guide to what may come.   —*Brooks Adams.*

The scholar who accumulates in himself the human past has something of that wisdom which goes, in individual life, with a long memory.   —*G. E. Woodberry.*

The free world must now prove itself worthy of its own past.
—*D. D. Eisenhower.*

Some are so very studious of learning what was done by the ancients that they know not how to live with the moderns.

—*Wm. Penn.*

The past is utterly indifferent to its worshippers.

—*William Winter.*

We ought not to look back unless it is to derive useful lessons from past errors, and for the purpose of profiting by dear bought experience. —*G. Washington.*

The past is the sepulchre of our dead emotions.

—*C. N. Bovee.*

The past always looks better than it was; it's only pleasant because it isn't here. —*F. P. Dunne.*

Our reverence for the past is just in proportion to our ignorance of it. —*Theodore Parker.*

The past is for us, but the sole terms on which it can become ours are its subordination to the present. —*R. W. Emerson.*

PATIENCE

Patience is passion tamed. —*Lyman Abbott.*

Patience and diligence, like faith, remove mountains.

—*Wm. Penn.*

To live in the presence of great truths, to be dealing with eternal laws, to be led by permanent ideals,—that is what keeps a man patient when the world ignores him, and calm and unspoiled when the world praises him. —*Francis G. Peabody.*

It is not necessary for all men to be great in action. The greatest and sublimest power is often simple patience.

—*Horace Bushnell.*

The marvel of all history is the patience with which men and women submit to burdens unnecessarily laid upon them by their government. —*William E. Borah.*

Adopt the pace of nature: her secret is patience.

—*R. W. Emerson.*

He that can have patience can have what he will.

—*B. Franklin.*

All things come round to him who will but wait.

—*H. W. Longfellow.*

Lack of pep is often mistaken for patience. —*Kin Hubbard.*

There is no great achievement that is not the result of patient working and waiting.   —*J. G. Holland.*

Patience is but lying to and riding out the gale.
                                                          —*H. W. Beecher.*

PATIENTS

A good patient is one who, having found a good physician, sticks to him till he dies.   —*O. W. Holmes.*

This sick economic world of ours is a patient in a hospital, not a subject for experimentation in a laboratory. —*B. M. Anderson.*

Doctors think a lot of patients are cured who have simply quit in disgust.   —*Don Herold.*

PATRIOTISM

Patriotism is the vital condition of national permanence.
                                                          —*G. W. Curtis.*

I only regret that I have but one life to give to my country.
                                                          —*Nathan Hale.*

There are no points of the compass on the chart of true patriotism.   —*Robert C. Winthrop.*

Our country right or wrong.   —*Stephen Decatur.*

Our country right or wrong! When right to be kept right; when wrong to be put right!   —*Carl Schurz.*

Swim or sink, live or die, survive or perish with my country was my unalterable determination.   —*John Adams.*

Every drop of blood in me holds a heritage of patriotism.
                                                          —*Elias Lieberman.*

Patriotism is easy to understand in America; it means looking out for yourself by looking out for your country.
                                                          —*Calvin Coolidge.*

Love of country is like love of woman—he loves her best who seeks to bestow on her the highest good.   —*Felix Adler.*

My country is the world; my countrymen are mankind.
                                                          —*W. L. Garrison.*

The name of AMERICAN, which belongs to you, in your national capacity, must always exalt the just pride of Patriotism.
                                                          —*G. Washington.*

The only sphere left open for our patriotism is the improvement of our children—not the few, but the many, not a part of them, but all.   *—Horace Mann.*

Protection and patriotism are reciprocal.   *—John C. Calhoun.*

Cut an American into a hundred pieces and boil him down, you will find him all Fourth of July.   *—Wendell Phillips.*

This heroism at command, this senseless violence, this accursed bombast of patriotism—how intensely I despise them!
—Albert Einstein.

The religion of Hell is patriotism, and the government is an enlightened democracy.   *—James Branch Cabell.*

I have tried to do good in the world, not harm, as my enemies would have the world believe. I have helped men, and have attempted in my humble way to be of some service to my country.
—J. P. Morgan.

With malice toward none, with charity for all, with firmness in the right, as God gives us to see the right, let us strive on to finish the work we are in.   *—A. Lincoln.*

It is no shame to a man that he should be as nice about his country as about his sweetheart.   *—J. R. Lowell.*

He loves his country best who strives to make it best.
—R. G. Ingersoll.

Whoever insults my state insults me.   *—Preston S. Brooks.*

A man's feet must be planted in his country, but his eyes should survey the world.   *—George Santayana.*

PATRIOTS
Delight—top gallant delight is to him, who acknowledges no law or lord but the Lord his God, and is only patriot to heaven.
—Herman Melville.

The man who loves his country on its own account and not merely for its trappings of interest or power, can never be divorced from it, can never refuse to come forward when he finds that she is engaged in dangers which he has the means of warding off.
—T. Jefferson.

No man can be a patriot on an empty stomach.
—W. C. Brann.

We can't all be Washingtons but we can all be patriots and behave ourselves in a human and Christian manner.

—Charles F. Browne.

PAYMENT

People who take pains never to do any more than they get paid for, never get paid for any more than they do. *—Elbert Hubbard.*

PEACE

We can have labor peace only through the long, slow and painful process of education. *—J. L. McCaffrey.*

If man does find the solution for world peace it will be the most revolutionary reversal of his record we have ever known.

—George Marshall.

There never was a good war nor a bad peace. *—B. Franklin.*

Even peace may be purchased at too high a price. *—Ibid.*

I have never advocated war, except as a means of Peace.

—U. S. Grant.

To be prepared for war is one of the most effectual means of preserving peace. *—G. Washington.*

The currency with which you pay for peace is made up of manly courage, fearless virility, readiness to serve justice and honor at any cost, and a mind and a heart attuned to sacrifice.

—Frank Knox.

Let us have peace. *—U. S. Grant.*

They have not wanted Peace at all; they have wanted to be spared war—as though the absence of war was the same as peace.

—Dorothy Thompson.

It must be a peace without victory. *—Woodrow Wilson.*

Peace must be planned on a global basis. *—Wendell L. Willkie.*

We shall point to the Pax Americana and seek the path of peace on earth to men of good will. *—W. J. Turner.*

Peace: in international affairs, a period of cheating between two periods of fighting. *—Ambrose Bierce.*

Man's greatest blunder has been in trying to make peace with the skies instead of making peace with his neighbors.

—Elbert Hubbard.

"Peace has its victories no less than war," but it doesn't have as many monuments t' unveil. *—Kin Hubbard.*

Peace is positive, and it has to be waged with all our thought, energy, and courage and with the conviction that war is not inevitable. —*Dean Acheson.*

Temporary peace will not become permanent except as men make the rich resources and technology, which today chiefly serve the few, the benefactors of all mankind. —*Norman Thomas.*

You don't get peace, you don't retain peace just by being peaceable. You get it, if it is worth having, by a constant willingness to work and sacrifice and risk for it. —*Frank Knox.*

Peace is the fairest form of happiness. —*W. E. Channing.*

Nothing can bring you peace but the triumph of principles.
—*R. W. Emerson.*

Let the bugles sound the Truce of God to the whole world forever. —*Charles Sumner.*

Peace is the healing and elevating influence of the world, and strife is not. —*Woodrow Wilson.*

The peaceful are the strong. —*O. W. Holmes.*

The blame for the danger to world peace lies not in the world population but in the political leaders of that population.
—*F. D. Roosevelt.*

PEACE-MAKERS

I have never known a peace made, even the most advantageous, that was not censured as inadequate, and the makers condemned as injudicious or corrupt. —*B. Franklin.*

PEDANTRY

When books absorb men, and turn them from observation of nature and life, they generate a learned folly, for which the plain sense of the laborer could not be exchanged but at a great loss.
—*W. E. Channing.*

Pedants are men who would appear to be learned, without the necessary ingredient of knowledge. —*George Bancroft.*

The most annoying of all blockheads is a well-read fool.
—*Bayard Taylor.*

PEN

A pen becomes a clarion. —*H. W. Longfellow.*

The pen is no formidable weapon, but a man can kill himself with it a great deal more easily than he can other people.
—*G. D. Prentice.*

Pens carry farther than rifled cannon.   —*Bayard Taylor.*

PENSIONS

We say to American industry, if you can afford to pay pension plans to people who don't need them, then by the eternal gods you are going to have to pay them to people who do need them, guys in the shop.   —*W. P. Reuther.*

The people now winning pensions will destroy or greatly cut their future value if they continue to vote for heavier spending and bigger debts.   —*E. T. Leech.*

PEOPLE

The genius of the United States is not best or most in its executives or legislatures, nor in its ambassadors or authors or colleges or churches or parlors, nor even in its newspapers or inventors . . . but always most in the common people.   —*Walt Whitman.*

God must have loved the plain people: He made so many of them.   —*A. Lincoln.*

The life of the common people is the best part of the world's life; the life of the common people is the life of God.
                                                        —*H. W. Beecher.*

The will of the people is the best law.   —*U. S. Grant.*

The people are the only sure reliance for the preservation of our liberty.   —*T. Jefferson.*

Government of the people, by the people, and for the people, shall not perish from the earth.   —*A. Lincoln.*

You can fool some of the people all of the time, and all of the people some of the time, but you cannot fool all of the people all of the time.   —*Ibid.*

The second, sober thought of the people is seldom wrong, and always efficient.   —*Martin Van Buren.*

Whatever you may be sure of, be sure of this, that you are dreadfully like other people.   —*J. R. Lowell.*

People are more fun than anybody.   —*Dorothy Parker.*

Most hard-boiled people are half-baked.   —*Wilson Mizner.*

The people's government, made for the people, made by the people, and answerable to the people.   —*Daniel Webster.*

One-third of the people in the United States promote while the other two-thirds provide.   —*Will Rogers.*

The people will have unbounded power, and the people are extremely addicted to corruption and venality as well as the great.
—*John Adams.*

People form the strength and constitute the wealth of a nation.
—*Patrick Henry.*

Governments are republican only in proportion as they embody the will of the people, and execute it. —*T. Jefferson.*

The people are to be taken in very small doses.
—*R. W. Emerson.*

It is through the instruments of politics that the people recognize themselves. —*Max Ascoli.*

A people like ourselves . . . must have freedom if we are to survive. —*H. S. Commager.*

I know of no safe depository of the ultimate powers of society but the people themselves, and if we think them not enlightened enough to exercise their control with a wholesome discretion, the remedy is not to take it from them, but to inform their discretion by education. —*T. Jefferson.*

I am a member of the rabble in good standing.
—*Westbrook Pegler.*

PERCEPTION

The heart has eyes that the brain knows nothing of.
—*C. H. Pankhurst.*

Simple people . . . are very quick to see the live facts which are going on about them. —*O. W. Holmes.*

PERFECTION

The maximums tell you to aim at perfection, which is well; but it's unattainable all the same. —*Bayard Taylor.*

If a man should happen to reach perfection in this world, he would have to die immediately to enjoy himself. —*H. W. Shaw.*

As we grow older and realize our inability to meet perfection, the happier we can and should be in everything that we do to make life a little better—to use the vehicles of science and cooperation to improve the lot of those who need it most.
—*F. D. Roosevelt.*

PERMANENCE

Religion means binding, and what is meant to last until the end of time must be bound religiously. —*Dagobert D. Runes.*

PERSECUTION

Whoever is right, the persecutor must be wrong. —*Wm. Penn.*

The history of persecution is a history of endeavor to cheat nature, to make water run up hill, to twist a rope of sand.
—*R. W. Emerson.*

The way of the world is to praise dead saints, and persecute living ones. —*Nathaniel Howe.*

Communism is neither disproved by constant aggression against Communists outside of Russia, nor proved by the persecution of non-Communists inside of Russia. —*H. M. Kallen.*

It is necessary . . . to defend the innocent, and to rescue the oppressed from the violent paws and jaws of oppressing persecuting Nimrods. —*Roger Williams.*

The whole earth (is) made drunk with the blood of its inhabitants, slaughtering each other in their blinded zeal, for conscience, for religion, against the Catholics, against the Lutherans. —*Ibid.*

A religion which requires persecution to sustain it is of the devil's propagation. —*Hosea Ballou.*

Persecution for the expression of opinion seems to me perfectly logical. —*O. W. Holmes, Jr.*

Persecution for the expression of opinion is, in the infallible, utterly illogical. —*H. M. Kallen.*

Persecution, wherever it occurs, establishes only the power and cunning of the persecutor, not the truth and worth of his belief. These develop only in freedom and through freedom. —*Ibid.*

Periodic outbursts of terror and hate have been directed in the course of our history against Mormons, Irishmen, the Latin immigrants, the free Negro, the German people, Catholics, foreigners once more, Communists, unbelievers. —*Ludwig Lewisohn.*

PERSEVERANCE

Perseverance is king. —*Josh Billings.*

The slogan "Press on" has solved and always will solve the problems of the human race. —*Calvin Coolidge.*

That which grows fast withers as rapidly; that which grows slowly endures. —*J. G. Holland.*

Do what you love. Know your own bone; gnaw at it, bury it, unearth it, and gnaw it still. —*H. D. Thoreau.*

Persistent people begin their success where others end in failures. —*Edward Eggleston.*

The conditions of conquest are always easy. We have but to toil awhile, believe always—and never turn back. —*W. G. Simms.*

When you get into a tight place, and everything goes against you, till it seems as if you could not go on a minute longer, never give up then, for that's just the place and the time that the tide will turn. —*H. B. Stowe.*

Consider the postage stamp, my son. It secures success through its ability to stick to one thing till it gets there. —*Josh Billings.*

We make way for the man who boldly pushes past us.
—*C. N. Bovee.*

A man in earnest finds means, or if he cannot find, creates them.
—*W. E. Channing.*

The practise of perseverance is the disciple of the noblest virtues.
—*M. L. Magoon.*

To run well we must run to the end. —*Ibid.*

It is not the fighting but the conquering that gives a hero the title of renown. —*Ibid.*

Persistency attracts confidence, more than talents and accomplishments. —*E. P. Whipple.*

PERSONALITY

Personality is to a man what perfume is to a flower.
—*C. M. Schwab.*

If you have anything really valuable to contribute to the world it will come through the expression of your own personality—that single spark of divinity that sets you off and makes you different from every other living creature. —*Bruce Barton.*

PESSIMISM

Pessimism is only the name that men of weak nerves give to wisdom. —*Bernard De Voto.*

The wages of pessimism are futility. —*Thurman Arnold.*

The world, life itself, is embittered to most of us, so that we are glad to have done with them at last. —*W. D. Howells.*

PESSIMIST

I am no pessimist as to this republic. I always bet on sunshine in America. —*Henry W. Grady.*

The man who is a pessimist before forty-eight knows too much; the man who is an optimist after forty-eight knows too little.
                                                    —*Mark Twain.*

PHILANTHROPY
Philanthropies and charities have a certain air of quackery.
                                                    —*R. W. Emerson.*

To pity distress is but human; to relieve it is Godlike.
                                                    —*Horace Mann.*

PHILOSOPHER
All are lunatics, but he who can analyze his delusions is called a philosopher.   —*Ambrose Bierce.*

There is no record in human history of a happy philosopher.
                                                    —*H. L. Mencken.*

The more conscious a philosopher is of the weak spots of his theory, the more certain he is to speak with an air of final authority.   —*Don Marquis.*

There are nowadays professors of philosophy, but not philosophers.   —*H. D. Thoreau.*

PHILOSOPHY
Philosophy asks the simple question: What is it all about?
                                                    —*A. N. Whitehead.*

It is a great advantage for a system of philosophy to be substantially true.   —*George Santayana.*

Philosophy: unintelligible answers to insoluble problems.
                                                    —*Henry Adams.*

Philosophy is a pseudo-knowledge which attempts to add a dimension to human capacity.   —*Leo Stein.*

The philosophy of one century is the common sense of the next.
                                                    —*H. W. Beecher.*

Philosophy: A route of many roads leading from nowhere to nothing.   —*Ambrose Bierce.*

Philosophy is the art of lying about the art of living.
                                                    —*D. G. Kin.*

Philosophy: Can never be defined because it is the search for the indefinable.   —*Dagobert D. Runes.*

PIONEERS

Conquering, holding, daring, venturing as we go the unknown ways,

Pioneers! O pioneers! —*Walt Whitman.*

A pioneer should have imagination, should be able to enjoy the idea of things more than the things themselves. —*Willa Cather.*

The great-grandchildren of the Middle Western pioneers are not easily persuaded that farming is an honorable calling.

—*Meredith Nicholson.*

We must face the fact that the splendid story of the pioneers is finished, and that no new story worthy to take its place has yet begun. —*Willa Cather.*

PITY

Pity costs nothing, and ain't worth nothing. —*Josh Billings.*

Pity and friendship seek different habitations.

—*Helen Hunt Jackson.*

Pity, if hard pressed, degenerates into contempt. —*J. G. Saxe.*

The great basis of the Christian faith is compassion.

—*Theodore Parker.*

There are two sorts of pity: one is a balm and the other a poison; the first is realized by our friends, the last by our enemies.

—*Charles Sumner.*

Compassion is the only one of the human emotions the Lord permitted himself and it has carried the divine flavor ever since.

—*Dagobert D. Runes.*

PLACE

Every place is under the stars, every place is the centre of the world. —*John Burroughs.*

PLAGIARISM

Our best thoughts come from others. —*R. W. Emerson.*

The only "ism" Hollywood believes in is plagiarism.

—*Dorothy Parker.*

Take the whole range of imaginative literature, and we are all wholesale borrowers. In every matter that relates to invention, to use, or beauty or form, we are borrowers. —*Wendell Phillips.*

When you take stuff from one writer, it's plagiarism; but when you take it from many writers, it's research. —*Wilson Mizner.*

Honest thinkers are always stealing unconsciously from each other. *—O. W. Holmes.*

There are thoughts always abroad in the air which it takes more wit to avoid than to hit upon. *—Ibid.*

A certain awkwardness marks the use of borrowed thoughts, but as soon as we have learned what to do with them, they become our own. *—R. W. Emerson.*

> Though old the thought and oft exprest,
> 'Tis his at last who says it best.
>
> *—J. R. Lowell.*

PLANNING

The twentieth century is certainly the Plan Age.
—George B. Galloway.

Regimentation of material and mechanical forces is the only way by which the mass of individuals can be released from regimentation and consequent suppression of their cultural possibilities.
—John Dewey.

Planning is not in itself socialism or capitalism or fascism. It is collectivism applied to the major processes of the economic system.
—Max Lerner.

The conflict in America is between two kinds of planning. It is privately planned economic scarcity by companies for profits or public planned economic abundance for people. That is really the struggle. *—W. P. Reuther.*

We have a choice only between democratic planning and totalitarian regimentation. *—A. H. Hansen.*

Is not civilization, with all it has accomplished, the result of man's not letting things alone, and of his not letting nature take its course? *—Lester Ward.*

Every step in the direction of planning for social ends must be a step away from capitalism, no matter how hard that word is defined. The more advanced stage of a planned society must be something closely akin to the broad ambition of socialism.
—George Soule.

Genuine planning on the part of society involves the ownership by society of the industry directed. *—H. W. Laidler.*

PLAY

Work consists of whatever a body is obliged to do, and Play consists of whatever a body is not obliged to do.   *—Mark Twain.*

The machine age has given us more leisure in which to play.
—Stuart Chase.

When the play, it may be the tragedy, of life is over, the spectator goes his way.   *—H. D. Thoreau.*

PLEASURE

Pleasure is more trouble than trouble.   *—Don Herold.*

The rule of my life is to make business a pleasure, and pleasure my business.   *—Aaron Burr.*

There is no pleasure in having nothing to do; the fun is in having lots to do and not doing it.   *—M. W. Little.*

A life merely of pleasure is always a poor and mirthless life and not worth the living.   *—Theodore Parker.*

I do not believe in doing for pleasure things I do not like to do.
—Don Herold.

The purest pleasures lie within the circle of useful occupations.
—H. W. Beecher.

The average man does not get pleasure out of an idea because he thinks it is true; he thinks it is true because he gets pleasure out of it.   *—H. L. Mencken.*

Whenever you are sincerely pleased you are nourished.
—R. W. Emerson.

There are two things to aim at in life: first, to get what you want; and, after that, to enjoy it. Only the wisest of mankind achieve the second.   *—Logan Pearsall Smith.*

Anything which makes one glow with pleasure is beyond money calculation, in this humdrum world where there is altogether too much grubbing and too little glowing.   *—David Dunn.*

PLEDGE

We mutually pledge to each other our lives, our fortunes, and our sacred honor.   *—T. Jefferson.*

POET

To have great poets, there must be great audiences, too.
—Walt Whitman.

All men are poets at heart.   —*R. W. Emerson.*

Next to being a great poet is the power of understanding one.
                                                —*H. W. Longfellow.*

All that is best in the great poets of all countries is not what is
national in them, but what is universal.   —*Ibid.*

A poet must needs be before his own age to be even with posterity.   —*J. R. Lowell.*

To the poetic mind all things are poetical.

                                                —*H. W. Longfellow.*

POETRY

Good poetry is the most scarce of all literary commodities.
                                        —*Charles Brockden Brown.*

Poetry is that thirst, or aspiration . . . for something purer and
lovelier, something more powerful, lofty and thrilling, than ordinary or real life affords.   —*W. E. Channing.*

I wanted, and still want, for poetry, the clear sun shining, and
forest air blowing—the strength and power of health, not of delir-
ium, even amidst the stormiest passions—with always the background of the eternal moralities.   —*Walt Whitman.*

> A poem should not mean
> But be.
>
>   —*Archibald MacLeish.*

It is never what a poem *says* that matters, but what it *is*.
                                                      —*T. S. Eliot.*

Publishing a volume of verse is like dropping a rose-petal down
the Grand Canyon and waiting for the echo.   —*Don Marquis.*

With me poetry has not been a purpose, but a passion.
                                                —*Edgar Allan Poe.*

The finest poetry was first experienced.   —*R. W. Emerson.*

Poetry is evidently a contagious complaint.

                                                —*Washington Irving.*

This class struggle plays hell with your poetry.   —*John Reed.*

Poetry is the utterance of deep and heart-felt truth.—The true
poet is very near the oracle.   —*E. H. Chapin.*

Poetry is something to make us better and wiser by continually
revealing those types of beauty and truth which God has set in
all men's souls.   —*J. R. Lowell.*

Only that is poetry which cleanses and mans me.

—*R. W. Emerson.*

POISE

One woman's poise is another woman's poison.

—*Katharine Bush.*

POLICY

We shall not, I believe, be obliged to alter our policy of watchful waiting. —*Woodrow Wilson.*

Peace is, indeed, our policy. —*John C. Calhoun.*

POLITENESS

Politeness is one half good nature and the other half good lying.

—*M. W. Little.*

There is no policy like politeness, since a good manner often succeeds where the best tongue has failed. —*E. L. Magoon.*

True politeness is the expression of good will and kindness.—It is a religious duty, and should be a part of religious training.

—*H. W. Beecher.*

Courtesies of a small and trivial character are the ones which strike deepest in the grateful and appreciating heart.

—*Henry Clay.*

Politeness looks well in every man, except an undertaker.

—*Josh Billings.*

Politeness is an easy virtue, and has great purchasing power.

—*A. B. Alcott.*

POLITICAL

A political war is one in which everyone shoots from the lip.

—*Raymond Moley.*

Political internationalism without economic internationalism is a house built upon sand. For no nation can reach its fullest development alone. —*Wendell L. Willkie.*

An empty stomach is not a good political adviser.

—*Albert Einstein.*

POLITICIAN

The most successful politician is he who says what everybody is thinking most often and in the loudest voice.

—*Theodore Roosevelt.*

A politician is like quicksilver; if you try to put your finger on him, you will find nothing under it. —*Austin O'Malley.*

The statesman shears the sheep, the politician skins them.
                                                            —Ibid.

A politician thinks of the next election; a statesman, of the next
generation.   *—J. F. Clarke.*

An honest politician is one who, when he is bought, will stay
bought.   *—Simon Cameron.*

I'm not a politician and my other habits are good.
                                                    —Artemus Ward.

We cannot safely leave politics to politicians, or political economy to college professors.   *—Henry George.*

You cannot adopt politics as a profession and remain honest.
                                                  —Louis Untermeyer.

Politician: any citizen with influence enough to get his old
mother a job as charwoman in the City Hall.   *—H. L. Mencken.*

It is good business men that are corrupting our bad politicians.
                                                    —Joseph W. Falk.

One plow is worth twenty politicians.   *—Henry W. Grady.*

POLITICS

Politics is the science of exigencies.   *—Theodore Parker.*

Practical politics consists in ignoring facts.   *—Henry Adams.*

In politics, merit is rewarded by the possessor being raised, like
a target, to a position to be fired at.   *—C. N. Bovee.*

There is no more independence in politics than there is in jail.
                                                        —Will Rogers.

Politics . . . are but the cigar smoke of a man.   *—H. D. Thoreau.*

Before you can begin to think about politics at all, you have to
abandon the notion that here is a war beween good men and bad
men.   *—Walter Lippmann.*

Modern politics is a struggle not of men but of forces.
                                                        —Henry Adams.

Once politics enters, the entire edifice of an enterprise built
upon expert skills becomes unsafe.   *—David E. Lilienthal.*

In the name of all that's American, how can any good citizen
feel superior to politics? We achieved our independence by politics.
We freed the slaves by politics. We are taxed by politics. Our businesses flourish or wither by politics.   *—Charles Edison.*

What is called politics is comparatively so superficial and inhuman, that, practically, I have never fairly recognized that it concerns me at all.   —*H. D. Thoreau.*

Politics makes strange postmasters.   —*Kin Hubbard.*

My politics are short and sweet, like the old woman's dance.
—*A. Lincoln.*

Politics is and has always been an imitation of war aimed at exorcising war.   —*Max Ascoli.*

Through politics, men can learn to use ballots instead of bullets, symbols instead of weapons.   —*Ibid.*

I tell you folks, all politics is Apple Sauce.   —*Will Rogers.*

The purification of politics is an iridescent dream.
—*J. J. Ingalls.*

Politics is but the common pulsebeat, of which revolution is the fever-spasm.   —*Wendell Phillips.*

My hat's in the ring. The fight is on and I'm stripped to the buff.
—*Theodore Roosevelt.*

As long as I count the votes what are you going to do about it?
—*W. M. Tweed.*

If you do not know how to lie, cheat and steal, turn your attention to politics and learn.   —*H. W. Shaw.*

No man should think himself a zero, and think he can do nothing about the state of the world.   —*B. M. Baruch.*

Our foreign dealings are an open book—generally a checkbook.
—*Will Rogers.*

POOR

One of the strangest things about life is that the poor, who need money the most, are the very ones that never have it.
—*F. P. Dunne.*

Bitter it is to be poor, and bitter to be reviled.
—*Herman Melville.*

When one starts poor, as most do in the race of life, free society is such that he knows he can better his condition. —*A. Lincoln.*

We have no reason to fear that the poor and unfortunate will ever receive too much attention either at home or abroad.
—*Mrs. E. C. Stanton.*

It's no disgrace to be poor, but it might as well be.
—*Abe Martin.*

The poor ye have with you always—but they are not invited.
                                                        —*Addison Mizner.*

Remember the poor—it costs nothing.   —*Josh Billings.*

POPULARITY

No popularity lives long in a democracy.   —*John Q. Adams.*

Avoid popularity; it has many snares and no real benefit.
                                                        —*Wm. Penn.*

Applause waits on success.   —*B. Franklin.*

The actor's popularity is evanescent; applauded today, forgotten
tomorrow.   —*Edwin Forrest.*

Avoid popularity if you would have peace.   —*A. Lincoln.*

POPULATION

An increase of population will of necessity increase the proportion of those who will labor under all the hardships of life, and
secretly sigh for a more equal distribution of its blessings. . . .
According to the equal law of suffrage the power will slide into
(their) hands.   —*James Madison.*

POSSESSIONS

Most writers regard truth as their most valuable possession, and
therefore are most economical in its use.   —*Mark Twain.*

One of the very best of all earthly possessions is self-possession.
                                                        —*G. D. Prentice.*

> They who have nothing have little to fear
> Nothing to lose or to gain.
>
>   —*Madison Cawein.*

All our possessions are as nothing compared to health, strength
and a clear conscience.   —*Hosea Ballou.*

POSTERITY

POSTERITY! you will never know how much it cost the present
generation to preserve your freedom!   —*John Adams.*

Think of your forefathers! Think of your posterity!
                                                        —*John Q. Adams.*

POTENTIALITY

What a man does compared with what he is, is but a small part.
                                                        —*H. D. Thoreau.*

POVERTY

The American people have decided that poverty is just as wasteful and just as unnecessary as preventable disease. —*H. S. Truman.*

Poverty is the step-mother of genius. —*Josh Billings.*

The child was diseased at birth, stricken with a hereditary ill that only the most vital men are able to shake off. I mean poverty —the most deadly and prevalent of all diseases.
—*Eugene O'Neill.*

The greatest man in history was the poorest. —*R. W. Emerson.*

That amid our highest civilization men faint and die with want is not due to the niggardliness of nature, but to the injustice of man. —*Henry George.*

Poverty is a soft pedal upon all branches of human activity, not excepting the spiritual. —*H. L. Mencken.*

There can be no perfect democracy curtailed by color, race or poverty. But with all we accomplish all, even peace.
—*W. E. B. Dubois.*

Poverty is very good in poems but very bad in the house; very good in maxims and sermons but very bad in practical life.
—*H. W. Beecher.*

Peace will never be entirely secure until men everywhere have learned to conquer poverty without sacrificing liberty to security.
—*Norman Thomas.*

Planning is essential . . . to prevent war and conquer poverty.
—*Ibid.*

I am a little impatient of being told that property . . . bears all the burdens of the state. It bears those, indeed, which can most easily be borne, but poverty pays with its person the chief expenses of war, pestilence and famine. —*J. R. Lowell.*

This association of poverty with progress is the great enigma of our times. —*Henry George.*

Poverty is not merely deprivation; it means shame, degradation.
—*Ibid.*

As society advances the standard of poverty rises.
—*Theodore Parker.*

There is nothing perfectly secure but poverty.
—*H. W. Longfellow.*

Poverty must have many satisfactions, else there would not be
so many poor people.   —*Don Herold.*

Poverty often deprives a man of all spirit and virtue; it is hard
for an empty bag to stand upright.   —*B. Franklin.*

The human race has lived for ages in a scarcity economy. Poverty, privation and hardship have been taken for granted. Machine
mass production opens up new social vistas. Poverty can be abolished.   —*Scott Nearing.*

Poverty . . . It is life near the bone, where it is sweetest.
                                                           —*H. D. Thoreau.*

POWER

We all love power—to be on the winning side. You cannot help
being there when you are fighting the slum, for it is the cause of
justice and right.   —*Jacob Riis.*

We cannot live by power, and a culture that seeks to live by it
becomes brutal and sterile. But we can die without it.
                                                           —*Max Lerner.*

Freedom is power, a concentrated, skilful capacity to act.
                                                           —*Max Ascoli.*

A friend in power is a friend lost.   —*Henry Adams.*

Let us not be unmindful that liberty is power, that the nation
blessed with the largest portion of liberty must in proportion to its
numbers be the most powerful nation upon earth.
                                                           —*John Q. Adams.*

Man is born to seek power, yet his actual condition makes him
a slave to the power of others.   —*Hans J. Morgenthau.*

The history of political thought is the history of the moral evaluation of political power.   —*Ibid.*

The arts of power and its minions are the same in all countries
and in all ages. It marks its victim; denounces it; and excites
public odium and the public hatred, to conceal its own abuses and
encroachments.   —*Henry Clay.*

Governmental power grows by what it feeds upon. Give an
agency any political power and it at once tries to reach out after
more.   —*Samuel Gompers.*

The question is not what power the federal Government ought
to have but what powers in fact have been given by the people.
                                                           —*Owen J. Roberts.*

Men . . . very naturally seek money or power; and power because it is as good as money. —*R. W. Emerson.*

The imbecility of men is always inviting the impudence of power. —*Ibid.*

I have never been able to conceive how any rational being could propose happiness to himself from the exercise of power over others. —*T. Jefferson.*

Power is ever stealing from the many to the few.
—*Wendell Phillips.*

The state's power extends to every regulation of any business reasonably required and appropriate for the public protection. —*Louis D. Brandeis.*

Increased wages, higher pensions, more unemployment insurance, all are of no avail if the purchasing power of money falls faster. —*B. M. Baruch.*

Printing of money is not the creation of purchasing power.
—*Bradford Smith.*

The sovereign power of all civil authority is founded in the consent of the people. —*Roger Williams.*

There must be, not a balance of power, but a community of power; not organized rivalries, but an organized common peace.
—*Woodrow Wilson.*

Power flows to the man who knows how. —*Elbert Hubbard.*

By moral power we mean the power of a life and character, the power of good and great purposes.—No other power of man compares with this. —*Horace Bushnell.*

All power is, if not really given, yet formally stolen.
—*John Wise.*

Pretension is nothing; power is everything. —*E. P. Whipple.*

Power is always right, weakness always wrong. Power is always insolent and despotic. —*Noah Webster.*

There is always room for a man of force and he makes room for many. —*R. W. Emerson.*

A power over a man's subsistence amounts to a power over his will. —*Alexander Hamilton.*

There is no knowledge that is not power. —*R. W. Emerson.*

PRACTICE

Some folks in this world spend their whole time hunting after righteousness and can't find any time to practice it.

—*Josh Billings.*

In our country we have those three unspeakably precious things: freedom of speech, freedom of conscience, and the prudence never to practice either. —*Mark Twain.*

PRAISE

God made man merely to hear some praise of what He'd done on those five days. —*Christopher Morley.*

Judicious praise is to children what the sun is to flowers.

—*C. N. Bovee.*

As the Greek said, many men know how to flatter; few know how to praise. —*Wendell Phillips.*

A man who does not love praise is not a full man.

—*H. W. Beecher.*

Our continual desire for praise ought to convince us of our mortality, if nothing else will. —*H. W. Shaw.*

Desert being the essential condition of praise, there can be no reality in the one without the other. —*Washington Allston.*

PRAYER

I pray every single second of my life; not on my knees, but with my work. —*Susan B. Anthony.*

The dull pray; the geniuses are light makers.

—*R. W. Emerson.*

Practical prayer is harder on the soles of your shoes than on the knees of your trousers. —*Austin O'Malley.*

Do not pray for easy lives; pray to be stronger men. Do not pray for tasks equal to your powers; pray for power equal to your tasks. —*Phillips Brooks.*

Prayer is not only worship; it is also an invisible emanation of man's worshipping spirit—the most powerful form of energy that one can generate. —*Alexis Carrel.*

Prayer is a force as real as terrestrial gravity. —*Ibid.*

Prayer is a binding necessity in the lives of men and nations.

—*Ibid.*

Whenever a man lives by prayer you will find that he eats considerable besides. —*R. G. Ingersoll.*

Let every man pray that he may in some true sense be a soldier of fortune; that he may have the good fortune to spend his energies and his life in the service of his fellow-men in order that he may die to be recorded upon the rolls of those who have not thought of themselves but have thought of those whom they served. —*Woodrow Wilson.*

People would be surprised to know how much I learned about prayer from playing poker. —*Mary Austin.*

A good deed is the best prayer. —*R. G. Ingersoll.*

The hands that help are holier than the lips that pray. —*Ibid.*

Between the humble and contrite heart and the majesty of heaven there are no barriers; the only password is prayer.

—*Hosea Ballou.*

A prayer, in its simplest definition, is merely a wish turned heavenward. —*Phillips Brooks.*

'Tis Heaven alone that is given away; 'tis only God may be had for the asking. —*J. R. Lowell.*

Prayers are all one whether read from the modern prayerbook or spoken from the heart. —*David Swing.*

No unsophisticated man prays to have that done for him which he knows how to do for himself. —*George Santayana.*

PREACHERS

I won't take my religion from any man who never works except with his mouth and never cherishes any memory except the face of the woman on the American silver dollar. —*Carl Sandburg.*

None preaches better than the ant, and she says nothing.

—*B. Franklin.*

The minister's brain is often the "poor-box" of the church.

—*E. P. Whipple.*

Alas for the unhappy man that is called to stand in the pulpit, and not give the bread of life. —*R. W. Emerson.*

All things with which we deal preach to us. What is a farm but a mute gospel? —*Ibid.*

Genius is not essential to good preaching, but a live man is.

—*Austin Phelps.*

PREDICAMENT

Life is not a spectacle or a feast; it is a predicament.

—*George Santayana.*

Life is a predicament which precedes death. —*Henry James.*

PREFERENCES

Deep-seated preferences cannot be argued about—you cannot argue a man into liking a glass of beer. —*O. W. Holmes, Jr.*

In a world as,cursed by prejudice and hate as ours we cannot afford to relinquish any heartfelt preferences and attachments of man or beast. —*S. Parkes Cadman.*

PREJUDICE

A prejudice is a vagrant opinion without visible means of support. —*Ambrose Bierce.*

It is never too late to give up your prejudices.

—*H. D. Thoreau.*

A great many people think they are thinking when they are merely rearranging their prejudices. —*William James.*

For those who do not think, it is best at least to rearrange their prejudices once in a while. —*Luther Burbank.*

There is nothing stronger than human prejudice.

—*Wendell Phillips.*

The prejudiced and obstinate man does not so much hold opinions, as his opinions hold him. —*Tryon Edwards.*

Prejudice assumes the garb of reason, but the cheat is too thin. —*H. W. Shaw.*

Prejudice is the twin of illiberality. —*G. D. Prentice.*

The time is past when Christians in America can take a long spoon and hand the gospel to the black man out the back door. —*Mordecai W. Johnson.*

PREPAREDNESS

We have had the lesson before us over and over again—nations that were not ready and were unable to get ready found themselves overrun by the enemy. —*F. D. Roosevelt.*

To be prepared for war is one of the most effectual means of preserving peace. —*G. Washington.*

We are the only nation in the world that waits until we get into a war before we start getting ready for it. —*Will Rogers.*

PRESENT

In our regrets and apprehensions, we miss the only eternity of which man can be absolutely sure, the eternal Present.
—*W. L. Phelps.*

In the parliament of the present every man represents a constituency of the past. —*J. R. Lowell.*

What is really momentous and all-important to us is the present, by which the future is shaped and colored. —*J. G. Whittier.*

One of the illusions is that the present hour is not the real decisive hour.—No one has learned anything rightly, until he knows that every hour is Doomsday. —*R. W. Emerson.*

Act—act in the living Present! Heart within, and God o'erhead!
—*H. W. Longfellow.*

PRESIDENT

I would rather that the people should wonder why I wasn't President than why I am. —*Stuart Chase.*

I would rather be right than President. —*Henry Clay.*

No man will ever bring out of the Presidency the reputation which carries him into it. —*T. Jefferson.*

If forced to choose between the penitentiary and the White House for four years, I would say the penitentiary, thank you.
—*W. T. Sherman.*

My movements to the chair of government will be accompanied by feelings not unlike those of a culprit who is going to the place of his execution. —*G. Washington.*

There's some folks standing behind the President that ought to get around where he can watch 'em. —*Kin Hubbard.*

When I was a boy I was told that anybody could become President; I'm beginning to believe. —*Clarence Darrow.*

PRESS

Better to lose a battle than to lose the advantage of the free press. —*William E. Borah.*

PRETENSION

Pretension almost always overdoes the original, and hence exposes itself. —*Hosea Ballou.*

When half-gods go, the gods arrive. —*R. W. Emerson.*

PRICE

All good things are cheap: all bad are very dear.

—*H. D. Thoreau.*

You can't have price-fixing in America under any law I know of. The only time you can set a price on an article is when it comes into free and open competition with others.   —*M. E. Tydings.*

PRIDE

The proud hate pride—in others.   —*B. Franklin.*

There is such a thing as a man being too proud to fight!

—*Woodrow Wilson.*

Pride is as loud a beggar as want, and a good deal more saucy.

—*B. Franklin.*

Pride is the master sin of the devil.   —*E. H. Chapin.*

A proud man is seldom a grateful man, for he never thinks he gets as much as he deserves.   —*H. W. Beecher.*

Pride eradicates all vices but itself.   —*R. W. Emerson.*

Pride ruined the angels.   —*Ibid.*

Pride that dines on vanity, sups on contempt. —*B. Franklin.*

Pride and weakness are Siamese twins.   —*J. R. Lowell.*

Some people are proud of their humility.   —*H. W. Beecher.*

Pride seems to be equally distributed: the man who owns the carriage and the man who drives it seem to have it just alike.

—*H. W. Shaw.*

Snobbery is the pride of those who are not sure of their position.

—*Berton Braley.*

There was one who thought himself above me, and he was above me until he had that thought.   —*Elbert Hubbard.*

When shall we learn to be proud? For only pride is creative.

—*Randolph Bourne.*

No man made great by death offers more hope to lowly pride than does Abraham Lincoln; for, while living, he was himself so simple as often to be dubbed a fool.   —*T. V. Smith.*

The prouder a man is, the more he thinks he deserves; and the more he thinks he deserves, the less he really does deserve.

—*H. W. Beecher.*

PRIESTCRAFT

The horrors of the Inquisition, the Massacre of St. Bartholomew, the atrocities of Laud, the abomination of the Scotch Kirk, the persecution of the Quakers had one object—the enslavement of the mind. —*Brooks Adams.*

PRIESTS

Once we had wooden chalices and golden priests; now we have golden chalices and wooden priests. —*R. W. Emerson.*

PRINCIPLES

If a principle is good for anything, it is worth living up to.
—*B. Franklin.*

Important principles may and must be flexible. —*A. Lincoln.*

We will hold firmly to the principle that those whom private industry cannot support must be supported by government agency, whether Federal or State. —*Wendell Willkie.*

Back of every noble life there are principles which have fashioned it. —*G. C. Lorimer.*

We may be personally defeated, but our principles never.
—*W. L. Garrison.*

Nothing can bring you peace but the triumph of principles.
—*R. W. Emerson.*

Principles have no real force except when one is well fed.
—*Mark Twain.*

Two principles . . . have stood face to face from the beginning of time. The one is the common right of humanity; the other, the divine right of kings. —*A. Lincoln.*

If we cherish the virtues and the principles of our fathers, Heaven will assist us to carry on the work of human liberty and human happiness. —*Daniel Webster.*

The great motors of the race are moral, not intellectual, and their force lies ready to the use of the poorest and weakest of all.
—*J. R. Lowell.*

The day has come when America is privileged to spend her blood and her might for the principles that gave her birth and the peace which she has treasured. —*Woodrow Wilson.*

Expedients are for the hour; principles for the ages.
—*H. W. Beecher.*

An army of principles will penetrate where an army of soldiers cannot.   —*T. Paine.*

PRINTING
The plainest print cannot be read through a gold eagle.
—*A. Lincoln.*

It is the mission of the printer to diffuse light and knowledge by a judicious intermingling of black and white.
—*Frederick Douglass.*

PRIVACY
The right to be alone—the most comprehensive of rights, and the right most valued by civilized men.   —*Louis D. Brandeis.*

No more privacy than a goldfish.   —*I. S. Cobb.*

PRIVILEGES
There must be no place in the post-war world for social privileges for either individuals or nations.   —*F. D. Roosevelt.*

PROCRASTINATION
Never leave that till tomorrow which you can do today.
—*B. Franklin.*

Procrastination is the art of keeping up with yesterday.
—*Don Marquis.*

Putting off an easy thing makes it hard, and putting off a hard one makes it impossible.   —*G. H. Lorimer.*

PRODUCTION
We must produce more—more goods, more services, more housing, more transportation—before we can expect to live better.
—*Mordecai Ezekiel.*

Mass production is production for the masses.   —*E. A. Filene.*

Improvement in the living standards of the workers must, in the main, come from increased productivity.   —*Sidney Hillman.*

Unless each man produces more than he receives, increases his output, there will be less for him and all the others.
—*B. M. Baruch.*

PROFANITY
The foolish and wicked practice of profuse cursing and swearing is a vice so mean and low that every person of sense and character detests and despises it.   —*G. Washington.*

Profaneness is a brutal vice. He who indulges in it is no gentleman.   —*E. H. Chapin.*

PROFESSIONALS

We forget that the most successful statesmen have been profes-
sionals. Lincoln was a professional politician.

—*Felix Frankfurter.*

PROFESSOR

Surely the nation which has built palaces for libraries, laboratories, and students will not permanently ignore the professor who
is in truth the institution itself.   —*Abraham Flexner.*

PROFIT

Profit is without honor except in our country—and even here
capitalists are beginning to look over their shoulders.

—*L. P. Shield.*

It is in the interest of the community that a man in a free business, in a competitive business, shall have the incentive to make as
much money as he can.   —*Louis D. Brandeis.*

If your earning capacity is the capacity to earn the public confidence you can go about your business like free men.

—*Woodrow Wilson.*

In business the earning of profit is something more than an incident of success. It is an essential condition of success; because
the continued absence of profit itself spells failure.

—*Louis D. Brandeis.*

When shallow critics denounce the profit motive inherent in our
system of private enterprise, they ignore the fact that it is an
economic support of every human right we possess and without it,
all rights would soon disappear.   —*D. D. Eisenhower.*

The day of large profits is probably past.   —*C. D. Wright.*

Children dying of pellagra must die because a profit cannot be
taken from an orange. And coroners must fill in certificates—died of
malnutrition—because the food must rot, must be forced to rot.

—*John Steinbeck.*

The organization of society on the principle of private profit . . .
is leading both to the deformation of humanity by unregulated
industrialism, and to the exhaustion of natural resources.

—*T. S. Eliot.*

PROGRESS

The test of our progress is not whether we add more to the abundance of those who have much; it is whether we provide enough for those who have too little.   —*F. D. Roosevelt.*

Every step of progress the world has made has been from scaffold to scaffold and from stake to stake.   —*Wendell Phillips.*

Westward the star of empire takes its way.   —*J. Q. Adams.*

Modern invention has banished the spinning-wheel, and the same law of progress makes the woman of today a different woman from her grandmother.   —*Susan B. Anthony.*

> New occasions teach new duties
>   Time makes ancient good uncouth;
> They must upward still and onward,
>   Who would keep abreast of truth.
>   —*J. R. Lowell.*

So long as all the increased wealth which modern progress brings, goes but to build up great fortunes, to increase luxury, and make sharper the contest between the House of Have and the House of Want, progress is not real and cannot be permanent. The reaction must come.   —*Henry George.*

It is not strange . . . that such an exuberance of enterprise should cause some individuals to mistake change for progress, and the invasion of the rights of others for national progress and glory.
                                     —*Millard Fillmore.*

The measure of the progress of civilization is the progress of the people.   —*George Bancroft.*

One of the fundamentals that has made America what it is today is our willingness to tear down and rebuild with the new and better, usually the bigger. To promote obsolescence is to accelerate progress.   —*A. P. Sloan.*

Our progress in degeneracy appears to me to be pretty rapid.
                                     —*A. Lincoln.*

Progress, the growth of power, is the end and boon of liberty.
                                     —*W. E. Channing.*

Progress is not an illusion but neither is it the habit of the universe.   —*Lyman Bryson.*

The life and the spirit of the American economy is progress and expansion.   —*H. S. Truman.*

Social progress does not have to be bought at the price of individual freedom.   —*John Foster Dulles.*

We must embark on a bold new program for making the benefits of our scientific advances and industrial progress available for the improvement and growth of underdeveloped areas.

—*H. S. Truman.*

The measure of the progress of civilization is the progress of the people.   —*George Bancroft.*

The truth that progress is the very end of our being, must not be received as a tradition, but comprehended and felt as a reality.

—*W. E. Channing.*

Progress is the activity of today and the assurance of tomorrow.

—*R. W. Emerson.*

Unquestionably, there is progress. The average American now pays out twice as much in taxes as he formerly got in wages.

—*H. L. Mencken.*

The direction of all true progress is toward greater freedom, and along an endless succession of ideas.   —*C. E. Bovee.*

No steps backward is the rule of human history.

—*Theodore Parker.*

The great thing in this world is not so much where we stand, as in what direction we are moving.   —*O. W. Holmes.*

I am suffocated and lost when I have not the bright feeling of progression.   —*Margaret Fuller.*

The natural progress of things is for liberty to yield and government to gain ground.   —*T. Jefferson.*

Moral excellence is the bright consummate flower of all progress.

—*Charles Sumner.*

We are either progressing or retrograding all the while; there is no such thing as remaining stationary in this life.

—*J. F. Clarke.*

The greatest evils of the world are goods that have refused to go on.   —*Julia W. Howe.*

I look forward to a time when man shall progress upon something worthier and higher than his stomach.   —*Jack London.*

The true law of the race is progress and development. Whenever civilization pauses in the march of conquest, it is overthrown by the barbarian.   —*W. G. Simms.*

Technological progress has merely provided us with more efficient means for going backward.   —*Robert M. Hutchins.*

PROHIBITION
Our country has deliberately undertaken a great social and economic experiment noble in motive and far-reaching in purpose.
—*Herbert Hoover.*

Prohibition has made nothing but trouble.   —*Al Capone.*

Adam did not want the apple for the apple's sake, he wanted it only because it was forbidden.   —*Mark Twain.*

PROHIBITIONISTS
Although man is already ninety per cent water, the Prohibitionists are not yet satisfied.   —*J. K. Bangs.*

PROMISE
Undertake not what you cannot perform but be careful to keep your promise.   —*G. Washington.*

Magnificent promises are always to be suspected.
—*Theodore Parker.*

PROOF
I am from Missouri. You have got to show me.
—*W. D. Vandiver.*

No way of thinking or doing, however ancient, can be trusted without proof.   —*H. D. Thoreau.*

PROPAGANDA
Propaganda replaces moral philosophy.   —*Hans J. Morgenthau.*

Both slogans, "Art is propaganda" and "Propaganda has no place in art," will be dropt hastily in the pail like fouled bandages when humanity, cured of its contemporary illness, takes the road again.
—*Max Eastman.*

PROPERTY
Man has no property in the generations which are to follow.
—*T. Paine.*

It is the right of the possessor of property to be placed on equal footing with all his fellow-citizens, in every respect. If he is not to be exalted on account of his wealth, neither is he to be denounced.   —*James F. Cooper.*

Property need not be made a tyrant in order to give men freedom and incentive to acquire it, own it and manage it and to unleash the great productive power of free enterprise.

—*W. O. Douglas.*

Whenever there is, in any country, uncultivated land and unemployed poor, it is clear that the laws of property have been so far extended as to violate natural right. —*T. Jefferson.*

It is best for all to leave each man free to acquire property as fast as he can. —*A. Lincoln.*

Property is the fruit of labor; property is desirable; is a positive good in the world. —*Ibid.*

Property, like liberty, thought immune under the Constitution from destruction, is not immune from regulation essential for the common good. What the regulation shall be, every generation must work out for itself. —*Benjamin Cardozo.*

The primary objective of government, beyond the mere repression of violence, is the making of rules which determine the property relations of members of society. —*Charles A. Beard.*

The supreme power cannot take from any man any part of his property, without his consent in person, or by representation.

—*James Otis.*

The instinct of ownership is fundamental in man's nature.

—*William James.*

Mine is better than ours. —*B. Franklin.*

Let not him who is houseless pull down the house of another, but let him work diligently and build one for himself, thus by example assuring that his own shall be safe from violence when built. —*A. Lincoln.*

The highest law gives a thing to him who can use it.

—*H. D. Thoreau.*

Property does become clothed with a public interest when used in a manner to make it of public consequence, and affect the community at large. —*Morrison R. Waite.*

Every man holds his property subject to the general right of the community to regulate its use to whatever degree the public welfare may require it. —*Theodore Roosevelt.*

Ultimately property rights and personal rights are the same thing. —*Calvin Coolidge.*

Few rich men own their property. The property owns them.
                                          —*R. G. Ingersoll.*

The property of the nation must be controlled by the nation.
                                          —*Albert Brisbane.*

PROPHECY

Don't ever prophesy—unless you know.   —*J. R. Lowell.*

Don't ever prophesy; for if you prophesy wrong, nobody will forget it; and if you prophesy right, nobody will remember it.
                                          —*Josh Billings.*

PROPHETS

To revere the prophets means to recognize the radical social implications of their message.   —*F. M. Isserman.*

The prophets, from Amos to Jesus, walked along the thorny road—enduring ostracism and martyrdom.   —*Ibid.*

The problems that faced the prophets face us.   —*Ibid.*

Prophets were twice stoned—first in anger; then, after their death, with a handsome slab in the graveyard.
                                          —*Christopher Morley.*

PROSPERITY

The best prosperity consists in right doing.

                                          —*Lyman Abbott.*

Not only the wealth but the independence and security of a country appear to be materially connected with the prosperity of manufactures.   —*Alexander Hamilton.*

The assertion that American prosperity is due to our great natural resources is only partly true. The fertile fields of the West would have brought us little wealth, but for mercantile science, and the development of agricultural machinery which eliminates waste in human labor.   —*Louis Brandeis.*

The less Government interferes with private pursuits, the better for the general prosperity.   —*Martin Van Buren.*

If it were true that we could create prosperity by making goods to give away, then we would not have to give them to foreign countries. We could accomplish the same result by making the goods to dump into the sea.   —*Henry Hazlitt.*

It requires a strong constitution to withstand repeated attacks of prosperity.   —*J. L. Basford.*

People who assume that we should always be prosperous unless some villain upset the applecart are reckoning without economic science. —*George Soule.*

If on this new continent we merely build another country of **great** but unjustly divided material prosperity, we shall have done nothing. —*Theodore Roosevelt.*

Of all the dispositions and habits, which lead to political prosperity, Religion and Morality are indispensable. —*G. Washington.*

To preserve the peace of our fellow citizens, promote their prosperity and happiness, reunite opinion, cultivate a spirit of candor, moderation, charity and forbearance toward one another, are objects calling for the efforts and sacrifices of every good man and patriot. —*T. Jefferson.*

To rejoice in the prosperity of another is to partake of it.
—*Wm. Austin.*

One is never more on trial than in the moment of excessive good fortune. —*Lew Wallace.*

PROVIDENCE

There are many scapegoats for our sins, but the most popular is Providence. —*Mark Twain.*

The Great Spirit does right. He knows what is best for His children; we are satisfied. —*Red Jacket.*

Without belief in Providence I think I should go crazy. Without God the world would be a maze without a clue.
—*Woodrow Wilson.*

God's providence is on the side of clear heads.
—*H. W. Beecher.*

Heaven trims our lamps while we sleep. —*A. B. Alcott.*

Providence is but another name for natural law.
—*H. W. Beecher.*

The superior man is the providence of the inferior. He is eyes for the blind, strength for the weak, and a shield for the defenceless.
—*R. G. Ingersoll.*

PRUDENCE

It is always the part of prudence to face every claimant and pay every just demand on your time, your talents, or your heart.
—*R. W. Emerson.*

It is by the goodness of God that in our country we have those three unspeakably precious things: freedom of speech, freedom of conscience, and the prudence never to practise either.

—Mark Twain.

Put all your eggs in one basket—and watch that basket.

—Ibid.

PUBLIC

The public is wiser than the wisest critic.   *—George Bancroft.*

The public good must come first.   *—Gifford Pinchot.*

The public be damned.   *—W. H. Vanderbilt.*

The public, with its mob yearning to be instructed, edified and pulled by the nose, demands certainties . . . but there are no certainties.   *—H. L. Mencken.*

To say that business is clothed with a public interest is not to import that the public may take over its entire management and run it at the expense of the owner.   *—Wm. Howard Taft.*

Those who feel themselves to be truly public servants will first bethink themselves of the public when in situations of public trust.

—James F. Cooper.

If there's anything a public servant hates to do it's something for the public.   *—Kin Hubbard.*

PUBLICITY

Modern business and persons and organizations that seek publicity must recognize their obligations to the public and to the press.   *—Henry F. Woods, Jr.*

Possessions, outward success, publicity, luxury—to me these have always been contemptible.   *—Albert Einstein.*

Business is a publicity, as well as an economic, game. We've learned to contact the moon, but we still have trouble contacting the public.   *—W. B. Weisenburger.*

When it comes to selling the business system, we get as drab as a crutch, as unexciting as a chorus girl in a flannel nightgown.

—Ibid.

PUBLIC OPINION

A Government can be no better than the public opinion which sustains it.   *—F. D. Roosevelt.*

PUBLIC SAFETY

There is no right to strike against the public safety by anybody, anywhere, anytime.　　　　　　　　　　　*—Calvin Coolidge.*

PUBLISHERS

Publishers are demons, there's no doubt about it.
　　　　　　　　　　　　　　　　　—William James.

PUN

Of puns it has been said that those most dislike who are least able to utter them.　　　　　　　　　*—Edgar Allan Poe.*

A pun is the lowest form of humor—when you don't think of it first.　　　　　　　　　　　　　*—Oscar Levant.*

PUNCTUALITY

Strict punctuality is a cheap virtue.　　　*—B. Franklin.*

Unfaithfulness in keeping an appointment is an act of clear dishonesty. You may as well borrow a person's money as his time.
　　　　　　　　　　　　　　　　　—Horace Mann.

Want of punctuality is want of virtue.　　*—John M. Mason.*

PUNISHMENT

The object of punishment is, prevention from evil; it never can be made impulsive to good.　　　　　　*—Horace Mann.*

The best of us being unfit to die, what an unexpressible absurdity to put the worst to death!　　　*—Nathaniel Hawthorne.*

Crime and punishment grow out of one stem.
　　　　　　　　　　　　　　　　　—R. W. Emerson.

Punishment is a fruit that, unsuspected, ripens within the flower of the pleasure that concealed it.　　　　　*—Ibid.*

We are not punished for our sins, but by them.
　　　　　　　　　　　　　　　　　—Elbert Hubbard.

Society does not punish those who sin, but those who sin and conceal not cleverly.　　　　　　　　　　　*—Ibid.*

This, it seems to me, is the most severe punishment—finding out you are wrong.　　　　　　　　　*—Walter Winchell.*

PURITAN

What the Puritans gave the world was not thought, but action.
—*Wendell Phillips.*

The great artists of the world are never Puritans, and seldom even ordinarily respectable.   —*H. L. Mencken.*

The objection to Puritans is not that they try to make us think as they do, but that they try to make us do as they think.   —*Ibid.*

We all have the potentiality of the puritan within us.
—*Randolph Bourne.*

The puritan gets his sense of power . . . in a crude assault on that most vulnerable part of other people's souls, their moral sense.
—*Ibid.*

The Puritans were in possession of everything necessary for the creation of living poetry, with the exception of the most important of all—a free soul. That their Calvinism crushed.
—*Charles Angoff.*

The Puritans were interested in the Word and that alone. They abhorred whatever smelled of the fine arts.   —*Ibid.*

PURITANISM

The ferment that produced Puritanism produced also the inquiring mind that denied the essential doctrine of all dogmatic faiths—universal conformity.   —*Charles and Mary Beard.*

The child of Puritanism is not mere Calvinism—it is the loyalty to justice which tramples under foot the wicked laws of its own epoch.   —*Wendell Phillips.*

PURITY

Purity in person and in morals is true godliness.   —*Hosea Ballou.*

Every pure thought is a glimpse of God.   —*C. A. Bartol.*

While our hearts are pure our lives are happy and our peace is sure.   —*William Winter.*

PURPOSE

The essence of freedom is the practicability of purpose.
—*A. N. Whitehead.*

Man's chief purpose . . . is the creation and preservation of values. —*Lewis Mumford.*

When you awake, resolve that it shall be to some faithful purpose. —*O. L. Frothingham.*

There is only one purpose to which a whole society can be directed by a deliberate plan. That purpose is war.

—*Walter Lippmann.*

Only the consciousness of a purpose that is mightier than any man and worthy of all men can fortify and inspirit and compose the souls of men. —*Ibid.*

Great minds have purposes, others have wishes.

—*Washington Irving.*

PURSUIT

The crowning fortune of a man is to be born to some pursuit which finds him employment and happiness, whether it be to make baskets, or broadswords, or canals, or statues, or songs.

—*R. W. Emerson.*

The rapture of pursuing is the prize the vanquished gain.

—*H. W. Longfellow.*

Q

QUACKERY

Take the humbug out of this world, and you haven't much left to do business with. —*H. W. Shaw.*

It would not be thought very just or wise to arraign the honorable professions of law and physic because the one produces the pettifogger and the other the quack. —*Henry Clay.*

Quackery has not such friend as credulity. —*Charles Simmons.*

Quackery is a thing universal, and universally successful. . . . No imposition is too great for the credulity of man.
—*H. D. Thoreau.*

QUALIFY

Christian morality is qualified to survive because love and agreement, which unite men, are stronger than hate and fear, which divide them. —*R. B. Perry.*

Submersion in war does not necessarily qualify a man to be the master of the peace. —*Ernie Pyle.*

When Nature has work to do she qualifies men for that and sends them equipped. —*R. W. Emerson.*

QUALITIES

Nothing endures but personal qualities. —*Walt Whitman.*

The first point of measurement of any man is that of quality.
—*J. W. Higginson.*

The finest qualities of our nature, like the bloom on fruits, can be preserved only by the most delicate handling.
—*H. D. Thoreau.*

The first of qualities for a great statesman is to be honest.
—*John Q. Adams.*

437

Moral qualities rule the world, but at short distances the senses are despotic. —*R. W. Emerson.*

Coolness and absence of heat and haste, indicate fine qualities. A gentleman makes no noise. A lady is serene. —*Ibid.*

The Christian churches have a special responsibility to keep alive now these attitudes and qualities of spirit that will make a just and constructive peace possible. —*H. E. Fosdick.*

QUALITY

It is futile, even silly, to suppose that some quality that is directly present constitutes the whole of the thing presenting the quality. —*John Dewey.*

It is a quality of revolutions not to go by old lines or old laws; but to break up both, and make new ones. —*A. Lincoln.*

The common people of America display a quality of good common sense which is heartening to anyone who believes in the democratic process. —*George Gallup.*

Everything runs to excess; every good quality is noxious if unmixed. —*R. W. Emerson.*

I think there is only one quality worse than hardness of heart and that is softness of head. —*Theodore Roosevelt.*

The rarest quality in an epitaph is truth. —*H. D. Thoreau.*

From the very beginning our people have markedly combined practical capacity for affairs with power of devotion to an ideal. The lack of either quality would have rendered the possession of the other of small value. —*Theodore Roosevelt.*

The quality of a teacher's life is a part of his professional equipment. —*A. Tompkins.*

The best is the cheapest. —*B. Franklin.*

Endurance is the crowning quality, and patience all the passion of great heart. —*J. R. Lowell.*

You cannot judge by outward appearance; the soul is only transparent to its Maker. —*Hosea Ballou.*

QUANTITY

Power obeys reality and not appearances; power is according to quality, and not quantity. —*R. W. Emerson.*

QUARANTINE

War is a contagion. . . . Quarantine the aggressors.

—*F. D. Roosevelt.*

QUARRELS

Every quarrel begins in nothing and ends in a struggle for supremacy.   —*Elbert Hubbard.*

Thrice is he armed that hath his quarrel just—and four times he who gets his fist in fust.   —*Artemus Ward.*

He that blows the coals in quarrels he has nothing to do with has no right to complain if the sparks fly in his face.

—*B. Franklin.*

. . . When chickens quit quarrelling over their food they often find that there is enough for all of them. I wonder if it might not be the same with the human race.   —*Don Marquis.*

A man may quarrel with himself alone; that is, by controverting his better instincts and knowledge when brought face to face with temptation.   —*W. E. Channing.*

QUARTER

Delight is to him, who gives no quarter for the truth, and kills, burns, and destroys all sin, though he pluck it out from under the robes of Senators and Judges.   —*Herman Melville.*

QUENCH

My love is such that rivers cannot quench.

—*Anne Bradstreet.*

QUEER

All the world is queer save thee and me, and even thou art a little queer.   —*Robert Owen.*

QUESTION

A child can ask a thousand questions that the wisest man cannot answer.   —*Jacob Abbott.*

The question of common sense is: what is poetry good for?—A question which would abolish the rose and be triumphantly answered by the cabbage.   —*J. R. Lowell.*

Civilization is becoming a hospital. You can hear Man moaning in the night, tossing in a fever of indecision, unable to come to

grips with the agonizing question of how to renew and reinstate his faith in life, to feel once more the illusion of life's significance.
—*Samuel D. Schmalhausen.*

We, upon many occasions, see wise and good men on the wrong as well as on the right side of questions, of the first magnitude to society. —*Alexander Hamilton.*

Ambition, avarice, personal animosity, party opposition, and many other motives, not more laudable than these, are apt to operate as well upon those who support, as upon those who oppose, the right side of a question. —*Ibid.*

The great question for all American radicals is that they must go back and reconsider the whole question of means of inquiry about social change and of truly democratic methods of approach to social progress. —*John Dewey.*

Only one fellow in ten thousand understands the currency question, and we meet him every day. —*Kin Hubbard.*

The labor question is beginning to open like a yawning gulf, rapidly widening every year. —*Walt Whitman.*

Is not marriage an open question, when it is alleged, from the beginning of the world, that such as are in the institution wish to get out, and such as are out wish to get in?
—*R. W. Emerson.*

QUESTIONABLE

We find no new truth because we take some venerable but questionable proposition as the indubitable starting point.
—*Will Durant.*

QUESTIONS

Man will not live without answers to his questions.
—*Hans J. Morgenthau.*

By nature's kindly disposition most questions which it is beyond a man's power to answer do not occur to him at all.
—*George Santayana.*

Absolute freedom of the press to discuss public questions is a foundation stone of American liberty. —*Herbert Hoover.*

We must not expect simple answers to far-reaching questions. However far our gaze penetrates, there are always heights beyond which block our vision. —*A. N. Whitehead.*

Shifts in attitudes toward economic questions are now occurring in the United States at a speed which is too dazzling to be comprehended. *—Kirby Page.*

Great political questions stir the deepest nature of one half of the nation; but they pass far above and over the heads of the other half. *—Wendell Phillips.*

QUICKEN

Ease, rest, owes its deliciousness to toil; and no toil is so burdensome as the rest of him who has nothing to task and quicken his powers. *—W. E. Channing.*

QUIET

To have a quiet mind is to possess one's mind wholly; to have a calm spirit is to command one's self. *—H. W. Mabie.*

God gives quietness at last. *—J. G. Whittier.*

Stillness of person and steadiness of features are signal marks of good breeding. *—O. W. Holmes.*

Vulgar persons can't sit still, or, at least, they must work their limbs or features. *—Ibid.*

QUOTATIONS

Every book is a quotation. *—R. W. Emerson.*

By necessity, by proclivity, and by delight, we all quote. *—Ibid.*

He presents me with what is always an acceptable gift who brings me news of a great thought before unknown. He enriches me without impoverishing himself. *—Ibid.*

The profoundest thought or passion sleeps as in a mine, until an equal mind and heart finds and publishes it. *—Ibid.*

To appreciate and use correctly a valuable maxim, requires a genius, a vital appropriative exercise of mind, closely allied to that which first created it. *—W. R. Alger.*

One must be a wise reader to quote wisely and well.
—A. B. Alcott.

Next to the originator of a good sentence is the first quoter of it.
—R. W. Emerson.

Now we sit through Shakespeare in order to recognize the quotations. *—Orson Welles.*

A great man quotes bravely, and will not draw on his invention when his memory serves him with a word as good.

—R. W. Emerson.

What he quotes he fills with his own voice and humor, and the whole cyclopedia of his table-talk is presently believed to be his own. *—Ibid.*

R

RACE

Today the notion of a master race is being revived, and most of us agree that it means the moral degradation of mankind.

—A. N. Whitehead.

Falseness dies; injustice and oppression in the end fade and vanish away. Greed, cruelty, selfishness, and inhumanity are short-lived; the individual suffers but the race goes on.

—Frank Norris.

In the gain or loss of one race all the rest have equal claim.

—J. R. Lowell.

Mere connection with what is known as a superior race will not permanently carry an individual forward unless he has individual worth.   *—Booker T. Washington.*

No race that has anything to contribute to the markets of the world is long in any degree ostracized.   *—Ibid.*

No race can prosper till it learns that there is as much dignity in tilling a field as in writing a poem. It is at the bottom of life we must begin, and not at the top.   *—Ibid.*

In the sciences and the arts and the letters, yellow men, black men, brown men, and red play on the teams on equal terms with white.   *—H. M. Kallen.*

A strong being is the proof of the race and of the ability of the universe.   *—Walt Whitman.*

The race to which we belong is the most arrogant and rapacious, the most exclusive and indomitable in history. All other races have been its enemies or its victims.   *—J. J. Ingalls.*

Human liberty may yet, perhaps, be obliged to repose its principal hopes on the intelligence and the vigor of the Saxon race.

—Daniel Webster.

Race phobia is as old as human nature and springs from the same primitive impulse: *We* are the People.

—*George A. Dorsey.*

The Americans, like the English, probably make love worse than any other race. —*Walt Whitman.*

Nobody has ever given satisfactory proof of an inherent inequality of races. —*Franz Boas.*

There are good and bad in all races. —*T. R. Garth.*

We cannot say that an idiot must of necessity be black or red, for in fact he may be white. —*Ibid.*

RADICAL

If a man is right, he can't be too radical; if he is wrong, he can't be too conservative. —*Josh Billings.*

A radical is a man with both feet firmly planted in the air.

—*F. D. Roosevelt.*

I am trying to do two things,—dare to be a radical, and not a fool; which, if I may judge by the exhibition around me, is a matter of no small difficulty. —*James A. Garfield.*

RADICALISM

The note of radicalism is a republican and individual note which cannot be too often sounded. —*Howard Mumford Jones.*

RADIO

Before the advent of the radio, there were advantages in being a shut-in. —*Don Herold.*

RAGE

Rage is mental imbecility. —*Hosea Ballou.*

RAIN

Into each life some rain must fall,
Some days must be dark and dreary.

—*H. W. Longfellow.*

The rain comes when the wind calls. —*R. W. Emerson.*

Rain is as necessary to the mind as to vegetation. My very thoughts become thirsty, and crave the moisture.

—*John Burroughs.*

RAINBOW

The rainbow—God's illumined promise. —*H. W. Longfellow.*

The rainbow—God's glowing covenant.   *—Hosea Ballou.*

RANK

What men prize most is a privilege, even if it be that of chief mourner at a funeral.   *—J. R. Lowell.*

A ploughman on his legs is higher than a gentleman on his knees.
—B. Franklin.

It is an interesting question how far men would retain their relative rank if they were divested of their clothes.
—H. D. Thoreau.

RASCAL

When a man makes up his mind to become a rascal, he should examine himself closely and see if he isn't better constructed for a fool.   *—Josh Billings.*

RATIONALISM

As rationalism sees it, the world is governed by laws which are accessible to human reason.   *—Hans J. Morgenthau.*

RATIONALIZING

Rationalizing is the self-exculpation which occurs when we feel ourselves, or our group, accused of misapprehension or error.
—James Harvey Robinson.

REACTIONARY

A reactionary is a somnambulist walking backward.
—F. D. Roosevelt.

READING

Read the best books first, or you may not have a chance to read them at all.   *—H. D. Thoreau.*

Reading is a dissuasion from immorality. Reading stands in the place of company.   *—H. W. Beecher.*

Many readers judge of the power of a book by the shock it gives their feelings.   *—H. W. Longfellow.*

Men must read for amusement as well as for knowledge.
—H. W. Beecher.

It is curious how tyrannical the habit of reading is, and what shifts we make to escape thinking. There is no bore we dread being left alone with so much as our own mind.   *—J. R. Lowell.*

Never read any book that is not a year old.   *—R. W. Emerson.*

Never read any but the famed books.   *—Ibid.*

Never read any but what you like. —*Ibid.*

In Hollywood the woods are full of people that learned to write but evidently can't read; if they could read their stuff, they'd stop writing. —*Will Rogers.*

Anybody that's got time to read half of the new books has got entirely too much time. —*Kin Hubbard.*

I divide all readers into two classes: those who read to remember and those who read to forget. —*W. L. Phelps.*

'Tis the good reader that makes the good book.

—*R. W. Emerson.*

A classic is something that everybody wants to have read and nobody wants to read. —*Mark Twain.*

REALITY

Whatever the mind demands for the satisfaction of its subjective interests and tendencies may be assumed as real in default of positive disproof. —*B. P. Boune.*

My greatest enemy is reality. I have fought it successfully for thirty years. —*Margaret Anderson.*

American realism is the realism of a spoiled child.

—*J. Donald Adams.*

I accept Reality and dare not question it. —*Walt Whitman.*

All literature tends to be concerned with the question of reality. —*Lionel Trilling.*

REASON

Our reasonings grasp at straws for premises and float on gossamers for deductions. —*A. N. Whitehead.*

We are a people with a faith in reason, and when we lose that faith and subtitute for it faith in weapons we become weak and are lost, even with our superatomic weapons.

—*David E. Lilienthal.*

Reason never has failed men. Only force and repression have made the wrecks in the world. —*William A. White.*

Socially useful reason is socially determined reason.

—*Hans S. Morgenthau.*

A man always has two reasons for doing anything—a good reason and the real reason. —*J. P. Morgan.*

If the animals had reason, they would act just as ridiculous as we menfolks do.   —*Josh Billings.*

If you do not hear Reason, she will rap your knuckles.
                                                          —*B. Franklin.*

We must ever be on our guard lest we erect our prejudices into legal principles. If we would guide ourselves by the light of reason, we must let our minds be bold.   —*Louis D. Brandeis.*

If I go to heaven I want to take my reason with me.
                                                     —*R. G. Ingersoll.*

Error of opinion may be tolerated where reason is left free to admit it.   —*T. Jefferson.*

If we believe in reasonableness we must follow wherever reason may lead.   —*A. Meiklejohn.*

An appeal to the reason of the people has never been known to fail in the long run.   —*J. R. Lowell.*

I have found some of the best reasons I ever had for remaining at the bottom simply by looking at the men on top.   —*F. M. Colby.*

Reason is a genius when it comes to solving problems in algebra. Reason is a good deal of an idiot when it comes to solving problems in human experience.   —*Samuel D. Schmalhausen.*

The more numerous an assembly may be, of whatever characters composed, the greater is known to be the ascendancy of passion over reason.   —*Alexander Hamilton.*

The Life of Reason is the seat of all ultimate values.
                                                    —*George Santayana.*

Reason of course, is weak, when measured against its neverending task. Weak indeed, compared with the follies and passions of mankind, which, we must admit, almost entirely control our human destinies, in great things and small.
                                                     —*Albert Einstein.*

REBEL

As long as our social order regards the good of institutions rather than the good of men, so long will there be a vocation for the rebel.   —*Richard Roberts.*

He is a rebel because he has a nobler social vision than our own.
                                                            —*Ibid.*

I am the sworn poet of every dauntless rebel the world over.
—*Walt Whitman.*

The rebel is a social outcast to be silenced at any cost.
—*V. L. Parrington.*

REBELLION

A little rebellion now and then . . . is a medicine necessary for the sound health of government. —*T. Jefferson.*

The only justification of rebellion is success. —*T. B. Reed.*

Rebellion against tyrants is obedience to God. —*B. Franklin.*

Remember the ladies . . . If particular care and attention is not paid to the ladies we are determined to foment a rebellion, and will not hold ourselves bound by any laws in which we have no voice or representation. —*Abigail Adams.*

When all other rights are broken away, the right to rebellion is made perfect. —*T. Paine.*

REBIRTH

Let us pray for a new birth, not as one experience, but as the perpetual experience of our lives. —*Phillips Brooks.*

It is slow work to be born again. —*H. W. Beecher.*

RECEIVER

A receiver is appointed by the court to take what's left.
—*Robert Frost.*

RECOLLECTION

The next thing like living one's life over again seems to be a recollection of that life, and to make that recollection as durable as possible by putting it down in writing. —*B. Franklin.*

RECOMMENDATION

The hardest thing is writing a recommendation for someone we know. —*Kin Hubbard.*

RECOMPENSE

There never was a person who did anything worth doing that did not receive more than he gave. —*H. W. Beecher.*

Soon or late, our Father makes his perfect recompense to all.
—*J. G. Whittier.*

RECONSTRUCTION

We must face the task of reconstructing our culture and creating our own design for living.—Until the culture makes the conservation of human values the dominant theme, the individual, cannot, or will not, find his fulfilment. —*Laurence K. Frank.*

RECREATION

Men cannot labor on always. They must have recreation.
—*Orville Dewey.*

To re-create strength, rest. Te re-create mind, repose. To re-create cheerfulness, hope in God, or change the object of attention to one more elevated and worthy of thought.
—*Charles Simmons.*

RECURRENCE

Our life is but a new form of the way men have lived from the beginning. —*H. W. Beecher.*

REDEMPTION

Christ is redemption to us, only as he actually redeems and delivers our nature from sin. —*Horace Bushnell.*

The satisfaction of Christ is to free us from misery; the merit of Christ is to purchase happiness for us. —*Jonathan Edwards.*

Welcome the hour that may put me where a man cannot take a dollar in exchange for a soul. —*John Wise.*

REFINEMENT

True refinement elevates the soul of man, purifying the manners by improving the intellect. —*Hosea Ballou.*

Refinement is the lifting of one's self upward from the merely sensual; the effort of the soul to etherealize the common wants and uses of life. —*H. W. Beecher.*

Refinement that carries us away from our fellow-men is not God's refinement. —*Ibid.*

REFLECTION

When I reflect upon the number of disagreeable people who I know have gone to a better world, I am moved to lead a different life. —*Mark Twain.*

Think twice before you speak, or act once, and you will speak or act, and you will think or act the more wisely for it.
—*B. Franklin.*

REFORM

Turn the rascals out. —*Charles A. Dana.*

I think I am better than the people who are trying to reform me.
—*E. W. Howe.*

Reform must come from within, not from without. You cannot legislate for virtue. —*James Gibbons.*

Every movement has a lunatic fringe. —*Theodore Roosevelt.*

Our first thought, in connection with a desired reform, is to get a law passed against the evil in mind and rely on the law.
—*J. Williams.*

Social reform is not to be secured by noise and shouting; by complaints and denunciations; by the formation of parties or the making of revolutions; but by the awakening of thought and the progress of ideas. —*Henry George.*

If trouble comes from having the light turned on, remember it is not really due to the light but to the misconduct which is exposed. —*Theodore Roosevelt.*

Reforms are made by the vigor and courage and the self-sacrifice and the emotional convictions of young men, who did not know enough to be afraid, and who feel much more deeply than they think. —*Lafcadio Hearn.*

Great reforms are not accomplished by reasoning, but by feeling. —*Ibid.*

At twenty a man is full of fight and hope. He wants to reform the world. When he's seventy he still wants to reform the world, but he knows he can't. —*Clarence Darrow.*

We are reformers in Spring and Summer; in Autumn and Winter we stand by the old; reformers in the morning, conservers at night. —*R. W. Emerson.*

The hole and the patch should be commensurate.
—*T. Jefferson.*

We are all a little wild here with numberless projects of social reform. Not a reading man but has a draft of a new community in his waistcoat pocket. —*R. W. Emerson.*

The American religion of social reform expressed itself in the . . . Marxian revolutionary creed and impulse.
—*Van Wyck Brooks.*

The value of reforms, as I see it, is that they fail to achieve what they are sanguinely intended to achieve; and in so failing they help make the system which they are intended to patch up only the more unpatchable. —*John Chamberlain*.

The reformation of politics and business by propaganda and political action was impossible. Nothing but revolution could change the system. —*Lincoln Steffens*.

A reformer is a guy who rides through a sewer in a glass-bottomed boat. —*James J. Walker*.

What is a man born for but to be a Reformer, a Re-maker of what man has made, a denouncer of lies; a restorer of truth and good? —*R. W. Emerson*.

There is no lantern by which the crank may be distinguished from the reformer when the night is dark. —*Heywood Broun*.

Reform must come from within, not from without. You cannot legislate for virtue. —*James Gibbons*.

The reformer is careless of numbers, disregards popularity, and deals only with ideas, conscience and common sense.
—*Wendell Phillips*.

One of the besetting fallacies of reformers is the delusion that their plans will be carried out by people who think precisely as they do. —*J. M. Clark*.

For the Puritan reformer the heart of Christianity was not in an institution or a potentate but in a Book. —*Elizabeth Jackson*.

Why do women reformers almost always worry about men?
—*Wilson Mizner*.

Nothing so needs reforming as other people's habits.
—*Mark Twain*.

REGIONALISM

I know no South, no North, no East, no West, to which I owe any allegiance. —*Henry Clay*.

REGRET

I only regret that I have but one life to lose for my country.
—*Nathan Hale*.

> For all the sad words of tongue or pen,
> The saddest are these: "It might have been."
> —*J. G. Whittier*.

O lost hours and days in which we might have been happy!
—*H. W. Longfellow*.

REGULATION

It is hardly lack of due process for the government to regulate that which it subsidizes. —*Robert H. Jackson.*

The general rule at least is, that while property may be regulated to a certain extent, if regulation goes too far it will be recognized as a king. —*O. W. Holmes.*

Government cannot take its hands off business. Government must regulate business, because that is the foundation of every other relationship. —*Woodrow Wilson.*

We cannot afford to let any group of citizens, any individual citizens, live or labor under conditions which are injurious to the common welfare. Industry must submit to such public regulation as will make it a means of life and health, not of death and inefficiency. —*Theodore Roosevelt.*

Regulation cannot make an inefficient business efficient.
—*Louis D. Brandeis.*

Regulation cannot overcome the anemia of wasting-sickness which attends monopoly. —*Ibid.*

RELATIVE

There is only one good substitute for the endearments of a sister, and that is the endearments of some other fellow's sister.
—*Josh Billings.*

Don't despise your poor relations; they may become suddenly rich someday, and then it will be awkward to explain things to them. —*Ibid.*

Visit your aunt, but not every day; and call at your brother's, but not every night. —*B. Franklin.*

The richer a relative is, the less he bothers you. —*Kin Hubbard.*
We call our rich relatives the kin we love to touch.
—*Eddie Cantor.*

Distant relatives are the best kind, and the further the better.
—*Kin Hubbard.*

God gives us our relatives; thank God we can choose our friends.
—*E. W. Mumford.*

RELATIVITY

Any selection and arrangement of facts, pertaining to any large area of history, either local or world, race or class, is controlled

inexorably by the frame of reference in the mind of the selecter and
arranger.   —*Charles A. Beard.*

Truth, after all, wears a different face to everybody, and it would
be too tedious to wait till all were agreed.   —*J. R. Lowell.*

What appears as reason to one group of men is condemned as
unreason by others.   —*Hans J. Morgenthau.*

RELIEF

The first responsibility of taking care of people out of work who
are lacking housing, clothing, or food—the first charge is upon
the locality; then, if the locality has done everything that it possibly can do, it is the duty of the State to step in and do all the
State can possibly do; and, when the State can do no more, then
it becomes the obligation of the Federal Government.

—*F. D. Roosevelt.*

Continued dependence upon relief induces a spiritual and moral
disintegration fundamentally destructive to the national fibre.

—*Ibid.*

RELIGION

Religion means faith that man's ideals are achievable and will
be achieved.   —*Jerome Frank.*

I say the real and permanent grandeur of these States must be
their religion.   —*Walt Whitman.*

Of all dispositions and habits which lead to political prosperity,
Religion and Morality are indispensable supports. —*G. Washington.*

Whatever may be conceded to the influence of refined education
on minds of a peculiar structure, reason and experience both forbid
us to expect that national morality can prevail to the exclusion of
religious principle.   —*Ibid.*

The war took it (religion) out of our generation, exhausting our
capacity for emotional and moral reaction to events.   —*Bliss Perry.*

I won't take my religion from any man who never works except
with his mouth.   —*Carl Sandburg.*

Religion flourishes vastly only in a world conceived in terms of
caste.   —*Max Eastman.*

Religion is life and life is love, and love is God, and the Christian
religion is God in human life.   —*Lyman Abbott.*

Religion is renunciation.   —*H. H. Tucker.*

We hold religion to be the supreme authority and guide of life.
—*John D. Rockefeller, Jr.*

Religion has not civilized man, man has civilized religion.
—*R. G. Ingersoll.*

Many people think they have religion when they are merely troubled with dyspepsia. —*Ibid.*

Religion has reduced Spain to a guitar, Italy to a handorgan and Ireland to exile. —*Ibid.*

The more spiritual is a man's religion, the more expansive and broad it always is. —*Phillips Brooks.*

Religion sees science doing its own work in its own field better than it can itself. —*H. M. Kallen.*

Essential religion is one of the world's supremest needs.
—*R. A. Millikan.*

The religion that sets men to rebel and fight against their Government, because, as they think, that Government does not sufficiently help some men to eat their bread in the sweat of other men's faces, is not the sort of religion upon which people can get to heaven. —*A. Lincoln.*

I, too, following many, and followed by many, inaugurate a a new religion. —*Walt Whitman.*

I must ever believe that religion substantially good which produces an honest life. —*T. Jefferson.*

I have ever judged of the religion of others by their lives. For it is in our lives, and not from our words, that our religion must be read. —*Ibid.*

In this industrial epoch it (religion) is the servant of the monster business. —*Lafcadio Hearn.*

True religion is far more a matter of character than a question of cult and creed. —*Isidor Singer.*

One of the great tasks of the twentieth century will be the reconciliation of Socialism and Religion. —*Ibid.*

My religion and my politics are one and the same.
—*George W. Norris.*

If men are so wicked with religion, what would they be without it? —*B. Franklin.*

Religion is nothing else but love to God and man.—*William Penn.*

The world is my country, all mankind are my brethren, and to do good is my religion.   *—T. Paine.*

Women are twice as religious as men, but are they better?
—O. W. Holmes.

The first and last lesson of religion is, "The things that are seen are temporal; the things that are unseen are eternal." It puts an affront upon nature.   *—R. W. Emerson.*

If thinking men would have the courage to think for themselves, and to speak what they think, it would be found they do not differ in religious opinions as much as is supposed.   *—T. Jefferson.*

Of all the dispositions and habits which lead to political prosperity, religion and morality are indispensable supports. In vain would that man claim the tribute of patriotism who should labor to subvert these great pillars of human happiness, these firmest props of the duties of men and citizens.   *—G. Washington.*

All religions, arts and sciences are branches of the same tree.
—Albert Einstein.

When a man says he can get on without religion it merely means he has a kind of religion he can get on without.   *—H. E. Fosdick.*

It seems to me that the chief danger to religion lies in the fact that it has become so respectable.   *—John Dewey.*

There are no atheists in foxholes.   *—William T. Cummings.*

REMEMBRANCE

If you tell the truth, you don't have to remember anything.
—Mark Twain.

Remember Babe Ruth and think about just one thing, hitting the ball.   *—W. M. Marston.*

If you have to keep reminding yourself of a thing, perhaps it isn't so.   *—Christopher Morley.*

Remembrance is a form of meeting.   *—Kahlil Gibran.*

REMORSE

Remorse is the pain of sin.   *—Theodore Parker.*

There are some people who are very resourceful
At being remorseful.

—Ogden Nash.

To be left alone, and face to face with my own crime, had been just retribution.   *—H. W. Longfellow.*

Remorse is virtue's root; its fair increase are fruits of innocence and blessedness.   —*Wm. Cullen Bryant.*

REORGANIZATION

"Regenerate the individual" is a half-truth; the reorganization of the society which he makes and which makes him is the other half.   —*H. D. Lloyd.*

REPARTEE

Repartee is what you wish you'd said.   —*Heywood Broun.*

Repartee: any reply that is so clever that it makes the listener wish he had said it himself.   —*Elbert Hubbard.*

Repartee is something we think of twenty-four hours too late.
—*Mark Twain.*

Repartee is a duel fought with the points of jokes.
—*Max Eastman.*

REPENTANCE

Most people repent of their sins by thanking God they ain't so wicked as their neighbors.   —*Josh Billings.*

True repentance also involves reform.   —*Hosea Ballou.*

Repentance is but another name for aspiration. —*H. W. Beecher.*

Our hearts must not only be broken with sorrow, but be broken from sin, to constitute repentance.   —*Orville Dewey.*

Repentance is something more than mere remorse for sins; it comprehends a change of nature befitting heaven. —*Lew Wallace.*

It is foolish to lay out money to the purchase of repentance.
—*B. Franklin.*

None but the guilty know the withering pains of repentance.
—*Hosea Ballou.*

REPOSE

Vulgar people can't be still.   —*O. W. Holmes.*

Something attempted, something done, has earned a night's repose.   —*H. W. Longfellow.*

God offers to every mind its choice between truth and repose. Between these, as a pendulum, man oscillates.   —*R. W. Emerson.*

The repose which comes from perfect achievement was never yet won in the struggle of life.   —*H. W. Mabie.*

There is a repose which comes from adjustment to present conditions, acceptance of present limitations, and victorious recognition of the far-off peace.   *—Ibid.*

The heart that is to be filled to the brim with holy joy must be held still.   *—C. N. Bovee.*

Repose and cheerfulness are the badges of the gentleman—repose in energy.   *—R. W. Emerson.*

Repose without stagnation is the state most favorable to happiness.   *—C. N. Bovee.*

REPRESENTATIVE

We have been taught to regard a representative of the people as a sentinel on the watchtower of liberty.   *—Daniel Webster.*

The representative who exceeds his trusts, trespasses on the rights of the people.   *—J. F. Cooper.*

REPROOF

Confront improper conduct, not by retaliation, but by example.
                                                      —John Foster.

The severest punishment suffered by a sensitive mind, for injury inflicted upon another, is the consciousness of having done it.
                                                     —Hosea Ballou.

REPUBLIC

A republican government is slow to move, yet when once in motion, its momentum becomes irresistible.   *—T. Jefferson.*

A monarchy is a merchantman which sails well, but will sometimes strike on a rock, and go to the bottom; a republic is a raft which will never sink, but then your feet are always in water.
                                                     —Fisher Ames.

It is of great importance in a republic not only to guard against the oppression of its rulers, but to guard one part of society against the injustice of the other part.   *—Alexander Hamilton.*

Republics exist only on tenure of being agitated.
                                                 —Wendell Phillips.

The Republic never retreats. Its flag is the only flag that has never known defeat.   *—Albert Beveridge.*

There are few positions more demonstrable than that there should be in every republic some permanent body to correct the prejudices, check the intemperate passions, and regulate the fluctuations of a popular assembly.   *—Alexander Hamilton.*

The early history of most of the world's republics is the best part of their history. —*Julius Kahn.*

REPUTATION

Reputation is what men and women think of us; character is what God and the angels know of us. —*T. Paine.*

Reputation: what others are not thinking about you.
—*Tom Masson.*

We are weary of the false coin of reputation that passes current in the market of vanity fair. —*Felix Adler.*

A woman can defend her virtue from men, much more easily than she can protect her reputation from women. —*Elbert Hubbard.*

To enjoy a good reputation, give publicly, and steal privately.
—*Josh Billings.*

Many a man's reputation would not know his character if they met on the street. —*Elbert Hubbard.*

A broken reputation is like a broken vase—it may be mended, but it always shows where the break was! —*Josh Billings.*

How many people live on the reputation of the reputation they might have made! —*O. W. Holmes.*

Associate with men of good quality, if you esteem your own reputation; for it is better to be alone than in bad company.
—*G. Washington.*

A thief breaks into your house, steals your watch, and goes to Sing Sing. The newspaper man breaks into the casket which contains your most precious treasure—your reputation—and goes unscathed before the law. —*Roscoe Conkling.*

The solar system has no anxiety about its reputation.
—*R. W. Emerson.*

REQUEST

Polite beggary is too common. —*W. R. Alger.*

RESEARCH

Research is an organized method for keeping you reasonably dissatisfied with what you have. —*C. F. Kettering.*

RESERVE

Reserve may be pride fortified in ire; dignity is worth reposing on truth. —*W. R. Alger.*

RESIGNATION

Life is easier to take than you'd think; all that is necessary is to accept the impossible, do without the indispensable, and bear the intolerable. —*Kathleen Norris.*

> For after all, the best thing one can do
> When it is raining, is to let it rain.
>
> —*H. W. Longfellow.*

There is no good in arguing with the inevitable. The only argument available with an east wind is to put on your overcoat.

—*J. R. Lowell.*

What is called resignation is confirmed desperation.

—*H. D. Thoreau.*

Obedience and resignation are our personal offerings on the altar of duty. —*Hosea Ballou.*

It is the highest exhibition of Christian manliness to be able to bear trouble than to get rid of it. —*H. W. Beecher.*

RESISTANCE

When wrongs are pressed because it is believed they will be borne; resistance becomes morality. —*T. Jefferson.*

Stand your ground. Don't fire unless fired upon; but if they mean to have a war, let it begin here! —*John Parker.*

RESOLUTION

Resolve and thou art free. —*H. W. Longfellow.*

Resolve to perform what you ought; perform without fail what you resolve. —*B. Franklin.*

> Clothe with life the weak intent,
> Let me be the thing I meant.
>
> —*J. G. Whittier.*

Men die that might just as well live if they had resolved to live.
—*George M. Beard.*

I am in earnest—I will not equivocate—I will not excuse—I will not retreat a single inch and I will be heard. —*W. L. Garrison.*

I propose to fight it out on this line if it takes all Summer.

—*U. S. Grant.*

We have to resolve to conquer or to die. —*G. Washington.*

RESPECT

One of the surprising things of this world is the respect a worthless man has for himself. —*E. W. Howe.*

RESPONSIBILITY

Responsibility is the thing people dread most of all. Yet it is the one thing in the world that develops us, gives us manhood or womanhood fibre. —*Frank Crane.*

Responsibility educates. —*Wendell Phillips.*

Responsibility walks hand in hand with capacity and power.
—*J. G. Holland.*

Every human being has a work to carry on within, duties to perform abroad, influence to exert, which are peculiarly his, and which no conscience but his own can teach. —*W. E. Channing.*

REST

He that can take rest is greater than he that can take cities.
—*B. Franklin.*

> Life's race well run,
> Life's work well done,
> Life's victory won,
> Now cometh rest.

—*E. H. Parker.*

Oh, how I long to be at rest and soar on high among the blest.
—*Anne Bradstreet.*

To will what God doth will, is the only science that gives us rest.
—*H. W. Longfellow.*

RESULTS

Results! Why, man, I have gotten a lot of results. I know several thousand things that won't work. —*Thomas A. Edison.*

RETIREMENT

Love prefers twilight to daylight. —*O. W. Holmes.*

RETREAT

There can be no retreat from mechanization . . . We must proceed to turn it to the service of man. —*C. Hartley Grattan.*

A great part of the happiness of life consists not in fighting battles, but in avoiding them. A masterly retreat is in itself a victory. —*H. W. Longfellow.*

He has sounded forth the trumpet that shall never call retreat.
—Julia W. Howe.

I shall never surrender or retreat.   *—W. B. Travis.*

Women never acknowledge that they have fallen in love until the man has formally avowed his delusion and so cut off his retreat.
—H. L. Mencken.

RETRIBUTION

Those who imprison the helpless are likely in the end to find themselves inside the walls they have erected.   *—Alan Barth.*

Retribution is one of the grand principles in the divine administration of human affairs. There is everywhere the working of the everlasting law of requital: man always gets as he gives.
—John Foster.

He that sows the wind ought to reap the whirlwind.
—R. D. Hitchcock.

Nemesis is one of God's handmaids.   *—W. R. Alger.*

Heaven never defaults. The wicked are sure of their wages, sooner or later.   *—E. H. Chapin.*

The law of consequence holds without variation or exception. "The day of reckoning is not far off," says the Jewish Agadin and men will learn that human action likewise reappears in their consequences by as certain a law as the green blade rises up out of the buried corn-seed.   *—John Haynes Holmes.*

REVELATION

Nature is a revelation of God; Art a revelation of man.
—H. W. Longfellow.

Let man learn the revelation of all nature, and of all thought to his heart—this namely: that the Highest dwells with him; that the sources of nature are in his own mind, if the sentiment of duty is there.   *—R. W. Emerson.*

Revelation, like creation, must be fluent.   *—Charles W. Eliot.*

REVENGE

Not to be provoked is best; but if moved, never correct till the fume is spent; for every stroke our fury strikes is sure to hit ourselves at last.   *—Wm. Penn.*

Revenge is often like biting a dog because the dog bit you.
—Austin O'Malley.

This nation is too great to look for mere revenge.

—James A. Garfield.

A spirit of revenge is the very spirit of the devil.

—J. M. Mason.

REVERENCE

Reverence the highest; have patience with the lowest. Let this day's performance of the meanest duty be thy religion.

—Margaret Fuller.

In a democracy both deep reverence and a sense of the comic are requisite. *—Carl Sandburg.*

Reverence is an ennobling sentiment.—He that has no pleasure in looking up is not fit so much as to look down.

—Washington Allston.

Only the ignoble mind feels reverence degrading; it escapes the sense of its own littleness by elevating itself into an antagonist of what is above it. *—Ibid.*

REVERIE

Sit in reverie and watch the changing color of the waves that break upon the idle seashore of the mind. *—H. W. Longfellow.*

Do anything innocent rather than give yourself to reverie.

—W. E. Channing.

Both mind and heart when given up to reverie and dreaminess, have a thousand avenues open for the entrance of evil.

—Charles Simmons.

There is no self-delusion more fatal than that which makes the conscience dreamy with the anodyne of lofty sentiments, while the life is groveling and sensual. *—J. R. Lowell.*

REVOLUTION

Revolution: in politics, an abrupt change in the form of mis-government. *—Ambrose Bierce.*

Philosophers are the pioneers of revolution.

—Robert G. Harper.

Revolutions are not made; they come. *—Wendell Phillips.*

This country, with its institutions, belongs to the people who inhabit it. Whenever they shall grow weary of the existing govern-

ment they can exercise their constitutional right of amending it, or
their revolutionary right to dismember or overthrow it.

—*A. Lincoln.*

No government provides for its own death; therefore there can
be no constitutional right to secede. But there is a revolutionary
right.   —*Wendell Phillips.*

The Declaration of Independence establish'es, what the heart of
every American acknowledges, that the people—mark you, the
people—have always an inherent, paramount, inalienable right to
change their governments, whenever they think that it will minister
to their happiness. That is a revolutionary right.   —*Ibid.*

No one denies the right of revolution.   —*Edward Everett.*

Any people anywhere being inclined and having the power have
the right to rise up and shake off the existing government, and
force a new one that suits them better.   —*A. Lincoln.*

This (right of revolution) is a most valuable, a most sacred right
—a right which we hope and believe is to liberate the world. —*Ibid.*

The old is cracking; something new is rising to take its place.

—*George Soule.*

For the next hundred or two hundred years the world will be in
the grip of revolution.   —*Paul Hutchinson.*

Revolution is a smashed, overturned, pulverized world.   —*Ibid.*

Every revolution was first a thought in one man's mind.

—*R. W. Emerson.*

If by the mere force of numbers a majority should deprive a
minority of any clearly written constitutional right, it might, in any
moral point of view, justify revolution.   —*A. Lincoln.*

Abuses are lopped by the sword of revolution where peaceful
remedies are unprovided.   —*T. Jefferson.*

The "idea of revolution," no matter where it explodes, can inspire the depressed and the deprived of other countries.

—*Lyman Bryson.*

They (revolutions) are become subjects of universal conversation, and may be considered as the order of the day.   —*T. Paine.*

All revolutions come from below.   —*Wendell Phillips.*

Political convulsions, like geological upheavings, usher in new
epochs of the world's progress.   —*Ibid.*

The world is in a revolution which cannot be bought off with dollars . . . A fire is gathering for a mighty effort.

—W. O. Douglas.

Whenever any government becomes destructive of these ends (life, liberty and the pursuit of happiness) it is the right of the people to alter or abolish it, and to institute a new government, laying its foundations on such principles, and organizing its powers in such form, as to them shall seem most likely to effect their safety and happiness. *—T. Jefferson.*

The right of revolution is an inherent one. When people are oppressed by their government, it is a natural right they enjoy to relieve themselves of the oppression, if they are strong enough, either by withdrawal from it, or by overthrowing it and substituting a government more acceptable. *—U. S. Grant.*

An oppressed people are authorized whenever they can to rise and break their fetters. *—Henry Clay.*

The most sensible and jealous people are so little attentive to government that there are no instances of resistance until repeated, multiplied oppressions have placed it beyond a doubt that their rulers had formed settled plans to deprive them of their liberties; not to oppress an individual or a few, but to break down the fences of a free constitution, and deprive the people at large of all share in the government, and all the checks by which it is limited.

—John Adams.

America was born because it revolted. It revolted because it condemned. *—Stuart P. Sherman.*

REWARD

The only reward of virtue is virtue. *—R. W. Emerson.*

The reward of a thing well done is to have done it. *—Ibid.*

No man who continues to add something to the material, intellectual, and moral well-being of the place in which he lives, is left long without proper reward. *—Booker T. Washington.*

RHETORIC

There is truth and beauty in rhetoric but it oftener serves ill turns than good ones. *—Wm. Penn.*

RICH

Rich men die but banks are immortal. *—Wendell Phillips.*

In all the wars of history there are very few instances of the rich meeting their death on the battlefield.   —*Charles T. Sprading.*

A man is rich in proportion to the number of things he can afford to let alone.   —*H. D. Thoreau.*

The man who dies rich dies disgraced.   —*Andrew Carnegie.*

I don't believe in a law to prevent a man from getting rich; it would do more harm than good.   —*A. Lincoln.*

It must be great to be rich and let the other fellow keep up appearances.   —*Kin Hubbard.*

It is not what we *take* up, but what we *give* up, that makes us rich.   —*H. W. Beecher.*

It is the heart that makes a man rich.   —*Ibid.*

He is rich or poor according to what he *is*, not according to what he *has*.   —*Ibid.*

He who knows the most; he who knows what sweets and virtues are in the ground, in the waters, in the plants, in the heavens, and how to come at these enchantments,—he is the rich and royal man.
—*R. W. Emerson.*

It ain't so much trouble to get rich as it is to tell when we have got rich.   —*Josh Billings.*

It is the wretchedness of being rich that you have to live with rich people.   —*Logan Pearsall Smith.*

If a man is wise, he gets rich, and if he gets rich, he gets foolish, or his wife does.   —*F. P. Dunne.*

Man grows rich by the use of his faculties, by the union of thought with nature.   —*R. W. Emerson.*

Liberty will ultimately make all men rich; it will not make all men equally rich.   —*Benj. R. Tucker.*

The pride of dying rich raises the loudest laugh in hell.
—*John Foster.*

It is the heart that makes a man rich. He is rich according to what he is, not according to what he has.   —*H. W. Beecher.*

Those who have had a stranglehold upon America have been served long enough.   —*Sherwood Anderson.*

RICHES

If your riches are yours, why don't you take them with you to the other world?   —*B. Franklin.*

The riches of a country are to be valued by the quantity of labor its inhabitants are able to purchase, and not by the quantity of silver and gold they possess.   *—Ibid.*

The use we make of our fortune determines its sufficiency. A little is enough if used wisely, and too much if expended foolishly.
—C. N. Bovee.

Ah, if the rich were rich as the poor fancy riches.
—R. W. Emerson.

That man is the richest whose pleasures are the cheapest.
—H. D. Thoreau.

Wealth is not his that has it, but his that enjoys it.
—B. Franklin.

RIDICULE

Resort is had to ridicule only when reason is against us.
—T. Jefferson.

Ridicule is the first and last argument of fools.
—Charles Simmons.

Ridicule may be the evidence of art or bitterness and may gratify a little mind or an ungenerous temper, but it is no test of reason or truth.   *—Tryon Edwards.*

RIGHT

Be always sure you're right—then go ahead.   *—David Crockett.*

With firmness in the right, as God gives us to see the right.
—A. Lincoln.

Let us have faith that right makes might, and in that faith let us dare to do our duty as we understand it.   *—Ibid.*

Right is more beautiful than private affection, and is comparable with universal wisdom.   *—R. W. Emerson.*

Always do right; this will gratify some people and astonish the rest.   *—Mark Twain.*

Let none falter, who thinks he is right, and we may succeed.
—A. Lincoln.

The right is more precious than peace.   *—Woodrow Wilson.*

I would rather be right than President.   *—Henry Clay.*

He will hew to the line of right, let the chips fly where they may.
—Roscoe Conkling.

They are slaves who dare not be
In the right with two or three.

—J. R. Lowell.

There is such a thing as a nation being so right that it does not need to convince others by force that it is right.

—Woodrow Wilson.

The right of private property, the fruit of labor or industry, or of concession or donation by others, is an incontrovertible natural right; and everybody can dispose reasonably of such property as he thinks fit. *—O. W. Holmes.*

Right is the eternal sun; the world cannot delay its coming.

—Wendell Phillips.

Heaven itself has ordained the right. *—G. Washington.*

No question is ever settled until it is settled right.

—E. W. Wilcox.

The right of the people to resist their rulers, when invading their liberties, forms the corner-stone of the American republics.

—David Ramsay.

The right to food, shelter and clothing at reasonable prices is as much an inalienable right as the right to life, liberty and the pursuit of happiness. *—Fiorello La Guardia.*

Our country, right or wrong. When right, to be kept right; when wrong, to be put right. *—Carl Schurz.*

Whenever they (the people) grow weary of the existing government, they can exercise their constitutional right of amending it, or their revolutionary right to dismember or overthrow it.

—A. Lincoln.

The right of every human being to himself is the foundation of the right of property. *—Henry George.*

Every man who strikes a blow for the right must be just as good an anvil as he is a hammer. *—J. G. Holland.*

The right of petition belongs to all. *—John Q. Adams.*

The gratifications of life grow from the virtue of doing right by the right principle. *—Dagobert D. Runes.*

It takes less time to do a thing right than it does to explain why you did it wrong. *—H. W. Longfellow.*

RIGHTEOUSNESS

If I must choose between righteousness and peace, I would choose righteousness.   *—Theodore Roosevelt.*

Those who put peace before righteousness, and justice, and liberty, do infinite harm and always fail of their purpose ultimately.
   —Frank Knox.

RIGHTS

A Bill of Rights is what the people are entitled to against every government on earth.   *—T. Jefferson.*

The Bill of Rights should contain the great principles of national and civil liberty. It should be unalterable by any human power.
   —Benjamin Rush.

There isn't a Parallel of Latitude but thinks it would have been the Equator if it had had its rights.   *—Mark Twain.*

The sacred rights of mankind are not to be rummaged for among old parchments or musty records. They are written, as with a sunbeam, in the whole volume of human nature, by the hand of the Divinity itself, and can never be erased or obscured by mortal power.   *—Alexander Hamilton.*

Government founded on a moral theory, on a system of universal peace, on the indefeasible rights of man, is now revolving from West to East by a stronger impulse than the government of the sword revolved from East to West.   *—T. Paine.*

Men, their rights and nothing more; women, their rights and nothing less.   *—Susan B. Anthony.*

Men have as exaggerated an idea of their rights as women have of their wrongs.   *—E. W. Howe.*

If some people got their rights they would complain of being deprived of their wrongs.   *—Oliver Herford.*

The true foundation of republican government is the equal right of every citizen, in his person and property, and in their management.   *—T. Jefferson.*

I believe each individual is naturally entitled to do as he pleases with himself and the fruit of his labor, so far as it in no wise interferes with any other man's rights.   *—A. Lincoln.*

From the equality of rights springs identity of our highest interests; you cannot subvert your neighbors' rights without striking a dangerous blow at your own.   *—Carl Schurz.*

Equality of rights, embodied in general self-government, is the great moral element of true democracy; it is the only reliable safety valve in the machinery of modern society.   *—Ibid.*

How can you have states' rights when you keep running to Washington for money?   *—B. M. Baruch.*

Equal rights for all, special privileges for none.   *—T. Jefferson.*

We hold these truths to be self-evident,—that all men are created equal; that they are endowed by their Creator with certain unalienable rights; that among these are Life, Liberty, and the pursuit of happiness.   *—Ibid.*

Among the natural rights of the colonists are these: First a right to life, secondly to liberty, thirdly to property; together with the right to defend them in the best manner they can. *—Samuel Adams.*

Wherever there is a human being, I see God-given rights inherent in that being, whatever may be the sex or complexion.
—W. L. Garrison.

Political equality calls for equal rights to participate in government, regardless of sex, color or economic status.   *—H. M. Groves.*

Property rights are legal rights . . . They exist only because government recognizes and protects them.   *—R. M. MacIver.*

No man has a natural right to commit aggression on the equal rights of another, and this is all from which the laws ought to restrain him.   *—T. Jefferson.*

The right of labor to organize, the right to strike—these are, beyond all question, fundamental human rights. *—Thomas E. Dewey.*

Free enterprise must be reinforced by the guardianship of the right to live.   *—H. E. Humphreys, Jr.*

He is the purest democrat who best maintains his rights.
—James F. Cooper.

No rights can be dearer to a man of culture than exemptions from unreasonable invasions on his time by the coarse-minded and ignorant.   *—Ibid.*

Every single right and protection the individual has in our society has been created legally. And it can be by the same process modified to meet our changing needs.   *—Donald Richberg.*

The right of the laborer to wages, the right of every innocent man to his own person, the right of all to equity before the laws,—these are no longer abstractions of speculative visionaries, no longer innovations, but the established rights of humanity.

—*W. E. Channing.*

RISKS

The willingness to take risks is our grasp of faith.

—*G. E. Woodberry.*

Risk is a part of God's game, alike for men and nations. —*Ibid.*

Government must enter fields where private finance cannot enter without assuming risks that are too great to take with other people's money. —*H. A. Wallace.*

RITUAL

Ritual is the art of the ordinary man, just as art is the routine of the superior man. —*Leon Samson.*

But just as the love of God demands a ritual of observance lest it die, so does love among people demand a ritual of friendship— a ritual of small attentions, services and remembrances which make one almost say that great love is verily a series of many little attentions. —*Dagobert D. Runes.*

Marriage and birth, confirmation of manhood, confirmation of womanhood, life as well as death rise to their significance when given the beauteous nimbus of religious symbolism and ritual.

—*Ibid.*

Symbols and rituals sustain the decorum of grace and reverence.

—*Ibid.*

ROMANTICISM

The coming of the machine age was the material spark that ignited the spiritual flame we call romanticism. —*Bernard Smith.*

ROOTS

John Brown has loosened the roots of the slave system. It only breathes—it does not live—hereafter. —*Wendell Phillips.*

ROSE

A Rose is a rose is a rose is a rose. —*Gertrude Stein.*

ROTARIAN

The first Rotarian was the first man to call John the Baptist Jack.

—*H. L. Mencken.*

ROUTINE

We are weary of the emptiness of routine. —*Felix Adler.*

RUIN

The road to ruin is always kept in good repair, and the travelers pay the expense of it.   *—Josh Billings.*

RULE

Any fool can make a rule, and every fool will mind it.
—H. D. Thoreau.

It has always been my rule never to smoke when asleep, and never to refrain when awake.   *—Mark Twain.*

If you would rule the world quietly, you must keep it amused.
—R. W. Emerson.

It's a good rule never to send a mouse to catch a skunk or a polliwog to tackle a whale.   *—A. Lincoln.*

No government rule ever can bring about dynamic use of individual freedom and of equality of opportunity.*—J. H. McGraw, Jr.*

Nowhere else does the captain of big business rule the affairs of the nation, civil and political, and control the conditions of life so unreservedly as in democratic America.   *—Thorstein Veblen.*

The propitious smiles of Heaven can never be expected in a nation that disregards the eternal rules of order and right, which Heaven itself has ordained.   *—G. Washington.*

Learn all the rules, every one of them, so that you will know how to break them.   *—I. S. Cobb.*

There are those whose sole claim to profundity is the discovery of exceptions to rules.   *—Paul Eldridge.*

Rule is evil, and it is none the better for being majority rule.
—Benj. R. Tucker.

RUM

Rum is good in its place, and hell is the place for it.
—Josh Billings.

We are Republicans, and we don't propose to leave our party and identify ourselves with the party whose antecedents have been rum, Romanism, and rebellion.   *—S. D. Burchard.*

RUSSIA

What a social revolution in Russia would portend transcends

human foresight, but probably its effects would be felt throughout the world.   —*Brooks Adams.*

RUT

The only difference between a rut and a grave is their dimensions.
—*Ellen Glasgow.*

You won't skid if you stay in a rut.   —*Kin Hubbard.*

S

SABBATH

Day of the Lord, as all our days should be.

—*H. W. Longfellow.*

> Some keep the Sabbath going to church;
> I keep it staying at home,
> With a bobolink for a chorister,
> And an orchard for a dome.

—*Emily Dickinson.*

He who ordained the Sabbath loves the poor.   —*J. R. Lowell.*

Sunday is the common people's great Liberty day.

—*H. W. Beecher.*

There are many persons who look on Sunday as a sponge to wipe out the sins of the week.   —*Ibid.*

SACRIFICE

In the perspectives of history the distinction of constructive and fruitless sacrifice is of utmost significance.   —*Corliss Lamont.*

Who lives for humanity, must be content to lose himself.

—*O. B. Frothingham.*

Good manners are made up of petty sacrifices.

—*R. W. Emerson.*

A bronco often becomes so attached to his master that he will lay down his life if necessary—his master's life, I mean.

—*E. W. Nye.*

An enemy is invented, an evil one, one upon whom both guilt and punishment can be rolled, who is both instigator and sacrifice, who both explains the moral torment in which men find themselves and expiates it for them.   —*Ludwig Lewisohn.*

This method of finding for an irresolvable moral conflict an outer instigator and sacrifice is as old as the world. Under this pretext Jews have been burned and heretics massacred from age to age. *—Ibid.*

In this world it is not what we take up, but what we give up, that makes us rich. *—H. W. Beecher.*

SADNESS

Our sadness is not sad, but our cheap joys.

—H. D. Thoreau.

Some people habitually wear sadness like a garment, and think it a becoming grace. God loves a cheerful worshipper.

—E. H. Chapin.

A feeling of sadness that is not akin to pain, resembles sorrow only as the mist resembles rain. *—H. W. Longfellow.*

Oftentimes we call a man cold when he is only sad.

—Ibid.

Of all the sad words of tongue and pen, the saddest are these: It might have been. *—J. G. Whittier.*

SAFETY

The safe man is the only free man; and it is not enough not to be in danger, one must not be in fear of danger. *—W. D. Howells.*

In skating over thin ice our safety is in our speed.

—R. W. Emerson.

They that give up essential liberty to obtain a little temporary safety deserve neither liberty nor safety. *—B. Franklin.*

Every man has a right to his own property; which means a right to be assured, to the fullest extent attainable, in the safety of his savings. *—F. D. Roosevelt.*

SAINTS

Saint: a dead sinner revised and edited. *—Ambrose Bierce.*

It is easier to make a saint out of a libertine than out of a prig. *—George Santayana.*

The highest holiness will not work miracles, but only do its duty. *—Phillips Brooks.*

SALVATION

Some of the most devoted and sacrificial efforts to change the world towards humaneness and brotherhood are going on outside the church, while within the church too many Christians settle down into well-adjusted conformity.   *—H. E. Fosdick.*

> Heaven's gate is shut to him who comes alone;
> Save thou a soul, and it shall save thy own.
>
>   *—J. G. Whittier.*

SARCASM

Edged tools are dangerous things to handle, and not infrequently do much hurt.   *—Agnes Repplier.*

Few things in the world are more wearying than a sarcastic attitude towards life.   *—Ibid.*

Sarcasm poisons reproof.   *—E. Wigglesworth.*

A sneer is the weapon of the weak.   *—J. R. Lowell.*

Sarcasms, bitter irony, scathing wit are a sort of sword-play of the mind. You pick your adversary, and he is forthwith dead, and then you deserve to be hung for it.   *—C. N. Bovee.*

SATAN

All religions issue Bibles against Satan, and say the most injurious things against him, but we never hear his side.

              —Mark Twain.

The Galilean was right. All history teaches that Satan cannot cast out Satan.   *—Jerome Davis.*

SATIETY

A full belly makes a dull brain.   *—B. Franklin.*

Expectation gives way to ennui, and appetite to satiety.

              —C. N. Bovee.

The flower which we do not pluck is the only one which never loses its beauty or its fragrance.   *—W. R. Alger.*

SATIRE

Satire is a lonely and introspective occupation, for nobody can describe a fool to the life without much self-inspection.

              —F. M. Colby.

Satire is the last flicker of originality in a passing epoch as it faces the onrush of staleness and boredom. Freshness has gone; bitterness remains.   *—A. N. Whitehead.*

Strange that a man who has wit enough to write a satire should have folly enough to publish it. —*B. Franklin.*

Satire that is sensible and just is often more effective than law or gospel. —*H. W. Shaw.*

All honor to him who makes oppression laughable as well as detestable. —*E. P. Whipple.*

Arrows of satire, feathered with wit, and molded with sense, fly home to their mark. —*Charles Simmons.*

SAVAGE

The savage state was more favorable to liberty than the civilized . . . it was only renounced for the sake of property which could only be secured by the restraints of regular government.

—*Gouverneur Morris.*

The leading characteristic of the savage state is its refusal or avoidance of industry. —*Arthur Brisbane.*

SCANDAL

Scandal died sooner of itself, than we could kill it.

—*Benjamin Rush.*

If hours did not hang heavy what would become of scandal? —*George Bancroft.*

The unsexed scandalmonger hies from house to house, pouring balm from its weeping eyes on the wounds it inflicts with stabbing tongue. —*E. P. Whipple.*

Old maids sweeten their tea with scandal. —*H. W. Shaw.*

SCEPTICISM

Scepticism is a barren coast, without a harbor or a lighthouse. —*H. W. Beecher.*

It is men of faith, not sceptics, who have made the world aware that they were in it. —*W. E. Channing.*

Scepticism has never founded empires, established principles, or changed the world's heart. The great doers in history have always been men of faith. —*E. H. Chapin.*

Imperfect knowledge is the parent of doubt; thorough and honest research dispels it. —*Tryon Edwards.*

The thorough sceptic is a dogmatist. He enjoys the delusion of complete futility. —*A. N. Whitehead.*

SCHOLARSHIP

The riches of scholarship and the benignities of literature defy fortune and outlive calamity.   —*J. R. Lowell.*

Historical scholars . . . ought to contribute powerfully to the opening up of a better political and social future for the nation at large.   —*Andrew D. White.*

The resources of the scholar are proportioned to his confidence in the attributes of the intellect.   —*R. W. Emerson.*

SCHOOL

The school is not the end but only the beginning of an education.
—*Calvin Coolidge.*

Schoolhouses are the republican line of fortifications.

—*Horace Mann.*

A Sunday school is a prison in which children do penance for the evil conscience of their parents.   —*H. L. Mencken.*

Political democracy, as it exists and practically works in America, with all its threatening evils, supplies a training-school for making first-class men. It is life's gymnasium, not of the good only, but of all.   —*Walt Whitman.*

The school of life embodies a compulsory education, that no man escapes.   —*G. E. Woodberry.*

SCIENCE

Every great advance in science has issued from a new audacity of imagination.   —*John Dewey.*

Science is a first-rate piece of furniture for a man's upper chamber, if he has common sense on the ground floor.

—*O. W. Holmes.*

Science is nothing but developed perception, interpreted intent, common sense rounded out and minutely articulated.

—*George Santayana.*

Don't hesitate to be as revolutionary as science. Don't hesitate to be as reactionary as the multiplication table.

—*Calvin Coolidge.*

Science . . . is not the enemy of religion . . . But it is often the antagonist of school divinity.   —*O. W. Holmes.*

The function of science . . . is to classify, which is simply and intimately to unify.   —*Charles Singer.*

The science of freedom is the equipment of the international mind. —*H. M. Kallen.*

Star-eyed Science brings us from its vast excursions only the tidings of despair. —*J. F. Clarke.*

Science is the topography of ignorance. —*O. W. Holmes.*

Science does not know its debt to imagination.
—*R. W. Emerson.*

Science is the natural ally of religion. —*Theodore Parker.*

Science has but one fashion—to lose nothing once gained.
—*E. C. Stedman.*

Our science, so called, is always more barren and mixed with error than our sympathies. —*H. D. Thoreau.*

Social science is scientific only under certain premises whose universal acceptance it presupposes but never achieves.
—*Hans J. Morgenthau.*

Science, accelerated by war, is changing the face of civilization before our very eyes. —*Charles A. Madison.*

The church saves sinners, but science seeks to stop their manufacture. —*Elbert Hubbard.*

Science is the century-old endeavor to bring together by means of systematic thought the perceptible phenomena of this world into as thorough-going an association as possible. To put it boldly, it is the attempt at the posterior reconstruction of existence by the process of conceptualization. —*Albert Einstein.*

The worship of the eternal truth and the burning desire to seek an ever-broadening revelation of it constitute what I call "Idealism in Science." —*Michael Pupin.*

It stands to the everlasting credit of science that by acting on the human mind it has overcome man's insecurity before himself and before nature. —*Albert Einstein.*

If Christian scientists had more science and doctors more Christianity, it wouldn't make any difference which you called in—if you had a good nurse. —*F. P. Dunne.*

SCIENTISTS

Look at those cows and remember that the greatest scientists in the world have never discovered how to make grass into milk.
—*Michael Pupin.*

SEASONS

Blessed is he who takes comfort in seed-time and harvest, setting the warfare of life to the Hymn of the Seasons.

—_Julia W. Howe._

Our constitution protects aliens, drunks and U.S. Senators. There ought to be one day (just one) when there is an open season on senators. —_Will Rogers._

SECRECY

Three may keep a secret if two of them are dead.

—_B. Franklin._

To keep your secret is wisdom; but to expect others to keep it is folly. —_O. W. Holmes._

If you would keep a secret from an enemy, tell it not to a friend.

—_B. Franklin._

Thou hast betrayed thy secret as a bird betrays her nest, by striving to conceal it. —_H. W. Longfellow._

A sekret ceases tew be a sekret if it iz once confided—it iz like a dollar bill, once broken, it iz never a dollar agin.

—_Josh Billings._

There is something about a closet that makes a skeleton terribly restless. —_Wilson Mizner._

You cannot hide any secret. —_R. W. Emerson._

Secrets are things we give to others to keep for us.

—_Elbert Hubbard._

SECURITY

The only lasting security for any of us lies in moving constantly forward. —_H. A. Wallace._

The greatest security to be found on earth is in the grave. And the next greatest security is to be found in the penitentiary.

—_Arthur Kudner._

Security is a spiritual experience. Security is a feeling—something inside. It's different for every situation . . . Security is faith.

—_W. F. Bennett._

Security is man at his best—working in freedom. —_Ibid._

This search for a state security—in the law or elsewhere—is misguided. The fact is security can only be achieved through constant change, through discarding old ideas that have outlived their usefulness and adapting others to current facts. —_W. O. Douglas._

Business has a moral obligation to provide a rich and satisfying social life for the people it has made dependent.

—L. J. McGinley.

In a free America no man should be fully relieved by others of the duty of providing for his future and that of his family. Congress recognized this principle in setting up our social security system. There the man and his employer share the cost together.

—C. B. Randall.

SEGREGATION

Segregation is rooted in fear and in doubt as to whether our democratic principles will really work.   *—W. H. Alexander.*

Minds broken in two. Hearts broken. Conscience torn from acts. A culture split in a thousand pieces. That is segregation.

—Lillian Smith.

SELF-ASSERTION

Insist on thyself.   *—R. W. Emerson.*

SELF-CONCEIT

Conceited men, by their overweening self-respect, relieve others from the duty of respecting them at all.   *—H. W. Beecher.*

In the same degree that we overrate ourselves, we shall underrate others; for injustice allowed at home is not likely to be corrected abroad.   *—Washington Allston.*

Whenever Nature leaves a hole in a person's mind, she generally plasters it over with a thick coat of self-conceit.

—H. W. Longfellow.

SELF-CONTROL

No man is such a conqueror as the man who has defeated himself.   *—H. W. Beecher.*

Self-control is promoted by humility. Pride keeps the mind in disquiet. Humility is the antidote to this evil.

—Lydia H. Sigourney.

Man's struggle with himself has become increasingly far-reaching and dangerous.   *—James H. Breasted.*

For me, life can hold no higher adventure than to see man learn to control his own nature as he now controls the atoms.

—Walter B. Pitkin.

SELF-DECEPTION

Who has deceived thee so often as thyself?   *—B. Franklin.*

Every man is his own greatest dupe. —*W. R. Alger.*

SELF-DENIAL

Only the soul that gives itself up forever to the life of other men finds the delight and peace which such complete self-surrender has to give. —*Phillips Brooks.*

Of all sorts of earthly good the price is self-denial.
—*R. D. Hitchcock.*

Every step in our progress towards success is a sacrifice. We gain by losing; grow by dwindling; live by dying. —*Ibid.*

Self-abnegation, that rare virtue, that good men preach and good women practice. —*O. W. Holmes.*

SELF-DEPENDENCE

There is no use whatever trying to help people who do not help themselves. You cannot push anyone up a ladder unless he be willing to climb himself. —*Andrew Carnegie.*

SELF-ESTEEM

The average man plays to the gallery of his own self-esteem.
—*Elbert Hubbard.*

SELF-GOVERNMENT

Allow all the governed an equal voice in the government, and that, and that only is self-government. —*A. Lincoln.*

SELF-IMPROVEMENT

Each year one vicious habit rooted out in time ought to make the worst man good. —*B. Franklin.*

SELF-INTEREST

We have always known that heedless self-interest was bad morals; we know now that it is bad economics. —*F. D. Roosevelt.*

A cow goes on giving milk all her life even though what appears to be her self-interest urges her to give gin. —*H. L. Mencken.*

SELFISHNESS

Selfishness is that detestable vice which no one will forgive in others and no one is without in himself. —*H. W. Beecher.*

> That man who lives for himself alone
> Lives for the meanest mortal known.
> —*Joaquin Miller.*

We have profaned the temple of this life by our selfishness
and heedlessness. —*R. Niebuhr.*

SELF-KNOWLEDGE

> Just stand aside and watch yourself go by,
> Think of yourself as "he" instead of "I".
> —*Strickland Gillilan.*

> I want to be able as days go by,
> Always to look myself straight in the eye.
> —*Edgar A. Guest.*

> Great God, I ask thee for not meaner pelf
> Than that I may not disappoint myself.
> —*H. D. Thoreau.*

SELF-LOVE

He that falls in love with himself will have no rivals.
—*B. Franklin.*

The finest bread has the least bran; the purest honey, the least
wax; and the sincerest Christian, the least self-love.
—*Anne Bradstreet.*

Self-love is a cup without any bottom; you might pour all the
great lakes into it, and never fill it up. —*O. W. Holmes.*

SELF-MADE

Everybody likes and respects self-made men; it's a great deal
better to be made that way than not to be made at all.
—*O. W. Holmes.*

A self-made man? Yes, and worships his creator.
—*Henry Clapp.*

Self-made men are very apt to usurp the prerogative of the
Almighty and overwork themselves. —*E. W. Nye.*

No self-made man ever did such a good job that some woman
didn't want to make a few alterations. —*Kin Hubbard.*

Our self-made men are the glory of our institutions.
—*Wendell Phillips.*

SELF-PITY

A capacity for self-pity is one of the last things that any woman
surrenders. —*I. S. Cobb.*

SELF-PRAISE

Most of our censure of others is only oblique praise of self.
—Tryon Edwards.

SELF-RELIANCE

If you would have a faithful servant, and one that you like, serve yourself.   *—B. Franklin.*

No external advantage can supply the place of self-reliance.
—R. W. Clark.

Doubt whom you will but never doubt yourself.

—C. N. Bovee.

The best thing that can happen to a man is to be tossed overboard and compelled to sink or swim for himself.
—James A. Garfield.

Don't give up the ship.   *—J. Lawrence.*

No man should part with his own individuality and become that of another.   *—W. E. Channing.*

No grace can save any man unless he helps himself.
—H. W. Beecher.

God gives every bird his food, but does not throw it into the nest.   *—J. G. Holland.*

Despair and postponement are cowardice and defeat. Men were born to succeed, not to fail.   *—H. D. Thoreau.*

The duty of America is to secure the culture and the happiness of the masses by their reliance on themselves.
—George Bancroft.

SELF-RESPECT

Self-respect is the gate of heaven.   *—H. T. Tuckerman.*

No more important duty can be urged upon those who are entering the great theatre of life than simple loyalty to their best convictions.   *—E. H. Chapin.*

Never violate the sacredness of your individual self-respect.
—Theodore Parker.

Be true to your own mind and conscience, your heart and your soul; so only can you be true to God.   *—Ibid.*

SELF-RIGHTEOUSNESS

You can always tell when a man is a great way from God—when he is always talking about himself, how good he is.
—Dwight L. Moody.

If you trust in your own righteousness then all that Christ did to purchase salvation is in vain.   —*Jonathan Edwards.*

SEMANTICS

We all declare for liberty, but in using the same word we do not all mean the same thing.   —*A. Lincoln.*

The sheep and the wolf are not agreed upon a definition of the word liberty.   —*Ibid.*

SENSE

Common sense is very uncommon.   —*Horace Greeley.*

Common sense does not ask an impossible chessboard, but takes the one before it and plays the game.   —*Wendell Phillips.*

Common sense is genius in homespun.   —*A. N. Whitehead.*

Common sense is the knack of seeing things as they are, and doing things as they ought to be done.   —*C. E. Stowe.*

Freedom of the press and freedom of the radio are the common means by which the common man gets his common information on which must depend his common sense.   —*S. M. Shoemaker.*

The moral sense enables one to perceive morality—and avoid it; the immoral sense enables one to perceive immorality—and enjoy it.   —*Mark Twain.*

Sense doesn't make sense in radio.   —*Fred Allen.*

There is more sophistication and less sense in New York than anywhere else on the globe.   —*Don Herold.*

Women have a wonderful sense of right and wrong, but little sense of right and left.   —*Ibid.*

If a man can have only one kind of sense, let him have common sense.   —*H. W. Beecher.*

SENSIBILITY

Laughter and tears are meant to turn the wheels of the same machinery of sensibility; one is wind-power; and the other water-power.   —*O. W. Holmes.*

SENSIBLE

It is easy enough to be sensible for other people.
                    —*W. D. Howells.*

SENSUALITY

The body of a sensualist is the coffin of a dead soul.

—*C. N. Bovee.*

I have never known a man who was sensual in his youth, who was high-minded when old.   —*Charles Sumner.*

SENTIMENT

He who molds public sentiment . . . makes statutes and decisions possible or impossible to be executed.   —*A. Lincoln.*

SERMONS

Sermons are like pie-crust, the shorter the better.

—*Austin O'Malley.*

The half-baked sermon causes spiritual indigestion.   —*Ibid.*

SERVICE

No man has ever risen to the real stature of spiritual manhood until he has found that it is finer to serve somebody else than it is to serve himself.   —*Woodrow Wilson.*

They also serve who only stand and cheer.   —*Henry Adams.*

We do not retreat. We are not content to stand still. As Americans, we go forward, in the service of our country, by the will of God.   —*F. D. Roosevelt.*

He profits most who serves best.   —*A. F. Sheldon.*

To be of service is a solid foundation for contentment in this world.   —*Charles W. Eliot.*

SERVILITY

A nod from a lord is breakfast for a fool.   —*B. Franklin.*

Servility is disgusting to a truly noble character, and engenders only contempt.   —*Hosea Ballou.*

SEX

Sex will be seen to be an important part of life, but not, the Freudians to the contrary notwithstanding, the whole of life.

—*V. F. Calverton.*

Sex has little significance unless it is treated in personally artistic, novelistic terms.   —*Randolph Bourne.*

With what bitterness the moral rigorists of all ages have con-

demned the impulse which attracts the sexes toward each other, and how often they have tried, though vainly, to crush it!
—*Felix Adler.*

Women are not much, but they are the best other sex we have.
—*Don Herold.*

The thing that takes up the least amount of time and causes the most amount of trouble is Sex.   —*John Barrymore.*

I don't wonder men can't understand women; they don't understand their own simple sex.   —*W. D. Howells.*

Man is always looking for someone to boast to; woman is always looking for a shoulder to put her head on.
—*H. L. Mencken.*

A person who despises or undervalues, or neglects the opposite sex, will soon need humanizing. What God hath joined together, let no man put asunder.   —*Charles Simmons.*

> Breathes there a man with soul so tough
> Who says two sexes aren't enough?
> —*Samuel Hoffenstein.*

Oh, what a tangled web we weave when first we practice to conceive.   —*Don Herold.*

SICKNESS

Sickness is a belief, which must be annihilated by the divine Mind.   —*Mary Baker Eddy.*

Some maladies are rich and precious and only to be acquired by the right of inheritance or purchased with gold.
—*Nathaniel Hawthorne.*

SILENCE

If you don't say anything, you won't be called on to repeat it.
—*Calvin Coolidge.*

Silence is often evidence of the most persuasive character.
—*Louis D. Brandeis.*

The only golden thing that women dislike is silence.
—*M. W. Little.*

Silence, when nothing need be said, is the eloquence of discretion.   —*C. N. Bovee.*

Let us be silent that we may hear the whispers of the gods.
—*R. W. Emerson.*

If a man keeps his trap shut, the world will beat a path to his
door.   —*F. P. Adams.*

Silence is a figure of speech, unanswerable, short, cold, but
terribly severe.   —*Theodore Parker.*

Silence is one of the hardest arguments to refute.
                                                     —*Josh Billings.*

Silence never makes any blunders.   —*Ibid.*

A man is known by the silence he keeps.   —*Oliver Herford.*

> These be
> Three silent things:
> The falling snow . . . the hour
> Before the dawn . . . the mouth of one
> Just dead.
>   —*Adelaide Crapsey.*

Teach your child to hold his tongue; he'll learn fast enough to
speak.   —*B. Franklin.*

Blessed are they who have nothing to say, and who cannot be
persuaded to say it.   —*R. L. Lowell.*

None preaches better than the ant and she says nothing.
                                                     —*B. Franklin.*

SIMILARITY

Whatever you may be sure of, be sure of this; that you are
dreadfully like other people.   —*Amy Lowell.*

SIMPLICITY

Nothing is more simple than greatness; indeed, to be simple is
to be great.   —*R. W. Emerson.*

The greatest truths are the simplest.   —*Hosea Ballou.*

Our life is frittered away by detail. Simplicity, simplicity, simplicity!   —*H. D. Thoreau.*

Simplicity is making the journey of this life with just baggage
enough.   —*C. D. Warner.*

In character, in manners, in style, in all things the supreme
excellence is simplicity.   —*H. W. Longfellow.*

SIN

No man ever inherited sin. There is not any original sin.
                                                    —*Lyman Abbott.*

Sin is not hurtful because it is forbidden, but it is forbidden because it is hurtful. —*B. Franklin.*

Every sin is the result of a collaboration. —*Stephen Crane.*

The besetting sin of philosophers is that, being men, they endeavor to survey the universe from the standpoint of gods.
—*A. N. Whitehead.*

After the first blush of sin, comes its indifference; and from immoral it becomes, as it were, unmoral, and not quite unnecessary to that life we have made. —*H. D. Thoreau.*

It is impossible to believe that the same God who permitted His own son to die a bachelor regards celibacy as an actual sin.
—*H. L. Mencken.*

Sin is forgiven only as it is destroyed by Christ—Truth and Life. —*Mary Baker Eddy.*

O sin, what hast thou done to this fair earth! —*R. H. Dana.*

> But he who never sins can little boast
> Compared to him who goes and sins no more!
> —*N. P. Willis.*

Never to have sinned is the unpardonable sin.
—*Paul Eldridge.*

It is both bad art and bad ethics to deny the existence of sins and sinners. —*Elizabeth Jackson.*

There is nothing complicated or mechanical or unnatural about the forgiveness of sin. There is only one thing that forbids it, it is the locked door of our own hearts. —*Francis G. Peabody.*

It is no sin to be tempted; it is to yield and be overcome.
—*Wm. Penn.*

Man-like it is to fall into sin; fiendlike it is to dwell therein.
—*H. W. Longfellow.*

Sin, every day, takes out a patent for a new invention.
—*E. P. Whipple.*

Only the sinner has a right to preach. —*Christopher Morley.*

Men who make no pretensions to being good on one day out of seven are called sinners. —*M. W. Little.*

Confess your sins to the Lord, and you will be forgiven; confess them to men, and you will be laughed at. —*Josh Billings.*

SINCERITY

Use no hurtful deceit; think innocently and justly, and, if you speak, speak accordingly.   —*B. Franklin.*

No man can produce great things who is not thoroughly sincere in dealing with himself.   —*J. R. Lowell.*

Sincerity is religion personified.   —*E. H. Chapin.*

Sincerity is no test for truth—no evidence of correctness of conduct.—You may take poison sincerely believing it the needed medicine, but will it save your life?   —*Tryon Edwards.*

SLANDER

A slander is like a hornet; if you cannot kill it dead the first blow, better not strike at it.   —*H. W. Shaw.*

Truth is generally the best vindication against slander.
                                                       —*A. Lincoln.*

No character, however upright, is a match for constantly reiterated attacks, however false.   —*Alexander Hamilton.*

Every calumny makes some proselytes, and even retains some; since justification seldom circulates as rapidly and as widely as slander.   —*Ibid.*

Believe nothing against another, but on good authority.
                                                       —*Wm. Penn.*

Liberty should not mean the right to foment wars by lies and slander.   —*Norman Thomas.*

Slander is a kind of lying which ought to be set apart for special censure.   —*W. Gladden.*

We cannot drive scientists into our laboratories but, if we tolerate reckless or unfair attacks, we can certainly drive them out.
                                                       —*H. S. Truman.*

Character assassination is at once easier and surer than physical assault; and it involves far less risk for the assassin. It leaves him free to commit the same deed over and over again, and may, indeed, win him the honors of a hero even in the country of his victims.   —*Alan Barth.*

SLANG

Slang is a language that takes off its coat, spits on its hands, and goes to work.   —*Carl Sandburg.*

Slang is the speech of him who robs the literary garbage cans on their way to the dump. —*Ambrose Bierce.*

SLAVERY

I can clearly foresee that nothing but the rooting out of slavery can perpetuate the existence of our union by consolidating it in a common bond of principle. —*G. Washington.*

Whenever I hear anyone arguing for slavery, I feel a strong impulse to see it tried on him personally. —*A. Lincoln.*

The compact which exists between the North and the South is a covenant with death and an agreement with hell.

—*W. L. Garrison.*

If slavery is not wrong, nothing is wrong. —*A. Lincoln.*

> Men! whose boast it is that ye
> Come of fathers brave and free,
> If there breathe on earth a slave,
> Are ye truly free and brave?
>
> —*J. R. Lowell.*

Slavery is a flagrant violation of the institutions of America— direct government—over all the people, by all the people, for all the people. —*Theodore Parker.*

There is no proportion between twenty pieces of silver and liberty. —*Samuel Sewall.*

If you put a chain around the neck of a slave, the other end fastens itself around your own. —*R. W. Emerson.*

The man who gives me employment, which I must have or suffer, that man is my master, let me call him what I will.

—*Henry George.*

Slavery and democracy—especially democracy founded, as ours is, upon the rights of man— would seem to be incompatible with each other. And yet at this time the democracy of the country is suffocated chiefly, if not entirely, by slavery. —*John Q. Adams.*

Where slavery is there liberty cannot be, and where liberty is there slavery cannot be. —*Charles Sumner.*

If you give up your convictions and call slavery right . . . you let slavery in upon you. —*A. Lincoln.*

Slavery stands in the way of that automatic instinct of progress which is eternal in the human race and irresistible in human history. *—Theodore Parker.*

I believe this government cannot endure permanently half slave and half free. *—A. Lincoln.*

Man is born a slave, but everywhere he wants to be a master. *—Hans J. Morgenthau.*

They are slaves who fear to speak for the fallen and the weak. *—J. R. Lowell.*

They are slaves who dare not be in the right with two or three. *—Ibid.*

In this world we must be conquerors or slaves. *—Phillips Brooks.*

SLEEP

Fatigue is the best pillow. *—B. Franklin.*

The only time most women give their orating husbands undivided attention is when the old boys mumble in their sleep. *—Wilson Mizner.*

Sleep lingers all our lifetime about our eyes, as night hovers all day in the boughs of the fir-tree. *—R. W. Emerson.*

There ain't no way to find out why a snorer can't hear himself snore. *—Mark Twain.*

SLOTH

Sloth, like rust, consumes faster than labor wears, while the used key is always bright, as Poor Richard says. But dost thou love life, then do not squander time, for that is the stuff life is made of, as Poor Richard says. *—B. Franklin.*

SMILES

A lot of men think that if they smile for a second, somebody will take advantage of them, and they are right. *—Don Herold.*

Wrinkles should merely indicate where smiles have been. *—Mark Twain.*

Something of a person's character may be discovered by observing how he smiles.—Some people never smile, they only grin. *—C. N. Bovee.*

The man worth while is the one who will smile when everything goes dead wrong. *—Ella W. Wilcox.*

SOCIALISM

Socialism is that contemplated system of industrial society which proposes the abolition of private property in the great material instruments of production, and the substitution therefore of collective property; and advocates the collective management of production, together with the distribution of social income by society, and private property in the larger proportion of this social income.
—R. T. Ely.

Socialism is a dead horse. *—Thorstein Veblen.*

The ideal of Socialism is grand and noble; and it is, I am convinced, possible of realization; but such a state of society cannot be manufactured—it must grow. Society is an organism, not a machine. *—Henry George.*

We are racing down a four-lane superhighway which terminates in Socialism whether you call it welfare state, collectivism or something else. *—H. F. Byrd.*

Socialism in America is doomed—unless it is linked up with the ideals of Americanism. *—Leon Samson.*

The American is an unconscious Socialist. *—Ibid.*

We are in for some kind of socialism, call it by whatever name we please. *—John Dewey.*

SOCIETY

Society will develop by living it, not by policing it.
—Anonymous (quoted by John Dewey).

Society is produced by our wants; government by our wickedness. *—T. Paine.*

Society is a hospital of incurables. *—R. W. Emerson.*

We have a society . . . whose symbol is the Public Relations Counsel. *—John Chamberlain.*

All society is a means of escape from personality, and its limitations of power and vision, into the larger communal life.
—G. E. Woodberry.

Society must see to it that it does not itself crush or weaken or damage its own constituent parts. The first duty of law is to keep sound the society it serves. *—Woodrow Wilson.*

The human imagination has already come to conceive the possibility of re-creating human society. *—Edmund Wilson.*

The only possibility left is that of a positive society.
—*T. S. Eliot.*

Society asks little more of its votaries than shining boots and a spotless shirt front. —*R. G. Ingersoll.*

Society is a masked ball, where every one hides his real character, and reveals it by hiding. —*R. W. Emerson.*

Help create a new society in which men and women the globe around can live and grow invigorated by freedom.
—*Wendell L. Willkie.*

SOLDIER

We are coming, Father Abraham, three hundred thousand more.
—*J. S. Gibbons.*

Every citizen should be a soldier. This was the case with the Greeks and Romans, and must be that of every free state.
—*T. Jefferson.*

I want to see you shoot the way you shout.
—*Theodore Roosevelt.*

SOLITUDE

Avoid the reeking herd,
Shun the polluted flock,
Live like that stoic bird
The eagle of the rock.

—*Elinor Wylie.*

The great man is he who in the midst of the crowd keeps with perfect sweetness the independence of solitude. —*R. W. Emerson.*

Solitude is as needful to the imagination as society is wholesome for the character. —*J. R. Lowell.*

I never found the companion that was so companionable as solitude. —*H. D. Thoreau.*

To go into solitude, a man needs to retire as much from his chamber as from society. —*R. W. Emerson.*

I have three chairs in my house; one for solitude, two for friendship, three for company. —*H. D. Thoreau.*

I live in that solitude which is painful in youth, but delicious in the years of maturity. —*Albert Einstein.*

All we ask is to be let alone. —*Jefferson Davis.*

Look at yourself from the far away pinnacle of aloneness, and your inner voices will tell you the right path to take henceforth.
—*Dagobert D. Runes.*

SOLVENCY

Solvency is entirely a matter of temperament and not of income.
—*Logan Pearsall Smith.*

SONG

I will make a song for these states that no one State may under circumstances be subjected to another State.   —*Walt Whitman.*

A love song is just a caress set to music.   —*Sigmund Romberg.*

A song will outlive all sermons in the memory.

—*Henry Giles.*

> Such songs have power to quiet
> The restless pulse of care,
> And come like the benediction
> That follows after prayer.

—*H. W. Longfellow.*

Song: the licensed medium for bawling in public things too silly or sacred to be uttered in ordinary speech.   —*Oliver Herford.*

SORROW

Sorrow makes men sincere.   —*H. W. Beecher.*

Into each life some rain must fall.   —*H. W. Longfellow.*

I do not know of a better cure for sorrow than to pity someone else.   —*H. W. Shaw.*

There can be no rainbow without a cloud and a storm.

—*J. H. Vincent.*

Out of suffering have emerged the strongest souls.

—*E. H. Chapin.*

Never a tear bedims the eye that time and patience will not dry.
—*Bret Harte.*

We may learn from children how large a part of our grievances is imaginary. But the pain is just as real.   —*C. N. Bovee.*

I shall not let a sorrow die until I find the heart of it, nor let a wordless joy go by until it talks to me a bit.   —*Sara Teasdale.*

SOUL

Was somebody asking to see the soul? See your own shape and

countenance, persons, substances, beasts, the trees, the running rivers, the rocks and sands.   *—Walt Whitman.*

It is in living wisely and fully that one's soul grows.
       —A. H. Compton.

Flowers are the sweetest things that God ever made and forgot to put a soul into.   *—H. W. Beecher.*

Immortality will come to such as are fit for it; and he who would be a great soul in the future must be a great soul now.
       —R. W. Emerson.

Drop an anchor anywhere and the anchor will drag—that is, if your soul is a limitless, fathomless sea, and not a dogpond.
       —Elbert Hubbard.

A man can't have his soul and save it too.   *—Don Herold.*

My soul has grown deep like the rivers.   *—Langston Hughes.*

Give the soul a new instrument, a spiritual body, and it will be seen that its power is the same as ever.   *—J. F. Clarke.*

Oh, let the soul alone! Let it go to God as best it may! It is entangled enough.   *—H. W. Beecher.*

If anything in the past is worth preserving, surely it is the history of the soul.   *—G. E. Woodberry.*

John Brown's body lies a-smould'ring in the grave.
His soul goes marching on.   *—T. B. Bishop.*

The one thing in the world, of value, is the active soul.
       —R. W. Emerson.

Self is the only prison that can ever bind the soul.
       —H. Van Dyke.

I loaf and invite my soul,
I lean and loaf at my ease, observing a spear of summer grass.
       —Walt Whitman.

> The windows of my soul I throw
> Wide open to the sun.
>
>   *—J. G. Whittier.*

The man who is always worrying whether or not his soul would be damned generally has a soul that isn't worth a damn.
       —O. W. Holmes.

The soul has more diseases than the body.
       —H. W. Shaw.

Everything but the soul of man is a passing shadow. The only enduring substance is within. —*W. E. Channing.*

As elemental and dominant as the passion of sex for physical union is the passion of the soul for spiritual union.

—*John Haynes Holmes.*

As the very atoms of the earth and the stars of the sky seek harmony with the system which binds them in a cosmic unity, so the souls of men seek harmony with the Spirit which makes them one. —*Ibid.*

What avail, O builders of the world, unless ye build a safety for the soul? —*Edwin Markham.*

SOVEREIGNTY

We are but the agents—the servants. The sovereignty resides in the people of the States. —*John C. Calhoun.*

My idea of the Sovereignty of the people is that the people can change the Constitution if they please; but while the Constitution exists they must conform themselves to its dictates.

—*James Madison.*

SPECIALTY

Let everyone ascertain his special business or calling, and then stick to it if he would be successful. —*B. Franklin.*

Keep to your speciality; to the doing of the thing that you accomplish with most of satisfaction to yourself, and most of benefit to those about you. —*Frances E. Willard.*

Keep to this (your speciality) whether it is raising turnips, or tunes, painting screens or battle-pieces. —*Ibid.*

SPECULATION

There are two times in a man's life when he should not speculate: when he can't afford it and when he can. —*Mark Twain.*

There will always be speculation of some kind. If you throw it out of an organized exchange, you throw it out into the street.

—*H. C. Emery.*

If there were no bad speculations there could be no good investments; if there were no wild ventures there would be no brilliantly successful enterprises. —*F. W. Hirst.*

Speculation is only a word covering the making of money out of the manipulation of prices, instead of supplying goods and services. —*Henry Ford.*

SPEECH

If a political candidate can't get up and make a speech of his own, if he has to hire a press agent to write it for him, then why not let the press agent be the candidate?   —*Raymond Clapper.*

This nation will survive, this state will prosper, the orderly business of life will go forward if only men can speak in whatever way given them to utter what their hearts hold—by voice, by posted card, by letter or by press.   —*William A. White.*

Never rise to speak till you have something to say; and when you have said it, cease.   —*John Witherspoon.*

Speak softly and carry a big stick.   —*Theodore Roosevelt.*

Speech is undoubtedly the supreme art of man.

—*Mathurin Dondo.*

Speech is better than silence; silence is better than speech.

—*R. W. Emerson.*

You will find half the battle is gained if you never allow yourself to say anything gloomy.   —*L. M. Childs.*

It usually takes more than three weeks to prepare a good impromptu speech.   —*Mark Twain.*

There is but one pleasure in life equal to that of being called to make an after-dinner speech, and that is not being called on to make one.   —*C. D. Warner.*

Half the world is composed of people who have something to say and can't, and the other half who have nothing to say and keep on saying it.   —*Robert Frost.*

Better say nothing than not to the purpose. And to speak pertinently, consider both what is fit, and when it is fit to speak.

—*Wm. Penn.*

If thou thinkest twice, before thou speakest once, thou wilt speak twice the better for it.   —*Ibid.*

I realize that there are certain limitations placed upon the right of free speech. I may not be able to say all I think, but I am not going to say anything I do not think.   —*E. V. Debs.*

Speech is power: speech is to persuade, to convert, to compel.

—*R. W. Emerson.*

For God's sake let us freely hear both sides!   —*T. Jefferson.*

Many public speakers are good extemporaneous listeners.

—*E. W. Nye.*

The obvious duty of a toastmaster is to be so infernally dull that the succeeding speakers will appear brilliant by contrast.

—C. B. Kelland.

Speech is human nature itself, with none of the artificiality of written language. *—A. N. Whitehead.*

There is a homely adage which runs, "Speak softly and carry a big stick; you will go far." *—Theodore Roosevelt.*

Free speech does not live many hours after free industry and free commerce die. *—Herbert Hoover.*

I have always been among those who believed that the greatest freedom of speech was the greatest safety, because if a man is a fool the best thing to do is to encourage him to advertise the fact by speaking. *—Woodrow Wilson.*

The most stringent protection of free speech would not protect a man in falsely shouting fire in a theater and causing a panic.

—O. W. Holmes, Jr.

Free speech is to a great people what winds are to oceans and malarial regions, which waft away the elements of disease, and bring new elements of health. Where free speech is stopped miasma is bred, and death comes fast. *—H. W. Beecher.*

SPEED

The eagle's wing is slow compared with the flight of love.

—David Swing.

In this world and in every-day affairs, you have got to run fast merely to stay where you are; and in order to get anywhere you have got to run twice as fast as that. *—Woodrow Wilson.*

SPENDING

Any government, like any family, can for a year spend a little more than it earns. But you and I know that continuance of that habit means the poor-house. *—F. D. Roosevelt.*

Along this road of spending the government either takes over, which is Socialism, or dictates institutional and economic life, which is Fascism. *—Herbert Hoover.*

There's too blamed many ways to spend money and not enough new ways to get it. *—Kin Hubbard.*

SPIRIT

The *spirit* only can *teach.* *—R. W. Emerson.*

Every spirit makes its house, but as afterwards the house confines its spirit, you had better build well.   —*Elbert Hubbard.*

There is only one thing that counts in this life, and it beats all the maxims ever penned—that is, for a man's spirit to be all right. If that is what it should be all the details of his life will fall into their proper places.   —*E. W. Bok.*

What is the glory of the midnight heavens to that of a great spirit which rises to truth and God, and lifts up nations with it?
—*J. F. Clarke.*

Whatever can't be done in the physical can be done in the spiritual. And in direct proportion as a man recognizes himself as spirit, and lives accordingly, is he able to transcend in power the man who recognizes himself merely as material.   —*R. W. Trine.*

What I admire most in any man is a serene spirit, a steady freedom from moral indignation, an all-embracing tolerance—in brief, what is commonly called good sportsmanship.
—*H. L. Mencken.*

It must be of the spirit if we are to save the flesh.
—*Douglas MacArthur.*

SPONTANEITY
All good conversation, manners, and action come from a spontaneity which forgets usages and makes the moment great.
—*R. W. Emerson.*

Nature hates calculators; her methods are salutory and impulsive.   —*Ibid.*

SQUARE DEAL
If elected, I shall see to it that every man has a square deal, no less and no more.   —*Theodore Roosevelt.*

STANDARDS
We cannot afford a double standard of morality in peace or in war. Our moral standing is among our most valuable assets.
—*Paul Hoffman.*

We are weary of the low standards by which actions are judged, and to which, to our dismay, we perceive our actions insensibly conform.   —*Felix Adler.*

You cannot choose your battlefield,
The gods do that for you,
But you can plant a standard
Where a standard never flew.

—Nathalia Crane.

STARS

Our stars—freedom, opportunity, faith—are ever constant.

—T. M. Wolff.

Though the star should be quenched in a moment forever, it is good that star should shine its brightest to the last.

—Phillips Brooks.

STARVING

We can plant wheat every year, but people who are starving die only once.   *—Fiorello LaGuardia.*

STATE

The state, which is the guardian of our liberties, must be exalted.

—A. Meiklejohn.

Wise and good men are the strength of a state; much more so than riches or arms, which under the management of ignorance and wickedness often draw on destruction, instead of providing for the safety of the people.   *—B. Franklin.*

The state is only a group of men with human interests, passions, and desires, or, worse yet, the state is only an obscure clerk hidden in some corner of a government bureau.

—W. G. Sumner.

It is not the function of the State to make men happy. They must make themselves happy in their own way, and at their own risk.   *—Ibid.*

The State . . . both in its genesis and by its primary intention, is purely anti-social.   *—A. J. Nock.*

The greatest violator of the principle of equal liberty is the State.   *—Charles T. Sprading.*

The outstanding political event of the century is the emergence of the United States of America as a superstate.

—Ely Culbertson.

At the best, the State or the government, is an instrumentality for making peace, not for the perpetuation of it.

—Thorstein Veblen.

The normal relation of the States is war.   —*Randolph Bourne.*

War is essentially the health of the State.   —*Ibid.*

Only when the State is at war does the modern society function with that unity of sentiment, simple and uncritical patriotic devotion, cooperation of services, which have been the ideal of the State lover.   —*Ibid.*

The state ought not to be that great leviathan before whom the free soul is compelled to bow down.   —*Howard Mumford Jones.*

STATESMANSHIP

In statesmanship, get the formalities right; never mind about the moralities.   —*Mark Twain.*

True statesmanship is the act of changing a nation from what it is to what it ought to be.   —*W. R. Alger.*

Honest statesmanship is the wise employment of individual meanness for the public good.   —*A. Lincoln.*

STATESMEN

Every man who looks at the Constitution in the spirit to entitle him to the character of statesman, must elevate his views to the height to which this nation is destined to reach in the rank of nations.   —*Henry Clay.*

The statesman shears the sheep, the politician skins them.
                                                          —*Austin O'Malley.*

The man who is dishonest as a statesman would be a dishonest man in any station.   —*T. Jefferson.*

Enthusiasm is good material for the orator, but the statesman needs something more durable to work in,—must be able to rely on the deliberate reason and consequent firmness of the people.
                                                          —*J. R. Lowell.*

Statesmen work in the dark until the Idea of Right towers above expediency or wealth.   —*W. E. Channing.*

You can always get the truth from an American statesman after he has turned seventy, or given up all hope of the Presidency.
                                                          —*Wendell Phillips.*

STATISTICS

Statistics are like alienists—they will testify for either side.
                                                          —*Fiorello LaGuardia.*

The federal government, unable to reconcile its laissez-faire philosophy with the exigencies of modern labor conflicts, compiles statistics and appoints fact-finding boards to collect more statistics. —*Hans J. Morgenthau.*

STOMACH

The size of a woman's stomach depends largely on her surroundings. —*Eugene Field.*

STORY-TELLING

Don't tell a good story even though you know one; its narration will simply remind your hearers of a bad one. —*E. W. Howe.*

The revulsion against story (in fiction) is a desire that experience be refined so far that it cannot be recognized. It is a desire in the void. —*Bernard De Voto.*

The fellow that tells a good story always has to listen to a couple of poor ones. —*Kin Hubbard.*

A good storyteller is a person who has a good memory and hopes other people haven't. —*I. S. Cobb.*

Stories now, to suit a public taste, must be half epigram, half pleasant vice. —*J. R. Lowell.*

STRANGER

Which of us not forever a stranger and alone.

—*Thomas Wolfe.*

STRENGTH

Let us preserve our strength . . . and not exhaust it in civil commotions and intensive wars. —*Patrick Henry.*

Be strong:
Sing to your heart a battle song.
—*Edwin Markham.*

Concentration is the secret of strength. —*R. W. Emerson.*

Without the protection of the law, the strong would oppress and enslave the weak. —*James F. Cooper.*

Don't expect to build up the weak by pulling down the strong.
—*Calvin Coolidge.*

It is only the strong who can promote and preserve a righteous peace. Idle and futile is the voice of the weak nation, or the craven nation, when it clamors for peace. —*Frank Knox.*

Only a strong state can maintain freedom and equality in any nation, or in the world as a whole.   —*A. Meiklejohn.*

The strength of a man consists in finding out the way God is going, and going that way.   —*H. W. Beecher.*

It has long been a grave question whether any government, not too strong for the liberties of its people, can be strong enough to maintain its existence in great emergencies.   —*A. Lincoln.*

I wish to preach not the doctrine of ignoble ease, but the doctrine of the strenuous life.   —*Theodore Roosevelt.*

STRIFE

Let us shrink from no strife, moral or physical, within or without the nation, provided we are certain that the strife is justified.
—*Ibid.*

STRIKES

There is no right to strike against the public safety by anybody, anywhere, anytime.   —*Calvin Coolidge.*

During strikes it must always be remembered that the public interest is paramount.   —*Fiorello LaGuardia.*

The right to strike is basic to a free society . . . for the prohibition of the right to strike is a long step on the road that leads to totalitarianism and complete regimentation of the economy.
—*A. J. Goldberg.*

I am glad to see that a system of labor prevails in New England under which laborers can strike when they want to. . . . I like the system which lets a man quit when he wants to.   —*A. Lincoln.*

The right of individuals to strike is inviolate and ought not to be interfered with by any process of government, but there is a predominant right and that is the right of the government to protect all of its people.   —*Woodrow Wilson.*

Any strike is of the nature of sabotage, of course. Indeed, a strike is a typical species of sabotage. . . . Strikes and lockouts are of identically the same character.   —*Thorstein Veblen.*

STUDENT

Don't despair of a student if he has one clear idea.
—*R. W. Emerson.*

STUDY

The world's great men have not commonly been great scholars, nor its great scholars great men.   —*O. W. Holmes.*

As turning the logs will make a dull fire burn, so change of studies a dull brain. —*H. W. Longfellow.*

The mind of the scholar, if he would leave it large and liberal, should come in contact with other minds. —*Ibid.*

STUPIDITY

Stupidity has no friends, and wants none. —*Horace Greeley.*
Stupidity—unconscious ignorance. —*H. W. Shaw.*

STYLE

One who uses many periods is a philosopher, many interrogations, a student; many exclamations, a fanatic. —*J. L. Basford.*

With many readers, brilliancy of style passes for affluence of thought. —*H. W. Longfellow.*

Readers mistake buttercups in the grass for immeasurable gold mines under ground. —*Ibid.*

He who thinks much says but little in proportion to his thoughts. He tries to compress as much thought as possible into a few words. —*Washington Irving.*

The secret of force in writing lies in having something that you believe to say, and making the parts of speech vividly conscious of it. —*J. R. Lowell.*

A chaste and lucid style is indicative of the same personal traits in the author. —*Hosea Ballou.*

Style is the gossamer on which the seeds of truth float through the world. —*George Bancroft.*

The style's the man, so books avow;
The style's the woman, anyhow.

—*O. W. Holmes.*

SUBLIMITY

One step above the sublime makes the ridiculous, and one step above the ridiculous makes the sublime again. —*T. Paine.*

SUBSIDIES

The man who pulls the plow gets the plunder in politics.
—*Huey P. Long.*

A subsidy is a formula for handing you back your own money with a flourish that makes you think it's a gift. —*Jo Bingham.*

The economy of no country can stand a kept agriculture for very long. —*Louis Bromfield.*

SUCCESS

Freedom from scruple, from sympathy, honesty, and regard for life may, within fairly wide limits, be said to further the success of the individual in the pecuniary culture.   —*Thorstein Veblen*.

Success is not always a sure sign of merit, but it is a first-rate way to succeed.   —*Josh Billings*.

It is not the going out of port, but the coming in, that determines the success of a voyage.   —*H. W. Beecher*.

The secret of success lies not in doing your own work, but in recognizing the right man to do it.   —*Andrew Carnegie*.

Be awful nice to 'em goin' up, because you're gonna meet 'em all comin' down.   —*Jimmy Durante*.

The gent who wakes up and finds himself a success hasn't been asleep.   —*Wilson Mizner*.

Nothing recedes like success.   —*Walter Winchell*.

The best way to get along is never to forgive an enemy or forget a friend.   —*Ibid*.

However things may seem, no evil thing is success, and no good thing is failure.   —*Samuel Longfellow*.

No man can stand on top because he is put there.
        —*H. H. Vreeland*.

Our business in life is not to get ahead of other people, but to get ahead of ourselves.   —*M. D. Babcock*.

The talent of success is nothing more than doing what you can do well; and doing well whatever you do, without a thought of fame.   —*H. W. Longfellow*.

One man of tolerable abilities may work great changes, and accomplish great affairs among mankind, if he first forms a good plan, and, cutting off all amusements or other employments that would divert his attention, makes the execution of that same plan his sole study and business.   —*B. Franklin*.

The penalty of success is to be bored by the attentions of people who formerly snubbed you.   —*M. W. Little*.

Success may go to one's head but the stomach is where it gets in its worst work.   —*Kin Hubbard*.

I have learned that success is to be measured not so much by the position that one has reached in life as by the obstacles which he has overcome while trying to succeed. —*Booker T. Washington*.

All you need in this life is ignorance and confidence, and then Success is sure.   *—Mark Twain.*

> Success is counted sweetest
> By those who ne'er succeed.
>   *—Emily Dickinson.*

If a man write a better book, preach a better sermon, or make a better mousetrap than his neighbor, though he build his house in the woods, the world will make a beaten path to his door.
                                        —R. W. Emerson.

Real success in business is to be found in achievements comparable rather with those of the artist or the scientist, of the inventor or the statesman.   *—Louis D. Brandeis.*

The successful businessman must be able to foresee possibilities, to estimate with sagacity the outcome in the future.
                                        —F. W. Taussig.

There's always something about your success that displeases even your best friends.   *—Mark Twain.*

With my own ability, I cannot succeed, without the sustenance of Divine Providence, and of the great free, happy and intelligent people. Without these I cannot hope to succeed; with them, I cannot fail.   *—A. Lincoln.*

Success don't consist in never making blunders, but in never making the same one the second time.   *—H. W. Shaw.*

Put all good eggs in one basket and then watch the basket.
                                        —Andrew Carnegie.

The thinking part of mankind will attach equal glory to those actions which deserve success, and those which have been crowned with it.   *—G. Washington.*

SUFFERING

Suffering is a part of the divine idea.   *—H. W. Beecher.*

No pain, no palm; no thorns, no throne; no gall, no glory; no cross, no crown.   *—Wm. Penn.*

Know how sublime a thing it is to suffer and be strong.
                                        —H. W. Longfellow.

SUICIDE

No man is educated who has never dallied with the thought of suicide.   *—William James.*

As men may be protected against murder, but cannot be guarded against suicide, so government may be shielded from the assaults of external foes, but nothing can save it when it chooses to lay violent hands on itself.   —*Daniel Webster.*

There is no refuge from confession but suicide; and suicide is confession.   —*Ibid.*

The fellow that tries to commit suicide with a razor, and fails, would fail at anything.   —*Kin Hubbard.*

Suicide is cheating the doctors out of a job.   —*Josh Billings.*

SUNRISE

The sunrise never failed us yet.   —*Celia Thaxter.*

Dazzling and tremendous, how quick the sun-rise would kill me, If I would not now and always send sun-rise out of me.
                                                        —*Walt Whitman.*

SUPERIORITY

We can all perceive the difference between ourselves and our inferiors, but when it comes to a question of the difference between us and our superiors we fail to appreciate merits of which we have no proper conceptions.   —*James F. Cooper.*

There are men too superior to be seen except by the few, as there are notes too high for the scale of most ears.
                                                        —*R. W. Emerson.*

It is a great art to be superior to others without letting them know it.   —*H. W. Shaw.*

SUPERSTITION

The amount of superstition is not much changed, but it now attaches to politics, not to religion.   —*W. G. Sumner.*

We are all tattooed in our cradles with the beliefs of our tribe.
                                                        —*O. W. Holmes.*

You cannot educate a man wholly out of the superstitious fears which were implanted in his imagination; no matter how utterly his reason may reject them.   —*Ibid.*

Men are probably nearer the central truth in their superstitions than in their science.   —*H. D. Thoreau.*

I would rather go to the forest . . . I would rather live there, with my soul erect and free, than in a palace of gold, and wear a crown of imperial power, and feel that I was superstitions's cringing slave, and dare not speak my honest thought.

—*R. G. Ingersoll.*

There is nothing people will not maintain when they are slaves to superstition; and candour and a sense of justice are, in such a case, the first things lost. —*George Santayana.*

SURGERY

Surgery is by far the worst snob among the handicrafts.

—*Austin O'Malley.*

SUSPICION

The less we know the more we suspect. —*H. W. Shaw.*

Ignorance is the mother of suspicion. —*W. R. Alger.*

Suspicion and persecution are weeds of the same dunghill, and flourish best together. —*T. Paine.*

Suspicion is no friend to virtue and always an enemy of happiness. —*Hosea Ballou.*

We are paid for our suspicions by finding what we suspect.

—*H. D. Thoreau.*

Discreet and well-founded suspicion avoids a multitude of evils, which credulity brings upon itself. —*Charles Simmons.*

Suspicions which may be unjust need not be stated.

—*A. Lincoln.*

SWAN-SONG

Whitman thought he was a rooster crowing at dawn, but actually he was singing the swan-song of the once triumphant antebellum democracy. —*T. K. Whipple.*

SWEARING

That unmeaning and abominable custom, swearing.

—*G. Washington.*

SWEETHEARTS

Love is said to be blind, but I know lots of fellows in love who can see twice as much in their sweethearts as I can.

—*Josh Billings.*

SWINDLE

There's a sucker born every minute. —*P. T. Barnum.*

SYMPATHY

Whoever walks a furlong without sympathy walks to his own funeral drest in his shroud.   —*Walt Whitman.*

Sympathy is two hearts tugging at one load. —*C. H. Parkhurst.*

Strengthen me by sympathizing with my strength, not my weakness.   —*A. B. Alcott.*

A crowd always thinks with its sympathy, never with its reason.
                                                        —*W. R. Alger.*

The secrets of life are not shown except to sympathy and likeness.   —*R. W. Emerson.*

The strongest bond of human sympathy, outside of the family relation, should be one uniting all working people, all nations, and tongues, and kindreds.   —*A. Lincoln.*

Personal magnetism is the conductor of the sacred spark that puts us in human communion, and gives us to company, conversation and ourselves.   —*A. B. Alcott.*

A sympathizer is a fellow that's for you as long as it doesn't cost anything.   —*Kin Hubbard.*

A helping word to one in trouble is often like a switch on a railroad track—but one inch between wreck and smooth-rolling prosperity.   —*H. W. Beecher.*

Happy is the man who has that in his soul which acts upon the dejected as April airs upon violet roots.   —*Ibid.*

Sympathy wanting, all is wanting.   —*A. B. Alcott.*

SYSTEM

Our political system is, in its purity, not only the best that ever was formed, but the best possible that can be devised for us.
                                                    —*John C. Calhoun.*

I'm sick of a system where the richest man gets the most beautiful girl if he wants her, while the artist without income has to sell his talent to a button manufacturer.   —*F. Scott Fitzgerald.*

The industrial system of a nation, like its political system, should be a government of the people, by the people, for the people. Until economic equality shall give a basis to political equality, the latter is but a sham.   —*Edward Bellamy.*

The existing system of businesslike control is obsolete.
                                                    —*Thorstein Veblen.*

T

TACT

Women and foxes, being weak, are distinguished by superior tact.
—Ambrose Bierce.

Tact is one of the first mental virtues, the absence of which is often fatal to the best of talents; it supplies the place of many talents.
—W. G. Simms.

Tact: the ability to describe others as they see themselves.
—A. Lincoln.

TAILOR

A young man of great judgment . . . knows how to choose his tailor.
—W. D. Howells.

TALENT

Talent is that which is in a man's power; genius is that in whose power a man is.
—J. R. Lowell.

In the battle of existence, Talent is the punch; Tact is the clever footwork.
—Wilson Mizner.

Talent is a cistern; genius a fountain.
—E. P. Whipple.

The world is always ready to receive talent with open arms.
—O. W. Holmes.

Talent, if sufficiently vital, can survive any thesis superimposed upon it.
—Leo Gurko.

Every man who can be a first-rate something . . . has no right to be a fifth-rate something; for a fifth-rate something is no better than a first-rate nothing.
—J. G. Holland.

Talent is worshipped; but if divorced from rectitude, it will prove more of a demon than a god.
—W. E. Channing.

The exaltation of talent, as it is called, above virtue and religion, is the curse of the age.
—Ibid.

Talent has always been able to break through class distinctions; in America it could conserve its energy for the tasks before it.
—*H. S. Commager.*

Talent for talent's sake is a bauble and a show. Talent working with joy in the cause of universal truth lifts the possessor to new power as a benefactor.   —*R. W. Emerson.*

TALES

Dead men sell no tales.   —*Carolyn Wells.*

TALKING

Don't talk about yourself; it will be done when you leave.
—*Addison Mizner.*

Never has there been so much patriotic talk as in the last twenty-five years and never were there so many influences at work strangling Republican institutions.   —*John P. Altgeld.*

Talking with your antagonist to avoid strife is a moral duty. Appeasement comes when, in order to avoid strife and to achieve a supposed security, you sacrifice a principle which you know to be a sacred right.   —*Brien McMahon.*

Every time I read where some woman gave a short talk I wonder how she stopped.   —*Kin Hubbard.*

People who have nothing to say are never at a loss in talking.
—*Josh Billings.*

Whether one talks well depends very much upon whom he has to talk to.   —*C. N. Bovee.*

In general, those who have nothing to say contrive to spend the longest time in doing it.   —*J. R. Lowell.*

When I think of talking, it is, of course, with a woman.
—*O. W. Holmes.*

Snobs talk as if they had begotten their own ancestors.
—*Herbert Agar.*

No man would listen to you talk if he didn't know it was his turn next.   —*E. W. Howe.*

War talk by men who have been in a war is always interesting; whereas moon talk by a poet who has not been in the moon is likely to be dull.   —*Mark Twain.*

A good talker or writer is only a pitcher. Unless his audience catches him with heart and mind he's defeated.   —*Wilson Mizner.*

There is only one rule for being a good talker: learn to listen.
—*Christopher Morley.*

I have never been hurt by anything I didn't say.
—*Calvin Coolidge.*

Drawing on my fine command of language, I said nothing.
—*Robert Benchley.*

TASK

The happiest and most honorable and most useful task that can be set by any man is to earn enough for the support of his wife and family, for the bringing up and starting in life of his children.
—*Theodore Roosevelt.*

The most honorable and desirable task which can be set by any woman is to be a good and wise mother in a home marked by self-respect and mutual forbearance. —*Ibid.*

TASTE

Bad taste is a species of bad morals. —*C. N. Bovee.*

I would rather be able to appreciate things I cannot have than to have things I am not able to appreciate. —*Elbert Hubbard.*

A refined taste easily degenerates into effeminacy.
—*H. D. Thoreau.*

Fine taste is an aspect of genius itself, and is the faculty of delicate appreciation, which makes the best effects of art our own.
—*N. P. Willis.*

There are tastes so entirely vitiated, as to perceive beauty in deformity. —*Benjamin Rush.*

TAXATION

Taxation without representation is tyranny. —*James Otis.*

For every benefit you receive a tax is levied. —*R. W. Emerson.*

In this world nothing is certain but death and taxes.
—*B. Franklin.*

The power to tax involves the power to destroy.
—*John Marshall.*

The excess profits tax exempts capital, and burdens brains, ability and energy. —*W. G. McAdoo.*

Our workers may never see a tax bill, but they pay. They pay in deductions from wages, in increased costs of what they may buy, or in unemployment throughout the land. —*F. D. Roosevelt.*

A tax . . . as used in the Constitution, signifies an exaction for the support of the Government. The word has never been thought to connote the expropriation of money from one group for the benefit of another.   —*Owen J. Roberts.*

War involves in its progress such a train of unforeseen and unsupposed circumstances that no human wisdom can calculate the end. It has but one thing certain, and that is to increase taxes.
—*T. Paine.*

The tax upon land values (Single Tax) is the most just and equal of all taxes. It is the taking by the community, for the use of the community, of that value which is the creation of the community.
—*Henry George.*

Taxation reaches down to the base; but the base is labor, and labor pays all.   —*Donn Piatt.*

The thing generally raised on city land is taxes. —*C. D. Warner.*

The income tax has made more liars out of the American people than gold has.   —*Will Rogers.*

In levying taxes and in shearing sheep it is well to stop when you get down to the skin.   —*Austin O'Malley.*

What is the difference between a taxidermist and a tax collector? The taxidermist takes only your skin.   —*Mark Twain.*

TEACHING

Knowledge exists to be imparted.   —*R. W. Emerson.*

The teacher is one who makes two ideas grow where only one grew before.   —*Elbert Hubbard.*

The object of teaching a child is to enable him to get along without his teacher.   —*Ibid.*

The teacher who can give his pupils pleasure in their work shall be crowned with laurels.   —*Ibid.*

There are men who teach best by not teaching at all.
—*Abraham Flexner.*

It is the true office of a teacher to show us that God is, not was; that he *speaketh*, not spake.   —*R. W. Emerson.*

Plodding and prodding is not the teacher's work. It is inspiration, the flashing of enthusiasm.   —*D. S. Jordan.*

A teacher is one who, in his youth, admired teachers.
—*H. L. Mencken.*

Thoroughly to teach another is the best way to learn for yourself.
—*Tryon Edwards.*

None can teach admirably if not loving his task. —*A. B. Alcott.*

TEAM-WORK

We all of us tend to rise or fall together. —*Theodore Roosevelt.*

If any set of us goes down the whole nation sags a little. —*Ibid.*

If any of us raise ourselves a little, then by just so much the nation as a whole is raised. —*Ibid.*

TEARS

The most efficient water power in the world—woman's tears.
—*Wilson Mizner.*

Tears are not the mark of weakness but of power. They speak more eloquently than ten thousand tongues. —*Washington Irving.*

The young man who has not wept is a savage, and the old man who will not laugh is a fool. —*George Santayana.*

Tears are a good alternative but a poor diet. —*H. W. Shaw.*

Tears may soothe the wounds they cannot heal. —*T. Paine.*

Tears are the tribute of humanity to its destiny. —*W. R. Alger.*

> Never a tear bedims the eye
> That time and patience will not dry.
>
> —*Bret Harte.*

Tears are often the telescope by which men see far into heaven.
—*H. W. Beecher.*

TEMPER

Nothing does reason more right, than the coolness of those that offer it: For Truth often suffers more by the heat of its defenders, than from the arguments of its opposers. —*Wm. Penn.*

A tart temper never mellows with age; and a sharp tongue is the only edged tool that grows keener with constant use.
—*Washington Irving.*

The man who rises in the morning with his feelings all bristling like the quills of a hedge-hog, simply needs to be knocked down.
—*J. G. Holland.*

Most nervous, irritable states of temper are the mere physical results of a used-up condition. —*H. B. Stowe.*

Men lose their tempers in defending their taste.

-R. W. Emerson.

TEMPERANCE

Every moderate drinker could abandon the intoxicating cup if he would; every inebriate would if he could.   -J. B. Gough.

The smaller the drink, the clearer the head, and the cooler the blood.   -Wm. Penn.

Abstaining is favorable both to the head and the pocket.

-Horace Greeley.

If it is a small sacrifice to discontinue the use of wine, do it for the sake of others; if it is a great sacrifice, do it for your own sake.

-S. J. May.

Eat not to fullness; drink not to elevation.   -B. Franklin.

If temperance fails, then education must fail.   -Horace Mann.

TEMPTATION

Every normal man must be tempted, at times, to spit on his hands, hoist the black flag, and begin slitting throats.

-H. L. Mencken.

As the Sandwich-Islander believes that the strength and valor of the enemy he kills passes into himself, so we gain the strength of the temptations we resist.   -R. W. Emerson.

> The Woman tempted me—and tempts me still!
> Lord God, I pray You that she ever will!
>
> -E. V. Cooke.

He who cannot resist temptation is not a man.   **-Horace Mann.**

Where there is no temptation, there can be little claim to virtue.

-William H. Prescott.

Do not consume your energy resisting temptation, else you will go to hell sure.   -Elbert Hubbard.

Why resist temptation—there will always be more.

-Don Herold.

If there were no evil in ourselves there would be no temptation from without, for nothing evil could seem pleasant.

-F. M. Crawford.

Temptations without imply desires within.   -H. W. Beecher.

Few men have virtue to withstand the highest bidder.

-G. Washington.

No degree of temptation justifies any degree of sin.

—N. P. Willis.

God is better served in resisting a temptation to evil than in many formal prayers.   *—Wm. Penn.*

Hard workers are usually honest. Industry lifts them above temptation.   *—C. N. Bovee.*

TENDERNESS

Do not keep the alabaster boxes of your love and tenderness sealed up until your friends are dead. Fill their lives with sweetness.

—H. W. Beecher.

I was never fit to say a word to a sinner, except when I had a broken heart myself.   *—Edward Payson.*

TEST

The real test of American citizenship . . . is the citizen's enthusiasm and determination to share in the everyday work of making the government of the United States serve its original purpose.   *—Robert La Follette.*

TEXTBOOKS

Most of our textbooks fail on two big counts. They are not sufficiently human, and their application is not sufficiently practical. Their tendency seems to be to look upon the whole process of education as a job of dull and uninteresting work—with the apparent argument that the duller and more uninteresting it is made the more credit there is for doing it.   *—Thomas A. Edison.*

THEFT

A man who has never gone to school may steal from a freight car; but if he has a university education, he may steal the whole railroad.   *—Theodore Roosevelt.*

For de little stealin' dey gits you in jail soon or late. For de big stealin' dey makes you emperor and puts you in de Hall o' Fame when you croaks.   *—Eugene O'Neill.*

To learn your offspring to steal, make them beg hard for all that you give them.   *—Josh Billings.*

It would be a swell world if everybody was as pleasant as the fellow who's trying to skin you.   *—Kin Hubbard.*

It is a mean thief, or a successful author, that plunders the dead.

—Austin O'Malley.

The least profitable profession in the world is that of a thief. There never was one who made a success at it.   *—E. W. Howe.*

Theft comes back to the thief as love returns to the lover.
                                                        —O. L. Triggs.

An hundred thieves cannot strip one naked man, especially if his skin's off.   *—B. Franklin.*

THEOLOGY

My theology, briefly, is that the universe was dictated but not signed.   *—Christopher Morley.*

Theology is the effort to explain the unknowable in terms of the not worth knowing.   *—H. L. Mencken.*

Theology is an attempt to explain a subject by men who do not understand it. The intent is not to tell the truth but to satisfy the questioner.   *—Elbert Hubbard.*

Let us put theology out of religion. Theology has always sent the worst to heaven, the best to hell.   *—R. G. Ingersoll.*

Theology is but a science of mind applied to God.
                                                        —H. W. Beecher.

THEORY

It is a condition which confronts us—not a theory.
                                                        —Grover Cleveland.

There can be no theory of any account unless it corroborate the theory of the earth.   *—Walt Whitman.*

THINGS

The sensual man conforms thoughts to things.
                                                        —R. W. Emerson.

Soft, sweet things with a lot of fancy dressing—that's what a little boy loves to eat and a grown man prefers to marry.
                                                        —Helen Rowland.

THINKING

The most necessary task of civilization is to teach man how to think.   *—Thomas A. Edison.*

Life consists in what a man is thinking of all day.
                                                        —R. W. Emerson.

Not only the tranquility of life, but the coherence of society itself, may hinge upon our ability to modify, more or less radically, our method of thinking.   *—Brooks Adams.*

When people think, they will nearly always think right. It is the thoughtless that are going astray.   *—Carrie Nation.*

We think in global terms. We inhabit a star, and we know it.
—J. W. Riis.

Our thinking and planning in the future must be global.
—Wendell L. Willkie.

If thinking men would have the courage to think for themselves, and to speak what they think, it would be found they do not differ in religious opinions as much as is supposed.   *—T. Jefferson.*

Thinking without constructive action becomes a disease.
—Henry Ford.

Where all think alike, no one thinks very much.
—Walter Lippmann.

Folks that blurt out just what they think wouldn't be so bad if they thought.   *—Kin Hubbard.*

As you think you travel; and as you love you attract.
—James Allen.

Some men think that being married to a woman means merely seeing her in the mornings instead of the evenings.
—Helen Rowland.

A "new thinker," when studied closely, is merely a man who does not know what other people have thought.   *—F. M. Colby.*

If you make people think they're thinking, they'll love you; but if you really make them think, they'll hate you.   *—Don Marquis.*

An Englishman thinks seated; a Frenchman, standing; an American, pacing; an Irishman, afterward.   *—Austin O'Malley.*

The person that always says just what he thinks at last gets just what he deserves.   *—Ibid.*

Men should not think too much of themselves, and yet a man should always be careful not to forget himself.   *—G. D. Prentice.*

Good thinking helps to make bearable irresponsible and vicious thinking.   *—Max Ascoli.*

Thinking is the hardest work there is, which is the probable reason why so few engage in it.   *—Henry Ford.*

THOUGHT

Thought is the measure of life.   *—C. G. Leland.*

To see what is general in what is particular and what is permanent in what is transitory is the aim of scientific thought.

—*A. N. Whitehead.*

The narrower the mind, the broader the statement.

—*Ted Cooke.*

The calmer thought is not always the right thought, just as the
distant view is not always the truest view. —*Nathaniel Hawthorne.*

Associate reverently, and as much as you can, with your loftiest
thoughts.   —*H. D. Thoreau.*

Nature, Scripture, society, and life, present perpetual subjects
for thought; and the man who collects, concentrates, employs his
faculties on any of these subjects for the purpose of getting the
truth, is so far a student, a thinker, a philosopher, and is rising to
the dignity of a man.   —*W. E. Channing.*

The happiest person is the person who thinks the most interesting thoughts.   —*W. L. Phelps.*

The tragedy of human thought is that the very process of thought
is self-betraying.   —*Charles Feideson, Jr.*

Thought itself is probably a superstition.   —*Don Herold.*

It takes a great deal of elevation of thought to produce a very
little elevation of life.   —*R. W. Emerson.*

It is only liquid currents of thought that move men and the
world.   —*Wendell Phillips.*

Thoughts are mightier than armies.   —*Wm. Paxton.*

Thought is the property of those only who can entertain it.

—*R. W. Emerson.*

The mind grows by what it feeds on.   —*J. G. Holland.*

Until there be correct thought, there cannot be right action and
when there is correct thought, right action will follow.

—*Henry George.*

Though the world exist from thought, thought is daunted in
presence of the world.   —*R. W. Emerson.*

Human thought is the process by which human ends are alter-
nately answered.   —*Daniel Webster.*

Thought takes man out of servitude, into freedom.

—*H. W. Longfellow.*

You are today where your thoughts have brought you; you will
be tomorrow where your thoughts take you.   —*James Allen.*

Our thoughts are the epochs of our lives; all else is but a journal of the winds that blew while we were here.   —*H. D. Thoreau.*

I cannot easily buy a blank book to write thoughts in; they are commonly ruled for dollars and cents.   —*Ibid.*

You must learn to put yourself in another's place, think his thoughts.   —*Gelett Burgess.*

The soul of God is poured into the world through the thoughts of men.   —*R. W. Emerson.*

As cloud on cloud, as snow on snow, as the bird rests on the air, and the planet rests on space in its flight,—so the nations of men and their institutions rest on thoughts.   —*Ibid.*

The person who really thinks learns quite as much from his failures as from his successes.   —*John Dewey.*

A man must link his written thoughts with the everlasting wants of men.   —*H. W. Beecher.*

The busiest of living agents are certain dead men's thoughts.
    —*C. N. Bovee.*

Thought means life. Thinking makes the man.   —*A. B. Alcott.*

The greatest events of an age are its best thoughts. It is of the nature of thought to find its way into action.   —*C. N. Bovee.*

A thought often makes us hotter than a fire. —*H. W. Longfellow.*

Spiritual force is stronger than material force; thoughts rule the world.   —*R. W. Emerson.*

THOUGHT-CONTROL

I have sworn upon the altar of God eternal hostility against every form of tyranny over the mind of man.   —*T. Jefferson.*

It were not best that we should all think alike; it is difference of opinion that makes horse-races.   —*Mark Twain.*

Where men cannot freely convey their thoughts to one another, no other liberty is secure.   —*W. E. Hocking.*

THOUGHT—FREE

If there is any principle of the Constitution that more imperatively calls for attachment than any other it is the principle of free thought—not free thought for those who agree with us but freedom for the thought that we hate.   —*O. W. Holmes, Jr.*

THREAD

There is no thread in life so narrow as the one which divides men—which separates those who win from those who lose.

—Gabriel Heatter.

THRIFT

There'll be no pockets in your shroud.   *—James J. Hill.*

TIME

Dost thou love life? Then do not squander time, for that is the stuff life is made of.   *—B. Franklin.*

In the end, time endorses God's evaluations.   *—H. E. Fosdick.*

If one thinks over the sort of life led in innumerable homes a generation ago, our immense speeding up in the process of living today is clear. People then, as we say, "had time." Now, no one "has time."   *—James Truslow Adams.*

Time is money and many people pay their debts with it.

—Josh Billings.

> Backward, turn backward, O Time in your flight;
> Make me a child again just for tonight.

—E. A. Allen.

Time is a great legalizer, even in the field of morals.

—H. L. Mencken.

> Time cuts down all,
> Both great and small.

—New England Primer.

Life and time are our only real possessions.   *—Ray L. Wilbur.*

The proper function of man is to live, not to exist. I shall not waste my days in trying to prolong them. I shall use my time.

—Jack London.

A woman on time is one in nine.   *—Addison Mizner.*

The trouble with life is that there are so many beautiful women —and so little time.   *—John Barrymore.*

God is the only being who has time enough; but a prudent man, who knows how to seize occasion, can commonly make a shift to find as much as he needs.   *—J. R. Lowell.*

I know I have the best of time and space, and was never measured and never will be measured.   *—Walt Whitman.*

The times are the masquerade of the eternities.

—*R. W. Emerson.*

We ask for long life, but 'tis deep life, or noble moments that signify. Let the measure of time be spiritual, not mechanical.

—*Ibid.*

As if you could kill time without injuring eternity!

—*H. D. Thoreau.*

Counting time is not so important as making time count.

—*James J. Walker.*

If you're there before it's over, you're on time.   —*Ibid.*

Faith loves to lean on time's destroying arm.   —*O. W. Holmes.*

It takes a lot of time to be sentimental.   —*Don Herold.*

Time is what we want most, but what alas! we use worst.

—*Wm. Penn.*

Time is an herb that cures all diseases.   —*B. Franklin.*

Time is like money; the less we have of it to spare the further we make it go.   —*H. W. Shaw.*

Time and tide wait for no man, but time always stands still for a woman of thirty.   —*Robert Frost.*

Since thou art not sure of a minute, throw not away an hour.

—*B. Franklin.*

Time was invented by Almighty God in order to give ideas a chance.   —*N. M. Butler.*

Lost, yesterday, somewhere between sunrise and sunset, two golden hours, each set with sixty diamond minutes. No reward is offered for they are gone forever.   —*Horace Mann.*

TIMES

The illusion that times that were are better than those that are, has probably pervaded all ages.   —*Horace Greeley.*

In times of grave crises, there are always some who fall a prey to doubt and unreasoning fear; some who seek refuge in cynicism and narrow self-interest; some who wrap themselves in the treacherous cloak of complacency.   —*Cordell Hull.*

If there is one thing which is taught us by our history, it is that in normal times of peace we never have thought of preparing for war.   —*Norman Thomas.*

We rise above our normal powers only in times of destruction.
                                                    —*Ernie Pyle*.

TITLES

Whilst another man has no land, my title to mine, your title to yours, is at once vitiated.   —*R. W. Emerson*.

Titles are valuable. They make us acquainted with many persons who otherwise would be lost among the rubbish.   —*H. W. Shaw*.

TOASTMASTER

Toast: Never above you. Never below you. Always beside you.
                                                    —*Walter Winchell*.

TOBACCO

Some things are much better eschewed than chewed; tobacco is one of them.   —*G. D. Prentice*.

What this country needs is a good five-cent cigar.
                                                    —*Thomas R. Marshall*.

TODAY

One today is worth two tomorrows.   —*B. Franklin*.

TOIL

The best things are all too cheaply purchased by a lifetime's toil.
                                                    —*A. B. Alcott*.

TOILERS

A genuine society of Nations may finally be evolved by millions of earth's humblest toilers, whose lives are consumed in securing the daily needs of existence for themselves and their families.
                                                    —*Jane Addams*.

TOLERATION

Tolerance is the positive and cordial effort to understand another's beliefs, practises and habits, without necessarily sharing or accepting them.   —*Joshua Loth Liebman*.

We are in favor of tolerance, but it is a very difficult thing to tolerate the intolerant and impossible to tolerate the intolerable.
                                                    —*G. D. Prentice*.

Unfortunately I have an open mind. I let down a window in my brain about six or seven inches from the top even in the bitterest weather.   —*Heywood Broun*.

This duty of toleration has been summed up in the words, "Let both grow together until the harvest."   —*A. N. Whitehead*.

It is the refusing toleration to those of a different opinion which has produced all the bustles and wars on account of religion.

—T. Jefferson.

To claim that the disappearance of witchcraft and slavery, and the introduction of religious toleration were the effects of Christian teachings does not stand inspection. *—James Harvey Robinson.*

The permission of other consciences and worships than a state professeth, only can (according to God) procure a firm and lasting peace. *—Roger Williams.*

Let us all resolve . . . to deem all fault-finding that does no good a sin. *—H. B. Stowe.*

What disturbs more and distracts mankind than the uncivil manners that cleave man from man? *—A. B. Alcott.*

How is it possible to imagine that a religion breathing the spirit of mercy . . . can be so perverted as to breathe the spirit of slaughter and persecution? *—Joseph Story.*

We anticipate the time when the love of truth shall have come up to our love of liberty, and men shall be cordially tolerant and earnest believers both at once. *—Phillips Brooks.*

He that is willing to tolerate any religion . . . Either doubts his own, or is not sincere in it. *—Nathaniel Ward.*

He that is willing to tolerate any unsound opinion, that his own may also be tolerated, though never so sound, will for need hang God's Bible at the Devil's girdle. *—Ibid.*

Corporal punishments . . . should not be tolerated in a free government. *—Benjamin Rush.*

Toleration in religion is absolutely the best fruit of all the struggles, labors and sorrows of the civilized nations during the last four centuries. *—Charles W. Eliot.*

TOMBSTONE

The tombstone is about the only thing that can stand upright and lie on its face at the same time. *—M. W. Little.*

TOMORROW

Never leave that till tomorrow which you can do today.

—B. Franklin.

Tomorrow will keep her unchanging appointment.

—Mary Siegrist.

TONGUE

A sharp tongue is the only edged tool that grows keener with constant use.   —*Washington Irving.*

There are many men whose tongues could govern multitudes if they could govern their tongues.   —*G. D. Prentice.*

TOWNS

The country is lyric,—the town dramatic. When mingled they make the most perfect musical drama.   —*H. W. Longfellow.*

Beside American towns, Paris must seem an unkempt village, Warsaw a dump-heap.   —*Waldo Frank.*

TRADE

No nation was ever ruined by trade.   —*B. Franklin.*

The greatest meliorator of the world is selfish, huckstering trade.
                                                      —*R. W. Emerson.*

Trade and commerce, if they were not made of India rubber, would never manage to bounce over the obstacles which the legislators are continually putting in their way.   —*H. D. Thoreau.*

World prosperity requires world trade.   —*Ben W. Lewis.*

TRADE-UNION

Every trade-union . . . vindicates the dignity of labor by reducing it to the lowest possible minimum, while increasing its wages to the maximum.   —*H. M. Kallen.*

TRADITION

Mankind is now in one of its rare moods of shifting its outlook. The mere compulsion of tradition has lost its force.
                                                      —*A. N. Whitehead.*

We should not forget that our tradition is one of protest and revolt, and it is stultifying to celebrate the rebels of the past . . . while we silence the rebels of the present.   —*H. S. Commager.*

The belief in the existence of opportunities to achieve economic equality has had a longer and more vital tradition in American history than has been the case anywhere else.   —*L. M. Hacker.*

The Transcendentalists at least escaped the life-hating Christian tradition sufficiently to attempt to achieve a new environment, misguided and essentially childish as those attempts now seem.
                                                      —*C. Hartley Grattan.*

Either traditionalism or revolt, when it reaches a high point, tends to discredit itself by its own excesses.   *—Henry Hazlitt.*

It takes an endless amount of history to make even a little tradition.   *—Henry James.*

Tradition is more than a school of crafts. It is a school of moods and manners.   *—Stuart P. Sherman.*

TRAINING

Training is everything: the peach was once a bitter almond; cauliflower is nothing but cabbage with a college education.

—Mark Twain.

TRANQUILITY

Be not disturbed at trifles, or at accidents common or unavoidable.   *—B. Franklin.*

Tranquil pleasures last the longest.   *—C. N. Bovee.*

There is majestic grandeur in tranquility.   *—Washington Irving.*

TRANSITION

The pangs of pain, of failure, in this mortal lot, are the birth-throes of transition to better things.   *—J. E. Boodin.*

TRAVEL

The man who goes alone can start today; but he who travels with another must wait till that other is ready.   *—H. D. Thoreau.*

The traveled mind is the catholic mind educated from exclusiveness and egotism.   *—A. B. Alcott.*

Travelers find virtue in a seeming minority in all other countries, and forget that they have left it in a minority at home.

—T. W. Higginson.

Only that traveling is good which reveals to me the value of home, and enables me to enjoy it better.   *—H. D. Thoreau.*

In America there are two classes of travel—first class, and with children.   *—Robert Benchley.*

There is a certain relief in change, even though it ebb from bad to worse; as I have found in traveling in a stagecoach, that it is often a comfort to shift one's position and be bounced in a new place.   *—Washington Irving.*

The time to enjoy a European trip is about three weeks after unpacking.   *—George Ade.*

Paper napkins never return from a laundry, nor love from a trip to the law courts.   —*John Barrymore.*

Travel is one way of lengthening life, at least in appearance.
—*B. Franklin.*

TREASON

An attack upon systematic thought is treason to civilization.
—*A. N. Whitehead.*

If this be treason, make the most of it.   —*Patrick Henry.*

We are a rebellious nation. Our whole history is treason; our blood was attainted before we were born; our creeds are infidelity to the mother church; our constitution treason to our fatherland.
—*Theodore Parker.*

Though all the governors in the world bid us commit treason against man, and set the example, let us never submit.   —*Ibid.*

A traitor is a good fruit to hang from the boughs of the tree of liberty.   —*H. W. Beecher.*

Caesar had his Brutus; Charles the First, his Cromwell; and George the Third—may profit by their example. If this be treason, make the most of it.   —*Patrick Henry.*

TREES

I like trees because they seem more resigned to the way they have to live than other things do.   —*Willa Cather.*

Many a family tree needs trimming.   —*Kin Hubbard.*

Tall oaks from little acorns grow.   —*David Everett.*

> Poems are made by fools like me,
> But only God can make a tree.
>
> —*Joyce Kilmer.*

When we plant a tree, we are doing what we can to make our planet a more wholesome and more happier dwelling-place for those who come after us, if not for ourselves.   —*O. W. Holmes.*

TRIALS

We are always in the forge, or on the anvil; by trials God is shaping us for higher things.   —*H. W. Beecher.*

TRIFLES

A small leak will sink a great ship.   —*B. Franklin.*

It is the little bits of things that fret and worry us; we can dodge an elephant, but we can't a fly. —*Josh Billings.*

The creation of a thousand forests is in one acorn.
—*R. W. Emerson.*

TROUBLE

There is trouble and sorrow enough in the world, without making it on purpose. —*W. D. Howells.*

There is always a comforting thought in time of trouble when it is not our trouble. —*Don Marquis.*

The price of progress is trouble. —*C. F. Kettering.*

I love the man that can smile in trouble, that can gather strength from distress, and grow brave by reflection. —*T. Paine.*

Do not anticipate trouble or worry about what may never happen. Keep in the sunlight. —*B. Franklin.*

If a man could have half his wishes, he would double his troubles. —*Ibid.*

Never bear more than one kind of trouble at a time. Some people bear three—all they have had, all they have now, and all they expect to have. —*E. E. Hale.*

Lots of people have matrimonial troubles and don't know it.
—*Oliver Herford.*

There are people who always anticipate trouble, and in that way they manage to enjoy many sorrows that never really happen to them. —*H. W. Shaw.*

Women like to sit down with trouble as if it were knitting.
—*Ellen Glasgow.*

I have had many troubles in my life, but the worst of them never came. —*James A. Garfield.*

Trouble is the next best thing to enjoyment; there is no fate in the world so horrible as to have no share in either its joys or sorrows. —*H. W. Longfellow.*

I am an old man and have known a great many troubles, but most of them never happened. —*Mark Twain.*

TRUE

Those who honestly mean to be true contradict themselves more rarely than those who try to be consistent. —*O. W. Holmes.*

Press through:
Nothing can harm if you are true.

—Edwin Markham.

He that feeds men serveth few;
He serves all that dares be true.

—R. W. Emerson.

TRUST

You may be deceived if you trust too much, but you will live in torment if you do not trust enough.   *—Frank Crane.*

Trust men and they will be true to you; treat them greatly and they will show themselves great.   *—R. W. Emerson.*

All that I have seen teaches me to trust the creator for what I have not seen.   *—Ibid.*

Trust everybody, but cut the cards.   *—F. P. Dunne.*

Sometimes it is said that man cannot be trusted with the government of himself. Can he, then, be trusted with the government of others?   *—T. Jefferson.*

Whenever the people are well-informed, they can be trusted with their own government.   *—Ibid.*

The powers of government are but a trust, and they cannot be lawfully exercised but for the good of the community.

—Daniel Webster.

Government is a trust, and the officers of the government are trustees; and both the trust and the trustees are created for the benefit of the people.   *—Henry Clay.*

When a man assumes a public trust, he should consider himself as public property.   *—T. Jefferson.*

Public office is a public trust.   *—Dan S. Lamont.*

The only way to make a man trust-worthy is to trust him; and the surest way to make him untrustworthy is to distrust him and show your distrust.   *—Norman Thomas.*

Let us trust God and our better judgment to set us right hereafter.   *—Patrick Henry.*

The only noble use of surplus wealth is this: That it be regarded as a sacred trust, to be administered by its possessor, into whose hands it flows, for the highest good of the people.

—Andrew Carnegie.

Trust thyself: every heart vibrates to that iron string.
—R. W. Emerson.

TRUSTS

Trusts are natural, inevitable growths out of our social and economic conditions. *—James B. Dill.*

The great corporations known as trusts are in certain of their features and tendencies hurtful to the general welfare.
—Theodore Roosevelt.

This is an age of combination, and any effort to prevent all combination will be not only useless, but in the end vicious, because of the contempt for law which the failure to enforce law inevitably produces. *—Ibid.*

Industrial combination is not wrong in itself. The danger lies in taking government into partnership. *—F. D. Roosevelt.*

TRUTH

Rather than love, than money, than fame, give me truth.
—H. D. Thoreau.

Truth crushed to earth shall rise again. *—Wm. Cullen Bryant.*

Truth is immortal; error is mortal. *—Mary Baker Eddy.*

Truth forever on the scaffold. Wrong forever on the throne.
—J. R. Lowell.

Every gaudy color is a bit of truth. *—Nathalia Crane.*

There are some truths like certain liquors, which require strong heads to bear them. *—Benjamin Rush.*

Fly for truth, and hell shall have no storm to crush your flight.
—E. A. Robinson.

Men in earnest have no time to waste in patching fig leaves for the naked truth. *—J. R. Lowell.*

The man who thinks to make much of the fuller truth to which he has come by upbraiding the partial truth through which he came to it, is a poor creature. *—Phillips Brooks.*

The greatest homage we can pay to truth, is to use it.
—R. W. Emerson.

Every violation of truth is a stab at the health of human society.
—Ibid.

Then to side with truth is noble when we share her wretched

crust, ere her cause bring fame and profit, and 'tis prosperous to be just. —*J. R. Lowell.*

Naked truth needs no shift. —*Wm. Penn.*

It takes two to speak the truth—one to speak and another to hear. —*H. D. Thoreau.*

Truth is stranger than fiction, but it is because Fiction is obliged to stick to possibilities; Truth isn't. —*Mark Twain.*

There is no fit search after truth which does not, after all, begin to live the truth which it knows. —*Horace Bushnell.*

There is nothing so powerful as truth; and often nothing as strange. —*Daniel Webster.*

Truth is the edict of God. —*H. W. Shaw.*

Truth is inclusive of all the virtues. —*A. B. Alcott.*

Let the truth fill your life. —*Phillips Brooks.*

The people have a right to the truth as they have a right to life, liberty and the pursuit of happiness. —*Frank Norris.*

The conception of truth as definite and therefore definable is misleading. —*Gelett Burgess.*

Truth is an abstraction, a hypothesis, as impossible to conceive as is the mathematical hypothesis of infinity. —*Ibid.*

Make use of truth as a tent in which to pass a summer night, but build no house of it, or it will be your tomb. —*Ernest Crosby.*

Truth gets well if she is run over by a locomotive, while error dies of lockjaw if she scratches her finger. —*Wm. Cullen Bryant.*

As scarce as truth is, the supply has always been in excess of the demand. —*Josh Billings.*

Defeat is a school in which truth always grows strong. —*H. W. Beecher.*

Truth is the property of no individual but is the treasure of all men. —*R. W. Emerson.*

Truth is such a precious article let us all economize in its use. —*Mark Twain.*

The passion for truth has underlying it a profound conviction that what is real is best; that when we get to the heart of things we shall find there what we most need. —*G. S. Merriam.*

Let me have truth at my tongue's root. —*Jay Davidman.*

Truth is ever incoherent, and when the big hearts strike together, the concussion is a little stunning.　　　　*—Herman Melville.*

The truth always matches, piece by piece, with other parts of the truth.　　　　*—Woodrow Wilson.*

Truth and sincerity have a certain distinguishing native lustre about them which cannot be perfectly counterfeited; they are like fire and flame, that cannot be painted.　　　　*—B. Franklin.*

Truth is stranger than fiction—to some people.　　*—Mark Twain.*

You can always get the truth from an American statesman after he has turned seventy, or given up all hope of the Presidency.
　　　　—Wendell Phillips.

Truth is not a diet but a condiment.　　　*—Christopher Morley.*

There are those who hold the opinion that truth is only safe when diluted—about one-fifth to four-fifths lies—as the oxygen of the air is with its nitrogen. Else it would burn us all up.
　　　　—O. W. Holmes.

Truth is tough. It will not break like a bubble at a touch; nay, you will kick it about all day, like a football, and it will be round and full at evening.　　　　*—Ibid.*

It is hard to believe that a man is telling the truth when you know that you would lie if you were in his place. *—H. L. Mencken.*

Scientific truth is marvellous, but moral truth is divine; and whoever breathes its air and walks by its light has found the lost paradise.　　　　*—Horace Mann.*

The firmest and noblest ground on which people can live is truth.　　　　*—R. W. Emerson.*

Truth should be the last lesson of the child, and the last aspiration of manhood.　　　　*—J. G. Whittier.*

Truth is a jewel which should not be painted over; but it may be set to advantage and shown in a good light. *—George Santayana.*

When in doubt, tell the truth.　　　　*—Mark Twain.*

The truth has always been dangerous to the rule of the rogue, the exploiter, the robber. So the truth must be suppressed.
　　　　—E. V. Debs.

I tell the honest truth in my paper, and I leave the consequence to God.　　　　*—James Gordon Bennett, Sr.*

There is not a truth existing which I fear, or would wish unknown to the whole world.　　　　*—T. Jefferson.*

Such is the irresistible nature of truth that all it asks, and all it wants, is the liberty of appearing. The sun needs no inscription to distinguish him from darkness.   —*T. Paine.*

TWO SIDES
He admits that there are two sides to every question—his own and the wrong side.   —*Channing Pollock.*

TYRANNY
Tyranny, like hell, is not easily conquered; yet we have this consolation with us, that the harder the conflict, the more glorious the triumph.   —*T. Paine.*

The accumulation of all powers, legislative, executive, and judiciary, in the same hands whether of one, a few, or many, and whether hereditary, self-appointed, or elective, may justly be pronounced the very definition of tyranny.   —*James Madison.*

Resistance to tyrants is obedience to God.   —*T. Jefferson.*

Arbitrary power is most easily established on the ruins of liberty abused to licentiousness.   —*G. Washington.*

As political equality is the remedy for political tyranny, so is economic equality the only way of putting an end to the economic tyranny exercised by the few over the many through the superiority of wealth.   —*Edward Bellamy.*

Tyranny is always weakness.   —*J. R. Lowell.*

TYRANTS
Every tyrant who has lived has believed in freedom—for himself.
                                                    —*Elbert Hubbard.*

With reasonable men, I will reason; with humane men, I will plead; but to tyrants I will give no quarter, nor waste arguments where they will certainly be lost.   —*W. L. Garrison.*

Whoever is right, the persecutor must be wrong.   —*Wm. Penn.*

When the will of man is raised above law it is always tyranny and despotism, whether it is the will of a bashaw or of bastard patriots.   —*Noah Webster.*

Any government is in itself an evil insofar as it carries within it the tendency to deteriorate into tyranny.   —*Albert Einstein.*

U

UGLINESS

Heaven sometimes hedges a rare character about with ungainliness and odium, as the burr that protects the fruit.

—*R. W. Emerson.*

There is a sort of charm in ugliness, if the person has some redeeming qualities and is only ugly enough.   —*H. W. Shaw.*

Ugliness without tact is horrible.   —*Nathaniel Hawthorne.*

Ugliness is a point of view: an ulcer is wonderful to a pathologist.

—*Austin O'Malley.*

Better an ugly face than an ugly mind.   —*James Ellis.*

ULTIMATE

The ultimate problem of production is the production of human beings.   —*John Dewey.*

Faith in freedom as a means and as an end must be the ultimate touchstone of American loyalty, of the loyalty of all free men.

—*Alan Barth.*

UMBRELLA

As history records the criminal blunder at Munich, it will record also the journeyings of a man with an umbrella.

—*A. Meiklejohn.*

The American people never carry an umbrella. They prepare to walk in eternal sunshine.   —*Alfred E. Smith.*

A widespreading, hopeful disposition is the best umbrella for this vale of tears.   —*W. D. Howells.*

UNBELIEF

Christian ethics are seldom found save in the philosophy of some unbeliever.   —*Heywood Broun.*

Doubt that creed which you cannot reduce to practice.
—Hosea Ballou.

Faith always implies the disbelief of a lesser fact in favor of a greater.   *—O. W. Holmes.*

In the hands of unbelief half-truths are made to do the work of whole falsehoods.   *—E. F. Burr.*

Unbelief is a confession of ignorance where honest inquiry might easily find the truth. 'Agnostic,' is but the Greek for 'ignoramus.'   *—Tryon Edwards.*

UNBOUND

Why bind oneself to a central or any other doctrine? How much nobler stands a man entirely unpledged, unbound.
—Margaret Fuller.

UNCERTAINTY

Freedom does not live on uncertainties: it clears up uncertainties. And we do not prove our freedom when we fall but when we make a choice.   *—Max Ascoli.*

Most men make the voyage of life as if they carried sealed orders which they were not to open till they were fairly in mid-ocean.
—J. R. Lowell.

What Shakespeare said of doubts is equally true of vacillation and uncertainty of purpose, that they make us lose the good we oft might win by fearing to attempt.   *—Charles Simmons.*

UNCOMPROMISING

I will be as harsh as truth, and as uncompromising as justice.
—W. L. Garrison.

UNCONSCIOUS

Nature's loveliness is an unconscious memory of the lost Paradise.
—H. Van Dyke.

UNDECORATED

Man today has become the undecorated animal, while woman flaunts the gay plumage.   *—Richard Burton.*

UNDERDOG

The underdog can and will lick his weight in the wildcats of the world.   *—Heywood Broun.*

The remedy for the evils of competition is found in the moderation and magnanimity of the strong and the successful, and not in any sickly sentimentalizing over the lot of the underdog.

—Irving Babbitt.

Those swarming spawning millions, the bottom layer of society, the proletariat . . . are by nature the peers of the boasted aristocracy of brains that now dominates society and looks down upon them.

—Lester Ward.

UNDERPRIVILEGED

The war on privilege will never end. Its next great campaign will be against the special privileges of the underprivileged.

—H. L. Mencken.

UNDERRATE

It is impossible to underrate human intelligence—beginning with one's own. *—Henry Adams.*

UNDERSTAND

For a man to pretend to understand women is bad manners; for him really to understand them is bad morals. *—Henry James.*

Most people are bothered by those passages of Scripture they do not understand, but . . . the passages that bother me are those I do understand. *—Mark Twain.*

Many a writer seems to think he is never profound except when he can't understand his own meaning. *—G. D. Prentice.*

He who does not understand your silence will probably not understand your words. *—Elbert Hubbard.*

Only themselves understood themselves, and the likes of themselves, as Souls only understand Souls. *—Walt Whitman.*

What is the spirit of moderation? It is the temper which does not press a partisan advantage to its bitter end, which can understand and will respect the other side. *—Learned Hand.*

It is difficult to get a man to understand something when his salary depends upon his not understanding it. *—Upton Sinclair.*

No man can understand why a woman should prefer a good reputation to a good time. *—Helen Rowland.*

UNDERSTANDING

There exists a passion for comprehension, just as there exists a passion for music.—Without this passion there would be neither mathematics nor rational science. *—Albert Einstein.*

We want an atmosphere of understanding.   —*John R. Mott.*

A world community can exist only with world communication, which means something more than extensive shortwave facilities scattered about the globe. It means common understanding, a common tradition, common ideas, and common ideals.
                                         —*Robert M. Hutchins.*

The things that a man does not say often reveal the understanding and penetration of his mind even more than the things he says.
                                         —*R. A. Millikan.*

Next to being a great poet is the power of understanding one.
                                         —*H. W. Longfellow.*

Utopian capitalism is a key to the understanding of America.
                                         —*Leon Samson.*

UNDERTAKER

Let us endeavor so to live that when we come to die even the undertaker will be sorry.   —*Mark Twain.*

UNDERTAKING

Democracy in any sphere is a serious undertaking. It substitutes self-restraint for external restraint.   —*Louis D. Brandeis.*

UNEMPLOYED

Mind unemployed is mind unenjoyed.   —*C. N. Bovee.*

UNEMPLOYMENT

The heavy, grinding, routine deadening jobs are the ones that machinery destroys.   —*R. A. Millikan.*

Taking the long-range view . . . there is no such thing as technological unemployment.   —*Ibid.*

Statistical evidence proves that wide-scale technological unemployment is imaginary.   —*Carl Snyder.*

UNFORTUNATE

The unfortunate do not pity the unfortunate.   —*H. W. Shaw.*

UNHAPPINESS

Unhappiness is not knowing what we want and killing ourselves to get it.   —*Don Herold.*

We degrade life by our follies and vices, and then complain that the unhappiness which is only their accompaniment is inherent in the constitution of things.   —*C. N. Bovee.*

Perfect happiness was never intended by the Deity to be the lot ·of one of his creatures in this world; but that he has very much put in our power the nearness of our approaches to it is what I have ·steadfastly believed. —*T. Jefferson.*

UNHISTORICITY

Viewed in relation to world history, America presents itself as a ·movement away from history, a vast historic unhistoricity.

—*Leon Samson.*

UNIFIED

Unless the people, through unified action, arise and take charge of their Government, they will find that their Government has taken charge of them. —*Alfred E. Smith.*

No completely unified, centrally planned productive system is tolerable for a free people. —*D. C. Coyle.*

UNIFORMITY

An enforced uniformity of religion throughout a nation or civil ·state confounds the civil and religious, denies the principles of ·Christianity and civility, and that Jesus Christ is come in the flesh.

—*Roger Williams.*

God requireth not a uniformity of religion to be enacted and enforced in any civil state; which enforced uniformity (sooner or ·later) is the great occasion of civil war. —*Ibid.*

UNINTERESTING

Waiting to be whipped is the most uninteresting period in boy-hood life. —*Josh Billings.*

UNION

My idea is that we should be made one nation in every case concerning foreign affairs, and separate ones in whatever is merely domestic. —*T. Jefferson.*

The local interests of a state ought in every case to give way to the interests of the Union; for when a sacrifice of one or the other is necessary, the former becomes only an apparent, partial interest, and should yield, on the principle that the small good ought never to oppose the great one. —*Alexander Hamilton.*

We must all hang together, or assuredly we shall all hang separately. —*B. Franklin.*

Union is the great fundamental principle by which every object of importance is to be accomplished.   —*Daniel Webster.*

UNION (LABOR)

The union of workingmen is not only a shield of defense against hostile combinations, but also a weapon of attack that will be successfully wielded against the oppressive measures of a corrupt and despotic aristocracy.   —*Ely Moore.*

The strongest bond of human sympathy, outside of the family relation, should be one uniting all working people, of all nations, of all tongues, and kindreds. Nor should this lead to war upon property, or the owners of property.   —*A. Lincoln.*

The pleas of trade unions for immunity, be it from injunction or from liability for damages, is as fallacious as the plea of the lynchers . . . We gain nothing by trading the tyranny of capital for the tyranny of labor.   —*Louis D. Brandeis.*

The trade union movement represents the organized economic power of the workers . . . It is in reality the most potent and the most direct social insurance the workers can establish.
                                                        —*Samuel Gompers.*

The union is a monopoly because it can and does raise the price of labor to levels which will in a competitive price system inevitably cause waste, unemployment, inflation, or all combined.
                                                        —*C. E. Lindblom.*

Rally around the standard of union—the union of states and the union of miners.   —*Ibid.*

Employers are forbidden to make contracts which would obligate them to hire or keep none but union members.
                                                        —*Felix Frankfurter.*

We have got to work to build, first a practical unity among American labor unions, and some day to have organic unity, one powerful union in America representing all the workers, and when we do that we will be in a position to do something that has to be done.   —*W. P. Reuther.*

The well-established union is, and has to be, as much concerned as the associated employers of an industry with the development of conditions which foster that industry's prosperity.
                                                        —*Ordway Tead.*

It is the mission of the trade unions to reform capitalism.
                                    —*Thomas Burns.*

Nothing must stop the work of organizing the unorganized in America—not even a great national emergency.   —*Philip Murray.*

As long as there are big corporations, there will be big unions. The economic power of big business will continue to be matched by the economic power of big unions.   —*M. C. Smith.*

UNION (NATIONAL)

We join ourselves to no party that does not carry the flag and keep step to the music of the Union.   —*Rufus Choate.*

If we do not make common cause to save the good old ship of the Union on this voyage, nobody will have a chance to pilot her on another voyage.   —*A. Lincoln.*

Liberty and Union, now and forever, one and inseparable!
                                    —*Daniel Webster.*

We have sown a seed of liberty and Union that will gradually germinate throughout the earth.   —*G. Washington.*

Now is the seed-time of continental union, faith, and honor.
                                    —*T. Paine.*

The government of the Union then, is emphatically and truly a government of the people.   —*John Marshall.*

Even if it were my own State should raise the standard of dissension against the residue of the Union, I would go against her.
                                    —*Henry Clay.*

The union of hearts, the union of hands, and the flag of our Union forever.   —*G. P. Morris.*

Perish the Union when its cement must be the blood of the slave.
                                    —*Wendell Phillips.*

You cannot have Union without meaning justice.   —*Ibid.*

No Union with slaveholders!   —*W. L. Garrison.*

That Union we reached only by the discipline of our virtues in the severe school of adversity.   —*Daniel Webster.*

The union of the States is indissoluble; the country is undivided and indivisible forever.   —*David Dudley Field.*

The union of the states (must) be cherished and perpetuated. Let the open enemy to it be regarded as a Pandora with her box

opened, and the disguised one as the serpent creeping with his
deadly wiles into paradise.   *—James Madison.*

We are not a nation but a union, a confederacy of equal and
sovereign states.   *—John C. Calhoun.*

Our Federal Union . . . must and shall be preserved.
                                          —Andrew Jackson.

UNITE

America was created to unite mankind by those passions which
lift, and not by the passions which separate and debase.
                                          —Woodrow Wilson.

We came to America, either ourselves or in the persons of our
ancestors, to better the ideals of men, to make them see finer
things than they had seen before, to get rid of the things that
divide and to make sure of the things that unite.   *—Ibid.*

Probably no deeper division of our people could proceed from
any provocation than from finding it necessary to choose what
doctrine and whose program public educational officials shall compel youth to unite in embracing.   *—Felix Frankfurter.*

It is for us to work with all our might to unite the spiritual
power of good against the material power of evil.
                                          —Helen Keller.

UNITED NATIONS

The United Nations is our one great hope for a peaceful and
free world.   *—Ralph J. Bunche.*

The United Nations is designed to make possible lasting freedom
and independence for all its members.   *—H. S. Truman.*

We have actively sought and are actively seeking to make the
United Nations an effective instrument of international cooperation.
                                          —Dean Acheson.

UNITED STATES

The United States themselves are essentially the greatest poem.
                                          —Walt Whitman.

Some day, on the model of the United States of America, will
be constituted the United States of Europe.   *—G. Washington.*

The United States is not a nation of people which in the long
run allows itself to be pushed around.   *—Dorothy Thompson.*

In the United States there is more space where nobody is than where anybody is. This is what makes America what it is.
—Gertrude Stein.

I pledge allegiance to the flag of the United States and to the Republic for which it stands; one nation, indivisible, with liberty and justice for all.   *—James B. Upham and Francis Bellamy.*

But mostly U.S.A. is the speech of the people.
—John Dos Passos.

The United States had got ahead wonderfully, but somehow ahead on the wrong road.   *—Willa Cather.*

The United States, as heir apparent to Britain, has not yet been able to assume the throne and play the role.   *—Allan Sproul.*

The United States is the Age of the Dynamo.   *—Isabel Paterson.*

The United States never lost a war or won a conference.
—Will Rogers.

The United States, as a first colony in modern history to win independence for itself, instinctively shares the aspirations for liberty of all dependent and colonial peoples. *—John Foster Dulles.*

UNITY

To unite our people in all that makes home pure and honorable as well as to give our energies in the direction of our material advancement, these services we may render. *—Benjamin S. Harrison.*

Whatever destroys a unity of interest between a government and a nation, infallibly produces oppression and hatred.
—John Taylor.

Men of widely divergent views in our own country live in peace together because they share certain common aspirations which are more important than their differences.   *—D. D. Eisenhower.*

We cannot be separated in interest or divided in purpose. We stand together until the end.   *—Woodrow Wilson.*

The free nations can win the peace only if they stand together, work together, and wage the peace together.   *—Paul Hoffman.*

The goals of business are inseparable from the goals of the whole community. Every attempt to sever the organic unity of business and the community inflicts equal hardship on both.
—Earl Bunting.

The great unity which true science seeks is found only by beginning with our knowledge of God, and coming down from Him along the stream of causation to every fact and event that affects us.
—Howard Crosly.

As governmental pressure toward unity becomes greater, so strife becomes more bitter as to whose unity it shall be.
—Felix Frankfurter.

By uniting we stand; by dividing we fall.   *—John Dickenson.*

One country, one constitution, one destiny.   *—Daniel Webster.*

UNIVERSAL

In all my travels the thing that has impressed me the most is the universal brotherhood of man—what there is of it.   *—Mark Twain.*

UNIVERSALISM

My country is the world; my countrymen are mankind.
—W. L. Garrison.

UNIVERSE

The universe is duly in order, everything is in its place.
—Walt Whitman.

A penny will hide the biggest star in the universe if you hold it close enough to your eye.   *—Samuel Grafton.*

Great is this organism of mud and fire, terrible this vast, painful, glorious experiment.   *—George Santayana.*

Every poet re-expresses the universe in his own way.
—Joel E. Spingarn.

Under every deep a lower deep opens.   *—R. W. Emerson.*

Every human being is born into this world, a potential universe. Prospectively, he is receptive of all sentient enjoyments; capable of all knowledge, and susceptible of all forms of virtue.
—Horace Mann.

An infinite universe is at each moment opened to our view. And this universe is the sign and symbol of Infinite Power, Intelligence, Purity, Bliss, and Love.   *—W. E. Channing.*

If this life be not a real fight, in which something is eternally gained for the universe by success, it is no better than a game of private theatricals from which one may withdraw at will.
—William James.

UNIVERSITY

The university most worthy of rational admiration is that one in which your lonely thinker can feel himself least lonely, most positively furthered, and most richly fed. —*William James.*

The task of a university is the creation of the future, so far as rational thought and civilized modes of appreciation can affect the issue. —*A. N. Whitehead.*

The great universities of the world have been more often fields of battle than ivory towers of contemplation. —*James Conant.*

Universities are full of knowledge; the freshmen bring a little in and the seniors take none away, and knowledge accumulates.

—*A. L. Lowell.*

The catalogue of a progressive institution of "higher learning" resembles nothing so much as a similar catalogue annually issued by Sears, Roebuck & Company. —*Everett Dean Martin.*

This institution will be based on the illimitable freedom of the human mind. For here we are not afraid to follow truth wherever it may lead, nor to tolerate error as long as reason is left free to combat it.

—*T. Jefferson.*

A senior always feels like the university is going to the kids.

—*Tom Masson.*

UNJUST

Nothing that is unjust can be eternal and nothing that is just can be impossible. —*Edward Bellamy.*

There never yet has been devised a scheme of emptying the pockets of one portion of the community into those of the other, however unjust or oppressive, for which plausible reasons could be found. —*John C. Calhoun.*

UNKINDNESS

There is nothing that needs to be said in an unkind manner.

—*Hosea Ballou.*

As unkindness has no remedy at law, let its avoidance be with you a point of honor. —*Ibid.*

UNLIMITED

The freedom which we seek is not the unlimited right of any man or nation to do as it likes. —*R. B. Perry.*

UNPARDONABLE

This is the unpardonable sin: to talk discouragingly to human souls hungering for hope.   —*Ella W. Wilcox.*

UNPOPULAR

Isn't it strange that I who have written only unpopular books should be such a popular fellow?   —*Albert Einstein.*

UNPROPERTIED

In future times a great majority of the people will not only be without landed, but any other sort of property . . . the rights of property and the public liberty will not be secure in their hands.
                                                —*James Madison.*

UNSAFE

It is unsafe to defer so much to mankind and the opinions of society, for these are always, and without exception, heathenish and barbarous, seen from the heights of philosophy.
                                                —*H. D. Thoreau.*

UNSELFISHNESS

The secret of being loved is in being lovely; and the secret of being lovely is being unselfish.   —*J. G. Holland.*

UNTRUE

Do not call things untrue because they are marvelous, but give them a fair consideration.   —*Wendell Phillips.*

UPLIFT

It may be conjectured that it is cheaper in the long run to lift men up than to hold them down, and that the ballot in their hands is less dangerous to society than a sense of wrong in their heads.
                                                —*J. R. Lowell.*

The happiest men I know in all this unhappy life of ours, are those leaders who, brave, loyal, and sometimes in tears, are serving their fellow men.   —*Lincoln Steffens.*

Your mind needs an uplift as well as your bust.
                                                —*Christopher Morley.*

UPRIGHT

The typical actor, at least in America, is the most upright of men; he always marries the girl.   —*H. L. Mencken.*

UPWARD

The great fact to remember is that the trend of civilization itself is forever upward. —*F. D. Roosevelt.*

USE

The use of philosophy is to maintain an active novelty of fundamental ideas illuminating the social system.

—*A. N. Whitehead.*

Science adapts nature to man's use. Art makes man more human to himself—it does not make nature more human to man.

—*James T. Farrell.*

The greatest homage we can pay to truth is to use it.

—*R. W. Emerson.*

When one devotes his property to a use in which the public has an interest, he, in effect, grants to the public an interest in that use, and must submit to be controlled by the public for the common good. —*Morrison R. Waite.*

Man has . . . the right to the use of so much of the free gifts of nature as may be necessary to supply the wants of (his) existence.

—*Henry George.*

The use of money is all the advantage there is in having money.

—*B. Franklin.*

To waste, to destroy, our natural resources, to skin and exhaust the land instead of using it so as to increase its usefulness, will result in undermining in the days of our children the very prosperity which we ought by right to hand down to them amplified and developed. —*Theodore Roosevelt.*

We are not weak if we make a proper use of those means which the God of Nature has placed in our power. —*Patrick Henry.*

The use of great men is to serve the little men, to take care of the human race, and act as practical interpreters of justice and truth. —*Theodore Parker.*

USEFULNESS

The usefullest truths are plainest, and while we keep to them, our differences cannot be high. —*Wm. Penn.*

I believe that the rendering of useful service is the common duty of mankind and that only in the purifying fire of sacrifice is the dross of selfishness consumed and the greatness of the human soul set free. —*John D. Rockefeller, Jr.*

Let us be ourselves, as God made us, then we shall be something good and useful.   —*J. F. Clarke.*

Usefulness is the great aim of human life.   —*Horace Mann.*

Have I done anything for society? I have then done more for myself. Let that truth be always present in your mind and work without cessation.   —*W. G. Simms.*

USELESS

It is useless to deny it: Democracy grows rankly up, the thickest, most noxious, deadliest plant of all.   —*Walt Whitman.*

USUAL

The foolish man wonders at the unusual, but the wise man at the usual.   —*R. W. Emerson.*

USURPATION

There are more instances of the abridgement of the freedom of the people by gradual and silent encroachments of those in power than by violent and sudden usurpation.   —*James Madison.*

USURY

Seven per cent has no rest, nor religion; it works nights, and Sundays, and even wet days.   —*Josh Billings.*

Usury is the serpent gnawing at labor's vitals, and only liberty can detach and kill it. Give laborers their liberty, and they will keep their wealth.   —*Benj. R. Tucker.*

Usury is the land-shark and devil-fish of commerce.
                                                    —*J. L. Basford.*

UTILITY

True art is but the anti-type of nature—the embodiment of discovered beauty in utility.   —*James A. Garfield.*

Truth and right are above utility in all realms of thought and action.   —*Charles W. Eliot.*

UTOPIANISM

History, with the utopian, disappears in ideas.
                                                    —*Leon Samson.*

American thinkers, no more than American plumbers, can escape the influence of Utopianism in the American atmosphere.
                                                          —*Ibid.*

The social standards of the New Deal appear utopian when contrasted with those of the early nineteenth century.
—*Charles A. Madison.*

The destiny of Western civilization is bound together with the most ambitious and perhaps utopian program of popular education ever contemplated. —*E. D. Martin.*

A people bent on a soft security, surrendering their birthright of individual self-reliance for favors, voting themselves into Eden from a supposedly inexhaustible public purse, supporting everyone by soaking a fast-disappearing rich, scrambling for subsidy, learning the arts of political log-rolling and forgetting the rugged virtues of the pioneer, will not measure up to competition with a tough dictatorship. —*Vannevar Bush.*

Puritanism is utopianism. The New England theocrats had about them all the traits of utopians. —*Leon Samson.*

Long before capitalism took root in the soil of America, it took root in the spirit of America. Therein lies its utopianism. —*Ibid.*

The rise of Marxism deprived utopianism of its appeal, since the workers, little attracted by social visions and interested primarily in increased wages and shorter hours, began to unite in their own behalf. —*Charles A. Madison.*

Utopianism is blueprintism, and no amount of weeping over the old arts and crafts will halt the march of America toward a paper-box civilization. —*Leon Samson.*

UTOPISTS

In the midst of suffering, confusion, and hopelessness they (the Utopists) rallied to a great standard, to the assertion that man could control the productive forces. —*Granville Hicks.*

UTTERANCE

Put fear out of your heart. This nation will survive, this state will prosper, the orderly business of life will go forward if only men can speak in whatever way given them to utter what their hearts hold—by voice, by postcard, by letter or by press.
—*William A. White.*

Whatever the speech, there is but one longing and utterance of the human heart, and that is liberty and justice.
—*Woodrow Wilson.*

V

VACATION

No man needs a vacation so much as the person who has just had one. —*Elbert Hubbard.*

If some people didn't tell you, you'd never know they'd been away on a vacation. —*Kin Hubbard.*

VACUUM

There is nothing in the nature of money to produce happiness. The more a man has, the more he wants. Instead of filling a vacuum, it makes one. —*B. Franklin.*

VAIN

Beauty that don't make a woman vain makes her very beautiful. —*Josh Billings.*

VALIDITY

All philosophies tend to elevate their truths into suppositions of absolute validity, based upon the authority of reason and claiming the objectivity of what the modern age calls science.
—*Hans J. Morgenthau.*

VALOR

True valor is like honesty; it enters into all that a man sees and does. —*H. W. Shaw.*

He fights well who has wrongs to redress; but vastly better fights he who, with wrongs as a spur, has also steadily before him a glorious result in prospect. —*Lew Wallace.*

Valor consists in the power of self-recovery. —*R. W. Emerson.*

There is always safety in valor. —*Ibid.*

Dare to do your duty always; this is the height of true valor.
—*Charles Simmons.*

VALUE

All that is valuable in human society depends upon the opportunity for development accorded the individual. —*Albert Einstein.*

I conceive that great part of the miseries of mankind are brought upon them by false estimates they have made of the value of things.
—*B. Franklin.*

It is the content of our lives that determines their value. If we limit ourselves to supply the means of living, in what way have we placed ourselves above the cattle that graze the fields?
—*A. H. Compton.*

None but they who set a just value upon the blessings of liberty are worthy to enjoy her. —*Joseph Warren.*

Religion is the sole technique for the validating of values.
—*Allen Tate.*

What we obtain too cheap we esteem too lightly; 'tis dearness that gives everything its value. —*T. Paine.*

The germs of war are all about us as in every society. Spiritual values—truth, justice, invincible goodwill, are the most certain anti-toxins. —*Jerome Davis.*

Each person is a temporary focus of forces, vitalities, and values that carry back into an immemorial past and that reach forward into an unthinkable future. —*Lewis Mumford.*

A man's opinions are generally of much more value than his arguments. —*O. W. Holmes.*

The value of a principle is the number of things it will explain; and there is no good theory of disease which does not at once suggest a cure. —*R. W. Emerson.*

VANITY

Men are vain, but they won't mind women's working so long as they get smaller salaries for the same job. —*I. S. Cobb.*

Vanity as an impulse has without doubt been of far more benefit to civilization than modesty has ever been. —*W. E. Woodward.*

There is nothing which vanity does not desecrate.
—*H. W. Beecher.*

Vanity is a strange passion: rather than be out of a job it will brag of its vices. —*H. W. Shaw.*

There is no restraining men's tongues or pens when charged with a little vanity. —*G. Washington.*

Never expect justice from a vain man. —*Washington Allston.*

Men that fight vanities are like men that fight midges and butterflies. It is easier to chase them than to hit them. —*H. W. Beecher.*

When a man has no longer any conception of excellence above his own, his voyage is done, he is dead—dead in trespasses and sin of blear-eyed vanity. —*Ibid.*

Vanity is often productive of good to its possessor. It would not be altogether absurd if a man were to thank God for his vanity, among the other comforts of his life. —*B. Franklin.*

Scarcely have I ever heard the introductory phrase, "I may say without vanity," but some striking and characteristic instance of vanity has immediately followed. —*Ibid.*

Vanity may be likened to the smooth-skinned and velvet-footed mouse, nibbling about forever in expectation of a crumb.
—*W. G. Simms.*

To be a man's own fool is bad enough; but the vain man is everybody's. —*Wm. Penn.*

VANQUISHED

The rapture of pursuing is the prize the vanquished gain.
—*H. W. Longfellow.*

VASES

Spoons and skimmers can be undistinguishably together; but vases and statues require each a pedestal for itself.
—*R. W. Emerson.*

VAST

All nature is a vast symbolism; every material fact has sheathed within a spiritual truth. —*E. H. Chapin.*

VEGETABLE

Cabbage: a familiar kitchen garden vegetable about as large and wide as a man's head. —*Ambrose Bierce.*

VEGETATION

Every green thing lives to die in bright colors.—It is not nature that is sad but only we. —*H. W. Beecher.*

Every plant is a manufacturer of soil. In the stomach of the plant development begins. The tree can draw on the whole air, the whole earth, on all the rolling main. —*R. W. Emerson.*

VEIL

Dignity is often a veil between us and the real truth of things.
—*E. P. Whipple.*

VENERY

Rarely use venery but for health and offspring. —*B. Franklin.*

VERACITY

In international affairs, as in other spheres of human relations, disregard of the truth is not sound strategy. —*Corliss Lamont.*

I had rather starve and rot and keep the privilege of speaking the truth as I see it, than of holding all the offices that capital has to give from the presidency downward.
—*Brooks Adams.*

VERBIAGE

Verbiage may indicate observation, but not thinking.
—*G. Washington.*

VERSE

Writing free verse is like playing tennis with the net down.
—*Robert Frost.*

Publishing a volume of verse is like dropping a rose petal down the Grand Canyon and waiting for the echo. —*Don Marquis.*

VETOES

No one of us ought to issue vetoes to the other, nor should we bandy words of abuse. We ought, on the contrary . . . to respect one another's mental freedom. —*William James.*

VIBRATION

Every action of our lives touches on some chord that will vibrate in eternity. —*E. H. Chapin.*

VICE

What maintains one vice would bring up two children.
—*B. Franklin.*

Human nature is not of itself vicious. —*T. Paine.*

Vice is a creature of such hideous mien that the more you see it, the better you like it. —*F. P. Dunne.*

Every vice was once a virtue, and may become respectable again, just as hatred becomes respectable in wartime.   —*Will Durant.*

There is no man who is not at some time indebted to his vices, as no plant that is not fed from manures.   —*R. W. Emerson.*

One big vice in a man is apt to keep out a great many smaller ones.   —*Bret Harte.*

It has ever been my experience that folks who have no vices have very few virtues.   —*A. Lincoln.*

There is never an instant's truce between virtue and vice. Goodness is the only investment that never fails.   —*H. D. Thoreau.*

We lament the virtue that is debauched into vice, but the vice that affects a virtue becomes the more detestable.   —*T. Paine.*

Man is my brother, and I am nearer related to him through his vices than I am through his virtue.   —*Josh Billings.*

There is no truth which personal vice will not distort.
—*J. G. Holland.*

This is the essential evil of vice: it debases a man.—*E. H. Chapin.*

It is but a step from companionship to slavery when one associates with vice.   —*Hosea Ballou.*

Vicious actions are not hurtful because they are forbidden, but forbidden because they are hurtful.   —*B. Franklin.*

VICTIM

The arts of power and its minions are the same in all countries and in all ages. It marks its victim; denounces it; and excites the public odium and the public hatred, to conceal its own abuses and encroachments.   —*Henry Clay.*

I do not believe government can run any business as efficiently as private enterprise, and the victim of every such experiment is the public.   —*Thomas E. Dewey.*

VICTORS

To the victors belong the spoils.   —*W. L. Marcy.*

When the victor is crowned, his path to the goal looks as plain and straight as the king's highway. Who could miss that road?
—*G. E. Woodberry.*

The aftermaths of great wars make it certain that the military victors become ultimately almost as impoverished and vanquished as those who have been beaten on the field of battle.

—Lewis W. Douglas.

VICTORY

Principles have achieved more victories than horsemen or chariots. *—W. M. Paxton.*

We must fight our way through not alone to the destruction of our enemies but to a new world idea. We must win the peace.

—Wendell L. Willkie.

Party-spirit is willing to pervert truth so it may gain the victory.

—Charles Simmons.

That we shall prevail is as sure as that God reigns.

—Woodrow Wilson.

Victories that are easy are cheap. Those only are worth having which come as the result of hard fighting. *—H. W. Beecher.*

We have met the enemy and they are ours. *—O. H. Perry.*

We should wage war not to win a war, but to win a peace.

—Paul Hoffman.

The army of the American revolution was a people's army. It was an army that suffered hunger, cold and defeat, but which fought on to victory. *—Philip S. Power.*

Whether in chains or in laurels, liberty knows nothing but victories. *—Wendell Phillips.*

VIEWS

Half of the secret of getting along with people is consideration of their views; the other half is tolerance in one's own views.

—Daniel Frohman.

Never will I be whipped by ministers or anybody else into views that do not commend themselves to my understanding as guided by the Bible and enlightened by the Spirit.

—John Humphrey Noyes.

Any views are unimportant, if they are held about women by a man past forty. *—Ben Hecht.*

I shall try to correct errors where shown to be errors, and I shall adopt new views as fast as they shall appear to be true views.

—A. Lincoln.

VIGILANCE

Eternal vigilance is the price of liberty.   —*T. Jefferson.*

Experience should teach us to be most on our guard to protect
liberty when the government's purposes are beneficent.
                                                  —*Louis D. Brandeis.*

Vigilance is not only the price of liberty, but of success of any
sort.   —*H. W. Beecher.*

There is a significant Latin proverb; to wit: Who will guard the
guards?   —*H. W. Shaw.*

Whilst on the one hand we should shun base women as a
pestilence of the worst and most dangerous kind to society, we
ought, on the other, to guard virtuous female character with vestal
vigilance.   —*Andrew Jackson.*

They that are on their guard and appear ready to receive their
adversaries, are in much less danger of being attacked than the
supine, secure and negligent.   —*B. Franklin.*

VILLAGE

The restlessness of women was the main cause of the development that was called Greenwich Village.   —*Robert Herrick.*

VILLAINY

The most natural man in a play is the villain.   —*E. W. Howe.*

VINEGAR

Put not your trust in vinegar—molasses catches flies.
                                                   —*Eugene Field.*

VIOLENCE

Degeneracy follows every autocratic system of violence, for
violence inevitably attracts moral inferiors. Time has proved that
illustrious tyrants are succeeded by scoundrels.   —*Albert Einstein.*

It is organized violence on top which creates individual violence
at the bottom.   —*Emma Goldman.*

All violence, all that is dreary and repels, is not power, but the
absence of power.   —*R. W. Emerson.*

Among political groups outbursts of violence are called revolutions; among nations they are called wars.   —*Max Ascoli.*

In 1940 the Alien Registration Act forbade all Americans to

teach or advocate the duty or necessity of overthrowing by force or violence a government created by just such advocacy.

—*Alan Barth.*

VIRGINIAN

I am not a Virginian but an American. —*Patrick Henry.*

VIRGINITY

Neither a fortress nor a maidenhead will hold out long after they begin to parley. —*B. Franklin.*

VIRTUE

Virtue does not consist in the absence of the passions, but in the control of them. —*H. W. Shaw.*

Home is the chief school of human virtue. —*W. E. Channing.*

Men are virtuous because women are; women are virtuous from necessity. —*E. W. Howe.*

Wisdom is knowing what to do next; virtue is doing it.

—*D. S. Jordan.*

Affectation hides three times as many virtues as charity does sins.

—*Horace Mann.*

Persistence is a great and necessary virtue. —*Louis D. Brandeis.*

It is with virtue as with fire. It exists in the mind, as fire does in certain bodies, in a latent or quiescent state.

—*Benjamin Rush.*

And what is a weed? A plant whose virtues have not been discovered. —*R. W. Emerson.*

Self-abnegation is a rare virtue that good men preach and good women practice. —*O. W. Holmes.*

The less a man thinks or knows about his virtues the better we like him. —*R. W. Emerson.*

The virtue most in request in society is conformity. Self-reliance is its aversion. —*Ibid.*

Virtue is self-subjection to the principle of duty, that highest law in the soul. —*W. E. Channing.*

There is no truth more thoroughly established, than that there exists in the economy and course of nature an indissoluble union between virtue and happiness. —*G. Washington.*

One's outlook is a part of his virtue. —*A. B. Alcott.*

There are those who have nothing chaste but their ears, and nothing virtuous but their tongues.   —*J. De Finod.*

The only reward of virtue is virtue.   —*R. W. Emerson.*

Virtue is an angel, but she is a blind one, and must ask of Knowledge to show her the pathway that leads to her goal.

—*Horace Mann.*

The choicest compliment that can be paid to virtue is that the best lies we have are those which most resemble the truth.

—*Josh Billings.*

Our vocabulary is defective; we give the same name to woman's lack of temptation and man's lack of opportunity.

—*Ambrose Bierce.*

Virtue is the adherence in action to the nature of things: the only right is what is after my constitution, the only wrong is what is against it.   —*R. W. Emerson.*

All virtue lies in strength of character or of moral purpose.

—*W. E. Channing.*

In the full enjoyment of the gifts of Heaven and the fruits of superior industry, economy, and virtue, every man is equally entitled to protection by law.   —*Andrew Jackson.*

Virtue has never been as respectable as money.   —*Mark Twain.*

Always in times of stress it is the simple virtues that really count.
—*John G. Winant.*

Peace is the soft and holy shadow that virtue casts.
—*H. W. Shaw.*

Have enough of little virtues and common fidelities, and you need not mourn because you are neither a hero nor a saint.

—*H. W. Beecher.*

Hast thou virtue? Acquire also the graces and beauties of virtue.
—*B. Franklin.*

No state of virtue is complete save as it is won by a conflict with evil.   —*Horace Bushnell.*

To be virtuous is to overcome our evil feelings and intentions.
—*Wm. Penn.*

Folks who have no vices have very few virtues.   —*A. Lincoln.*

Virtue is not hereditary.   —*T. Paine.*

Few men have virtue to withstand the highest bidder.
—*G. Washington.*

That virtue we appreciate is as much ours as another's. We see so much only as we possess. —*H. D. Thoreau.*

We love to talk of virtue and to admire its beauty, while in the shade of solitude and retirement; but when we step forth into active life, if it happen to be in competition with any passion or desire, do we observe it to prevail?

—*Hector St. Jean de Crèvecoeur.*

VISION

The lunatic's visions of horror are all drawn from the materials of daily fact. Our civilization is founded on the shambles, and every individual existence goes out in a lonely spasm of helpless agony. —*William James.*

Rouse up my slow belief, give me some vision of the future.

—*Walt Whitman.*

I would give all the wealth of the world, and all the deeds of all the heroes, for one true vision. —*H. D. Thoreau.*

Life itself is only a vision, a dream . . . Nothing exists save empty space—and you. —*Mark Twain.*

Puritanism . . . was an endeavor to fulfill the vision of the ideal Christian Church, as men derived that vision from the Bible.

—*H. H. Sanderson.*

Where there is no vision a people perish. —*R. W. Emerson.*

The life of the young man is his visions, hope of the future, plans of achievement and success for himself. —*Arthur Brisbane.*

No man that does not see visions will ever realize any high hope or undertake any high enterprise. —*Woodrow Wilson.*

VISITORS

Strange is our situation here on earth. Each of us comes for a short visit, not knowing why, yet sometimes seeming to divine a purpose. —*Albert Einstein.*

Fish and visitors smell in three days. —*B. Franklin.*

VITALITY

The well-springs of our vitality are not economic. They go deeper still; they are ethical and spiritual. —*David E. Lillienthal.*

VOCATION

Every man, in whatsoever condition, is to be a student. No

matter what other vocation he may have, his chief vocation is to Think.   —*W. E. Channing.*

Vocational education . . . is a threat to democracy because it tends to make the job-trained individual conscious only of his technological responsibilities but not of his social and moral responsibilities.   —*Sidney Hook.*

A truly liberal, and liberating education would refuse today to isolate vocational training on any of its levels from a continuous education in the social, moral and scientific contexts within which wisely administered callings and professions must function.
—*John Dewey.*

He that hath a trade hath an estate, and he that hath a calling hath an office of profit and honor.   —*B. Franklin.*

VOICE

The human voice is the organ of the soul.   —*H. W. Longfellow.*

The poet's voice need not merely be the record of man, it can be one of the props, the pillars to help him endure and prevail.
—*William Faulkner.*

Great truths always dwell a long time with small minorities, and the real voice of God is often that which rises above the masses, not that which follows them.   —*Francis Lieber.*

To be positive: to be mistaken at the top of one's voice.
—*Ambrose Bierce.*

The ideal voice for radio may be defined as having no substance, no sex, no owner, and a message of importance to every housewife.
—*H. V. Wade.*

In a free and republican government, you cannot restrain the voice of the multitude. Every man will speak as he thinks, or, more properly, without thinking, and consequently will judge of effects without attending to their causes.   —*G. Washington.*

It is the still small voice that the soul heeds; not the deafening blasts of doom.   —*W. D. Howells.*

VOLUME

To produce a mighty volume you must choose a mighty theme.
—*Herman Melville.*

Every man is a volume, if you know how to read him.
—*W. E. Channing.*

Although volume upon volume is written to prove slavery is a very good thing, we never hear of the man who wishes to take the good of it by being a slave himself. —*A. Lincoln.*

VOTE

Always vote for a principle, though you may vote alone, and you may cherish the sweet reflection that your vote is never lost.
—*John Q. Adams.*

A straw vote only shows which way the hot air blows.
—*O. Henry.*

Bad officials are elected by good citizens who do not vote.
—*George Jean Nathan.*

The future of this republic is in the hands of the American voter.
—*D. D. Eisenhower.*

VOYAGE

It is not the ship so much as the skillful sailing that assures the prosperous voyage. —*G. W. Curtis.*

VULGARITY

There are no people who are quite so vulgar as the over-refined ones. —*Mark Twain.*

Vulgarity is more obvious in satin than in homespun.
—*N. P. Willis.*

W

WAGES

No matter how hard the times get, the wages of sin are always liberal and on the dot. *—Kin Hubbard.*

No business which depends for existence on paying less than living wages to its workers has any right to continue in this country. *—F. D. Roosevelt.*

The high wage begins down in the shop. If it is not created there it cannot get into pay envelopes. There will never be a system invented which will do away with the necessity for work.
—Henry Ford.

One of labor's long-range objectives is to achieve in every basic industry a guaranteed annual wage so that the consumers of this country can have a sustained income month in and month out, because only on that basis can we sustain an economy of full employment and full production and full distribution.
—W. P. Reuther.

Labor is most productive where its wages are largest. Poorly paid labor is inefficient labor, the world over. *—Henry George.*

If we retrench the wages of the schoolmaster, we must raise those of the recruiting sergeant. *—Edward Everett.*

We declare war with the wages system, which demoralizes alike the hirer and the hired, cheats both, and enslaves the workingman.
—Wendell Phillips.

Wages is a cunning device of the devil, for the benefit of tender consciences, who would retain all the advantages of the slave system, without the expense, trouble and odium of being slaveholders. *—Orestes A. Brownson.*

WAITING

Learn to labor and to wait. *—H. W. Longfellow.*

The greatest lesson which the lives of literary men teach us is told in a single word: Wait! —*Ibid.*

All good abides with him who waiteth wisely. —*H. D. Thoreau.*

It is a good thing that life is not as serious as it seems to a waiter. —*Don Herold.*

Some folks get what's coming to them by waiting, others while crossing the street. —*Kin Hubbard.*

Everything comes to him who waits except a loaned book. —*Ibid.*

WANT

The seeds of totalitarian regimes are nurtured by misery and want. They spread and grow in the evil soil of poverty and strife. —*H. S. Truman.*

Our necessities never equal our wants. —*B. Franklin.*

The keener the want, the lustier the growth. —*Wendell Phillips.*

Nature has provided for the existence of privation, by putting the measure of our necessities far below the measure of our wants. —*C. N. Bovee.*

What man wants: all he can get; what woman wants: all she can't get. —*G. D. Prentice.*

WAR

War is low and despicable, and I had rather be smitten to shreds than participate in such doings. —*Albert Einstein.*

The man who enjoys marching in line and file to the strains of music falls beneath my contempt; he received his great brain by mistake—the spinal cord would have been amply sufficient. —*Ibid.*

In modern war there is nothing sweet nor fitting in your dying. You will die like a dog for no good reason. —*Ernest Hemingway.*

The American people will not relish the idea of any American citizen growing rich and fat in an emergency of blood and slaughter and human suffering. —*F. D. Roosevelt.*

There's many a boy here today who looks on war as all glory, but, boys, it is all hell. —*William T. Sherman.*

War is hell. —*Ibid.*

Economic warfare in uncontrolled markets can be as devastating as military warfare. —*Ben W. Lewis.*

We Americans cannot conceive a war without a moral background.   *—W. E. Woodward.*

If war were fought with push-button devices, one might make a science of command. But because war is as much a conflict of passion as it is of force, no commander can become a strategist until first he knows his men.   *—Omar N. Bradley.*

I know war as few other men now living know it, and nothing to me is more revolting. I have long advocated its complete abolition, as its very destructiveness on both friend and foe has rendered it useless as a means of settling international disputes.
                                                    —Douglas MacArthur.

War is the science of destruction.   *—J. S. C. Abbott.*

What distinguishes war is, not that man is slain, but that he is slain, spoiled, crushed by the cruelty, the injustice, the treachery, the murderous hand of man.   *—W. E. Channing.*

There never was a good war or a bad peace.   *—B. Franklin.*

War is as much a punishment to the punisher as to the sufferer.
                                                            —T. Jefferson.

Modern warfare is an intricate business about which no one knows everything and few know very much.   *—Frank Knox.*

> Ez for war, I call it murder,—
>   There you hev it plain and flat;
> I don't want to go no furder
>   Than my Testyment for that.
>
>   *—J. R. Lowell.*

> And this I hate—not men, nor flag, nor race,
> But only War with its wild, grinning face.
>
>   *—J. D. Miller.*

If there are to be no more wars the men and women of the world must put their hearts and minds to the task of bringing us all into comradeship this side of Jordan.   *—Heywood Broun.*

War is the desperate, vital problem of our time.
                                                    —Thomas A. Edison.

War will never be made impossible until men are convinced by definite demonstration that it is impossible.   *—Ibid.*

More than an end to war, we want an end to the beginnings of all wars.   *—F. D. Roosevelt.*

The surest way to prevent war is not to fear it.
—*John Randolph.*

War means fightin' and fightin' means killin'. —*N. B. Forrest.*

The real war will never get in the books. —*Walt Whitman.*

War is the concentration of all human crimes. It turns man into a beast of prey. —*W. E. Channing.*

Wars are over before they are fought. —*Gertrude Stein.*

Wars are not "acts of God." They are caused by man, by man-made institutions, by the way in which man has organized his society. What man has made, man can change. —*Fred Vinson.*

The war of the poor against the rich . . . will come, and come with all its horrors. —*O. A. Brownson.*

If the happiness of the mass of mankind can be secured at the expense of a little tempest now and then, or even of a little blood, it will be a precious purchase. —*T. Jefferson.*

I have seen war. I have seen war on land and sea. I have seen blood running from the wounded. I have seen men coughing out their gassed lungs. I have seen the dead in the mud. I have seen cities destroyed. I have seen 200 limping, exhausted men come out of the line—the survivors of a regiment of 1,000 that went forward 48 hours before. I have seen children starving. I have seen the agony of mothers and wives. I hate war. —*F. D. Roosevelt.*

Older men declare war. But it is youth that must fight and die. And it is youth who must inherit the tribulation, the sorrow, and the triumphs that are the aftermath of war. —*Herbert Hoover.*

War is the health of the state. —*Randolph Bourne.*

WASTE

Waste neither time nor money, but make best use of both. Without industry and frugality, nothing will do, and with them everything. —*B. Franklin.*

The waste of life occasioned by trying to do too many things at once is appalling. —*O. S. Marden.*

WATER

A drop of water has all the properties of water but it cannot exhibit a storm. —*R. W. Emerson.*

Water, taken in moderation, cannot hurt anybody.
—*Mark Twain.*

Never drink from your finger bowl—it contains only water.
—Addison Mizner.

WE

There are just two people entitled to refer to themselves as "we";
one is the editor and the other is the fellow with a tapeworm.
—E. W. Nye.

Only presidents, editors and people with tapeworm have the
right to use the editorial "we".   *—Mark Twain.*

WEAKNESS

Better make a weak man your enemy than your friend.
—Josh Billings.

Our strength grows out of our weakness.   *—R. W. Emerson.*

We cannot complain if the weakness of our political position
reflects the weakness of our thinking.   *—Max Ascoli.*

The weakest spot with mankind is where they fancy themselves
most wise.   *—Charles Simmons.*

Weakness ineffectually seeks to disguise itself—like a drunken
man trying to show how sober he is.   *—C. N. Bovee.*

We must have a weak spot or two in character before we can
love it much.   *—O. W. Holmes.*

WEALTH

Private wealth I should decline, or any sort of personal possession, because they would take away my liberty.
—George Santayana.

God shows his contempt for wealth by the kind of person he
selects to receive it.   *—Austin O'Malley.*

I am poor, and I am glad that I am, for I find that wealth
makes more people mean than it does generous.   *—Josh Billings.*

He is only rich who owns the day.   *—R. W. Emerson.*

If Rockyfeller could eat he wouldn't be so rich. *—Kin Hubbard.*

There's nothing so comfortable as a small bankroll. A big one is
always in danger.   *—Wilson Mizner.*

Man is not a savage or a pauper by the inexorable fatality of
his nature. He is surrounded with every form of the truest and
noblest wealth;—wealth, or well-being, for the body, wealth for
the mind, wealth for the heart.   *—Horace Mann.*

The greatest wealth you can ever get will be in yourself.

—Horace Bushnell.

Superfluous wealth can buy superfluities only. Money is not required to buy one necessary of the soul.   *—H. D. Thoreau.*

Surplus wealth is a sacred trust which its possessor is bound to administer in his lifetime for the good of the community.

—Andrew Carnegie.

If you would be wealthy, think of saving as well as of getting.

—B. Franklin.

The ideal social state is not that in which each gets an equal amount of wealth, but in which each gets in proportion to his contribution to the general stock.   *—Henry George.*

The advantages of wealth are greatly exaggerated.

—Leland Stanford.

The generality of men are worse for their riches.   *—Wm. Penn.*

Wealth is the least trustworthy of anchors.   *—J. G. Holland.*

Wants keep pace with wealth always.   *—Ibid.*

Wealth is not his that has it but his that enjoys it. *—B. Franklin.*

Without a rich heart wealth is an ugly beggar.

—R. W. Emerson.

Wealth may be an excellent thing, for it means power, it means leisure, it means liberty.   *—J. R. Lowell.*

Great wealth . . . ought to be taken away from its possessors on the same principle that a sword or pistol may be wrested from a robber.   *—Thomas Skidmore.*

Wealth tends to corrupt the mind and to nourish its love of power, and to stimulate its oppression. History proves this to be the spirit of the opulent.   *—Gouverneur Morris.*

On the theories of the social philosophers . . . we should get a new maxim of judicious living: Poverty is the best policy. If you get wealth, you will have to support other people; if you do not get wealth, it will be the duty of other people to support you.

—W. G. Sumner.

Recognition of the falsity of material wealth as the standard of success goes hand in hand with the abandonment of the false belief that public office and high political position are to be valued only by the standards of price, of place and personal profit.

—F. D. Roosevelt.

The way to wealth is as plain as the way to market. It depends chiefly on two words, industry and frugality.   —*B. Franklin.*

The real wealth, not only of America, but of the world, is in the resources of the ground we stand on, and in the resources of the human mind.   —*Norman Cousins.*

I hope and believe that great unregulated concentrations of wealth, with their enormous power for evil, will no longer be allowed to exist.   —*Gifford Pinchot.*

Inherited wealth is an unmitigated curse when divorced from culture.   —*Charles W. Eliot.*

The great war that education has to carry on in society is a war against the brutal self assertion of great wealth. —*Carl Schurz.*

What a man does with his wealth depends upon his idea of happiness.   —*E. P. Whipple.*

The corrupt use of wealth is undermining our institutions, debauching public officials, shaping legislation and creating judges who do its bidding.   —*John P. Altgeld.*

The eminently successful man should be beware of the tendency of wealth to chill and isolate.   —*Otto H. Kahn.*

Labor alone produces all the wealth.   —*Daniel De Leon.*

A man is rich in proportion to the number of things he can afford to let alone.   —*H. D. Thoreau.*

WEATHER

If you don't like the weather in New England, just wait a few minutes.   —*Mark Twain.*

Everybody talks about the weather but nobody does anything about it.   —*C. D. Warner.*

Don't knock the weather; nine tenths of the people couldn't start a conversation if it didn't change once in a while.   —*Kin Hubbard.*

Some are weatherwise, some are otherwise.   —*B. Franklin.*

WEDLOCK

In modern wedlock, too many misplace the key.

—*Tom Masson.*

WELFARE

Never in the history of man has there been so splendid a spec-

tacle of widely diffused and steadily increasing material welfare as America has displayed during the last hundred years.
—C. E. Norton.

A welfare state should be the goal of everyone who calls himself a liberal.
—H. A. Wallace.

The sound direction of the counter movement to communism in the democracies . . . is the creation of the human welfare state — the great political invention of the twentieth century.
—W. O. Douglas.

The man who holds that every human right is secondary to his profit must now give way to the advocate of human welfare, who rightly maintains that every man holds his property subject to the general right of the community to regulate its use to whatever degree the public welfare may require it.   *—Theodore Roosevelt.*

WELL-BEING
In this critical time in the affairs of the world, it is vital that the democratic nations show their concern for the well-being of men everywhere and their desire for a better life for mankind.
—H. S. Truman.

WEST
Go West, young man, and grow up with the country.
—Horace Greeley.

If you have no family or friends to aid you, and no prospect open to you there, turn your face to the great West, and there build up a home and fortune.   *—Ibid.*

American democracy is fundamentally the outcome of the experience of the American people in dealing with the West.
—F. J. Turner.

There were thousands of Americans who heard voices calling them westward and who banded together to find "a land of equal laws and happy men."   *—H. W. Schneider.*

Here in the Great West if anywhere must arise the Kingdom of God foretold by ancient prophets and foreseen by countless generations of seekers and wanderers. These were the latter days, the end of man's pilgrimage on earth.   *—Ibid.*

The Middle West is the apotheosis of American civilization.
—Randolph Bourne.

I must walk toward Oregon, and not toward Europe. And that way the nation is moving, and I may say that mankind progresses from East to West.   —*H. D. Thoreau.*

WESTERN CIVILIZATION
The greatest problem of Western civilization is that it is breeding from the bottom and dying from the top.   —*Will Durant.*

WHIGGERY
For a capitalistic society Whiggery is the only rational politics, for it exalts the profit-motive as the sole object of parliamentary concern.   —*V. L. Parrington.*

WICKEDNESS
The world loves a spice of wickedness.   —*H. W. Longfellow.*

I's mighty wicked; anyhow I can't help it.   —*H. B. Stowe.*

It is a statistical fact that the wicked work harder to reach hell than the righteous do to enter heaven.   —*H. W. Shaw.*

It isn't the wicked people who do the harm.   —*W. D. Howells.*

WIDOW
So far as is known, no widow ever eloped.   —*E. W. Howe.*

To be two years a widow exceedeth a college education.
                                                —*Gelett Burgess.*

A widow of doubtful age will marry almost any sort of a white man.   —*Horace Greeley.*

Easy-crying widows take new husbands soonest; there's nothing like wet weather for transplanting.   —*O. W. Holmes.*

Rich widows are the only second-hand goods that sell at first-class prices.   —*B. Franklin.*

Grass widow: the angel a man loved, the human being he married, and the devil he divorced.   —*Helen Rowland.*

WIDOWERS
Some widowers are bereaved; others, relieved.   —*Ibid.*

WIFE
Wife: a former sweetheart.   —*H. L. Mencken.*

It is better to have loved your wife than never to have loved at all.   —*Edgar Saltus.*

Men's wives are usually their husbands' mental inferiors and spiritual superiors; this gives them double instruments of torture.
—*Don Herold.*

No family can long remain harmonious if a wife always gives her husband just what he deserves! Generous portions of forgiveness and forbearance and sacrificial loyalty are required.
—*Kirby Page.*

There is one thing more exasperating than a wife who can cook and won't, and that's the wife who can't cook and will.
—*Robert Frost.*

She is but half a wife that is not, or is not capable of being a friend. —*Wm. Penn.*

An undutiful daughter will prove an unmanageable wife.
—*B. Franklin.*

The world well tried—the sweetest thing in life
Is the unclouded welcome of a wife.
—*N. P. Willis.*

The dearest object to a married man should be his wife but it is not infrequently her clothes. —*J. M. Bailey.*

Heaven will be no heaven to me if I do not meet my wife there.
—*Andrew Jackson.*

An ideal wife is any woman who has an ideal husband.
—*Booth Tarkington.*

Ne'er take a wife till thou hast a house (and a fire) to put her in.
—*B. Franklin.*

In choosing a wife, a nurse, or a school-teacher, look to the breed.—There is as much blood in men as in horses.
—*Charles Simmons.*

Everything in life is fairly simple except one's wife.
—*Don Herold.*

Probably a widower enjoys a second wife as much as a widow enjoys her husband's life insurance. —*E. W. Howe.*

The only time some fellows are ever seen with their wives is after they've been indicted. —*Kin Hubbard.*

There is one advantage in a plurality of wives; they fight each other instead of their husbands. —*Josh Billings.*

Of all the home remedies, a good wife is the best.

—*Kin Hubbard.*

I will be so polite to my wife as though she were a perfect stranger.   —*R. J. Burdette.*

Try praising your wife, even if it does frighten her at first.

—*Billy Sunday.*

It is a very rare thing to find a man preferring his neighbor's son or daughter to his own, but not his neighbor's wife.

—*G. D. Prentice.*

WILL

If the expressed will of the people is scorned and scorned again —then the popular government fails, then government of the people, by the people, and for the people is at an end.

—*Robert M. LaFollette.*

There exists in the world today a gigantic reservoir of good will toward us, the American people.   —*Wendell L. Willkie.*

Man is the will and woman the sentiment.   —*R. W. Emerson.*

Man has his will,—but woman has her way.   —*O. W. Holmes.*

The man that leaves no will after his death had little will before his death.   —*Austin O'Malley.*

The education of the will is the object of our existence.

—*R. W. Emerson.*

Most men fail, not through lack of education, but from the lack of dogged determination, from lack of dauntless will.

—*O. S. Marden.*

When there is no will, there is no way for the lawyers.

—*Austin O'Malley.*

A boy's will is the wind's will.   —*H. W. Longfellow.*

A tender heart, a will inflexible.   —*Ibid.*

Where there's a will, there's a lawsuit.   —*Addison Mizner.*

The saddest failures in life are those that come from not putting forth the power and the will to succeed.   —*E. P. Whipple.*

To will what God wills is the only science that gives us rest.

—*H. W. Longfellow.*

WIN

Each wellborn soul must win what it deserves. —*Ella W. Wilcox.*

Anybody can win, unless there happens to be a second entry.

—*George Ade.*

WINE

No nation is drunken where wine is cheap.   *—T. Jefferson.*

That is a treacherous friend against whom you must always be on your guard. Such a friend is wine.   *—C. N. Bovee.*

WISDOM

The art of being wise is the art of knowing what to overlook.
   —William James.

It is wisdom to believe the heart.   *—George Santayana.*

A grain of gold will gild a great surface, but not so much as a grain of wisdom.   *—H. D. Thoreau.*

I doubt the wisdom of being too wise, and I see much wisdom in some folly.   *—Elbert Hubbard.*

The masses have political wisdom because the life of the people is the life of the state.   *—G. E. Woodberry.*

Wisdom is never dear, provided the article be genuine.
   —Horace Greeley.

The wise people are in New York because the foolish went there first; that's the way the wise men make a living.   *—F. P. Dunne.*

A wise man does not waste so good a commodity as lying for naught.   *—Mark Twain.*

It is a characteristic of wisdom not to do desperate things.
   —H. D. Thoreau.

Wisdom consists in perceiving when human nature and this perverse world necessitate making exceptions to abstract truths.
   —Wendell Phillips.

Any boy can see an abstract principle. Only threescore years and ten can discern precisely when and where it is well, necessary, and right to make an exception to it. That faculty is wisdom; all the rest is playing with counters.   *—Ibid.*

The heart is wiser than the intellect.   *—J. G. Holland.*

Nine-tenths of wisdom consists in being wise in time.
   —Theodore Roosevelt.

The rights and interests of the laboring man will be protected and cared for—not by the labor agitators, but by the Christian men to whom God, in his infinite wisdom, has given control of the property interests of the country, and upon the successful management of which so much depends.   *—George F. Baer.*

Wisdom is of the soul, is not susceptible of proof, is its own
proof.   —*Walt Whitman.*

The doors of wisdom are never shut.   —*B. Franklin.*

Much of the wisdom of the world is not wisdom.
                                                    —*R. W. Emerson.*

Cunning is the dwarf of wisdom.   —*W. R. Alger.*

The invariable mark of wisdom is to see the miraculous in the
common.   —*R. W. Emerson.*

Many a crown of wisdom is but the golden chamberpot of
success, worn with pompous dignity.   —*Paul Eldridge.*

The use of the head abridges the labor of the hands.
                                                   —*H. W. Beecher.*

A man doesn't begin to attain wisdom until he recognizes that
he is no longer indispensable.   —*Richard E. Byrd.*

If a man empties his purse into his head, no one can take it from
him.   —*B. Franklin.*

Wisdom is the abstract of the past, but beauty is the promise
of the future.   —*O. W. Holmes.*

Much of the wisdom of one age is the folly of the next.
                                                   —*Charles Simmons.*

The wise potter who would fashion a new vessel knows the clay
with which he has worked and must work.   —*Charles A. Beard.*

It's a wise man who profits by his own experience, but it's a good
deal wiser one who lets the rattlesnake bite the other fellow.
                                                   —*Josh Billings.*

He who devotes sixteen hours a day to hard study may become
as wise at sixty as he thought himself at twenty.   —*M. W. Little.*

Every man is a damn fool for at least five minutes every day;
wisdom consists in not exceeding the limit.   —*Elbert Hubbard.*

A man cannot learn to be wise any more than he can learn to
be handsome.   —*H. W. Shaw.*

Wisdom deprives even poverty of half its power.   —*Ibid.*

What we call wisdom is the result of all the wisdom of past ages.
                                                   —*H. W. Beecher.*

Wisdom comes by disillusionment.   —*George Santayana.*

The older I grow, the more I distrust the familiar doctrine that
age brings wisdom.   —*H. L. Mencken.*

WISHES

If a man could have half his wishes he would double his troubles.
                                                            —*B. Franklin.*

A man will sometimes devote all his life to the development of one part of his body—the wishbone.   —*Robert Frost.*

Many of us spend half our time wishing for things we could have if we didn't spend half our time wishing.
                                                    —*Alexander Woollcott.*

WIT

Wit is the unexpected explosion of thought.   —*E. P. Whipple.*

The next best thing to being witty one's self, is to be able to quote another's wit.   —*C. N. Bovee.*

Avoid witticisms at the expense of others.   —*Horace Mann.*

Wit marries ideas lying wide apart by a sudden jerk of the understanding.   —*E. P. Whipple.*

Wit implies hatred of folly and crime; produces its effects by brisk shocks of surprise, uses the whip of scorpions and the branding-iron, stabs, stings, pinches, tortures, goads, teases, corrodes, undermines.   —*Ibid.*

Wit must be without effort. Wit is play, not work.
                                                            —*C. N. Bovee.*

Less judgment than wit, is more sail than ballast.   —*Wm. Penn.*

Where judgment has wit to express it, there is the best orator.
                                                                    —*Ibid.*

Wit makes its own welcome, and levels all distinctions. No dignity, no learning, no force of character, can make any stand against good wit.   —*R. W. Emerson.*

WITCHES

The wretches have proceeded so far as to concert and consult the methods of rooting out the Christian religion from this Country, and setting up instead of it, perhaps a more gross diabolism than ever the world saw before.   —*Cotton Mather.*

WOLF

The shepherd drives the wolf from the sheep's throat, for which the sheep thanks the shepherd as his liberator, while the wolf denounces him for the same act, as the destroyer of liberty, especially as the sheep was a black one.   —*A. Lincoln.*

WOMAN

Woman: the peg on which the wit hangs his jest, the preacher his text, the cynic his grouch, and the sinner his justification.
—*Helen Rowland.*

I don't know of anything better than a woman if you want to spend money where it'll show.   —*Kin Hubbard.*

The taste forever refines in the study of women.   —*N. P. Willis.*

The woman who is known only through a man is known wrong.
—*Henry Adams.*

The way to fight a woman is with your hat. Grab it and run.
—*John Barrymore.*

Woman would be more charming if one could fall into her arms without falling into her hands.   —*Ambrose Bierce.*

Th' woman that tries t' keep up with th' procession don't see near as much as her husband who stands on th' curb.
—*Kin Hubbard.*

A woman, like a cross-eyed man, looks one way, but goes another—hence her mysteriousness.   —*Austin O'Malley.*

If there be any one whose power is in beauty, in purity, in goodness, it is a woman.   —*H. W. Beecher.*

A tender woman, if she be gripped by some strong emotion, fright or eagerness to save her child, may suddenly become strong as a giant.   —*Frank Crane.*

If men knew how women pass the time when they are alone, they'd never marry.   —*O. Henry.*

Women are getting dumber as they grow smarter.
—*Mary Garden.*

Informal's what women always say they'll be and never are.
—*Christopher Morley.*

They govern the world, these sweet-lipped women, because beauty is the index of a larger fact than wisdom. —*O. W. Holmes.*

The typical modern American woman tends to deny her responsibility as a wife, toward society, husband or child. She owns only a duty to herself to live for her own good, her guide being her own judgment.   —*Brooks Adams.*

The test of civilization is the estimate of woman. —*G. W. Curtis.*

Earth's noblest thing, a Woman perfected.   —*J. R. Lowell.*

The brain woman never interested us as much as the heart woman, white roses please less than red. —*O. W. Holmes.*

Would you hurt a woman worst, aim at her affections.
—*Lew Wallace.*

Women are just like elephants to me; I like to look at them, but I wouldn't want one. —*Kin Hubbard.*

Woman, like gold, is legal tender the world over, no matter what image or superscription is stamped on it by the national mint.
—*H. W. Beecher.*

Even a simple woman, that was wise, by her wisdom saved the city. —*B. Franklin.*

The growing freedom of women can hardly have any other outcome than the production of more realistic and more human morals. —*John Dewey.*

Women give us solace, but if it were not for women we should never need solace. —*Don Herold.*

From the day on which she weighs 140, the chief excitement of a woman's life consists in spotting women who are fatter than she is. —*Helen Rowland.*

Every man wants a woman to appeal to his better side, his nobler instincts and his higher nature—and another woman to help him forget her. —*Ibid.*

Women can instantly see through each other, and it's surprising how little they observe that's pleasant. —*Wilson Mizner.*

A woman's whole life is a history of the affections. The heart is her world: it is there her ambitions strive for empire; it is there her avarice seeks for hidden treasures. —*Washington Irving.*

There is in every true woman's heart a spark of heavenly fire, which beams and blazes in the dark hours of adversity. —*Ibid.*

Lord, spare me from sickly women and healthy men!
—*Don Herold.*

A man's ideal woman is the one he passes with a worshipful bow—when he's on his way to call on the other woman.
—*Helen Rowland.*

Divination seems heightened and raised to the highest power in woman. —*A. B. Alcott.*

When men and women agree, it is only in their conclusions; their reasons are always different. —*George Santayana.*

On one issue at least, men and women agree; they both distrust women.   —*H. L. Mencken.*

WONDER

Wonder is prophetic.   —*C. H. Parkhurst.*

Men love to wonder and that is the seed of our science.
—*R. W. Emerson.*

God works wonders now and then; behold, a lawyer, an honest man.   —*B. Franklin.*

WORDS

God wove a web of loveliness, of clouds and stars and birds, but made not anything at all as beautiful as words.
—*Anna H. Branch.*

Although words exist for the most part for the transmission of ideas, there are some which produce such violent disturbance in our feelings that the role they play in transmission of ideas is lost in the background.   —*Albert Einstein.*

There ain't but one word wrong with every one of us in the world, and that's Selfishness.   —*Will Rogers.*

One of our defects as a nation is a tendency to use what have been called "weasel words." When a weasel sucks eggs the meat is sucked out of the egg. If you use a "weasel word" after another there is nothing left of the other.   —*Theodore Roosevelt.*

Through all varieties of creeds, through the thousandfold forms of mythology and theology, through the systems of philosophers and the visions of poets, has spoken more or less audibly one Eternal Word.   —*W. E. Channing.*

Many a treasure besides Ali Baba's is unlocked with a verbal key.
—*H. Van Dyke.*

> Go put your creed into your deed,
> Nor speak with double tongue.
>
> —*R. W. Emerson.*

Words once spoken can never die; they will turn up on the day of judgment, like things of life, and will either acquit or condemn.
—*Edward Everett.*

Words are deeds. Words are wonder-working acts. Words create things which otherwise could not exist.   —*Mathurin Dondo.*

Nothing, surely, is more alive than a word. —*J. Donald Adams.*

Some of mankind's most terrible misdeeds have been committed under the spell of certain magic words or phrases.

—James Conant.

The safest words are always those which bring us most directly to facts. *—C. H. Parkhurst.*

Words are often seen hunting for an idea, but ideas are never seen hunting for words. *—H. G. Shaw.*

It makes a great difference in the force of a sentence whether a man be behind it or not. *—R. W. Emerson.*

I would rather speak the truth to ten men than blandishments and lying to a million. *—H. W. Beecher.*

Words are weapons, and it is dangerous in speculation, as in politics, to borrow them from the arsenal of the enemy.

—George Santayana.

He can compress the most words into the smallest ideas of any man I ever met. *—A. Lincoln.*

WORK

We work and that is God-like. *—J. C. Holland.*

Work brings a man into the good realm of facts.

—Phillips Brooks.

Men who do their work without enjoying it are like men carving statues with hatchets. *—Ibid.*

Work is a form of nervousness. *—Don Herold.*

Life is work, and everything you do is so much more experience. *—Henry Ford.*

Work is power, and the modern trend is of necessity to subject power to increased social regulation and supervision.

—H. P. Fairchild.

Happiness lies not in the mere possession of money; it lies in the joy of achievement, in the thrill of creative effort. The joy and moral stimulation of work no longer must be forgotten in the mad chase of evanescent profits. *—F. D. Roosevelt.*

Work is the greatest thing in the world, so we should always save some of it for tomorrow. *—Don Herold.*

No man is born into the world whose work is not born with him. *—J. R. Lowell.*

Work is something you want to get done; play is something you just like to be doing.   —*Harry Leon Wilson.*

The world is full of willing people; some willing to work, the rest willing to let them.   —*Robert Frost.*

There will never be a system invented which will do away with the necessity for work.   —*Henry Ford.*

Wanting to work is so rare a want that it should be encouraged.
                                                                —*A. Lincoln.*

The race is over, but the work never is done while the power to work remains.   —*O. W. Holmes, Jr.*

God does not charge for His work, neither can I in working with him.   —*George W. Carver.*

Work is work if you're paid to do it, and it's pleasure if you pay to be allowed to do it.   —*F. P. Dunne.*

A man can be freed from the necessity of work only by the fact that he or his fathers before him have worked to a good purpose.
                                                                —*Theodore Roosevelt.*

See only that thou work, and thou canst not escape the reward.
                                                                —*R. W. Emerson.*

Whether thy work be fine or coarse, planting corn or writing epics, so only it be honest work, done to thine own approbation it shall earn a reward to the senses as well as to the thought.
                                                                —*Ibid.*

The reward of a thing well done is to have done it.   —*Ibid.*

I have succeeded in getting my actual work down to thirty minutes a day. That leaves me eighteen hours for engineering.
                                                                —*Charles Steinmetz.*

What no wife of a writer can ever understand is that a writer is working when he's staring out the window.   —*Burton Rascoe.*

I never did anything worth doing by accident, nor did any of my inventions come by accident; they came by work.
                                                                —*Thomas A. Edison.*

Handle your tools without mittens.   —*B. Franklin.*

Heaven is blessed with perfect rest but the blessing of earth is toil.   —*H. Van Dyke.*

When large numbers of men are unable to find work, unemployment results.   —*Calvin Coolidge.*

Work is the meat of life, pleasure the dessert.   —*B. C. Forbes.*

The fellow who isn't fired with enthusiasm is apt to be fired.
—*Ibid.*

The man flaps about with a bunch of feathers: the woman goes
to work softly with a cloth.   —*O. W. Holmes.*

My father taught me to work; he did not teach me to love it.
—*A. Lincoln.*

One machine can do the work of fifty ordinary men. No machine
can do the work of one extraordinary man.   —*Elbert Hubbard.*

The work you began in the fog you continue in the sunlight.
—*Max Otto.*

If you do your work with complete faithfulness, . . . you are
making as genuine a contribution to the substance of the universal
good as is the most brilliant worker whom the world contains.
—*Phillips Brooks.*

> Thank God for a world where none may shirk—
> Thank God for the splendor of work!
> —*Angela Morgan.*

Find your place and hold it: find your work and do it. And put
everything you've got into it.   —*E. W. Bok.*

I don't pity any man who does hard work worth doing. I admire
him. I pity the creature who doesn't work, at whichever end of the
social scale he may regard himself as being.   —*Theodore Roosevelt.*

When God wanted sponges and oysters, He made them, and
put one on a rock, and the other in the mud. When He made man,
He did not make him to be a sponge or an oyster; He made him
with feet, and hands, and head, and heart, and vital blood, and a
place to use them, and said to him, "Go, work!"   —*H. W. Beecher.*

WORKERS

Betterment for workingmen must come primarily through workingmen.   —*Samuel Gompers.*

Freedom for workers is in turn conditioned by freedom for
enterprise.   —*William Green.*

The builders of any desirable future must be the workers in the
fullest and richest sense of the word.   —*Norman Thomas.*

The workingmen have been exploited all the way up and down
the line by employers, landlords, everybody.   —*Henry Ford.*

The American worker enjoys an economic, political and social status . . . Labor has become a full partner in our economy.
—*H. S. Truman.*

The complete organization of the workers of America is a basic necessity, not only for the protection of the immediate interests of labor but as one of the instrumentalities essential for a planned economy.   —*Sidney Hillman.*

The workingmen are the basis of all government, for the plain reason that they are the most numerous.   —*A. Lincoln.*

The workers are the saviors of society, the redeemers of the race.
—*E. V. Debs.*

WORKS

Faith without works is dead, because it is out of work that faith is born.   —*D. S. Muzzey.*

WORLD

Our real world is enough.   —*George Santayana.*

There is much disease and chaos and ugliness in the world. Yet is there a stream of love, of health and beauty-making power, flowing through the all.   —*J. E. Boodin.*

The free peoples of the world look to us for support in maintaining their freedom.   —*H. S. Truman.*

I am interested now in world planning for the welfare of the whole world.   —*Ibid.*

Not until this generation, roughly this century, have people here and elsewhere been compelled more and more to widen the orbit of their vision to include every part of the world. —*F. D. Roosevelt.*

We all, whether we know it or not, are fighting to make the kind of a world that we should like.   —*O. W. Holmes, Jr.*

To accept the world as it comes to our hands, to shape it painfully without regard to self—that brings the soul to peace.
—*Robert Herrick.*

The world after 1865 became a bankers' world.
—*Henry Adams.*

The whole world broke in two in 1922 or thereabouts.
—*Willa Cather.*

In this world nothing is sure but death and taxes.
—*B. Franklin.*

When a resolute young fellow steps up to the great bully, the world, and takes him boldly by the beard, he is often surprised to find it come off in his hand, and that it was often tied on to scare away timid adventurers. —*O. W. Holmes.*

O world, I cannot hold thee close enough.
—*Edna St. Vincent Millay.*

The world is God's workshop for making men. —*H. W. Beecher.*

The world gets better every day—then worse again in the evening. —*Kin Hubbard.*

The axis of the earth sticks out visibly through the center of each and every town or city. —*O. W. Holmes.*

The world is to each man according to each man.
—*R. G. Ingersoll.*

The world is not made for the prosperous alone, nor for the strong. —*G. W. Curtis.*

Man can only live in a cultural world which he himself creates and imposes upon himself. —*Lawrence K. Frank.*

The world always had the same bankrupt look, to foregoing ages as to us. —*R. W. Emerson.*

We Socialists are the builders of the world that is to be.
—*E. V. Debs.*

WORLDISM

The era is worldistic. As soon as humanity adjusts itself to this patent fact it will find peace and abundance in a world community.
—*Scott Nearing.*

Worldism, as a cultural stage, will be reached when the dominant activities of mankind take place on a world scale. —*Ibid.*

There can be no secure peace now but a common peace of the whole world; no prosperity but a general prosperity.
—*James Harvey Robinson.*

We are all so pathetically and intrinsically interdependent that the old notions of noble isolation and national sovereignty are magnificently criminal. —*Ibid.*

Hearken, my America, imperious is your errand, and sublime. 'Tis yours to build the world-state in your dream. To strike down Mammon and his brazen breed. Yours to shape the mighty deed, to build the brother-future.—America, rise to your high-born part!
—*Edwin Markham.*

The earth to be spann'd, connected by network,
The races, neighbors, to marry and be given in marriage,
The oceans to be crossed, the distant brought together,
The lands to be welded together.

—*Walt Whitman.*

The world is my country.   —*T. Paine.*

WORRY

The freedom now desired by many is not freedom to do and dare but freedom from care and worry.   —*James Truslow Adams.*

There are two days about which nobody should ever worry, and these are yesterday and tomorrow.   —*R. J. Burdette.*

Keep cool: it will be all one a hundred years hence.

—*R. W. Emerson.*

I have lost everything, and I am so poor now that I really cannot afford to let anything worry me.   —*Joseph Jefferson.*

The reason why worry kills more people than work is that more people worry than work.   —*Robert Frost.*

It's a funny thing that when a man hasn't got anything on earth to worry about, he goes off and gets married.   —*Ibid.*

Worry and hurry insure a short life and anything but a merry one. We can't all be Napoleons or Edisons.   —*R. C. McCaughan.*

The round of a woman's daily life may be characterized as one part work, three parts worry.   —*Marion Harland.*

Most parents don't worry about a daughter till she fails to show up for breakfast, and then it's too late.   —*Kin Hubbard.*

Marriage, like death, is nothing to worry about.   —*Don Herold.*

It is not work that kills men; it is worry. Worry is rust upon the blade.   —*H. W. Beecher.*

If you live your life amongst your family and your nation you must bear the worries that are love's inescapable companions.

—*Dagobert D. Runes.*

WORSHIP

Work and worship are one with me.   —*Susan B. Anthony.*

It is only when men begin to worship that they begin to grow.
—*Calvin Coolidge.*

What greater calamity can fall upon a nation than the loss of worship?   —*R. W. Emerson.*

Man cannot live all to this world. If not religious, he will be superstitious. If he worship not the true God, he will have his idols.
—*Theodore Parker.*

WORTH

Human worth knows neither Jew nor Gentile, rank nor caste.
—*V. L. Parrington.*

Appreciation of distinctions of worth is an essential of a liberal education, as it is of the whole spiritual life of man.
—*E. D. Martin.*

I believe in the supreme worth of the individual and in his right to life, liberty, and the pursuit of happiness.
—*John D. Rockefeller, Jr.*

The smile that is worth the praises of earth is the one that shines through tears.   —*Ella W. Wilcox.*

The life that is worth the honor of earth is the one that resists desire.   —*Ibid.*

For anything worth having one must pay the price; and the price is always work, patience, love, self-sacrifice.
—*John Burroughs.*

At its present cost, life is worth about thirty cents on the dollar.
—*Don Herold.*

There is worth enough in any rascal to cost the spilling of the Precious Blood.   —*Austin O'Malley.*

I am not sure that God always knows who are His great men. He is so very careless of what happens to them while they live.
—*Mary Austin.*

WRATH

In the souls of the people the grapes of wrath are filling and growing heavy, growing heavy for the vintage.   —*John Steinbeck.*

The bow of God's wrath is bent . . . and it is nothing but the mere pleasure of God . . . that keeps the arrow from being made drunk with your blood.   —*Jonathan Edwards.*

Many men want religion as a sort of lightning-rod to their houses, to ward off, by and by, the bolts of divine wrath. —*H. W. Beecher.*

WRITE

You don't write because you want to say something; you write because you've got something to say.   —*F. Scott Fitzgerald.*

WRITERS

Those of our writers who have possessed a vivid personal talent have been paralyzed by a want of a social background.

—*Van Wyck Brooks.*

A serious writer is not to be confounded with a solemn writer. A serious writer may be a hawk or a buzzard or even a popinjay, but a solemn writer is always a bloody owl.   —*Ernest Hemingway.*

Shakespeare was a dramatist of note;
He lived by writing things to quote.

—*H. C. Bunner.*

A good many young writers make the mistake of enclosing a stamped, self-addressed envelope, big enough for the manuscript to come back in. This is too much of a temptation to the editor.

—*Ring Lardner.*

The writers who have nothing to say are the ones you can buy; the others have too high a price.   —*Walter Lippmann.*

In Hollywood the woods are full of people that learned to write, but evidently can't read. If they could read their stuff, they'd stop writing.   —*Will Rogers.*

There seems to be no physical handicap or chance of environment that can hold a real writer down.   —*Kathleen Norris.*

There is no luck, no influence, no money that will keep a real writer going when she is written out.   —*Ibid.*

Writers cannot write good books at any level of excellence if they are badgered to death by economic worries.

—*C. Hartley Grattan.*

Talent alone cannot make a writer. There must be a man behind the book.   —*R. W. Emerson.*

Writers seldom write the things they think. They simply write the things they think other folks think they think.

—*Elbert Hubbard.*

A man may write himself out of reputation when nobody else can do it.   —*T. Paine.*

Somebody who wants to do his country a good turn should start a society to drive the ghost writer out of politics.

—*Raymond Clapper.*

WRITING

All writing comes by the grace of God, and all doing and having.

—*R. W. Emerson.*

The search for depth results merely in obscurity.

—*H. E. Luccock.*

The art of writing is the art of applying the seat of the pants to the seat of the chair.

—*M. H. Vorse.*

If you want to get rich from writing, write the sort of thing that's read by persons who move their lips when they're reading to themselves.

—*Don Marquis.*

You must write to the human heart, the great consciousness that all humanity goes to make up.

—*Willa Cather.*

Writing is like religion. Every man who feels the call must work out his own salvation.

—*G. H. Lorimer.*

Writing or printing is like shooting with a rifle; you may hit your reader's mind or miss it.

—*O. W. Holmes.*

The problems of the human heart in conflict with itself alone can make good writing because only that is worth writing about, worth the agony and the sweat.

—*William Faulkner.*

People do not deserve to have good writing, they are so pleased with the bad.

—*R. W. Emerson.*

Poetry and science were written in great part by the same people and appeared in the same books.

—*Max Eastman.*

Art (literature) is not a branch of pedagogy.

—*James Branch Cabell.*

The worst thing that ever happened to writing is that it became a business.

—*Dagobert D. Runes.*

WRONG

Woe to that people which would found its prosperity on wrong!

—*W. E. Channing.*

There is no war so brilliant as a war with wrong.

—*Horace Bushnell.*

Truth forever on the scaffold, wrong forever on the throne.

—*J. R. Lowell.*

Manly regret for wrong never weakens, but always strengthens
the heart.   —*H. W. Beecher.*

As some plants of the bitterest root have the sweetest blossoms,
so the bitterest wrong has the sweetest repentance, which, indeed,
is only the soul blossoming back to its better name.   —*Ibid.*

Wrong no man and write no woman.   —*Elbert Hubbard.*

The only right is what is after my constitution; the only wrong
what is against it.   —*R. W. Emerson.*

It is vain to trust in wrong; it is like erecting a building upon a
frail foundation, and which will directly be sure to topple over.
                                                    —*Hosea Ballou.*

Hatred of wrong can become a consuming and overpowering
passion, destroying sleep and health and overriding all the natural
human desires. In sane men it becomes madness.
                                              —*Elizabeth Jackson.*

X

XERXES

It is not a great Xerxes army of words, but a compact Greek ten thousand that march safely down to posterity.　　*—J. R. Lowell.*

Y

YARDSTICK

Do not take the yardstick of your ignorance to measure what the ancients knew and call everything which you do not know lies.

—*Wendell Phillips.*

YAWP

I sound my barbaric yawp over the roofs of the world.

—*Walt Whitman.*

YEARNINGS

A woman is never too old to yearn.   —*Addison Mizner.*

Our yearnings are homesickness for heaven.   —*H. W. Beecher.*

Those who have been bruised and distorted by culture yearn neurotically for a (bestial) freedom that neither they nor others could ever enjoy.   —*Laurence K. Frank.*

YEARS

The years teach much which the days never know.

—*R. W. Emerson.*

We do not count a man's years until he has nothing else to count.

—*Ibid.*

It is but a few short years from diapers to dignity and from dignity to decomposition.   —*Don Herold.*

YEOMAN

The yeoman and the scholar . . . are two distinct individuals, and can never be melted or wedded into one substance.

—*Nathaniel Hawthorne.*

YES

One half the troubles of this life can be traced to saying "yes" too quick, and not saying "no" soon enough.   —*Josh Billings.*

YESTERDAY

Most people put off till tomorrow that which they should have done yesterday. —*E. W. Howe.*

There are two days about which nobody should ever worry, and these are yesterday and tomorrow. —*R. J. Burdette.*

YIELD

If you want to get a sure crop, and a big yield, sow wild oats.
—*Josh Billings.*

The sun does not willingly shine upon you to give you light to serve sin and Satan; the world does not willingly yield her increase to satisfy your lusts. —*Jonathan Edwards.*

YOKE

What boots it that I am crushed by no foreign yoke, if through ignorance and vice, through selfishness and fear, I want the command of my own mind? —*W. E. Channing.*

No more is God a stranger: he comes as Common Man, at home with cart and crooked yoke. —*Edwin Markham.*

YOU

There is enough power in you to blow the city of New York to rubble. —*N. V. Peale.*

If there is literally enough force in you to blow up the greatest city in the world, there is also literally enough power in you to overcome every obstacle in your life. —*Ibid.*

You cannot play the hypocrite before God. —*H. W. Beecher.*

When you see what some girls marry, you realize how they must hate to work for a living. —*Helen Rowland.*

No matter what party you support, no matter what men you elect, property is always the basis of your governmental action.
—*Orestes A. Brownson.*

There is no use whatever trying to help people who do not help themselves. You cannot push anyone up a ladder unless he be willing to climb himself. —*Andrew Carnegie.*

If anyone corrects your pronunciation of a word in a public place, you have every right to punch him in the nose.
—*Heywood Broun.*

Accustomed to trample on the rights of others, you have lost

the genius of your own independence and become the fit subjects
of the first cunning tyrant who rises among you.   —*A. Lincoln.*

You can have no wise laws nor free enforcement of wise laws
unless there is free expression of the wisdom of the people—and,
alas, their folly with it.   —*William A. White.*

You say that freedom of utterance is not for time of stress, and
I reply with the sad truth that only in time of stress is freedom
of utterance in danger.   —*Ibid.*

Whoever you are, to you endless announcements!
                                        —*Walt Whitman.*

The independence and liberty you possess are the work of joint
councils and joint efforts—of common dangers, sufferings, and
successes.   —*G. Washington.*

The ideal with which you go forth to measure things determines
the nature, so far as you are concerned, of everything you meet.
                                        —*H. W. Beecher.*

Your superior mental powers impose upon you a responsibility to
make the most of them.   —*Granvelle Kleiser.*

Ye that oppose independence now, ye know not what ye do: ye
are opening a door to eternal tyranny, by keeping vacant the seat
of government.   —*T. Paine.*

If you help run our government in the American way, then there
will never be danger of our government running America in the
wrong way.   —*Omar N. Bradley.*

Knowing you, persuades me more than the Bible of our immortality.   —*Herman Melville.*

If you wish to lower yourself in a person's favor, one good way
is to tell his story over again, the way you heard it. —*Mark Twain.*

YOUNG

Much of what the young learn from their elders they acquire at
their peril.   —*J. M. Brown.*

It is not book learning young men need, nor instruction about
this and that, but a stiffening of the vertebrae which will cause
them to be loyal to a trust, to act promptly, concentrate their
energies, do a thing—"carry a message to Garcia."
                                        —*Elbert Hubbard.*

To be seventy years young is sometimes far more cheerful and
hopeful than to be forty years old.   —*O. W. Holmes.*

Whenever a man's friends begin to compliment him about looking young, he may be sure that they think he is growing old.

—*Washington Irving.*

Young man, if she asks you if you like her hair that way, beware; the woman has already committed matrimony in her heart.

—*Don Marquis.*

Nothing seems so tragic to one who is old as the death of one who is young, and this alone proves that life is a good thing.

—*Zoë Atkins.*

Gossip is always a personal confession either of malice or imbecility and the young should not only shun it, but by the most thorough culture relieve themselves from all temptation to indulge in it. —*J. G. Holland.*

Young men think old men fools, and old men know young men to be so. —*Richard Metcalf.*

The darkest hour in the history of any young man is when he sits down to study how to get money without honestly earning it.

—*Horace Greeley.*

One of the many things nobody ever tells you about middle age is that it's such a nice change from being young.

—*Dorothy Canfield.*

It is by the promulgation of sound morals in the community, and more especially by the training and instruction of the young, that woman performs her part towards the preservation of a free government. —*Daniel Webster.*

It is the intimations of mortality, not immortality, that devastate parents in the presence of their young. —*J. M. Brown.*

Do not fear to put novels into the hands of young people, as an occasional holiday experiment, but above all, good poetry in all kinds,—epic, tragedy, lyric. —*R. W. Emerson.*

If we can touch the imagination (of youth) we serve them; they will never forget it. —*Ibid.*

An art school is a place for young girls to pass the time between high school and marriage. —*T. H. Benton.*

She was only sixteen; but what does that matter when one is young. —*Gelett Burgess.*

The sweetest roamer is a boy's young heart. —*G. E. Woodberry.*

When one becomes indifferent to women, to children, and young people, he may know that he is superannuated, and has withdrawn from whatsoever is sweetest and purest in human existence.

—*A. B. Alcott.*

Courage is a virtue that the young cannot spare.

—*H. Van Dyke.*

If we keep well and cheerful we are always young, and at last die in youth, even when years would count us old.

—*Tryon Edwards.*

Every young man would do well to remember that all successful business stands on the foundation of morality.   —*H. W. Beecher.*

YOUNGEST

By the time the youngest children have learned to keep the place tidy, the oldest grandchildren are on hand to tear it to pieces again.   —*Christopher Morley.*

YOUR

Give your heart to the hawks.   —*Robinson Jeffers.*

YOURSELF

I only am he who places over you no master, owner, better, God, beyond what waits intrinsically in yourself.   —*Walt Whitman.*

First find the man in yourself, if you will inspire manliness in others.   —*A. B. Alcott.*

YOUTH

The day will come when youth will listen with respect to the teachings of the old and look with love and reverence upon the unselfishness of the old.   —*Arthur Brisbane.*

Young men have a passion for regarding their elders as senile.

—*Henry Adams.*

> One may return to the place of his birth,
> He cannot go back to his youth.

—*John Burroughs.*

It is not possible for civilization to flow backwards while there is youth in the world.   —*Helen Keller.*

Youth has steadily gained on the enemy . . . through it alone shall salvation come.   —*Ibid.*

Youth, though it may lack knowledge, is certainly not devoid of intelligence; it sees through shams with sharp and terrible eyes.

—H. L. Mencken.

Older men declare war. But it is youth that must fight and die.

—Herbert Hoover.

Youth is impulsive. When our young men grow angry at some real or imaginary wrong, and disfigure their faces with black paint, it denotes that their hearts are black. *—Chief Seattle.*

In youth we run into difficulties, in old age difficulties run into us. *—Josh Billings.*

Youth today must be strong, unafraid, and a better taxpayer than its father. *—H. V. Wade.*

A youth with his first cigar makes himself sick; a youth with his first girl makes other people sick. *—M. W. Little.*

Flaming youth has become a flaming question. And youth comes to us wanting to know what we may propose to do about a society that hurts so many of them. *—F. D. Roosevelt.*

Reckless youth makes rueful age. *—B. Franklin.*

The world's tragedy is that it must be grown up; in other words, that it must be run by men who, though they know much, have forgotten what they were in their youth. *—J. M. Brown.*

You have elevated the desire for health, youth and longevity to the position of a religion. *—Stephen S. Wise.*

Fewer pillories and whipping posts, and smaller gaols, with their usual expenses and taxes, will be necessary when our youth are properly educated. *—Benjamin Rush.*

Youth does not get ideas,—ideas get him! *—Randolph Bourne.*

The virtue of youth in art, as it is the virtue of youth in life, is sincerity to put the right questions and passionately to keep on demanding the right answers until they are given.

—Howard Mumford Jones.

I, for one, hope that youth will again revolt and again demoralize the dead weight of conformity that now lies upon us. *—Ibid.*

Youth rebels because by the mere fact of being young, it is nearer heaven than are the aging. In fact, youth rebels, even to destruction. *—Ibid.*

Youth must be optimistic. Optimism is essential to achievement and it is also the foundation of courage and true progress.

—N. M. Butler.

Keep flax from fire, youth from gambling.   *—B. Franklin.*

Morbid impulses are one of the luxuries of youth.

—W. D. Howells.

What one knows is, in youth, of little moment; they know enough who know how to learn.   *—Henry Adams.*

I have never known a man who was sensual in his youth, who was high-minded when old.   *—Charles Sumner.*

In many ways youth has more to teach its parents than to learn from them. The real savages are the old, not the young.

—J. M. Brown.

Marriage is a mistake of youth—which we should all make.

—Don Herold.

Age and youth look upon life from the opposite ends of the telescope, it is exceedingly long; it is exceedingly short.

—H. W. Beecher.

The boy gathers materials for a temple, and then when he is thirty concludes to build a woodshed.   *—H. D. Thoreau.*

Praise begets emulation—a goodly seed to sow among youthful students.   *—Horace Mann.*

If youth be a defect, it is one that we outgrow only too soon.

—J. R. Lowell.

Z

ZANZIBAR

It is not worth while to go round the world to count the cats in Zanzibar. —*H. D. Thoreau.*

ZEAL

The greatest dangers to liberty lurk in insidious encroachment by men of zeal, well-meaning, but without understanding.
—*Louis D. Brandeis.*

Zeal is the fire of love, active for duty—burning as it flies.
—*W. R. Williams.*

A meek soul without zeal, is like a ship in a calm, that moves not as fast as it ought. —*J. M. Mason.*

It is a coal from God's altar must kindle our fire; and without fire, true fire, no acceptable sacrifice. —*Wm. Penn.*

Never let your zeal outrun your charity. The former is but human; the latter is divine. —*Hosea Ballou.*

The whole earth (is) made drunk with the blood of its inhabitants, slaughtering each other in their blinded zeal.
—*Roger Williams.*

True zeal is a strong, steady, uniform, benevolent affection; but false zeal is a strong, desultory, boisterous, selfish passion.
—*Nathaniel Emmons.*

To be furious in religion is to be irreligiously religious.
—*Wm. Penn.*

We often excuse our own want of philanthropy by giving the name of fanaticism to the more ardent zeal of others.
—*H. W. Longfellow.*

The weakness of human nature has always appeared in times of great revivals of religion, by a disposition to run into extremes, especially in these three things: enthusiasm, superstition, and intemperate zeal.   —*Jonathan Edwards.*

Ye ministers of the gospel . . . Let your zeal keep pace with your opportunities to put a stop to slavery.   —*Benjamin Rush.*

ZEALOTS

Often a convert is zealous not through piety, but because of the novelty of his experience.   —*Austin O'Malley.*

A zealous soul without weakness, is like a ship in a storm, in danger of wrecks.   —*J. M. Mason.*

Zealots have an idol, to which they consecrate themselves high priests, and deem it holy work to offer sacrifices of whatever is most precious.   —*Nathaniel Hawthorne.*

When we see an eager assailant of wrongs, a special reformer, we feel like asking him, What right have you, sir, to your one virtue? Is virtue piecemeal?   —*R. W. Emerson.*

ZERO

Naivete in art is like zero in a number; its importance depends on the figure it is united with.   —*Henry James.*

ZEST

Forbid a man to think for himself or to act for himself and you may add the joy of piracy and the zest of smuggling to his life.
                                                      —*Elbert Hubbard.*

Mirth is the sweet wine of human life. It should be offered sparkling with zestful life unto God.   —*H. W. Beecher.*

ZIONISM

Zionism was the will of the Jewish people to re-create its life through a national homeland.   —*Stephen S. Wise.*

Empires live in terms of centuries. Millennia have witnessed Israel's sufferings, and shall yet crown the triumph of Israel's hope.
                                                                —*Ibid.*

ZONE

Commerce defies every wind, outrides every tempest, and invades every zone.   —*George Bancroft.*

ZOROASTER

Zoroaster said, when in doubt, abstain, but this does not always apply. At cards, when in doubt, take the trick.   —*H. W. Shaw.*